QMW Library
23 1101816 4

D1615253

# THE PUBLICATIONS OF THE Northamptonshire Record Society

FOUNDED IN DECEMBER, 1920

VOLUME XXXVI

FOR THE YEAR ENDED 31 DECEMBER 1988

**Earl and Countess Fitzwilliam, monument in Marholm Church.**

# THE CORRESPONDENCE OF LORD FITZWILLIAM OF MILTON AND FRANCIS GUYBON, HIS STEWARD 1697–1709

Edited by
D. R. HAINSWORTH
and
CHERRY WALKER

Northampton
1990

ISBN 0 901275 54 9

Published by the Northamptonshire Record Society,
Delapré Abbey, Northampton NN4 9AW

Typeset by BP Integraphics Ltd., Bath, Avon
Printed in Great Britain at Bookcraft Bath Ltd.

# CONTENTS

| | Page |
|---|---|
| Abbreviations | vi |
| Introduction | |
| The Fitzwilliam estate | vii |
| The letters and their authors | x |
| Milton and its surroundings | xvi |
| Taxation and coinage reform | xix |
| The archive | xxi |
| Note on editorial method | xxii |
| Acknowledgements | xxii |
| The Text of the Letters | 1 |
| Index | 297 |

# ILLUSTRATIONS

| | | |
|---|---|---|
| 1 | Earl and Countess Fitzwilliam, monument by James Fisher in Marholm church | *frontispiece* |
| 2 | Lord Fitzwilliam to Francis Guybon, NRO, F(M)C 1286 A (letter no. 291) | *facing p. 132* |
| 3 | Francis Guybon to Lord Fitzwilliam, NRO, F(M)C 651 A | *facing p. 133* |
| | Pedigree of the Fitzwilliam family | *page viii* |
| | Map of Milton and its surroundings | *page xvii* |

# ABBREVIATIONS

| | |
|---|---|
| Baker | Anne E. Baker, *Dictionary of Northamptonshire Words and Phrases*, 2 vols (1854) |
| Bridges | J. Bridges, *The History and Antiquities of Northamptonshire*, 2 vols (1791) |
| *Complete Peerage* | G.E. Cockayne, *The Complete Peerage*, rev. edn. 12 vols in 13 (1910–59) |
| Disbursements 74 | Guybon's accounts of disbursements 1700–10, NRO, F(M)Misc. vols. 74 |
| Disbursements 790 | Guybon's accounts of disbursements 1684–1700, NRO, F(M)Misc. vols. 790 |
| F(M)C | NRO, Fitzwilliam (Milton) correspondence |
| LRS | Lincoln Record Society |
| Longden | H.I. Longden, *Northamptonshire and Rutland Clergy from 1500*, 16 vols (Northampton, 1938–52) |
| NRO | Northamptonshire Record Office |
| NRS | Northamptonshire Record Society |
| O.E.D. | *Oxford English Dictionary* |
| Pevsner | N. Pevsner, *The Buildings of England Bedfordshire, The county of Huntingdon and Peterborough* (1968) |
| *The Commons 1660–1690* | B. Henning (ed.), *The House of Commons 1660–1690*, 3 vols. (History of Parliament Trust, 1983) |
| *The Commons 1715–1754* | R. Sedgwick (ed.), *The House of Commons 1715–1754*, 2 vols. (History of Parliament Trust, 1970) |
| *VCH* | *Victoria County History* |
| Washington | J. Washington, *An Exact Abridgment of all the Statutes . . . to the end of the last session of parliament, April the 34rd 1704* (London, 1704) |

# INTRODUCTION

## *The Descent of Lord Fitzwilliam and His Estate*

William Fitzwilliam, third Baron Fitzwilliam, created first Earl Fitzwilliam in 1716, was descended from Sir William Fitzwilliam, a wealthy London alderman, a Merchant Taylor and Merchant of the Staple of Calais, who converted the profits of trade into landed wealth chiefly in Northamptonshire and Essex.[1] The Northamptonshire manors were in the Soke of Peterborough, on land lying between the rivers Welland in the north and the Nene to the south. This was not fenland, but well watered valuable land, gently undulating as it trended down toward Peterborough where the fens began. Here in 1502 Sir William purchased the manors of Milton, in the parish of Castor, and Marholm, together with the advowson of Marholm and of the chantry of St Guthlac in Marholm parish, and with fishing and wharfage at Gunwade ferry on the Nene.[2] By his death in 1534 Fitzwilliam had further acquired two more manors in Castor parish, and the manor and advowson of Etton and the manor of Northborough, both a few miles to the north of Milton, together with half the manor of Woodcroft in Etton parish. Perhaps to symbolise the transformation of his family from merchants to landowners Fitzwilliam ordered that at his death his corpse must be expensively and ceremonially transported from London for burial in Marholm church, an ancient building on which he had bestowed a beautifully proportioned chancel.[3]

Unfortunately for the fortunes of his eldest son, Sir William Fitzwilliam II, the Founder left many children and much of the landed property was divided among younger sons who were unable to capitalise on their inheritance so that much of the scattered property was alienated by the next generation. These included in the Soke of Peterborough the manor of Northborough. However, the core of the Peterborough manors, Milton, Marholm and Etton, descended to Sir William II and remained in the family. Containing much land frequently enriched by the overflowing of the Welland and the Nene, with Milton mainly enclosed at the time of its purchase, and wholly enclosed by 1576, this was a landed estate of considerable potential value.[4] Nevertheless the withdrawal of the Fitzwilliams from the mercantile to the landowner class meant that Sir William's eldest son never commanded his father's wealth and his attempts to increase the estate by savings from its income proved unavailing.

[1] The early history of the Fitzwilliams of Milton and their estate has been splendidly analysed in Mary E. Finch, *The Wealth of Five Northamptonshire Families 1540–1640* (NRS, xix, 1955), pp. 100–134. It will be accorded only the briefest summary here. For Lord Fitzwilliam's posterity reference has been made to E. A. Smith, *Whig Principles and Party Politics: Earl Fitzwilliam and the Whig Party 1788–1833* (London, 1975) and to Graham Mee, *Aristocratic Enterprise: The Fitzwilliam Industrial Undertakings 1795–1857* (London, 1975).

[2] Finch, p. 101.

[3] For a description of the church and its monuments see Pevsner, p. 289, and see below, pp. xvi–xix.

[4] Finch, pp. 103–4.

# FITZWILLIAM FAMILY TREE

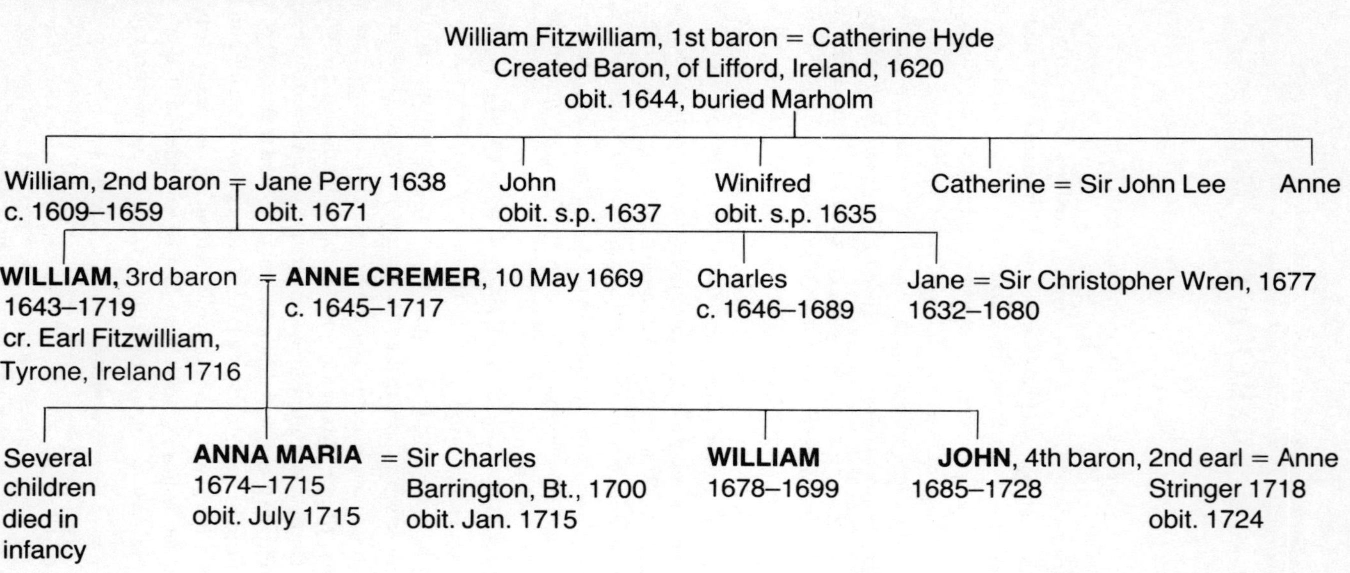


**Highlighted names are of those frequently occurring in the correspondence.**

His son and heir, Sir William III sought his fortune at court, a venture which was to be aided in the long term by his marriage to the sister of Sir Henry Sidney and the marriage of his first cousin to Sir William Cecil. Under Elizabeth he commenced a career in Ireland which was to continue with few breaks until a few years before his death, being successively Vice-Treasurer, Lord Deputy (1571–5 and 1588–1594), and general commanding the army in Ireland. Between 1575 and 1588 he was in England and as Keeper of Fotheringay Castle was responsible for the imprisonment of Mary Queen of Scots until her trial and execution. Although Sir William was probably extravagant in Ireland, and was certainly a remarkably poor bookkeeper, his frequent complaints from Ireland of impending ruin have to be weighed against the fact that in 1572 and 1576 his son bought on his behalf two manors in Helpston, Clapham's and Woodhall, with other lands for £1,600 and £500 respectively. In 1577 Fitzwilliam made further purchases in Etton, Helpston and Woodcroft, all helping to consolidate his estate. He also at a date unknown built the manor house at Milton, of which only the splendid north front survives today. Whether it was built in his Fotheringay period or after his retirement in 1594 is unknown.[5]

The Lord Deputy's eldest son, Sir William Fitzwilliam IV, was also a courtier. He exploited the perquisites of office until shortly after the accession of James I and then retired from public life and kept himself moderately prosperous by astute estate management and by exploiting his demesne lands as sheep pastures at a time of high wool prices. His son, Sir William Fitzwilliam V, succeeded in 1618 and in 1620 was created first Baron Fitzwilliam of Liffer in the Irish peerage. Declining wool prices ended sheep farming in favour of a resort to rents. However, an extravagant way of life which far exceeded his annual income, gradually drove the first Lord Fitzwilliam further and further into debt, and to mortgaging his estate to the point where the estate's income could not sustain the interest payments. Parts of the estate were sold, and the second Lord Fitzwilliam entered on a dismal inheritance in 1644 with most of the estate depleted and most of it heavily mortgaged. However, his father had married him to a wealthy widow, a member of a notable merchant family in London, and by the skilful use of her wealth, which was managed in her interest by members of her own family, and by transferring virtually the whole of the estate to trustees acting for his wife, the second baron gradually and painfully paid off his father's debts prior to his own death in 1659. When his son, the author of this correspondence, came into his inheritance the estate had been restored to modest prosperity without the extinction of his mother's personal wealth and, even more remarkable, without debilitating sales of land although the holdings in Castor and Ailesworth had been reduced, and substantial holdings in Helpston had been alienated.[6]

Under the third Lord Fitzwilliam and his steward Francis Guybon, the authors of the correspondence edited here, the estate in the Soke of Peterborough slowly began to increase in size. Northborough was recovered in 1681,[7] and the manor of Maxey was added, and part of the Lolham estate during the period the letters

[5] Pevsner, pp. 291–2.
[6] Finch, pp. 132–4.
[7] For Northborough, *VCH Northamptonshire*, ii. 509.

cover. While the accounts Guybon kept were primitive, even by the standards of the seventeenth century, it would seem that Fitzwilliam had an income from all sources, including sales of wood, of more than £3,000 a year, although the habit of at least some of his tenants of permitting their rents to run long in arrears must have seriously weakened Fitzwilliam's liquidity. Moreover his insistence on living in London, a notoriously expensive choice in the long term, put the estate and its steward under constant financial stress. Nevertheless Fitzwilliam's estate in the Soke of Peterborough, supplemented by his holding through his wife of several manors in Norfolk, provided him with an income thought sufficient to sustain an Irish earldom which was conferred on him in 1716, a reward for consistent Whiggery.[8]

His only surviving son, John, married in 1718 Anne Stringer of Sutton-on-Lound, Nottinghamshire. Although he only lived until 1728 he left a son and three daughters, the eldest of whom married Lord Godolphin. The son, another William, was the first Fitzwilliam to achieve an English peerage, being created a baron in 1742 and advanced to an English viscountcy (Milton) and earldom (Fitzwilliam) in 1746, a reward for consistent loyalty to Sir Robert Walpole and his Whig successors. It was this first Earl of the English creation who took the decisive step which later enormously increased the wealth of the family by marrying Anne, elder daughter of Thomas, first Marquess of Rockingham. Since Anne's brother, the second Marquess died without heir, the Rockingham and Fitzwilliam estates were united in 1782 and Charles Wentworth-Fitzwilliam, third earl of the English creation became the owner of Wentworth Woodhouse in South Yorkshire as well as Milton in Northamptonshire. This inheritance not only gave the family the Wentworth and Malton estates but along with them the Rockingham interest in Yorkshire and Whig politics to add to their control of elections in Peterborough and Higham Ferrers. Both the fourth and fifth earls sat (as Lord Milton) as M.P.s for Malton during the nineteenth century. The Fitzwilliam line ended with the tenth earl who died without heir male in 1979.

## *The Letters and their Authors*

Lord Fitzwilliam was a magnificent letter writer. He is always spontaneous, down-to-earth, and, despite occasional errors of sentence structure, syntax or grammar as his fertile mind ran ahead of his scratching quill, he displays a natural mastery of the English language. It is unfortunate that the editors have been compelled by the sheer size of the correspondence to calendar in whole or in part a majority of the letters, but many have been left partly or wholly uncalendared to give the reader rich examples of his style, and every effort has been made in calendaring to retain something of the flavour of the originals. There are here no formal circumlocutions, no 'business' or 'civil service' style as opaque filters between the writer and his message. He wrote as he thought, and he wrote what he thought, and therefore there is no barrier between the reader and the man who is writing. We

[8] Viscount Milton, Co. Westmeath; Earl Fitzwilliam, Co. Tyrone.

can follow his train of thought even to the extent of picking up odd associations of ideas so that although occasionally a letter hops backwards and forwards between unrelated topics, the reader has little difficulty in following the writer's train of thought. To a remarkable degree, therefore, the Fitzwilliam correspondence permits us to get inside the head of an English nobleman living in the second half of the seventeenth century.

Those who still assume that history concerns itself chiefly with the motives and actions of men at the centre of public life might consider this nobleman a person of no particular historical importance. Although he represented Peterborough in the House of Commons in the Cavalier Parliament from November 1667, was re-elected in March 1679 and to the short-lived Oxford parliament of 1681, he was never more than a back bench local member. His other public activities also largely fall outside the period covered by these letters: a long serving member of the Commissions of the Peace for Peterborough, Northamptonshire and Norfolk, at various times a Commissioner for the Assessment for both Northamptonshire and Norfolk, and Deputy Lieutenant for Northamptonshire from 1666–78, and from 1715 until his death.[9] As a Whig he would have welcomed the Revolution but displays little enthusiasm for William III.

Essentially Fitzwilliam during the dozen years covered by the correspondence was a private country gentleman, concerned about his estate, his neighbours, his tenants, their health, their prosperity or lack of it; taxes and their local impact; births and deaths; the prices of stock, of feed, of crops, of wool; the prices of land; the progress of his deer park; the renovation of his mansion and its outbuildings; the maintenance of his political interest in Peterborough; and the gradual increase of the extent of his estate; and the difficulties involved in transferring the income of his estate to London. We know all this because Fitzwilliam was a figure of paradox. He was a countryman with a countryman's store of knowledge of farming, of forestry, of gamekeeping, of fishing, and of estate management, perpetually fascinated by every detail concerning his seat, his estate and the affairs of his neighbours. Yet during the whole course of this correspondence he never once visited Milton. He remained throughout an absentee landlord, permanently resident in London, dependent on his increasingly aged steward, Francis Guybon, for the administering of his estate. For the detailed news of his estate and region which he craved he had to depend on Guybon's letters and on conversations with tenants and other locals who visited him in London, or whom he tracked down by riding out to the fattening paddocks in Islington Fields as they arrived with droves of sheep or cattle. Every year he announces his intention of 'coming down'. On his instructions beer is brewed, rooms and beds are aired, and housemaids are hired and a fellow for 'drudging work' and to watch the gates at night. Every year the beer goes stale, the extra servants are paid off, and the Fitzwilliams remain in London. The excuses vary, the result is always the same. Fitzwilliam is like a reverse image of Chekhov's *Three Sisters* who talked endlessly of visiting a capital they are doomed never to see. It is this paradoxical behaviour that provides us today with this almost unbroken series

[9] He was also Custos Rotulorum of Peterborough for the last four years of his life: *House of Commons 1660–1690*, ii. 328–9. See also E. G. Forrester, *Northamptonshire County Elections and Electioneering 1695–1832* (Oxford, 1941).

of letters covering a rich mix of topics and furnishing the modern historian of the social life of late Stuart England with a wealth of invaluable data. Fitzwilliam chose to live the life of a country gentleman vicariously and we are the richer for it.

This is all the more true because the correspondence is entirely composed of letters between a landowner and his steward. The seventeenth century estate steward has attracted little attention from historians in the past, although his eighteenth century and nineteenth century equivalents have received some attention.[10] The evidence of the substantial estate archives which have survived from the second half of the seventeenth century suggests that estate stewards were increasingly crucial figures, not mere rent collectors, seekers of tenants and keepers of manorial courts, but actively engaged in seeking to expand and improve their masters' estates. Moreover they were an important part of the social machinery for they linked capital and provinces, rural society and metropolitan society, gentle and simple, landlords and tenants, landlords and clergy, and, for that matter, landlord and landlord.[11] All this led to a developing role for many as parliamentary election agents in county and borough elections. By comparison with many of his contemporaries Francis Guybon was a less active steward, partly because his master's estate was far less complex than those of such landlords as the Cholmondeleys of Cheshire or the Lowthers of Cumberland and Westmorland or the Leveson-Gowers of Staffordshire, and partly because in the period covered by these letters Guybon was advancing into old age and was inevitably less active. Nevertheless the rich variety of topics covered by the correspondence, ranging from the impact of the reform of the currency to the cultivation and mobilisation of the Fitzwilliam political 'interest' in the Parliamentary borough of Peterborough, from the difficulty in finding suitable tenants to the problems of returning rural income to an absentee landlord, from tax evasion to the social problems caused by rural poverty, from the impact of the war to the impact of death and disease on family and neighbours, all serve to demonstrate that even a Guybon had a variety of functions to perform. One of the most important in his master's eyes was the provision of intelligence not just about the estate and its affairs but of the district and its inhabitants. Since most of the surviving letters from 1697 to 1709 are from Fitzwilliam to his steward, rather than the reverse, it is Fitzwilliam's questions and commentary on the information he receives as well as the instructions he issues that make these letters a particularly rewarding source for the social historian of the era of the later Stuarts.

Fitzwilliam himself emerges from his letters as a complex man with a remarkably sympathetic personality even to twentieth century eyes. Warm hearted, intensely interested in other people and their affairs, deeply concerned about the health and welfare of his relations and friends, neighbours and servants, he is in marked contrast to such near contemporaries as the terrible tempered, callous and self absorbed second

[10] For the seventeenth century see D. R. Hainsworth, 'The essential governor: the estate steward and English society 1660–1714', *Historical Studies*, 21 (1985); 'The Estate Steward' in Wilfrid Prest (ed). *The Professions in Early Modern England* (London, 1987), where footnotes 2 and 3 contain bibliographical information on publications relating to stewards. Dr Hainsworth is currently engaged in writing a monograph on the social role of the estate steward in England during the second half of the seventeenth century. For the eighteenth century see, among others, Joan Wake and Deborah Champion Webster (eds.), *The Letters of Daniel Eaton 1725–1732*. (NRS, xxiv, 1971).

[11] For this mediating role see Hainsworth, 'The Mediator: a link between national and provincial society in seventeenth century England' in *Parergon*, n.s. no. 6, 1988, Festschrift for Sir Geoffrey Elton.

Viscount Cholmondeley or the icily detached Sir John Lowther of Whitehaven.[12] In a patriarchal age in which fathers and sons were often on bad terms, Fitzwilliam and his wife appear to have maintained a loving family relationship with their surviving son and daughter, and regarded their long serving steward Francis Guybon more as an old family friend, indeed more as a member of their family, than as an employee. Fitzwilliam could be bad tempered on occasion, easily offended, angered at what he perceived as disloyalty or bad friendship, and determined to have his way in the face of recalcitrant tenants. However, his bark was very much worse than his bite, and where tenants are concerned it is often amusing to see his resolute declarations not to give an inch succeeded by gradual yieldings (always accompanied by further assertions that no further point shall be conceded) and this in turn succeeded by still further concessions until the tenant has extracted virtually all the terms he had aimed at all along.

If these characteristics render Fitzwilliam a figure more attuned to the new age of sensibility and more enlightened, more affectionate, social and family relationships which some authors consider to have been an eighteenth century phenomenon, his political views belong to an age we have been assured had passed away.[13] Essentially a Whig, Fitzwilliam tended to support at Peterborough and for the county candidates who were personally known to him and preferably neighbours, rather than men chosen for their party label.[14] Like other men of his station he had no love for electoral 'contests', and believed that in boroughs the voters should vote according to the direction of those to whom they owed loyalty, whether because they were tenants, frequently employed tradesmen, estate or household servants (or their connections). Fitzwilliam uttered the classic statement of this conviction during the Peterborough election of January 1701.[15] The tanners who bought his bark, the brazier who mended his kitchen utensils, the plumber who leaded Milton's roofs, the carrier who transported his goods, the waterman who moved his coal from Lynn, the saddler who caparisoned his horses, the man who yearly bought his rushes and a mason occasionally employed on the fabric of his mansion, were all in his eyes legitimately part of his electoral interest, as were his debtors. 'I . . . shall take it ill if any that works for mee and takes my money or that owes mee any money will not vote for my freinds' he declares during the same election.[16] In such matters Fitzwilliam may sound to modern ears extraordinarily arrogant but he was merely expressing the deeply held beliefs and assumptions of all men of his rank in the

[12] Cited here because both Cholmondeley and Lowther left archives which contain extensive correspondence with their stewards much of which overlaps in time Fitzwilliam's correspondence with Francis Guybon; for Cholmondeley see the correspondence files in the Cheshire County Record Office, Chester; for Lowther the correspondence files in the Lonsdale Archives, Cumbria County Record Office, Carlisle, and Hainsworth (ed.), *The Correspondence of Sir John Lowther of Whitehaven 1693–1698: a Provincial Community in Wartime* (London, 1983). Fitzwilliam's concern for the health of his household, tenants and neighbours is so intense that his letters are a valuable source for students of medical history.

[13] On family relationships see particularly Lawrence Stone, *Sex, Marriage and the Family in England 1500–1800* (London, 1977), and on political views Mark A. Kishlansky, *Parliamentary Selection: Social and Political Choice in Early Modern England* (Cambridge, 1986).

[14] 'I declare I am for Mr Wortley and Mr St John . . . for Mr Dolbin I have not the good fortune to be knowne to him and being a stranger to him I shall sooner be for my acquainteance and good neighbours then him', 5 December 1700 (**165** below).

[15] See **163**, 26 November 1700.

[16] See **165**, 5 December 1700.

seventeenth century. However, we must be careful not to confuse Fitzwilliam's assumptions with the realities of political and social life. In the election referred to here Fitzwilliam's friend St John was defeated by Dolben, the candidate Fitzwilliam had coldly dismissed as not personally known to him. In fact Fitzwilliam had got wind of some symptoms of disobedience (as he saw it) before the result and tended to blame his steward for sloth rather than accept that his assumptions were not shared by those he regarded as his political 'interest'. Guybon had claimed to have done all he could but

> 'how does this appeare when Peter Rainsford and his sonn and Mr Willis and my sadler Bates and Mr Pendleton's nephew vote for Mr Dolbin? Positively I shall take it so very ill of these and of some others if they give not one vote for Mr Wortley, or else go out of the towne the day of the election and vote for nobody, I shall not be easily reconciled to them . . .'[17]

The truth is that the political hegemony of the landed elite was not unchallenged by those over whom it was asserted and indeed it is precisely because of this that during the half century following the Restoration we can see emerging that increasingly significant political figure, the election agent. Very often the agent and the estate steward were one and the same for apart from some country attorneys and an occasional large scale borough tradesman there was no-one better placed to fulfil such a role, nor anyone in whom the landowner could so implicitly trust. The 'interest' could not be taken for granted. It had to be massaged, cajoled and, finally, bribed, to follow the landowner's lead.[18] Fitzwilliam was too casual and too remote to be a successful political manager. The statement that after the Restoration 'for two hundred years there was always a Fitzwilliam or a Fitzwilliam nominee sitting as a member for Peterborough' is not applicable to the period observed in this correspondence.[19] It implies a degree of control Fitzwilliam was incapable of exercising even
if he had wished to. Friends, men he approved of, might represent the borough but their successful candidature did not depend on that approval, let alone his nomination.

The limits of his hegemony in the borough can be seen in the county election of 1705. In January Fitzwilliam instructed his steward to speak to those tenants who were freeholders on behalf of Lord Mordaunt, and to tell others not his tenants that he would 'take it kindly' if they would cast their vote for this soldier son of the Earl of Peterborough. Guybon must 'do him what service lies in your power both in my severall townes, likewise in Peterborough and elsewhere. Speak to all the ministers and they will secure their parishioners.' Assuming Guybon tried to carry out this order the result can have given Fitzwilliam little satisfaction. In Peterborough of thirty-seven who voted only three cast a vote for Mordaunt, whereas thirty-three voted for Sir Justinian Isham and Thomas Cartwright (both Tories who served Northamptonshire for long periods). Another voter cast a single vote for

[17] See **168**, 26 December 1700.

[18] The role of the steward as election agent is discussed at length in Dr Hainsworth's forthcoming monograph on the social role of the estate steward.

[19] Herbert F. Tebbs, *Peterborough: a History* (Cambridge, 1979), p. 94.

Cartwright.[20] Several men who had voted for Isham and Cartwright in 1702 did not vote in 1705, including such Fitzwilliam friends as Seth Meek, Thomas Deacon and Charles Parker, but it is extremely doubtful, indeed highly unlikely, that this failure to vote had any connection with Fitzwilliam's enthusiasm for Mordaunt. In Fitzwilliam's 'towns' things went no better. In 'Marham cum Milton and Gunworth Ferry-House' of fifteen who voted only five voted for Mordaunt; in Helpston only two out of eleven; in Etton one out of two; in Maxey things went better with seven out of ten for Mordaunt including John Catlin, Fitzwilliam's understeward; in Castor five out of ten (including Joseph Chamberlaine, Fitzwilliam's tenant and gardener) and the best result was in 'Peakirk cum Waldrum Hall' with two out of two.

If Fitzwilliam's claim of a right to direct voters connected to him was as ineffective in practice as it was all embracing in theory, he was remarkably lacking in vindictiveness to those who crossed him, whether politically or otherwise, at least in his actions if not his words. Certainly it would be difficult for readers of his letters to find an example of his using his power as a nobleman and landlord as a weapon although they might find threats to do so. More typical is his treatment of 'little Joe', a juvenile household servant who is sent back to his innkeeper father at Peterborough because he is a drunkard and a thief. Fitzwilliam claimed he dare not keep him in London lest his opportunities for crime bring about his destruction, but instructed Guybon that the boy's father must never learn of his son's ill behaviour for fear of what he might do to him. When he was old enough Fitzwilliam would provide money to meet the cost of binding him as an apprentice. This was a remarkable but nevertheless typical example of Fitzwilliam's intense concern for the welfare of members of his household.[21] It is the supreme Fitzwilliam paradox that this prototype of Squire Allworthy was simultaneously an absentee landlord.

Francis Guybon (pronounced Gibbon) is an obscure figure. He was probably a member of a cadet branch of the armigerous Norfolk family of that name, but it has proved impossible to trace precisely from which branch he sprang. At least as early as 1669 he was employed as an estate servant on the Norfolk estate at Setchey which Lady Fitzwilliam inherited from her father for accounts in his hand survive from that date. It is not certain when he took up his duties at Milton but it was certainly prior to 1678, the date of the earliest surviving letter he wrote from Milton to Lord Fitzwilliam. If he ever married there are no references to a wife in his surviving correspondence from the thirty or more years he served at Milton. When Fitzwilliam's sons William and John were boys they spent months at Milton in the care of Guybon and a housekeeper, and the Fitzwilliam brothers together with their surviving sister, Lady Barrington, were as devoted to Guybon as were their parents and regularly sent him affectionate messages by their father or wrote to him themselves and complained when he was tardy in replying. Paid a salary of £40 a year, with allowance for his and his servant's diet and his horse (a typical

[20] For these and the following figures see the Northamptonshire poll book for 1702 and 1705 in the Northampton Library. We are grateful to Victor Hatley for sending us a xerox of the pages covering the Soke of Peterborough. Fitzwilliam's letters for the summer of 1702 may not be quite complete but those which survive contain no references to the election, held in July, save for a vague expression of satisfaction that the election at Peterborough was over (**227**).

[21] 'I dare not write thus much to his father because he is so passionate he may mischieve the boy but must pretend the towne aire does not agree with him, or some such excuse' (**71**, 30 July 1698).

emolument for a steward in this period) Guybon no doubt had other sources of income both from the perquisites of office and from sources outside the estate. Certainly his relatives believed him possessed of considerable substance and the news of his death aroused considerable interest among those who might have expectations under his will.[22] In general he belonged to that class of stewards who, although of 'gentle', not 'simple', origins, tended to share the outlook and interests of the tenants, or at least strongly to sympathise with them and to plead their cause, rather than fight single mindedly on behalf of his master's pecuniary interest. He was ageing and doubtless little inclined for conflict and hard bargaining. As a consequence Guybon is usually found advocating reduced rents (to make easier the task of finding new tenants or even hanging on to old tenants), better leasing terms (particularly where ploughing was concerned), and is far too inclined to permit the poorer tenants to drift into long arrears, stretching back into years. In an age when there was a shortage of tenants and landlords were competing with each other for them it was very difficult for stewards to maintain estate rentals, let alone increase them, but even by the standards of the times Guybon seems to have been lax and easy going.[23] However, Fitzwilliam was himself much to blame for his own financial problems in leaving his estate unvisited year after year.

### *Milton and Its Surroundings*

Milton was bought as we have seen by the first Sir William Fitzwilliam, clothier of London, in 1502. With it he acquired fishing rights in the River Nene (still possessed by this Lord Fitzwilliam and referred to in the letters) and wharfage rights at Gunwade Ferry. Gunwade was near the head of navigation on the Nene, which explains the presence of warehouses there, and meant that its importance in the history of local transportation far transcended the ferry itself. Milton now stands in a park of about 1,000 acres and cannot be seen from any of the roads which follow the park wall because of the great stands of trees which surround it. However, during the seventeenth century a road ran past the house itself which explains how travellers who had not called at the house could report to Fitzwilliam in London that the stable yard clock had lost its hand or that the roof over the chapel at the north west end of the mansion needed slating. The deer park, so frequently referred to by Fitzwilliam, lay to the north of the mansion. The large stable block, dated 1690, and running at right angle to the east end of the north front of the mansion was not the work of Talman but of John Sturges. It survives today, although in 1720 John, second Earl Fitzwilliam, built a back range to the stable yard which was given an octagonal tack room in its centre. In Lord Fitzwilliam's time the private chambers of the family were in a wing which ran at right angle to the main axis of the house, as did also the kitchen and pantry wing. Nothing of this mansion survives today except, remarkably, the exterior north wall of the late sixteenth century block with its great bays and oriel windows and two storey porch. This wall was allowed

[22] See Thomas Guybon to Fitzwilliam, 18 September 1710, referring to 'the expectation of the rest of the relations running pretty high from the common report of my uncle dying very rich': F(M)C, Box 22, Unnumbered corr. 1710–1744, no. 85.

[23] For the problem of falling rents see M. G. Davies, 'Country gentry and falling rents in the 1660s and 1670s', *Midland History*, 4 (1977), pp. 86–96, although the phenomenon persisted much longer than this article suggests.

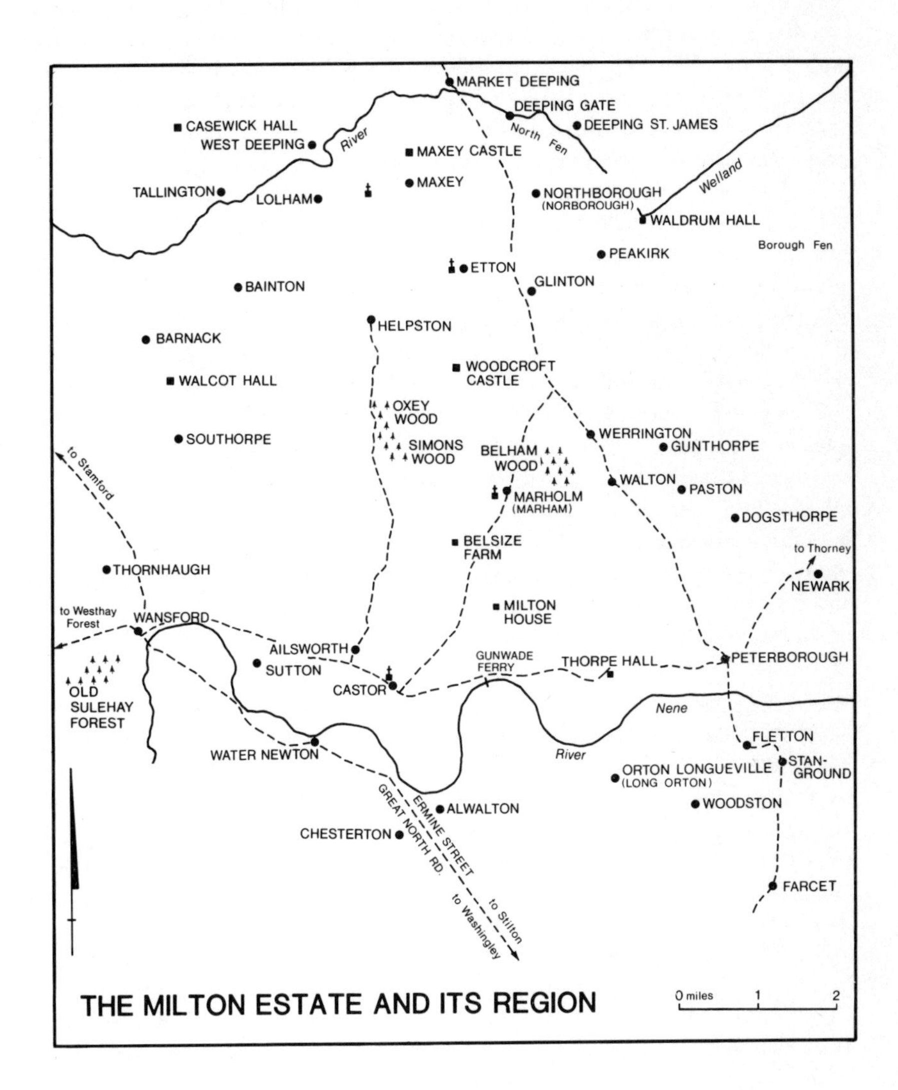

THE MILTON ESTATE AND ITS REGION

to survive when about 1750 (according to Pevsner) the house was demolished and replaced by an eighteenth century mansion. The architect was Flitcroft, his work being supplemented later (c 1800) by Chambers who supplied the dormer or attic bedroom windows in the mansard roof which are a conspicuous feature of the north side above the battlemented sixteenth century facade.

Due south of Milton is Gunwade Ferry and two miles southwest the village of Castor with its remarkable Norman church and some houses which would have stood in Fitzwilliam's lifetime. However, Castor was largely owned by the Dean and Chapter of Peterborough, Fitzwilliam having only a few tenancies there, and the property known as 'Thorold's Manor' (held by the Fitzwilliams since 1534) together with some tenancies in the nearby hamlet of Ailsworth.[24] Fitzwilliam's properties were more to the north and west of his mansion in the villages of Marholm, Northborough, Etton, Helpston and Maxey. Marholm Church has a Norman tower, the nave and chancel arch are thirteenth century but the chancel itself is a magnificent light, airy structure, disproportionately large because it was built by the first Sir William Fitzwilliam to serve as the pantheon of his posterity. Among others it contains the tomb of Sir William Fitzwilliam I and of his grandson, Sir William III, Elizabeth's commander and Lord Deputy in Ireland, and, most prominent of all, the standing monument with near-life-size figures of the author of these letters and his wife by James Fisher of Camberwell. In Marholm village can be seen what Pevsner describes as Marholm Farm and local people refer to as Manor Farm, a seventeenth century house dated 1637, which may well have been the farm leased by Mrs Bull, a friend and neighbour of the Fitzwilliams who acted as a sort of honorary housekeeper.

About five miles north of Marholm lies Northborough where the manor house and farm were leased in Fitzwilliam's time by Marmaduke Tomlinson (the 'Duke of the letters). Pevsner describes it as a 'remarkable survival of hall and gatehouse of a major manor house of c. 1330–40.'[25] The manor was owned by the Claypole family after 1563 and it was John Claypole, the husband of Oliver Cromwell's daughter Elizabeth, who sold it to Lord Fitzwilliam in 1681. The manor of Maxey, which lies to the west of Northborough, was given by Queen Elizabeth to William Cecil, first Lord Burghley. From him it passed to the Howards, Earls of Berkshire, and two daughters of that house, Anne, widow of Sir Gabriel Sylvius, and her sister Dorothy, wife of James Graham, sold it to Lord Fitzwilliam in 1699, a transaction well documented in these letters. By the time of that transaction Maxey Castle (actually a manor house which had been embellished with battlements in 1374–5) may well have disappeared. References to the castle in this correspondence are to Maxey Castle farm, a later structure. Beyond Maxey lies Deeping Gate, a small village on the edge of the fens, dependent on Maxey manor, in which Fitzwilliam was chief landlord. To the east of Northborough, but at one time forming part of the manor of Maxey, was Waldrum Hall, once a medieval manor house, but by Fitzwilliam's time no more than a crumbling farmhouse attached to a ferry across the Welland. The farmhouse was rebuilt by Fitzwilliam in the course of this correspondence. A ruin by 1903 it has since disappeared.

Etton, the village from which came the family of Daniel Defoe, is a small village

[24] *VCH Northamptonshire*, ii. 474.
[25] Pevsner, p. 297 ('Northborough Castle').

on the road from Marholm to Maxey. It was sold to Sir William Fitzwilliam in 1514. The church, of which Fitzwilliam's chaplain, the Rev. Jeremiah Pendleton was pluralist for he also held Marholm, is described by Pevsner as 'memorable as a completely thirteenth century church'.[26] Between Etton and Marholm is Woodcroft Castle, the remains of a once substantial thirteenth century castle which had a design similar to that encountered on the Welsh Marches, together with a range of Elizabethan buildings. This manor had formed part of the Fitzwilliam estate since the mid sixteenth century.[27] Close to Etton on the south west lies Helpston, which like Maxey, Marholm and Castor, has a church with a Norman tower. The township contains two ancient manors, Clapham, sold by Thomas Clapham to William Fitzwilliam in 1572, and Woodhall, sold with a mill and three dovecots to Sir William Fitzwilliam in 1576.[28] The right of presentation to the church at Helpston from the fourteenth to the nineteenth centuries was held by Christ's College, Cambridge.

It is difficult to estimate the precise extent of Lord Fitzwilliam's estate in the Soke of Peterborough but his descendant, the fourth earl, is said to have inherited 20,000 acres about Milton when he succeeded his father in 1756,[29] and it does not appear that there had been large acquisitions in the Soke during the intervening half century.

### *Taxation and the Reform of the Coinage*

There are frequent references to taxation, particularly national taxes, in the Fitzwilliam letters. They are in themselves a valuable source for any student seeking to explore attitudes towards and perceptions of William III's and Anne's wartime taxation measures.[30] The principal tax which confronted Fitzwilliam at regular intervals through the correspondence is the Land Tax, which, despite the name it soon acquired, was a tax on property of various kinds, not just the annual value of land. The taxation measures of William III's government although innovatory in their frequency and regularity, and in their capacity to raise large sums of money for the prosecution of the war, were the fruit of the fiscal experiments of Charles II's government, and particularly the Subsidy Act of 1671. It was in Charles II's reign that the power to appoint taxation commissioners passed from the Commons to the Crown, that a central Tax Office was set up, that it was firmly established that most forms of personal wealth should be taxed, not simply land, that the old Poll Tax was adapted for this purpose on the principle of a pound rate, and that the tax should be on the gross value and not simply the 'spareable part' (that is, what was left after all expenses and costs of living had been deducted). Moreover it was Charles II's government which devised and William III's government which inherited the system by which every county was given a quota of a total national sum which it must raise, distributing its quota among the hundreds into which

[26] Pevsner, p. 241.

[27] *VCH Northamptonshire*, ii. 487; Pevsner, p. 367.

[28] *VCH Northamptonshire*, ii. 496.

[29] Graham Mee, *Aristocratic Enterprise: the Fitzwilliam Industrial Undertakings 1795–1857* (London, 1975), p. 1.

[30] No more than a very brief summary can be given here. The reader is referred to C. D. Chandaman, *The English Public Revenue 1660–1688* (Oxford, 1975), chapter V, *passim*; W. R. Ward, *The English Land Tax in the Eighteenth Century* (Oxford, 1953); and for a general summary David Ogg, *England in the Reign of James II and William III* (Oxford, 1955), chapter XV, *passim*.

the county was divided. This system was employed in 1697, although Ogg points out that it was not until 1698 that William III's government was 'sufficiently established to make the quota system a permanent one'. In that year a specific amount of tax was levied from each district on the basis of the assessments of 1693, and at a rate of 3s in the pound. The tax included within its scope the profits of office, other than military or naval, as well as shares in public companies. Stock, merchandise and money were assessed, nominally at least, on their capital value and the tax was levied on six percent of that value. The tax was therefore intended to be a property tax, as had been intended by Charles II's government earlier. The problem was that evasion of the 'personal' property provisions was so much easier than was evasion of the provisions applying to rents that, just as in Charles II's reign, the tax became primarily a land tax and thus acquired the name by which it became famous (or infamous) in the eighteenth century.

There are references in the Fitzwilliam letters to the machinery of collection. In general commissioners were appointed for each county or borough by the act authorising the aid, the commissioners being chosen by the Crown. The commissioners announced the rate, determined the quota of each hundred or other division, and charged property owners to truly certify their property to the assessors. The commissioners authorised and sent out the assessors to inform themselves of the full yearly value of all property in the various hundreds who in turn issued their assessments to the collectors who actually levied the tax.

During the following letters readers will observe Fitzwilliam seeking to frustrate the collectors by minimising the tax on his lands (see particularly **6** and **8**). At the same time his sense of duty towards his neighbours suggested he should help his hundred meet its quota obligations by paying his 'personal' tax—tax on money at interest, stocks held, etc—in the country rather than in London (the choice was his). This sense of duty was tempered by a natural desire to pay whichever assessment was lower. If the country assessors would assess him lower than the London assessors he would pay at Milton; if not, he wished to pay in London. He remarked to Guybon on 1 April 1697 (**12**) that he must now be taxed for his personal estate in London, but would have been glad to hear how the country commissioners would have dealt with him, and asked how 'they deale by other people especially the rich men of Peterborough, and if the Lord Exeter be taxed for his sonn's lady's portion.' A fortnight later Guybon had clearly answered the query about his master's assessment for (**14**) Fitzwilliam sourly observed: 'I perceave by yours they would have been Jewish with me.' Nevertheless in the end Fitzwilliam paid at least part of his personal tax in the country (see **17**). In 1698 he again divided the payment of his personal tax between London and Milton, paying tax on £1,000 in the country after his lawyer, Roger Pemberton, assured him this would make the 'rest of the towne very easy ... and that very summe of £9 would do the business'; (i.e. 3s in the pound on £1,000, see **68**). Meantime Guybon must send up a certificate to say this has been done for his London parish had been assessed some hundreds of pounds and without it he might be assessed for that £1,000 in order to make up that quota.

In the early letters Fitzwilliam issues detailed instructions to his steward about what coin he should employ in paying taxes, and what coins he should send up for Fitzwilliam to dispose of in London. These instructions were inspired by the aftermath of the celebrated reform of the coinage undertaken by William III's government in 1696. This was a remarkable reform to undertake whilst Britain was heavily engaged in war with France, but was brought to a triumphant conclusion in little more than eighteen months although the transition period was to bring great distress to many of the poorer and less well informed of the king's subjects. By the measures taken the old badly clipped silver coins were to be exchanged for new milled silver coins, issued at provincial mints as well as the London mint, and the difference in value would be a cost borne by the tax payer (through a window tax). By the beginning of 1697 this process had largely occurred, and the Treasury was only accepting 'old' silver money for taxes by weight at 5s 8d an ounce, whilst by law old money in all other transactions passed by weight at a rate of 5s 2d an ounce. This provided an opportunity for men of property to make a profit by 'buying' old money at 5s 2d and paying their taxes at 5s 8d (see **1, 8, 13**). However, there was a time limit: old money was not to pass in any transactions after 2 June 1697. The reform of the coinage greatly affected the value of guineas. One of the motives for the reform was provided by the lower value of silver in England against gold compared with other Western European countries, particularly Holland, which tended to encourage clipping and the illegal export of silver. This in turn tended to inflate the value of gold coins, and when William Stout of Lancaster visited London in 1695 he was as astonished as delighted to discover that the guineas he had brought with him, bought for 22s or 23s a piece, were there worth from 28s to 30s.[31] The reform ensured that the exchange rate of gold and silver more closely matched that of Holland, gold lost its inflated value and the exchange rate of guineas against the new silver coins was much lower than against the old clipped currency. This fall in value caught Fitzwilliam by surprise in October 1697 (see **36**).

## *The Archive*

The Fitzwilliam Papers are held at the Northamptonshire County Record Office, Northampton. The surviving estate correspondence of the third Lord Fitzwilliam amounts to approximately 1,100 items. It includes letters from the stewards of the Norfolk manors (but none from him to them) and a few miscellaneous letters to or from other individuals, but the bulk of the correspondence is made up of letters from Francis Guybon at Milton to his master in London during the period 1678–1709, and letters from Fitzwilliam to Guybon between 1694 and 1709. However, no Fitzwilliam letters have been discovered earlier than 1 February 1694 and only 14 letters from then to the date this edition begins, 16 January 1697. Between January 1697 and April 1709 there are 536 Fitzwilliam letters, the bulk of the correspondence calendared or edited here. For the period 16 January 1697 to September 1709 barely 50 Guybon letters have survived compared to 136 letters from the period 1678 to 1696 (of which only four are dated earlier than 1687.)

In brief the Fitzwilliam–Guybon correspondence is heavily imbalanced. It is not unusual in seventeenth century estate correspondence for only the lord's letters to the steward to survive, or for only the steward's letters to the lord to survive, but in the Fitzwilliam correspondence there is first a long and substantial run of steward's letters with almost no surviving replies, followed by a long and still more

[31] *The Autobiography of William Stout of Lancaster*, ed. J. D. Marshall (Manchester, 1967), pp. 113–14

substantial run of the lord's correspondence punctuated occasionally by a steward's letter.

In addition some of Guybon's accounts have survived, including disbursements for the period 1684 to 1710 but receipts only to October 1700.[32]

## *A Note on the Editing*

In those letters which are in whole or in part transcribed the editing has been governed by the principle of doing as little violence to the original as possible and we have been guided by the methods set out in the British Records Association's pamphlets *Notes for the Guidance of Editors of Record Publications* (1946) and its updated successor, R. F. Hunnisett's *Editing Records for Publication* (1977). The original spelling has been retained throughout the transcribed letters, but contractions have been expanded and intrusive capitals have been reduced to lower case, except for titles (e.g. the Earl of Exeter, but 'my lord' and 'the bishop'). The editors have used the modern spelling of place names in the calendared versions of the letters and in footnotes (e.g. Marholm for 'Marham' and Northborough for 'Norborough'). Lord Fitzwilliam used the word 'countrey' in three senses, that is, for England, for the provinces as distinct from metropolitan London, and for 'county'. In calendared letters we have retained 'countrey' (in inverted commas) where Fitzwilliam meant 'county' in the original. Punctuation has been cautiously modernised, save where the meaning is ambiguous and the insertion of a comma or full point would arbitrarily determine the sense. The dates on letters are standardised, but the practice of dating the beginning of the year from the 25th of March, Lady Day, has been retained so that all dates between 1 January and 24 March give both the old and the new year, whether the author did or not (e.g. 26 February 1701/2).

In letters or portions of text printed in full all editorial interpolations (as with damaged words or words omitted in error) are enclosed in square brackets. All calendared letters or portions of letters are indented and all editorial interpolations are enclosed in square brackets. In the interests of readability as well as clarity all calendared letters, or parts of letters, are expressed in direct speech, our model being G. Dyfnallt Owen's admirable edition of the Sydney Papers for the Historical Manuscripts Commission. However, where letters have been badly damaged or are simply repetitive parts or all have been more briefly summarised in indirect speech and these letters or parts of letters are enclosed in round brackets. The principle observed in calendaring the letters was to retain all matter provided by the original, except on very rare occasions in the briefly summarised letters where lengthy repetition is omitted and a brief indication of topic and a reference to the earlier letter is footnoted.

## *Acknowledgments*

The editors wish to thank the Countess Fitzwilliam for agreeing to the publication of these letters and to warmly acknowledge her kindness, together with her daughter, Lady Hastings, in welcoming Dr Hainsworth to Milton in October 1987 and guiding him through its treasures. They also acknowledge with gratitude the assistance they

[32] F(M)Misc. Volumes 21, 27, 74, 790.

have received from Edmund King, General Editor of the Northamptonshire Record Society, Victor Hatley and Bruce Bailey, who furnished many suggestions, advice and information helpful in preparing the scholarly apparatus of this edition. They wish to thank the University of Adelaide and its Council for making it possible for Dr Hainsworth to visit Milton in pursuit of materials connected with this edition, and Irene Cassidy, the University of Adelaide History Department's permanent Research Officer in London, for first discovering and photocopying the correspondence on their behalf, and they warmly thank Marion Pearce, Marilyn Denholm and Roslyn Mitchell for many hours of difficult word-processing in the preparation of the manuscript. They would like to thank Mrs Chris Crothers for preparing a map of admirable simplicity and clarity. Finally the editors thank their respective spouses, Margaret Hainsworth and Owen Slight, for enduring the presence of Lord Fitzwilliam and his concerns in their households with admirable patience.

# THE CORRESPONDENCE OF LORD FITZWILLIAM OF MILTON AND FRANCIS GUYBON, HIS STEWARD 1697–1709

## 1 FITZWILLIAM TO GUYBON

*London, 16 January 1696/7; F(M)C 976*

Francis Guybon, by the late act of parliament for remedeing the coine of the nation it is ordered that all old money both little and great shall go for five shillings twopence an ounce till the first day of next February and no longer and the time now drawing neare I thought convenient to give you notice of it that you should take no more and gett ridd of what you have before that time.[1] The King's officers are obliged to take it for taxes and any other duties till that time and no longer. If you could contrive to send any provisions up to us in a box the next weeke I would have you send me up in it the money I left with you in the blew bagg and send me up what guyneas and broad gold you have by you or can gett up against that time. Pray send it me up the next weeke or the weeke after at farthest.[2] The little hogg man[3] has not paid me any money since the first £50. I have no money left and shall breake all my creditt for want running in debt to everybody. Therefore pray take care of me. In hast I am your loveing freind, W. Fitzwilliam. [P.S.] If I can gett no money I must leave the towne and live upon the tennants in the countrey.

[1] See above Introduction, p. xxi.

[2] '25th Jan. Returned my lord by John Clarke [carrier] 50 guinieas', Guybon's accounts of Disbursements 1684–1700, F(M) Misc. Vols. 790, henceforth 'Disbursements 790'.

[3] Rowland Morrice of Peterborough.

## 2 FITZWILLIAM TO GUYBON

*London, 21 January 1696/7; F(M)C 977*

Mr Phillips' £100 bank note I send you to return to him because I need money and the bank will not pay it. I wonder you would take it and put me to the postal charge when I told you in the country I would not meddle with them, and you told me nobody would. Hogman Morrice paid me £30 for William Sergeant but had no orders to pay me Duce's £50, the remainder of Thomas Freeman's £100. Duce's man was in town with beasts, and could have paid if his master had wished it. Tell Freeman how his chapman Duce 'baffles' in these payments. I have no reason to wait so long for my rent which I relied on receiving when he promised it. [P.S.] I am sorry my Cousin Bellamy is not well.[1]

[1] 'Cousin' Bellamy, used indiscriminately by Fitzwilliam to describe his wife's cousin, née Tryce, who was married to John Bellamy of Farcet, Huntingdonshire, or to describe Bellamy himself. She was the sister of Henry Tryce, usually referred to by Fitzwilliam as 'Cousin Harry Tryce'. They had a son Fitzwilliam refers to as Thomas. *VCH Huntingdonshire*, iii. 168.

## 3 FITZWILLIAM TO GUYBON

*[London,] 29 January 1696/7; F(M)C 978*

I received the bag of money in the basket. The silver wants 5s of the 'taile' (tally) I left with you and of the note you enclosed, but I will have it 'told' again.[1] Mr Thacker's bill on Mr Horseley of Cliffords Inn he returned, but hoped to pay it soon after term. If he does not soon pay I will return it. Mr Winkles has paid £100, and a Mr Henry 'Hawkin'[2] paid yesterday £22 8s 3d on Mr Brecknocke's account and £20 2s 6d on Mr Kingston's.[3]

[1] Silver was passing by weight, not face value, see Introduction, p. xxi.
[2] Hankin, a salesman and proprietor of The Angel, Islington, but originally from Northamptonshire.
[3] Both paid by Guybon between 8th and 16th February, Disbursements 790.

## 4 FITZWILLIAM TO GUYBON

*London, 5 February 1696/7; F(M)C 979*

Francis Guybon ... we were late last night with the c[or]poration[1] of adventurers to gett the countrey's greivances rem[ed]ied in a faire way without the charge of goeing into Parliament and I hope we have done it if they will but honestly performe those orders they have made and entred in their books. I have lett Mr Ash[2] and the [rest] of them have £20 for the countrey's service. You must take care to g[et] it againe.

I hear nothing of Morrice's £50 nor Hewson's £20. Horsley still puts off paying Mr Thacker's £9 bill. You say it will be hard getting it from him if I send it back. If you knew his condition to be desperate I wonder you would trust him with money before hand. I am sorry poor Clarke the carrier[3] is broke. He owes me £23 10s for the two horses but has paid almost half. Get him to set our reckoning straight and give a receipt for what he has carried which will lessen my debt, for if they take out a statute of bankruptcy against him they will compel me to pay all my carriages which we agreed in the bond was to be let off. If he gives me a receipt before the statute his debt will be less, and I'll give my word not to molest or sue him but I hope he will pay me when he can. Date the receipt a few days before January 27, the date Brown seized his wagon. I had the silver 'told' at Heriot's[4] again, and sold it for £22 10s, 5s 6d an ounce, but must wait 12 months for payment. Clean all the gutters fortnightly, especially over the chapel chambers for fear they be flooded at (the thaw). [P.S.] Will Mrs Bull have 'Burmerhurne'[5] to plough? What has Wright done about wainscoting the two new rooms? Get Pendleton[6] and Wright to measure exactly the two chimneys there for I think to have marble chimney pieces, hearths and sides.

[1] Entrepreneurs involved in fen drainage.
[2] William Ash of Paston, acquired the manor of Paston (or Peverels) c. 1680 through his wife Elizabeth, widow of Sir Henry Massingberd. Ash was still in possession of the manor in 1720; *VCH Northamptonshire*, ii. 514.
[3] John Clarke, see **1** note 2.
[4] James Heriot (died 1705, see **358**), goldsmith, The Naked Boy, Fleet Street, descendant of George Heriot of Edinburgh, goldsmith to James I prior to his accession: F. G. Hilton Price, *A Handbook of London Bankers* (London, 1890–1).
[5] A field name.
[6] The Rev. Jeremiah Pendleton, born Lancashire, admitted sizar at Emmanuel College, Cambridge, 11 March 1667, B.A. 1671, deacon 1671, priest 22 December 1672 (Peterborough); instituted Rector of Marholm 26 February 1676; instituted Rector of Etton 17 May 1698; died 24 August 1704: Longden, iv. 235.

## 5 FITZWILLIAM TO GUYBON

*London, 11 February 1696/7; F(M)C 980*

Tell Mr Wright[1] I do not intend hangings for the two chambers over the store room or the laundry but only a handsome painting. Tell Mrs Bull[2] I will not let Burmer Hurne under £17 for ploughing, or under £14 for grazing. If it proves dear at £17 she must 'stand to my curtesie' for 20s a year. If she ploughs, that last crop should be 'Saint Foile grass'[3] and be laid three years before it returns to my hands. I expect rent fowls besides. If she declines let it elsewhere. The bed for the drying yard hedge should be two feet not one and a half feet and set in a deep border. If the orchard won't supply enough bring some rich earth, once sawdust, from the saw pits in Meadow Close. The border should stand 10 inches or a foot high. Tell Mr Parker[4] and they who came up about the fens that we are put off for the second time since they left and cannot be heard for 10 days so it's well they left when they did. Tell Mr Wright I intend no marble on the chimney's within side because 'marble is very deare by reason of the warr'. [P.S.] Mr St John[5] has had a dangerous apoplectic fit taking away his eyesight and all his senses for a considerable time, but he came to himself again.

[1] Robert Wright of Castor (c. 1661–1736). A master carpenter and builder Wright also acted as an architect and became surveyor to the Dean and Chapter of Peterborough, making a survey of the cathedral's fabric in 1734. In 1688 he was setting a wooden balustrade on Charles Bertie's house, Uffington, near Stamford, where the steward considered him 'a very prettie ingenious workman and one that understands all things belonging to any building'. At Milton in 1689 Wright agreed to build the new stable wing, much of which survives, to a design by John Sturges (not Talman as is often believed). In 1726 he was one of the contractors who agreed to make the Nene navigable, the work having been completed as far as Oundle by 1730. See Howard Colvin, *A Biographical Dictionary of British Architects 1600–1840* (London, 1978), p. 932. Colvin states that Wright lived at Castor during the latter part of his life, but in fact he was living there throughout the period covered by these letters.

[2] A prominent tenant, probably of the farm now known as 'the Manor Farm', Marholm, about a mile from Milton. A friend and confidant of both Fitzwilliams, and an 'honorary' housekeeper of Milton at need, Mrs Bull was a widow with an adult son, Joseph, himself a tenant of another farm, and several daughters.

[3] Sainfoin.

[4] Probably Mr Charles Parker of Burghberry Hall, Peterborough (c. 1663–1730), who inherited part of Thurlby estate, Lincs. from an uncle in 1672; M.P. for Peterborough 1710–22, Sheriff of Northamptonshire 1726–7.

[5] Francis St John of Thorpe Hall, Longthorpe, near Peterborough (1634–1705), son of Oliver St John famed as the defender of John Hampden and the prosecutor of the Earl of Strafford. A confirmed Whig, he voted for the Exclusion Bill, presumably welcomed the Revolution but only sat in one parliament after 1681 and that was for Peterborough in 1698. He was defeated in the election of 1700. *The Commons 1660–1690*, iii. 381–2.

## 6 FITZWILLIAM TO GUYBON

*[London,] 18 February 1696–7; F(M)C 981*

Duce's £50 and Howson's and Horsley's money are all unpaid. The King's surveyor will pay LePlaw's money as soon as he can. Had I not received money from Norfolk[1] these disappointments would have put me to 'great streights'. I am sorry to hear the smallpox is so rife. God keep them from Mrs Bull's family. If she refuses 'Burmore hurne' on my terms let it elsewhere but not for ploughing.

You must be thinking how to mannage yourselfe about this tax. The King names commissioners for the levieing of it. I heare Mr Noah Neale of Stamford is the only commissioner for our liberty, and it's discoursd they will be very severe, and therefore it behoves us not to owne how much the tennants payes. You must speake to all the tennants not to owne the full of their rents by a fourth or fi[f]th part; they cannot punnish them for denieing their rent, but they may punnish you that are the steward by fineing you. Therefore, I am advised, if they send to you for a rentall, to go to them but pretend some business made you forgett it. If they aske you what such and such tennants paies, pretend your memory is bad, you cannot remember. Be sure not to name anything, for if you name less then any tennant paies, they will make me pay treble the tax, if they can contradict us. Be sure to remember nothing that they aske you, pretend you are antient, and your memory much failes you. If they tax my lands at a venture, and it does not exceed my rents, we must be contented, but if it does, we have liberty to appeale within tenn daies, therefore give me notice every question they ask and I will send you fresh instructions what to do every post. The commissioners must name assessors out of the severall townes, and they are to be the collectors of the tax payable out of their own townes. They are to receave a small allow[ance] in the pound for their paines, but I would not perswade any of them for the hopes of gain[ing] twenty shillings [to] go to disoblige all their neighbours, that they must live all their lives [near?] them just to serve the King who will hardly thanke them. The assessors must owne what rents they pay, but they may pretend ignorance what other men pay in the p[lace?]. This tax is but three shillings in the pound. If the commissioners will be content to have the severall townshipps tax't at the vallew they were in the 4s in the pound tax, and then abate one shilling in the pound out of it, we will willingly be content to pay that; else lett them tax what they will, we will owne nothing, for this may prove a tax of dangerous consequence hereafter. It is not for this yeare only, but may be for ever. Discourse of this with Mr Selby, Mr Forster and the neighbours at Etton, Helpston and Norborough[2] and tell them, if they are to be trusted, what I say.[3] Do not loose this letter but laiy it by. You may have occasion to read it over and over againe. If they will tax me moderately for money,[4] I will pay there; else here . . . [P.S.] My wife is very ill.

[1] Referring to Fitzwilliam's Norfolk estates at West Winch and Setchey.

[2] The village of Northborough was called 'Norborough' in this period and was invariably so spelled by the correspondents here.

[3] In fact Mr Selby, along with William Serjeant, both of Castor, were the assessors for Milton in 1697. Serjeant was a Fitzwilliam tenant, Selby was tenant to the Bishop of Peterborough. On 14 August Guybon paid them £64 14s for a year's tax of the Milton estate, the woods, and Fitzwilliam's personal estate, Disbursements 790.

[4] By 'money' Fitzwilliam means money invested, out at loan, money in the bank, etc, which was all part of his taxable wealth: see Introduction, p. xix–xxi.

## 7 FITZWILLIAM TO GUYBON

*London, 25 February 1696/7; F(M)C 982*

Francis Guybon . . . [I] am sorry to heare Mr Turner of Peterborough[1] is so ill. You may be sure whatever dammage you come to by my direction either in this bussiness of the tax or any other, I will be sure to beare you harmless, and I will give you instructions from time to time how you are to act, though you may aske Mr Pemberton's[2] advise, who I am sure will carry the act of parliament downe with him. I know not certainly how often I may have occasion of writeing to you about this matter therefore leave word with Nell Rainsford[3] that she sends to the post house every time the post comes in to see for your letters and send them to you with what convenient speed she can. Mr Noah Neale of St Martins is the only commissioner for our liberty who is a sober and a moderate man and I hope will do things fairly. I have complemented him already upon it. He goes out of towne this day so on Munday I suppose he will begin to act and by Wensday night post if not sooner you shall be sure to have a letter from mee how you shall carry yourselfe.

> I received £20 by Howson's order, and Duce's £50 from Rowland Morrice. Has drying yard hedge been set?

[1] Turner was an innkeeper in Peterborough. A former tenant of Fitzwilliam's, his wife had served as housekeeper in the 1680s when Fitzwilliam's sons were resident at Milton (see Guybon's letters to Fitzwilliam for the year 1688, *passim*).

[2] Roger Pemberton of Peterborough was Fitzwilliam's lawyer.

[3] In business with her husband in Peterborough.

## 8 FITZWILLIAM TO GUYBON

*London, 4 March 1696/7; F(M)C 983*

> I sent the bills you enclosed to the person who is to pay them who says they deceived me if I expected payment on sight for 'by way of trade' they always had two months after sight to pay. Knowing him to be punctual, having had payments from him from my Norfolk concerns, I accepted the delay and will be paid £40 on May Day. I have Mrs Horsley's £9. For Mr LePlaw's money the man keeps the bill another week. It depends on the King's pay, for Mr Buckle is Surveyor to the King's Stables. He is promised £4,000 or £5,000.

As to the tax, I heare the commissioners in the towne and the countreys round intend to lay the tax as it was in the last yeare, and to abate a 4th part of it; and for money just the same. If Mr Neale and our commissioners will take the same method, it will be the more easie to every body, and save them a great deale of trouble. I am advised that neither you nor any of the tennants, if they should be so troublesome to examine, should owne any thing but pretend ignorance, that you cannot remember what the rents are; they cannot fine you by the act, but they may fine you and the tennants very severely if you tell them the rents, and then can prove upon inquiry that you have told them false. Pray informe all the tennants what I write and charge them to say nothing if they [sic] assessors or commissioners examine them. Lett them tax them as they please, if any of them are over tax't, then they may appeale to the commissioners within a certaine time, and then must be forc't to declare their rents so as to be eased. If any of the tennants are made assessors, then they are bound to declare their owne rents truely, but for any of their neighbours, they are not bound to tell the truth of their rents. I thinke I can give you no further instructions. If I can learne anything betweene this and the next post, I will be sure to write, therefore leave orders with Nell Rainsford to send your letters to you in time, if there be any. When the tax is gathered, you may pay it all in old money at 5s 8d an ounce but you are not bound to take it at above 5s 2d per ounce. If you have as much as will pay the whole yeare's tax you may pay alltogether as you did last [year?], and if you want old money I can send you some downe. For you must know no old is to go at all neither to the King, nor in any other payments after the 2nd day of next June, therefore pray be wary what you take unless you can putt it off againe within that time ...

## 9 FITZWILLIAM TO GUYBON

*London, 11 March 1696/7; F(M)C 985*

I am glad the tax will be settled without trouble to poor people and for my personal estate if the commissioners will not be content to tax me there as I was last year I can be taxed here at that rate and please all people very well and myself too. Mr Buckle offered me £40 in old money by the ounce but I would not take it since he would not offer the whole £50 and no part new milled money. If I have no hopes of him in a week I will return the bill. Phillips only offers me a bank bill and his bond to make it good which I am unwilling to take, lacking money at this time. My wife wishes you to give Mrs Bull money to go to Mid Lent Fair[1] with Goody Freeman[2] to help her buy seven or eight pairs of sheets for coachmen and grooms' beds and cloth for eight or ten pairs of finer sheets for 'better' servants. Get me what money you can in new money or the greatest part at worst. [P.S.] Phillips says five or six acres of plashing is needed next the Werrington wheat field this year. If he gives up his 60 acres next Glinton cow pasture raise the rent; it is let too cheap by 12d an acre.

[1] At Stamford, see **11**.
[2] Wife of Thomas Freeman, substantial tenant and gamekeeper.

## 10 FITZWILLIAM TO GUYBON

*London, 18 March 1696/7; F(M)C 986*

I received no letter from you last week so hope all is well. Yesterday I received Mr Exton's[1] £50 but nothing from Mr Phillips of Walton who left me his bank bill to see if anything would be got of it and said he would give you a bond for £100 at six per cent. Take his bond until he can pay his rent though I would rather have the money. Go on with the 'ceylings' in the new buildings. Let that floor be 'ceyled'[2] in the room Wright is wainscotting. The walls in those rooms need not be plastered for they must be either hung or wainscotted. Next they must do the storeroom, then laundry, then the paved dairy. If Wright thinks the morning frosts will do no harm to the sealing order the slaters to come. [P.S.] Let me hear what is done in the tax. Everybody tells me I must pay for my money here.

[1] A frequent 'returner' of Fitzwilliam money. Often, as here, spelled 'Exon' by Fitzwilliam, but sometimes 'Exton'. Guybon invariably uses 'Exton' in letters and accounts so we consistently use that form in calendared letters.
[2] It was then the practice in the Midlands to lay plaster floors: Edward Dobson, *Rudiments of the Art of Building* (1871), p. 122. See **512**.

## 11 FITZWILLIAM TO GUYBON

*[London,] 25 March 1697; F(M)C 987*

I wonder that Mr Wright is so backward in wainscoting, though I don't wish more 'hast then good speed', but if he will be two months at it those rooms shall not be sealed until after harvest. Hot weather will crack the ceilings, so let them do the storeroom, passage and dairy. I fear Mr Wright's men 'lumbering over head' will crack the ceilings, and they may fall down. If Tidd and his son cannot be got at once, employ others. I don't care who if they are good workmen, can burn my lime, work by the day and 'by great',[1] and find their own drink. I wonder you cannot find enough plaster to finish that room. Mr Phillips must pay rent in money for bank bills grow worse and worse, are sold for £24 and £25 loss 'and will yett rise higher'. I am sure you can raise the rent on Phillips' 60 acres. Werrington men or some thereabouts would give more for it 'but you had rather pleasure James Dove'.[2] The land I think is let for 6s 8d an acre. I am sure you could get 7s for it. It is as good as most around it which is let for 8s. What you write about stock giving no price is a mistake. It never sold better here than it does now. Horner, Mr Phillips' salesman, told me last week when he brought Mr Exton's £50 that Phillips' beasts sold for a very good price, saying the countryman was never satisfied but only (complained) purely to try to lower rents. Beef and mutton sell dearer by a halfpenny in the pound than it has sold all winter. I will not let Burmer Hurne under the price I set. Let Mrs Bull use her own discretion whether she takes it. I would have Meadow Close let this year to graze but not to mow. I shall only need hay for the deer this year and you must supply them other than by keeping so great a ground in hand. Take care Manton leaves all the fences, gates and stiles in repair. If he takes it again let it only from year to year. Tell him it won't be taken out of his hands until I use the ground myself but he shall not mow this year because he mowed it last. I will not let Burmer Hurne to John Rycraft to plough. He may have it to graze at that rent if Mrs Bull will not. I wonder you let the barn at Chiseldine's fall down. I warned you when last at Milton to have it propped. The roof might have stood many years had the walls been repaired but nothing is mended if I am not there to look after things. Be getting stone for it when the ways are good enough to carry loads. Take the rest down to save the timber and let me know what size of barn you will build. Let me know quickly what the commissioners say to what the assessors intend and then I will consider where to pay. [P.S.] My wife would know what Mrs Bull paid for the cloth at Stamford.

[1] By great, at a fixed price for the task.
[2] A Fitzwilliam tenant.

## 12 FITZWILLIAM TO GUYBON

*[London,] 1 April 1697; F(M)C 988*

Francis Guybon, I have received no letter from you this weeke and much wonder I do not heare from you what the commissioners do in your parts. I must now be taxed here in towne for all is pass't with us. I should have been glad to have knowne how they intended to have used me. Pray lett me heare how they deale by other people especially the rich men of Peterborough, and if the Lord Exeter be tax't for his sonn's lady's portion.[1] Lett me know if they make an alteration in the tax upon land or not and how much they vallew Thomas Freeman's stocke at. What they assess you for wages and money and lett me know who are the assessors and collectors for Castor and if the new Commission of the Peace is come downe for our hundred and Peterburgh. I am now in some want of money for my tax will run pretty high. I understand there is a likely young man (one Healy by name) that is in your debt for wood, as likewise for the rent of the close next Walton feild, a considerable summe. I understand his circumstances are very bad, haveing spent and morgaged all. His land is morgaged to Mr Lawrence of Walton. You must take a very speedy course with him for I heare he is neare running away, therefore you must loose no time. Do not take notice how you come by your information but I say be very quicke with him or all is losst. I have given you formerly warning of your long forbeareance of them that owe you money. I will not loose through your sloth and negligence. I keep you in the countrey to gather up my rents not to loose them for want of calling on and therefore expect them from you if it appeares they are loss't through your carelessness.

I want money. Mr Buckle has not yet paid David 'LePlaw's' £50 bill. [P.S.] You may pay the tax for my land all at once in old money at 5s 8d an ounce which you take only at 5s 2d an ounce. After the tax is paid take as little of the old money as you can for there will be a loss at last. Therefore keep no money but return it and pay it away as fast as you receive it. Answer every particular of my last two letters.

[1] John Cecil, 5th Earl of Exeter, of Burleigh House (died 1700). His son was John Cecil, Lord Burleigh, subsequently 6th Earl (died 1721), who married firstly Annabella, daughter of John Bennett 1st Lord Ossulston (on 9 February 1697); she died July 1698. *Complete Peerage*, v. 219–20.

## 13 FITZWILLIAM TO GUYBON
*London, 8 April 1697; F(M)C 989*

Francis Guybon ... As to the tax I am sorry to heare they intend to be so very severe with me. Lett mee know what quantity of old money you have by you and are like to have as neare as you can guess, that we may consider how to dispose of it. Paying the whole yeare's tax together for my land will go off with a good quantity and we shall gett sixe pence an ounce by it, for the King must take it at 5s 8d and we receave it but at 5s 2d,[1] so that if you thinke you may want old money with you I can send you some downe purposely to gett sixe pence per ounce by it which will pay well for the carriage of it downe, but I beleive you will not want. Have a care of haveing to much of it for feare we should not have occasion to part with it all before the first of June next. Lett me heare as soone as you can how they tax my personall estate in the countrey but I must pay it here because I am taxt already and it must be paid before that in the countrey else I had rather our assessors should gett the money by us.

John Webdale paid me £50 and with much ado I got £25 from Mr Buckle who promises the rest this week if I may believe him. I shall be glad of Mr Sowgate's £50. I am glad your tenant Healey pays rent well and wish you would make William Carnell and others pay equally well. Let the 'slaterers' come as soon as they can work but I fear this frosty weather is not good for 'sealeing work'. I had rather Tidd and his son did all or most of the work with labourers to mix their mortar. Many bad hands will make haste but I fear will not do it well. Let the Deeping masons do the coachhouse and other partitions, and by the time they are finished Mr Wright will be ready for them to do the ceilings in those chambers. But I only expect the Deeping men to partition below stairs and the work in the henhouses. I am sorry you can get no plaster for the floors, but seek some out. How do you intend to sell the bark this year for leather is extraordinarily risen here and will be higher, I am informed, so bark should be a higher price than formerly. I am glad you have let James Dove the 60 acres because he is a good tenant, though I hoped for a higher rent. I don't doubt you will do the same for Burmer Hurne. If you cannot get the rent I would like I hope you will raise it somewhat but I wish it let. I think you propose well having Chisseldine's barn as big as you mention. Tell Mr Selby they may tax me for £3000 or £4000; it may be the commissioners (whatever they say) may be content to let it go at that. Secure my rent of William Carnell and let it from him to another tenant. We must not trust such poor men too far and the like with others in arrear. Take care of all things ...

[1] Under the rules governing the reform of the coinage landowners could pay their royal taxes in 'old money' at a higher rate (5s 8d an ounce) than silver was passing in general circulation (5s 2d or even less), which was profitable so long as they did not acquire more old money than they owed in taxes: see below **15**.

## 14 FITZWILLIAM TO GUYBON

*London, 15 April 1697; F(M)C 990*

Francis Guybon ... I am tax't here in towne and must pay here and expect every day when they will call for my money, for they are most daies in the streets about us; but we that pay good summs they gather ours last. I had a mind to know how the commissioners would have dealt by me, but now it's to[o] late. I perceave by yours they would have been Jewish with me. I perceave by Mr Sowgate, Mr Dreydon[1] is not tax't at all for money. Mr Sowgate paid me no more then forty seaven pounds, and for that told me he would take old money of you in the countrey, haveing an opportunity to dispose of it. I would have you pay the King's tax no further then your old money will go for I perceave you have but little of it. What we are to pay in new money we can stay till the time of payments come, which will be monethly, and every 3 moneths. If your old money be brass, the King's receivers will certainly not take [it]; that which is sterling they dare not refuse. Be sure you gett ridd of all before the time.

I will speak with the dean[2] about Paradise lease. It is locked up with my Northborough writings but I will be in the country before the time of renewing. Renewal every seven years would cost more for the seal than the fine, so we renew every 17 or 18 years. I am sure it is not so long since I renewed, which was after I bought Northborough estate. Agree with Mr Feary the carrier about 'my carriages'. I would give 6s a cwt as I always did from Lady Day to Martinmas; 7s in the winter; 8s a buck, 5s a doe; 8s each for servants going down in his wagon. I would be grateful if you got them cheaper. Mr Buckle failed to pay the remaining £25. I do not wish more bills charged on this 'very shuffling man'. [P.S.] Let the slaters employ only very good workmen to work with them. I hope your Deeping masons are 'teareing'[3] the partitions in the new stables, henhouses, etc.

[1] John Dryden of Chesterton, Huntingdonshire, son of Sir John Dryden and first cousin of the poet, M.P. for Huntingdonshire from 1690 until his death in 1707, apparently a friend of Fitzwilliam *VCH: Huntingdonshire*, ii. 34, and see **93**.

[2] Samuel Freeman, Dean of Peterborough 1691–1707: Longden, v. 129–31.

[3] Plastering.

## 15 FITZWILLIAM TO GUYBON

*London, 22 April 1697; F(M)C 991*

Francis Guybon . . . I cannot send downe my certificate to sattisfie the commissioners there. I have paid here till such time as the collectors gather up our moneys which I doubt heare they will do very speedily, in regard it's a business very tedious and long before it can be dispatcht but so soone as I have it I will send it downe. As to the £100 in old money I do not want to pay my tax for we can buy old money for 4s 10d or 11d what quantity we want but if you have £100 in old money more then you thinke you can putt off to pay my land taxes with in the countrey, for the whole yeare, I am ready to receave it if you will send it me up by the carrier next weeke. Lett the countrey beleive what they will, the King's receivers are bound to take all our old money that is sylver at 5s 8d per ounce for the taxes; lett it be little or broad it must all be melted downe and by weight it's all alike to the King. But if the £100 worth of money be Burmingham or brass do not send it up to me for I shall returne it back upon your hands. I have none by mee but what is in Mr Herriott's hands and so soone as yours comes it shall be sent to him . . . to see if it weighs 100 li or not at 5s 2d an ounce. Therefore pray weigh it before you send it and picke out all the false peices for Mr Heriott will pick them here. I will take care to see this done myselfe and you shall have no wrong done you for what ever ill peices there are they shall be laid by till the good money be weighed and then we will weigh the bad and so see if both together they make up the same quantity of ounces you send me word they weigh in the countrey. If you have more then one hundred pounds of this money I can putt it off to my tradesmen if it comes quickly, but what money you have now by you, pray send it mee up next weeke for I expect everyday when I shall pay my tax and you must agree with Feary for the carriage of it for Clarke made me pay very unreasonably for the £100 you sent me up last summer and I brought it backe againe when I came downe. Therefore without you can send it me up in a box with something else out of the countrey you had better agree with him for 10s the £100 which I thinke is enough.

(Hopes they have had London's good rains. Guybon to let Burmore Hurne at old rent rather than fail. Wishes slaters to secure roof to prevent rain spoiling new ceilings, and Old Tidd to be rebuked for using filling in cracks which the rain had washed away. The nursery staircase should be plastered but only after leaks above have been filled. Deeping masons must finish henhouses, then begin on the coachhouses and stables. Hopes Mrs Pendleton has dried herbs for his son William's eyes as in former years. Must be done before they are 'full blowne out in the flower'. John Webdale tells him Jackson has sold his farm to a Mr Kettleborough for £1,300. Guybon should have secured the purchase for Fitzwilliam at that price. Displeased that Mr Snow [Jackson's lawyer] would let it be sold to another when he had told Snow he would pay that price but sees 'what all the world is'.)

## 16 FITZWILLIAM TO GUYBON

*London, 6 May 1697: F(M)C 992*

Francis Guybon ... I am glad the tax is settled but you do not mention that they have tax't me for any money. If you have no more old money then one hundred pounds do not send it me up for you will want that or rather more to pay the whole yeare's tax with you and I can have here what I will and gett 7d or 8d an ounce by it. The £100 you mention will come to very little more then £60 for the £35 that I putt off came but to £22 at 5s 6d per ounce. I find you will not lett Burmore hurne but lett me loose the rent of it rather then the tennants' cattle you may lett it too should trespass upon Mrs Bull's grounds but if it cannot be lett soone I will order to take in joicers.[1] I am glad to heare Nanny Bull[2] is married. I wish her and her mother much joy. I heare barke is like to be a good commodity. They export a bundance of leather ready dresst that it sells very deare as I heare. I hope you will take the advantage of it as other men do. Pray lett me heare what prizes it gives with you and what you are offered. I want money and should be glad you could help me to some ...

[P.S.] Mr Buckle has paid me the remaining £25 on David LePlaw's bill.

[1] Cattle taken on agistment.

[2] 'Nanny' (probably Anne) Bull was married to a Mr Hunt and died after childbirth in 1698, see below 63.

## 17 FITZWILLIAM TO GUYBON

*London, 22 May 1697; F(M)C 994*

I have not seen or heard of Mr Newcomb whom you promise will pay £60 or £80. I thought I had left enough lime in the new stable to have finished the wing next 'the Great House', but see you have burned a 'kill'[1] this week and are to burn another next. Burn no more until I come down. Mr Brogden paid the £40 bills soon after May Day. I hope the Deeping masons have finished the hen house floors so they will be dry and usable when I come. I shall ask Mr Pidgeon if Lady Sylvius really intends to sell all or part of Maxey estate.[2] I have not yet paid my tax as I am to receive £150 in old money next Wednesday to pay with so cannot yet send you the certificate. Tradesmen must take the remainder at 5s 2d an oz.

Before I finish this letter I intend to speake with the collectors of our parrish and settle matters so with them if I can that you may pay it in the countrey for the whole yeare together in old money at 5s 8d an ounce. If so be you can send me up a certificate in due time to sattisfie the commissioners here I have paid there, that so, my owne neighbours may receave the benefitt the act of parliament allows. Since I writt the fore part of this letter I have agreed with the collectors and they will stay for my certificate from you till the middle of the next weeke after this that is comeing, till about the 3rd or 4th of June, so you may pay the whole yeare for £1000 which is £12 10s and send me up a certificate from the commissioners that I have paid it and your affidavitt must be writt at the bottome of the certificate as it was the last yeare before a justice of the peace for the liberty as Mr Noah Neale who is both a commissioner and justice who must sett to his hand that you made affidavitt before him. Lett it be drawne right as it should be and not force me to send for another.

[1] Kiln.

[2] Pidgeon was lawyer to Lady Sylvius, widow of Sir Gabriel Sylvius, and, with her sister Dorothy, owner of the manor of Maxey: see Introduction, p. xviii.

## 18 FITZWILLIAM TO GUYBON

*London, 10 June 1697; F(M)C 996*

Francis Guybon ... Your letter with the inclosed certificate I received last weeke ... I am ashamd to thinke that a man of your yeares and long experience should be so much imposd upon as you are not only in this business of the tax at present but in all other businesses to my great loss and cost. Mr Mathews the head collector and all others that acquainted you what you have writt to me are very dishonest to deale so by you and had you had but common foresight you might have contradicted them. I do tell you the act expressly saies the land and money at interest paies no more then 12 moneths to the yeare, but the capitation upon people's heads, servants' wages, and stocke upon land paies 13 moneths to the yeare. Lett them tell you what they will £1,000 paies no more then twelve pounds tenne shillings per annum, that is, twenty five shillings for every £100 by the yeare. I have not time to gett a certificate this post but I will send one ready filld up the next post therefore pray send on Munday morning for my letter or order Peter Rainsford to send it to you. It must be attested by 2 commissioners and you must make oath before one of them that is a justice of peace that you see them signe it. I have heard nothing of Mr Matthews about the money being weighed in the Exchequer. Mr Selby and Serjeant must give you a receit by itselfe that they have received of you so much money for a £1000 I have at interest which must be given the collectors here and they give it the commissioners to sattisfie them I have paid in the countrey. What else is taxt upon the famiely is nothing to the commissioners here for that ought to be taxt in the countrey but this £1000 I am taxt here and so must have a certificate I have paid there otherwise I must pay it here. I have here inclosed sent the certificate backe againe and Mr Mathews' note.

You inform me you have let Burmore hurne but not who to or for what rent.

## 19 FITZWILLIAM TO GUYBON

*London, 12 June 1697; F(M)C 997*

> I enclose two certificates which you must see signed by two commissioners, the second one being a justice of the peace, though you ride several miles to get it done, so that you can make affidavit that you saw the commissioners sign. I have considered it will be best to pay for the whole year at once (rather than in three instalments) which is only £12 10s for £1000, so you will not have to make three journeys to the commissioners. Although Mr Selby has only

paid in 4 months to the head collector he can take the rest and give you a receipt for the whole and pay the head collector at the due dates. This to save trouble.

Now I would know how they tax me at £7 13s 11d for I have advised upon the act of parliament with councell as likewise with gentlemen that are tax't for money and they assure me they pay no more then £12 10s for a £1000 for the whole yeare which is twentyfive shillings for £100. My capitation money for my head, my wife and children, together with the rest of the family I pay here and so must not pay in two places and for my stock I have none but the cart horses which they cannot vallew much. Deare in the parke are not to be taxt by the act, nor goods in a house, only stocke on ground and I have none ... I feare your imprudence has caused all this trouble. Therefore lett it be rectified and take two receipts from Mr Selby and Serjeant, that is one for £12 10s for a whole yeare's pay for the £1000 and another receipt for the rest of the family which you must keep by you and send me up that for the money ...

[P.S.] Mr Newcomb has yet paid no money. I wonder you should let me want so long after I wrote that my money was all gone.

## 20 FITZWILLIAM TO GUYBON
*London, 22 June 1697; F(M)C 998*

(Hopes he can pass certificate Guybon sent. Ashamed it is no better finished. Newcomb has not come to pay. Fears he is like Buckle who took five months to pay £50. Never needed money more. Guybon to go to apologise to Dean of Peterborough for Fitzwilliam's failure to renew Paradise lease, taking with him Pendleton, who, as a clergyman, could 'word it better with them'. Fitzwilliam had also sent his apologies by Mr Bleckington whom he met by chance at the house where 'my sonns board'. Since Pendleton had said slaters would soon have finished the roofs, they must finish the floor over the last new stable and the barn where timber was stored, and then the garrets overhead which are floored with plaster. Guybon must burn another kiln of lime if necessary.)

## 21 FITZWILLIAM TO GUYBON
*London, 26 June 1697; F(M)C 999*

My wife would have Mrs Bull buy at the fair what bowls are needed for kitchen and washhouse, and anything else we need. Whatever she cannot get we will buy here. Robert Newcomb has paid £20 and hopes to pay £20 next week. John Webdale's[1] drover paid me only £28 0s 8d. Morrice has gone, paying nothing and Mr Sowgate I cannot hear of. These small sums keep me from starving but will not pay my debts. Return money quickly for if I had it now I need not stay here another fortnight ...

[P.S.] I have writt this night to James Ullitt's mother that he is like to do very well; the 16th day is over.[2] He would not lett me write sooner for feare his mother should come up to him and neglect her business at home and could do him no good.

[1] Spelled both Webdale and Webdell by Guybon in Disbursements 790, but certainly the same man.
[2] Ullitt had smallpox. His mother, a widowed tenant, came to London anyway, see below **23, 25**.

## **22** FITZWILLIAM TO GUYBON

*London, 8 July 1697; F(M)C 1000*

I have received by Mr Kingston £29, but none from Mr Deacon's agent so I am again quite destitute of money unless you have ordered me any tomorrow market. Send me by Fearey's coach or wagon those guineas you intended to send by Mr Whinyates. With them I could come away a week earlier. My man sought Robert Newcomb's corn factor but his wife knew of no order her husband had to pay me money, and he only had exchequer bills which go under £7 or £8 per cent loss. Get back the money you paid beforehand for there is no likelihood of my getting money from his correspondent. I fear Mr Newcomb may be worsted dealing so much with the King whose debts are very ill paid and only in exchequer bills. If there are fat bucks send one next week by Fearey's coach. [P.S.] A Mr Cloathier, a surveyor here, is building a house in Lincolnshire and goes by Milton shortly. I wish him to spend a day there. Have Mr Pendleton show him the house and leads to see how to secure it from rain.

## **23** FITZWILLIAM TO GUYBON

*London, 22 July 1697; F(M)C 1002*

(Complains of lack of payments from Webdale and Newcomb. Guybon must recall money entrusted to Newcomb for Fitzwilliam would only get exchequer bills from his agents. If Guybon lacked exchequer notes to pay the King's taxes he would send some for 'we are forct to take them here for desperate debts'. Sir John Brownlow had 'pistolld himselfe being destracted[1] so his estate is now come to Robert Newcomb's master'.[2] His wife wishes Mrs Pendleton to pickle six pounds of walnuts. Hopes Ullitt and his mother got well home.)

[1] Sir John Brownlow of Belton, Lincolnshire, 3rd bart., M.P. for Grantham, shot himself at the house of his uncle, Thomas Freke, M.P. at Shroton, Dorsetshire, on 16 July 1697; *The Commons 1660–1690*, i. 736.
[2] Possibly an ironic reference to the king, a suicide's estate being usually forfeit to the Crown, although not on this occasion for his great wealth passed to his four daughters.

## **24** FITZWILLIAM TO GUYBON

*London, 27 July 1697; F(M)C 1003*

(Glad that everyone is so well except 'Cousin' Bellamy who they fear 'will never be a well woman more'. John Webdale's drover Broughton brought £38 9s 3d. If Newcomb had had money in town Fitzwilliam would have sent for it for 'people must be dunnd that are to pay money'. He stays only to pay his debts. The 'slaters' must buy enough plaster at Stamford Fair to do that last garret floor, hopefully at the old price of 4d a cwt. Glad the Ullitts got safely home.)

## 25 FITZWILLIAM TO GUYBON

*London, c. 3 August 1697; F(M)C 1004*

(Has received no money from Newcomb, as expected, and no venison arrived on the Peterborough coach, as ordered. Buck to be sent next week. His daughter wishes to know if Mrs Ullitt delivered Guybon her letter. Fitzwilliam asks after Ullitt; is his face 'tollerable'?)

## 26 FITZWILLIAM TO GUYBON

*London, 7 August 1697; F(M)C 1006*

I received your letter yesterday by Mr Fearey and 40 guineas, the sum you told him was enclosed in the sealed paper, but afraid of being robbed he left them in the country and paid the money here by way of return.[1] When I told him there were 50 in the paper he said he would pay the other 10 next week. I received yesterday £22 by John Webdale's drover William Broughton. Contrary to my expectations I have received by a Mr Warner's order £20 for Robert Newcomb. I perceive by the note that Warner, his corn factor, advances the money for him. I hope now to be speedily at Milton. The buck came sweet and good but not as cleanly killed as Thomas Freeman used to kill them. Send another next week, clean dressed, the shoulders fairly cut. [P.S.] Thank God we are all in good health.

[1] 1 Aug. 'Returned my lord by Mr Ferie, £55', Disbursements 790.

## 27 REV. JEREMIAH PENDLETON TO FITZWILLIAM

*Milton, 7 August 1697; F(M)C 1005*

(Has little to write, the slaters having worked a week at Etton, and then for Mrs Watts at the ferry. Gives details of the work remaining which will soon be done when they 'settle to work'. 80 cwt of plaster had come for the 'reeded' floor of the garret. The joiners would finish in a fortnight. Mrs Pendleton had found the walnuts too old to pickle. Asks Fitzwilliam to receive £40 on his behalf from his brother-in-law and to direct Guybon to repay it there. Mr Ballet,[1] his son-in-law and two gentlemen had called to see the house and gardens. They had dined at 'Mr Drayton's',[2] spent the night at Mr Checkly's, then on to Spalding. Asks for notice of Fitzwilliam's coming so that he and his wife can remove to other quarters. Guybon had fallen very ill for two days but is now 'indifferent well againe' but he wrote this without Guybon's order.)

[1] Almost certainly the armigerous lawyer Charles Ballett, late of Clements Inn, whose marble monument stands in the church of his ancestors at Strubby, Lincolnshire, although Fitzwilliam's acquaintance lived further south at Spalding. Fitzwilliam's Ballett and this Charles Ballett died in the last week of January 1704 so their identity can be assumed. W. J. Monson, *Lincolnshire Church Notes* (LRS, xxxi, 1936), p. 347.

[2] Probably the Mr 'Dreydon' (ie. John Dryden of Chesterton) referred to in **14** above.

## 28 FITZWILLIAM TO GUYBON

*London, 19 August 1697; F(M)C 1007*

I received the remaining 10 guineas and gave my receipt. The buck came also, a very good one, but had 'much adoe' to be sweet. The wagon does not bring it as well as the coach used to do. Consult with Mr Fearey that it may come up behind his coach as formerly and in the middle of the week. Sunday is not so convenient a day to feast on as a week day. Send a good buck next Monday or Tuesday, whichever day the coach leaves to be here next Wednesday. If it cannot come to be here the middle of the week be sure to let me have it on Saturday by the wagon, though it can hardly come sweet. Cut the shoulders fairly out. My wife hopes Mrs Bull has taken up her bees before this; if not, she desires it may be done out of hand and wishes Mrs Pendleton to pickle her some mushrooms, at least a peck. I shall be very glad when Mr Ash pays his money. I find Ballett will always be troublesome. I told him before he left town I did not design for Milton this summer because I would not be troubled with his company when he returned from Lincolnshire. Tell Mr Pendleton I hear nothing yet of the business he wrote about.

## 29 FITZWILLIAM TO GUYBON

*London, 26 August 1697; F(M)C 1008*

(Has heard nothing yet of Pendleton's £40.) I am glad to hear from him the garret floor is run with the Stamford plaster. What is left lay aside, together with a bushel of plaster ready burned in 'a great 2 eared baskett' in the granary over the wash house, for I will use it when I come down. Ash has paid nothing yet but John Webdale's drover, Goodman Broughton, has paid £75. I am sorry you have so unseasonable a harvest time, the weather here being tolerable, only a shower now and then. Keep the gutters swept clean or the rain will spoil the house. Do no 'ceileing' work on the great staircase in the new building until I come down. James Ullitt's nurse, they tell me, brought his greatcoat here about a fortnight since. Return money as you get it for my wife and daughter, being to be left here in town, will need it. The hen house floors must be left until I come for the experienced women here differ in opinion with yours in the country. It would be too long to write their several sentiments.

## 30 FITZWILLIAM TO GUYBON

*[London,] 2 September 1697; F(M)C 1009*

I enclose three warrants for the three forest walks in Lady Westmorland's[1] jurisdiction. Send the warrant which you think will be best served so that I may have a buck next week, and ask the keeper to shoot it so that it will come up better.[2] My daughter has been very ill of a fever caused by violent toothache but is a little better. I hear nothing of Pendleton's business, nor has Ash paid any money. [P.S.] Give one of the warrants between Cousin Harry Tryce,[3] his sister Bellamy, Mr Lowrey and Robert Newcomb; let them have a piece [of venison] each. I give half the other to you, the side or haunch to Pendleton and the other piece to Charles Duce.

[1] Referring to the Dowager Countess of Westmorland, Apethorpe Hall, Northamptonshire, mother of Vere Fane, 5th Earl of Westmorland (1679–98), a minor. Apethorpe Hall was about 10 miles from Milton. The forest walks were probably Sulehay, Morehay and either Morehay Lawn or a walk Fitzwilliam refers to as 'Cross-a-hand', all in Rockingham Forest.

[2] 10 September 'Gave Mr Brutnall his fee for a buck and his man's, 15s', Disbursements 790.

[3] Cousin to Lady Fitzwilliam and brother to Mrs Bellamy of Farcet.

## 31 FITZWILLIAM TO GUYBON

*London, 9 September 1697; F(M)C 1011*

(Encloses the other warrant [for the buck] which Guybon is to divide between Mr Whinyates, Mr Roger Pemberton and any two other 'of our friends' Guybon chooses. Has been ill but now much better. His daughter not yet perfectly well. Hopes they are having London's fine harvest weather.)

## 32 FITZWILLIAM TO GUYBON

*London, 16 September 1697; F(M)C 1012*

I have received £10 0s 5d from Mr John Mapletop's salesman, £19 paid by Mr Duce's order and £14 1s 10d by Mr Ash's order. I hear nothing of John Webdale's man. I shall be very glad if Mr Duce keeps his promise to pay me £60 or £80 this week or next but I fear he is unreliable.

I received a letter this weeke from Mrs Ullitt of Thorpe about her sonne James. Lett me know by your next how he is, if he be not much deformed, if his eye is not a great blemmish to him, for I would not have unsightly servants, and if he is not very much growen for if he be to tall he will not be fitt for a footman. His father was a very propper man. You may tell her I would have him stay with her till I go into the countrey or if it be not soone I will send for him up for I cannot be long without him or some body else. My wife would have you tell Mr Turner that if he has a mind to part with his sonne Joseph and will provide him with that linnen my wife told him last yeare was necessary for him to have he shall come up to her along with James Ullitt. He has linnen enough that was his wife's to do more then these small matters. He must have a surtout coate and some other cloathes to weare a mornings when he goes to schoole. Pray lett me have his answer soone ... [P.S.] I am glad to heare you are all in good health. Thanke God we are all very well againe.

## 33 FITZWILLIAM TO GUYBON

*[probably 23 September 1697]; F(M)C 1013*

William Crosen has paid £30 for Mr Duce. Write out all your accounts for me, and the rent rolls for Michaelmas and Michaelmas 1696 that I may set my rentals right. Let me know how forward Mr Wright and his joiners are in their work, and what the slaters have done and are doing. I will inform you when I receive Mr Pendleton's money so that you can repay him there. [P.S.] Let me know if the farmers got their white corn in before the rains, and if Mrs Bull and Mr Forster[1] got in theirs. I hope you keep the leads and gutters clean.

[1] A substantial tenant in Marholm, a village close to Milton and containing many of the Milton estate farms.

## 34 FITZWILLIAM TO GUYBON

*London, 30 September 1697; F(M)C 1014*

Francis Guybon, Yours of the 28th I received yesterday and by it perceave Mr Wright has [ha]de a long time to wainscoate 2 roomes. What would he do if there was a great deale more of it? I am glad to heare the slaterers have done all but the great staires in the middle of the building and the porter's lodge. I am not in hast of haveing them done, and those staires shall be the thing last finished. The clossetts in Mr Pendleton's old chamber that are fallen, pray lett the materialls be laid up dry. If I had been at home and knowne they had been so neare falling they should have been taken downe long since, and wonder you could not write me word of it. I knew not but Mr Pendleton might make use of the chamber and clossett in the daytime though he lay in the head house a nights.[1] If he goes not into the chamber pray lett the slates and the roofe be taken downe and the boards of the floore taken up and laied up dry, as likewise the wainscoate and all the other materialls that will take despaire in the weather. What plaister there is lett it all be pickt up cleane and laied into some dry place where it may be secured, as in the porter's lodge, or a corner of one of the coach houses. The boards you may carry up into the great granary and the wainscoate also. Pray lett the glass be taken downe and laied by carefully in the great roomes over the great parlour where the other glass lies, and if you think the gable ends, and the walls, will not stand they must be taken downe so low as is convenient, but not so low as people may gett over. If the stone windowes be taken downe, lett it be done with care that they may not be broken, and laied severally in parcells together that we may know how to sett them up together againe upon occasion.

I have received no money last week or this so am now in straits again. You mentioned John Webdale's drover should pay some. He is the surest paymaster but has paid none this month. I will send for James Ullitt soon, if I don't go down myself.

[P.S.] Lett the sparrs and joice of Mr Pendleton's building be laied together by themselves, and lett the boards of the old porter's lodge be taken up and laied up dry. The hearth of Mr Pendleton's old chamber chimney is right marble. Lett that be taken care of likewise. Mr Wright you sayes there wants but 3 chimney peices; but if he reckons the roome that I call the steward chamber there will be 4; and Mr Pendleton and he both sent me a measure of that likewise, but we could not very plainly understand them. I want the notes of the meaddow both for 1696 and '97. Pray lett your last yeare's accompts be writt out for if I go downe I shall stay but a short time. If I go not downe I shall send for them up soone. Mr Pendleton may make use of the nearest clossett to the nursery in the new building to putt his books in, and make a study of it, or any other place in the great house that he likes better for that purpose. I find by my wood bookes Mr Wright owes a considerable summe to me for timber both in Oxey Wood and other sales since. I do not remember when we reckoned with him that any summs were chargd upon him for wood. Pray pay not money to him over fast that we may have roome to sett that off with him.

[1] Pendleton's former quarters were in the old gatehouse of the manor, long since disappeared. On 9 December Guybon paid John Wilkinson £1 'for taking down the building at the gate', Disbursements 790.

## 35 FITZWILLIAM TO GUYBON

*London, 7 October 1697; F(M)C 1015*

I have received £31 from John Webdale by drover William Broughton. Charles Duce's agents have paid nothing yet. I sent to Duce's salesman, Horner, thinking he might have money 'as those sort of people usually make use of other men's money a weeke or a fortnight together' but he protested he had none and knew of nothing Duce had 'upon the road'. Do not depend on Duce or Newcomb for speedy returns. I am sure they will fail me. Send pigeons and partridges, though in this extraordinary rainy weather I fear nothing will be good. I received Pendleton's £40 for his use so repay him there in milled money or guineas for I received it here in extraordinary good money. Let him report how my new building does, and if it has rained in for in early summer he wrote that Old Tidd would undertake to cure all the 'lewcombs'.[1] Let me know if the drain keeps the cellar dry, and how the drying yard hedge grows. Mr Pendleton may use any of the closets or rooms in the new building nearest the nursery for his books. He may inform me how the great clock goes, and whether the kitchen chimney is cured of smoking.

[1] Lewcombe is a dialectal form of lucarne, a form of window, dormer or skylight. However, judging by a more explicit reference in **445** below, Fitzwilliam uses it to refer to the roofing of the seven two-storey oriel windows which project from the front of Milton (and perhaps the roof of the two storey projecting porch). The Tidds, father and son, were plasterers.

## 36 FITZWILLIAM TO GUYBON

*London, 14 October 1697; F(M)C 1016*

No letter this week but I expect one with the pigeons by the carrier on Saturday. Duce and Newcombe have paid me no money. Neither are to be relied on. 'Honest Mr Ash of Paston' paid me £18 18s by one Richard Ette, who also paid £10 on his own account which you are to pay him there. Take care I be supplied by reliable returns. Guineas are now fallen again to 21s 6d and it's believed they will fall to 21s, so I advise you receive none and put off what you have as fast as you can before it be known the price alters. I refused them myself at 22s although in need of money. I fear they will be carried into the country to impose upon the ignorant. I warn you, therefore, and whisper it into the tenants' ears that they may not be 'imposed upon' at Saturday market. I received Pendleton's £40 in guineas which I thought very good pay then and now am like to lose almost 20s by them.[1]

[1] For guineas see Introduction, p. xix–xxi.

## 37 FITZWILLIAM TO GUYBON

*London, 21 October 1697; F(M)C 1017*

I am sorry I cannot accommodate Mr Thompson for this is the worst time of the year for money with me, as you might have told them, knowing how I press you for money whenever I write. On the 18th I received £54 in good money by order of Mr Kingston and one Meares, but not a penny from your other two friends. With the rentals send also the Northborough estate rentals for 1696 and 1697, and any alterations between them and Lady Day 1696 and 1697.

I received Mr Pendleton's letter ... I perceave by it Mr Wright has ordered the roomes he has wainscoated to be painted which I am angry at. I suppose he did it that I should not see what sorry boards he used and what bottching worke he has made of it, which the paint will hide. The painter shall never be paid for it by me, nor for nothing he does, without my particular order. Nor would I have you pay Mr Wright any money in payment of it till I see it which will now be the spring of the yeare first, for I feare I shall find a sorry peice of worke of it, otherwise he would not have coulourd it over so soone but to hide faults. Pray lett Mr Turner know I received his letter and have not time to answer it now but you may lett him know my wife is willing to have little Joe if he will be at the charge of his carriage up and will buy him those other little necessaries, and then he may come up along with James Ullitt, but if he is unwilling to be at that charge I will write to Jame[s] Ullitt to come away next Thursday with the waggon. But if the little boy comes then he shall stay a weeke longer for him unless Mr Turner can buy his things so soone as they may both come next Thursday.

Send James Ullitt to go to the post next Monday morning to pick up a letter for you and another for him. I cannot write them now, the post just going.

## 38 FITZWILLIAM TO GUYBON

*London, 28 October 1697; F(M)C 1018*

Glad to hear you are all well, and have taken care to supply money.

I have received a particular here in towne of some closes my Lady Sylvius has a desire to sell me, lieing in Etton parrish (vizt) Tindalls[1] or Tinshaw pasture grounds conteineing as they say 68 acres and well wooded, together with one acre of arrable land lieing over against the gate or way that leads to the said pasture. One other close calld Norborough Hills in the same parrish, well wooded, conteining as they say 45 acres. Pray take some understanding countrey man with you and ride over the grounds and observe what sort of land it is and what it will rent, for a holding rent. Francis Freeman lives just upon those closes and knows every inch of them and what sort of stocke they will beare and what they are worth to a very small matter to hold the rent. Pray send me an exact account as soone as you can, both what rent each ground will give and how many acres each ground conteines. I take them to be much such sort of cold spewy ground as Francis Freeman hires of Mr Phillips that we used to ride thorough to Etton. They offerre me likewise 7 acres of meadow in Bainton meddow lett to James Horwood at £5 per annum and three acres in the same meaddow lett to Thomas Beaver for £1 15s per annum. You may inquire if this meadow is lett at this rent here mentioned and will hold that rent or what it is really lett for, and if these acres lie in a good place or bad place in the meadow, that is whither it be in a high part of the meadow or the very sincke of it where the water lies a great while on it, for there is a great deale of difference in the lieing of meddow. I will not buy this meddow if I can help it, because I have nothing else there, unless it lies convenient for my Maxey farme but it may fall out they will not sell me one without I buy the other and therefore lett me know the worth of it to a tittle, and if you can, lett me know all this next weeke for they will expect my answer soone. Tindalls they tell me was lett for 3 lives to one Alice Townesend and two of the lives are dead. Inquire of this also and how much cheife rent they pay for this Tindalls to the lord of Maxey and how old that person is whose life is still in being. It may be there is 2 lives in being; it's good to know all.

My wife will not have the honey come up yet. Ask Thomas Freeman if the does are fat and ready to be sent for, and how many he can spare me this season.

[1] An earlier name for Clapham's manor.

## 39 FITZWILLIAM TO GUYBON
*London, 4 November 1697; F(M)C 1019*

The two boys came well to town last Saturday. By William Ash's order I received £32 9s, and from Mr Miller £43 16s 4d. Return me money weekly, 'it runns away apace'. Tell Mr Turner I received his letter and will speak to Sir Robert Cotton, but he must provide very good security, 'for ordinary security will not pass for such an imployment'.[1] I enclose warrants for forest does but don't know whether they are good enough to kill. Tell Thomas Freeman to kill a very good doe from my park and send it clean dressed next week in a flag basket[2] and don't let the carrier know what it is. I would have you send a doe each week as long as they last in season. I received the accounts from James [Ullitt] but have no wood books for the last two winters. Let them be writ out. Mr Turner writes that Mr Wells is in prison and Hinton 'in a declineing condition'. I hope you have received the rent for the fishing. I only received two guineas for one year's rent due four or more years ago. Mr John Mapletopp, Mr Wells and the Registrar[3] all promised to pay their parts so call for that rent.

[1] A postmastership at Peterborough.
[2] A basket woven from rushes or 'flags'.
[3] Mr Maidwell, see below **54**.

## 40 FITZWILLIAM TO GUYBON
*London, 11 November 1697; F(M)C 1020*

The partridges were all old. You let Mr Leafield and Captain Styles poach so about my lands that I cannot have a young partridge for my own eating; and Claypoole, when he is sent for, will not lose his labour, but catches the old ones and so the breed will be destroyed. The doe was good, as sweet as ever I had. Send another next week. Let Freeman 'shoote it dead at first'.[1] I am glad to have so particular an account of the estate I enquired after. I wish we could learn where in town this Alice Townesend, or Warwicke lives. Surely John Blackborne or one of the Bells could tell us who collects their rent, and he would know where she is. So long as Mr Forster of Marholm has such good crops and corn sells so dear I think the land well worth the rent he pays, but if he paid my arrears I would be the more kind to him for 'that money in my pockett would bring me in something to make me amends for abateing the rent'. Some wood for fencing I might be induced to give him. Ensure he new thatches his barn and out buildings and keeps all in repair. You may 'run that floore' now if you can buy plaster, but use it speedily, don't let it rot in the rain.[2]

Pray tell Mr Turner I received his letters and went purposely to the post office and spoke to Sir Robert Cotton about him but it seemes he is ingaged if Hinton goes off. For Mr Wortley[3] wrote a letter to him sixe weekes since which he shew me in behalfe of young Edward Tinkerson and he is promist it if the other goes off. Butt Hinton has wrote to him that his unckle Wells whome he trusted in the mannagement of it has not done his part as he should have done by him, and that from henceforward he is resolved to take care of all things himselfe, his unckle being now in prison. So for the present Hinton is like to be postmaster. The little boy Joe Turner yesterday and this day is much troubled with the gripes and saies he used to have them at home. I would know what they used to give him that did him most good. It may be it's the change of aire and drincke may be the reason of it at first and for want of goeing abroad. He shall want for nothing.

Guineas are 'in better reputation', about £1 1s 10d, but will certainly fall to £1 1s 6d after Christmas so do not take them.

[1] Killed instantly rather than allowed to run wounded, since Fitzwilliam believed flesh heated by exertion would taint sooner.

[2] Guybon paid John Christopher £1 4s for 64 cwt of plaster at 4½d a cwt.

[3] Hon. Sidney Wortley Montagu of Hinchingbrooke, Huntingdonshire, and Wortley, Yorkshire (1650–1727) the second son of Edward Montagu, first Earl of Sandwich; *The Commons 1660–1690* , iii 759–60; *The Commons 1715–1754*, ii. 557

## 41 FITZWILLIAM TO GUYBON

*London, 18 November 1697; F(M)C 1021*

The doe came sweet, but not as good as the last. Send a very good doe next week. Only send partridges if they are young. My wife loves woodcocks beyond anything and we never have any sent up, nor snipe. The people of Peterborough would be glad to have all my game to themselves, but I think it's fitter for myself than them so let me have it. Let those who poach in my royalties be punished according to the late act of parliament, Captain Styles, Mr Leafield or any other.[1] They have often been warned and I never gave them leave. John Webdale called, gave me an account of Tindall's [estate] but left no money.

Richard Ettee has paid £30, but nothing has come from Morrice. Call on the tenants for money and return as fast as you can.

[1] Fitzwilliam probably refers to the act of 1697 (8 and 9 William III, c. 11) which provided that the plaintiff might not only recover damages but also costs of suit if the trespass was 'wilfull and malicious'; P. B. Munsche, *Gentlemen and Poachers: the English Game Laws 1671–1831* (Cambridge, 1981), p. 185.

## **42** FITZWILLIAM TO GUYBON

*London, 25 November 1697; F(M)C 1022*

Send up another doe next Monday. Order Freeman to very fairly shoot and dress a prime good one for it is to be given to particular friends. If you have caught no partridges buy from Fearey or any of those people. Buy four partridges, three woodcocks, four snipe, four duck and mallard, four teal and two dozen larks—or three or four dozen if they will keep well—otherwise I will buy larks here at 12d a dozen. If Robert Holmes has shot you some pheasants send them up, but do not buy any. I am again in great need of money. The £20 the Stamford hogman is to pay will only go a little way, and I do not depend on Charles Duce's £60 next week for it may not be paid for a month or six weeks. If you have bought the plaster for Chisseldine's [farm] let it be run with all speed but let nobody walk on the floor for two weeks for it must be seasoned. I am dissatisfied with the rent set down for Chisseldine's. I am confident I let him it for 40s more than Mr Exton paid, and 20s a year for a court dinner, so give him no receipts in full for his rent. John Webdale will speak to Mr Lawson at Bourne who will inform you where Mrs Warwicke lives in town.

I am extreame glad to heare Joseph Bull[1] is so well married. Pray God send she may prove so good a fortune as you mention, but I never heard Benjamin Johnson died halfe so rich a man as you mention. I understand old Mr Standish of Peterborough[2] is dead. Etton liveing I intend for Mr Pendleton but till matters can be settled you must order the church wardens to take care the liveing be supplied every Sunday with sermon and praiers and Goodman Chamberlaine[3] the tennant must pay tenne shillings a Sunday which must be allowed him in his rent by the next incumbent. I will have sermon and praiers every Sunday morning and praiers after dinner. You may lett Goodman Chamberlaine know I would have him go on in manageing the tyeth and gleab as he did for one yeare longer, for whoever has the liveing cannot mannage it themselves so soone. I will take care he shall not sufferre by goeing on with the farme for one yeare . . .

[P.S.] I understand the new great clock at Milton does not go well. Take care Watts puts it right rather than waiting until I come. The clock has been made six years, and set up four and might go well in that time.

[1] Son of Mrs Bull, the Fitzwilliams' friend and tenant at Marholm.

[2] Francis Standish (1627–97), minor canon of Peterborough, rector of Etton 1656–97, of which Fitzwilliam held the advowson; member of a family which provided clergy for the Peterborough diocese over several generations: Longden, xiii. 37–8.

[3] George Chamberlaine, see **49**.

## 43 FITZWILLIAM TO GUYBON

*London, 2 December 1697; F(M)C 1023*

The doe I received was very good, but very badly killed and had it not been frosty would not have come up sweet. Send another next week, but since you have not sent the fowl I ordered do not send them next week. I shall not need them. I have received £20 from a Thomas George by William Sheate's order. Take order Etton living is supplied on Sundays as in Mr Standish's time until I can present Mr Pendleton it, unless Pendleton can supply both Marholm and Etton himself. I should be glad to save him that money. The ministers supplying Etton should be allowed the rate Mr Standish allowed. How many good does may I have out of my park?

## 44 FITZWILLIAM TO GUYBON

*London, 9 December 1697; F(M)C 1024*

Acknowledges receipt of doe. Warrants for forest deer to be distributed one between Henry Tryce and Mr Lowrey; one half between Charles Duce and Robert Newcomb, and Cousin Bellamy the other; the third between Guybon and Pendleton. If Mr Wortley of 'Walcott'[1] needs our assistance for Peterborough election ask all 'our freinds' to support him. Keep all gutters clean at Milton for a terrible thaw has followed a great snow. Tell Mrs Bull Roger Pemberton has shown me two copies and surrenders of [her daughter] Nanne's husband and his brothers in 'Awkenberry Westonburt'[2] which I think 'fully worded' and 'safely done'. Neither Duce nor Wright have paid anything so I am in 'great streights'.

[1] Walcot Hall in Barnack was acquired by Wortley Montagu from Sir Hugh Cholmondeley who had built it in 1671. Montagu sold it to John Noel about 1703.

[2] Alconbury Weston, Huntingdonshire.

## 45 FITZWILLIAM TO GUYBON

*London, 16 December 1697; F(M)C 1025*

Has received £31 15s by John Horner 'the salesman' for Thomas Wright; £50 of Rowland Morrice, the 'hoggman', for Duce, and £20 on 'his own account'. These so long delayed that he was in debt so hopes Guybon will supply him in good time in future. Needs wood books to correct his own copies: Oxey Wood, second sale 1693; Belham Wood first sale 1693, 1694. Has Belham Wood second sale, and all woods sold since, except Simonds Wood second sale last winter. Guybon must give to the 'townes' as formerly at Christmas.[1] It's reported the northern post boy was drowned. Hopes not true but letters due previous Monday were not there.

[1] On 27 December Guybon recorded he had paid 6d each to 40 poor of Castor, to 12 of Ailsworth, 32 of Helpston, 6 of Etton and 1 of Northborough. He made similar payments each Christmas, Disbursements 790.

## 46 FITZWILLIAM TO GUYBON

*London, 6 January 1697/8; F(M)C 1026*

Received yours with the wood book mentioning I was to receive money from Duce three weeks since, but I hear nothing of it. I wonder you trust to a man that never keeps his promise and refuse other proffered returns, the money for which lies dead here.

I was told last Sunday by a drover of Eye (that knew me not) that Mr Mappletop proffered you £100 here in towne that lies in the salesman's hand and you would not accept of it. And the drover had a great drove of sheep of Mr Exton's and Mr Panck's that he wanted a returne for. You cannot but thinke I am in great want of money, not haveing received any from you but that money Rowland Morrice paid about a moneth since, and I was indebted at least halfe of that before I received it. Therefore, you may judge how much I may owe now. You must take better care of me then to returne moneys by these uncertaine paymasters. For Mr Bell's oates, it's well if he be paid for them by Easter, therefore trust not to that. I know how all the corne factors pay, wittness the £50 Mr Wright was to pay me by a bill from David LePlaw last spring, that I waited at least 5 moneths for. There is no returnes so certaine as by the beast and sheep droves that I receave certainly in a weeke's time after promise, at least most may be exactly at the time. Therefore, pray trust to no other, for you may have them if you please, and pray lett me have that £100 of Mr Mappletop's which I am confident is yett to be had being in George Mawre's hand as salesman. Thomas Freeman must sell his wooll. I cannot spare my rent any longer. I thinke he was very well offered; 24s 6d was a good price for wooll this yeare. He sold but 25s last [year], and I heare by all the countrey men ... they could not sell their wooll this yeare but at 1s the todd[1] less then they had last yeare, and why should he thinke himselfe wiser then all the countreys round besides? So pray spirr him on to sell for I must have my money. I am sorry to heare the floods have done so much harme.

Keep Milton leads and gutters clean. God send you a merry new year. My wife has been very ill but much better now. [P.S.] White Hall is all burned down except the 'banquetting house' and some inconsiderable buildings.[2] Did Pendleton receive my last letter about six weeks ago which largely answered his?

[1] Tod: a weight of wool, usually 28 pounds but varying locally.

[2] Designed by Inigo Jones for James I and decorated by Rubens for his successor, the Banquetting Hall survives today.

## 47 FITZWILLIAM TO GUYBON

*London, 13 January 1697/8; F(M)C 1027*

Yesterday I received Mrs Bull's kind present to my wife of a chine and puddings. We are sorry to hear of Mrs Hunt's[1] illness. Milton air always recovered her and I believe would again if we were in the country to entertain her. Sorry also to hear of Joseph Chamberlaine's wife but hope they will both do well again. Duce has paid nothing. Henry Hankin paid £35 18s 5d for Brecknock.

Pickering's £50 is uncertain. Mr St John said he might need £50 in the country, and would pay me if he did.

Mr Wortley told me Peter Rainsford and his two sonns would not give him their voices at the next election. Pray tell Peter I shall take it very ill from him if they all three do not give their voices for him. He has taken care to gett between £300 and £400 out of the Exchequer to pay all the arreares due to the inns and alehouses for soldiers being quartered at Peterborough which will be sent downe forthwith, and Peter shall be sure to be paid as soone [as] anyone. I would have you see amung my owne tennants or else at Etton or Warmington if there be ever a horse that is fitt to make me a good coach horse for I want one. He must be fifteene hands and an inch high and a blaze of white in his face and take care he has good feet and limbs. I care not how leane he is in flesh, I shall soone raise him with my keeping. I know horses are very cheap at this time which makes me send that you may see out for one or two for mee but I would not have you buy till you send me word what sizes and what sort of horses you can have and the lowest prizes and the ages of the horses.

Return me what money you can and hasten the tenants to pay their rents.

[1] Mrs Bull's married daughter.

## 48 FITZWILLIAM TO GUYBON

*London, 27 January 1697/8; F(M)C 1028*

Mr St John ordered £50 to be paid to Heriot whose note I suppose you received and paid Pickering. I received £19 from Morrice, £10 of it for Joseph Chamberlaine's hogs, the rest by return. Mrs Bull's horse is too small to match mine. I must have blazes in their faces, so must stay till Oundle fair. All well save my wife has had a sore leg for a month or more which still pains her greatly.

## 49 FITZWILLIAM TO GUYBON

*London, 3 February 1697/8; F(M)C 1029*

Mr Miller came but told me he could not pay the £200 before Friday week. I perceive he has paid others but I must be last.

It is now almost time for me to thinke of disposeing Etton liveing but before I do it I would know how much the liveing is lett for to George Chamberlaine or his sonne. I would have you both aske them and one of Mr Standish's sonns likewise, for Chamberlaine may say less then it is purposely to abate the rent but Standish will tell the truth. Then I would have you advise and consider (when you know certainely what it is lett for) how much the liveing is worth to one who lives upon the spott and mannages it as a farmer does his farme and as Mr Standish did when he lived at Etton before he removed to Peterburgh. Then lett me know in what condition the house is in at the parsonage, the barnes etc, and what it may cost to putt them in a condition for a minister to live comfortably in it. I desire to be sattisfied of these particulars very exactly and that you would write me your answer next Tuesday's post at furthest, for next Satturday at markett or Sunday or Munday at Etton you may learne all that I here require of you . . .

## 50 FITZWILLIAM TO GUYBON

*London, 17 February 1697/8; F(M)C 1030*

> I would have written last week but my wife has been so extremely ill we feared for her. She is something better. I received the four pheasants last week and three this by the carrier with the very good chine of pork for which I kindly thank you.[1] Miller paid £182 1s 9d and a note for the rest from selling some hogs. Miller's brother Mr Newcomb could leave me no money.

As to the hedge in Ladyleas I know it wants plashing but I am not willing it should be done unless Thomas Freeman and Bates both laied their Ladyleas to mow for it utterly destroyes quick to have it cropt by sheep and I know Thomas Freeman is not to be trusted. He will promise faire but never performe. I remember how he served mee when I plasht the hedge in the cowclose next to Ladylees. If I durst trust him, and Goodman Bates will but promise to lay his ground, I would have you plash halfe that hedge this yeare and the other halfe another yeare, for all the hedge together will fill the yard too full with faggotts that they will lie and rott before we have occasion to use them. Therefore I would have but halfe plasht at a time, and pray imploy some of the Thorpe men to do it who are the best plashers in our parts, and that hedge lies neare them, but I feare the season is too farr advanc't to do it this yeare. As to my fishing Robert Newcomb spoke to me for it but I had rather Mr St John had it. Agree with Mr Pickering to give me tenne pykes, well feed, every yeare for it, that shall not be less then twenty five inches long, and I will send for them as I have occasion to spend them. If I have them not all one yeare he shall make them up the next so that I expect 30 pykes for the terme of three yeares, and upon those termes Mr St John shall have it before any one else. If you agree with Mr Pickering for it, have some writeing or a short agreement made for it. But before you make a noise of letting it, gett my rent that is due to me from Hinton and his partners and lett them know nothing of your letting it from them till you have gott all your money. I received a letter from Mr Forster of Marrham wherein he acquaints me of his haveing laied his compass on my land and that you promised to allow him for it if he went off and that he agreed with you for £45 per annum for the farme, I suppose for show sake because he ownes it was just before the tax was laied. I have not yett answered his letter but intend very speedily to do it, but if he is urgent to know my mind from you, you may tell him that so long as he plowes my land you beleive I expect the same rent he has all along paid from the beginning, but so soone as he leaves off plowing I shall make a considerable abatement . . . [P.S.] Mr Roger Pemberton shew me a coppy of Benjamin Johnson will. I do not like it much. Mr Whinyates has made mistakes. You must give Charles Duce good words to make the matter easie to Jo[seph] Bull, else if he should be vexatious, the young woman will not prove so good a fortune.

[1] Guybon paid a Thomas Southwell 10s for catching 30 partridges and 4s for two brace of pheasants on 7 February, Disbursements 790.

## 51 FITZWILLIAM TO GUYBON

*London, 3 March 1697/8; F(M)C 1031*

> I am very sorry to hear of Mr Pendleton's illness. I hope he is much better. Let me hear how he is. I have received no money since the £48 by Mr Miller's order.

... be earnest with the tennants for their rents. I am sure they never had better prizes for everything. All sorts of graine is very deare, beefe at 4d per pound, mutton at 4½d and 5d a pound, and veale at 6d and better. All sorts of woollen commodities are very deare, and in conclusion everything that comes out of the countrey. We are like to have a tax of 3s in the pound upon land this year, to be assessed by our owne commissioners, as formerly, and not by the King's as last yeare. As to Maxey I know nothing of it. Mr Boreman[1] makes no inquiry into it upon my account. I would have bought Tyndale's and those lands of them that lie in Etton parrish, but my Lady Sylvius's mind is now altered and she will not sell: this they told me. It may be Mr Boreman has yett a better chapman for all together. Pray learne the truth of it out, if possible, for I have a mind to the whole if it must be sold, but my lady's councell tell me otherwaies. ... [P.S.] My wife is very ill still, though thanke God much better then she was. My daughter remembers herselfe very kindly to you.

[1] Subsequently referred to by Fitzwilliam as Burman.

## 52 FITZWILLIAM TO GUYBON

*London, 24 March 1697/8; F(M)C 1033*

> My not being well prevented my answering your letters. Horner paid me £51 11s 2d for Mr Wright on the 15th, but I have received nothing since. I have no money to lend Mr Hunt[1] for this is a very expensive year. I owe money before I receive it but I will not be in debt on any account. Let the Meadow Close and the Old Park, but let them both be fed or not [let] at all. I had as good mow them myself as let another do it and the hay will serve my deer and stables. Inform me who wants them and what they offer, but clear the grounds of stock until you have my answer. I shall be glad to see Captain Selby and John Webdale. Lady Sylvius' counsel says Maxey will not be sold, not even the land they offered me last summer. Let me know the price of bark this year, and who you think to sell to.

[1] Probably Mrs Bull's son-in-law.

## 53 FITZWILLIAM TO GUYBON

*London, 31 March 1698; F(M)C 1034*

> (Selby had paid Thomas Manton's £31 4s 1d. Fitzwilliam had agreed to take £30 8s from Rowland Morrice for Guybon to repay at Milton. Wright's and Miller's money would be welcome for this was the season new clothes were bought. Complains that Guybon has not said what is due from Hinton and his partners who he hears are destroying all the fish in the river. Would prefer St John [as tenant] if he would give so many pikes yearly for rent. The others had

sent fish to Milton when he was there and he and his family had always had liberty to fish with 'cast netts, angles and troleing lines', a liberty he would 'never be debarred from'. Guybon to report what Pickering, St John's steward, said and he would decide whether to let the old tenants continue. Sorry Mr Ireland the tanner was dead who was the most substantial buyer of his bark. Guybon must enquire the 'condition' of other tanners, and if dissatisfied, seek security, for bark brought considerable sums which were only paid months later, or half down and the rest on trust. If Mr Bellamy of Fletton stood surety he would be less fearful. Guybon must ask the 'noblemen's bailiffs' how bark would sell this year.) You may let Joseph Chamberlaine the Old Park, but Thomas Freeman only takes Meadow Close to feed Brookfield which he has ploughed 'out of hart', and then late in the year will 'teare' it all up with horses. If he will feed it and undertake to put no horses on it after Christmas he could have it before anyone at £28 and 5s to buy my wife a couple of geese. He must undertake to spend all the hay he mows on the Meadow Close on that ground, and leave fences, gates and stiles in repair. If Mrs Bull is sure that hemp and flax was 'well got' last year my wife wishes her to buy at Stamford Midlent Fair enough linen cloth to make 10 pairs of such sheets as are on your and Mr Pendleton's beds, and ten pair of coarser sheets as lie upon the ordinary servants' beds, as grooms, maids, etc, unless linen is extraordinarily dear. Tell the Pendletons about gathering the herb for my son William: it must be got very dry, before the flower appears, as near full moon as possible, but rather than have it gathered near full moon if the bud or flower be blown my wife would rather have it near the new moon with the bud unblown. If the flower is out pick it early next week if the weather is dry. If not my wife would not have it gathered until one, two or three days before full moon. Read this to the Pendletons carefully. We are glad he is pretty well again. Thank you for the pheasants.

## 54 FITZWILLIAM TO GUYBON

*London, 7 April 1698; F(M)C 1035*

Today Nicholas Phillips brought £47 12s for Mr Miller of Thorney. If Mr Wright's salesman is John Horner, a Quaker, his money will not be paid for some time. He will not return from Newmarket this week, if next. If Mr St John will not pay for the fishing the rent you asked I had rather Robert Newcomb had it, for he asked for it first. Know Pickering's mind quickly. I am glad the barkmen, the brothers Andrews, are so substantial.[1] Let Thomas Freeman have the Meadow Close (on the terms set down before) with no horses on it during the last 3 months. Secure my [fishing] rent from Hinton. I don't know why you did not demand it half yearly as my other tenants. He took it with Mr Mappletop and the Registrar Mr Maidwell, and told me Mr Bell would be a fourth. I care not who the partners were if Hinton pays the rent. If not I shall look to them for it.

[1] The brothers Andrew and Ireland may have been partners for Guybon had received £21 from 'Mr Ireland, Thomas Andrew and Charles Andrew for 3 score and 12 yards of bark ... out of Brakes Wood and the first sale of Simonds', Milton Receipts 1693–1700, F(M) Misc. Vols. 73.

## 55 FITZWILLIAM TO GUYBON

*London, 14 April 1698; F(M)C 1036*

Horner, Wright's salesman, paid £115 for him. I am sorry Mr Pendleton does not come this week. Next week is so near the 'Holydaies' I fear most officers through whose hands his business must go (if not the bishops themselves) may be going out of town for a week to make merry so he will be kept longer in town.[1]

[1] A reference to Pendleton's admission to Etton rectory.

## 56 FITZWILLIAM TO GUYBON

*London, 21 April 1698; F(M)C 1037*

Mr Pendleton arrived well, but we will keep him longer than Mrs Pendleton would have him stay, because of a qualification I hoped he would bring with him, and because many of the noblemen are out of town and he must stay their return. I have received £15 6s 5d from Henry Hankin, salesman, for Mr Brecknock, so am able to pay all my debts. I am sorry Widow Ullitt's barn is damaged by flood. I hope the roof stands though the mud be washed from the studwork. You had best repair that wall with stone. I hope to be there soon to decide what is fitting, but meantime, when the ways are passable have the widow's teams carry stone to the work.

As to the 2 brother Prestons' houses in Norborough there has been so much money laied out upon them within these few yeares that I will have nothing more done at them till I see them. They never keep them with thacking as other tennant do, that the raines rott both my timber and walls. Where I find tennants do their parts it does not trouble me to do for such men, but they that expect all from their landlords I care not how few such men I have live upon my holds. I will build nothing at Goodluck's house. If he will marry his children so young he had need keep them at home with him to looke after them.[1] I meane Thomas Freeman: would any body but he thinke of marrieing a boy of 19 or 20 yeares of age? Lett me know by the next post how many coles your warehouse at the ferry will hold more then what is now in it, that I may write to Beales to buy them for mee before the act passes that laies the imposition of 5s per chalder upon them.

You do not write whether Mr St John will take the fishing nor reply to my complaint that you did not call for Hinton's rent with the rest of the tenants. Mind my letters and let me have an answer to every particular henceforward.

[1] Fitzwilliam declines to build a house on the Goodlucks land for Thomas Freeman's recently married son to inhabit.

## 57 FITZWILLIAM TO GUYBON

*London, 28 April 1698; F(M)C 1038*

Prop up the Widow Ullitt's barn roof to prevent it settling for I think to build the walls up to the same roof but do no repairs until I come down in a fortnight's time. If you have as much rain there as we have here there will be no carting stone to Etton or Northborough, unless half loads which is not in my interest.

I will decide the fishing [lease] when I come. I had intended coming this week but was hindered by Pendleton's business, which 'runs more cross' than we expected. I am sorry to hear of William Carter's death, and not glad to hear of John Freeman's marriage. I think it's too soon by six or seven years but 'its fitt everyone should do what they thinke and like best on.' Pendleton is very well, has received a £20 bill from Duce but not yet the money. He wishes you to get Gascoigne or anybody to preach for him at Marholm next Sunday. [P.S.] Pendleton says the ceilings and wainscoting in the new building 'tooke despaire'. Order Willis to glaze that wing with all speed next week.

## 58 FITZWILLIAM TO GUYBON

*London, 26 May 1698; F(M)C 1039*

(Hopes Pendleton got well home, and has been inducted at Etton. Fitzwilliam's homecoming has been delayed but not for long.) Begin necessary repairs when weather is fitting, but there will be no carting in that 'deep countrey' unless I suffer from small loads, so only do what is absolutely necessary. Ash paid Heriot £50 but the (messenger) did not know whose account it was for. Ash must sign the back of the note and I will order it placed to my account.

I much wonder the countrey commissioners (or at least some of them who have often occasions of comeing to towne) will not consult with the commissioners in these parts to learne what methods they take, when an act of parliament is not rightly word[ed]; for the Parliament never intended to raise above 3s in the pounds as lands were lett in that yeare of 1694 if I am not mistaken, or '93. The commissioners hereabouts charge every towneship and parrish with the same summe as was laid upon it in that yeare and then abate just a 4th part of it. This is the reall way they proceed by here, for I talke both with the commissioners and assessors of the parish where I live, which is St Giles's in the Feilds, where is to be raised £10,000 and some odd hundred pounds for this tax. If our commissioners do not take the same method they will bring a very great charge upon the countrey that will never be gott off againe for the court will certainely make a precedent of it and expect the same for the future, and it's a very hard case that the citty of Peterborough should have two such Parliament men as have no estates neare us and care not how the taxes fall upon us: for if their concernes were amungst us they would for their owne sakes send downe directions how they ought to act in the countrey. If the commissioners will tax me for £1,000 personall estate as formerly you may lett me be tax't; if more, I will be tax't here. ... [P.S.] There are so few printed certificates this yeare I could not gett one right to my mind, so I borrowed an old one from one of the officers of St Giles parish and writt it out and left blancks for the commissioners to fill up. You may have it writt over handsomer if this is not likt. You must take care the justice of the peace before whome you make oath be not one of those commissioners that signs this certificate. Lett this be dispatcht as soone as possibly and sent up that I may have it ready to produce so soone as I am call[ed] on least I be forct to pay in both places. And you had best pay for the whole yeare together that I be not troubled to have more of the certificates. I shall want more money soone.

## 59 FITZWILLIAM TO GUYBON

*London, 28 May 1698; F(M)C 1040*

Francis Guybon, Since I writt my last to you on Thursday the collectors for the taxes came to mee yesterday and told me unless I paid here for my personall estate since I had lived 3 yeares amungst them they would returne me into the Exchequer. So finding they had assess't me moderately I paid them and so will send a certificate downe very speedily to sattisfie the commissioners in the countrey I have paid here. I thought fitt to give you this timely notice that you may proceed no further with that certificate I sent downe inclosed in your letter on Thursday last, for I will not be assess't and pay in both places. We are all extreamely concerned to heare by Mrs Pendleton's letter of Mrs Hunt's condition, but while there is life, there's hope. So we hope for the best, but my wife is sorry she is not in the countrey for she fancies she knows of something that would save her ... [P.S.] I did not thinke the commissioners and the rest had been so forward about their taxes, for they never were with me but once about them so I could not avoid paying here without I had a certificate ready to produce.

## 60 FITZWILLIAM TO GUYBON

*London, 31 May 1698; F(M)C 1041*

Francis Guybon, Mr St John was with me this morneing, desireing a returne for fifty pounds. Pray acquaint Mr Pickering he may have it, and pay it him when he demands it. Mr St John told me of another sturgeon that was taken in the river lately in my part of the river. Lett me know in what part of the river it was taken in and how it came to pass that Mr St John had it carried home to his house without your knowledge or consent, not that the thing is so valewable, but I must not loose my royalty, for the deane and chapter hereafter will pretend a claime to these royall fish. We very much long to receave a letter from you about Mrs Hunt to know whither she be dead or alive, which if you nor no body else has writt already about it, pray lett us heare by the very next post. If she be dead you must lett us know when she died, and when and where she is buried; if she be alive, how she is and if there be hopes of her. We suppose she lies in at her mother's at Marrham. I hope Mr Pendleton is inducted into his liveing before this....

[P.S.] Hope you received my letter intimating I had been forced to pay for my personal estate here and forbidding you paying it there.

## 61 FITZWILLIAM TO GUYBON

*London, 10 June 1698; F(M)C 1042*

Received Ash's note for £60 signed on the back. What was the price and carriage of the 10 chalder of coals sent by Mr Beales? Where was the sturgeon caught by Tobie? Was it got in that cut from Castor Mill to the main river or the river itself? Ride to the mill, taking with you one of the fellows that helped kill it, and see the very place. I have a reason for this but don't let them know anything but that it is only your curiosity to see the place and the manner how they killed it.

We are extreamely concerned here for Mrs Hunt's illness. If Mrs Bull will write my wife ... a true account of her condition, what advise can be had here in towne shall immediately be gott, and what things shall be prescribed shall forthwith be sent downe if they are to be had for money. We hope Mrs Bull received my daughter's letter which she writt by my wive's order yesterday was sennight by the post. Pray lett us heare twice or thrice a weeke how she does, and if Mrs Bull wants anything for Nanne, do you, or Mrs Pendleton write to us about it for her.

Tell Pendleton Mr Ballett described to me Dr Hascard's case who, as Dean of Windsor, succeeded to a country living which was let to a farmer, as Etton is, near the half year's rent day, and Hascard recovered the half year's rent. Ballett wishes to know when the farmer entered, Lady Day or Michaelmas, and whether the payments are equally divided, £34 each.

**62** FITZWILLIAM TO GUYBON
*London, 16 June 1698; F(M)C 1043*

Francis Guybon, As to the taxes, I acquainted Mr Pemberton and Mr Whinyates the reason how I came to be tax't here which could not be avoided. They will tell you when they are in [the] countrey the manner of raiseing the tax in the countries round about here and that we shall pay no more then 3s in the pound, lett the summe laied upon the severall towneships amount to what they will. We must run the hazard of being returned into the exchequer rather then pay above 3s in the pound, and appeale to the next parliament whither we ought to pay more or not, when the parliament gave the King no more then 3s in the pound. But then we must sweare our estates to be so as that we pay to the full of our rents 3s in the pounds. I thinke you may safely sweare the full rents of Milton lordship that we are over taxt there, but remember that much the greatest part of Stoney Goodlucks and a good bitt of Doves, Goodlucks and a little parcell of Middle Goodlucks are in Marrham lordship, and Gunnard Hill and Milton Holme are in Castor. For Marrham, Etton, Woodcraft and Norborough we will not complaine of them and so there will be no occasion to sweare upon that accompt, but if they should raise the taxe upon those townes, lett me immediately know what it is, that we may compute the rents before we complaine if taxt above 3s or not. Upton in Castor parrish is very much under rated in all taxes and that may be raised to ease the rest of the parish and lett them sweare it off.

I have received from John Cole by John Horner £30 7s 4d. If those horses are so very fat sell them if for a good price but if not we need them continually when I am there carting mortar, stones and coal. I leave it to you. We are extraordinarily troubled about Mrs Hunt's condition. Pray God restore her, but by Mrs Pendleton's letter she must be departed before this, else we would have sent prunes and 'prunelloes' down today, though my wife says they cannot be good for her in her condition. I am sure Mrs Bull cannot take more on for her than my poor wife, who is very ill herself.

## 63 FITZWILLIAM TO GUYBON
*London, 18 June 1698; F(M)C 1044*

Francis Guybon, Wee are extraordinarily troubled here for the loss of Mrs Hunt, and my wife was so much concerned that she fell into her fitts upon heareing the newes of it by Mr Pendleton letter. I am sure her owne mother cannot be more concerned then she is, and I do not remember her to have had fitts these many yeares before. Pray go as often to her [Mrs Bull] as possibly you can to comfort her up, and whatever you can do for her to putt off her melancholly pray do it . . .

[P.S.] Desire Mr and Mrs Pendleton to go often to comfort Mrs Bull. My wife would know where Mrs Hunt is buried. I hope our heavy rain did not reach you and the meadows are safe.

## 64 FITZWILLIAM TO GUYBON
*London, 21 June 1698; F(M)C 1045*

I received your letter with the dean's enclosed. I have written to him saying that Paradise lease is locked away so you could not get it until I came, and so I desired a power left in two or three of the prebends nearest to Peterborough to renew it next Michaelmas. Also that there were 18 years expired at the last renewal, for at a £4 rent it was unreasonable I should renew every seven years when the charges for sealing and lease would be more than the fine. I said I hoped he would remit most of the next fine since I must spend near £40 building a house on it. You must be in the same story I am as to the building cost and the rent, which is near enough considering my own intermingled land makes up the rent Oagle pays me. If they ask what fine I paid last say you believed under £20 but you are not positive after so long a time. The more you write about Mrs Hunt the more we are troubled. Comfort Mrs Bull all you can.

## 65 FITZWILLIAM TO GUYBON
*London, 30 June 1698; F(M)C 1046*

John Horner, the salesman, paid me £23 13s 4d for Mr Ash and £21 7s 10d for Cole. 'If you have not settled the duplicates for the taxes of Milton, Castor etc. I am willing to pay 3s in the pound for £1,000 as . . . formerly rather then have the tax raised higher upon the rest of the parrish.' If all is settled say nothing but otherwise pay and send the certificate signed by the commissioners. I hope your repairs go well this fine weather.

## 66 FITZWILLIAM TO GUYBON
*London, 2 July 1698; F(M)C 1047*

I am uncertain whether I asked you to pay Mary Tomlyn's[1] mother 10s, but if not do it quickly, for Mary spoke of it three weeks ago and I always forgot. The woman had a pretty livelihood from the town toll which has been taken from her. If you can, help her to it again by speaking to your friends there. My wife would have written about it but is too ill. She wishes you and the Pendletons to go to Mrs Bull as often as convenient 'to comfort her up'. Tell her my wife received her letter and is sorry she is so ill. She will write to her when she is able but meanwhile if she thinks anything in town will do her good if she writes to my wife we will send it as soon as it can be got.

[1] Probably Lady Fitzwilliam's maid. Guybon paid her on 8 July, Disbursements 790.

## **67** FITZWILLIAM TO GUYBON

*London, 7 July 1698; F(M)C 1048*

Have had no letter this fortnight so hope you are in good health and all goes well. 'My wife desires to know how long Mrs Pendleton has to reckon'[1] and how Mrs Bull and family are. What have you done about the tax?

[1] Until her baby is born, see below **74, 75**.

## **68** FITZWILLIAM TO GUYBON

*London, 14 July 1698; F(M)C 1049*

Francis Guybon, ... as to the tax, I spoke with Mr Roger Pemberton about it and told him what I writt to you concerning paying for a thousand pounds in the countrey though I do pay here, rather then make so great a confusion in the parish rates as will be if I do not pay it. He told they could not tell which way to raise that summe and earnestly desired me to lett it be paid which would make the rest of the towne very easy for he had been examining the severall rents in the townes of Castor, Aylesworth etc, and they were in much disorder about it, and that very summe of £9 would do the business. I hope you pay no more then 3s in the pound for the rents of Milton in this tax and the same for the £1,000 personall estate, which 3s ... for the personall estate amounts to £9, which ... I would have you pay at 4 payments and not all together as formerly ... Pray send me up a certificate next weeke that you have paid the 4th part of what I am charged with for my personall estate in the countrey that I may produce it here in towne if occasion be, for we want some hundreds of pounds in the parish I live in here and they talke of a review and I may be tax't for £1,000 more to help to make up the summe, so if I have a certificate ready by me I may shew it if I am so served.

I am glad all neighbours are in good health. Do not depend on Newcomb, who has so often failed, but find others to supply me. Writs for a new parliament go to the sheriffs this post. Secure Mr Wortley's interest as much as possible. Mr St John is surely safe enough. The election for knights is Thursday week. I am sorry you have so much rain. Here is fine haying weather, and rain will do no damage, the hay being mostly in 'the great cocke.' I have enquired of the drovers that come up our roads who say there are no floods on Stamford River and only a little one at Wainsford. I hope your meadows are all mown. [P.S.] I am not 'fond' of paying for this £1,000 if the tax is settled and you and my friends think it needless. I can send a certificate that I have paid here but wait to hear what you have done.

## 69 FITZWILLIAM TO GUYBON

*London, 21 July 1698; F(M)C 1050*

Mr Newcomb paid me £10 which served to go to market with on Saturday, and if none is paid tomorrow 'must run a trust ... next markett'. I am glad the tax is settled.[1] I hope you take two receipts, or express in one how much is paid for Milton rents, how much for personal estate for fear in time it may be seen as all due from rents. 'When I have disposed of my personall estate ... the lordship may be abated that money'. I am glad the Peterborough election is so near, thereby avoiding trouble and charge. I hope my friends carry it. Surely Mr St John will succeed. Let me know the result and whether Lord Exeter's 'baily' or the dean and chapter's made the return. If the weather be temperate send up a fat buck next week. Feary's coach is quickest. Let me know when in the afternoon it arrives.

[1] On 19 July Guybon paid Robert Wright and William Serjeant, assessors for 'Castor-cum-Milton', £17 3s 1½d for 'the first quarterly payment' for Milton manor and the woods, £2 5s for Fitzwilliam's personal estate, and £4 12s 7¾d for Marholm for Fitzwilliam, Mrs Bull and Thomas Freeman; Disbursements 790.

## 70 FITZWILLIAM TO GUYBON

*London, 28 July 1698; F(M)C 1051*

I received your letter and the enclosed papers which I like, as also the venison, pretty sweet, well killed and fat. I am sorry you only have one buck more. I used to have four or five a season, and wonder they should be so 'killed downe in my absence that I can have but a brace this yeare'. I am in great straits for my house and other expenses. I am extremely glad of the Peterborough result. Give my particular respects to all my friends there and my thanks for their kindness to my friends.[1] I enclose two warrants for my fee does.

[1] The successful candidates were Wortley Montagu and Francis St John: Bridges, ii, 540.

## 71 FITZWILLIAM TO GUYBON

*London, 30 July 1698; F(M)C 1052*

Francis Guybon, I received yesterday by order of Mr Kingston of Thorney the summe of £30. I intend God willing next Munday by the carrier to send downe Joe Turner to his father againe. I may say it to you I dare keep him no longer for feare he should gett into company here as will bring him to an untimely end soone. He is of himselfe so addicted to theiveing he is not fitt to be in my house and whatever he steales he converts into money and drinkes it presently. He has all manner of ill qualitys besides, as sweareing and lieing, for which he has been corrected both by myselfe and his schoole master, butt all to no purpose. He seemes hardened in his wickedness. I desire he may not come neare Milton. If he cannot steale anything handsomly he sells his cravatts rather then he will want strong drincke. His father keeping a publique house has been his ruine. His shirts being worne out my wife intends to buy him some when we come into the countrey for we dare not keep him another weeke for feare of greater mischeife, otherwaies he should carry some downe with him. I dare not write thus much to his father because he is so passionate he may mischeive the boy, but must pretend the towne aire does not agree with him, or some such excuse ... [P.S.] I have hereunder writt the other 2 warrants which I would have sent for as I shall direct hereafter.

## 72 FITZWILLIAM TO GUYBON

*London, 4 August 1698; F(M)C 1054*

I have received £20 from Kingston by Laxton, his Thorney neighbour, and £25 17s from Horner for Ash. I hope little Joe Turner got safe home to his father ... The carrier had a great charge of him, and money paid him to bear his charges home. Send another buck by Feary's coach. I hope you have a good 'haysell' time and a good harvest.

## 73 FITZWILLIAM TO GUYBON

*London, 16 August 1698; F(M)C 1055*

Today I received a bill from Mr St John for £100 on Mr Sheppard and partners, goldsmiths of Lombard Street. Pay Pickering on sight or carry the money to Thorpe when you receive this. If Mr St John needs money at any time pay him before hand for I don't doubt the payment of it here. Give a warrant to Cousin Harry Tryce, Cousin Bellamy, Mr Lowrey and Mr Newcomb, letting them choose their own pieces, but if they disagree let Tryce and Lowrey have the two sides, and the others the two half haunches. Divide the other between yourself, Pendleton, Robert Pemberton and Whinyates. Let me have a buck next week by the third warrant.[1] I despair of getting the fourth this year, but Lord Exeter has given me a warrant for Burghley Park which I won't send yet. I hope Ballett will settle matters between Pendleton and Standish.

[1] Guybon paid keepers' fees of 15s each on 22 and 29 August, the latter to Exeter's keeper, Disbursements 790.

## 74 FITZWILLIAM TO GUYBON

*London, 25 August 1698; F(M)C 1056*

Francis Guybon ... I do much admire at the great confidence of Mr Ballett. I gave him a side of venison here in towne and told him I had no venison in the countrey but if he stayed a few daies at Mr Checkley's I would order him a fawne. He said he should not stay but one night so I never writt to you about it. He shall never have any venison more from mee and you served him very well, for so impudent and intrudeing a man I never knew the like. He does nothing for me but what he is paid 2d for every pennyworth of service.

I received the buck, sweet and handsome. I have had better from Mr Waller's walk. I enclose Lord Exeter's warrant. Send it next week by the coach. Ask Mr Dowsett, the keeper, to shoot it so it comes better. Mr Tanner tells me he never saw such thick, fat venison as is in Lord Exeter's park. [P.S.] I hope Ballett well advised Pendleton about his case with Standish. Let me know how the case goes, or if it is accommodated. My wife wishes all pigeons that are fit to send to come next week by the coach, but consult Mrs Pendleton and Mrs Bull if they will come sweet this warm weather. 'Thanke God we have brave harvest weather'. How near her time is Mrs Pendleton? How are Mrs Bull and her family? Also Cousin Henry Tryce, his sister Bellamy, the Lowreys and Mrs Watts? My wife has just ended drinking the waters.

### 75 FITZWILLIAM TO GUYBON

*London, 1 September 1698; F(M)C 1057*

I received by Mr Brecknock's order £35 18s 9d and £12 by Mr Ash's order. The Peterborough coach brought a very good buck. We are very sorry to hear how ill a time Mrs Pendleton has had but hope she is better every day. We wish them much joy of their daughter. We hope that as Mr Pendleton saw here all contrivances for curing smoking chimneys care has been taken to cure the kitchen chimney.

[P.S.] My wife cannot write for she is very ill with a lame legg since she dranke the waters. She remembers herselfe very kindly to Mr and Mrs Pendleton and bidds you tell them if the child is not christened and they are not provided with godmothers, my wife will make one, if they will accept of her; and Mrs Bull must stand for her and you must give Mrs Bull just as much money to give the midwife and nurse and maide as I ordered you to give for me when the boy was borne.[1] They may please themselves for the name.

[1] 'Gave Mrs Bull to give to the midwife, nurse and maydes at Mrs Pendleton's christening, £1 10s', 13 September, Disbursements 790.

### 76 FITZWILLIAM TO GUYBON

*London, 8 September 1698; F(M)C 1058*

Yesterday arrived a flag basket with three dozen pigeons. Today John Horner paid me £25 2s 6d for Mr Ash.

### 77 FITZWILLIAM TO GUYBON

*London, 29 September 1698; F(M)C 1059*

The letter with the pigeons was never delivered. Your two letters of 14th and 18th arrived with Mr St John's bill for £50 enclosed. The servants who went for the money lost their labour twice 'for the old gentleman his baily'[1] was out of town, but will return once the harvest is in. You wrote a Mark Simpson of Allerton should pay me £100 or £120 by Michaelmas but has not done so. Inform my wife whether Mrs Pendleton suckles her child herself or who is her wet nurse, and who her dry nurse if she has one. You need send no more tax receipts for my personal estate. I pay my poll tax here. Tell Pendleton not to conclude with Standish unless he gives him a good round sum to make habitable the parsonage at Etton for [Pendleton] can be assured that neither myself nor children, nor the incumbent after him will be satisfied unless it is left in very good order.

Have a care of sending up bills of exchange in letters, for since I received Mr St John['s] bill to old Mr Bennett the northerne letters have been twice robbed, opened and the bills taken out and the money received by those rougues, that it has been a great loss to severall merchants and gentlemen. I know not what course we must take. The westerne post and Norwich post are very often robbd, but I never knew the northerne maile robbd before this.

I hope the pigeons are better now than last time and that you will send some when they are good, but let me know the post before they come. My wife has been ill but is pretty well again. She wishes to know how are Mrs Bull and family, and if Joseph Bull's wife is with child how near her time she is; if Betty Bull is at home and how long she has been there. Let us know how are Mr and Mrs Henry Tryce, the Bellamys, the Lowreys, Mrs Watts, the Selby family and all other friends and neighbours. Send what country news you have.

[1] 'Old' Mr Bennett.

## **78** FITZWILLIAM TO GUYBON
*London, 6 October 1698; F(M)C 1060*

I have received Mr St John's £50, and £100 from William Checkley on account of Mark Stevenson[1] for Thomas Freeman's wool, and £31 3s 5d from Horner for a Matthew Pickering.[1] Since Mrs Bull paid 10s to Mrs Pendleton's nurse of the 20s you gave her, give Mrs Bull 10s more so she can pay the midwife 20s as I did last year, that is 30s amongst them. Was the nurse Goody Watson or Mother Butler? Mrs Bull could have told you whether Joe's wife is with child. [P.S.] Write out this year's accounts, and the wood book, for I shall soon send for them.

[1] Probably the Mark Simpson of **77** above is meant.
[2] 'Returned my lord by Mr Pickering, £31 3s 5d, 10 October, Disbursements 790.

## **79** FITZWILLIAM TO GUYBON
*London, 17 November 1698; F(M)C 1062*

I am not well enough to write more than that last week I was extremely ill with a fever, and write now in 'great paine of blisters that are running upon mee.' I hope the worst is past with no relapse. A porter has brought £54 for John Cole of Northborough. I hear nothing of the doe from the carrier's inn. Their wagons sit on the road unable to pass for frost and snow. My wife would know if Mrs Bull received the basket and its contents safely. [P.S.] I hear nothing yet of Maxey particular[1] which you said would come this week. If Pemberton or Whinyates do not bring it to me I shall not receive it soon being confined to my house. I can do nothing about that purchase until I see it.

[1] A detailed description of the Maxey estate.

## **80** FITZWILLIAM TO GUYBON
*London, 24 November 1698; F(M)C 1063*

Received yours from Whinyates but am still too 'faint and out of order' to look over the enclosure.[1] Mr Ash's £60 14s 5d was paid today. I am sorry Mr Turner is in prison. I received two letters from him during my sickness about his little boy.[2] I dare not take him again into my house without 'a manifest danger' to myself. His faults are in his nature; I dare not trust to promises. As soon as he is old enough to be apprenticed I will give 'a piece of money' to help bind him out. I have nothing to say about William Turner. He is big enough to go to service. Send up a doe from my park next week. The last deer's haunch had a great hole as if bitten by a dog. Let the next be shot and not hunted. In the Maxey particular I find a query in Pendleton's hand against William Exton who in the leases for two lives has a tenement with a yard, 1 rod pasture, 2 rods meadow, 8 acres arable. Present rent: £1 6s; improved £4 10s. What is the doubt? Then a query by you against Thomas Ewin of Deepingate: 7 acres 3 rods in Deepingate Meadow, 33 acres 1 rod in Deepingate Field. Present rent £4 5s 8d; improved rent £15 13s 4d. Were your doubts concerning the rent, or the quantity held, or what? Roger Pemberton queries Thomas Field, for three lives, particularly Bridge Gate Close with a barn, present rent £2, improved rent £7. What is his query?

[1] The description of the Maxey estate.
[2] 'Little' Joe Turner.

## 81 FITZWILLIAM TO GUYBON

*London, 13 December 1698; F(M)C 1064*

The bishop's Mr Baxter has paid Heriot £100 for Charles Duce. Captain Styles of Walton has begged venison of me this winter and since the occasion is extraordinary, and he has never asked before, let him have half a doe. Take the other half yourself, using one of the warrants. Go as soon as possible to Walton to ask the captain when he would have it. For the other warrants: give half a doe to Cousin Harry Tryce, and a piece each to Mr Lowrey and Cousin Bellamy. The third divide between Roger Pemberton, Whinyates, Charles Duce and Pendleton. Divide the fourth amongst our Peterborough friends.

## 82 FITZWILLIAM TO GUYBON

*London, 22 December 1698; F(M)C 1065*

The bill you enclosed from Mr Ash should have his name signed on the back because they write a receipt of the money just above the name but I will get somebody to do it for him. Thank you for your kind present of partridges, rabbits and pheasant. This morning arrived two pheasants, four partridges and two stock doves. John Horner paid me £67 11s 7d for Matthew Pickering. My wife is very ill of a cold, the rest of us in reasonable health. [P.S.] Give to the poor of the several parishes as in former years. Is the kitchen chimney quite cured of smoking?

## 83 FITZWILLIAM TO GUYBON

*London, 29 December 1698; F(M)C 1066*

Lady Sylvius's counsel[1] has set down for me £15 a year for Dr Wigmore's rent, whereas in the particular I sent you it was set down £4. It's among the rack rent tenants, 15 acres of meadow or pasture. Robert Smith is tenant. Ask him what he pays 'to a farthing' either to Wigmore or his heirs, and if it will hold that rent, and if any of it lies in Deepingate Meadow. Dr Wigmore's lease ends next Lady Day, whereas when you returned the particular Pendleton interlined there was 12 years to run. Ask Mr Smith about it also. The counsel says the cowpasture leases expire within four years. Go to Maxey and Deepingate and satisfy me about these particulars by Tuesday's post. Is the kitchen chimney cured since Robert Bursnoll made the holes in it?

[1] Mr Pigeon.

## 84 FITZWILLIAM TO GUYBON

*London, 5 January 1698/9; F(M)C 1067*

I am glad you wrote to me what Smith told you of Dr Wigmore's meadow. I fear all the meadow in the rest of [Maxey] estate in Deepingate Meadow can only be valued at 6s an acre. If so there must be a great deduction made throughout the particular. In the particular I sent down a Widow Anne Cooke pays £1 per annum for a Northborough cottage but Pendleton writes in the margin that it is now let for 5s. Let me know the true value, where it stands, what land belongs to it. The widow may have paid a fine at first and had the rent reduced. Let me know the annual value of the Cowpastures if they were out of lease, and what they are generally let for. Send Mary Tomlyn's mother half a crown from her daughter.[1]

[1] Paid 27 January, Disbursements 790.

## 85 FITZWILLIAM TO GUYBON

*London, 19 January 1698/9; F(M)C 1068*

I received your answers about Maxey estate. Mr St John has repeatedly asked me if you had paid £50 to Mr Pickering, offering to pay it here. If you can spare it pay the £50 which I suppose he needs in the country.[1] It may do them a kindness. John Horner has paid me £44 5s 6d for Mr Ash, but have not yet heard from Thomas Fuller who was to pay £33 from Ash's wool money. I asked where he lived, but you have sent no answer. I am sorry to hear of the mischief by the great floods but the adventurers of Deeping Fen are justly served for their only care is to secure their land though the common be drowned, when their land was given them for draining that common. Mr Pigeon insists that Waldrum Hall,[2] grounds and ferry let with it, is worth upon the rack £10 a year, whereas I only value it at £6 or £7 at most. I would be glad to know the rack rent value. Matthew Hycklin pays now £2 and has one life in it. I believe it's all meadow and subject to be drowned with the meadows. Consult with Pendleton and Wright about the kitchen chimney in spring for there's no living for me at Milton if it continues to smoke. I hope to be down in May.

[1] Guybon paid St John on 27 January, Disbursements 790.
[2] See Introduction, p. xviii.

## 86 FITZWILLIAM TO GUYBON

*London, 26 January 1698/9; F(M)C 1069*

We return our thanks for your kind present of pheasants for my wife which came sweet and very good, and my wife sends her thanks to Mrs Bull for a chine and black puddings, for she is not well enough to write yet. I have not seen her so ill for many a day as lately. We are sorry Mrs Bull still mourns her daughter. She must take care of herself for her younger children's sake. I am sorry for the great mischief done by the mob in Deeping Fen, although the adventurers deserve no better.[1]

[1] On these riots see M Beloff, *Public Order and Popular Disturbances 1660–1714* (1938), pp. 79–80, and for the problem in general, *The Agrarian History of England and Wales* , vol. 5, 1640–1750, pt. ii, ed. Joan Thirsk (Cambridge, 1985), pp. 312–14.

## 87 FITZWILLIAM TO GUYBON

*London, 2 February 1698/9; F(M)C 1071*

I think I have agreed for Maxey. Enquire of Ewing of Church Hall if he has a life in being, for in the particular he was among the rack rents at £15. Now they place him among the leaseholders with one life. He has a messuage of 40 acres arable, 3 acres 3 rods meadow, a close called The Fox 2 acres 2 rods. Reserved rent £7, improved rent £15. Also for a messuage and 2 barns 16 acres 3 rods arable, 3 rods meadow, 2 acres pasture inclosed, etc. Reserved rent £2 2s 8d, rack rent £7 10s. Ask if he pays the reserved rent; if not, how much, and if the land will yield £15 and £7 10s on the rack, if he has a life in being in both, and if a new lease lies with Mr Burmer of Stamford until he pays his fine. All this they tell me. When I hear you have paid the £50 to Mrs St John or to Pickering for her use I will inform Mr St John.[1] I shall want a great deal of money to pay for Maxey, though I never had more by me than now.

[1] Paid 4 February, Disbursements 790.

## 88 FITZWILLIAM TO GUYBON

*London, 9 February 1698/9; F(M)C 1072*

The brace of hares came up sweet. Our agreement for Maxey is not fully made, but they must accept my offer for nobody else will be so mad as to offer so much. They haggle for trifles which I will never condescend to. They sent to me yesterday but I would not go near them. Mr St John knows his wife had £50 from you, and will pay me soon. The other £50 he paid on the 26th. Mr Kingston's salesman, Henry Hankin, paid me £13, all he had left after paying the Duke of Bedford's rent.

We had a terrible storme of wind here in towne yesterday and the day before that has done much harme to the house besides the killing and wounding severall people and horses. The Earle of Cardigan had a great deliveringe. A stack of chimneys fell over his house and broke downe into the roome where he was standing by the fire talking with people and one man in the company who stood but one yard from my lord was knockt downe, his collar bone broke and three of his ribbs, and otherwise so bruised and wounded his life is despaird off. They were forc't to breake downe the wall to gett my lord out. This was in his owne house in Lincolnes Inne Feilds. Abundance of mischeife was done. I hope it has not reacht you in the countrey but I heare it was twenty miles off. God preserve us from such stormes, many trees are blowne up by the rootes in St James Parke etc. . . .

## 89 FITZWILLIAM TO GUYBON

*London, 16 February 1698/9; F(M)C 1073*

> I am sorry the wind went as far as you. I hear the same out of Norfolk. It was very terrible here and has killed many. I am glad Milton House and the ferry escaped damage. Since it blew down that old building at Helpston it had best be rebuilt between the head house and the great barn, so as to fence that ground they wish to make into an orchard but not too near the house for fear of fire. I hope you have no cause to fear my losing Maxey. It will be my own fault if I do.

## 90 FITZWILLIAM TO GUYBON

*London, 2 March 1698/9; F(M)C 1075*

> I have received £30 by Mr Phillips' order. Today Mr Ash's woolman, Thomas Fuller, paid me £23 and a bank bill for £10.

Harry Watts takes this opportunity of his comeing to see his freinds here in towne to make complaints of his ferry boate, of his warehouses being ready to fall and of the old house being much decayed, the water running quite through it these wett seasons. As to his warehouses I told him I should do nothing at them for if he would be so careless as not to keep them well thatcht on the backe side of them and the dyke there not well scowred to secure the thacke that was on them, whereby the wett soakt the wall and rotted it, it was a signe the warehouses were of little use to him and so lett them fall; they were putt into repaire when his father tooke his lease and that I expect he should uphold and leave them so to mee. For the old ferry house, if it was of no use to the ferry, I was content it should go downe. I meane the middle part of it but for the old stable and the brewhouse, they must be kept up being necessary for the new house, and so he must repaire them according to his lease. If he is willing to lett the middle part of the old house go downe, pray lett the boards of the floores of the chambers, the doores, shutters and the timber of it be carried to Milton and laied up dry. For the ferry boate, that I heare both by your letter, and him also, is quite woren out. I much wonder at it because we never had a boate yett but what lasted 12 yeares at least and this I am sure is not so old by a yeare or two, for it was made the summer or winter before this king came in.[1] It either must be ill kept and repaired by him or else the timber was not well seasoned nor substantiall enough that it was made on, and I remember this was made of our owne timber which ought to be a warneing to us not to doe the like againe. I hope I shall be downe in 2 moneths time and beleive the boate may last so long well enough and then we may all consult together with Mr Wright what is best to be done: whither to use our owne timber againe or else to have it made at Peterborough by the boaterights with their plancke and timber if they have that which is thoroughly seasoned which I much fe[are] they have not, being most of them poore fellows and have not store by them.

> We must be prudent now we are about it. 'I hope a little time will breake no squares for what is once well done is twice done'. Only Maxey settlement keeps me here. Mr Pigeon their counsel says it will be completed in about a month. Mr Clitheroe,[2] who owns Lolham, has a lease for three lives in Maxey. Ask John Webdale what Maxey lands Clitheroe holds. They tell me it lies so intermixed with Lolham lands that they cannot be without it. Write what Webdale says and if it disagrees with the particular show him it and note his reply. Learn the truth of it for Mr Clitheroe, who had intended to bid for Maxey, is willing to sell Lolham and we have already discoursed about this. Keep this to yourself. Harry Watts brought an account which I refused to read, being determined not to pay it, for repairs to the [ferry] boat, and for the window tax which the act expressly states the tenant must pay. I will allow no tenant it, nor does any landlord. When the season permits, if Watts has stone dug at the nearest quarry to the ferry I will lend my horses and tumbril to bring the stone to those areas at the horse ferry the rains have turned to quicksands [P.S.] Tell old Mr Vaughan and his son Harry that they shall have the same charge of Maxey as under Lady Sylvius, and that they should let to the best advantage any lands which come out of lease this Lady Day, especially Dr Wigmore's meadow and Waldrum Hall. Learn from Matthew Hicklyn what rent he pays Mr Bertie for his ferry right, and, if he can remember, how long he has paid it for I think to have it paid no longer.

[P.P.S.] Pray consult with Old Mr Vaughan likewise what is fitt to be done when Markett Deeping faire is kept, for Harry Vaughan tells mee Mr Bertie has sett downe 2 posts and a chaine to hinder carts from comeing over the bridge into the meadow where we have a royalty and can take a tole for laying downe of timber or earthen ware and other commodities, and if we can mannage our business well I hope in time to bring that faire into our meadows as it is at Peterborough brigg faire.[3] The bridge foot of Deeping stands upon an acre of my meadow belonging to Norborough estate and I will throw up the bridge if they stop that way over. Pray consider seriously of this with Mr Vaughan and if you thinke fitt you may have Mr Pendleton by, and Mr Burman the steward too, who I intend shall keep the courts still and likewise Norborough.

[1] Fitzwilliam's recollection was correct. Guybon paid John Andrews £10 for making the ferry boat on 6 February 1688, Disbursements 790.

[2] Possibly a member of the wealthy London family of Clitherow of Boston House, Brentford, descended from Sir Christopher Clitherow, who was Lord Mayor of London in 1635. Elsewhere, however, it is stated that Lord Fitzwilliam had bought the manor of Lolham from John Claypole on 20 February 1681. (*VCH Northamptonshire*, ii, 504, which cites a deed then at Milton Hall.) The Claypoles had raised money on the manor from a John Clitherowe about 1669. The Clitherowe name does not appear on the deed transferring the manor to Fitzwilliam, but their connection must have been more than temporary for Bridges states that in 1720 John Clitherowe was 'possessor' of the manor and Lolham House. Possibly Fitzwilliam and Clitherowe owned different parts of Lolham as neighbouring landlords.

[3] The Bridge or 'Brig' fair is referred to throughout the letters. It was held at Peterborough four times a year: 29 June (St Peter and Paul); mid-Lent; 5 August (St Oswald); 21 September (St Matthew); *VCH Northamptonshire*, ii. 427.

## 91 FITZWILLIAM TO GUYBON
*London, 23 March 1698/9; F(M)C 1077*

Francis Guybon, I saw John Webdale twice and had a great deale of talke with him about the faire you mention in the meadows.[1] I bad him consult with Mr Bimrose and other knowing men on that side the countrey to know when they thought it might be a propper time to have the faire on, for they must consider harvest is alwaies inned later on that side the countrey[2] which lies low and cold ground then it is with us about Castor and those towns, and also round Peterborough, and if harvest is not in sometime before the faire it will not be so great a conveniency to that side the countrey, and if we have a charter it must be kept before Peterburgh bridgg faire. You did very well to threaten to pull downe Deeping bridge, for it stands on my meadow and I am sure does me a great deale of mischeife. It may frighten them into a compliance to leave the way open. If so, Deeping faire will soone remove into our meadows as at Brigg faire where there is roome enough for all things that come.

I have discoursed Mr Wortley and Mr St John about this land tax to prevent the imposing on our hundred £200 more than before. They take little notice of it. Having only small estates in our hundred they are little concerned for us. Mr Wortley does not intend to present the petition the hundred sent to Mr St John, which I signed. I have received no money since Mr Ash's wool money on March 3rd. Return me what you can so that I can pay for Maxey, which I hope will be dispatched by Easter. My wife would have Mrs Bull buy her cloth at Stamford Fair for eight or 10 pair of sheets of two or three sorts of cloth.

[1] Fitzwilliam appears to mean Maxey (see **92** below).
[2] By 'country' Fitzwilliam here probably means 'district' rather than, as so often, 'county'.

## 92 FITZWILLIAM TO GUYBON
*London, 30 March 1699; F(M)C 1078*

Francis Guybon, Yours of the 26th I received last Munday and as to the new faire I thinke it will be too soone to have it in August but rather the first Munday in September which will [be] but one weeke longer and then harvest will be more inned every where and consequently more people may come to it. And that time will be also before either Spalding, Peterborough or Deeping but I immagined you designed cheifly to have it a day or two before Deeping faire[1] to have the benefitt of everything that was to come to that faire and so the faire would last 3 or 4 daies. After all I fancy there being no accomodation of inns and alehouses in Maxey and if the faire be kept in the meadows, the towne of Markett Deeping being so neare that towne will receave more benefitt then we shall at Maxey unless it be a little money will be spent in the booths, for where there is best accomodation, there the money will be spent. We have time enough to consult of this matter when I go downe. I thought the £200 would be levied upon the Soake since I perceaved the parliament men for Peterborough were so indifferent and careless in lookeing after it. I could but putt them in mind of it, but their estates being small in the hundred, their parts will be but small they must pay of it, and so they were the more remiss. Pray take care there be as little as may be laied of it upon the townes belonging to my estate. I suppose Joseph Chamberlaine is tennant for the Old Parke so he may have it againe this yeare, but for the Meadow Close I am not free to lett it unless they raise rent upon it which they may afford as times now are, and besides I will have it fedd this yeare. Lett me know who is tennant and what rent they pay and if it was fedd or mowed. I thinke Thomas Freeman is tennant and paid £29 last yeare and mowed it besides. Lett me know if I am right. Pray returne mine and my wive's kind thanks to Mr and Mrs Pendleton for their very good chine and sawciges which we receaved yesterday by the carrier. And pray tell Mrs Pendleton my wife desires she would gett some more of the herbs this spring that my sonn William used to weare in a bagg. It must be gott in dry weather and not washt after, no not so much as the root of it. It must be gott in the budd before it be blowne out to a flower and my wife desires it may be gott on Munday and Tuesday if dry weather and not [after?] Tuesday because of the full of the moone. My wife had rather it should all be gott dry if possible . . .

[1] The fairs at Market Deeping, Lincs, were on the first Wednesday in May and on 10 October for cattle according to Lewis, *A Topographical Dictionary of England* (London, 1844).

## **93** FITZWILLIAM TO GUYBON

*London, 13 April 1699; F(M)C 1079*

If the Meadow Close hedge 'be plasht' the ground must be mowed this year.[1] Let me know if Milton Field is fallow this year, or what field is. You mention that £28 is the old rent of Meadow Close. Not so, the old rent was £32 and it was never let for less than £30 until Thomas Manton had it for less because of the trespasses committed when we were building there. It's a bargain at £30 a year considering the prices wool, beef, lamb and mutton bring. If Thomas Freeman won't pay it I can mow it myself, needing hay for my stables and park. Since he is tenant to it he can have it at £30, otherwise I will not let it to anyone at any rent. Mr St John will pay the money you have now returned when I inform him of it. He has been ill and staying at Sir Walter St John's. Joe Chamberlaine may hold the Old Park this year again at the old rent. I am glad Mr Dreydon[2] is chosen at Huntingdon. Get me quickly all the returns you can.

[1] Plashers cut small branches and stems half through, and wove and interlaced them with twigs to form a low, close hedge or fence.

[2] John Dryden of Chesterton, M.P. for Huntingdonshire (**14** note 1).

## **94** FITZWILLIAM TO GUYBON

*London, 20 April 1699; F(M)C 1080*

Goodman Thomas Freeman must pay £30 this year for Meadow Close. Let him not deceive himself by saying he will 'stand to my curtesie'.[1]

I am sorry to heare the distemper amungst horses reaches to your countrey. We have had it here almost these 3 weekes, not one horse escapes but thanke God very few die except old decayed jades here and there one. I thinke when they are recovered it does them a great deale of good for they purge very much at the nose. We are very much frightened with the report that is spread abroad that beast and sheep are infected with a malignant distemper. If so, Lord have mercy on us, for we must all expect to be infected with our daily food and it's reported the doctors have advised that no beef nor mutton should be killd these 2 moneths till the malignancy be over. Pray send mee word if it be true or not that beefe and mutton are infected and how my deare stand in the parke. Thanke God the towne is yett very healthfull and not any symptome of a contagious distemper as we heare off.

Remind Mr Duce of his promise to return £100. Don't let him 'forfeit his word' as he has often done formerly for the time of payment for Maxey is now very near. Do all you can to get what money you can among the tenants and return it [P.S.] Tell Mr Pendleton I received his letter advising that arches and a false back be made if we pull down and new build the kitchen chimney. Tell him there is a false back already, and there were holes in it which drew the smoke very well. I do not remember why they were walled up, but they could be quickly opened, and the space between the false and other chimney cleared of its soot and rubbish fill. If this fails, the chimney must be pulled down and rebuilt.

[1] Maintaining the rent at its old level but permitting the tenant to pay a lower rent for that year.

## 95 FITZWILLIAM TO GUYBON

*London, 4 May 1699; F(M)C 1081*

Mr Vaughan of Maxey writes he has not yet let the Cowpastures, but says he will let them but leave me to fix the rent when I come down. He claims they have been let dear. Safely convey the enclosed reply to him, which tells him that when his son Harry was in town he told me the cowpastures and all other Maxey properties would hold their rents, and this encouraged me more than any other report to pay a high price. He and his father had managed the Maxey estate many years and must know the value better than any neighbour. I told Vaughan I would entrust the estate to him and I take it the worse that he should have deceived me about the value. Speak with both Vaughans and hear what they say to it. Dr Wigmore's meadow's lease expired last Lady Day. Find out if they have let it and for what, and if not, what they think it will bring. It's 15 acres and Harry assured me he could get £12 a year. 'I am sorry to heare of the loss of so good a tennant as William Wade, but his wife is so discreet a woman that I do not doubt but she will gett another good husband soone'. I hope young George Chamberlaine will do well again, and am glad you have arranged for a return by Henry Wingfield. If you have pigeons send some up.

## 96 FITZWILLIAM TO GUYBON

*London, 18 May 1699; F(M)C 1082*

I am glad Vaughan has let the Cowpastures. I would have Dr Wigmore's meadow let this year but tell Mr Smith I won't decide whether to lease it until I come down. Tell Vaughan to let it to the best chapman, that I may see its worth, for Smith undervalued it when he offered only £4 a year for Henry

Vaughan claimed he could get £12. I am sorry you have let the yards become so overrun with vermin that there are no pigeons. Set traps to destroy them for there is no living in the country without a dovecote and poultry in the yard. Is there likely to be much wall and other fruit in the gardens? What price will bark bring this year, and which tanners do you sell to?

## 97 FITZWILLIAM TO GUYBON

*London, 1 June 1699; F(M)C 1083*

Francis Guybon, I was sorry to heare by a former letter of yours of the death of William Wade of Woodcraft. My Lord of Exeter's John Carter comeing to towne at that time and telling me he had left my lord's service[1] and intended to settle himselfe in a good farme as soone as any of my farmes fell, I told him of this, and that the woman[2] also would make him a good wife. He seemed to be very well pleased with it and said he would see after it and speake with you about it. I told him also of John Holman['s] farme in Castor because I have not a very good account of Ned Holman['s] mannagement. He [Carter] likes much better I find to be settled about Castor, Ailesworth or Milton because he was borne at the ferry and bred up in the parrish. Pray lett me heare if he has been with you and what he resolves on.

John Horner has paid me £80 1s 4d for William Miller.

My wife fell ill of a feaver last Satturday night and has been very ill ever since. Sometimes she is better and sometimes worse, that we know not yett what may become of her, though we hope the best, but she is in great danger and we are the more apprehensive because the feaver carries off many persons of quality that are young people, as my poore Lord of Westmorland[3] and others. Pray God keep us all from the malignancy of the distemper. All the rest of us thanke God are in good health, only my sonne William who we feare is farr gone in a consumption, for he is much altered within these 2 moneths as can be ... [P.S.] Pray lett me heare if you have had any raine about you. We have had none neare London, God knows when, and we have such hott weather we know not how to beare it.

[1] As coachman.
[2] The widow of William Wade.
[3] Vere Fane, 5th Earl of Westmorland, of Apethorpe Hall, Northants. (1678–1699), *Complete Peerage*, xii. 2, pp. 572–3.

## 98 FITZWILLIAM TO GUYBON

*[London,] ? June 1699; F(M)C 1084*

(Letter partly destroyed. References to his need of money because of his son's illness and (probably) because of Maxey purchase. Sends a certificate concerning the taxation of his personal estate. Mrs Bull to buy for Lady Fitzwilliam at Peterborough sufficient cloth to make six long hall cloths, six dresser cloths and six towels, of the quality she bought before. Also enough cloth to make four dozen napkins for the hall, which last time cost 8½d or 9d a yard.)

**99** FITZWILLIAM TO GUYBON
*London, 29 June 1699; F(M)C 1086*

Neither Mr Duce nor Mr St John has yet paid any money either to me or Mr Heriot.

My wife has been so very ill for these last tenne daies that she was given over, and yesterday we were out of all hopes but thanke God this day she is finely well if it holds. My sonne William sometimes give us great hopes of his recovery and sometimes in halfe a daie's time is at death's doore againe. I much feare the worst. I wish he were well at Milton but know not which way to gett him thither. He seemes rather willing to ride but I doubt he cannot ride above 10 miles a day, and for the coaches, he is so very leane he is not able to sitt so long together upon their hard seates. God Almighty, fitt us all for our Great Change ... [P.S.] I hope Mr St John is safely home ...

**100** FITZWILLIAM TO GUYBON
*London, 6 July 1699; F(M)C 1087*

I expect no money from Duce who never yet kept his word about returns. My business will certainly be dispatched next week, and so could come down then if my wife was in a condition to travel. We hope she is recovering but often relapses and my poor son William is as he was. I would have sent him this week but my wife hopes to be able to travel soon so that we can all come together. My wife would have Mrs Bull check the pewter chamber pots, and replace any broken, so that there be twelve sound and good. Next week brew a hogshead of ale and two of small beer from 10 strike of malt fit to be drunk in two or three weeks. Allow eight strike for the ale and two for the small beer which with the help of the ale grains should make good beer. Have Mrs Bull when most convenient for her air all the beds and blankets at our end of the house and in the matted chambers. Mrs Pendleton can remain in the nursery. Find us a fellow to keep the gates, sweep out the house and heat the ovens, even though you pay dear for him until Michaelmas. We may hire him or another cheaper afterwards.

**101** FITZWILLIAM TO GUYBON
*London, 18 July 1699; F(M)C 1088*

John Horner has paid £71 for John Cole. Don't depend on Duce who has paid none. I have sent hair brooms and brushes down by Feary's wagon. Send for them to make clean the house. I don't understand 'how I can justifie paying the countrey's money to help to pay taxes with. If Mr Neale will ingage to see mee paid this money againe I am willing to lay it downe till it be allowed mee by the freeholders'. My wife is recovering but my son very ill. I wish he were at Milton.

## 102 FITZWILLIAM TO GUYBON

*London, 26 July 1699; F(M)C 1089*

I am sending four warrants by Mr Ballett for my fee deer this summer. I offered him one but he tells me there is a restraint on our forest this year, which I hope is untrue, having heard it from nobody else. Dr Hascard told him but perhaps that was so he would not beg any venison of him. If there is no restraint let Ballett have one warrant. If there is let him have a side of venison from my park to present to Mr 'Dreydon'.[1] Kill a buck next week, therefore, and send the other side, the haunches and shoulders to me by Feary's coach. Robert Feary has asked me for some money on account, so pay him £7 and I will settle the rest when I come down. I hope you have not brewed yet for I cannot come down very soon. Duce has paid £50 of the £100 he promised. I don't expect the remainder soon. Ask Mr St John or Mr Pickering to write to his old gentleman[2] to pay me the £50 you paid Mrs St John a month since. Let me know how many bucks I can have this year but let Mr Ballett know of no more than a brace. My wife asks if Mrs Pendleton is with child and how near her time she is. My wife wishes her, when she is able, to visit Stamford in search of chests of drawers. We shall need four or five and if they can make good ones would rather buy there than pay the carriage and risk the damage of carrying them down. I hope you have found a fellow to heat ovens, clean the house and do other drudging works while I am at Milton which will be not much before harvest. We must have an ordinary wench to help the cook and other ordinary work, as washing bucks, etc. [P.S.] Could not finish my letter in time for Mr Ballett so I will bring the warrants, save Ballett's. Don't let Ballett know when I intend for Milton for I would not be troubled with him at his return. The best way to find out if there is a restraint on the forest is to send young Joseph Chamberlaine on Sunday morning next to the head keeper to ask if the bucks are fat, telling him I intend to send a warrant on the Monday. If the keeper does not tell him of a restraint, Joe must not tell him of it.

[1] John Dryden, see note to **93** above.

[2] Bennett, St John's steward. Pickering was his local steward.

## 103 FITZWILLIAM TO GUYBON

*London, 3 August 1699; F(M)C 1090*

(Has received a buck and fawn by Feary's coach; orders another for the following week, but none thereafter as will be down soon.)

I would have replied to Pendleton's letters earlier but I have been so 'tormented with this troublesome business of Maxey' now for the past 12 months that I have had no leisure for anything else. I was about to seal the purchase when their counsel claimed a Mr William Griffin's Northborough rent had been omitted (16s 8d) and I should allow for it. It's claimed to be a reserved rent granted for three lives: Daniel Blackbourne of Pilsgate, his wife Margaret and John Wildbore, son of John Wildbore of Glinton, gentleman. The lease dates from

Charles I's reign, and they believe it long expired; yet by Vaughan's receipts Griffin paid the rent during the past three years. The lease contains one acre pasture, Northborough Fields; three acres pasture Northborough Cowpasture, five and a half acres of Northborough Long Meadow. I fancy these parcels are already in the particular under Randall Cole and Robert Burley. I fear they try to impose on me, but if not God forbid I should not allow for it. I am for all things that is fair and honest. Go to Maxey, taking Pendleton if you think fit, and examine the matter with Vaughan and Mr Bimrose; talk to the old men of Northborough and see if any can remember this Blackbourne, his wife and young Wildbore. Enquire if Wildbore was he that was hanged for Parfaite's murder 10 years ago; if Griffin is landlord or tenant to it at present; the value of the land; what it will yield annually. It's at least 50 years since the lease was granted. Old John Burley may remember it. Stephen Brightman has only lived in Northborough 30 years, but being sensible may be helpful. Reply by Tuesday's post for I cannot conclude without it. When I have paid for Maxey I shall be £300–£400 in debt so make what returns you can. Send word how old and new oats and beans sell . . .

[P.S.] Pray acquaint Mr Roger Pemberton that Mr Pendleton has acquainted mee by his letter how kindly he expresst himselfe upon the bench in behalfe of the towne of Marrham concerning Tom Tympany's maide, which business I never heard off before. Lett him know I take it extreamely kindly from him and will not die in his debt for any service he does us. I wonder you should never write me word of it, that I might have thankt him here when he was in towne. Pray lett there be great care taken of it next sessions and wonder you tooke no better care of it all this while. At first, if wisely mannaged, all this might have been prevented.

## 104 FITZWILLIAM TO GUYBON

*London, 10 August 1699; F(M)C 1091*

The buck came very sweet and clean dressed but I regret it was no fatter because I intended it for particular friends. So you must send another, the best you have, next week. The lease granted to Blackbourne in 1651 mentions no house as yours does. If this house that Ward lives in is certainly part of Griffin's estate learn if it is a new erection, and if it has right of common which it might if built on an old toft or foundation of an old house. Was that John Wildbore mentioned in the lease the one that was hanged or the Peterborough draper dead four or five years ago? I don't understand by your letter whether the enclosed pasture is worth 20s or 30s a year and unenclosed worth 6s or 9s a year. Satisfy me in this. I shall want money very much before Abraham Ree pays me that £100. [P.S.] Ask Mr St John to order his correspondent to pay me the £50 you paid them last. My wife wishes Mrs Bull and Mrs Pendleton to take up the bees. Does my cousin Henry Tryce live still at Peterborough or at Clenchwharton?[1]

[1] Clenchwarton, Norfolk, village 3 miles west of King's Lynn.

## **105** FITZWILLIAM TO GUYBON

*London, 17 August 1699; F(M)C 1092*

(Encloses warrant for first of his summer bucks. Repeats his query of Letter **104** concerning the annual rental value of Griffin's pastures. St John's agent has not paid the £50, and he is in great need of money. Would have warrant served next Saturday and the buck sent up next week, but if it cannot be served so soon, then week after.) We have found Griffin's lease among Mr Pigeon's writings, which mentions no house but refers to another acre of Northborough pasture. Ask Vaughan about it and discover its annual value. It's 50 years since Blackbourne took his lease and I really fancy he built that house Edward Ward lives in upon that acre. If not then this acre must be discovered for it's in the lease and must not be lost. I hope to finish Maxey business this week. The buck you send me next week I desire to be a very good one for it's to be presented to extraordinary friends. If the keeper will not serve the warrant send one from my park, but shot, not hunted, for otherwise it will not come sweet. I wish you good harvest weather.

## **106** GUYBON TO FITZWILLIAM

*22 August 1699; F(M)C 1093*

Received yours of the 17th. Griffin's pasture is let for 20s enclosed and for 6s unenclosed. Have visited Northborough and Maxey but nobody can identify that single acre. Old Burley and all neighbours say it must be the acre the house stands on, which Burley says was built about the time of the lease [i.e. 1651]. Have sent a forest buck. Have spoken to Pickering and Mr St John is much troubled his steward[1] has not paid the £50, having written three times about it. Mr Ree will pay the £100 this week and I will send more as fast as I can get returns. Mrs Bellamy, who is still very bad, sends her humble duty. I hope Mr William is better. We should be very glad to see him here for after harvest is the time for setting, coursing and hunting. I hope we shall see you all here soon.

[1] Mr Bennett.

## **107** FITZWILLIAM TO GUYBON

*24 August 1699; F(M)C 1094*

Received yours of the 22nd but too late for I have paid for Maxey, Griffin's land and all, so we must contrive to get up money to repay what I have borrowed. I suppose harvest is in, or almost, so ride among the tenants and get up what money you can. Thomas Freeman and the rest must sell their wool for ready money for I cannot forbear. It gives a good price so they may keep it to their loss and my inconvenience so press them. If Mr St John needs another £50 let him have it for his correspondent may as well pay me £100 as £50. I would have had it already but the 'old gentleman his steward' has a great harvest and cannot come to town yet. The buck came sweet but I prefer my own. I give the Cross-a-hand warrant to yourself, Pendleton, Cousin Tryce and his sister Bellamy.

I understand there are severall royalties due to the Castle of Maxey, as presents of pepper etc, from severall townes round about it and especially from the Deepings, which Sir Gabriell Sylvius and his lady, being low, durst not insist upon. I would not have you pretend ignorance but you may be asking Mr Vaughan about it to try if he be honest and remember what he tells you and sett it downe in writeing. If you thinke fitt you may sett Mr Pendleton to sift it out of him. I intend against I go downe to be instructed in the whole. My sonne William continues as he was. I hope to come downe soone and bring him with mee to try if the countrey aire will help him but I feare nothing will doe.

[P.S.] If the beer and ale won't keep a fortnight longer bottle the ale.

## **108** FITZWILLIAM TO GUYBON
*[London, ? August 1699]; F(M)C 1096*

I understand [Abraham] Rees' money is paid to another person so don't depend on that £100. This means I cannot leave town next week, wanting money to discharge my debts. I shall receive £40 by Pickering's order and Mr St John's £50 next week but these will not near pay my debts so I cannot stir without further supply. [P.S.] Mr Morrice's money came in good time. Pay him on sight.[1]

[1] Guybon paid Morrice £23 on 2 September. He also paid £100 to 'Abram Ris' the 30 August, although it is not clear why he would have paid in advance. Ris or Rees had in fact paid £100 at Heriot's about 30 August, see Letter **110** below; Disbursements 790.

## **109** FITZWILLIAM TO GUYBON
*London, 31 August 1699; F(M)C 1095*

Neither Mr Rees nor Mr St John's agent has paid as yet. I wonder Mr St John should be so backward. I am glad you are returning by other hands. I hope to be down next week if my son is fit to travel.

## **110** FITZWILLIAM TO GUBYON
*London, 14 September 1699; F(M)C 1097*

Have received no letter from you this fortnight, and have little to report save that Abraham Ree paid £100 about August 30 which I only learned 4 or 5 days ago, and Mr St John's £50 is paid. I hope you have distributed that warrant for Westhay Walk among our Peterborough friends. I know not when I shall come down since my son is somewhat better and winter so near at hand. [P.S.] Return money as fast as you can for I am to pay £1,300 next term, a mortgage on Maxey estate I cannot pay off sooner, and I am unwilling to pay interest since I hope to get enough ready money if you are 'quicke' on the tenants. We would be glad of some partridges and pigeons. Send word if Mr St John is at Thorpe and when he comes to town, and if his sons are yet gone into Holland.

### 111 FITZWILLIAM TO GUYBON

*London, 21 September 1699; F(M)C 1098*

I am glad Pendleton can recover the beer and ale since it's been kept too long although at worst it could have been new brewed with the addition of a little water and malt. I am glad you know where to get a she ass, but I can buy cheaper here and drive her down. If the militia is to be called out have the black colt handled; he will pass muster for one. Mr Clitheroe[1] must send his horse this year. Last time I sent three and will only send two this time. Maxey finds no militia horse at all but do not mention this to anybody. 'A blott is not a blott while it's hitt'[2] as the old saying is. My wife will have no pigeons or partridges till the weather cools. Tell Mr Pendleton if Mr Standish will come to a reference there is not a more understanding man than Mr Ballett to advise him, and he will be in the country on Monday. I have consulted two or three London lawyers but they claim not to understand the business and insist Pendleton come up to state it, but I think that not worth his time so never mentioned it before. [P.S.] I enclose a letter for old Mr Vaughan how to order himself at next Deeping Fair which he must do something about two or three days before, so carry it to him next Monday and discuss it together if health and business will permit. Have the beds of my dressing room, Lady Newburgh's chamber,[3] Mrs Forster's chamber and Mrs Lewellin's chamber very well aired the beginning of next week for I may come down a week or fortnight hence. I would have nobody know it. I will write a post or two before I go down. If I do not write by a Thursday's post I will direct it to be sent from Peter Rainsford's. If you can inform yourself write by the next post what day Lord and Lady Exeter come up for their Italian journey. I charge you not to let Mr Ballett, or anyone else know I design to come down.

[1] See **90** above.

[2] An expression from backgammon in which a single 'man' is a 'blot'. If an opponent plays to it he 'hits a blot', takes it up, puts it on 'bar'. A blot is not a blot while it's hit, therefore, means immobilised, removed from play. However, here Fitzwilliam seems to mean that a blot is not a blot while it is concealed.

[3] More correctly Lady Barrett. Lady Newburgh was Fitzwilliam's maternal grandmother, who married as her second husband Lord Barrett of Newburgh, Co. Fife. She married two further husbands before her death in 1674, and may have spent her last years at Milton.

### 112 FITZWILLIAM TO GUYBON

*London, 23 September 1699; F(M)C 1099*

The weather is now so very cold and my son William so very tender and ill that I darc not stir out of town. Do not air the beds until further order. [P.S.] The buck you and Thomas Freeman think can be spared from my park give to Peterborough [friends].

### 113 FITZWILLIAM TO GUYBON

*London 28 September 1699; F(M)C 1100*

Francis Guybon, I received no letter from you this weeke nor any money as yett paid mee. Pray speake with Mr Roger Pemberton and desire him to looke amung his father's papers for my courts, for that I have writt this post to Mr Burman of Stamford to keep my court of Maxey and I would have Mr Pemberton keep a court for mee at Norborough the same day and, after the charge given, adjourne the jury to Maxey and so dine all together at Maxey Castle. I have reason for what I write and will write both to you and Mr Pemberton about it the next post and leave order with Peter Rainsford to send the Sundaie's letter to you. I have not time to explaine myselfe now, the post being just goeing away . . .

[P.S.] Let Mr Pemberton and Mr Burman agree together what day to keep the courts that may best suit their occasions.

## 114 FITZWILLIAM TO GUYBON

*London 30 September 1699; F(M)C 1101*

Francis Guybon, I have writt this post to Mr Roger Pemberton to keep Norborough court the 12th of the next moneth and last Thursday I writt to Mr Burman about what he shall propose that day both to the jury of Maxey and Deeping Gate as likewise to Norborough jury for I have ordered the jury of Norborough after the court is over, which will not last above an howre, their business being little, to go dine at Maxey. Pray lett Mr Vaughan know of it in time and provide a good dinner for at least 40 or 50 people and we had best this time have the company dine at Maxey Castle being the propperest place especially since it's the first court kept in my name. Hereafter it may be kept at Mr Vaughan's as formerly but now there will not be roome at his little house for all the company that will be there, as I conjecture. Mr Burman haveing appointed Thursday the 12th of October to keep Maxey court I have directed him after dinner when the company is a little merry with good liquour to move them now at my first court to make a present to mee as their cheife lord of that little liberty; and that which will be most acceptable to mee will cost them nothing and signifie nothing to any of them. I desire they would give mee twenty acres out of the North Fenn and I would have it lie round Waldrum Hall. I have some reasons why I would have it there and if you read Mr Pemberton's letter I have writt a little more fully to him but not so fully as I shall write to you about it afterwards. Pray perswade Mr Pemberton to dine that day at Maxey, he and Mr Burman together may do more then one of them only. If the business succeeds that I have that land, you may assure Mr Pemberton from me he shall have tenne guyneas for his good will and assistance, and if he finds the commoners in a good humour he may run them up and say from himselfe that since my lord is so moddest a gentleman to aske so small a present as 20 acres, the commoners can do no less then present him with tenne more acres, out of their good will, but Mr Pemberton must do this with great wariness for it may be this may spoile all if he finds the commoners not well inclined, and if he can mannage the affaire so well as to gaine me thirty acres he shall have twenty guyneas. If things succeed, he may have some small writeing ready for them to sett their hands to, as are present, least they forgett their promise afterwards. Pray invite Stephen Brightman and 3 or 4 more of Norborough cheife men, unless they be upon the jury, and picke up some out of Deepingate and Maxey that are leadeing men, besides the jury, and lett Mr Vaughan know as neare as you can what company he is like to have that he may provide accordingly, and lett John Webdale likewise be there.

He may do us some service by his talkeing with some of them. I have not writt as yett to Mr Vaughan about it but you may acquaint him with my designe and heare what he saies to it and who he thinks may be propper persons to help to forward the business, but after all, the business must not be made publike or knowne till the very day, but only to some few persons that you are sure will hold their tongues. If you find Mr Pemberton coole in this busieness do not shew this letter to him. You may consult also with Mr Pendleton. It may be he may assist you with his advice, or otherwise. I have not time to inlarge more at present, the post staying, but hope you will altogether mannage things with that prudence and circumspection as to gaine my point, and you will oblige your loveing freind ... [P.S.] I have spent all my money and heare nothing as yett of Mr Pickering's money or his salesman.

## 115 FITZWILLIAM TO GUYBON

*London, 5 October 1699; F(M)C 1102*

> Today Horner paid me £36 2s 9d for Matthew Pickering. In mid November I must pay £1,300 remaining of my purchase money for which I have not £200 as yet, and am loath to borrow. Be very earnest with my tenants and bespeak what returns you can.

I hope you have consulted with Mr Roger Pemberton about the twenty acres I desire may be laied out of the North Fenn to Waldrum Hall, and should be glad to heare by next post what your opinions are of it, which I will answer by next Tuesdaye's post and would have you send for the letters on Thursday morneing before you go to Maxey court, for I would have you be there by all meanes to see what is done and incourage this business what you can. If you find any leading man that has a considerable interest averse to it you may whisper them in the eare and tell him he shall be no looser, that I will make him a present when I come into the countrey, and thus to every one that you find peevish and averse, but never tell this to any one before another person, but privately in his eare. Pray acquaint Mr Vaughan also of my designe for I have not yett writt to him about it haveing been hindred by other business but it's very likely I may the next post if not this. If I do not write lett him know I received his last letter giveing me an account that he could do no good as to the removeing the post Mr Bertie sett downe in the middle of Markett Deeping New Bridge to hinder carts comeing into my meddow with timber etc. Lett him know I understand there are many people out of the Deepings and other townes that are bound by the tennure to do suite and service at Maxey, and bring pepper and other acknowledgements. That I do expect at my first court they all come and do their fealties, upon the forfeiture of their estates if they do not. If you thinke Mr Pendleton can do us any good at Maxey court gett him to go along with you thither ...

> [P.S.] Send the enclosed to Mr Vaughan which I fear otherwise may not reach him from Stamford in time to provide for the court dinner. Learn how I must send to him by the post hereafter.

## 116 FITZWILLIAM GUYBON
*London, 12 October 1699; F(M)C 1103*

Mr Pickering's salesman has paid £29 15s 3d.

I am sorry for what you write that what I expect from the commoners out of the North Fenn will not be acceptable to them. The thing is so small a matter amungst them all and would be so convenient for mee to make that little farme more commodious that I could not expect but they would have granted it mee readiely. When I go into the countrey if I can find the like number of acres belonging either to Maxey, Norborough or Deeping Gate that can be conveniently parted from any of my farmes I will exchange it freely or I will give them the vallew of it in money meerly for the conveniency of it. I do not expect to have it for nothing for had they freely presented mee with it I should at one time or other have returned them as much for it. I have not heard either from Mr Pemberton or Mr Burman about it. I hope they are of another opinion from you otherwise they would have writt to mee before now. If I heare not from them by the post tomorrow I will write to them about what you say next post. It may be vogued[1] how that the Soake presented my Lord of Exeter with 100 acres out of the Great Fenn, and I am as much lord paramont over the North Fenn as my Lord Exeter was over the Great Fenn. Pray consider of what I write to you and consult with Mr Pemberton whose advise and assistance I rely on as much as of any one's ... [P.S.] Thanke God we are all in good health except my poore sonne William who is very ill at this time and yesterday as finely chearfull as could be and eates heartiely most an end but his great affliction is a tormenting cough that much hinders his sleep a nights. I hope he will be pretty well againe in a day or two. James Ullitt had a mind to go see his mother for a weeke. He went from hence last Munday sennight. If he is not come away already pray hasten him up. Lett his mother know he is a very idle fellow and I am afraied will never come to any thing. She may do well to give him good advise for if he continues as he is he is [not] like to continue long in my service. I sent downe by him my young greyhound that I have bred in the house. He carried him to my Cousin Bellamie's[2] who I hope will take care of him and enter him well with his doggs. He is as hopefull as can be. I would have sent him to Milton but heare a certaine woman there loves not doggs so I would not trouble her.[3] The dogg's name is Smugg which was the name of the greyhound that was pictured with mee in the picture in my bed chamber at Milton and this dogg is very like him. If you write to mee by the next post of anything that relates to this busieness of Maxey I can answer it by the post after which you will receave on Thursday morning before you keep Maxey and Norborough courts if you send to Peterborough for the letters. I heare the ferry boate is past the best. You may do well to consider where to have a new one built that may do us the best service. Write mee your opinion of it before you bespeake it and heare what Mr Lowrey and Robert Newcomb saies to it because they are masters of ganges of boates. Heare where they say it's best to build them, whither at Peterborough or any of the Deepings and who has the most seasoned timber for such a use.

[1] The meaning here is probably 'spread' or 'noise abroad'.
[2] At Farcet, south of Peterborough.
[3] Presumably Mrs Pendleton is meant.

## 117 FITZWILLIAM TO GUYBON

*London, 26 October 1699; F(M)C 1105*[1]

Am sorry you did not think fit to pursue my proposal for a 'decoy' at Waldrum Hall. Peakirk is the nearest town but it's fully half a mile away, and if I had 20–30 acres more about that land I already have it would do my business well enough. I told Mr Ash of my design who said he would accompany you there any time and give his best judgment. However, the plan is lost for now. When I come down I will go over and consider what to do.

As to the new boate I thanke Mr Lowrey for his good advise. Pray follow it and if you thinke it will be best for [us] to cutt our owne timber and season it this winter season, pray lett it be done for I [do] not vallew a little barke since I may be made amends in the goodness of my [b]oate, but you may aske Mr Lowrey's advise againe whither it may be best for [m]ee to find my owne timber or lett them find it and I agree with them so much [fo]r a boate of such and such scantlings. If I find timber then you are to agree [w]ith them for sawing out the timber and makeing the boate up and doeing all [th]ings to it to fitt it for the water, and you must be carefull they do not aske [fo]r more wood then is necessary and so cheate you of the rest. Be sure to imploy the best boatewrights and inquire of Mr Lowrey who they are, whither at Peter[bo]rough or at one of the Deepings. You must enter into articles with them [who]ever does it and lett all your several scantlings be expresst.

Give Mr Pemberton 10s for keeping Northborough court. I don't know how I shall pay the £1,300 for Maxey. Mr St John's £50 will only meet expenses. I used to receive £200–£300 from Thomas Freeman at this season and other rents in great sums. I must pay in three weeks. Use all possible means to supply me. Write out and send your accounts for the two years past, each year separately.

[1] Edge of letter destroyed. Letters and words in brackets reconstructed.

## 118 FITZWILLIAM TO GUYBON

*London, 2 November 1699; F(M)C 1106*

I have overwritten two more warrants for my does. Send a doe every week, in flag baskets to save the extraordinary carriage fee. How many good does may I have from my park? Don't mention the 'decoy' since we don't pursue it. If we can spare our own timber for the boat I am ready to save my money. Two shillings a day for boatwrights is a great rate, besides a groat a day a man for ale. Try others to see what they will do; Deeping men, for Peterborough men will go home every night and perhaps come later in the morning, we having nobody to supervise them. Deeping men must stay at the ferry and are sooner at work. Yet it may be my best course to pay the 2s 4d a day a man if I cannot do it cheaper. Make returns by the 20th; otherwise I must borrow. I am glad you are returning £50 by Mr St John although I hear nothing yet of the £50 you last paid him. Ask them to write to old [Bennett] whenever you pay them money. My daughter asked me to inform you James Ullitt came here safe. I hope the boy will mend his manners. If so I shall not part with him, but I fear he gets now and then into bad company which will ruin him ... His mother would do well to write to him occasionally with good advice.

### 119 FITZWILLIAM TO GUYBON

*London, 9 November 1699; F(M)C 1107*

Send two more does from my park, and distribute the warrants among Peterborough friends. Be sure Cousins Tryce and Bellamy are well served, with a warrant between them. The other give to Roger Pemberton, Lowrey, Duce and Newcomb. You and Pendleton shall have a doe from my park. Send the first doe loose and the second in a flag basket so I can compare how they travel—the last by basket was moist, ugly and ill killed. Since you have timber felled and hard to sell, bring it to the sawpit. I think it very dear to allow the Deeping boatwrights seven groats a day a man and diet besides. I never heard of diet before. Harry Watts allowing it is no precedent to me. He might allow it to a man for a day or two for it's not worth bringing victuals for so short a time. When they are to work weeks together it's another matter. Inform yourself as I shall also. Let me hear from you about it and I shall let you know what I learn, for I cannot believe it's a common practice. I will rather employ Peterborough men and save their diet, which will be considerable. Mr Bennett has paid me £50. I was not sure whether you had paid £50 more but he said when he heard he would pay it as soon as he got up the money.

### 120 FITZWILLIAM TO GUYBON

*London, 16 November 1699; F(M)C 1108*

For the ferry boat I am indifferent whether you use Peterborough or Deeping men since the wages are alike. I am for employing the best workmen but you had better not begin till the days be long enough for the men to work from six to six. Three weeks or a month 'will breake no squares' and the men will dispatch it in time and cheaper. If not, they will use fewer days. I thank Mr Lowrey for his kind intention of coming occasionally to see the work and give directions. My money must be paid next Wednesday without fail, and since I am unlikely to receive more than £100 from you, I must borrow a great deal at interest and, besides, be forced to keep it six months. Mr St John keeps no cash in town. When you pay him any he orders [Bennett] to raise it among his tenants, which requires time.

### 121 FITZWILLIAM TO GUYBON

*London, 28 November 1699; F(M)C 1109*

Francis Guybon, On Satturday night last between 11 and 12 it pleased God to take my deare sonne William out of this world. He died with great patience and resignation, and at noone there was very little appeareance of death in him, for he dined below staires with us that day and we imagined he might have lived these 3 moneths; but the great change happened within 2 houres before his death. God fitt us all for himselfe, for there is great uncertainty in this world. His body will be sent out of towne next Thursday morneing very early, in order to be buried at Marrham on Satturday, by foure of the clocke after dinner. Therefore, immediately after receipt of this, order the vault to be opened, that it may be cleane and sweet against the time.[1] The herse and coaches that attend him will go through Peterborough about 2 of the clocke on Satturday, not dareing to send them over the ferry for want of a boate. Pray desire my cozen Henry Tryce, my cozen Bellamy, Mr Hacke, young Mr Roos, [and] Mr Leaffeild's sonne, to be bearers of the pall, and a sonne of Mr Ap Price's[2] of Washingly will make up the sixth, who will meete them at Stilton. My cozen Tryce and Bellamy being married men must hold up the pall at the head, young Mr Price and Mr Hacke in the middle, Mr Roos the younger and Mr Leaffeild's sonn at the feet. If any of these cannot be there, supply their places with others. Yourselfe, Mr Pendleton, and these bearers, must meete the corps at Woodson[3] by twelve of the clocke, or at farthest by one, for it's better you should stay for the corps then they for you. The coffin is very heavy being lined with lead, therefore you must appoint eight strong men to carry it, as Adam Johnson, Goodman Wootton, and sixe others like men, who must be at Woodson with you and the other gentlemen to attend the corps. These must have gownes sent downe and velvett capps and long blacke staves, and must walke on foote round the hearse from Woodson to Marrham to keep off the mobb, and if the waies are durty woud do well to have bootes. Pray aske Mr Pickering that the hearse and coaches may go through Mr St John's ground, and I choose that way for them to go by Milton to Marrham, because it's most greensword all the way. Aske leave of Mr Pendleton to breake a gapp in his hedge for the body to be carried through by the bearers, because the little gate I used to light at in the church meddow is not wide enough for the bearers to go through with the body.

By all meanes buy yourselfe a sute of mourneing, which I will allow you for, and lett it be made up against the time, for you and my sonn's gentleman, that comes downe in the coaches, must be cheife mourners, and there will be a long cloake for you sent downe. Therefore, you must go into the coach at Woodson, and my sonn's footman shall ride your horse. There must be some streamers and other trophies hung up in the chancell, so there must be a lather[4] gott ready to hang them up with. I have ordered some gloves to be sent downe, that if any gentlemen in the neighbour[hoo]d comes in to the funerall, or the tennants, they may have each a paire of gloves, but I do not meane to give to all the mobb that are not my tennants. There will be some escutcheons, 3 dozen, sent downe to be left with you to give away to my cheife tennants and neighbours. The eight silke escutcheons on the pall, 6 must be given to the 6 gentlemen bearers, and [for] the other 2, one you may keep yourselfe and send backe the other. Mr Pendleton will have cloath and 8 escutcheons on his pulpitt; the cloath to make him mourning with afterwards; besides the escutcheons about the hearse which I suppose the mobb will make sure off. You are to be at no mannor of expences, not so much as a pott of ale, for as soone as the body is buried the hearse and coaches come away to towne. I agree with them for all. They are not to stop at all at Milton. There must come a man 2 or 3 houres before the body to hang the chancell with mourneing, etc., therefore the clarke must be there ready with a ladder or two to help him and one or two more if occasions serves. What is spent at Woodson while you waite for the hearse take care to pay for.[5] I am in hast, your loveing freind, W.

Fitzwilliam. [P.S.] You shall have a mourning hattband sent downe by the coaches.

[1] 'Dec. 3: Gave Robert Bursnoll for opening and covering the vault, 4s'; Disbursements 790.

[2] Apreece (variously spelled in the letters Ap Rice, Price, etc) was Robert Apreece of Washingley, Huntingdonshire (1638–1723), M.P. for Huntingdonshire: *House of Commons 1660–1690*, i, 540–1.

[3] Woodston, Huntingdonshire, south of Peterborough across the Nene.

[4] Ladder.

[5] 'Dec. 3: Spent at Peterborough and Woodson when we went to meet the hearse, 10s', Disbursements 790.

## 122 FITZWILLIAM TO GUYBON
*London, 30 November 1699; F(M)C 1110*

Francis Guybon, The three coachmen that attends the body downe undertooke to mee this morneing to lie at Stilton tomorrow night. They sett out halfe a howre after five this morneing from hence. Pray be all ready at Woodson soone after twelve a clocke next Satturday for I chargd them not to be there sooner and they are to returne to Stilton againe the same night after the service is over. The coffin being covered with vellvett and lined with lead and quilted with silke within side contrary to the act of parliament in that behalfe, pray acquaint Mr Pendleton with it and pay him 50s to distribute amungst the poore of Marrham and lett me have his certificate least I be tax't here againe for the same.[1] We intend to send some things downe by the carrier next Munday, therefore pray lett some body be sent for them next Wednesday ... [P.S.] My wife is so afflicted I wish it does not put her into a fitt of sickness. I will send Mr Pendleton some cloath downe for mourning, for the cloath sent downe to cover the pulpitt must continue to be putt on every Sunday for some time. I will send word when it may be taken away for good and all. In the mene time, after service is over on Sundays after dinner it must be taken downe and brusht and laied by till next Sunday. I meane the fines[t] of the cloath not the baies. The baies and estchuchions in the chancell must continue up [the whole] yeare. There will be amungst other things sent downe next Wensday some women's gloves which we had not time to send downe by the hearse. Pray have some body ready against service is over at the funeral to shew the coachmen the way backe to Peterborough by Walton because that is the nearest way though I would have them come by Thorpe and Milton way because it's cleane that way ...

[1] 'Dec. 3: Gave Mr Pendleton to distribute among the poor of Marham, 50s'; Disbursements 790. The act of 1678 provided that 'no corpse of any person (except those who shall die of the plague) shall be buried in any shirt, shift, sheet or shroud of anything' other than woollen cloth, and coffins were to be lined with sheep's wool only. The penalty for non-compliance was £5, half to be distributed to the poor and half to any informer. Gentlefolk who wished to avoid restriction therefore informed on themselves and thus had only to pay £2 10s; W. E. Tate, *The Parish Chest* (Cambridge, 1957), p. 66–8.

## 123 FITZWILLIAM TO GUYBON
*London, 7 December 1699; F(M)C 1111*

Francis Guybon, My wife has been so much troubled that we have sent nothing downe yett for Mrs Bull and Mrs Pendleton but they shall not faile of it the next weeke on Satturday by the carrier. There will be cloath sent downe to be at Petterborough next Wednesday for old Joseph and his sonne Joseph Chamberlaine to make each of them a coate and paire of breeches, 4 yards and a quarter each man, and then will be 3 yards more of the same cloath to make John Wattson a coate only. It may be at the same time we may send some cloath for Mr Pendleton, if not at farthest on Satturday when the women's things will be sent downe. Pray send me word if you have bought yourselfe any cloath yett. Lett me know by the next post, that if you have none I will send you some downe with the women's things. My wife would not have Mrs Pendleton and Mrs Bull go to church nor any where abroad till they have their mourning. Lett mee know if there has been any paper escutcheons sent downe since the buriall was over because I understand those that should have been putt up on the mourning round the chancell were loss't and then those I designd for you to give away to the cheife of my tennants were forc't to be putt up in the chancell in their place. As soone as these paper eschutcheons comes, lett me know how many they be.

> Notwithstanding that you wrote I should receive so many hundred pounds I have received nothing since Webdale's drover, Broughton, paid some,[1] and [Mr Bennett] paid £50 last week. Having extraordinary occasions you should be earnest with those who promised returns not to fail their times and with the tenants for rents. [P.S.] Next Monday have the escutcheons round the chancel and pulpit taken down and dispose of them among the best of my tenants, for they will spoil if they hang there longer.

[1] Guybon paid Webdell £80 in the last week of November, Disbursements 790.

## **124** FITZWILLIAM TO GUYBON

*London, 14 December 1699; F(M)C 1112*

> (Has sent down mourning in two boxes by Fearey's wagon, one containing clothes for Mrs Pendleton, Mrs Bull and Goody Butler; the other cloth not made up: 4½ yards fine, 7 quarters wide, for Mr Pendleton's gown; 3 yards coarser for a loose coat for his clerk, 'yung Wattson'; 8½ yards to make coats and breeches for the [two Joseph] Chamberlaines, 4¼ yards each. £25 0s 10d paid by order John Featherstone and £64 7s 8d by Pickering's bill on Sir Francis Child.)[1] [Bennett] does not pay as soon as he should; I have waited three months for £50 paid in the country. He paid £50 on the 2nd, but I believe another £50 is owed which you paid before Mr St John came to town. When you pay them money take a receipt. When they pay they send mine or my goldsmith's receipt to you, and you deliver them their receipt again. Then there can be no mistake. Tell the Chamberlaines I have sent the cloth that they may buy black buttons, etc, at Peterborough on Saturday so they may be made up for Christmas, and Watson the same.

I am very much concerned for my greyhound dogg and wish I had sent him to Milton, where you might have bought things that were necessary for him. The dogg was sound enough when he went from hence and was not fatt in the least but in good tune for sport. If he was rotten which I cannot beleive, it must be by drinkeing butter milke and whey, which putt him into a looseness and so carried him off. I wish I had never sent him to them. My sonne is very desirous to know what day of the moneth he died off, if they can recollect themselves. He was the hopefullest young dog in England and of the best breed both by dogg and bitch.

I shall never have the like againe. I could have had a very good horse in exchange for him. . . .

[P.S.] We have wet, warm, unhealthy weather. Keep the leads swept and the pipe heads clean. If you feed the pigeons in hard weather buy offal corn, but destroy the vermin about the yards or there will be no pigeons left.

[1] Both sums repaid 21 December, Disbursements 790.

## **125** FITZWILLIAM TO GUYBON

*London, 4 January 1699/1700; F(M)C 1113*

Your letter three weeks ago said I should receive £300 that week but have only received £40 by Edward Checkley's order, and £100 paid to Heriot by your and Whynyates' order. The person paying Checkley's money said one person 'was broke' who should have paid more, so it would not be paid before spring. If it was for Thomas Freeman's wool he should take care how he deals with them, for I hear the £100 William Checkley paid me last year for that year's wool is yet unpaid, he having borrowed on bond. If your payments are not more certain I shall not know how to live. I had to buy Christmas provisions from my main stock, some principal having been accidentally paid. My son is much troubled you did not answer my query as to the exact day my greyhound died. If that cannot be remembered he would know if it was before his brother's corpse was interred. There was no intention of sending down gloves for the tenants' wives. That is not proper upon a man's death.

## **126** FITZWILLIAM TO GUYBON

*London, 1 February 1699/1700; F(M)C 1114*

I told you in my last that Mr Seth Meares of Thorney paid £67 19s 10d on January 11th, and £160 on the 29th.[1] For the £34 0s 5d mistakenly paid Sir Francis Child's shop by James Dove and William Ashly send me the note they gave you otherwise they will not repay me for although Heriot will trust me, goldsmiths I deal with but little will not. I ordered Mr Russell the undertaker to send down two dozen paper escutcheons to hang around the chancel to replace those which were lost. Pin them to the baize hanging there. Let me know Fearey's charge for carriage and I will make Russell allow for it. I ordered Mr Vaughan to pay Maxey rents to you. He writes that some tenants make waste on their land and desires a note of the covenants in the leases, but I cannot send them yet, Mr Pigeon being dead and his executors having not yet acted. Explain this to him and discover which tenants commit waste and what waste it is. As I remember their leases the tenants must commit no waste and are obliged to plant so many young trees yearly. Let their wastes be set down in writing for memory's sake. I would know if Mr Clitheroe has other land belonging to Lolham Estate than what John Webdale rents from him; who are tenants to it, and their rent. Vaughan or Webdale could inform you, but ask this 'as it were accidentally in discourse and not as if I bid you do it'. My wife is often ill and my son not as healthy as he was. I hope the country air may do him good. [P.S.] When do you intend to begin the new ferry boat?[2] Let the days be first of 'handsome' length and employ the best workmen.

[1] Fitzwilliam's previous letter has not survived. He probably wrote two letters during January which are lost. Guybon paid £100 to Mr 'Whingates' on 6 January, £67 19s 10d to Mr Seth Meares on 11 January, £100 to Mr Dews (and the £40 to Mr Checkley) on 16 January, and £68 12s to Mr Exton on 23 January, and the further £160 to Seth Meares on 29 January; Disbursements 790. All these sums Guybon would not normally have repaid until his master had informed him that he had received the sums in London.

[2] In fact Guybon had paid 'Goodman Ricroft' and his son £2 13s for 26½ days 'sawing and hewing wood for the boat' as early as mid December, Disbursements 790.

## 127 FITZWILLIAM TO GUYBON

*London, 8 February 1699/1700; F(M)C 1115*

(Has received the notes he had asked for in the previous letter but will not present them at Sir Francis Child's until Guybon explains why one note for £10 19s 9d 'paid by William Ashley's order' is endorsed on the back by James Dove by mark 'in parte of my halfe yeare's rent due Lady Day '99'. May be correct if Ashley and Dove are partners in that ground, but if wrong note has been endorsed must be corrected or will confuse Guybon's accounts. Again requests information about Clitheroe's holdings of Lolham land.)

## 128 FITZWILLIAM TO GUYBON

*London, 15 February 1699/1700; F(M)C 1116*

(Reiterates query about notes. Thomas Wright has paid £22 9s 1d to Heriot. Guybon must dun Mr Checkley to pay Thomas Freeman's wool money). Let me know if the escutcheons are painted as handsomely as the rest were that went down with the hearse and the cost of carriage. Pin them on the breadth of the baize around the chancel for they must hang for a year.

## 129 FITZWILLIAM TO GUYBON

*London, 29 February 1699/1700; F(M)C 1117*

(Regrets escutcheons not yet arrived. They were delivered to Peterborough carrier in Aldersgate Street. Must inquire further. Had ordered Vaughan to pay Guybon Maxey rents as he received them.[1] Guybon to report what Vaughan has paid, and all further receipts as they occur.) Tell Mrs Bull my wife would have her buy coarse linen at Stamford Midlent Fair for sheets for the under-servants' beds, for hall and dresser cloths, towels, etc. Some must be as fine as that she used for your and Pendleton's beds, enough for five or six pairs, and that for the under-servants must be coarser, six or seven pairs. Supply her with money but she need not buy if there is no linen 'to her mind'.

[P.S.] Thank Mrs Bull for the chine and black pudding and to yourself for the hare and pheasant.

[1] Guybon had received £48 from Vaughan in part of Maxey rents on 3 February and received further sums during the year, Receipts 16 Nov. 1699–15 Oct. 1700, F(M) Misc. Vols. Vol. 27 (hereafter Receipts 27).

## 130 FITZWILLIAM TO GUYBON

*London, 7 March 1699/1700; F(M)C 1118*

I am glad the escutcheons are come.[1] If there are only 23 perhaps the carrier has cheated you of one for himself. There should have been eight buckram escutcheons for round the pulpit but they are not needed now. Get Mrs Bull to direct their pinning at equal distance round the chancel. Were they as well painted as the buckram? They need not be gilded but the arms must be painted like the others. My wife believes there is not enough cloth at Milton to make up the sheets she requires and would have the rest bought at Midlent fair. She believes linen will be good and cheap since hemp and flax were got so well and dry last summer, and it has been a fine 'open' winter to work it in. We leave it to Mrs Bull's prudence. Richard Ettee has paid £36 10s for Mr Exon, and says he will pay more this week for James Dove. I need a considerable sum to lend to a person who wants £600 of it paid at Stamford. In what time could you get me such a sum out of my rents? Meantime you can borrow part of it from Mr Lowrey and some of our Peterborough acquaintances and from Mr Kettleborough at Stamford, and if you cannot repay them in a month or six weeks I can repay them here if they need it. It will be a good time next week to begin the ferry boat. Employ those reputed the 'honestest' and best workmen. Let them live where they will, 'the best are the best cheape.' I shall be obliged if Mr Lowrey steps over now and then to see they work well.

[1] On 3 March Guybon paid Fearey 6d for bringing down 23 paper escutcheons, Disbursements 790.

## 131 FITZWILLIAM TO GUYBON

*London, 14 March 1699/1700; F(M)C 1119*

I have received £21 15s 4d from James Dove, and £16 15s 4d by Thomas Ashly, and £20 4s 6d from William Ash. These small sums help little when I am paying great sums. I can pay the loan here but it would be a kindness to the borrowers to pay so much in the country. If you cannot pay £600 let me know what you could pay. I am glad Mrs Bull has bought linen. My wife wishes to know what kinds, in what quantity, and the prices.[1] The boat-builders must be looked after at the beginning and ending of the day. [P.S.] Is the kitchen chimney cured of smoking; does the clock go and the hands with it as they should; do the new building garrets no longer leak, and what lime have you in the lime house or the new stables.

[1] Guybon paid Mrs Bull £1 19s for 42¾ yards of cloth at 11d a yard, and £1 9s 2d for 35½ yards at 10d a yard, Disbursements 790.

## 132 FITZWILLIAM TO GUYBON

*London, 28 March 1700; F(M)C 1120*

(Has received £43 2s by Horner for a Mr Baily, and £52 12s 2d for Mr Wright and £43 9s 8d for Mr Pickering.[1] The person holding the money at Stamford can return it to London as Guybon wishes, that loan being presently at a standstill.) For Milton repairs I ordered you last spring to stop your hand only because I expected to be down to see what needed to be done. You might have reminded me last August for after harvest is a good time for such work. Let me know what needs to be done. I am glad Mr Willis has glazed all the new buildings save the stables and barn. They can wait until I come down to advise about the placing of the casements, of which there must be several, some with leaden panes not glass. I am sorry the kitchen chimney is as bad as ever. I must have advice more expert than Wright's, and not rebuild it without curing it. [P.S.] Ask Mr Lowrey if he has a dependable correspondent at Lynn to supply French wine. I must have both white and red before I come down. If he knows nobody to trust ask him if he ever goes to Lynn, for I could have him choose me some from Charles Turner's vaults, who tells me he has as good as any comes to England but I don't know how to credit him unless Lowrey tasted it and took care to send it away safe so that the watermen could not drink it and fill it up with water again for that's the great danger.

[1] Guybon did not repay Baily until 21 May, whereas Thomas Wright and Matthew Pickering were repaid on 8 April, so perhaps Guybon did not know him either; Disbursements 790.

## 133 FITZWILLIAM TO GUYBON

*London, 4 April 1700; F(M)C 1121*

I am sorry to hear of the deaths of my old friends Mr Denham and Mr Hawkins, but they died in good old age. I am more sorry for Thomas Freeman who is not at their great age, but I hope he will recover if he and his wife 'have the heart' to provide what is fitting—the advice of a good physician and good cordials, etc, from the apothecary suitable to his distemper. Advise his wife not to neglect him for her and her children's welfare depend on his life. His son is yet an ignorant boy, unfit to manage a farm of £20 a year. I would not have neglected that Preston's house at Northborough if you had reminded me, as is your duty, for I have business enough here to put things out of my head which I do not daily see. Wright could go with you to Northborough to advise how to repair it. You may shore up the roof and rebuild the decayed wall. I will build no new stable at Helpston; the new stable at the end of the great barn is enough for that farm. The hay barn should be built between the wheat barn and the house partly to fence that ground we designed for an orchard. Repair the wheat barn but build no buildings which are needless charge to me to build and for the tenant to keep repaired. [P.S.] Who is this Baily who paid me £43? I fancy he is a fenman about Thorney who paid at a venture knowing you would repay it on my note which he has not yet brought you. Let me know if this be so.

## 134 FITZWILLIAM TO GUYBON

*London, 11 April 1700; F(M)C 1122*

I received the hares but it's a pity to kill more for one was a doe with milk in her teats, and consequently out of season. You have not informed me whether the boat-building goes well, and whether Mr Lowrey is so kind as to come over to check the work. I hope you ensure they do a good day's work keeping the correct times. Are they Deeping or Peterborough workmen? I can say little at this distance to Mr Ewing's offer to sell his land, but if I can have it at a pennyworth and it holds its rent you may buy it. Consult with Mr Bimrose or William Day or especially with Carter, tenant to my farm in Maxey with the slate house that belonged to Northborough purchase. Know if [Ewing's] land could be attached to his farm and how much lies in the field where he wants land most, or whether it would be better attached to Drewry's little farm. I would like to increase Carter's farm by as much land as would bring the rent to £40 or £35 a year, and to Drewry's as to make it £15 or £20. If Ewing's meadow lies in Deepingate Meadow remember we let our meadow there at only 6s an acre. Find out what another tenant would rent it for, and be sure no encumbrance, by mortgage, statute or judgement, lies on it, and what chief rent it owes for Ewing is no lord and must hold of some manor and so owe an acknowledgement, though only a peppercorn. Let me know all before you make a bargain. I am sorry Ewing runs in your debt. Secure what you can for I fear all will be 'nought' with him soon. John Mappletopp paid Heriot £40 for Henry Phillips April 2nd. Shore up the floors and roof of Preston's former Northborough house and repair the walls well. Even Milton could have its walls rebuilt if the roof and floors were propped. If Wright cannot advise how to do it and the workmen don't know how, let it alone; I will bring a man down with me to direct it. Build a pretty handsome hay barn at Helpston, but for calves houses and hogsties tenants used to set up little 'leane-too's' at their own charge against a fence wall, etc. We built nothing of that kind ourselves and I will not begin now. You say no farm in Helpston lies as mine does. I hope you mean for the best, for I have spent much money on it. If for the worst, it is due to your carelessness in not ensuring the tenant maintains it properly for it was in repair when he entered. I am heartily glad Thomas Freeman is like to do well again. '*Pray call upon his wife to keepe home and not gad abroad but mind her husband*'.[1] Captain Styles was in town to renew a lease with the bishop. I lent him £7 6s 8d, but do not call on him for it. He will pay the first money he gets.

[1] Words in emphasis an insertion not by Fitzwilliam but by Guybon himself, perhaps indicating that he intended to read the letter aloud to Mrs Freeman in their cottage, and felt that if she believed that the words came from Fitzwilliam they would have greater effect. See also postscript to Fitzwilliam's letter of April 27th (**136** below).

## 135 FITZWILLIAM TO GUYBON

*London, 18 April 1700; F(M)C 1123*

If you see Captain Styles at Peterborough on Saturday tell him I received the £12 from the goldsmith he wrote of. Pay him £4 13s 4d, which settles that debt. He owes for tithe wood but will pay when he can. I suppose Mr Wingfield will pay me a good sum as he used to do. It will be welcome. No letter this post so hope you are well.

## 136 FITZWILLIAM TO GUYBON

*[London,] 27 [April] 1700; F(M)C 1124*[1]

I suppose this comes soon enough to show the enclosed (tax certificate) to Mr Neale next week. The King's collector came for money for my son's death the next week after, but I did not pay him for some time being dissatisfied when and what I must pay.[2] Being advised I must pay in the parish where he died, and the collector bringing the act and the rate schedules I paid and took this receipt, which I wrote myself, not liking his (version). My house stands in St Giles' parish, Drury Lane division. Having shown it to Mr Neale keep it safe. I am glad the boat goes on and that Mr Lowrey sees it is well done, but it cannot take as long as you write unless too few are employed or they do not keep to their work. Let me know how many hands are constantly engaged. I long for Mr Wingfield to bring me the money yours mentions.

[P.S.] I hope Tom Freeman is quite well againe *and that his wife keepes home and take[s] care of him.*[3]

[1] On cover 'to be sent from Peter Rainsford's with speed.'

[2] The tax was £15 on the death of the eldest son of a baron, imposed from May 1695; Washington, pp. 455–6.

[3] Words emphasised added by Guybon (see **134** above and note).

## 137 FITZWILLIAM TO GUYBON

*London, 9 May 1700; F(M)C 1125*

Francis Guybon, ... As to Mr Ewen's land and the particular, I know he is too cunning for us to deale with and am much affraied some of it is my owne land already, part of the lease for one life. If I could be assured it was no part of the lease land and that his deeds could make out there's so many acres of it and that it was all freehold land and paid no rent to no lord whatsoever I would give him 20 yeares purchase for it at the rates as lands goes in the places where it lies, but he setts downe in Deepingatefeild his land at 9s the acre where I lett my meddow but at 6s, and againe in Grass Crofts which I suppose is baulks between the arrable land that he vallewes at 16s an acre which I suppose is very much over vallewed. You must be very carefull how you deale with him. I had rather have you lett it alone till I come into the countrey which will be in 3 weekes or a moneth at farthest, by midsummer the longest day. And then if he will sell me his lease for a life and this land altogether I will be his chapman for the whole. However, keep his particular and if he is unwilling, take a coppy of it before you part with it. Henry Wingfeild paid mee last Fryday just one hundred pounds and there has been none paid since. Pray make it your business to gett us some servants against we come downe. There must be a fellow to looke after the gates, to make cleane the house, heate the ovens, and to do the other drudging worke about the house. There must be two maides, one for the kittchin that can roast and boile meate cleanely and do the other worke in the kittchin, and the other maide must make cleane the house and wash, and wash bucks, and do any other business that is to be done about the house fitt for a maide servant to doe. Pray gett Mrs Bull to help you to these maides, or any body else that you thinke can do it, and do not neglect to do this thinking Goody Buttler may serve for one. We will not have it so. She must go home and will have worke enough to do to wash for the famiely ... [P.S.] In my next I will order when you shall brew.

## **138** FITZWILLIAM TO GUYBON

*London, 16 May 1700; F(M)C 1126*

Let Mr Wortley dig what gravel he pleases, but warn him it is not a good binding gravel, nor well coloured.

My wife is very earnest that you and Mrs Bull should help her to two workeing maides, one for the kittchin and the other for the house for this summer, for we must be in towne againe the latter end of October. Such sort of maides are not worth our time and charge to carry up and downe. Neither will the maides in this towne do such sort of worke. They are too fine fingred for countrey business. Do all that possibly you can to help us to such maides and also a man as I told you off in my last.

[P.S.] I believe Mr Beales[1] must send to [Milt]on for one of your horses for their muster on Tottenhill Heath, June 17th. Let which you think fit of either the Norfolk gelding or the black colt be shod and trimmed ready about a week before. If you cannot get two maids help us to one, but better two.

[1] Steward of Fitzwilliam's Norfolk estate.

## **139** FITZWILLIAM TO GUYBON

*London, 21 May 1700; F(M)C 1127*

Horner has paid £57 0s 1d for Mr Exton, £18 2s 6d for Matthew Pickering. We are heartily sorry to hear of Cousin Bellamy's[1] death. Thank you for advertising me of the sale of Lolham estate, although Sir Thomas Trollop being a relation will be preferred unless I offer unreasonable terms. I have bid Mr Clitheroe 21 years' purchase, but don't mention this for Sir Thomas does not know. (Asks again about unknown Baily's £43.)[2] Don't neglect getting maids and a man able to heat ovens. We come down sooner than you think.

[1] Perhaps the wife of the John Bellamy mentioned later as the Cousin Bellamy who is to visit Milton with his son Thomas.

[2] See **132** note and **133** above.

## 140 FITZWILLIAM TO GUYBON

*London, 6 June 1700; F(M)C 1128*

Francis Guybon, My daughter is married and has been so ever since last Munday was sennight.[1] I designed she should have the same person but not so soone. However, the young folks thought otherwise and so made an end of the business. You must imagine this is a chargeable time and it has run mee quite out of cash. I desire therefore you will gett mee up all the moneys possibly you can and returne it as soone as ever you can for my stocke is now very low, nay, should be in debt if I should pay my bills.

Am glad the boat is like to be finished before you get this. [P.S.] Have spoken to Clitheroe and believe I have outbid his kinsman Sir Thomas Trollop, to whom, as you informed me, he offered it first, but keep this to yourself. Mr Hide absolutely refused it. Clitheroe is buying land near his home.[2]

[1] To Sir Charles Barrington, Bart., of Hertingfordbury, Hertfordshire.

[2] The postscript refers to sale of lands in Lolham, the lands of which manor may have been part owned by Fitzwilliam, part by Clitheroe (see note to **90** above). The Mr Hide referred to was probably William Hyde (died 8 May 1703 aged 43), the eldest son of William Hyde snr (died 1694) and his wife Mary, daughter of Sir Thomas Trollope, 1st bart. (died 1654) whose grandson, the 3rd baronet is referred to here. Hyde and Trollope were, therefore, cousins, and Clitheroe was probably their cousin also since Trollope's grandmother was Mary Clitheroe.

## 141 FITZWILLIAM TO GUYBON

*London, 13 June 1700; F(M)C 1129*

Get all things ready speedily for some of us will come down if not all together. Get your brewing vessels ready and brew four hogsheads small beer and two of ale. I allow 20 bushels of malt, 16 for the ale and four for the beer. Hop them so they can be drunk within a month from today. Don't let the drink want hops, yet not too bitter. I hope you have hired a man for the gates, etc, ready to come at three days warning. Likewise two maids, one for the kitchen as good as possible, the other a good working servant. Send money speedily for I am in want on such an expensive occasion. [P.S.] Thoroughly air all the beds and clean the rooms at the great end, at the matted end, and at our end of the house.

## 142 FITZWILLIAM TO GUYBON

*London, 26 June 1700; F(M)C 1130*

Sir Charles Barrington[1] intends not to build yet but something will be done hereafter. Mr Wright may be sure I will be mindful of him. Nobody has paid me money since yours of the 10th so I am in need. I will decide about Griffin's land when I come down, but if one house is burned and the other worthless he asks twice the value. I shall certainly be there before you keep courts. What is done about Paradise lease? Lose no time in brewing. My wife is much concerned that Mrs Bull parted with the maids before sending word. We had rather have paid wages than parted with them if worth keeping. Do all possible to get us a kitchen maid and one for washing bucks, and other necessary work about the house. Try at Stamford, Peterborough or anywhere else you think likely. Be sure to get a manservant as I have ordered before. My wife wishes Mrs Bull to buy her enough soap at Petermass Fair to last until Brigg Fair, or else agree with Mr Duce to supply us for that time at a price. If she cannot agree with Mr Duce then with anyone at Peterborough. We believe we will need about a firkin or firkin and a keg. If Mrs Bull thinks the house lacks anything, pewter, brass, wooden or earthenware, which will be cheaper at this fair than after we come down, let her buy it. If cloth was not bought for kitchen towels, hall cloths, kitchen cloths, last year buy them now. Read this to her and give her money. By Sunday's post write what is bought and about the maids. Mrs Bull should supply as many chamber pots and basins as are needed. If the venison is fat send me up a buck with shoulders by the Peterborough coach next week. I have bought extraordinary fat venison here so surely there are good deer at Milton after this fine winter. Is the ferryboat finished?

[1] Fitzwilliam's new son-in-law, see **140** above.

## **143** FITZWILLIAM TO GUYBON

*London, 27 June 1700; F(M)C 1131*

Vaughan has written about one Rippon's death, and my reply requires haste, so send it from Peterborough on Saturday if any there will deliver it safely that night. Otherwise send Thomas Wootton with it on Sunday morning. Send a buck next Saturday if they are fat for Sir Charles loves a shoulder of venison beyond anything.

## **144** FITZWILLIAM TO GUYBON

*London, 4 July 1700; F(M)C 1132*

Have visited Heriot's and find £28 9s 3d has been paid for Mr Exton and £36 18s 10d for John Coles. I would have expected such small sums to be paid at my house. It's very strange my venison should be so backward, and we have so much in town. I fear you overstock the park with horses. The carthorses might be kept in the woods. This open winter the grass has grown all the while so that the venison should be more forward than ordinarily. I am glad you have brewed and that you were so merry at the 'lanceing your frigott'.[1] Thank Mr Lowrey from me for his care and kindness in overlooking the work. Son John must drink ass's milk in the country so hire one for four months, which I hope you may do for 20s since I keep her and her foal besides. I am unwilling to buy one just for that time for we have enough about town.

[1] Launching the new ferry boat. Guybon had paid the boatwrights John Andrew senior and John Andrew junior £15 10s on 22 June for building the ferry boat; and the same day had paid Goodman Rycroft and his son 8s for four days work in making 'rowles' (rowlocks?) and for helping to take the old boat to pieces.

## 145 FITZWILLIAM TO GUYBON

*London, 25 July 1700; F(M)C 1133*

Pickering's money was paid at Heriot's—unexpectedly because Horner, having quarrelled with Heriot, always paid here. My wife says she will try to obtain a cook maid here but does not believe she can for town maids worth anything care not to live in the country, and if they are good for nothing are not worth carrying down. Let Mrs Bull do all she can to find one. I fear before Mr Exton can pay I shall want money, for my daughter is a great charge, and I don't know where to get money for her necessaries. Send me a buck next week if the weather is cool and let me know the hour the coach passes through Welwyn or Hatfield for hereafter I must have venison left there for Sir Charles.

## 146 FITZWILLIAM TO GUYBON

*[London,] 1 August 1700; F(M)C 1134*

I enclose three warrants. Send me a buck from the forest next week by the wagon. I send for venison from my park at this season because the weather being hot the forest venison will not keep as sweet being killed a day earlier, and they hunt them a little whereas ours is shot dead and dressed cool and so come up better. However, I will try this time for an experiment. Have heard of no money from Exton or Ash but they may have paid at Heriot's.

Mr Clitheroe was with mee yesterday and brought mee a particular of Lolham. He saies John Webdale paies him £145 per annum and a fatt turkey. The odd £5 was in consideration of the great repaires he has been at in the farme. Know of him if this be true. He saies Widdow Curtis of Westdeeping paies him £6 13s 4d per annum. Learne of him what that is for and also if R. Turnhill paies him 30s a yeare and for what. One William Bucke paies him yearly 20s a yeare. For what learne also, and if one Mr Stevens paies him 5s 6d a yeare for a cheife rent. Be sattisfied in all these points of John Webdale as soone as possible you can for I promisd he should know my mind in a very little time. Pray keep this very secrett from any body else but John Webdale who we may confide in. He vallewes his timber and his wood growing which all his tennants have planted and do plant yearly. Ride over all the grounds and observe what timber there is and what other young wood is growing and give mee the vallew of it and know of John Webdale what and how many trees he is obliged to plant yearly. You may take Mr Pendleton along with you if you thinke fitt . . .[1]

[1] Guybon drafted a reply on the verso stating that the keeper had failed to supply the buck but he could send venison from the park.

## 147 FITZWILLIAM TO GUYBON

*London, 3 August 1700; F(M)C 1135*

Today I received Ash's £39 from Mr Robert Arrasmith, a jobber. Nothing from Exton yet.

The venison came up this morneing very early but it stuncke as they tell mee for I gave it away and had none but the shoulder which we made a shift to eate. I hope the halfe of it that was left at Welling for Sir Charles Barrington yesterday was sweeter otherwise I shall be very sorry. The carrier formerly usd to lay it out every night a cooleing and had beaten pepper every night to season and preserve it if he thought good, but by this, my man found it packt up in a hamper amungst pigeons and they all stuncke and I beleive infected the venison. I write this purposely that you should give a strickt charge about this bucke that I expect next weeke and pray order it be putt in a hamper by itselfe and not amungst pigeons which heate and corrupt sooner then any other fowle.

Half of next week's buck leave at Welwyn for Sir Charles with a shoulder, which you can get for half a crown, for he loves shoulders more than any other cut. Tell Pendleton I hear nothing of his money yet. If Sir Charles Barrington's servant does not meet the wagon let the whole buck come to London.

### 148 FITZWILLIAM TO GUYBON
*London, 8 August 1700; F(M)C 1136*

I fear the venison will not come sweet because of the excessive hot weather. If it cools send another next week from my own park for I must give some away soon. For Lolham, inform me the name and acreage of the close John Webdale ploughs; if he is obliged to sow grass seed at the end of his time of ploughing; where and how much is the house and land Mr Stevens rents for 5s 6d. The £2 Clitheroe pays me is a reserved rent on his lease.

### 149 FITZWILLIAM TO GUYBON
*London, 10 August 1700; F(M)C 1137*

I am much concerned at the disappointment of the [forest] venison, for Sir Charles sent his man to meet it. Let the best buck in my park be killed, and a shoulder and a half be left at The Swan in Welwyn for him. The fee deer are never due before July 15th, and would not have been served sooner. I sent a fortnight after but surely all the deer are not killed in that time. It's a lame excuse. We are mightily concerned at Mrs Bull's illness. God send her health again. Let us know by next post how she does. My wife leaves it to her to choose when to take up the bees.

### 150 FITZWILLIAM TO GUYBON
*London, 15 August 1700; F(M)C 1138*

Received only a side and a half haunch yesterday. If you sent the shoulders the coachman must be answerable to his master for it. I sent James Ullitt for the venison and, knowing him to be a careless fool, fancied he left it behind so sent a more trustworthy footman who was told by the innkeeper and the ostler that only a side and half haunch had come. Perhaps the coachman, carelessly laying it out at Huntingdon, had it stolen from him. Your note to the carrier said how many pieces Sir Charles should have but not how many there were for me. Pray investigate. Horner has paid Heriot £60 for John Bolton of Northborough so repay him. Tell Vaughan I received his letter about Mr Ewing's death, but I don't reply because I am near coming down. Until then will resolve nothing about his house and land come to me by his death for we must contrive how to improve John Carter's farm. Vaughan has a 21 year lease from Lady Sylvius. I am not obliged to build or repair for him during that time unless he surrenders and takes a fresh lease from me, whereupon I would accommodate him on reasonable terms. Otherwise I have only to receive his rent half yearly. Now my daughter is married I must give her what venison I can spare so my friends must excuse me. However, give one warrant amongst them—my Cousin Henry Tryce and Mr Lowrey the sides and the two haunches to Roger Pemberton and who else in Peterborough deserves it most. Send a forest buck next Thursday and let me know how many I can expect from my park. I have not seen Clitheroe this fortnight but expect him daily. You say all the wood [on Lolham] is not worth £30 besides the pollards which are only good for fencing. If Clitheroe should insist on having the pollards valued guess at their worth if cut down for firing.

## **151** FITZWILLIAM TO GUYBON

*London, 22 August 1700; F(M)C 1139*

Francis Guybon, Yours of the 20th I received yesterday and much wonder to heare I can have but one bucke more out of my owne parke. I used to have often 5 and 6 bucks in one yeare and never less then 4 and now I can have but 3 that I cannot beleive I have faire play. They must either be stole, given away or losst through carelessness. Tom Freeman is growne now too rich and too lazy to looke after anything but his owne stocke. They are neglected in winter in the fothering of them and the ground is overstock with horses both winter and summer that I cannot have my venison so soone by two moneths as others have out of private parks. Tom Freeman letts my deare be losst in winter for want of lookeing after the pales as he should do and when you are abroad at the other end of my estate he may shoote my venison and dispose of it unbeknowne to you for all I know for I find by yours I am like to have no venison either the next yeare or yeare after for if there be but one sore,[1] that will be all the bucks will be next yeare, and if (as you say) there is but one sorell[2] that will be all the bucks that will be this time two yeare. So consequently here must be a great many young deare loss't within these 2 last yeares through some carelessness or other or knavery.

I know Mr Clitheroe will insist on the wood so take Mr Wright one day and value all timber save hedges and trees of three or four years' growth. Value all fit for timber or firewood, valuing separately the timber, the good pollard trees and the rotten pollards fit only for firing, so I can judge what to allow for and what to refuse.

[1] A buck in its fourth year.
[2] A buck in its third year.

## 152 FITZWILLIAM TO GUYBON

*London, 24 August 1700; F(M)C 1140*

(Regrets venison not coming up because of Barrington's disappointment. Wishes Guybon could get a shoulder of venison for his son-in-law; would willingly pay 2s 6d for it.)[1]

[1] Guybon paid 2s 6d for a shoulder of venison on 3 September, Disbursements 790.

## 153 FITZWILLIAM TO GUYBON

*London, 29 August 1700; F(M)C 1141*

(Sorry they had once more been disappointed about venison for Barrington, but glad Guybon had earlier sent him a shoulder. Would not disappoint him again so a buck in the park must be killed and sent up, half for himself, half for Barrington. Webdale's man had paid £70 18s 11d. Nothing since from Vaughan or Bimrose.) You talk of my sparing my venison two or three years. God knows who may live so long. I cannot spare any. Try Westhay Walk warrant. The restraint is not to be for ever, and I think I have had none from there these five or six years.[1] Keep the leads very clean or this rain will damage the rooms. I hope the wheat is all secured in your parts.

[1] 'Sept. 3 Paid Mr Brutnall his fee and his man's for a buck, 15s', Disbursements 790.

## 154 FITZWILLIAM TO GUYBON

*London, 12 September 1700; F(M)C 1142*

On Friday Rowland Morrice, the little Peterborough hog man, would needs pay me £43 which came luckily, for I was drawn very low, and it's all gone so hope you have another supply ready. Our venison came well. Will reserve the remaining buck in Milton Park for next year. I am glad you have a good harvest. God send you rain for your edishes.[1] Ask Pendleton if he has observed how the cellar well keeps its water in dry years, and report it in your next.

[1] Eddish, grass that grows again; an aftergrowth after mowing.

## 155 FITZWILLIAM TO GUYBON

*London, 19 September 1700; F(M)C 1143*

I understand Brigg Fair is on Saturday. Send me the price of best hops there. So the keepers shall not say I sent too late I shall enclose one or two of my doe warrants. Speak with the keepers at Brigg Fair and know when is a good time to present them. Learn the price of shoulders also. I hope the beer is not spoiled. My son and I intend to be down soon but shall not stay long.

## 156 FITZWILLIAM TO GUYBON

*London, 26 September 1700; F(M)C 1144*

(Sorry well in new cellar dry. Mr Apreece reported that when he was at Milton in the summer it held two feet. No doe venison will be served until November. To consult with Mrs Bull and Adam Johnson, who understand these matters about re-brewing the beer gone stale.) Begin at once as I will be down suddenly. 'As to the burgessing busieness I will neither meddle nor make amungst them, they are all my good freinds'.[1] William Miller has paid by Henry Hankin £29 10s; John Webdale by Richard Bramson £23 17s. Hope you have had as much rain at Milton as we have had here. Keep leads and gutters clean.

[1] A reference to the parliamentary election of 1700.

## 157 FITZWILLIAM TO GUYBON

*London, 10 October 1700; F(M)C 1145*

Have received no more from Webdale and none from John Clarke of Glinton; Horner has paid Herriott £63 3s 9d for Mr Eddins and £85 0s 10d for John Cole.

I have ordered Mr Burman and Mr Vaughan to keep Maxey court when Mr Burman is best at leisure. I remember Mr Pemberton was telling last winter that he thought there was a coppyholder or two dead belonging to Norborough mannor. If it be so and that there is a reall occation I would have Mr Pemberton keep Norbrough court the same day as Maxey is kept that he may have a dinner at Maxey when he keeps it, but if there be no admittance nor no advantage like to come to mee, I will not be at the charge of keeping a court this yeare at Norborough. You may order Harry Vaughan to inquire who is dead within these 2 yeares that has any coppyhold estate in those parts that holds of the mannor of Norborough. If you do keep court at Norborough do not invite the jury there to dine at Maxey as they did last yeare. I do not intend to use them to it for I invited them last yeare upon another occation, but you may give them something to drinke as we used to do . . .

## 158 FITZWILLIAM TO GUYBON

*London, 17 October 1700; F(M)C 1146*

(Will have nothing done about Maxey Mills or Mrs Ewin's farm until he comes down. Does not know where to send to 'this Fuller' for Mr Ash's money. Since there are partridges in the mew his wife would have some sent.)

## 159 FITZWILLIAM TO GUYBON

*London, 24 October 1700; F(M)C 1148*

John Edins has paid Heriot by Horner, £64 6s. I see Maxey court is to be kept on November 4, but I suppose you won't keep Northborough court. I would be at no charge of keeping court there unless a copyholder dies or there is any other great occasion. Being subservient to Maxey, where a court must be held yearly, a court will rarely be needed there. Ask Vaughan in what condition Richard Ewing has left his widow. If so well that we may venture to let her continue the farm, she may stay a year for £25.[1] If Vaughan is apprehensive let Mr Bimrose be bound for the rent since he interceded for her. I will only let it for a year until I have considered it further. It's time the winter corn was sown and I shall not be soon out of town. Learn what land belongs to Maxey mills, how many acres of arable, meadow and pasture, and yearly value with the profit of the mills if it were let upon a rack rent. I received a letter from his widow, old Goodman Hippwell's daughter[2] wishing to admit her three children's lives to it. I cannot answer until I know the value. Be not partial and undervalue it for the widow's sake but let me know the truth. I will not resolve speedily and will know it perfectly before I do anything. I have fair offers made me from a brother at Lolham Mills but will prefer the widow and her children if they will give as good a price. I am sorry you understand so little as to mention a fine of a year and a half's purchase to admit three lives to an estate that is quite fallen. Had there been two lives in being you had been near the mark but as it is I expect a great many years' purchase. When I know the value I will resolve how many years' purchase I expect. I would have been down before this but Sir Charles Barrington and my daughter have been with me and we don't know when they will leave. The rain this month makes me fear the roads will be extremely bad, especially about Northborough and Maxey. Sweep the gutters and leads clean or the house will be utterly spoiled. Remember how much mischief was done when the pipe beside the great staircase next the partridge room was stopped. Get somebody with good eyes with you to inspect the pipes on the yards and garden side and see the walls are not wet. I will send the warrants when the keepers tell you they will be served. Send word if Lord Exeter be buried 'and if a great funerall or not',[3] and how the election goes on at Peterborough. I hope Mr Wortley and Mr St John will be chosen.

[1] Guybon overwrote £28.

[2] Alice Rippon (see below **161**). Richard Hippwell was Fitzwilliam's bailiff or under-steward for Northborough until his accidental death by drowning in 1687, his duties being taken over by Guybon; Guybon to Fitzwilliam, 12 and 17 April 1687, F(M)C 564, 567.

[3] John Cecil, 5th Earl of Exeter (1648–1700).

## **160** FITZWILLIAM TO GUYBON

*London, 31 October 1700; F(M)C 1149*

Francis Guybon, I received your letter dated the 22th of this moneth and sent on Satturday to the carrier's inne to inquire after the flagg baskett wherein were the partridges and hare you designed to send mee up, but heard nothing of them and moreover said they could not tell whither any waggon would come up the waies being so bad with wett. However I sent againe on Munday morneing to the same inne and they denied any thing was there or that any wagon came up. Whereupon my servant went to drinke at Luff's house hard by the inne who in his life time was Fearey's porter. There he was directed to go into Spittle Feilds by great accident where he found the baskett and understood it came to towne on Fryday night before. It had been so wett and so hott a weeke that they all stuncke and, except a few partridges, were throwen away. The hare was worst of all being I suppose a stale one. Fearey must make sattisfaction for this loss for if he changes his inne he ought to give notice as likewise to the porters that if things are not sent for in time they ought to take care to carry them according to directions. Pray take care that Fearey paies for this loss. On the 25th Mr Thomas Ewin of Deeping Gate paid £23 and John Sisson of Northborough paid £57; John Horner has paid at Heriot's £59 12s 8d for Mr Ash, and £28 10s 10d for Mr Matthew Pickering. The Barringtons have been with me a month or more so fear I shall not get down this winter. Those Northborough and Maxey affairs must be settled by letter. Dispose of the drink you brewed me, and write up and send me this year's accounts, and the wood books for 1699 and this year. Let me know when I may have venison sent up, but I will not be at the charge and fees if the wet season has spoiled them.[1]

[1] Fitzwilliam copied out a warrant to the keepers of Sulehay in the royal forest of Rockingham for his fee doe for that year because, since his earlier warrants were dated before All Saints, he did not know if they were still valid.

## 161 FITZWILLIAM TO GUYBON

*London, 7 November 1700; F(M)C 1150*

Mr Vaughan has sent an account of what [Maxey] Mills have been let for, with the Mill Holmes[1] which is not copyhold, but I know not what they are let for now. Mr Burman says the widow [Rippon] has let them but could not tell for what. I cannot set a fine till I come down for there are several things that I must learn which cannot be done by letter, so the rent must be paid to me until we agree it. The widow shall have it before another if she can pay the fine which I believe will be some hundreds of pounds if she puts in her children's lives, but I cannot be positive until I see for myself. I hear Mrs Ewen's condition is very 'sadd' so I have no mind she should [keep] her farm at all. How could she pay the rent if she has not a full stock to make the best of it? 'The land must run out of heart and the buildings out of repaire.' Mr Bimrose might pay the rent, but he would be unwilling to maintain the buildings. I will not reduce £28 rent, but so she is not destitute of a habitation she shall continue the farm a year until she can provide otherwise. If I hear when I come next spring that she can deal with it I may let her continue, taking a lease but I will promise nothing. (Encloses deer warrant. Hears nothing of Fuller who is to pay Ash's £64. Will have no venison until has agreed with the new carrier.) Talk to the horse carriers that go over the ferry. They used to take but 5s a cwt for carriage of goods, and since I will send up nothing heavy this winter they could carry it. What are their inns in town? [P.S.] I wonder we can have no pigeons from our dovecotes two summers together. Go soon with Vaughan to view the wood growing on Mrs Ewin's farm that you may know if she commits any waste in the future.

[1] Probably an area of ground by the millpond, now become a field name.

## 162 FITZWILLIAM TO GUYBON

*London, 21 November 1700; F(M)C 1151*

Mr Ash's friend, the Essex man Fuller, has paid the £64. I have asked Vaughan to consider how to dispose of Maxey mills which I will lease upon lives. I perceive the widow [Rippon] is unable to pay a fine suitable to three lives unless she has any estate to sell to raise the money. The miller of Lolham mills wrote to me for them and may be discoursed with if the poor woman cannot purchase them. Mrs Ewin's farm must be disposed of likewise for she will not give £28 per annum for it as you wrote others would. Consult with Mr Vaughan how to let these two farms to my best advantage.

## 163 FITZWILLIAM TO GUYBON

*London, 26 November 1700; F(M)C 1152*

Francis Guybon, I have some reason to feare Mr Wortley[1] may loose the election at Peterborough by what I am informed and therefore pray do him the best service you can but privately. Mr Charles Parker will show you a list of those persons' names who can vote for this election and I would have you at the same time looke over your wood booke and see which of them owe mee any money and sett their names downe in the paper that you may speake to them. Gett as many single votes for him as you can and when his election is secured lett all my freinds vote for Mr St John though I am sattisfied he is secure enough. Haveing seen Mr Wortle[y]'s list of the scott and lott[2] votes I tooke this inclosed note of the names of some of my freinds that I wonder have not promised their votes for Mr Wortly, as Bates, and Mr Willis my saddler and plummer, Charles Duce and Peter Rainford, William Briers that rents my rushes, Thomas Stamford that brings up my coales; the Andrews, both brother[s] that buys my barke; Mr Pendleton's nephew, and Robert Fearey the carrier; our Mr Turner, and Howson my brasier; John Deborough one of my masons, and Seeth Meekes my old freind. Pray speake to every one of these to give one vote for Mr Wortley or I shall take it unkindly of them and I know you may influence Mr John Dickenson for one vote, and by his meanes, Docter Lee. Use all your interest possible to secure Mr Wortley but do it without any noise for I would have no notice taken that I concerne myselfe. By Thursday night we shall certainly know if the Parliament will be dissolvd and till that is certaine I would not have you speake to any body, but have your note of the names ready that you may speake to them on Satturday, and if you know any of my tennants that have an influence over any of the voters pray lett them all be for Mr Wortley, and, to be sure, many of the inhabitants of Peterborough owe my tennants money either for corne, malt or one thing or other. The yeare of mourning being now expired you may order the mourning in Marrham chancell next weeke to be taken downe. The baies belongs to the clerke and the escutcheons you may dispose off among the poorer sort of my tennants that have not yett had any. I understand Mr Fearey is become our carrier againe. If so, pray send me up a fatt doe by him as soone as you can if worth sending. If it comes out of my owne parke lett the shoulders be sent up also and send it up in a flagg baskett. Give me notice before, by the post, when I may expect it. I heare Mr William Parker of the Minster paies scott and lott in the towne. If so, pray lett him know I shall take it kindly he will give a single vote for Mr Wortley. Tell Peter Rainsford his sonne that lives in Brigg Street I expect should vote for Mr Wortly as well as himselfe, and pray neglect not to press every one you have an influence over to vote for Mr Wortley and one single vote is worth 3 others but do not refuse any. I heard this day by Mr Whinyates the ill newes of good Mrs Lowrey's death. Pray when you see him remember us kindly to him and that we heartily condole his great loss. A better woman could not live then she was. At the same time lett him know his waterman Stamford is against Mr Wortly. I leave all these matters to yours and Mr Charles Parker's mannagement ... [P.S.] If you thinke you cannot prevaile with Mr John Dickenson never speake to him. Try allso the Standishes.

[1] Wortley Montagu.

[2] Peterborough was one of 37 boroughs 'where the right of voting was in inhabitants paying scot and lot, that is in inhabitant householders who paid the poor rate', E. and A. E. Porritt, *The Unreformed House of Commons* (Cambridge, 1903), i. 30.

## 164 FITZWILLIAM TO GUYBON

*London, 28 November 1700; F(M)C 1153*

Do Mr Wortley the best service you can, getting him single votes where you can, and those you cannot so persuade, let them give one vote for Wortley and another for Mr St John. Use all the industry imaginable for there will certainly be a new parliament although I have not heard it positively. I am heartily sorry for poor Mrs Lowrey. Tell Mr Pocklington I received his letter and when his money is paid to me I will be sure to tell you to pay him again there. I am sorry for Mrs Watts. Comfort her for it's a sad accident. Send me a doe by Fearey, which if I like I will send for more. Otherwise you shall dispose of the rest there.

## 165 FITZWILLIAM TO GUYBON

*London, 5 December 1700; F(M)C 1154*

Francis Guybon, I received a letter from you yesterday and as to the election I declare I am for Mr Wortley and Mr St John and was so all along, and for Mr Dolbin,[1] I have not the good fortune to be knowne to him, and being a stranger to him I shall sooner be for my acquainteance and good neighbours then him, and shall take it ill if any that works for mee and takes my money or that owe mee any money will not vote for my freinds. I do not heare at present that there is a likelyhood of a new parliament that it's time enough to consider of this matter but we may know more by the next post.

Tell Mr Pocklington I have not received his money yet nor any other returns from you since Ash's £64. Give to the poor of the towns as we used to at Christmas.[2] I enclose an urgent answer to a letter from Mr Vaughan for you to send to him by some of the market people on Saturday. Vaughan writes that he cannot let Mrs Ewen's farm for £28, being bid only £25 and that by John Carter, not Mr Richard Ewin[3] as yours mentioned. He believes there is a confederacy among the neighbours to beat down the rent because we are straitened for time because of ploughing it, and that you both think if I kept it in hand a year I would make more of it. I will be content with what you both decide. However, remember I won't make as much as a tenant, and it's not certain we will get £28 next year. It would vex me to hold it a year and then let for less. If Vaughan thinks it worth £28 I will plough it for a year. Otherwise try to let it for 20s less. We regret Mrs Watts[4] is so ill, and hope she mends but there is great danger for one of her years. I wish Harry was well married. [P.S.] We hear my daughter is pretty well. Go speak with Vaughan on Monday for I would not lose time in ploughing it. Send another doe next week if it's worth it, otherwise carry it to my Peterborough friends. Let Cousin Henry Tryce and Mr Lowrey have their choice.

[1] Gilbert Dolben, who was to defeat Francis St John in the election.

[2] Once again Guybon gave 6d each to 40 poor of Castor, 12 of Ailsworth, 30 of Helpston, six of Etton and one of Northborough, Disbursements 1700–1710, F(M)C Misc. Vol. 74 (hereafter Disbursements 74).

[3] There were two Richard Ewings. Richard Ewing's death is referred to in **150**, **159** above. For Richard 'Ewen' of Maxey, see **281** note, and index.

[4] Mother of Henry Watts, who rented the Gunwade ferry and 'ordinary' there.

## **166** FITZWILLIAM TO GUYBON

*London, 12 December 1700; F(M)C 1155*

Morrice the hogman paid me £20 for William Serjeant. He could have paid me £50 or £60 but you told him you had no occasion. I hear nothing of Pocklington's money nor of Mr Wright of Woodson who you wrote some time ago was to pay me money. I hope all goes well at Peterborough for Mr Wortley and Mr St John. Parliament is not yet dissolved, but all believe it will be soon. I hope to receive venison by Saturday's wagon. If I like it you shall send a doe to Sir Charles Barrington next week to be left at the Swan at Welwyn for his man to collect. Let me know what time on Friday the wagon passes there. Next week my wife wishes you to send up all the honey made at Milton this summer, marking the pot or pots which is virgin honey, for she has a particular use for it.

[P.S.] I heare my daughter is very ill at Hertingfordberry Parke and has no manner of stomach, and my sonne was last night so ill of a feavour we were all scared but thanke God he is better all this day and if he hold out well all day to morrow we shall be out of our paine. It came as we thinke with a great cold. If Mr Fearey has any waggon or pack horses that come out next Munday we would have the honey sent up then as soone as you can possibly.

## **167** FITZWILLIAM TO GUYBON

*London, 14 December 1700; F(M)C 1156*

Received partridges and venison, but latter so thin will have no more. Carrier insisted on 5s 10d, a penny a pound. Guybon to send no more by him but by horse carriers who go over the ferry at 5s a 'pound'.[1] Glad Mrs Ewen's farm is let. Hopes Mrs Watts will recover.

[1] Sic, probably an error for hundredweight. See **176**.

## **168** FITZWILLIAM TO GUYBON

*London, 26 December 1700; F(M)C 1157*

I am glad you sent no venison to my daughter since it was so indifferent, and hope you paid no fees for it. Thanks for the pheasants but send no more by the Peterborough carrier. Employ the horse carriers, and write what they will charge me and what is their inn here. A John Wright, I suppose of Woodson, has paid Heriot's £28 13s 4d; Webdale paid [Heriot] only £50, not the £100 yours mentioned; and John Sisson for himself and the two Bolton brothers paid me £78 17s, Oliver Bolton paying only £6 odd.[1]

You mention you have done all you can to serve Mr Wortly and Mr St John in the election. How does that appeare when Peter Rainsford and his sonn and Mr Willis and my sadler Bates and Mr Pendleton's nephew vote for Mr Dolbin? Possitively I shall take it so very ill of these and of some others if they give not one vote for Mr Wortley, or else go out of the towne the day of the election and vote for no body, I shall not be easily reconciled to them and you may lett Mr Willis know I have been (and my tennants also) as good customers to him as Mr St John and therefore expect one of his votes before Mr Dolben, or that he votes for no body and go out of the way. The election is now neare at hand and therefore loose no time nor opportunity to serve Mr Wortley as you vallew the freindship of your loveing friend . . .

[1] 'Oliver' is perhaps an error for Guybon entered that he had repaid £79 17s (not £78) by Sisson, John Bolton and Alexander Bolton, Disbursements 74.

## **169** FITZWILLIAM TO GUYBON

*London, 2 January 1700/1; F(M)C 1158*

My father sold Barnigham's farm. It belonged I think to a Mrs Palmer. It was let when I was last there for £17 a year. Joseph Chamberlaine lived there and can tell you the value and number of acres of meadow, pasture and arable in each field. See how well repaired are the buildings. I hope to buy it for 18 or 19 years purchase.

Since you informe me of Mr Selby and some others in Castor their designe to alter the tax, I suppose you meane the towne assessments for church repaires and other towne duties, for the King's tax is settled by the pound rate already for Milton paies so. I will write a letter to Mr Selby about it as likewise to Mr Pemberton and Mr Noah Neale and have spoke to Mr Appreece to be at the sessions which I suppose will be held the Thursday after Plow Munday.[1] By that time he will be in the countrey and pray do you speake to Mr Dreydon[2] to be there who is also a justice of the peace in our liberty, and present my service and tell him the whole matter and wherein it will be a prejudice to mee. I beleive Mr Dolbin is not in [the] commission of the peace but Mr Pemberton can better sattisfy you. Speake to Mr Dickenson about our business also and desire his assistance. I cannot immagine how the alteration of the tax from a 15th to a pound rate should be a prejudice to mee since Milton paies by the pound rate unless the tax would fall higher on my farmes in Castor. If it be so, pray neglect not to oppose it all that ever you can and lett mee know wherein Mr Selby will be a gainer by it, for he being a farmer there as well as Holman and Joseph Chamberlaine why should he be advantaged by it and they prejudic't? And to the Peterborough business, I should be sorry either of my 2 freinds should loose the election and those that you cannot gett to vote for them lett them know I should take it as kindly of them if they contrivd business to go out of towne the day of the election and so vote for no man, as if they stayed and voted for my freinds, but of their goeing out of towne that day they must acquaint no man with, nor their wives . . .

[P.S.] What day is Peterborough election? See someone carries my letter to Mr Selby for he knows not of it. I have also writ to Mr Pemberton.

[1] Thursday 13 January.
[2] John Dryden, M.P.

## 170 FITZWILLIAM TO GUYBON

*London, 9 January 1700/1; F(M)C 1159*

I am concerned to hear Mr St John lost the Peterborough election. I imagined his interest was so good there was no fear of his losing. I have written to Mr Neale asking his assistance next sessions in the Castor business. Who is the doctor you say always opposes my interests? If Dr Woolsey I am confident he would not be against me if the matter was rightly stated to him, for I always took him for my friend. If it is him go give him my service, tell him the whole matter and that I wish it delayed until I come down. Then I may hear it all and what I think fit to be done can be done without making a 'sessions business' of it. If you think fit I will write to Dr Woolsey before the sessions begin. We have had great frost, snow and now a thaw. Keep leads and lucarnes clean and when it thaws clear the pipe heads of frost or they will drown the house.

## 171 FITZWILLIAM TO GUYBON

*London, 23 January 1700/1; F(M)C 1160*

Yours of 21st came late this evening. The floods are so great the post could not pass. Mr Pemberton, while acquainting me with what passed at the sessions, writes it will be determined when I come down; you write it will be determined next sessions. Which of you is right? If any Castor inhabitants oppose Selby's design carry them to Pemberton and discuss what will be the inconveniency of his proposed method, and how much they are prepared to contribute to the cost of a *certiorari* that will remove the case to Westminster Hall. I believe it dangerous to alter old customs in a parish, and the judges will never suffer it if it comes before them. I never knew more snow and rain than this three weeks past. Take care of the house. I would be glad of more money if the ways are such that you may ride out. Kind respects to all friends and especially thank Mr Dickenson for his care of our business at the sessions. You write several banks are broke but not where. Hope my land in James Deeping is not drowned.

## 172 FITZWILLIAM TO GUYBON

*London, 13 February 1700/1; F(M)C 1161*

Francis Guybon, As to this business of the chayce which you mention in your letter, I never heard of such a place before and if there be such a roade why must it just belong to Norborough, Glinton and Deepingate only, and not to Maxey,

Ashton, Bainton, Barnack, Pilsgate, St Martin's and Wothrope if they drive into the Great Fenn by that chaice.[1] If they never make use of the fenn it's another matter. They ought not to pay to the repaire of a roade they never make use off. I understand they have levied a distress upon Sutton for the same. I will joine with the parrish of Castor against such a distress for if it does not belong to those townes of Stamford Barron etc. it cannot belong to Castor parrish who I beleive drive alwaies into the fenn by Werrington and never come neare the chaice. To avoide all suites at law amungst us I am of opinion the best way will be to have it repaired out of the publick stocke of the hundred which you receave every yeare for to my knowledge many a hundred pounds has been laied out for such purposes about the fenns and why not for this. Pray propose it to Mr Neale and the rest and tell them it's my opinion and withall that I must defend those townes where my estate lies from being oppress't.

Henry Hankin has paid Heriot's £40 for James Dove and Thomas Ashley. More will be welcome. We thank Mrs Bull very kindly for her chine and puddings and all her former presents, and regret her poor health. Tell Mr Dickenson 'I much condole with him' in his great loss. God maintain your good health and 'send us good times for there is a melancholy prospect before us'.

[1] The fens provided coarse grazing for geese, cattle, horses and sheep, 'usually in common, and frequently by intercommoning townships. ... townships for miles around sent their stock down to the fens along grassy droveways radiating from them ... thirty or forty towns depastured in Peterborough Fen. ... Concentric rings of towns fed their stock in Marshland and Farcet fens.' Eric Kerridge, *The Agricultural Revolution* (New York, 1968), pp. 139–40.

## 173 FITZWILLIAM TO GUYBON

*London, 15 February 1700/1; F(M)C 1162*

Francis Guybon, This morning John Mappletopp who married the widdow at Oxney farme was with mee and is very earnest I should lett him Kenwicke farme in Marshland[1] and all the grazeing land belonging to it though it were 4 or 500 acres. He pretends he must leave Oxney because his sonne in law is now of age and will mannage it himselfe. Pray lett mee know what Mr Mappletopp is for a tennant, if he be understanding in the way of grazeing and if he has gott money by it and what his substance is for I should be loath to trust a good farme in a maggott pated fellow's hands and if he be poore besides. Informe yourselfe as soone as you can of Mr Phillips, John Webdale or Mr Ash or of any body else that you thinke knows his ability as to meanes and substance and his understanding in countrey affaires, and know why he left his farme at Estree so soone that I feare he is fickle and cares not to stay long in a place. Pray lett mee know every thing as soone as you can for he seemes to be very pressing with mee for an answer ...

[1] Part of Fitzwilliam's Norfolk estate.

## 174 FITZWILLIAM TO GUYBON

*London, 27 February 1700/1; F(M)C 1163*

Your account of Mapletop is useless at present as Mr Beales tells me Kenwicke Farm comes not into my hands this Lady Day. Mr Pancke, the Peterborough hogman, told me last week his correspondent would pay my goldsmith £120.

He said you had told him you could repay only £50, but asked me to take the £120, and would wait for the rest. If you cannot repay in a reasonable time see him next Saturday and he will order matters with his correspondent. My wife is ill of a cold, and we hear my daughter has not been 'breeding' since she was married and is much troubled with a pain in her breast which the women fear may turn to a cancer.

## 175 FITZWILLIAM TO GUYBON

*London, 13 March 1700/1; F(M)C 1164*

Pancke's correspondent did not pay the £120 so suppose you stopped the payment on receiving my letter.

This being the time of yeare that I make my new liveries James Ullitt told my wife there should be made none for him for he would not stay and because this last twelve moneth or more he has much neglected my service being often out and takeing ill courses, he has been admonished for it many times, that I the more freely part from him. However, because his mother desired mee at first to have him pray lett her know so much that she may consider what to advise him for he is become a very idle druncken fellow and extravagant. He was advised by us to write his mother word he was to leave our service but he said what should he trouble himselfe for that; he was old enough now to take care of himselfe without her. His mother may do well to advise him soone for though he is at present in my house as soone as ever he is out, forty to one but he may be press't to go to sea for they take up all loose fellowes that are out of service and many servants also . . .

## 176 FITZWILLIAM TO GUYBON

*London, 3 April 1701; F(M)C 1165*

We are all well although I have had some 'lamenesses' this spring which I fear will turn to the gout. Mr [William] Miller of Thorney Fenn has paid £60; Mr Pancke £120; Mr Pickering's man £36 8s 11d; and a man unknown[1] paid by your order £50; all at Heriot's. I need a good sum by three weeks or a month. The ways being now good I shall be sending goods down every week. Learn whether Fearey will carry for 5s or 5s 6d or at most 6s. Otherwise I will send heavy things by sea,[2] and lighter things by the Lowth and Lincoln carriers who come over the ferry and charge but 5s a cwt. I will write Mr Pemberton about Castor business but he tells me it will be put off until midsummer sessions by which time I will be down. As for 'the chayce' I wonder Mr Neale would put the country to the expense of a trial at assizes, when all the hundred would be willing to repair it from the public stock, as they have done other ways leading into the fens, that money being for such purposes. I asked Mr Pemberton to tell Mr Neale this, but fear he has not, 'lawiers being willing to have suites go on it being for their profitt'. Present my service to Mr Neale and say I desire he would not put the 'country' to a cost of lawsuits when [the road] can be repaired from the public stock with damage to none. If there is no money we can raise it by letting out a piece of the common. My tenants and I will consent to it. I will be down by midsummer sessions and will satisfy him there should be no alteration in Castor assessment, so ask him to put it off, and be my friend in it, which I shall always deem a particular favour. [P.S.] James Ullitt's mother wrote about her son for she never hears from him. Tell her he is well and still in my house until he gets a place, which I hope he will soon and we shall part very fairly. I believe he regrets going from me but I have another in his room . . .

[1] In fact Mr Panke, the Peterborough hogman, Disbursements 74.

[2] That is to King's Lynn by sea, and thence by river boat to Gunwade Ferry via the Great Ouse, the fenland waterways and the Nene.

## 177 FITZWILLIAM TO GUYBON

*London, 17 April 1701; F(M)C 1166*

Since I wrote last Mr William Ash has paid £34 11s 9d, Mr Matthew Pickering £37 12s, and Rowland Morrice paid £30 on April 9th, promising another £20 from his correspondent but I hear nothing yet. I hear nothing of Mr Fearey. Discover the lowest prices of the horse carriers that go over the ferry. They once proffered to carry for 5s a cwt, and would bring the horses to my house to weigh the goods. I will speedily send the heavy goods by sea, and my light goods and boxes by the Lowth and Horncastle carriers. Those carriers carry considerable sums for me yearly by return so I know them to be 'safe men'. However, let us first agree with them. We are all in pretty good health. My lameness has worn off. I believe it is scurvy which comes for want of country air.

## 178 FITZWILLIAM TO GUYBON

*London, 8 May 1701; F(M)C 1167*

I was glad to hear from Mr Ash who dined with me today of all your good healths. I am sorry the towns concerned to repair the chase[1] should be 'so oppositious' as to put themselves to such charges in the sessions. I hear by Mr Ash it's a 'perfect highway that belongs to those townes to repaire and every towne must mend its owne highwaies.' Persuade them to peace and to not lose the opportunity of this dry season to do it. I am glad you intend me money for I greatly need to make up a sum. [P.S.] My daughter is in town in good health and remembers herself very kindly. I wish you would agree with Fearey for our carriages for he never comes to me.

[1] To chase is to drive cattle; thus the chase and 'chaice highway' means a drove road.

## 179 FITZWILLIAM TO GUYBON

*London, 22 May 1701; F(M)C 1168*

Francis Guybon, I received your letter of the 6th instant by which I am sorry to heare there has been so much money expended on account of the chaice high way and like to be a great deale more. Advise the townes to consider if it be not a high way belonging to those townes to repaire and if they have not done it formerly;

and for them to object that Stamford Baron, Barnicke and the rest of the townes drive through it to the fenn and ought to contribute, the roade to London may as well be repaired by all the waggons and coaches as drive through it as well as the towneshipps adjoineing, so that can be no presedent. I am sorry these townes should be so unadvised, because I am concerned in most of them. I wish Mr Stamford who lives at Maxey does not foment this difference for his owne sake.

I am glad you intend returns by Mr Edins and Cole. My lame leg, came with a strain, but it may be the gout or scurvy.

## 180 FITZWILLIAM TO GUYBON

*London, 12 June 1701; F(M)C 1169*

I have not seen Mr Fearey. I wonder he should increase the carriage. I never paid him more than 6s in the summer, 7s in the winter, and he carried my things to Milton into the bargain when in quantity. He only had that trouble once or twice a year. Little parcels and boxes we fetched ourselves, or had them brought by a tenant's wagons at the market. Make an exact bargain so that I can send down my things by degrees. I don't know what has been paid Heriot's because my continuing lameness prevents my going there. Harry Vaughan lately came up to pass his accounts with Lady Sylvius and myself, and she so scrupulous about some arrears he had to return for his father's books. He has no horse fit for the journey so borrow one for him from Stephen Brightman's son-in-law, or any tenant or neighbour. He is light, not apt to ride fast so should do the horse no mischief. Failing a horse from around Northborough, Maxey or my own tenants, let him have my bay if shod and not too fat. My daughter desires to be kindly remembered, and reminds you to answer her letter. How is my venison to come and when can I expect it?

## 181 FITZWILLIAM TO GUYBON

*London, 26 June 1701; F(M)C 1170*

The borrowed horse brought Vaughan very well. Since Fearey so imposes on me I will send less down and have wine from Lynn rather than from here. You wrote he asked 6s 6d, but I never paid him above 6s in summer and corn, horse meat and hay were never cheaper, and the roads never better. Ask him finally if he will not abate of 7s. Take off as many female fawns from the does as you and Tom Freeman think prudent so we may have some barren does in winter. Let me know how the bucks do and when I may send for a fat one. I shall be down soon so be prepared for brewing before 'haysell' begins, the vessels well 'binged' and seasoned. Hop it well because the season is very hot. Mr Gascoigne paid at Heriot's £64 10s, and someone paid by your order £37 14s 6d and £14 15s 3d. Money will be badly needed to pay bills before leaving town and my daughter is to have a great deal. Mr Davies of Wattlington who married the daughter of Mr Bermey of St Mary's Hall buried her last week. Ill all winter, she came to town for better advice, and intended to go to the Bath but one of her doctors persuaded her to use the Cold Bath which 'strucke her into convulsion fitts' of which she died in a few days. An extraordinary good woman and much lamented by all that knew her. [P.S.] Brew next week two hogsheads of ale, four of small beer, with the allowance for malt I ordered last year, 16 strikes for two hogsheads of ale, two or three strikes for the beer.[1]

[1] Guybon paid Mathew Buninge £2 6s 8d for 20 strike of malt, and 4s 8d for 4 cwt of hops on 9 July, Disbursements 74. Several Fitzwilliam letters between **181** and **182** may be missing.

## 182 FITZWILLIAM TO GUYBON

*London, 31 July 1701; F(M)C 1171*

I have received no letters for many a day nor any money. Burton has paid none. I wrote Pendleton a week ago for a buck this week, but none came. Send one next week by the coach without fail. Address a side, half haunch and a shoulder to my daughter marked 'carriage paid'; the rest to me. Send another thus divided the following week. Charge the coachman to take out the venison every night and lay it on a cold floor. John Carter, Lord Exeter's coachman, called yesterday and told me the whole story of the robbery near Maiden's Grave. It's a great loss but I hope the country will not be forced to pay it.[1]

[1] Hundreds were collectively responsible for losses by highway robbery if no hue and cry was raised after the thieves. Maiden's Grave is a cowpasture in Thornaugh parish between Wansford and Stamford: *VCH Northamptonshire*, ii. 530. See also below **185**, **219**, **220**.

## 183 FITZWILLIAM TO GUYBON

*London, 7 August 1701; F(M)C 1172*

(To send no venison until cooler weather. Wishes to know if county is likely to be sued for the stolen money.)

## 184 FITZWILLIAM TO GUYBON

*London, 9 August 1701; F(M)C 1173*

The buck came well this cooler weather. If it continues send another by Thursday's wagon, directing a half with shoulder to my daughter. Mr Ballett will be at Peterborough on Tuesday night. Carry a warrant there for I have promised him half a buck, and give the other side to Cousin Harry Trice, and the half haunch to Robin Newcomb. I have given away the Cross-a-Hand warrant. My good friend Mr 'Price' [Apreece] of Washingly has much 'good company' of his daughter-in-law's relations. Carry a warrant there, pay my respects, and whisper to Mr Apreece that if he wants any venison before his company leaves, I have ordered him a buck or a half buck. If he takes only the half, give Mr Whinyates and Mr John Dickinson the other two pieces. He has had a warrant from me already.

## 185 FITZWILLIAM TO GUYBON

*London, 14 August 1701; F(M)C 1174*

The venison came well but I only saw the shoulder, the rest being given away before I came home. Mr Pickering's £60 was paid the 5th or 6th. Hankin paid Duce's £50 today. I hope you have visited Mr Apreece, and saw Mr Ballett before he left for Spalding. I purposely told him I would not be at Milton this summer that he might not come back our way, for he is very troublesome. I am sorry the country is burned for lack of rain. Keep only deer in the park; turn my horses into the woods or fens. I hope Lord Exeter will not 'sue the countrey'.[1] How many chalder of coals are in the warehouse at the ferry?

[1] For the robbery, see **182**, **183**. There is no record of any payment from Guybon on behalf of Fitzwilliam toward the loss in Disbursements 74. Oddly, although it is never referred to in the letters, Guybon did make such a payment in June 1700: 'Paid Mr Wythe for a robbery done upon Barnock Heath, £14 18s 6d.' Similarly in July 1697 Guybon had paid Wythe £3 4s 4d 'by an order of Langdyke Court for a robery', Disbursements 790. However, it is possible that the hundred was not compelled to reimburse the loss until the following year when Fitzwilliam agreed to lend the hundred £50 to assist in recompensing a robbery, see **219** and **220**.

## **186** FITZWILLIAM TO GUYBON

*London, 19 August 1701; F(M)C 1175*

(Complains of quality of his venison. That delivered to his daughter had been given to the poor. High time he investigated his affairs when he could not have two bucks from his park. Guybon had sealed venison in earlier years but not this, so he fears the carriers changed it. Guybon to send a forest buck next week and supply hay to the deer. 'Lett it cost what it will the poore dumb creatures must not be starved'. Complains of drought in Northamptonshire while they have heavy rain in London. Guybon must have burned much lime or he would have more than five chalders of coal. Guybon to say how high the river is for he will have coal brought from Lynn.)

## **187** FITZWILLIAM TO GUYBON

*London, 28 August 1701; F(M)C 1176*

I am troubled at the drought. The poor deer must be 'fodered'. Heriot was paid by your order £28 16s 6d, but the £60 I said was paid by Pickering came from Mr Beales by another hand. I shall be glad of all you can return.

## **188** FITZWILLIAM TO GUYBON

*London, 30 August 1701; F(M)C 1177*

The buck proved the best warrant buck ever, and I wish my daughter could have had half. Try to procure Lord Exeter's buck for next week, and if very good direct half to my daughter. Go over to Burleigh with my service and if his lordship has gone hunting wait his return even if to six o'clock. I hear from Beales the steeple at North Runcton has fallen on the church, laying it a heap of ruins with only the chancel standing.[1] I fear we must have a gathering to raise it again. [P.S.] Many thanks for the partridges. They came up cooler in the oyster barrel than they would have in a basket. How does the dovecote thrive and are any pigeons to be had?

[1] North Runcton was part of Fitzwilliam's Norfolk estate of which Beales was steward. By 'gathering' Fitzwilliam presumably meant a public subscription. The church was rebuilt between 1703 and 1713, and

is attributed to Henry Bell of King's Lynn who certainly contributed to the cost: N. Pevsner, *North West and South Norfolk* (London, 1962), p. 274.

## 189 FITZWILLIAM TO GUYBON

*London, 6 September 1701; F(M)C 1179*

My daughter designs the half buck for a Mr Shales[1] here in town. Direct it to the King's goldsmith in Lombard Street, over against the church near the Post House. I am sorry my dovecotes are destroyed in my absence. I shall send some things down in Fearey's wagon on Monday week. It is wonderful you have a drought and we little showers keeping the ground green.

[1] Charles Shales, goldsmith to four successive monarchs. His premises were The Unicorn, Lombard Street. See further F.G. Hilton Price, *A Handbook of London Bankers*, London, 1890–1.

## 190 FITZWILLIAM TO GUYBON

*London, 18 September 1701; F(M)C 1180*

The venison, partridges and pigeons came up well. Thank you for your care of us. John Cole paid by Horner £27 or £28 at Heriot's. I have not gathered sufficient things to make it worth Fearey sending a cart to Milton, but by Monday week I should have near a wagon-load. He must be careful loading them for there will be hampers of wine, boxes of china and pictures and cabinets, that must not take wet besides other boxes. Put the wine in the new cellar if you can lock it. Don't mix the bottles from the different hampers. If Brigg Fair be next Monday I may write again by Saturday's post.

## 191 FITZWILLIAM TO GUYBON

*London, 25 September 1701; F(M)C 1181*

You will receive on Wednesday a considerable weight of boxes, and hampers of wine, which I suppose Fearey will bring to Milton by wagon. Have two very strong men help unload them without jumbling them. Have them weighed. Let Joseph Chamberlaine and yourself note the weights. If not delivered until Thursday charge Fearey's people to keep them well covered from the rain. I hope you have some in the country but I hear from Norfolk it has not rained there for three or four months. In the hamper marked '1' are 39 quart bottles of white wine; in '2' are 39 quart bottles of French claret; in '3' are 39 bottles Canary, and in '4' nine bottles French claret, 10 Canary and 10 white wine; in all 12 dozen and two bottles. Sort them and set them together. John Horner has paid £27 1s 8d for John Cole and £56 1s for Mr Ash. I shall need more before I leave town.

[P.S.] Pray let old Joseph Chamberlaine save mee about halfe a bushell of the outward green rine of the wallnutt and lett him steep it in something with man or woman piss.

## **192** FITZWILLIAM TO GUYBON

*London, 'Munday morneing', 29 September 1701; F(M)C 1182*

This morning I have sent down by the carrier seven boxes, four cases of pictures, four hampers of wine. Among them the old box of plate but take no notice of it. I don't wish it to be known the plate is in the house. Carry all boxes up into Lady Newburgh's chamber, but if that room will not conveniently hold the picture cases take them up the Great Stair into the Great Dining Room and place them where the rain does not come in. [P.S.] Tuesday, 30 September. The carrier dared not take this as it was sealed. My man returning it told me one case holding a cabinet had to be left in the warehouse for next week. Weigh the six that come for my man did not see them weighed there. I shall send more next Monday and I believe some more wine. Mr Ballett came up, and says he heard in Peterborough all were well at Milton, and the small pox in Peterborough has improved, only a few houses infected, which I was glad to hear. Heriot has received no money lately. Have you any good does in the park? When may I send for forest venison? I hope you have a man in your eye for seeing to the gates, heating ovens and other drudgery about the house.

## **193** FITZWILLIAM TO GUYBON

*London, 9 October 1701; F(M)C 1183*

I am glad the things arrived safe but sorry the great box of pictures was broken. Let me know if any have taken wet, for it rained the night they got to Peterborough. I don't agree with Pendleton about keeping the wine in the hampers for at this time of year wine is 'upon the frett' and if one bottle should 'fly' it may break several others packed together. Set upon the ground a little apart one may 'fly' and not harm the rest. Pendleton believes they would be warmer in the hampers, but to preserve them from the cold winter get some sand for them to stand on and stop up all windows with straw or horse 'mucke' which will keep out the frost and let them have a little air when it is more temperate. Send for the box containing the cabinet, which I suppose went down on Monday. Send the weight of it, so I may compare their weighing with yours. The weights you sent me are heavier than theirs by which I perceive Joseph Chamberlaine forgot to weigh them. You wrote the park is overstocked with deer, as it may be since you sent me few last year intending to preserve them and now there is little grass to feed them. They must increase at this rate and I never the better. You killed fawns purposely this year that I might have good winter venison and now I can have none. I will thin them next summer, so that if you can carry 'brouse' enough to keep them this winter I will save you that labour another winter. I hear John Horner has paid in £70 odd, probably Ash's money and Cole's. I have not seen Mr Ballett since I had your letter but it's like him; 'he is a sharking old theife as any is in England'. Pendleton may lay his coal in the coalhouse. Tell Mr Mappletopp there is two or three years to run in Kenwicke Farm lease but when it is free he may have it, or any other in the meantime. I fancy young Stephen Brightman will do no good at Northborough; that may fit Mappletopp when it falls, or Woodcraft Farm.

Send a forest doe next week, half to me, half to my daughter, but if not warrantable send it back.

## 194 FITZWILLIAM TO GUYBON

*London, 16 October 1701; F(M)C 1185*

John Horner has paid at Heriot's £71 4s 6d for Mr Ash; also £21 8s 11d for John Collins; £16 4s 10d for John Eddins. Business will keep me here during the term and after I may find it too late to go down, so use the small beer. Ask Adam Johnson if he thinks the strong beer will keep. Send word if the cabinet is arrived, and its weight, and whether the pictures took wet.

## 195 FITZWILLIAM TO GUYBON

*London, 23 October 1701; F(M)C 1186*

I am glad the box arrived safe, and that I am likely to have some venison for my daughter. In former years the keepers used to blame me for sending so late, saying the venison would have been better earlier. Now they blame me for sending too soon. I wonder they need more room for the wine than the still house and inner still house under the great stairs. I had rather store it there than in the new great cellar for fear it may be too cold this winter. If you can seal the window and yard door with horse muck, lay sand under the bottles and in frosty weather throw straw over the bottles, that will preserve the wine in any vaulted cellar. I suppose all the doors have locks and bars. My vintner Field has a mortgage on Mr Levett's Deeping Gate land, granted by Widow Levett's [second] husband, Norton. Speak to Pemberton, who does Field's business, and ask him to be at Maxey court. Field complains that Robert Smith, 'the great fatt man at Deeping Gate', threatens to sue a tenant of Field for a small piece of land which the tenant has 'enjoied time out of mind', as all the neighbours know, especially William Day. It's not worth a lawsuit, barely 12d a year, so let the Maxey court jury view it, hear the neighbours and decide the matter. Let some one with an interest with Smith speak to him. Did Johnson hop last summer's ale well enough to keep until spring?

## 196 FITZWILLIAM TO GUYBON

*London, 30 October 1701; F(M)C 1187*

I have received £52 of John Sisson of Northborough, and the £60 bill in favour of Mr Walter Slye you enclosed. It lacked his signature on the back, but Mr Petty at Bedford House had separate advice and will pay it but insists on ten days. Send up a doe next week. Our thanks for the partridges and pigeons. Spend the strong drink as fast as you can, bottling that which will not keep. I would not have brewed these past two years if I had not intended to come down but business prevented it. Draw your accounts, rentals and wood books and send them up by Pemberton or Whinyates this term. We have frosty weather here. Dung up the cellar windows that the wine may not be too chilled. [P.S.] The sink in the new cellar may be done with dung but be careful if the sink runs it does not block the drain. Let Joe Chamberlaine pour water down the pipes and keep the lucarnes and gutters clean.

### **197** FITZWILLIAM TO GUYBON
*London, 6 November 1701; F(M)C 1188*

Mr Petty paid the £60 bill with a 'world of scruples' because Slye had not signed the back. I hear nothing of Sisson of Northborough but may tomorrow after market. I need a large sum so call upon the tenants and return speedily.

### **198** FITZWILLIAM TO GUYBON
*London, 13 November 1701; F(M)C 1190*

The half doe came up very sweet but the other half was directed to Sir Charles Barrington when I ordered it to be directed to my daughter. Henceforth direct them to her. Send up a [fee] doe next week and the other the week following, but if the warrants are ill served give them to Peterborough friends, they paying the keeper's fees. If not worth the fees let the keepers take them. When sending a whole doe use a flag basket to save on carriage, but send halves loose. I am glad the wine is secure against frost, but write how many bottles arrived and of what sorts. I will not pay the vintner until you send an account. We are likely to have a new parliament. If Mr St John stands I hope he has better luck. [P.S.] If any tenants or neighbours, as John Webdale and others, have any young black stone horses fit for the coach, although lean, let me know their heights, markings and prices asked.

### **199** FITZWILLIAM TO GUYBON
*London, 20 November 1701; F(M)C 1191*

Since the wine is still in the hampers leave them until I consult Mr Field. Vaults are warm if air cannot enter. I hear nothing of Sisson who was to pay last Monday.

Wee heartily condole with my Cousin Harry Trice for the losse of his wife. It's a great and a suddaine change. Pray God preserve the poore little children. So I perceave the small pox is not yett out of your towne of Peterborough. I perceave nobody stands there but Mr Wortley and Mr Dolben. Pray do you appeare for them since I had a letter from Mr Pemberton to desire it and, withall, to acquaint mee it's rumoured about the towne that I intended to send Jacke downe to stand. I had no such thoughts in the least.

(Reiterates instructions concerning the next fee does.)

### **200** FITZWILLIAM TO GUYBON
*London, 27 November 1701; F(M)C 1193*

The venison, hare and pheasants came well. The venison had begun to change but 'spent well in a pasty'. I hope we don't lose the half doe to my daughter this week. She writes she must join her husband for his election in Essex. It was rumoured here yesterday that Peterborough election was over last Monday and Mr St John defeated again. I never heard that he stood, but if so am sorry he lost. He was ill advised to stand when they used him so ill before. Let me know how matters went. I hear nothing of Sisson's money unless he paid at Heriot's where I have not been these three weeks. Tell Mr Vaughan I will lease the cowpastures again when the leases expire, and would know when that will be, I suppose next Lady Day. Learn as from yourself how much fine each man pays per 'cow common'. Charge him to secure Waldrum Hall against falling, and discover whether Alice Rippon can pay the fine for Maxey Mill. If not I must turn her out and let to another. I hope you call on him for Maxey rents. Leave no money in his hands for he is 'antient' and I don't know their 'ability'. This to yourself. Let me know what sums you have received from him from the first and the dates. [P.S.] Ask him how Maxey is taxed for the militia. I hear only a third part of a horse. Ask if there are no lives fallen since Ewing and Rippon died, and if any fines were paid at last court.

## 201 FITZWILLIAM TO GUYBON

*London, 4 December 1701; F(M)C 1194*

The venison, pheasants and hares came up, but we are quite tired of hares so send no more. Yesterday at Mr Heriot's they said no money was paid in. If any have paid since October 24th last let me know what each man paid and the dates of the notes Mr Heriot gave them. This you always ought to do, and then no man can 'cozen' me though I believe Mr Heriot is an honest man. Yet when you have the goldsmith's notes you should acquaint me the sums and the dates. I am sorry Peterborough is so set against Mr St John though I hear he did not stand this time but only some hot heads made a show of it without his order. I am sorry to hear by Mr Pemberton that his [St John's] old servant Mr Pickering is dead. Send no more venison unless extraordinarily good. Keep all leads and gutters clean this winter. [P.S.] We are all in pretty good health except my wife who is seldom very well. I am glad you are all well. It were well if Mrs Pendleton['s] children have got over the small pox. Better have them now than hereafter.

## 202 GUYBON TO FITZWILLIAM

*9 December 1701; F(M)C 1195*

I have acquainted Mr Vaughan you will lease out the cowpastures again. They don't 'come out' until Lady Day 'come twelve month', but they lease them the Lady Day before, each paying per 'cow comon' 30s fine and 12¼d a year rent. Vaughan says they never paid more. Alice Rippon goes on with the mill. Nothing will be done there until you come. Vaughan says my lady [Sylvius] paid 40s the last time the militia was out which he believes a little hard. Since Sisson paid you £121 Ette has paid Heriot near £100, but they have not yet brought their notes. More should be paid this week for Mr Edings, and by Mr Panke for William Serjeant. I was glad Sir Charles was elected again. [P.S.] Shall I give to the poor of the 'neighbour townes' this Christmas as before?

**203** FITZWILLIAM TO GUYBON
*London, 11 December 1701; F(M)C 1196*

Received yours of the 9th yesterday. If the fines for Maxey cowpastures be no more than 30s for 21 years I will not renew but take the hazard of letting them yearly. I had thought they could not be less than £4 for each cow common. Have Vaughan discover if that is the most they will give, for I shall end those leases. I am not in such want of money to miss about £200 for such a small fine. That does not make above half a crown a year per common, far short of what we let them at yearly. Give to the poor of those towns at Christmas as formerly. Mr Pocklington of Castor wrote concerning the churchwardens' levy for their new ring of bells. I forget how much it was but think it unreasonable that to please Mr Wright and one or two others the whole parish should be assessed so great a sum, and Wright did it for himself for I believe he hung the bells. But since it's done let me know how much Milton is assessed and if not too unreasonable you shall pay it. Hasten returns for I shall soon need money. Speak with Vaughan about the cow commons, and also with intelligent men about Northborough, John Sissons and others that have no Maxey concerns, and you may learn their full worth. I fear Mr Vaughan may too much side with his neighbours, being concerned himself. Smith the fat man of Deeping Gate is an understanding man, able to advise if no way concerned himself, or the little man, Goodman Day.

**204** FITZWILLIAM TO GUYBON
*London, 23 December 1701; F(M)C 1197*

Let Tom Freeman kill my best doe, and send it my daughter but only if it prove well. Direct it only to her by 'Welling'. My wife has been ill and kept her chambers a fortnight. When able she will thank Mrs Bull for her kind present. [P.S.] Return money as fast as you can.

**205** FITZWILLIAM TO GUYBON
*London, 3 January 1701/2; F(M)C 1198*

Francis Guybon, ... I will rather run the hazzard of letting the cow commons at Maxey yearly then take so inconsiderable a fine as 30s apeice. I am not in such want of money as to loose above £40 yearly for the sake of £200 ready money. I thinke of makeing a farme of them and lett them out to some sufficient man at the racke rent by lease. I know in wett yeares they must be worth 10s or 12s a peice when Deeping fenn is under water. You had best pay the church levy at Castor being £5 14s.[1] I thinke it's hard upon the parrish they should be putt to so great a charge for two or three whimsicall fellows' fancys. I am sorry to heare Mr Willis is dead.[2] I feare it will be hard to make out his reckoning now he is gone and much apprehend you have paid him more money then is due to him. There was paid me yesterday by one Paule of Peterborough by your order and Goodman Serjeant's and Mr Pancke's £30, and this day Mr Henry Hankin paid me more by Mr Panck's order and yours £36 6s 9d. I heare nothing yett of Mr Ree.[3] I hope you have sent my daughter this weeke a good doe, or none at all.

My wife can by no meanes enjoy her health perfectly. The rest of us, thanke God, in very good health, only I have had of late now and then great dizzinesses in my head which I feare was a little apoplecticall. Thanks be to God I have not this last fortnight had any simptomes of it. Mr Whinyates is gott very well againe and intends next Munday for the countrey. . . .

[1] Guybon paid a Mr Death 'to a leavey for new casting the bells at Castor, £5 14s' on 15 January, and a levy of £2 17s for repairs to the church for the previous two years; Disbursements 74. There are six bells, all cast by Henry Bagley of Ecton, dated 1700 (according to *VCH Northamptonshire*, ii. 481).

[2] A local glazier.

[3] '15 Jan. Returned Mr Heriott by Mr Abraham Riss, £100', Disbursements 74.

## **206** FITZWILLIAM TO GUYBON

*London, 8 January 1701/2; F(M)C 1200*

We return our thanks for your kind New Year's gift to my wife. All the things were very good in their kind. My daughter was well pleased with her doe. Mr Heriot's accounts show several sums of money paid in which I did not know of. I always desired when you received Heriot or his man Barrett's notes that you give me notice of dates and amounts, otherwise I might lose money if they were not honest. They were by John Cole's order £36 19s 2d, of a Mr Tomlin £34 6s 6d; by Thomas Rudkins £13 3s 3d; by John Shelton £12 7s 2d, all on 25 November. Not knowing the last three named inform me whether they were paid by your order. On 15 December Joseph Webdale paid £7 14s 6d; on the 18th John Cole £18 3s 10d; 1 January Mr Burton £12 4s 1d; yesterday Mr Abraham Ree £100. These sums you have had no notice of from me, although you should, and likewise I from you, or we can never keep true accounts. Wishing you and all friends a merry New Year.

## **207** GUYBON TO FITZWILLIAM

*15 January 1701/2; F(M)C 1196 [verso]*[1]

Received yours of the 8th. There are a brace of good does here. Those people who paid in money by my order are all neighbours and tenants and I have repaid them that have brought their notes. I enclose the measurements of the glass at Milton done by Mr Willis. Mr Wright and Willis's son measured it at Mrs Willis's desire, she hoping there would be much money due; I fear there will be little. Mr Lawrence desires you would divide his ground with a 'quick' or by a dike, which being large would be better.

[1] A draft, written on the reverse of Fitzwilliam's letter of 11 December 1701 ( **203** above).

## **208** FITZWILLIAM TO GUYBON

*London, 22 January 1701/2; F(M)C 1201*

I received yours enclosing the measurements of the glazing in the new Milton buildings and can only hope you did not pay more beforehand than is due. Pay no more until I come down and look at the agreement with Willis. Since you 'cracke so much' of your venison send a whole doe in a basket so they won't know what it is. I would not have Mr Lawrence dike out his ground this winter but wait until I come down. If I find it convenient I may have it done next winter, but not before. My wife, we hope, mends a little, but has long been ill and often troubled with toothache. Return money speedily.

## 209 FITZWILLIAM TO GUYBON

*London, 29 January 1701/2; F(M)C 1202*

I shall have business of concern to write about next post so go yourself to Peterborough without fail for it on Monday and give me a speedy answer.

## 210 FITZWILLIAM TO GUYBON

*London, 31 January 1701/2; F(M)C 1203*

Francis Guybon, Pray lett me desire you to write to my daughter and inclose my letter, here sent you, in it, and send it to her by Mr Roger Pemberton and gett him to deliver it to her with his owne hands. For I can not write to her by the post but her letters are intercepted,[1] and this way it may go without suspition. I send the letter open that you may read it and then pray putt a little wax under the seale to close it up. I received the venison this day and would have thankt you had you eate it or given it away and not putt mee to the charge of bringing it up. I had not sent for it, neither did I want it, but you writt word they were so good, encouragd me to send for it. My sonn is sorry for the loss of his old horse but old freinds must part. I rest in hast ... [P.S.] Mr Pemberton I heare is expected in towne this day sennight. Pray loose not the opportunity of sending this letter by him, but don't lett him know that I have a letter inclosed. Desire him to give it to her when they two are alone and that none of the servants or any other person is by.

[1] Possibly because Lord Fitzwilliam and his son-in-law Sir Charles Barrington were in disagreement over financial matters relating presumably to the marriage settlement, traditionally a fertile source of disagreement (see **226** below), and any letters from father to daughter might be considered to contain useful information. In a letter of 2 May 1702 Richard Butler (possibly a lawyer) wrote to Lord Fitzwilliam, 'I am extreame glad to heare there is now an end in the affair between your lordshipp and Sir Charles Barrington without suit.' F(M)C 1213.

## 211 FITZWILLIAM TO GUYBON

*London, 5 February 1701/2; F(M)C 1204*

John Horner has paid £16 2s 1d and Henry Hankin has paid £34 13s 2d for a William Whittmore, a fenman. Were these sums paid by your order? Had today a kind of offer of the Aylesworth farm old William Burton always rented. I don't know whether it was in earnest. However, inform yourself about it but very privately. I would not have it known until we have done it, but I may hear no more of it. Ask his son who rents Wildbore's farm from us what rent his father pays 'in ordinary discourse' not as if you came on purpose to ask it, and set others to 'sift the rest' from him 'over a pott of ale'. Learn how many acres of meadow and pasture there are to it, and where they lie, and if any Lammas land belongs to it, and if any small rent is paid out of it, and, if so, to whom, and everything else proper to know. Learn the field names where the land lies; which is the best field, which the worst. I have much ado to write having sprained my thumb. I hope you received the enclosed letter and sent it away.[1]

[1] Referring to the letter he wished Pemberton to carry secretly to his daughter.

## 212 FITZWILLIAM TO GUYBON

*London, 14 February 1701/2; F(M)C 1205*

Francis Guybon, I should not have given myselfe the trouble, nor you neither, of sending my daughter's letter for you to convey to her if I had not immagined you had knowne where she lived and had an influance over Mr Pemberton to go to her with it. He has brought the letter up to towne and now askes mee where she is. She lives upon the roade up to towne and nothing could have been a more specious pretence then for him as he came up to make her a short vissitt and so have brought us a true account of the state of her health. It's just 4 miles out of the roade which could not have taken him up much time and it fell out he came to towne last Satturday at 11 of the clocke in the forenoone that he could not pretend he wanted time, and by the directions of sending the venison to her you could not but know where she lived and Mr Pemberton ownes he was at Mr Clerke's, who lived at Dosthorp,[1] who now lives within less then two miles of her.

Fearey the carrier brought his bill which I thought extraordinary and full of mistakes. I have not had time to compare it with my book but let him have £8 or £9 on account. He had £7 from you about two years since. John Webster offers to be my coachman. I shall not take him if you don't think it convenient and fear he will be troubled by creditors when we are down there. Pray advise me. [P.S.] Note my daughter lives at Hertingfordbury Park, within a mile from Hertford, within four miles of Welwyn on the carriers' road, within four miles of Ware on the post road. Mr Pocklington brought a letter from Mr Pendleton who writes Pocklington was to pay me money but I think mistakenly for he said nothing of it. He leaves for Castor on Monday.

[1] Dogsthorpe, a hamlet of Peterborough.

## 213 GUYBON TO FITZWILLIAM

*28 February 1701/2; F(M)C 1206*

Yours of the 14th received. Mr Burton's Aylesworth farm has 68 acres land[1] and 7 acres meadow belonging to it; rent: £30 a year. Eight cottages in Aylesworth belong to it with 66 acres of land and meadow belonging to them let for £25 5s a year, and in Castor there are three cottages with 10 acres and 1 rod of land let for £6 4s a year. The land lies well for you, among your own in many places. I know not what to say for John Webster. If he be a good husband he will do well enough. I do not hear of many creditors. I hope Mr Mapletoft and Mr Edings have paid you money this week. I will return as fast as I can get returns.

[1] By 'land' Guybon meant arable, as Fitzwilliam indicated when he jotted down these statistics again in a marginal note.

## 214 FITZWILLIAM TO GUYBON

*London, 5 March 1701/2; F(M)C 1207*

Yours of the 28th received. Nothing has been paid by your order save £27 7s 6d by John Horner for Mr Mapletoft on the 27th. I should be glad of more for these five little sums don't amount to much more than £100 in a month, and I have spent much more in that time. I delivered the letter Pemberton brought up to my daughter's own hands. For Burton's Aylesworth land I like the farm and the land belonging to the cottages but disapprove of the cottages. 'They are only a shelter for poore people who when they die leave their houses out of repaire', a great charge to their landlord. My father sold his Castor cottages for that reason. However, get the tenants' names, the rent each gives, and the acres of arable, pasture and meadow belonging to each cottage. The land may be well to lay to my farms. I understand John Webster is indebted to some Peterborough people by bond, so believe I won't take him lest he be troubled when he is my servant. Buy me 12 or 15 quarters of malt next Saturday before the tax is laid on it and store it for my brewing next summer and strong beer at Michaelmas. If cheap and good buy 20 quarters. Buy some of Mr Whinyate's coke dried malt, for he, Mr Deacon and Mr Parker make the best and buy the best corn for [malting]. Buy choice and take samples. Old Joseph and young Joseph Chamberlaine understand [malt] as well as any.

## 215 GUYBON TO FITZWILLIAM

*17 March 1701/2; F(M)C 1208*

Yours of the 5th I received but none since. I hope you will have a good deal of money paid this week. I enclose the names of the tenants in the Aylesworth and Castor cottages and their rent, and how many acres of arable, pasture and meadow belong to each. The cottages are in pretty good repair but if they were all down the land would give the rent. Many tenants would be very glad of it. The King's death 'have put a dampe upon every thinge in the countrey'.[1] Nothing gives any money. Trading is very dead, the people much dejected and cast down.

[1] William III had died on 8 March 1702.

## 216 FITZWILLIAM TO GUYBON

*London, 19 March 1701/2; F(M)C 1209*

Received yours of March 10 and 17. I am a little concerned you have not bought the malt. Your reasons are convincing. Edins and Horner paid me on the 10th only £21 11s 6d. I am well satisfied with your particular of Aylesworth and Castor cottages, save that I wish to know how much of John Palmer's 20 acres land is arable, pasture and meadow. Be very exact so that I may judge the true worth when it is offered me. You mention Richard Hullicke's cottage has 6 acres arable, 4 meadow and a close. How many acres is the close? By your estimate of these cottages and their lands, I cannot believe the lands are worth the price asked without the houses, and these houses will be a 'hard pennyworth' considering they are poor tenants, and their houses will cost much to repair 'if they die insolvent as most poore tennants do'. We are all extremely sorry at the loss of our King but must be contented with God's will. 'We have a gracious Queene in his roome who gives us great hopes of her goodness by her declaration'. We don't doubt she will perform her promises so let all men's minds be satisfied and I don't doubt trade will 'have its due course' again. [P.S.] My daughter sends her remembrances.

## **217** GUYBON TO FITZWILLIAM

*24 March 1701/2; F(M)C 1210*

Yours of the 19th received. I hoped to hear you received more money than you have. I hope it will be paid this week. Mr Thomas Barrett's receipt [at Heriot's] shows £22 11s 6d paid by Mr Edings. Mr [Thomas] Bevill holds Barrett's receipt for £24 6s 2d paid on 7 February. Please confirm these amounts. For the cottages, John Palmer has 18 acres 1 rod of arable and 1 acre 3 rod of meadow; Richard Hullock has 6 acres arable, 4 meadow and a close of 4 acres. 'Besides his homestead, head house he have none, it was burnt many years agoe'. These tenants wish to continue and would give the rent if there were no houses upon it. The cottages are mostly in good repair.

## **218** FITZWILLIAM TO GUYBON

*London, 2 April 1702; F(M)C 1211*

Francis Guybon, On Wednesday last weeke being Our Ladyday I was seizd with a violent feavour which had like to have turned to appoplectick fitts and would infallibly have taken mee off had not it been diverted (through God's blessing) by the meanes of the physitian. The feavour fell afterwards into my legg in a St Anthony's fire[1] which has kept mee in bedd ever since, but thanke God I am much recovered and in a very hopefull way.

Mr Heriot's man was mistaken in the account he gave me of Edins' payment which was £22 11s 6d by John Horner, so you see how necessary it is for you to let me know what sums are set down in the goldsmith's receipts that I may compare them with their books; then I cannot be wronged. I thought I had confirmed Bevill's payment by Horner long since.[2] 20 March Henry Hankin paid Heriot by your order £11 5s 1d; 21 March, Rowland Morrice paid at my house £40; 24 March, by your and John Webdale's order was paid here by Francis Hoare and Hubbord, two salesmen, £84. I think you have satisfied all my queries about Aylesworth and Castor lands. If I buy the tenants can be sure of what they have if they maintain the cottages. Only Burton's farm was offered me by Mr Whittwell of Oundle. I did not know the cottages also belonged to him. If offered together, or if either are offered singly, I will buy.

[1] St Anthony's fire: erysipelas, a local febrile disease causing inflammation.
[2] 3 April 1702: 'Returned Mr Heriott by Mr Thos. Bevill Feb. 7, '70, £24 6s 2d', Disbursements 74.

**219** FITZWILLIAM TO GUYBON

*London, 16 April 1702; F(M)C 1212*

I am daily mending in strength, but my fever, falling into my leg as a St Anthony's fire, kept me in bed until five or six days ago. Although it's pretty well, I have still such pains in the leg that I cannot leave my chamber nor write without trouble. Heriot informs me Mr Edins paid him £49 6s on the 9th.

As to lendeing the countrey money to pay off the robbery money[1] I could very ill spare it at this time being forc't to make use of all my money at this time and more then all, but the countrey shall not want money from mee if they cannot as easily gett it from another hand, for it's much better to pay a little interest till the rents will pay it off then to make an assessment in the Soake which will come hardly from the tennants. Pray recollect what the countrey owes mee at this time if not lately repaid. I remember one summe which was about £14 or £15 that Mr Neale wrote a letter to you to desire me to lay it downe out of the countrey's money which I ordered you to doe though at that time you said you had none of the countrey's money in your hands nor had not of a great while. That money was laied downe upon the score of a taxe one yeare for Sutton or Aylesworth, which had I not done it, the duplicates of the whole Soake must have been altered and a new levy made to raise it which would have caused great confusion. It's about 2 or 3 or 4 yeares since almost.[2] I have Mr Neale's letter to produce if occasion be. If I must lend this money pray take bond for it of 6 or 8 of the cheife tennants and gentlemen such as John Webdale, Bimrose and such like men as I used to have when I formerly lent the countrey money, and lawfull interest for it, and if you lay downe £140 now add whatever other summs the countrey owes mee and putt all into the bond, but still I had rather Mr Lowrey or any other honest man woud advance the money at this time for the reasons afore mentioned. My poore daughter is just come this evening to towne. She is still very ill and cannot presently recover her late miscarriage. She remembers her kindly to you....

[P.S.] Send what money you can spare. Let my wife know by Sunday's post which way Mrs Bull comes up, and what inn she comes to so we can send someone to meet her.

[1] See **182** above. It is not certain that this refers to the robbery of the previous year for which the hundred had now been made responsible, but this seems the most likely explanation.

[2] Guybon noted under 28 February 1702 that he had 'layd downe for the towne of Sutton money paid over and above the discharge layd upon the towne, £12 16s 10d'. In the margin he wrote 'Landike' referring to the hundred court (see note to **220** below); Disbursements 74.

**220** FITZWILLIAM TO GUYBON

*London, 7 May 1702; F(M)C 1216*

Today Mr Ash brought a letter from Langdike jury[1] desiring I would lend them £50 at interest until moneys come in from rents to reimburse it. He believes they will want a great deal more but that is the sum they request so let them have no more without my further order.[2] Tell them they would oblige me if they borrowed elsewhere because I need money greatly at present, and I only do it because the 'countrey' shall not lack money for their occasions while I live. If you give up your accounts next Tuesday to the 'countrey' I don't know what you can do without the last accounts which are locked in my closet at Milton. You may remember how the account was stated and what you have done since. Messrs Ash, Parker and Deepup had £20 of me three or four years ago, and you paid £13 or £14 on a letter from Mr Neale for a deficient tax for Aylesworth or Sutton. Recollect all other sums you have received or paid on that account that neither I nor the country be wronged. I hear of no more money paid at Heriot's. Take the wine from the hampers to set on the cold stones. Open the great case when Mrs Bull comes down to air the pictures. She and Betty [Bull] are well and will be with you soon.

[1] The jury of Langdyke Court, the court of the hundred. It consisted of 'Michael Selby, William Exton, John Buning, Richard Buddle, Thomas Lawrence, Joseph Bull, William Sargent, Nicolas Thougood, Robert Henry, Daniell Burbidge, Thomas Laxton, Lawrance Pilbort, Eddward Clark, Robert Denham, John Burrows' as is shown on a sheet of paper filed with the correspondence at F(M)C 1215. Langdyke Bush at the junction of the parishes of Ufford, Upton and Helpston was the traditional meeting-place of Nassaborough Hundred and the hundred court: *Place Names of Northamptonshire*, p. 223. The court held on 4 May dealt with the recent highway robbery (see **219**) and the compensation for which the hundred was liable.

[2] On 2 June Guybon noted 'My lord lent the countrey £50'; Disbursements 74.

## **221** FITZWILLIAM TO GUYBON

*London, 28 May 1702; F(M)C 1217*

From Heriot's book I find Edings paid £32 15s 4d on the 19th. We are happy Mrs Bull and Betty got down safely. I am glad the country does not call on you for money. I need all you can get me so call on the tenants and return it as fast as you can. Rowland Morrice paid £40 on the 21st. I thought Belsis lease was not up for twelve months. Advise with Mr Pemberton and insist on a £50 fine. It never paid more until Mr Bleckington became a prebend. You must own the rent we receive to be no more than £60, for which I am willing to pay £50 fine. If the dean and prebends consider I pay £6 and a mark chief rent, and the great taxes, and how good a tenant I have been in building a great barn with other buildings, they could not in conscience ask more. When the new lease is sealed Pemberton can hold it until I surrender the old which is locked away. Buy a new lock for the drying yard door. My fruit trees there must be come to some perfection before this, so let Old Joseph lock it up and keep the key. Let all the yards be made handsome forthwith, for I believe I may be down by midsummer and will order beer brewed within a week. I hope you have taken the wine from the hampers. I hear there is good wine to be had at Stamford. Let me know if so for I shall need a great deal. I hope all the gutters and pipes are cleaned, and would know if there is a good plumber now about Peterborough or must we send further. You don't mention whether your spectacles 'fitt your eyesight'. I got Mr Heriot who is 73 years of age to try them. 'If they be not old enough for you I will gett an older man to try them' and bring another pair down with me.

## 222 FITZWILLIAM TO GUYBON

*London, 4 June 1702; F(M)C 1218*

I hope the country calls on you only for the £50 you have let them have and that you have bond for it. I am glad you have returned money by Morrice and Edins. Let the drought or weather be what God pleases I must go into the country soon for my health requires it. I cannot live in this town long. The meadow hay must all be kept for I must keep five or six horses in the house besides yours. Lock the drying yard and clip the hedge handsomely. Let no horse but my own come into the park, for the poor deer need all the grass this dry time. Put my horses, all but your own, in the woods. We had rain but there is a drought again, the wind changing easterly once more. I hope you had some rain for I heard from some drovers it reached Biggleswade. Only pay a £50 fine for Belsis lease. We will pay £60 if they won't take £50 but it shall not be said we pay contentedly.[1] [P.S.] I will bring down a watering pot for Old Joseph.

[1] Guybon paid £60 on 24 June; Disbursements 74.

## 223 FITZWILLIAM TO GUYBON

*London, 18 June 1702; F(M)C 1219*

The money Mr Edins and Morrice were to pay me last week is still unpaid. I am sorry to hear of your drought. Here has been rain enough these three weeks but too late for they cut hay soon. I hope rain will bring down the price of cock hay. The price yours mentions is as dear as here. Buy as cheap as possible for I must have it, and let it stand where it is until I give notice of my coming down. Inquire what land it grew on and whether it was well 'inned'[1] last summer. Observe if the cock is well enough made to take no harm last winter. Inquire for more if that will not suffice which I fear it will not. I will see what Mr Eldred says about this money you mention he is to return for me. My wife desires Mrs Pendleton would pickle her some walnuts, if not grown too big. My son and daughter remember them kindly to you. My daughter was very ill two days this week but is very well again. [P.S.] Ask Mrs Bull and Mr Wright to open the other cases of pictures I sent last summer for fear they should be mouldy. Stand the pictures leaning against a wall in a dry room and air them on 'a fine sunshiny day' by opening the casements; the room to be kept locked.

[1] Harvested.

## 224 FITZWILLIAM TO GUYBON

*London, 28 June 1702; F(M)C 1221*

Yours of the 23rd I received but yesterday. It should have been with me on the 24th. If you send your letters by such uncertain ways I cannot answer them to your expectation. If there are but 10 loads in the haycock I fear you have over bid. It can only be worth £20 however dry a year it is, but since you have bid £25 I will not be worse than your word. If he refuses that price

I will run the hazard and buy as I can when I come down. You must have had rain by now for we have it every day, sometimes very heavy. There will be no lack of hay here nor in your parts as I hear from people from thence. Neither Mr Edings nor Morrice has paid anything, and Mr Eldred says his cannot be depended on. Seek other returns for I shall be in great want in a fortnight's time. I spoke with Mr Whinyates in the Hall last Thursday, who told me the 'countrey' need several hundred pounds. I told him I could not lend it needing money for my own business, but if anyone would lend it now I would repay them when I could spare it. Tell Lowrey or anyone that has money what I have written. The security is as good as any in England as Mr Whinyates can show. Tell Holmes the hempdresser's kinsman, the Northborough man—I cannot remember his name, his younger brother lives in Parfaite's house—that I have ordered Mr Burman to sue for arrears of quit rents and amercements for Maxey manor amongst which he is concerned.[1] I must pay Lady Sylvius and I would not have the tenants troubled so speak to him and persuade him to pay it quietly, for I will not lose it and he knows I am able to contend with him. If they tax my personal estate there at £1,000 as in the past I will pay there to 'ease the countrey' but must have a certificate to show here for I am taxed where I reside. Don't be forward to say I will be taxed there for the tax is not settled in our parish here so I don't know how much they will assess me. If it's very considerable I must not be taxed in the country also. I will write next week by which time perhaps I shall know what is best for me. I will do what I can for the 'countrey'.

[1] Bolton of Northborough (see below **225**).

## **225** FITZWILLIAM TO GUYBON

*London, 9 July 1702; F(M)C 1222*

Francis Guybon ... I beleive the reason why I received no money from you of so long time is because I understand that John Horner the Quaker is broake who us't to receave and pay away all the money from your parts and I understand poore Joseph Bull is concerned amungst the rest. He offerrs a noble in the pound as they tell mee but there's no manner of reason they should abate anything to him being he received all the money and could not pretend to have any loss and has broake out of downe right knavery.

Hope you have had rain for here we pray for fair weather. What have you done about the hay? I am willing to pay the tax there for I find they will deal favourably with me here. I hope for venison from the park this year, for they say venison will be fattest in dry years. There has been abundance of fat venison here. I have received nothing from Mr ,[1] the Deeping attorney, who I suppose has left town, so return me speedily all you can.

[P.S.] Pray call often of old Mr Vaughan for Maxey rents. Leave not moneys in his hands. He is antient and I know not his condition and his sonn's. I would know if you have spoke with Bolton of Norborough about Lady Sylvius' cheife rent and amerciaments. Those moneys I must not loose for I have paid the full worth of them. My wife would desire Mrs Pendleton to preserve her 2, 3 or 4 pounds of wallnutts. They are to be eaten as a cordiall and physicall, not as a sweate meate, therefore she would have them done with powder sugar of Lisbon if she can gett it, of 8d, 9d or 10d price, or 11d, but if she never did any they may lett alone. I hope she has pickled up some wallnutts that I writt about 3 weekes agoe to have done. My wife desires you would tell Mrs Bull if she has not aired the house very well very lately she would gett her to do it now before hay[s]ell beginns, and desires the bedds and blancketts may be thoroughly aired.

[1] Blank in original. Probably Mr Eldred of Deeping is meant, see **224** above.

## **226** FITZWILLIAM TO GUYBON

*London, 16 July 1702; F(M)C 1223*

I have still received no returns. Glad to hear of the rain which should fatten the deer and all else. I cannot come down for three weeks at soonest. I am sorry Mr Lowrey has no money to lend the 'countrey'. It's as good a security as any in England. I cannot spare any, for I am paying my daughter's portion and must borrow some of that. Mr Richard Dickenson or Mr Thomas Deacon or any of those great Peterborough maltsters must have money. Mr Lawrence of Walton and several others are never without one or two hundred pounds by them. It's a disparagement to our 'countrey' if we have to 'run out of the Soake for money'. Grass, hay and grain are plentiful here. We have had rain every day for six weeks and yet the hay 'is well gotten' though with more charge. [P.S.] I hear a Mr Ash has paid £19 8s at Heriot's.

## **227** FITZWILLIAM TO GUYBON

*London, 23 July 1702; F(M)C 1226*

Francis Guybon, I received yours and am glad to heare Mr Ash will pay me more money next weeke. I want a great deale to help to pay my daughter's portion which must be now paid as soon as writeings are ready which will be in a fortnight I hope. I am glad the election is over at Peterborough and am obliged to Mr Deacon and Mr Pemberton for their kind intentions to my sonn. I do not heare of any removall like to be amung the judges as yett. Pray tell Hicklin of Waldrum Hall I will stand by him in anything I can justifie for as yett I know not my owne strength not having lookt much into the writeings, but he may be sure nobody can go over in his ferry boate without paying whither I have a charter or not, for he may chuse whither or no he will carry them in his boate. When I go downe I shall looke better into things there. If the drought continues I thinke you had best buy the haycocke you writt to me off. Pray stand hard at £25 or £26 or £27 but if those summs will no[t] do, you must then give him £28 as you mentioned he was willing to take. You do not lett me know whose haycocke it is nor where it stands. If you buy it, don't lett it be stirred till I order it. My daughter remembers her kindly to you and saies she has received no letter from you off some time....

## 228 FITZWILLIAM TO GUYBON

*London, 30 July 1702; F(M)C 1224*

(Has paid tax there favourably so will pay tax on personal estate in country. Has Guybon got the Belsis fine reduced £10 at the audit?[1] Mr Ash dined previous Sunday. He was to pay Fitzwilliam a return next day but feared the markets would be bad. He only paid £30 at Heriot's rather than the £60–£80 Guybon had mentioned. Has underwritten warrants. Hears of no restraint on Lord Exeter's 'walke'; knows no reason he should lose a buck a year because Exeter's keepers are knaves who sell his venison.)

[1] Guybon had not been successful, see above **222** note.

## 229 FITZWILLIAM TO GUYBON

*London, 13 August 1702; F(M)C 1225*

Yours of the 4th I received the 10th. I don't know how you send letters, but some have arrived a week late. When you don't write by Sunday's post better send by 'Waternewton', giving them to 'Old Joseph'[1] whose grandson will carry them there. I am sorry your drought continues, we had rain last Wednesday and Friday 'that went thoroughly to the roote'. Have you bought the haycock? I wonder there should not be a good buck in the park. Send a warrant into the Forest and send a buck next week and another the week following. Mr Whittfield, an Oundle attorney, offered me Barningham's farme but insists on £400. I offered £340 which at £17 rent is just 20 years' purchase. The houses about it are ready to fall and I suppose the land 'out of heart' for the tenant is poor. You may offer £350. If refused 'lett whosoever will buy it. I will not buy gold to[o] deare'. Possibly Mr Bloofield has the selling of it who seldom comes to town and employed Mr Whittfield to come to me who I know very well. He is here constantly every term. However, I fancy you may buy it cheaper of Mr Bloofield than of [Whittfield] who probably expects a gratuity. Tell Mr Burman, Lord Exeter's steward that I hope Lord Exeter will give me a buck out of his park if he will not serve my Westhay Walk warrant.

[P.S.] There goes a strong report about towne and is in every body's mouth but I hope it is not true, that my Lord Exeter's lady has stabbed one of her women servants who they say is dead and buried. Pray lett us know by your next the truth of it, and if it be true, when it happened and what they say was the occasion of it, but take no notice of my writeing to you about it but inquire of it as from yourselfe but mention not my name in the least. Lett me know if it is her woman or chambermaid, or who and what her name was.

[1] Joseph Chamberlaine the elder.

## 230 FITZWILLIAM TO GUYBON

*London, 27 August 1702; F(M)C 1227*

(Buck came Saturday only moderately sweet the weather being very hot the two days it was on the road. Guybon to send up a buck from the park the next week. Glad Exton is to pay him money. Wonders at Guybon's not returning earlier, knowing of Ash's disappointing payment and his need when coming out of town. Guybon to report when harvest will be in, and when the 'statutes'[1] begin so he may order servants hired. [P.S.] His daughter very ill of a cold caught coming hot out of the playhouse.)

[1] A gathering or fair held annually in certain towns and villages for hiring servants.

## 231 FITZWILLIAM TO GUYBON

*London, 29 August 1702; F(M)C 1228*

(His wife, fearing the 'statutes' were near, wishes Guybon and Mrs Bull to hire a cook-maid, handy about the kitchen under a housekeeper, and a house-maid, handy about washing ordinary linen. Also wishes Mrs Bull to pickle 'a pecke of cowcumbers' and Mrs Pendleton to pickle 'abundance' of mush-rooms. If Mrs Bull knows good servants leaving their places she should hire them, not wait for the statutes. Exton has paid £132 'very seasonably'. Buck came very sweet. To send another from the park, or the warrant buck from Cross-a-Hand Walk.)

## 232 FITZWILLIAM TO GUYBON

*London, 3 September 1702; F(M)C 1229*

Let me have a buck from Burghley Park next week if Mr Burman[1] comes home. I fear I cannot pleasure my Peterborough friends with venison this season for my daughter has most of that you send up, and I have had little or none from my park this year or two past. My wife wishes Mrs Bull next Saturday to observe at Mr Duce's and elsewhere how much the best capers and anchovies sell for per pound; if they have good ones, and whether they will have better at next Brigg Fair. Also whether Mrs Bull can buy sugar as good as she bought in town, and its price. I shall be glad when I hear from the Cambridge woolman who bought Marholm wool and who is to pay me money.[2]

[1] Lord Exeter's steward.
[2] Halstead.

## 233 FITZWILLIAM TO GUYBON

*London, 5 September 1702; F(M)C 1230*

The buck arrived sweet but not so fat as the two before so I will have no more from my park this year. I think it very hard I can have no more venison than I have had this year and last, but must take a better course henceforward. If you can have a buck from Burleigh let four of my friends around Peterborough divide it. Let Cousin Harry Tryce have a piece and take one yourself, and the rest give away where you think fit. You need not give Mr Pendleton any for I believe they do not value it. We are sorry we cannot have the man Mrs Bull thought so fit for us, but hire another for us.

We should be glad you could help us to a good cooke maide because they are all here such slutts or whores or theives or druncken beasts that we dare hardly bring any of them downe, that we must desire you and Mrs Bull to do your uttmost to help us to a good cooke maide if you can. You shall be sure to have a fortnight's notice of our comeing downe because of brewing, but I hope there needs no notice for anything else because I hope the yards and gardens and all things else are kept handsome as they should be. And for hay getting in, I will have none gott home till I am there unless one loade for present use and some straw which may be putt over the carter's stable ... [P.S.] Pray lett me heare by the next if you can what you and Mrs Bull have done at Helpston statutes about a man and maides.

### 234 FITZWILLIAM TO GUYBON

*London, 10 September 1702; F(M)C 1231*

I hear nothing of the Cambridge woolman (Halstead), and don't expect to until he has sold his wool at 'Sturbitch'[1] Fair. Then I may if he prove honest. If I cannot have a buck from Burleigh Park send the Westhay warrant, demand it before Holyrood Day, and divide it among my Peterborough friends. I hear of no restraint on the Walk and I have no obligation to the family[2] to lose a buck and doe every year because they say there is a restraint. Give the warrant to Robert Newcombe who will certainly demand it and if he succeeds let him have a piece and the rest give to Peterborough friends. I wish I had venison enough for all my friends but after this warrant I must give to none lest by giving to some I disoblige others. If the keeper should pretend there is a restraint tell Robert Newcombe to demand they show it. I am sure they cannot since the Queen has not named a new justice in eyre, and the last is 'out', of course, upon the King's death. I can send my servants to kill a buck if the keeper refuses to serve my warrant unless they produce a restraint. If they do, let Newcombe examine the date to see if it has not expired. I need no venison here for my daughter has gone to Essex. Divide Cross-a-Hand warrant as you see fit. (His wife wishes to know if she can rely on the maids Mrs Bull hired at Helpston, and what places she hired them for. Hopes Guybon also hired a man.)

[1] Stourbridge, the great Cambridge Fair.
[2] The Cecil family, who controlled Westhay walk in the forest of Rockingham.

### 235 FITZWILLIAM TO GUYBON

*London, ? September 1702;[1] F(M)C 1232*

(Repeats his wish to know what places maids have been hired for so his wife will know what others to bring down. Maids to be paid from time they were hired.)

[1] Day left blank.

### 236 FITZWILLIAM TO GUYBON

*London, 17 September 1702; F(M)C 1233*

I hear nothing of the Cambridge woolman [Halstead] but glad you have disposed of the warrants.

As to Adam Johnson's sonne I can say nothing against him, not haveing knowne them since they were boyes. I remember one of them was a very unhealthy boy, it was the least in growth though I thinke he was the eldest sonne. I thinke if you tooke a man whose freinds lived further off then Marrham it might be better, for feare he should be runing home often and it may be on nights, he keeping the gates, when nobody can know it, but I leave it to your prudence to take such a one for me as you thinke may do my service well and that is rightly honest. He must understand heateing ovens well and do the other worke about the house that you know we shall want him for.

Buy the haycock rather than lose it but I hope for less than yours mentions. Hay is very much fallen in price about London. I will name no attorney to Joseph Bull. The two you named are both very good men; let him please himself. I understand Deeping Fen supplies all the country with fodder, which brings down the price, for that is as nourishing for cattle as hay. Let Mrs Bull have money to buy things for the house at Brigg Fair. Let me know the lowest price of hops at Brigg Fair and I will write how many Mrs Bull shall buy.

## **237** FITZWILLIAM TO GUYBON

*London, 24 September 1702; F(M)C 1234*

Today Mr Halstead paid me £160 on account of the tenants' wool at Marholm; and £40 by Mr William Ash's order which you must repay him there. He wishes you to inform Ash the money is paid, and the Marholm tenants that he will be there next Tuesday or Wednesday to weigh their wool. George Woodcocke has paid £33 8s 9d for three Northborough and Maxey tenants. I have no business in the term nor in parliament to hinder my coming this winter, which will be best for my business, nobody coming at me to hinder my taking accounts. I am sorry Mr Lowrey could not get the warrant served. Hops are much cheaper in town than you speak of and sending from here may be worth more than the carriage. My wife would know what wages the maids are to have and what Mrs Bull bought at the fair. My wife is very ill at present, but all the rest reasonably well.

## **238** FITZWILLIAM TO GUYBON

*London, 1 October 1702; F(M)C 1235*

My wife will not part with the maids so their wages may begin next Monday, but let them stay with their friends a fortnight longer. We shall certainly be down this month. A few weeks' wages is no loss. George Woodcocke the drover brought me £56 1s 4d. Mr Eddins must be paid of it £34 0s 7d, John Bolton £8 16s 4d, John Cooke £4 0s 10d, and a John Carborough £9 3s 7d.[1] Repay these three Northborough men. [P.S.] My wife wishes Mrs Bull to thoroughly air the house a week or 10 days before we come. Get pump and vessels ready for brewing.

[1] Guybon noted these amounts and gave totals in the margin. Guybon repaid them 6 October. 'Carborough' was really 'Scarbrow', Disbursements 74.

## 239 FITZWILLIAM TO GUYBON

*London, 8 October 1702; F(M)C 1236*

I have paid away all my ready money and am in debt. Ride among the tenants and tell them they must supply me now, it being an extraordinary occasion. Have all things ready about the brewhouse for in a week I shall write ordering you to brew. Have the vessels well 'binged',[1] the pump put in order and pipes mended so the water may come into the kitchen, larder and washhouse. Hoop well and sweeten the hogsheads, and keep account of what is done. Let me know in your next whether they can mash and cool three hogsheads of ale at the same time as they brew six hogsheads of small beer, and I will order what I want brewed. Get samples of malt from Messrs Whinyates, Parker, Deacon and John Dickenson, and you and the Joseph Chamberlaines decide which is best. I will then send word what quantity of malt I want brewed. [P.S.] Have Adam Johnson view the malt mill and see if it wants more than just the 'pecking'[2] of it.

[1] Binge, to soak, Baker.
[2] To clean it by gouging out any clogging dust, etc.

## 240 FITZWILLIAM TO GUYBON

*London, 15 October 1702; F(M)C 1237*

(George Woodcocke has brought £25 15s 2d: £16 19s 6d of it for John Bolton of Northborough and £8 15s 8d for John Watson, a Glinton butcher. John Cole of Northborough's money will be very welcome.)

## 241 FITZWILLIAM TO GUYBON

*[London, 17 October 1702]; F(M)C 1238*

Our business about paying Sir Charles Barrington's debts is so tedious and troublesome that I know not how long it will detain me. Return what money you can. [P.S.] I have underwrit two warrants for my does. Ask Tom Freeman how many I may expect from the park.

## 242 FITZWILLIAM TO GUYBON

*London, 5 November 1702; F(M)C 1239*

(Hopes only lack of business causes Guybon's three week silence. Hears nothing of George Woodcocke, but hopes Guybon will return money. Lady Fitzwilliam wishes to know how the maids were disposed of. Since he is unlikely to leave town before spring Guybon must take care of the wine sent last year. If Mrs Bull has not cleansed the pipes and leads it must be done, the wet season having begun. Sends a warrant for Westhay in his next; encloses Cross-a-hand. If fat enough Guybon to send a doe next week from forest or park.[1] His daughter's business keeps him in town so Guybon to send up the past year's accounts by Pemberton.)

[1] On 11 November Guybon paid Mr Arney and his man a keeper's fee for a doe, 10s; Disbursements 74.

## 243 FITZWILLIAM TO GUYBON

*London, 12 November 1702; F(M)C 1240*

(October 30 £29 5s 1d paid at Heriot's at Guybon's order; 9 November John Sesson of Northborough paid him £7 2s 6d. Halstead the woolman has paid nothing since the £100 on 24 September, and he knows not where to send to him. Understands Mrs Bull paid off the maids but not how much she paid. Guybon says the man will expect something but had never said he had hired one, only mentioned a son of Adam Johnson's whom Fitzwilliam disliked as having friends so near.)

I am heartily sorry to heare of poore old Joseph Chamberlaine's misfortune. Lett not his sonn Joe neglect any meanes that may be used for his recovery, though I feare through his great age he will hardly ever recover his eye sight againe. Pray do you and his other acquaintance go often to see him for it's a great comfort to have one's freinds come often to see them, for it may be his children may not be kind to him now they find he can do them no more service and he has been a thorough paines taker for them all, therefore they are obligd to be kind to him. I hope he will live till I come into the countrey that I may see him once againe and in every letter you write lett me know how he does. Aske Joe Chamberlaine if he will take care of the garden that I may know what to trust to. There's little to be done this winter more then pruneing the trees and bareing the rootes of such trees as do not beare well.

(Encloses Westhay warrant. Wishes another doe next week. The Pendletons may store their coal in his coalhouse for he is unlikely to be down before spring.)

## 244 FITZWILLIAM TO GUYBON

*London, 14 November 1702; F(M)C 1241*

(Had received the doe. Had never seen a worse; could hardly believe Guybon had sent it. In future Guybon must put his seal on every piece. If Guybon received any more as bad he must send them back, the keepers taking it for their fee, or must give them to Peterborough people. Send only very good, for he is ashamed that anyone should see his venison when there was good fat venison in town hanging up at every cook's shop. Guybon can send a doe from the park when Freeman thinks they are at their best.)

[P.S.] Every time you write, pray lett me heare how poore old Joseph Chamberlaine does and if we can heare of any thing here in towne that may do him good, he shall be sure to have it. Lett me know what they intend to do with him in the countrey, what meanes they intend to take and be sure you perswade him to make his will, and gett for Joe what you can. Lett me heare what Joe Bull and Mr Deepup have done about that business.

## 245 FITZWILLIAM TO GUYBON

*London, 21 November 1702; F(M)C 1242*

(Doe by the carrier was very good. Will have another next week. Guybon to remove shoulder bones only, with no fat at all, so the sides would be better. Have had abundant rain all that week so must kill their venison soon or that weather would 'wash all the fatt of[f] their backs'. Guybon to send for the fee deer soon or give the warrants away. Should give the man he engaged what he thinks fit though he would have lost no time but laboured for his father until he found a place. Supposes this was Adam Johnson's sickly son, for he heard the other was married and lived about Holme side. Had heard old Mr Vaughan had been very ill. Guybon to investigate and collect Maxey rents for he did not care to have money long in such people's hands. Hears nothing of [Halstead] or of other money and wonders that he receives none when Guybon knows his great need. [P.S.] The leads and pipes to be cleaned. He always found them full of leaves and dirt at this time after the high winds.)

## 246 FITZWILLIAM TO GUYBON

*London, 28 November 1702; F(M)C 1243*

The two does arrived sweet and good. Send another next week. Dispose of my other warrants as you think fit, but let Robert Newcombe and Mr Pemberton each have a piece. The 3s for Adam Johnson's son seems too little; give him 5s.[1] I hear nothing yet of Mr Baxter's £100. He came up with Mr Pemberton who delivered your accounts.

I cannot yett heare of any thing that may doe good on poore old Joseph Chamberlaine's eyesight. When I tell them his age, which as neare as I can guess, is at least 85, they tell me 'tis in vaine to do anything. You do not mention in any of your letters how his blindness happened whither all of a suddaine which may happen by a cold takeing, or else by degrees which if the last is impossible then to find releife because it must be old age. However, comfort him up and lett him make his will . . .

[1] 'Young Adam Johnson' was paid 5s for 'the loss of his time being hired to come to Milton' on 18 November, Disbursements 74.

## 247 FITZWILLIAM TO GUYBON

*London, 5 December 1702; F(M)C 1244*

The doe arrived today 'extraordinary good'. Let me have another next week, the last for this season. I hear nothing of Baxter's £100. I wish you could get a more certain return. Get up what money you can for I am considerably in debt. Call on Vaughan for Maxey rents. I have heard Lady Sylvius complain of his using her money which I don't like. He has not paid you near so much as he ought. Tell him I am angry and he must get it in faster and pay it because I have great occasion. I still don't hear what he did about Maxey mills and what he has received of them since Alice Hipwell's husband[1] died. Is there a possibility of her paying enough to put in her children's lives? If not, she must provide for herself, for there she must not continue. I am sorry Old Joseph[2] is so wilful as not to make his will. If he dies without one his other children's children will have equal share with Joe.

[1] Ripon or 'Rippon', the late Maxey miller.
[2] Chamberlaine.

## **248** FITZWILLIAM TO GUYBON

*London, 12 December 1702; F(M)C 1245*

(Halstead had brought the £8 and Hankin had paid £10 12s 3d for James Dove's rent. Did not believe Mr Baxter would pay anything but hoped Duce, who used to be unreliable with returns, would keep his promise.)

I find by your accompts you are to[o] forbeareing of the tennants. Old Joseph Chamberlaine I find much in arreare and also Mr Forster of Marrham, the warrenar at Helpston and Mrs Temple,[1] Edward Holman of Castor and Henry Watts at the ferry, who used to pay very well till now of late, and many others. You had best lett Mrs Temple['s] closes from her. It's a shame to thinke how you forbeare people and never write to me about them to know my pleasure. Adam Johnson of Marrham I find not any thing you receave of him. Pray lett most of his closes away from him this next Ladyday, as likewise the same from other tennants that are in arreare as I find many, and I beleive the same in the wood booke, and at this rate what must become of me if a great part of my rents become desperate debts for want of calling for them and your too great mildness. Mr Vaughan I find makes bad payments. Pray lett him know how ill I take it he payes you no more money yearly. Those tennants have no reason to complaine, because their rents are small, haveing fined of the [rents]. He must be quicker upon them or I must use some other course. Mr Collins the painter of Peterborough has sent me a letter and bill in it which comes to five pounds and better. I know not how it should be. There's nothing done by my order or consent. If it be for the wainscoate primeing in the new buildings, I was utterly against it, being desirous to have seen the worke before it was done over, for the painting is only to hide faults. He must forbeare his money till I come into the countrey and see what he has done for it, being very much against the thing doeing, but for the casements doeing, that's a thing I must be willing too and likewise some iron worke coulouring about the coach house doores, which altogether is about 13s or 14s. For the rest, Mr Wright sett him to worke, to hide his bottching worke I suppose.

I may send for that other doe shortly, but Tom Freeman to report whether I may have as many yearly as I have had [this season] or if I shall 'wrong the breed' by taking so many.

[1] On 14 January Guybon paid 16s for 'taking a letter of administration of Mrs Temple's goods', Disbursements 74.

## 249 FITZWILLIAM TO GUYBON

*London, 17 December 1702; F(M)C 1246*

I hear nothing from Duce or Baxter. Rowland Morrice brought me £34 and Heriot has received £37 5s from John Cole. Give to the poor of the towns this Christmas as before. My poor daughter is very ill of a miscarriage, her second in less than a year. My wife continues very ill. I am troubled with the stone. [P.S.] Pay 20s off Mr Collins the painter's bill. I will not pay for the wainscot until I see it measured, being done against my will. Get Mr Wright to prop that place in the Stone Gallery that Mrs Bull tells me is ready to fall. Secure everything and if I live I will take care of everything next summer.

## 250 FITZWILLIAM TO GUYBON

*London, 31 December 1702; F(M)C 1247*

I wonder you trust to Mr Duce or Mr Baxter for returns. Baxter will sooner accommodate the Bishop of Peterborough than you, and Duce never kept his promises. He and Robert Newcombe always failed you. He has his sheep and beasts here every market, but pays to them he respects more than us. I hear nothing of Phillips, Ashly or Dove. If you had not discouraged George Woodcocke the drover he would have continued to bring me money weekly, as he did until you forbade him. I am much in debt so use more certain methods, like Mr Miller and several of Thorney who were very punctual. Quicken up tenants in arrear. I am not obliged to let Mr Forster of Marholm run seven years in arrear.[1] I wonder you whom I entrust with my concerns would suffer it. If I siezed all he had I doubt it would pay three years' rent and then how would the rest be got? You are much to blame to suffer me to be so great a loser. As for abating his rent, he may be sure I will not so long as he ploughs the land. When he lays it down I will consider how far to be kind. I am sorry your and Pendleton's warrant was ill served. My daughter mends daily but my wife's illness wears her so much that I fear for her.

[1] Guybon's accounts of receipts after 1700 do not appear to have survived, but the account to 1700 shows that Fitzwilliam does not overstate Forster's arrears. Thus on 11 May 1700 Forster paid £25 for half a year's rent due Lady Day 1695. Looking back through the account he seems to have paid rent fairly regularly but always for earlier years, never for the year then current; F(M)C Misc. Vols. Receipts Vol. 2 1692–1700.

## 251 FITZWILLIAM TO GUYBON

*London, 7 January 1702/3; F(M)C 1248*

Henry Hankin has paid Heriot for Henry Phillips £26 10s 10d; for Thomas Ashly £9 18s 3d and for James Dove £8 3s 9d. A William Brimble has paid £14 17s 10d for Richard Burton of Marholm. Such sums amount to little considering my great debts, but Mr Ree's[1] [return] will do me some service. Hasten Vaughan for Maxey rents and all tenants. Thank God my daughter is quite well but my wife continues ill, though a little better. [P.S.] Keep leads and gutters clean. It rains every day. I here sad complaints from Norfolk but thank God I have had no breach yet. We desire to know how Mrs Pemberton and her daughter got home.

[1] 'January 14: Returned Mr Heriott by Mr Riss, £153 10s', Disbursements 74.

## 252 FITZWILLIAM TO GUYBON

*London, 14 January 1702/3; F(M)C 1249*

Joseph Bull writes that James Dove of Marholm, having leased some fen land from the Earl of Torrington gives up next Lady Day the 60 acres, formerly Mr Phillips' and before him John Webdale's. Bull hopes he may have the 60 acres at the old rent. I have not replied, wishing to consult you first. If you think you cannot get more from another, and are not engaged elsewhere, we ought to prefer Joe Bull as both a servant and a tenant's child. However, if you think he cannot manage both Belham Field and this 60 acres together you must do what is prudent. If he takes this and throws up Belham Field then you would have to find a tenant for it and perhaps at a lesser rent. Do what is most prudent for my interest, always regarding old tenants and servants' children so long as they can manage, and will pay the same rent as others. I will not come in for composition with Mr William Parker, but he need not fear me. I will not be very severe on him nor trouble him unless I find he intends to play the knave with his creditors.

## 253 FITZWILLIAM TO GUYBON

*London, 21 January 1702/3; F(M)C 1251*

(Sums paid into Heriot's: by Freeman for Guybon £50; £14 16s 11d by Joe Bull's order; £9 7s 3d by Thomas Ashley's order. Paid Fitzwilliam directly: by George Maure for Thomas Burton of Marholm £12 8s 8d; William Brimble for Richard Burton of Marholm £24 5s. Asks whether the Burtons and Ashley are tenants at Marholm; where they live; what grounds they hold.) I will not prefer Joe Bull for the 60 acres if he will not give the same price, but I see you are engaged to another and would not have you break a promise but hope you will get 8s an acre. Bull wishes you to fulfil your promise to repair a fence in Belham Field, next Werrington Field (now in wheat), having lost £5 this year by trespass. It could not be done in a better year than when Werrington Field is in wheat. 'Pleasure' Joe Bull in any way you can conveniently without prejudice to me.

## 254 FITZWILLIAM TO GUYBON

*London, 28 January 1702/3; F(M)C 1252*

George Woodcocke has brought me £28 16s 10d for Mr Eddings. Get up all the money you can. I had rather be there when Belham field is fenced because I would have the best 'plashers'[1] to do it, and would be assured Joe Bull would maintain the fence after bestowing that charge on it. I will take no land from Goodman Dove he wishes to hold. When I plash Belham field fence I will go on to plash all the outside of Marholm as far as Glinton cow pasture. My wife was well recovered for ten days, but took cold and had a fit of ague but we hope to hear no more of it. [P.S.] My daughter is well again, has read your letter and is glad you are in health. The rest of us are well.

[1] See **93** note 1.

## 255 FITZWILLIAM TO GUYBON

*London, 11 February 1702/3; F(M)C 1253A*

Having received no letter this fortnight I hope you are well. Your tenant Chisseldine of Etton writes that he has lost his wife and is in great perplexity about a reckoning, and that he and his brother would come up to reckon with me. I wrote by Peterborough bag that they would lose their labour for I lacked papers which were at Milton, and if I had them could do nothing without your presence, so wished him to wait until I came down next April and no wrong would be done him. Meantime you should find out his taxes before I come down. Have some Etton or Glinton neighbours call at the post house and carry the letter to him. There is a man in town famous for curing smoking chimneys. I would know from Mr Pendleton when it smokes worst, with the wind from the east, west, north or south, and I will then advise with him. If he cannot cure it I must pull it down and build anew, for I cannot have the house 'smoakt' when I am there. Heriot reports £17 18s 10d paid in by your order,[1] and no more paid since the 20th of January. I am in great want so be earnest with the tenants to supply me. I fear Joe Chamberlaine neglects the gardens, having much business of his own which he will surely not neglect. I hope the wall fruits are pruned and the orchards, and that he takes care to have pot herbs and other necessaries for the house for I shall be down in April, God permitting. I believe I have bought 'Barnisham's'[2] farm, Castor, to enter next Lady Day. I have not £50 so hope you will supply me by the latter end of this month when I am to pay for it. [P.S.] We hope my wife will do well again who has been extraordinarily ill these eight or nine weeks together.

[1] Returned by James Dove, February 5, according to Guybon, Disbursements 790.
[2] See below **259**.

## 256 REV. JEREMIAH PENDLETON TO FITZWILLIAM

*Milton, 16 February 1702/3; F(M)C 1253B*

Right Honourable, This is to let your honour understand that your kitchin chimny refuseth to carrie smoak [n]or will not let the same goe upward cheifly when the wind is south for that wind especially in wett, misty, darke weather blows it down the shafts into the kitchin and so into the great hall and passidges and over all the house where it can gett in. The said chimney will smoak sometimes when the wind is somewhat inclineing from the south to the east or to the west, if the wind be very high, but that signifies little. If it can be secured from the south wind the others will do no hurt but I am afraid there will scarce be any remedy found but takeing it down and building it new with a better draught for the smoak unless a weather-cock (which I think was never yet tryed) do help it. As to Milton house, it wants your honour mightily to repair both the old and new buildings. Neither are the gardens what I have known them, though young Goodman Chamberlaine does what hee can and has dessed[1] and pinned up most of the wall fruit trees. But of all Milton I myself am the worst, so overrunn with scorbutick paines and weakness that I am scar[c]e able to walke to Marham and back againe so that I cannot expect to be long for this world, and yet have very little to leave my poor wife and children which is a great trouble to me but why should I trouble your honour with it?

[1] Sic *for* dressed?

## 257 FITZWILLIAM TO GUYBON

*London, 18 February 1702/3; F(M)C 1254*

Francis Guybon, ... I received yesterday ... one from Mr Pendleton about Milton kittchin chimney about which I will take immediate care. He makes great complaints to me of his owne state of health and being much troubled with the scurvey, and inquireing of Mr Pemberton and others of all your healths, he gave me so good an account of Mr Pendleton's that I cannot conjecture but he is much troubled with the spleene and melancholly and fancies himselfe worse then he is. Pray lett me know your apprehensions of him, if he be really so much overrun with the scurvey, or has the spleen much and so is melancholly and conceits himselfe ill, or it may be he has both spleen and melancholly. If so there is no remedy so good for him as rideing out with you every day for good company will take off his melancholly and rideing will cure his spleen.

The £20 bill you enclosed I sent to Mr Brooks the merchant who, notwithstanding the mistake, says he will pay it the 3rd. I will not buy anything so far from Milton as the estate of 'Champion Dymocks'.[1] Heriot says only a small sum has been paid by your order since Thursday, but knew not how much, his man being from home. Halstead the Cambridge woolman came last Monday and offered a £40 bill on Mr Ash's account drawn on a merchant in 'Moore's Feilds' unknown to me and I to await the money until April next. I refused because you should not pay Mr Ash before I received it and knew not when that would be. My wife supposing Mrs Bull has taken up bees at Milton, desires some honey by the carrier, three pots of three or four pounds. If there is no honey let me know before you send anyone else's honey. I want money extraordinarily. [P.S.] If you have no honey write to me at what (price) you can have good virgin honey[2] there.

[1] Guybon must have reported that a part of the estate of the Dymokes of Scrivelsby, Lincolnshire, might be for sale. The family traditionally provided the King's Champion at coronations. Charles Dymoke, 22nd squire of Scrivelsby, who had been Champion at the coronation of William and Mary, had died on 17 January; see *Burke's Landed Gentry*, 17th ed. London 1952, i, 'Dymoke'.

[2] Honey which flows first from the combs.

## 258 FITZWILLIAM TO GUYBON

*London, 25 February 1702/3; F(M)C 1255*

If Mrs Bull thinks the honey taken up 'last Michaelmas was a twelve moneth' is fit to eat my wife would have you send up eight to ten pounds. The 13th Heriot's received £39 8s 5d and £11 16s 5d.[1] Consider the straits I am in and supply me. [P.S.] My wife is very much recovered.

[1] Returned respectively by Thomas Whitehead and John 'Hincon', Disbursements 790.

## 259 FITZWILLIAM TO GUYBON

*London, 11 March 1702/3; F(M)C 1256*

Received the basket with the hare and honey pots safe and sound last Saturday. Received with some trouble the £20 on the bill on Mr Brookbancke. Am in great need for money to pay for Barningham's Castor farm on Lady Day. Do all you can to supply me.

## 260 FITZWILLIAM TO GUYBON

*London, 18 March 1702/3; F(M)C 1257*

I received yours of 16th enclosing Mr Halstead's note to Mr Ash, and today Mr Halstead's man brought me £40 and I surrendered the note. Rowland Morrice has told an untruth in telling you he paid me or Heriot money. He has paid nothing for months, and only does so when he cannot get returns elsewhere. There is no depending on him. I still lack money and am told by Peterborough men of good credit that you need lack no returns. Last term some of them wanted returns of £500 and £600. Send for my letter by next post for I cannot write more now.

## 261 FITZWILLIAM TO GUYBON

*London, 20 March 1702/3; F(M)C 1258A*

Take Meadow Close in hand at Lady Day to be in hay for the stables and the deer. Joseph Chamberlaine may hold the Old Park this year but only if he mows it for there is a bad fence between it and the Meadow Close. Otherwise I will take Old Park in hand also. Let the yards and gardens be made handsome for I may be down sooner than you expect. No sheep must be kept in the yards or park, and no stock allowed in the park save your and my horses and the deer. Pray take grounds away from tenants that run in arrear and let them to others. I wrote you about Adam Johnson, Carnell and others and their arrears. I hope you have secured those rents and relet the lands. Seek old hay for me which I suppose is cheaper than it was at the beginning of winter, the season having been so favourable. Find me a plumber, for new pipes must be cast and much lead work done about Milton this summer, and pipes to the kitchen when I am down. A man has paid £42 for Rowland Morrice. I gave two receipts: to Thomas Toll for £22; to Jonathan Roberts for £20. How are old Joseph Chamberlaine's eyes? Need I buy anything for the garden? [P.S.] How are old Mr Vaughan and Harry. Tell them when Maxey cowpastures' leases expire this Lady Day they must be let at the full rent. Tell them I need returns, can forbear no rents and they must be earnest with the tenants for them.

## 262 FITZWILLIAM TO GUYBON

*London, 1 April 1703; F(M)C 1259A*

(Had received letter from Guybon enclosing a letter from Vaughan.[1] Wonders Old Park had been taken from 'Old' Chamberlaine who had been long its tenant, but Mr Pendleton could hold it this year so long as he fenced it from Meadow Close. If not he would take it in hand.)

[1] Vaughan had reported that John Webdale had cut trees down claiming a right under his lease from Mr Clitheroe (the former tenant in chief), had ploughed 10 acres of pasture and sowed flax last year and cole seed this, which Vaughan believed his lease would not permit without Fitzwilliam's permission. He wished Fitzwilliam to see the lease Clitheroe had received from Sir Gabriel and Lady Sylvius. Vaughan to Fitzwilliam 27 March 1703, F(M)C 1258B.

## **263** FITZWILLIAM TO GUYBON

*London, 8 April 1703; F(M)C 1260*

We are all sorry to hear of the death of Tom Freeman.[1] Comfort the poor woman and assist her with advice. I should be glad to hear how he left matters. Rowland Morrice has paid £41. Let Etton Meadow for surely Meadow Close will provide hay enough for a year and more. Quicken returns for I would settle a debt before I leave town, which I should shortly, hoping my wife may soon undertake a journey.

[1] A major tenant, and Fitzwilliam's part time keeper.

## **264** EDWARD VAUGHAN TO FITZWILLIAM

*[Maxey,] 15 April 1703; F(M)C 1261B*[1]

(Had received Fitzwilliam's letter. The pasture land John Webdale had ploughed, and the trees he had cut up by the roots, is on Fitzwilliam's land, lying by itself near the Lolham road. It did not lie in the middle of the 'grat ground' for it was not hedges Webdale had cut but many trees. Webdale claimed a lease from Clitheroe which permitted this, which Vaughan could hardly believe. Had been among the tenants about the cowpastures but they would only give 6s 8d a lease as last year. What further measures shall he take in this? He had no money in his hands save what he had paid Guybon. Was endeavouring to get in more, but all things were at 'so low a rate' people were in great straits to get money.)

[1] On the cover Fitzwilliam noted: 'Aprill 15th 1703: Mr Vaughan's letter acquainteing me what waiste of cutting up wood & trees is done by John Webdale in my grounds at Lolham & pretending he has authority by his lease for so doeing. He plowes up the land also and sowes it with cole seed etc; and tenn acres are plowed and sowen with hemp & flax. Mr Clitheroe by his last lease . . . is tyed from ploweing and soweing meadow & pasture on the penalty of £4 per acre each yeare he plowes.'

## **265** FITZWILLIAM TO GUYBON

*London, 22 April 1703; F(M)C 1261C*

Francis Guybon, Your letter of the 13th I received last Fryday being the 16th. As to Widdow Freeman I am very willing she should hold all the land this yeare because I know her stocke cannot be in a condition to putt off at this time of the yeare and besides, her stocke haveing been on the ground ever since Ladyday, there's no reason I should take my land into my hands now. I am willing to do the poore woman what kindness I can and if she finds herselfe able to manage the farme I am willing she should continue it, or a part of it. I have received no money from Mr Church nor any one else since I last writt to you and am in great streights for want of some haveing borrowed £70 of Mr Heriott for my occasions and am much in debt otherwise, some of which I would willingly see cleared before I leave the towne. I am very glad to heare old Joseph Chamberlaine has so much sight againe as that he can come up to Milton alone. I hope it will grow better still this summer but he must not expect it long by reason of his great age. ... [P.S.] Thanke God we are all now in pretty good health. Daughter Barrington recommends herselfe kindly to you, to Mr Pendleton and his wife and is glad to heare of Old Joseph's seeing againe. Pray take care of money for me.

### **266** FITZWILLIAM TO GUYBON

*London, 29 April 1703; F(M)C 1262*

Francis Guybon, Yours of the 27th I received yesterday with the inclosed bill which I sent immediately to Mr Dillingham's and the £50 was brought me this morning by himselfe.[1] I gave my receipt writt upon the backe part of the bill. If you have but money you need not want returns in Peterborough, if I may credit what they themselves have told me. I am glad you intend me some more next weeke for I am in great want being the tradesmen dunn me for money and I am forc't to putt them off with excuses like other broaken gentlemen. I thanke God I never did so before. If I had goods ready to send downe I should chuse rather to send them by the carrier then any countrey waggon for they know how to packe up goods safe and deliver them carefully then any countrey man can, though I wish I had knowne of John Wricraft's comeing up a weeke sooner for then I might have had somethings ready that could not well have miscarried by him. I am sorry he neglects his farme so as to undertake such journeys. This time of the yeare is usually a busie time with the farmers for after seeds time is over they usually breake up their fallows. Wricraft will ene do as John Webster and Woollaston did to gett ready money, carted away their time and neglected their farmes which made them have bad cropps and so were undone, and beggered my farmes besides. John Webster died last Munday night, I beleive poore enough though I understand he left wherewithall to be buried decently. No body knew where his sister lived here in towne to see him buried, that 'twas done altogether by strangers ...

[1] 'Returned my lord by Mr Church, £50', Disbursements 74.

### **267** FITZWILLIAM TO GUYBON

*London, 13 May 1703; F(M)C 1263A*

> Yours of the 11th received but not a penny from anybody. These little sums, and not above one of them in a fortnight or three weeks, do not supply provisions for the house so how should I get out of debt to tradesmen, pay for house rent, clothes, and everything else most needed at this season, liveries, etc.? I never was so long in debt to Mr Heriot before and all for necessaries, besides what I owe to others upon bond at interest. Take care of me and call earnestly on the tenants for money for I cannot forbear them. Corn rose very much last Monday at 'Bare Key'[1] and oats rose 12d a quarter. We have had abundant rain and I hear by Mr Pemberton you have also, and Beales writes the same from Norfolk. About a month since I paid for Barnsham's Farme so next Michaelmas rent is due to me. He pays half the King's taxes. His lease expires in a year or two's time. Helpston tithes are now offered me that old Bellus

rented. Give me your opinion of it. My grandfather sold it. It pays the parson Mr Ixom[2] a great sum yearly and the college rent is pretty considerable, but how much I know not, besides a fine every seven years. Discover very exactly what it is rented for, and what rents are paid out of it. The farm was very much out of repair in old Thomas Bellus's time. How is it now? What fine is paid at 'reviewing' [sic] the lease and what college is it held of? It's in Cambridge I believe.[3] My daughter is gone out of town for the summer. We are all in good health; I hope you are also.

[1] Bear Quay in Thames Street.
[2] Thomas Ixem was vicar of Helpston from 1683 to 1703, acting as curate at Etton in 1692 and 1696. *Longden*, vii. 235.
[3] Guybon noted in the margin that annually the parson received £32, and Christ's College received £13 annually and a fine of about £60 every seven years. 'Henry Walkin payes yearly £100'.

## 268 FITZWILLIAM TO GUYBON
*London, 27 May 1703; F(M)C 1264*

(Reiterates complaints that no money has been paid him, and that Guybon does not use surer methods of returning small sums weekly so that he avoids running into debt for 'meate and drincke'.) Get my gardens and yards fit for my coming down, not letting Mrs Pendleton's sheep run all over them and spoil my laurel trees. I will 'joice'[1] nothing in my park. Take care that Mrs Pendleton's stock don't break into the Meadow Close from the Old Park. [P.S.] I hear £40 has been paid into Heriot's, probably Andrews the thatchers' money.[2]

[1] Agist.
[2] In fact from Thomas and Charles Andrews, repaid 19 May, Disbursements 74.

## 269 GUYBON TO FITZWILLLIAM
*9 June 1703; F(M)C 1265*

There has been a fire at Paradice, Northborough which burned down the hovel and all things in the yard, so that the poor man is almost undone. They say it was caused by a bad chimney. They saved a few goods. I have got him to a neighbour until I know whether you will have the house rebuilt. He must have a house and he is a good tenant. Helpston tithes pays annually the parson £32, Christ's College £13 one year with another, fine about £60 every seven years. It is let for £100 a year, but pays no taxes, town charges nor repairs. The gentlemen have laid out much money on it this spring, and by next spring will be as well repaired as any house in town. Mr Buninge is said to think of buying it if you don't. Hope Miller and Ash have paid some money by now.

## 270 FITZWILLIAM TO GUYBON
*London, 10 June 1703; F(M)C 1266*

Francis Guybon, ... As to John Hullocke he is come to towne and came to me last Munday. I find he has a good opinion of himselfe and is much conceited. He thinks he can drive a coach as well as anyone because he understands a waggon but there is much difference as he will find. It will not be an easie thing to gett him a place who is fitt for nothing but husbandry, and till he can better dispose of himselfe I advised him to go worke at hay worke with Mr Hankin at the Angell at Islington, who came out of our parts, till he can heare of something, for people that have husbandry are not destitute of servants at this time of the yeare especially, and it may be his father may send for him againe, and while he is at worke there, he is free to returne at a weeke's warning and if he getts a place he is then tyed for a time and cannot returne. As to moneys, there has been none paid but £13 by Morrice his order last Satturday for all you have mentioned so many severall summs I should receave.[1] If I am to depend upon money from the cornfactors I may stay long enough for it for I know how I used to be paid by Mr Newcomb's correspondent at Barekey where I stayd above 4 moneths for one £50 and sent I know not how often for it besides. If Mr Miller of Toneham has no other way to returne the money for you then this way pray don't depend on it for I am in great want of some at present and I am sure you will have time enough to gett up money to pay Mr Miller before I am like to receave his from those cornfactors that will not pay it possibly before Michaelmas next. Pray lett Mr Lowrey know I wish him much joy of his new wife. I am sorry to heare Mr Dickenson is dead but he has lived to faire age . . .

[1] According to Guybon's accounts he returned during June £18 19s 5d, £11 5s 11d and £15 7s 8d by Mr William Miller, £30 by Rowland Morrice, and £50 by Mr Miles Bevis, Disbursements 74.

## 271 FITZWILLIAM TO GUYBON

*London, 12 June 1703; F(M)C 1267*

Francis Guybon, I am sorry to heare by yours of the 9th the mischance that happened at Norborough by fire. I suppose Robert Oagle is the tennant there still of the house called Parradice, and do beleive it must be through his or his wive's great carelessness that this mischeife happened for though the house was an old house, yett I never heard the chimney was dangerous and if people will be careless it may so fall out in a new house. We alwaies designed to build a new house up there as you well know but could never agree where to place the house but now we must settle that matter for we must gett another up as soone as possible with convenience. It falls out very unluckily this rainy season because of carting both wood and stone for the waies cannot but be extreame bad about Norborough and all the waies up to the stone pitts. I feare there will [be] nothing done before harvest be in, for we cannot in prudence go now to worke the waies being unpassable, unless we shall be contented with halfe loades which I am very much against though I am desirous it should be new built. The best way to place the house is to build it faceing the road, which, to the best of my remembrance, is the highest ground. I meane the front of the house to be against that ground of mine that has the barne in it. Barton hurne or some such name it's calld. I designe not to have too great a house, only two roomes (vizt) a house and parlour and a little place for a buttry[1] where they sett their milke. The chimney I would have built with stone for security sake and the walls to be off stone as high as the cattle rubb. I suppose you will answer this before you possitively resolve of anything. When you see Mr Vaughan next tell him I would have him send me word what he has done with the cowpastures at Maxey.

Brew two hogsheads ale and four small beer allowing per hogshead eight strike of malt for ale, one and a half for beer. Let the brewer hop it well this hot weather, though I design to be down by 'haysell'. I have only to pay my debts which you must enable me to do by returns. Hear nothing of Ash or Miller but one Nunnery yesterday paid £15 for Mr Eddins.

[1] Buttery, a pantry of a cottage or farm house.

## 272 FITZWILLIAM TO GUYBON

*London, 19 June 1703; F(M)C 1268*

Francis Guybon, Yours of the 17th I received yesterday. As to John Hullocke he is a haymakeing with Mr Hankin at the Angell Inne in Islington. He dines with us on Sundaies so I heare of him how he proceeds. He cannot heare of a place, nor I neither, for him. I endeavour to perswade him to returne home to his father or if not thither to go worke at day worke about home till he can gett himselfe a place at the statutes.[1] Since the waies are so very bad you have thought of a good expedient to rebuild Parradice with the barne in Barton hurne ground. It's of little use to the tennant I suppose since his hay may stand as well in a cocke. Thanke God the weather has taken up this day or 2 that I hope the waies will mend in case there should not be stone enough at the barne for this new house. I would have the chimney all stones and the walls the same above the reach of cattle rubbing themselves but I hope the stone of the old house and the barne together may do it well enough. Now you are about it make them a good convenient little house and since I perceave by yours there will be more then enough of materialls lett what you have to spare be laid by that there be no waist of it and then it's ready for another job in that towne to which place you know it's very bad carting most part of the yeare.

(Is glad they have good grass and more coming. Would know when Meadow Close will be mowed, although expects to be at Milton by then. Enquires when park and forest deer will be fat, and who looks after the deer at Milton since Tom Freeman's death, and can kill and cut up venison. Has received no money from Miller of Toneham or Church of Maxey and the Peterborough attorneys know of none to be paid him which surprises him considering his frequent requests.[2])

[1] See note to **230** above.

[2] Since Guybon repaid some of these returns in late June (see note to **270** above), Fitzwilliam's letter acknowledging their receipt must be missing.

## 273 FITZWILLIAM TO GUYBON

*London, 29 June 1703; F(M)C 1269*

I heartily congratulate you on the return of your health. I am obliged for Mr Pendleton's giving me an account almost every post of how you were. Repay him the cost of those letters I charged to him. I am sorry you have paid off Mr Grosvenor.[1] I think it was a little too soon for fear of a relapse which is often dangerous. Be careful of your diet. Eat no 'flesh meats' and take no strong drink for a fortnight and don't go abroad too soon. The weather we hope is settled fair so you will mow the Meadow Close in a week or 10 days, but don't venture out too soon; get somebody else to look after the people. Any hay not carried into the park cock up on dry ground near the house near the stables. I hope to come down in a fortnight. We all pray for your daily recovery.

[1] Apparently Guybon's medical consultant.

## 274 FITZWILLIAM TO GUYBON

*London, 8 July 1703; F(M)C 1270*

We all heartily rejoiced to see a letter from you, and congratulate the return, in some measure, of your health. Be careful of your health and sparing of your diet until your fever is quite gone, 'least falling ... on meate dietts' brings back the fever, perhaps more dangerously than at first. Set somebody to look after your [haymakers] in Meadow Close, and don't venture out too soon for I had rather suffer a little than that you should run any hazard. I am in great want of returns so send somebody among the tenants to tell them to bring the money to you. My wife and son daily pray for you and your full recovery. [P.S.] Hope for a good 'haysell' for it's been fine here a fortnight.

## 275 FITZWILLIAM TO GUYBON

*London, 15 July 1703; F(M)C 1271*

Francis Guybon, I received yours of the 11th last Munday and am glad to find you daily abroad. I perceave you were taken in the same manner as I was last Ladyday was twelve moneth only the swelling did not come into your legg as soone as mine did for want of the pitch plaisters being applied to the bottome of your feet as mine was the next moment after I was taken which by the next day drew it out of my head into my legg and there it proved a Saint Anthonie's fire for almost 6 weeks and kept me in my bed all that time with great paine and trouble but I did nothing to it but anointed it with oiles that were cooleing till the paine went away and the swelling is not yett gone. It never proved a sore. You must take some gentle purgeing as I did to carry off the humour. Since I perceave by yours that your head is not yett quite right you had best be cupt in your necke and shoulders and take away about some 6 or 7 ounces of blood as they did from me, for the first blooding in my arme did not quite sett my head to rights therefore I advise you the same and in the necke and shoulders which draw most from the head. Mr Ridley the surgeon, he can cup you to be sure, and I am thus cuppt every 6 moneths by way of prevention.

As your health permits return me money. None has been paid since Miller. I suppose the venison is as fat as it will be so if you have someone who knows how to shoot and dress a buck properly send one up next week in the wagon. My wife wishes Mrs Pendleton to preserve her a good many green walnuts this year.

## **276** FITZWILLIAM TO GUYBON

*London, 17 July 1703; F(M)C 1272A*

Send this warrant to the Sewley Walk keeper. Send half after Mr Ballett to Spalding and give a side to Mr Lowrey and half haunch to Robin Newcombe. Mr Ballett will gratify the keeper for carrying the half buck to Spalding. Let Mr Pendleton meet Ballett at Mr Dryden's at Chesterton at dinner next Tuesday and tell him what care I have taken to have the venison come to him in time.

## **277** FITZWILLIAM TO GUYBON

*London, 29 July 1703; F(M)C 1273A*

The venison came much spoiled by the hot weather. I fear it was not as well killed and dressed as Tom Freeman used to do it. Then again I fear the carrier did not lay it out at night in cool cellars, and pepper it, as should be done in hot weather. You should have sent word to him for he is young and does not understand the way of it, and his servants, though the same old ones, are careless without his orders. Sending the next by the coach might be better, for it comes a day earlier, but the coachman must lay it out and pepper it at nights, and pack it in clean straw in the morning. If there will be little advantage I had rather have it by Chatteris[1] because I would help a 'young beginner', and then he carries somewhat cheaper. I leave it to you, but send no more this hot weather. I received today £50 by Mr Bevis' order, but hear nothing of the other sums yours mention but they would be welcome to help me out of town. I am glad most of the hay is in the great cock. We have had abundant rain yesterday and today. I hope you missed it. Keep leads and gutters clean. I received a letter from a Mr Gabriell Barber of Stamford with a particular of Smith's hold in Aylesworth and Castor, but I don't see Palmer's cottage and land there which is one of the best.[2] Let me know if that is sold away from the rest whether this Mr Barber is the owner of the land or an attorney employed to sell it. I have referred that matter to my coming down. I hope you get strength every day and can ride a little, the air will do you good, but be careful what you eat and drink until you are quite well ... [P.S.] When you send venison charge them to hang up every piece every night and to stuff with clean straw the holes from which the shoulder is cut for there it soonest taints being always full of blood and consequently moist.

[1] Mr Chattris of Longthorpe 'now the Peterborough carrier'; so described in a rough account of his services and charges dated July 1703, drawn up by Fitzwilliam; F(M)C 1275v.

[2] The letter of 24 July offered Fitzwilliam several properties in Castor and Ailesworth, annual rent roll £56 5s, at about 21 years' purchase although no specific price was mentioned; F(M)C 1272B.

## **278** FITZWILLIAM TO GUYBON

*London, 5 August 1703; F(M)C 1274*

(Miller's salesmen, Hankin and Price, have paid at Heriot's £11 5s 11d and £15 7s 8d. Weather too hot for sending venison. Wishes them as good weather for the harvest. Is sorry Guybon does not recover his strength quickly. Wife very ill but he hopes she and Guybon will do well again.)

## **279** GUYBON TO FITZWILLIAM

*10 August 1703; F(M)C 1275*

(Has received Fitzwilliam's of 5th; sends no venison; fears for deer although they have grass enough; hopes worst of Lady Fitzwilliam's illness is past; can recover his strength but little; Mr Bevis promises a return.)

## **280** FITZWILLIAM TO GUYBON

*London, 12 August 1703; F(M)C 1276A*

(Regrets Guybon regains his strength so slowly. Wife better but still much troubled with gripes in the stomach. Heat abated so expects buck next week; hopes Bevis will pay good sum. Meadow Close must be well fenced, especially against Old Park.)

## **281** FITZWILLIAM TO GUYBON

*London, 19 August 1703; F(M)C 1277*

I am sorry to hear of old Mr Vaughan's death. I wrote today to Henry Vaughan, asking him to receive my rents and to pass them to you as he received them. Another wrote me seeking to supplant him but if young Vaughan makes me fair account and endeavours to 'exert my interest' nobody shall put him out.[1] I wonder you should send a note for me to receive money next October as if I was resolved to stay in town this winter. I will be down sooner than you expect. Keep the mourning rings till we come. I shall be glad of Mr Bevis's money, and of the venison next Saturday, this fine temperate weather.

[1] The letter was from Richard Ewen at Maxey, dated 16 August 1703, reporting Vaughan's death, offering to serve Fitzwilliam in his place, promising to come to London whenever Fitzwilliam required it, and asking that nobody should be informed he had made this approach if it proved unsuccessful; F(M)C 1276B.

## **282** FITZWILLIAM TO GUYBON

*London, 26 August 1703; F(M)C 1278A*

Francis Guybon, Yours dated the 24th I received yesterday with the bancke bill inclosed and that we reckon alwaies ready money. For your bucke that I received last Satturday it was so small and withall soe farr from being fatt that I was ashamed to give any of it away. I wonder I can have but one good bucke in a yeare out of my parke when I used to have alwaies 4, sometimes 5 or 6, in a yeare and much of the same size and goodness. This cannot be without foule play and I am sure the parke must be robbd every yeare or else the deare must be starved for want of winter meate and neglected as I most feare they are, that we must have some body else to looke after them and not trust to Freeman's people who for their owne sakes neglect them either through lazyness or coveteousness because the more dies the more skins they have. Every yeare you write me word that the next yeare there will be pretty many bucks but I find that yeare is to come yett. There being no seale nor direction upon any peice of the last bucke made me beleive the carrier or the porter that brought it to my house had changd it for a worse.

Hear nothing of Mr Bevis. I intend down shortly, and since I suppose harvest is over, as I hear it mostly is within 100 miles of London, let Mrs Bull hire us two maids as she did last year. Have Mrs Bull write my wife about them before she 'absolutely' hires them. Get a man to look after the gates and drudging work. I hope you take care of the eddish in Meadow Close, see the fences are well kept, and well fence the hay cocks if they stand on the ground, so that the eddishes may be let to the best advantage. [P.S.] I give you and Mr Pendleton a warrant for a forest deer, half each. Another warrant divide between Cousin Harry Tryce, Mr Whinyates (the two sides), Mr Bellamy, and Robin Newcomb. Dispose the West Hay Walk warrant to four of my friends that you think have 'a creditt at Burleigh that it may be servd out of my lord's parke.'

**283** FITZWILLIAM TO GUYBON
*London, 2 September 1703; F(M)C 1279A*

I did not say the bank bill was paid but is passable and as good as ready money and Mr Heriott allowed it. Young Bevis of Peterborough paid me £100 yesterday, £50 by your order, and £50 he had to spare, which I took knowing you often lack returns.[1] Next week send up the best buck the park affords. If you give West Hay warrant to Peterborough friends let Richard Dickenson and Charles Duce have a share, and perhaps some of them may have credit to get it by means of a friend at Burleigh. I am glad Mrs Bull can get maid servants any time but my wife will take it ill if she is disappointed, and would rather be sure beforehand. I am sorry the eddishes are bad in your parts. Never were better hereabouts. After harvest let Adam Johnson taste the beer and ale that I may direct what's to be done.

[1] Guybon must have paid Mr Miles Bevis in advance for the first £50 for he listed the payment at 1 September; the second £50 he repaid on 4 September, Disbursements 74.

**284** FITZWILLIAM TO GUYBON
*London, 16 September 1703; F(M)C 1280A*

(Buck arrived well killed, dressed, not fat but 'pretty meate'. Rowland Morrice paid £30 on 3rd, and £15 14s on 4th. Has told Mrs Bull to see what is wanting at Milton and buy it at Brigg Fair, so Guybon to supply her with money. Wishes to know what has been done at burned Paradise Farm.)

**285** FITZWILLIAM TO GUYBON
*London, 24 September 1703; F(M)C 1281A*

(Glad to hear will be supplied with money for wishes to get out of debt before leaving London.) I wrote two or three weeks ago that Adam Johnson should taste the drink brewed last midsummer and if it will not do it must be reboiled with some fresh malt, for I must have drink against my coming down which I resolve to do although the winter advances. Since nothing has been done at Paradise House begin nothing now for what is done at this season will be unfit for anyone to go into this winter. 'I only writt about it because I knew not how the poore people can dispose of themselves to live; if they are but provided for I care not.' I am sorry Mrs Bull and family are ill and that it is a sickly time there, but it generally is at this season and I hope they may do well again. [P.S.] Let me know by your next how the drink is and how Mrs Bull and her family are.

### **286** FITZWILLIAM TO GUYBON

*London, 30 September 1703; F(M)C 1282A*

Dr Barber and I have been treating by letter for his estate and for the estate of Mr Weaver, his brother-in-law, both in Castor and Aylesworth. The particulars I here underwrite:

| | £ s d |
|---|---|
| *Dr Barber's* | |
| Benjamin Burton's farme per annum | 30 00 00 |
| Widdow Healey's cottage and land | 04 00 00 |
| John Cross his cottage etc | 01 10 00 |
| John Walton's cottage etc | 00 18 00 |
| Tottall | *36 08 00* |
| *Mr Weaver's* | |
| Thomas Bates senior | 03 10 00 |
| Thomas Tippins late Thomas Bates junior | 01 03 00 |
| Josiah Serjeant | 03 05 00 |
| Griffin Popely | 02 00 00 |
| Richard Eades | 02 00 00 |
| Richard Hullocke | 06 00 00 |
| and John Burton your tennant rents 45 acres calld Blackelands under Hanglands Wood for | 02 00 00 |
| Tottall | *19 18 00* |
| Dr Barber's per annum | 36 08 00 |
| Mr Weaver's per annum | 19 18 00 |
| Both yearly | *56 06 00* |

I hope you have now so good health as to be able to ride abroad and pray do so much as to speake with every one of these tennants and know if their rents be the same as I have here above writt them downe and which of them paies less, sett it downe and lett me have a speedy account of it by next Tuesdaie's post if you can possibly. I am informed that severall of Mr Weaver's cottages paies all the Parliament's taxes and have leases. Pray know which they are that pay all the taxes and which of them have leases, and for how many yeares they have remaineing in their leases, and if they will be willing to renew their leases againe upon the old rents when their leases expire. We are very neare a conclusion, the writeings being sent up to towne for councell to peruse. Therefore pray be as speedy as you can in your answer to this. The owners of Manton's farm late Lea's sent me a particular about a fortnight since of that estate which I intend likewise to purchase if we can agree for it but I have not since heard of them and suppose they have been lately at Castor to see and gather up their rents and that I may heare suddainly againe of them. Pray inquire first if one Mr Colcutt has been lately at Manton's and if he has ordered the spinney behind the house to be cutt downe, and if [he] has not been there inquire what rent the two cottages are lett for that belong to that farme. One stands by Old Joseph Chamberlaine's house where young Toby the miller lived, and the other was that where Old Widdow Lea did live and lies between my farme yard where Serjeant lives and Jeffrey Graie's old house. They vallew the whole at [£]27 per annum, vizt £23 ... the farme and 40s a yeare each of the cottages. Old Joseph can tell you the full worth of this estate and send me an answer about it.

I fear this business will keep me in town longer than expected, and my wife's health is very bad so spend the drink lest it spoil. George Woodcocke's salesman has paid £37 9s 2d for Mr Edins, Mr Lawrence and others. We are glad Mrs Bull's family are pretty well againe. Let me know when the does in the park will be fit for sending. [P.S.] Take care of that place in the Stone Gallery that rains in; just over the door going down to the matted chamber from the great stairs. Prop it for it bears part of the wall belonging to the turret and its fall may cause the fall of the turret. About eight years ago the pipe from the turret next the old partridge room was blocked, and damaged that wall and my wife's linen then kept in the candle chamber. Take care of this and clean all lucarnes, pipes and gutters.

## **287** HENRY VAUGHAN TO FITZWILLIAM

*[Maxey], 4 October 1703; F(M)C 1282C*

(Maxey Court is on 21st and Vaughan seeks Fitzwilliam's commands about what he shall do and whether he shall follow the 'old waye and custome'. Will endeavour to take care of fines and the amercements which had not been paid since Fitzwilliam bought Maxey but now he would 'bring them all upon the stage befor them all and will tell them what thaye must trust tow' and he hoped this would prevent trouble thereafter. Was trying to get up other arrears as fast as possible.)

## **288** FITZWILLIAM TO GUYBON

*London, 7 October 1703; F(M)C 1283A*[1]

(Guybon having written that the rent of Burton's farm in Aylesworth was too high Fitzwilliam had informed Dr Barber that he would reduce his offer by £50. However, Guybon must investigate further because 'Old Burton' had rented the farm to Fitzwilliam's knowledge for 40 years which he would hardly have done if it was unprofitable. John and Henry Holland had paid £62 4s on 2 October.)

We are all heartily sorry to heare of poore old Joseph Chamberlaine's death. We had great hopes he might have lived till we had come into the countrey but God's will be done. I am glad he left Joe so well. I hope all the rest of yee are pretty well and that the countrey are the same and the sickly time over with them. My poore wife is much out of order with the cholicke in her stomach but she has intermissions and is now and then pretty well. Pray send me up what moneyes you can. I heard by John Hullocke that Mr Wright the carpenter was taken very ill at March in the fenns and was in great danger but I hope it is not true because you make no mention of it in any of your last letters ... [P.S.] When we heare from my daughter Barrington she alwaies inquires of your health and recommends herselfe kindly to you. In your next lett me know how long Joseph Chamberlaine lay sicke before he died or if he died suddainly and if he left Richard Edwards[2] his children anything.

[1] Letter damaged so first paragraph briefly summarized.
[2] Probably a son-in-law.

## 289 FITZWILLIAM TO GUYBON

*London, 21 October 1703; F(M)C 1284*

> Glad to hear you are all well and Mr Wright and family likely to do well again. John Sisson of Northborough last week paid £28 1s 6d for Marmaduke Tomlin[son] and others. Today the son of Mr Halstead, the Cambridge woolman, brought £12 due on Mrs Bull's note. I little thought when you sent that note two months ago that I would still be in town when the money was paid but God disposes all. My wife has been very ill these two months and I see no likelihood of our leaving town this winter. I shall need a good sum to pay off a debt due on the 12th.

I have been in treaty some time with Dr Barber of Stamford for his and his brother Weaver's estates in Castor and Ailesworth and we came to a summe, that is, I offered him £1,150 for the whole estate together and they demanded about £6 and odd shillings more. I thought that was a summe we should hardly breake off about and I writt him a letter of my offerre this day was sennight last Thursday and I have not since heard from him whereby I conclude he will not take my money or else that he is fallen ill. You may inquire at a distance next Satturday of any of the Stamford people that know him how he does and possibly you may learne whither he be about selling it to another though I would not have it taken notice off that I am either about it or am fond of it and so pray have a care how you aske the question.[1] Here came to me this morning one Mr Willson if I mistake not his name with a note from Mr Barlow, I suppose the naileman of Stamford, for £2 9s. I knew nothing of it or if there be any thing due to him upon a reckoning. If he is never paid he can be no looser for both myselfe and mother before me have been good customers but I designe no such thing for when I am in the countrey whatever appeares to be due to him shall be honestly paid him. In the meane time the summe is not so great but he may forbeare it a little longer.

> I received a bill for £5 from Mr Collins, the Peterborough painter, for painting Mr Wright's wainscot in the new buildings. I did not order it, nor, I think, did you. I would have preferred it uncoloured so I could inspect Wright's work. I don't know what it really comes to but since he is afraid of being sued you had best pay him £3.[2] He owes me 12 or 13 years pepper rent in right of his wife. Pepper is now 2s a pound, so there will not be much more due him even by his own reckoning, which may be less when we measure it. I enclose a note of money due Mr John Whittaker, an acquaintance here, who owns

my Ld August 11: 88;

yor Honrs of ye 2d instant wth one inclosed to mr Pendleton I recd, mr Tallman ye Surveyor came to milton last monday about ten a clock: & stayed there yt night. & ye next day after diner, went to Norbrough, & from thence to Burley: I suppose mr Pendleton have given yor Honr an account of his being here, before this, yor Honr will have a Buck out of mr Arneys walke, shall come up by Gregory next tuesday, shoulders an all; the Bishopp have beene about his Diocesse this fortnight: for mr Hake have done nothing yet in his businesse, he profferes to morgage ye house he lives in, for 200l: to renew his Lease, till he can raise moneys to redeeme it againe, masters thanke god are very well, & desires to have their humble duty presented to yor Honrs & their loves to miss. mr Turner & mrs Turner desire to have their humble duty presented to yor Honrs & to miss & soe doth

yor Honrs

most dutifull &
obedient Servant
Fra: Guybon



Letter of Francis Guybon to Lord Fitzwilliam, 11 August 1688.

Fra: Guybon,

London Novemb.r 4th 1703

Yo.rs of the 2d instant Rec'd: yesterday. The 25th of the last month Mr Church of Maxey paid me Fifty Pounds And on the 1st of this month Geo: Woodcocke the Drover, paid me on the account of John Cole Marmaduke Tomlyn & Rudkin of Northborough 30=17=05: And at the same time paid me on his owne account Twenty Pounds for which I gave him my Receipts. I am sorry to heare of Mr Burman's death, which Mr Pemberton gave me notice of the last Weeke & I have given him Maxey Court. Mr Wrights coming up will signifie nothing I suppose he is overpaid already: but before I part with any money more his Worke shall be measured: however, if he has any other business here I should be glad to see him & speake with him: but not to come on purpose. With all our kind Loves to Mr & Mrs Pendleton, & all our ffriends I am in hast

Yo.r Loving ffriend

Fitzwilliam

Pray neglect no opportunity of getting up, & returning me what money you can, with all the speed you can.

Letter of Lord Fitzwilliam to Francis Guybon, 4 November 1703 (no. 291).

the late Mr Thomas Griffin's estate held of my manor of Maxey. He offers to sell it but since I presently lack money will keep it until I can buy it. In return for this kindness I have agreed to receive his rents. Call on the tenants for their arrears and your receipts shall be their discharge. Whittaker has written asking the tenants to send their rents up but they take not notice. Mr Burman used to collect the rents but his 'gratification' took too much of the rent. When you have received the rents I will pay them here.

[1] The purchase was concluded in May 1704, see **311**, **316**, **317**, **318** below.
[2] Guybon paid Richard Collins the painter on October 23, presumably the same day he received Fitzwilliam's order; Disbursements 74.

## **290** GUYBON TO FITZWILLIAM

*2 November 1703; F(M)C 1285*

My lord, Your honour's of the 21 of October I received. I hope Mr Church have paid your honour some money before this. Benjamin Burton of Ailesworth tells me that all the boards in the garretts through out the house are his and the hovells in the yards given him by his father long since for they were never fixt to the free hold and the hovells sett upon stones soe that he can take the boards and hovells away with him if he leaves the farme. I suppose your honour heare that Mr Burman is dead, buried last Thursday. He was ill and could not keepe Maxey court. It was kept by his sonne. I have speake with Mr Whittaker's tennants and one of them have paid there rent to Mr Burman as your honour may see by this inclosed receit and Joe Clarke will pay his rent to me when I goe to Norbrough. The houses are pettifull old thinges, little worth and much out of repaire. Mr Eldred an attorney that lives at James Deepin[1] desires that your honour would be pleased to lett him keepe Maxey court. Mr Pemberton keepes all your honour's other courts when kept and I suppose shall this. I am sorry that my lady continue ill still ... [P.S.] Mr Wright intend to come up to London soone to waight upon your honour about a reckoning. He wants money and to stopp his journey your honour had better order me to pay him 30 or 40 pounds.

[1] Deeping St. James.

## **291** FITZWILLIAM TO GUYBON

*London, 4 November 1703; F(M)C 1286A*

Yours of 2nd received yesterday. Mr Church of Maxey has paid me £50 and George Woodcocke the drover £30 17s 5d for John Cole, Marmaduke Tomlyn [sic, Tomlinson] and Rudkin of Northborough and £20 on his own account. I am sorry for Mr Burman's death. I heard of it from Mr Pemberton to whom I have given Maxey Court. Wright's coming to town will signify nothing. I think him overpaid already. Before I part with more his work shall be measured. If he has other business I should be glad to see him but not to come on purpose. [P.S.] Neglect no opportunity of returning money.

## 292 FITZWILLIAM TO GUYBON

*London, 25 November 1703; F(M)C 1287*

I have not written every week having no business but want of money which you said you would return as fast as possible. I have been forced to borrow £60 for the use of my house and owe much to tradesmen. You let the tenants run too much in arrear. Glad to hear you are all well at Milton. We are reasonably well here save for my poor wife who is much afflicted with the colic. Pemberton brought your papers but I still lack your wood books, your rent rolls for five years past, and papers showing how the meadows have been let. I have written three warrants for my fee does. Mr Colcutt came about selling his farm[1] but he knows not what to do with the money, and I have none to buy it with now so we agreed to wait two years and then agree for it. Meantime he asked that you would receive the rent. He says his brother Manton is a great knave to him and he would turn him out and let it to Boare of Ailesworth. Manton owes two years rent and commits waste. When you ride that way look into it, see what repairs are done of those he claims, see how everything is and let us know, but what I here write keep to yourself; don't let Manton know it. See that he does not impose on Mr Colcutt. Ask to see his bills for repairs and taxes.

[1] Manton's farm, Castor.

## 293 GUYBON TO FITZWILLIAM

*30 November 1703; F(M)C 1288*

Yours of the 25th received. I hope Mr Parsons, the bishop's gentleman, has paid you money before this. I have received the warrants for fee does but I fear they will not be worth their fees, having had so much wet which has 'basht' them much. I would not have you send a Westhay warrant for it will not be served.

Wee had last Friday night a very great stormey windey night which have made worke for the slater, thacker, carpenter and glasior. It have done much harme all the countrey over, blowne downe many houses, hovells and trees.[1] £10 will not make the pales good againe about the parke and gardens. One week of the slater will make our houses good againe at Milton.

Goodman Manton promised me he would send his landlord an account of what he laid out on repairs and taxes. Will you give to the poor this Christmas as before? Joe Clarke has paid me his year's rent due Michaelmas last to Mr Whitaker as you may see by this enclosed receipt.[2] Ward's house in Northborough about two or three years ago was burnt and Mr Griffin ordered Ward in my hearing to buy some wood and get it repaired and he would allow them a year's rent although two years' rent would not do it, but as yet they have been allowed nothing. I let them have wood but it is owing for still. I desire you would get a year's rent from Mr Whitaker for them and let it not fall upon the poor people for it would ruin them.

[1] The Great Storm of 26–27 November 1703 was one of the most devastating ever to strike England, resulting in loss of life and great damage on land and even worse losses at sea. The Royal Navy lost

1,500 seamen and 15 warships, besides smaller craft, and the losses to the merchant service, although never computed, must have amounted to several hundred of all sizes. G. M. Trevelyan, *England under Queen Anne*, i (1930), pp. 307–11.

[2] Receipt signed by J. Whitaker for £6 written on verso.

## **294** FITZWILLIAM TO GUYBON

*London, 2 December 1703; F(M)C 1289*

You enclosed a receipt for Clark's taxes but not how much rent you received which I must pay Whitaker here when I have money, for at present I live upon credit. I will endeavour what I can with Whitaker on Ward's behalf about building his house but I fear he will be hard with him. I expect no money from the bishop's man, Parsons. When I sent to him he replied he had a bill on Mr Baxter's account but did not know if it would be accepted. He would send word only if it was. This is the fourth day so I suppose I shall hear no more. I have been served thus before by Baxter so I wonder you would trust to him. Dispose of the fee doe warrants among my Peterborough friends, and let Mr Richard Dickenson have a piece in place of his deceased uncle. You and Pendleton take one or dispose of it also at Peterborough. Ask Mr Parker and Mr Deacon if they will accept any but warn them does will not be fat this wet season. Give to the poor as you did last year. I am sorry about your Northamptonshire storm, although what I read in letters from the country it was not so violent as here and in Lincolnshire it was nothing. Ride through the estate noting what trees are down. Have them valued and sold to the best chapman. Let me know exactly what other damage is done. Here, thank God, we are all well escaped, although much frightened. It lasted seven hours. Did you let the eddishes in the Meadow Close, and if so, for what rent? Are they well fenced from cattle? Let all storm damage at Milton be mended, and the pales, and I hope care has been taken to keep the deer in, which can easily be done by hanging red and white rags in the gaps. We remember ourselves kindly to you and all our friends and hope we all live to see one another in a few months time. [P.S.] If possible send a doe from the park next week. Put in the basket the two mourning rings for Mr John Dickenson which Mr Richard (Dickenson) left with you.

## **295** GUYBON TO FITZWILLIAM

*7 December 1703; F(M)C 1290*

Received yours of 2nd. I received £4 16s of Joe Clarke and £1 4s allowed for a year's tax, making his full rent due Michaelmas past. Mr Bevis will certainly pay you £100 this week. I shall trust Mr Baxter no more. Two or three trees were blown down at Etton on John Chiseldine's ground which I have brought to Milton to make pales for the park, and three or four at Wood Croft and two in Edward Holman's ground; all these shall be sold. Much harm is done among the houses and hovels in the 'country'. I let the Meadow Close eddishes for £9 and have let it again until Lady Day for £3. The hay cocks are well fenced and thatched. If they stood three or four years they would take no harm. I cannot send a doe this week for the pales are not set up and killing a deer would drive the rest out of the park. I have had four carpenters working since the storm making posts, pales and rails[1] and next week we should be able to send a doe, although I fear you will not like it.

[1] On 4 January Guybon paid John Wilkinson and Edward Rycraft £6 0s 6d for setting up 201 yards of park pales at 6d a yard; also 5s 4d for helping to get the wood to the sawpit; and then a further 4s for four days mending the pales 'next Gunworth Ground and the garden'; Disbursements 74.

## 296 FITZWILLIAM TO GUYBON

*London, 9 December 1703; F(M)C 1291*

Yours of 7th received. I will pay Whittaker the £4 16s. Glad trees have suffered so little. I believe I can spare Meadow Close next year since the hay you got this summer from it will last two years in the stables, so you may rent it from Lady Day to Goody Freeman or another. Since the does are so indifferent send none up for I do not desire to pay the carriage of lean venison but I very much wonder that I neither can have summer nor winter venison. Something must be the matter. I am sure there are not many of my own horses in the park to hinder the deer and there never was more grass than this year. When then must I expect fat venison? Be very earnest with the tenants for my arrears. I must pay my debts. I will not pay interest to pleasure the tenants and forbearance does them more harm than good. You must furnish me with £400 or £500 by the beginning of [January] for I am engaged to pay a very large sum then, and will suffer a great loss without it. Send up the rentals, woodbooks, and meadow rentals when it will cost nothing. Send the mourning rings with them for if we wear them it should be 'within the yeare'.

## 297 FITZWILLIAM TO GUYBON

*London, 16 December 1703; F(M)C 1292*

(One Read, correspondent of Miles Bevis, has paid £60 and promises about £40 more when he gets it up, probably next week. Does not know where to send to Mr Colcutt, whose rents Guybon is collecting. When Fitzwilliam has funds Guybon must write to ask Colcutt to call on Fitzwilliam to be paid, and also inform Colcutt of the state of repair of the cottages and what storm damage his timber suffered about his house or on his land near Belsis. His wife continues ill of the colic. Enquires about Guybon's memory of outbuildings at Setchey 'great house'.[1] Letter damaged.)

[1] Guybon appears to have been steward at Setchey manor, near King's Lynn, early in his career. Setchey came to Fitzwilliam through his marriage.

## 298 FITZWILLIAM TO GUYBON

*London, 30 December 1703; F(M)C 1293*

(Conjectures will receive no more from Bevis's man Read from whom he has not heard. The Hollands have paid £50. Needs returns quickly. To send a park doe if 'tollerable good', with Guybon's papers and mourning rings. Wishes box marked 'M & W' he sent down Michaelmas 1701 to be sent up with the carrier charged to keep it dry. Wine to be kept warm and cellar windows stopped with straw. If deer escaped when the pales were down let them be watched and recaptured. When Guybon sees Cousin Bellamy of 'Fawsett' [Farcet] he must thank him for the swan and turkey sent up for Christmas which proved 'extraordinary good', and his daughter sends her thanks for the same present sent to her. The venison to be sent up in a flag basket; the carriers must not be told the contents.)

## **299** FITZWILLIAM TO GUYBON

*London, 8 January 1703/4; F(M)C 1295*

(Has received box and bundle. Hears nothing of Bevis's £40. Guybon not to rely on Duce who has failed Fitzwilliam so often. To send no venison since it's so poor, but to recover deer escaped after the storm. Mr Thomas Barrett has left Heriot who has taken his son Harbord Heriot into his 'shop' in his place.)

## **300** FITZWILLIAM TO GUYBON

*London, 20 January 1703/4; F(M)C 1297*

Have heard nothing of the £40 from Mr Bevis's friend. Colcutt's son came for the £42, and for the second time I could not pay because of lack of returns. It's strange you neglect me when I told you a month or six weeks since that I was obliged to pay a great sum on the 25th, and I have not had a penny since. Even if Duce should be punctual he won't pay by Tuesday and I must take up money for six months at interest because of your slackness in getting returns. Tell John Rycraft, or any other, that I will allow no man to plough any enclosure on my estate until I am down there to decide which is fit to be ploughed.

## **301** FITZWILLIAM TO GUYBON

*London, 25 January 1703/4; F(M)C 1298*

Francis Guybon, Yours I received yesterday and am much surprized to heare of the misfortune of poore Harry Vaughan.[1] I never designed to keep a bailiffe for a constancy in that towne, only continued him and his father in till I went into the countrey and then intended to settle a young man under you to ride about and save you that labour. Pray go to his house and take Mr Pemberton, or if he is not to be gott, any other sensible person, as Mr Curtis the minister,[2] or Mr Bimrose or Mr Richard Ewen, along with you. Demand the books and rentalls belonging to the manor as he has severall and what other papers there is that may be useful to give any one a light into the estate and lett them be brought to Milton and laied carefully by themselves. If any people are solicitous to have the place you may give them hopes for then they will be the readier to assist you and tell you of many things that without it you would not heare off, and particularly learne how the cowpastures were lett the last yeare and who had them. Without doubt he writt their names downe in a paper. I reckon Mr Richard Ewin may give you more knowledge of the affaires then Bimrose who I heare is become a drunken man of late yeares and grows fatt and careless in most matters. However advise with them both but lett it be singly for they do not care for one another. Ewin has a mind to the place. He wrote to me about it when Old Vaughan died but take no notice of what I write to him, only, if he should speake to you about such a thing, give him hopes by telling him you know I have a kindness for him but that you beleive I will not promise the place till I am in the countrey and that you expect me downe every moneth. Bimrose I dare say will not accept of it but if he does give him hopes for these two men are only able to advise you and without them you will be much to seeke. They will tell you how to make the best of the cow commons and every thing else, in hopes of being imployed and I wish I be not forc't to imploy one of them for a time. Pray recommend me to the poore widdow. Lett he[r] know how sorry I am for her great loss, as well as my owne, that I shall be ready to do her any kindness I can at any time. What money she has of mine, demand it of her and give her your receipt. Learne all you can of her how affaires stand with every one of the tennants, and of the cowpastures. If she be a notable woman she may tell you many things. If she deales ingeniously with you and tells you all she knows you may assure her I shall be the kinder to her. I have not time to write any more this post but shall by the next as things come into my thoughts. Pray secure all the books and papers as soone as you can and lett them be laied by safe. Yesterday Henry Hankin's man brought £48 9s 5d (vizt) on Joseph Bull's account £10 3s 7d, on Mr Bevill's £24 16s 2d, on Mrs Anne Bonnor's £13 9s 8d ... [P.S.] I would know where the body was found whither in my manor or where else.

[1] Bailiff of Maxey, killed by a fall from his horse.

[2] Possibly Henry Curtis is meant, appointed Vicar of Maxey in 1678, although according to Longden (iii. 323) he resigned in 1691.

## **302** JOHN CATLIN TO FITZWILLIAM

*Maxey, 25 January 1703/4; F(M)C 1299*

May it please your lordship, I, one of your tenants in Maxey, do beg the favour of your lordship in the behalfe of the balifship of Henry Vaughan (which as he was coming from Stamford market on Friday last fell from his horse and dyed and was buried last Sunday) and most of your honour's tennants in Maxey doth desire that if your lordship is not provided that you would bestow the same upon me and I would be content with what sallery you please to order. I have done several busieness for the town these four or five years and I know all your tennants that belongs to the court in Maxey. I am at the age of twenty eight years. My substance may be worth about an hundred pounds or better. I was borne in Maxey and never was above two years from it. I have learned arithmatick and if I might be admited could balance your lordship's accounts. I have a coppy of all the tennants and rents belonging to the court as freeholds, coppieholds, leasholds, tenants at will, and cowpastures having helpt Henry Vaughan in his life time and many of your tennants have given me encuragement to write. If your lordship be pleased to grant me the office I shall be exceeding thankfull and very diligent in your lordship's business.

## 303 FITZWILLIAM TO GUYBON

*London, 27 January 1703/4; F(M)C 1300*

Francis Guybon, Goodman Dove was here yesterday with me and desires to plow but I told him I would not consent to it till I was in the countrey and then I would view the ground and consider what was best to be done. He paid me no money haveing sold his beasts by the way, nor have I received any from either Mr Duce or any other by your order. Pray be circumspect what you do at Maxey. I am affraied it will appeare Mr Vaughan is in my debt a very considerable summe. Therefore, under hand, be very inquisetive what stocke he has and in what condition he died. Richard Ewin may be usefull to you if you mannage him right. He is a prying, inquisitive man and by him you may learne much. Therefore give him very good words and hopes if you find him desirous to succeed Vaughan. Pray remember me kindly to Mr Pemberton. Lett him know I received his letter about Mr Vaughan's death and that I thanke him for his good advise therein. Pray take all possible care you can to returne me money . . .

[P.S.] Sorry to hear Pendleton's arm so bad. I paid Mr Colcutt's son the £42 you received of his father's Castor rents because they had called two or three times for it, although I could ill spare it.

## 304 FITZWILLIAM TO GUYBON

*London, 3 February 1703/4; F(M)C 1302*

Have heard nothing from you since you wrote of Henry Vaughan's death. Are all his books and writings in your hands? Duce paid £100 at Heriot's only today. Had not Mr Ballett died[1] last week the very day I was due to pay him a great sum of money I should have been much disappointed for want of it sooner. Send more returns for Ballett's executors meet next week and will receive my money. [P.S.] My wife is troubled still with her old complaint, the colic. Write word how my cousin Trice does, if he is to marry and who it is.

[1] Mr Charles Ballett died 27 January 1704.

## 305 FITZWILLIAM TO GUYBON

*London, 10 February 1703/4; F(M)C 1305*

When the Vaughan matters are settled get all books and papers relating to the estate. I know nobody in Maxey I like better (for bailiff) than Mr Richard Ewen, but will not decide now. Get returns quickly. Mr Pemberton has been too busy to relate what you and he did at Maxey, save to say the widow is a cunning woman who advises with Sharpe of Deeping and 'your' Richard Ewen.[1]

[1] This suggests Guybon favoured Ewen's appointment.

## 306 FITZWILLIAM TO GUYBON

*London, 17 February 1703/4; F(M)C 1309*

(Glad you are returning me money as I shall greatly need it at Lady Day. Henry Hankin has paid Heriot's £45 3s 3d for a Mr Whitehead[1] and £42 10s 5d for Mr Pancke; Hankin bringing me Heriot's receipt for £87 13s 8d, I giving him receipts for both sums. Hankin has also paid £12 17s for a Thomas Lawrence of Walton. I yet hear nothing of Bevis' and Rycraft's money.

I received a letter last Munday from one Mr Cozens, a grocer in Stamford, with an abstract inclosed of Mr Vaughan's accompts and withall offering me his service to collect all the arreares due from the tennants.[2] This person I find the widdow imploies to settle his [sic] husband's accounts and he has done them very well and writes an excellent hand. I answered his letter and desired the particulars at large which he offered to send me if I pleased. If he should speake to you to intercede with me in his behalfe that he may be imployed you may returne him for answer you shall be ready to do him any friendly offices; that I have already writt you word I resolved not to nominate any to that place till I came into the countrey myselfe which now you expected in May at farthest; that in the meane time the fairer and clearer he made the accompts to me it would be the greater inducement to me to have the more favourable opinion of him and that to your knowledge I had named no body yett that should succeed Mr Vaughan; that if the widdow dealt well by me in delivering all things up of papers and books relateing to the estate and made the accompts true and honest I should be alwaies her freind and take care nobody else should wrong her. With all pray lett them know, and I hereby order you to receave all those arreares of rents and lett not the tennants offerre to pay them to any one else. I understand by private letters out of the countrey that the widdow and his brothers['] and sisters[']³ children intend to divide the estate amungst them: I meane his personall estate. Pray take care before anything of that kind be done or anything removed off the ground that my accompts be all cleared first, and speake with all the tennants and lett them produce their last receipts from him that you may see what moneys they have paid that you may know the better how to charge the widdow. I suppose Mr Leaffeild the coroner sate upon his body and found the horse as guilty of his death. That horse is forfeited to me as lord of the manor you writeing me word his body was found within Maxey mannor. Therefore pray lett the horse be secured and before you mention this my demand you had best learne from some of the neighbours what sort of horse or mare he rode out off that day that they may not impose upon you and give you a worse. Pray act in this matter with all the prudence and circumspection you can.

[P.S.] This Mr Cosins as an admirable accountant. You may use him for I believe he has drawn up the three years accounts very well. I find Vaughan has received no rents for this last year. Pray examine them, keep a copy and send me the original by the carrier or by a friend coming up on other business. You must be thinking of letting the cow commons for next summer but be sure the last year's rent be paid before you let it again. Nobody shall rent next year who is [in arrear]. Let this be a consta[n]t rule as also in Etton Meadow.

[1] Thomas Whitehead according to Disbursements 74, 19 February.

[2] Cosins had written 12 February (F(M)C 1306r) that Widow Vaughan had asked him to draw up her husband's and father-in-law's accounts. He wrote on the verso (F(M)C 1306v) an abstract of the accounts for three years ending Michaelmas 1702. He offered his services as bailiff. He wrote again 20 February (F(M)C 1310) saying that some alleged that Vaughan had received part of Lady Day 1703 rents although no rental had been found. He had heard Fitzwilliam did not intend to replace Vaughan at Maxey but rather employ someone generally to assist Guybon and offered himself for the position.

[3] Not known whether singular or plural is meant.

## **307** FITZWILLIAM TO GUYBON

*London, 24 February 1703/4; F(M)C 1311*

I must pay a considerable sum on Lady Day so hasten returns. I have received no money since my last.

When you have an opportunity pray inquire, but do it privately, what this Mr John Cozens the grocer of Stamford is; whither he be rich or otherwise; if he has a good reputation in the world as to his honesty, for the Widdow Vaughan I find trusts wholly to him in settling her accompts, and so when I heare the character of the man I shall be the better judge if her accompts are fairly given up or otherwise. I perceave there is at least 6 or 700 pounds due to me from the tennants of that manor. Therefore I desire you would be speedy in gathering up those rents and reckon with all the tennants there, and lett them produce their last acquittances, that so I may know how to charge the widdow, and before the estate be divided, for feare there should not be enough to make me sattisfaction. I understand you have a great many out lieing deare since the pales have been blowne downe about the parke. You may do well to have a leap or two made, for the deare come home anight and strive to get in as they alwaies used to and if there be a leap they may gett in againe, otherwise never. If you sett downe a new leap you must be sure the ground be low on the parke side least the deare within side leap out that way, and the leap must be all covered with sadds[1] of earth. John Wilkenson can remember how the last was made and where it stood . . .

[P.S.] My daughter asks to be remembered, and wonders that she can never receive a letter from you.

[1] Sods.

## **308** FITZWILLIAM TO GUYBON

*London, 2 March 1703/4; F(M)C 1314*

I received yours enclosing Mr Halsted's note for £66 due to Mr Exton for wool money, payable about Lady Day. When I receive the money I will give you notice to repay Exton. George Woodcocke has paid £18 for Joe Chamberlaine and £13 10s 5d for John Watson of Glinton; and Henry Hankin brought £6 5s 5d, an odd sum he owed Exton. If you see Cousins on Saturday tell him his letter last post did not mention sending Vaughan's accounts, nor to which carrier I am to send for them. I am glad we have lost no deer. A week ago I sent a 'turk's head'[1] for Mrs Bull to clean the house, but forgot to mention it. I was sorry to hear of John Burton of Ailesworth's death, but am offered a very good tenant for it, paying a higher rent. Give me your advice in it for I suppose he has left nobody who can manage the farm for the children. Should Ben Burton take it you would then lack a tenant for his farm, and I doubt he would be as able to manage it.

[1] 'Turk's head', a round, longhandled broom. (This usage pre-dates the *O.E.D.*'s example by 150 years).

## **309** FITZWILLIAM TO GUYBON

*London 9 March 1703/4; F(M)C 1316*

I received a letter from a troublesome fellow at Ketton, a son of Arnold Wilkenson the freemason, who so duns me for a bill of £4 19s 6d for paving the cellar, laundry, etc., since I left the country, that I am ashamed of myself. He sets Mr Bertie to speak to me who tells everybody round the town of it. Were it not that I scorn to hinder the labourer of his hire I would not pay him a penny, and it shall be the last he ever has of me. I am sure he has (overcharged) by 40s so [I] will not clear his bill until I come down. However, pay him 40s and take his receipt in part of it. I am glad you intend me more money for I shall need it at Ladyday. I have heard nothing of Mrs Vaughan's accounts yet which Mr Cozens told you he had sent up. There is at least £500 or £600 owing to me out of Maxey which you must gather speedily because I cannot know how to reckon with the widow until that is done. Therefore reckon speedily with every tenant, because that which Henry Vaughan had in his hands must be paid me out of his personal estate before it be divided between his wife and his heirs. They write he died worth £300 and no more. You sent me no account of it. Let me know how you proceed for this matter must not be delayed. The person I proposed for a tenant for John Burton's farm is young Gardiner of Sutton, recommended by Mr Henry Hankin of the Angel Inn, Islington. He says he will lend him £100 if he needs it to stock the farm. Mr David Standish of Peterborough has played the knave with him for Gardiner trusted Standish to renew his lease on the great farm at Sutton and Standish took it in his own name so now he is destitute and would willingly take [my farm].[1] I don't know Gardiner's condition and whether he can manage this farm. You must inquire among the neighbours and discover if he is an honest man. I told Hankin I must have £50 per annum for the farm. They seem very fond of it because it's near to where he lived last. He has a brother-in-law, one Sisson, a great farmer in Rutland who can assist him, as well as Hankin. I will have the rent advanced. If you cannot get £50 I will not take less than £48 per annum. 'Corne is like to give a great price in this warr'. I am not against that man you are treating with. Take the most substantial and most honest man who will pay the most rent whom we can safely deal with. The tenant must take a lease for six, nine or 12 years, whichever you think best. Do not forget six boon days yearly and two fat geese or 5s at my pleasure; the lease shall not be assigned to another without my consent, etc., and he to pay for drawing it. Be circumspect and careful of my interest ... [P.S.] Do not lose this letter. You may need it as a reminder of what I would have done. The tenant of Burton's farm shall be debarred from ploughing up any enclosure or meadow ground at a penalty of £5 per acre. I will have nothing ploughed but the farm's field land.

[1] The letter is damaged at this point.

## 310 FITZWILLIAM TO GUYBON

*London, 16 March 1703/4; F(M)C 1318*

I am glad you take care of me for money. Although Halstead's bill is made payable at Lady Day, I will do well if it is paid a month after, because Halstead paid me what he owed Mr Ash for wool last year six weeks late. When I receive it I will give you notice to repay Exton.[1] I am sorry young Gardiner's circumstances are too low for him to manage that farm. 'He's of an honest breed and our neighbour'. I don't know what other men are. I am sorry you have not raised that rent at least 40s. Corn has doubled its price and likely to retain it during the war. Since you give this King so great a 'character' we will try him for three years and see how we like him. Mrs Bird tells me she has that money in her hand but no orders to pay it me, so if Mr Whinyates has not disposed of it elsewhere get him to write to her. That £100 would save me borrowing as much next week.[2] I have hay enough for one year so let Meadow Close at LadyDay.

[1] Guybon repaid Exton on 29 April, Disbursements 74.
[2] Repaid Whinyates on 21 March, *ibid.*

## 311 FITZWILLIAM TO GUYBON

*London, 23 March 1703/4; F(M)C 1319*

On the 17th Halstead paid the £66 he owed for Exton's wool, and on the 18th Hankin paid £62 10s 4d for Exton's beasts. On Tuesday Mrs Bird paid the £100 at Heriot's on Whinyate's order. These sums save borrowing because in a fortnight I must pay 'Dr Barber, etc' for their estate in Castor and Aylesworth and any returns before then would be welcome. Be earnest with Maxey and other tenants for their arrears.

If you say William Gardiner of Sutton be a poore fellow I do not care to deale with him though Mr Hankins tells me he was at Sutton last summer and he thought there was a very good stocke on his farme which farme is esteemed worth £50 per annum but he knew not what he might owe on it. He told me he would lend him £100 but I question whither he will be so good as his word if he heares he is in debt. There is a brother-in-law of Gardiner's a rich farmer in Ruttland.[1] If he will be bound to see my rent paid then you may safely accept of him especially if Hankin will lend him £100. Corne rises much here. We transport abundance every day to Portugall and Holland that the farmers must have a good time of it. Our bread is now very deare in this place ... [P.S.] I hope you have lett the Meadow Close and that you will dispose well and soone of this farme at Ailesworth.[2]

[1] Sisson.
[2] Burton's farm.

## 312 FITZWILLIAM TO GUYBON

*London, 30 March 1704; F(M)C 1320*

Francis Guybon, Yours of the 28th I received yesterday. I wonder you should lett the new tennant so long a terme in Burton's farme when I writt you word I would not lett it at the old rent from 3 yeares to 3 yeares. I will never seale his lease but upon such a terme though possibly I may never turne him out, but I will have it in my power. Twelve yeares may be longer by much then I may live and I will not tie up my sonn's hands. I would have the draught of the lease sent up to me before it is ingross't that I may putt in or out what I thinke fitt. If your tennant King does not like the farme upon my termes he is at liberty. If he will give £48 a yeare for it, etc., he shall have it for either 3 or 6 yeares but no longer for the reasons above. I will not pay one penny towards the lease. I thinke you have lett the Medow Close too cheap by 40s a yeare but because it is to Joseph Chamberlaine I am content it should go so for the yeare. I suppose he paies a New Yeare's gift besides. Do not forgett returns . . .

[P.S.] We have had abundant rain. I hope you keep the leads and gutters clean.

## 313 FITZWILLIAM TO GUYBON

*London, 13 April 1704; F(M)C 1321*

Your letter dated 4th did not arrive until Friday 7th, too late to answer for you to receive on Saturday at market. You may let Maxey cowpastures this year at the same rent as last, but I hope when I come down to find a way to raise them. They are too cheap at 6s 8d each. Sorry Mrs Dove is dead, but she lived to a good age.

I know not what you meane by granting a certificate to Sowgate of Marrham upon his removeing to Allerton. Pray advise with Mr Pemberton . . . and lett the towne do nothing of that kind, if possible, that may bring a future charge upon us . . . [P.S.] One John Cattlin of Maxey has writt me 2 letters both importing his desire of serveing under my cheife steward and that he has a promise from some sufficient neighbours they will be bound with him for his truth and honesty.[1] In his last letter he writt me an account of a rentall he transcribd for Henry Vaughan being Ladyday rent 1702 and some other things of moment wherein it appeares by his account that Mr Cozens and Mrs Vaughan would have couzened me in that rentall neare £20, for by Cattlin's account that halfe yeare came to £164 4s 3¼d and Mr Cozens' account saies it's no more then £146 1s 9d. Besides he[2] saies she is disposeing of all things so as if she intended to run away or at least as if I should have nothing to seize on so I may become a great looser if you and Mr Pemberton don't take [pains?] to secure me what lies in your power. I have writt an answer to John Cattlin's letter wherein I incourage him to be true and honest to me and whatever he can discover to acquaint you with it and I have here inclosed it because no body should know I write to him, so you may give him it yourselfe when you see him.

[1] See above **302**.

[2] Catlin.

### 314 JOHN COSINS TO FITZWILLIAM
*Stamford, 22 April 1704; F(M)C 1322*

According to the instructions in your first letter I have fairly transcribed the rents of Maxey from Lady Day 1700 to Michaelmas 1702; set down the arrears due at Michaelmas 1699, and each succeeding half year; with disbursements for repairs, taxes, etc; and then the two next half year rentals, the last, Michaelmas 1703, amounts to £238 6s 6d 'by the improvements of the cow pastures they being out of lease'. (Seeks authority to negotiate cowpasture leases; will send transcripts or keep until Fitzwilliam comes down as directed.)

### 315 FITZWILLIAM TO GUYBON
*London, 27 April 1704; F(M)C 1323*

Mr Hankin has paid £22 19s for Mr Exton; £5 19s 4d for Mr Bevill. George Woodcocke drove up their sheep. Received nothing since although yours mentioned more to come last week. These 'little dribbling summs don't find bread for the house'.

I am very sorry to heare by yours of Mr Pendleton's illness. Mr Roger Pemberton assured me last terme he was in a fine way, was not so fatt and could ride very well. If he has a dizziness he must loose immediatly 10 or 12 ounces of blood by cupping neare his necke between his shoulders. That eases the head the most of anything and takes off the drowsiness. That under God preserved me in my last distemper and I was taken then before my appoplecticke fitt came just in the same manner with dizziness and drowsiness. Therefore lett him prevent it in time. If Mr Riddley has but the new instruments for cupping it will do much better then the old way for it's a surgeon's bussiness rather then an appothecary's. I am forc't to be bleeded thus spring and fall by way of prevention but in cases of necessity we may take away blood at any time either by cupping or the lancett. I should be glad to heare what you have done at Maxey about the cow commons, if all the old ones are paid for and how you have lett the new ones for this yeare; what you have done about the arreares for there was at least £500 due when Harry Vaughan died and I desire they may be gathered up with all speed because of my great want of money and likewise the other rents of the rest of the estate ... [P.S.] Thanke God we are all in reasonable good health. My wife is the worst but at this time is better then usually. John Cattlin may be made very usefull to us provided no body knows we imploy him, for if it were knowne no body else would serve us who now may be in hopes of the imployment when I come into the countrey.

### 316 FITZWILLIAM TO GUYBON
*London, 4 May 1704; F(M)C 1324*

Have received no money since the £28 paid me for Exton's and Bevill's sheep which George Woodcocke brought up three weeks since. When I told you how I needed money you answered you could get no returns so I have found you one for £250. Dr Barber and his son of Stamford and some others from Cambridgeshire will be here tomorrow night to convey that Castor and Aylesworth estate. Barber wishes some of the money paid at Stamford, so when the writings are sealed I will give him a note on you for either £200 or £250. He says he will take it as you can gather it in a fortnight or three weeks, and you can pay it £50 or £100 at a time. When all is paid take up the note and his receipt.

### 317 FITZWILLIAM TO GUYBON

*London, 11 May 1704; F(M)C 1325*

Francis Guybon, I signed the writeings with Dr Barber and others the last night and paid them £900 here and charged a bill upon you for two hundred and fifty pounds more which you are to pay at Stamford to the doctor or his order in a fortnight or three weekes time. He will not be at Stamford till tomorrow sevennight. His sonne and you will settle the payments.[1] I received not your letter the last weeke till Fryday which was the cause I did not answer it this day sennight. George Woodcocke paid me last Fryday £55 12s 4d, but I heare nothing of Mr Duce unless he has paid his money in at Mr Heriott's. For the inne at Markett I vallew not much, it being out of my mannors and in another countrey,[2] though if I had money to spare I might thinke of it. It may be my freind Mr Charles Bertie may buy it, and may take it ill if I should bid a price for it, he being lord of the manor but this is only my conjecture. We are extreame glad to heare Mr Pendleton is better. Pray God continue it and send him quite well again ... [P.S.] My daughter goes out of towne next Thursday and I thinke to be goeing downe to Milton now very speedily.

[1] Guybon paid Dr Gabriel Barber on 23 May, Disbursements 74.
[2] Probably Market Deeping, the other 'countrey' being Lincolnshire.

### 318 FITZWILLIAM TO GUYBON

*London, 25 May 1704; F(M)C 1326*

No money has been paid since Woodcocke paid me that £55 for [Henry] Thompson of the fens. Duce cannot be depended on. I don't know Stinton of Allerton. I am sorry for Eddins of Glinton. On his death there will be alterations which may stop the sending the beasts up. I am sorry that £20 odd of Marmaduke Tomlinson's of Northborough which is in Hankin's hands is not paid me. Hankin will pay nothing without Duke's written order, though he had it by word of mouth from Woodcocke. Money is needed for fitting ourselves and servants with new clothes and getting ready to come down. Be earnest with the tenants for arrears. We are all well, my wife better than any time this winter. My daughter has left town for the summer. Am sorry to hear of Pendleton's continuing illness. Glad Dr Barber is paid.

### 319 FITZWILLIAM TO GUYBON

*London, 8 June 1704; F(M)C 1327*

Yours of 30th not received until 2nd. I suppose you sent it to the ferry in time and they could not get a passenger to carry it sooner. The sums you said we would receive last week are unpaid. Mr Whittacre sends this enclosed letter by which you see that Ward was satisfied for rebuilding his house in Mr Griffin's lifetime, and has paid several half years' rents to Mr Griffin before he died and since the house was burned. Whittacre wishes me to buy these two farms or cottages but I don't know if I will. Let me have a true account of them: if there be two houses or not; are they in repair; what land to each; what arable and what grass; where they lie and whether in a good part of the fields and town, and the rent and whether likely to hold constantly. I understand Joseph Clarke lives in my farm that Anthony Preston lived ; . Is his cottage empty or does he let it to another poor man? If so, can the tenant pay the rent and keep the cottage repaired? What would it cost to repair it? Colcutt's son came to ask me to find out from you if, as his father had heard, Thomas Manton would go off the farm. Let Joseph Chamberlaine privately inform himself if Manton has begun to plough the fallows, for if not Mr Colcutt must take care to have them ploughed, and also to enter upon the meadow. If Manton ploughs the fallows we would not have him know we enquire after it for then he must hold for another year ... [P.S.] You shall brew before h[aysell] begins ...[1]

[1] Foot of letter damaged.

## 320 GUYBON TO FITZWILLIAM
*15 June 1704; F(M)C 1329*

Yours of the 8th received. I have obeyed your commands, and Mr Colcutt's and Mr Whitaker's. Thomas Manton has ploughed and mucked his fallows, and does not intend to leave his farm as I hear. If he did I don't know where Mr Colcutt would find such another tenant, for they say he pays dearly for it, and is a good honest tenant. As for Clarke's and Ward's houses you must rebuild them if you buy them. £50 would hardly repair them. Clarke's house and homestead is ½ an acre with ½ an acre of grass, 10 acres of arable. It's good land and he pays £6 14s a year rent. He has a tenant in it. Ward's house and homestead is 1 acre, with 5½ acres meadow, 1½ acres enclosure, 1½ acres cow pasture; £8 rent. They will continue at that rent if the houses are repaired, otherwise not. They pay no King's taxes. Clarke owes half a year's rent, Ward a year. They will pay in a month but cannot now. If you please we will brew next week but hope we shall not keep it until it spoils as formerly. Mr Pendleton continues ill.

## 321 FITZWILLIAM TO GUYBON
*London, 17 June 1704; F(M)C 1330*

Received yours of 15th yesterday. Brew whenever convenient before 'haysell' begins. Let the drink be handsomely hopped, and the hogsheads well hooped. I promise you the drink shall not spoil this year for want of spending in time. I will allow 16 bushels of malt for the two hogsheads of ale and six for the four of small beer. Not Duce nor Edins' beasts nor anybody has paid a penny since the 27th May when Mr Holland paid £70[1], so I want a speedy supply. Sorry to hear Mr Pendleton continues ill. I hope he does not keep his bed.

[1] There is no reference to Holland in Guybon's accounts but only a payment of £70 3s 1d 'returned by Mr Edins', Disbursements 74.

## 322 FITZWILLIAM TO GUYBON

*London, 22 June 1704; F(M)C 1331*

Have still received none of the payments yours mentioned three weeks ago, save Mr Hankin paid £20 at Duce's order upon John Rycraft's account. I only write to enclose this to Joseph Clarke from Mr Whittacre who wonders at your writing the two houses would cost £50 to repair when £50 would build two such houses; and Ward's house was new built five years ago. Have a carpenter view them and let me know the true cost of repairing them. We are all well save my poor wife.

## 323 GUYBON TO FITZWILLIAM

*27 June 1704; F(M)C 1332*

Clarke has replied to Whitaker this post. Hope you received mine of 22nd with bill enclosed. Could not speak with Henry Holland on Saturday, he being not in town, but I left word for him to send or order you £50, which I hope he or some of the neighbours will do. The two cottages in Northborough will cost £50 to put in repair. Ward's house was new built but was burned. If the cottages are not repaired the tenants will leave. If you buy them and pay Whitaker what is due from the tenants they will pay you within a month. Mr Pendleton is something better but cannot get to church yet.

## 324 FITZWILLIAM TO GUYBON

*London, 29 June 1704; F(M)C 1333*

(Received letter of 22nd enclosing bill on Mr Brogden for £27 10s. Last Friday Hankin paid Heriot £20 for Duce. Only one business holds him here which he hopes to clear in a fortnight. Glad Pendleton is better and hopes he will be able to get to church soon. [P.S.] They have had a hot week for brewing which he fears has spoiled the drink. Will observe Guybon's directions if he deals with Whittacre but not sure he will.)

## 325 FITZWILLIAM TO GUYBON

*London, 6 July 1704; F(M)C 1334*

(Has heard nothing of Holland's money or any other save £31 10s paid at Heriot's by a Gregory Alexander. Brogden's £27 10s unpaid but has no fear for it. Concerning claims of Deeping St James 'officers', 'The Parks' had never been assessed for the poor or the church in that parish and never would be without lawsuit. If they distrained, goods must be replevied. Imagines the other gentlemen's parks around were also exempt, so all must join in case of a suit. Guybon should consult them. Extremely sorry for Pendleton, and prays he may recover. Lady Fitzwilliam much afflicted by colic. If they brewed the last week asks how many days Johnson worked, how many hoops per hogshead.)

**326** GUYBON TO FITZWILLIAM
*11 July 1704; F(M)C 1335*

(Surprised Holland had paid nothing; but having never heard of Gregory Alexander, believes the £31 10s must have been paid for Holland.[1]) Richard Stasey will pay £100 next week without fail. Johnson brewed four days, using 19 hoops on the hogsheads (24 the brewing before); and 22 strike of malt at 3s 3d (22 strike at 2s 4d before); six bushels of hops at 5s 5d (7s 6d before). You may kill a brace or two of bucks, although they will be better in a fortnight because of the very dry summer. Marholm and Milton will cut little hay, the meadows are 'light'. They would bring Marmaduke [Tomlinson] in for repairs to Northborough church. I think they cannot for you have part of it for your own use, and keep it in repair without charge to them, so why should they bring you into their charge? 'James Deepin' [Deeping St James] would bring The Parkes in to pay constables' charges. Mr Pendleton continues ill.

[1] Top of letter damaged so beginning only briefly summarised. The Alexander return was from Edmund Beales in Norfolk, see **328** below.

**327** GUYBON TO FITZWILLIAM [draft]
*18 July 1704; F(M)C 1334v*

(Had received no letter the last week but glad to hear from Pemberton that all were in good health. Hopes Richard Stasey has paid some money. The sooner Fitzwilliam sends for bucks the better for they have little grass and water. Such a dry time never was known. People forced to fodder cattle already. Pendleton continued ill.)

**328** FITZWILLIAM TO GUYBON
*London, 20 July 1704; F(M)C 1336*

(Had not written previous week because had received neither letter nor money, Guybon's of the 11th not coming until Friday the 14th, not Wednesday the 12th as it should. Alexander's £31 10s had been returned by Mr Beales. Had now received by Guybon's and John and Henry Holland's order £43 17s 6d, and from John Marshall by Guybon's and Stacey's order £80, not £100 because they had other occasions for the money. The 'Great House in Norborough'[1] never paid church repairs because of the chapel he maintained there, nor never should. At Deeping St James he never paid any town charges and never would unless compelled by law. Pemberton had promised to take care of it. Weather too hot for venison, but venison usually fatter in dry years than in wet. Had underwritten two warrants.)

[1] Northborough Castle, leased by Marmaduke Tomlinson.

## **329** FITZWILLIAM TO GUYBON

*London, 27 July 1704; F(M)C 1337*

Nothing prevents my coming down but the need for a good sum of about £150 to be returned to pay my expenses down and clear my debts in town. I rely on your rents for this for without it I am 'directly windbound'.[1] (Weather is milder so would have a buck sent up the next week, pieces 'superscribed' to prevent changing, and the carrier to lay them out each night.)

[1] Detained by contrary winds.

## **330** GUYBON TO FITZWILLIAM

*1 August 1704; F(M)C 1338*

[I will do my best to return you some money next week for I would not have you 'windbound'. Thursday I will send a buck by Fearey's wagon, arriving Saturday morning. Mr John Bellamy and his son called yesterday. They said you were all well and would soon be down; God keep you in that mind. Joe Clarke and Edward Ward have paid Mr 'Whittaker's' Lady Day rent but he demands a further half year from Clarke, claiming he owed it Mrs Griffin, but Clarke paid it to Mr Burman and has his receipt. He went to Burman's but Mrs Burman could give him no satisfaction, her son being in London. It would be very hard if Clarke should pay twice. [P.S.] Mr Pendleton continues ill. Doctor Wright being in the country he has him as his physician now.

## **331** FITZWILLIAM TO GUYBON

*London, 10 August 1704; F(M)C 1339*

Yours of the 1st and 8th received. The venison came up very sweet, extremely good but so young I conclude it was only a 'sore'. I wonder you have no bigger bucks. Send another next week. I am sorry I am to have no money this week for I am reduced to the last penny. Sorry also Mr Pendleton is no better, and the drought continues. Yesterday we had a few showers. God send more soon. Drovers tell me harvest will be in soon so have Mrs Bull seek two maids, and find us a drudging man for the gates etc. [P.S.] Cousin Thomas Bellamy was here last Sunday and told me of his Milton visit, that you looked well, but he was mistaken if he told you we were all in good health for my poor wife is seldom well 24 hours together.

## **332** FITZWILLIAM TO GUYBON

*London, 17 August 1704; F(M)C 1340*

(Wonders Guybon had not received his letter of 10th but glad no buck sent in the heat. Had received £2 19s 9d and £6 10s 4d for James Dove and Richard Burton but these 'driffletts' did him no good. Tenants must pay a good sum or he could not stir. Might send boxes down the next Monday.)

## 333 FITZWILLIAM TO GUYBON

*[London,] 26 [August] 1704; F(M)C 1342A*

Francis Guybon, I received both [your letters and am] much concerned to heare by the last of poore Mr [Pendleton's dea]th.[1] I had great hopes I might have seen him before his death, but we must all submitt. Pray be very obligeing and kind to the poore widdow and fatherless, and countenance her all you can. As to the liveings, I shall not in hast dispose of them. When I come into the countrey I shall informe myselfe what young ministers there are that deserve my kindness. I shall not dispose of them to boyes as yours mention. Pray remember me kindly to Mr Selby[2] and lett him know I received his letter and will consider of his proposall and will give him my answer by word of mouth when I see him in the countrey, and in the meane time will not dispose of either of the liveings.

> The buck came, sweet but neither fat nor large. I suppose you only have 'sores' in the park for they are very small. Send another next week. Yours of the 23rd said several sums would be paid this week, and your former letter said some would be paid the previous week but nothing has been paid me yet. I wonder you would take no better care of me. I am forced 'to run a ticke' for 'drincke, meate and lodgings', something I have never done before. You mention moving the baker's oven from Castor to Maxey but not whether it is a baker that desires it. He may be a fanciful man, thinking to hire someone to carry on a trade he understands little about and may be mistaken. The oven stands in a likely place for trade, but if you think well of the Maxey man I have no objection so long as I am at no charge.

[1] Pendleton died on 24 August 1704, Longden, iv. 235. Letter damaged; words in square brackets reconstructed.

[2] Christopher, son of Michael Selby of Castor, gentleman, deacon 25 September 1698; licensed to curacy at Marholm church 26 September 1698; curate of Framlingham, Suffolk, 1704; Vicar of Grantchester, Cambridgeshire, 1707–16; Longden, xii. 109.

## 334 FITZWILLIAM TO GUYBON

*London, 31 August 1704; F(M)C 1343*

Francis Guybon, Yours of the 29th I received yesterday and likewise another from Mrs Pendleton about her sonne being putt into the Charter House. I am none of the governors and so cannot help her but the governors give their turns of presenting to their servants who sell them for £30 or £40 for each boy comeing in, and then she must be obligd to live in London to looke after him, though I beleive it may be her best course so to doe for the education of her children, and here is cheape enough liveing for retired private people. Pray read thus much of this letter to her. Since I writt last Mrs Mary Gascoigne, sister to the minister,[1] brought me £50; it was on Tuesday last, and yesterday Mr Hankin's man brought me a receipt by which it appeared he had paid to Mr Heriott the 27th instant £37 5s 4d on Tom Lawrence's account so I gave him my receipt and tooke up Mr Heriott's. I heare nothing of Sissenar of Norborough who I should be glad to speake with. Dispose of my forrest bucks amungst my freinds and neighbours as you thinke fitt and either gett me a fatt bucke from Lord Exeter in liew of my fee bucke out of Westhay or give the warrant to 3 or 4 in Peterborough who have an interest in Burley and lett them divide it amung themselves. Mr Whinyates will go neare to procure it but for feare he should not reserve one peice out of the other warrants for him. Keep one peice for yourselfe, or more, if you have a mind. My cozens Trice and Bellamy must not be forgott. Send me word who you most approve for Etton liveing and likewise for Marrham for I intend to part them and whoever has Etton shall be obliged to reside upon the place and build a good house. It shall not be neglected as it was in Mr Standish his time, and the last,[2] had he lived he should have gone thither. For the oven at Castor, if the man you speake of at Maxey will be at the charge of takeing it downe, carrieing it to Maxey and setting it up there on my ground and leaving it in repaire whenever he leaves the towne and farme, I shall consent to it, but lett him consider if he is sure of a good trade to answer his charge. With all our kind respects to Mrs Pendleton ... [P.S.] If Mrs Pendleton will not be at the charge of putting her sonn into the Charter House, Peterborough or Stamford are good schooles, but still London are better. [P.P.S.] Mrs Pendleton writes to me in behalfe of her cozen Forster[3] for Marrham and saies he has gained so good an opinion among the inhabitants there that they intend to petition me in his behalfe. Pray lett them not give themselves that trouble for I am as good a judge as they are of preaching and will be sattisfied my selfe who is fitt to preach before me. Since I writt this I mett George Woodcocke in Islington Feilds with a drove of beasts and tells me he is not to pay me any money and that he mett Sissenar on the roade goeing backe. Don't forgett to send me some more money and soone and by Sissenar, if you can, and if he comes up againe.[4] You may take halfe a bucke of this venison to yourselfe if you would make a present of it to any person.

[1] Probably George Gascoigne is meant, originally of Market Deeping, Rector of Paston 1691, died February 1705. Longden, v. 183. In Fitzwilliam's terms 'Mistress' Gascoigne could have been either Gascoigne's sister or sister-in-law.

[2] I.e. Mr Pendleton.

[3] In fact Mrs Pendleton's nephew. Forster was acting in place of Pendleton at Marholm. Possibly either Richard or William Forster both of whom had graduated B.A. early in 1704; Longden, vol. 5, Forster. For Fitzwilliam's views on Forster see below **355**, **356**.

[4] 'Goodman Sissenar' returned £13 17s 6d but not before October, or at least Guybon did not repay him until 8 October; Disbursements 74.

## **335** FITZWILLIAM TO GUYBON

*London, 5 September 1704; F(M)C 1344*

The venison came up well last Saturday. Contrive to send me a buck so that it is here before 'Holy Rood Day'[1] when my daughter needs a half. If it's the only buck in the park send it, and then I am beholden to none. If you have none in the park ask Lord Exeter if he will give me one in exchange for a fee deer. [P.S.] I hope you ensure that the cures are performed at Marholm and Etton. Pay the preachers and let me know their names. I hope Fearey has packhorses or a coach coming up early next week, but if not, rather than use another's coach, send the buck by the wagon as formerly even if it arrives a little after Holy Rood Day.

[1] 14 September.

**336** FITZWILLIAM TO GUYBON
*London, 7 September 1704; F(M)C 1346*

I am glad there is good venison in the park. If a buck cannot come by Holyrood Day do not fail of the Saturday after. Mr Whittacre came for his rents which you said you had collected. He said £8 was due from Ward and £3 from Clarke which I paid. He promised to reimburse me if there is any mistake, of which inform me. If there is any mistake I can thank you for it for you always write your letters too short, saying you received the rent but not how much, so I pay 'at all adventures'. Thank you for your good advice about the livings. I will consider it.

**337** FITZWILLIAM TO GUYBON
*London, 14 September 1704; F(M)C 1348*

Francis Guybon, Yours of the 12th I received yesterday. I am sorry you can not remember what money you received of Mr Whittacre's tennants at Norborough without first consulting with them for I immagined you sett downe every summe in your pockett booke that you received daily from the tennants and after you came home entred them in your account booke. Without such a method you must have all things in great confusion I feare. I am glad to heare of some venison. I mett George Woodcocke this afternoone in the Feilds[1] who told me he had 15 sorry sheep of old Mr Lawrence's to sell which money he was ordered to pay me, but no other though he has a great many more to sell. I am sorry I heare of no other summe because I have nothing more to do but to pay my bills and come away. I forgott to write you word a moneth since that I had sent downe another box of pictures which I hope are safe at Milton before this though you have never mentioned it to me in any letter. Pray lett the box be weighed and see what it comes too and then lett Mr Wright open the box and part the pictures carefully and lett them be sett up one by one against a dry wall that they may take aire, otherwaies they will turne yellow. I shall not consent that Goodman Dove should plow up the 11 acres without he be willing to advance five pounds a yeare for every yeare he plowes it and that he laies it downe againe with grass and afterwards give the old rent for it for 3 yeares before he leaves it. If he thinks £5 a yeare is to much to advance for plowing lett him send me word what he is willing to give for I will not consent to plow without a handsome advance of rent. Last Fryday young Mr Lawrence of Walton paid me £30 for which I gave him my receipt but pray lett me have a further and greater supply so fast as you can possibly for that's the only thing I stay for. [P.S.] I was glad to heare last Sunday by Mr Pemberton of your good health. If there be anything wunting (sic) in any part of the house lett Mrs Bull provide it now at Bridge faire; I meane in the kittchin, larders, washhouses and brewhouse, and the chambers for chamber potts, brass or pewter.

[1] Islington Fields.

## **338** FITZWILLIAM TO GUYBON

*London, 21 September 1704; F(M)C 1349*

Have received no letter from you this week. The venison arrived sweet, tender and ate well. George Woodcocke brought me £6 for Mr Henry Lawrence and I persuaded him to let me have £25 of his own – with much ado because he was to pay it away last Monday, and feared you might not repay him in time and his credit would 'be broke' with his customers. I assured him you would and hope you have. Lawrence paid on the score of wood money owed you. We are making haste to get down, having only to pack and buy some winter clothes. Get all the house clean and fit for us. Joseph Chamberlaine must lay his fruit in the appointed chambers, i.e. in that great lower room in the new building I call the barn, where the timber lies, for we must use the room over the new laundry and dairies where the apples used to lie to dry linen this winter. He can get to them by the stair under the clock. His 'codlins' and early fruit already in the drying room he can leave there, for he will have ample time to clear them before we need it. Send all money you can for I must not leave town in debt. I need £150 to clear me.

## **339** FITZWILLIAM TO GUYBON

*London, 28 September 1704; F(M)C 1351*

We all rejoiced to receive your letter yesterday for I had accidentally learned at Islington that you had been very ill for a week. I wonder you would let nobody write to me. I hope this finds you much better, for we all desire to see you and God grant we may all meet once again, and soon for we have only to pack and pay reckonings. My wife was so afflicted for fear you might be dead that we could not pacify her, and had we not received your letter would certainly have been at Milton tomorrow night to see you. Take care and do not stir out. Send Joseph Chamberlaine or Goodman Wootton with your note to tenants you know to have money for you. If God lets me live to come down we will contrive to ease you of so much riding about. Meanwhile let me know if the pictures came, their weight, and the amount you received from Whittacre's tenants. [P.S.] My wife and son wish you a speedy recovery. Take care that there are prayers and preaching at Etton and Marholm every Sunday. Mr Church may supply Etton on the same terms Pendleton allowed him, and whoever serves Marholm shall have 10s paid him every Sunday. Mrs Pendleton must allow for what was paid before Michaelmas, for she shall enjoy the profits of both livings until then.

## **340** GUYBON TO FITZWILLIAM

*3 October 1704; F(M)C 1353*

I am much better than I have been, and intend for Maxey and Northborough tomorrow. I hope Mr Thomas Wright of Woodson will pay you £100 next week. Ward, Mr Whittacre's tenant paid me on 22 July £6 8s in full of his year's rent, £1 12s allowed him for tax; and Joe Clarke paid £2 8s, his half year's rent, allowing 12s for tax. No more due until Lady Day 1705 for they pay only once a year. The pictures came safe but the case was too large to weigh on our scales. Etton and Marholm are well supplied every Sunday for prayers and preaching by (respectively) Mr Church and Mr Forster.[1] Mrs Bull will hire no maids until she hears certainly when you are coming. She says her ladyship must bring a cookmaid down with her for there is not one to be had in the country now.

[1] Mrs Pendleton's nephew.

## **341** FITZWILLIAM TO GUYBON

*London, 5 October 1704; F(M)C 1354*

I am glad you recover more and more but sorry you venture out so soon for fear of a relapse. You could send Joe Chamberlaine or Goodman Wootton with a note to any of the tenants and they would pay without your venturing abroad, for the weather is cold although very fair. I am sorry I did not know earlier the rents you received for Whittaker who had £11 from me. Write what weight the carrier sets down for the pictures box. Don't let him know we cannot weigh it there for he may impose on us. I have sent two hampers of wine. Let Joe Chamberlaine weigh them and get the weights from the carrier. They told us they weighed 2 cwt 13 q 12 lbs. I have seen neither George Woodcocke nor Sisson[1] so hope Mr Wright pays the £100 next week. I will bring a cookmaid but Mrs Bull must be sure of the others. [P.S.] Write each week whether there is business or not to let us know how you do. My wife is ill.

[1] It is clear from Guybon's accounts and **342** below that Goodman Sissenar of Northborough is meant.

## **342** FITZWILLIAM TO GUYBON

*London, 12 October 1704; F(M)C 1356*

I hope your health is better every day, hearing nothing to the contrary. Glad the wine arrive safely. John Sisson paid me £13 7s 6d[1], but I hear nothing yet of Woodcocke or Wright. I cannot say if the post fine you sent from Mr William Leafield is correct because I could not find my attorney today but will send word next week. Send the enclosed from Mr Whittacre to Joe Clarke and send up their receipts for taxes from the collectors for last year. If Clarke pays you that half year's rent due Mrs Griffin remind him to set off the taxes and enclose that receipt also. There may be a whole year's tax due for taxes are allowed but once a year. Sorry to hear about your sad accident last Sunday.[2]

[1] Guybon's accounts show a repayment of the return of £13 17s 6d to 'Goodman Sissenar'; Disbursements 74.

[2] Probably the loss by fire of Joe Chamberlaine's house, see **344** note and **345** below.

## **343** FITZWILLIAM TO GUYBON

*London, 19 October 1704; F(M)C 1357*

I am glad Mr Wright has promised to pay me money this week for I never needed it more. I have heard nothing from him yet. Mrs Pendleton came unexpectedly last Tuesday night. Her business was to get both livings for her cousin which I refused. At that she was content to accept Etton but I refused that too which she took very ill. She left here this afternoon. Her cousin the minister never visited me.[1] I am sorry you are not yet perfectly well. Only stir abroad on warm days, and with very warm clothes to keep out the cold. Have somebody with you to help you on and off your horse. If the weather is fine go to Northborough and Maxey when the courts are kept, but neglect going rather than endanger your health. While you are forced to stay indoors write out your accounts for the last year, and the Meadow and Wood Books for when I come down. I hope you get me some more money and very soon.

[1] Mr Forster, see **334** notes 2 and 3 above.

## **344** GUYBON TO FITZWILLIAM

*24 October 1704; F(M)C 1358*

I hope Wright has paid this week. Richard Stacy will pay you £60 or £80 and John Watson will pay some. George Woodcock drives Stacy's beasts up. I will return money as fast as I can but never knew it so hard to get. Have enclosed Clarke's and Ward's receipts, and an unsealed letter for Mr 'Whittaker' from Clarke which he wishes you to read. Mrs Pendleton got home Saturday.[1]

[1] Fitzwilliam's marginal note: 'To write to him about paying the fine to Mr William Leaffeild. About Joe Chamberlaine's house being burnt.'

## **345** FITZWILLIAM TO GUYBON

*London, 26 October 1704; F(M)C 1359*

Received yours of the 24th and am glad Mrs Pendleton got well home. One Marshall has paid £14 11s 11d for a John Wattson. Mr Wright has not sent to me yet. I greatly need that £100. Tradesmen dun me for money. I have not been so served since I came into this house and am quite ashamed. They that promise you returns never pay for a fortnight or three weeks after the day, which is inconvenient for I often appoint that day for tradesmen to come for their money. I have given Whittacre Joe Clarke's letter who says God forbid he should expect half a year's rent twice over, and promises to write to Mrs Burman of Stamford. I hope Clarke has Mr Burman's receipt safe for it is his discharge. Whittacre must make good that rent to his aunt, for Whittacre, not the aunt, employed Burman as receiver. I enclose Mr William Leafield's bill for the fine of the land I bought from Dr Barber, which is very right, so pay him 45s.[1] Mrs Pendleton told me of poor Joseph Chamberlaine's loss by fire, which we are sorry for, but would not advise his rebuilding for he will never live there again. It will only harbour a poor tenant who may burn it again. I will buy from him the ground it stood on with the yard and garden to join to Manton's farm. I hope that farm did not suffer by the fire. My wife would have Goody Butler lie in your chamber on a pallet or truckle bed[2] for fear you should be ill in the night.

[1] Paid 13 January; Disbursements 74.

[2] A truckle-bed, a low bed running on 'truckles' or castors; a pallet, a small bed.

## 346 FITZWILLIAM TO GUYBON

*London, 2 November 1704; F(M)C 1361*

I have not yet heard of Wright but to my relief honest George Woodcocke came with £82 3s 1d for a Mr Stacy.[1] Otherwise I would have been forced to borrow to supply the house. I am sorry you are disappointed in returns, and hope you will supply me better in the future. I am glad Joe Chamberlaine's loss is only one of those cottages by the 'berristead'.[2] Mrs Pendleton said it was that house by Manton's farm. I would certainly cast the mud from the moat this dry season if I were there, or had somebody to look to the labourers, but your health and your need to ride about on business not permitting, the labourers could not be trusted since they work by the day. However, I am glad you put me in mind of the dry season, so get some labourers to cleanse the house-well under the pump, the brewhouse moat and that part of the moat beneath the houses of office[3] from the wall of the new drying yard to the bridge into the new orchard. Also the drain under the drying yard to the back of the old stable and slaughter house, and the piece of moat dividing the orchard from the horse pond and lane. The mud from the two latter sections of moat should be thrown on the garden to improve the soil. If the weather continues dry I intend to have the fish ponds cleaned, especially that which we draw water from for the washing or other needs of the house, and that pond next the garden gates and wood yard which was never cleaned in my memory. If any of the Castor people like John Palmer or Holman that rent land near the Milton moat will be at the charge of cleaning the moat for the benefit of the mud I will not hinder them so they may lay the muck on my land, beginning at the dovecote and going as far as they can while the weather lasts. Mr Selby has land near there and though it is not mine he may carry what he pleases, but be sure they make all clean as they go. If the pales round the garden and orchard are rotten, have workmen repair them as fast as they can with new pales to work in with the old, beginning at the old drying yard end at the chapel end of the house. The moat being dry at this time they may stand both sides. If you need wood for pales cut it from nearby trees, for there are so many there they hinder each other.

[1] Guybon calls him Richard Stacey without the 'Mr', Disbursements 74.

[2] Berryingstead is an obsolete word for a threshing floor. However this may be reference to an ancient place name for a document of 1650 concerning the manor of Castor refers to 'the site of the said manor commonly called Berrysteed': *VCH Northamptonshire*, ii. 474.

[3] A privy.

## 347 FITZWILLIAM TO GUYBON

*London, 9 November 1704; F(M)C 1362*

I was very angry with myself that I forgot to thank you for the swan you sent. It proved very young, tender and good meat and we drank your health over it. By good fortune the carrier came in so early that I was able to send my daughter her swan before the market people were gone home. She sends her thanks; it proved very good. I am glad I am to have money this week. The last was quickly paid away to settle debts. I presume Mr Wright will not pay me that money now. Do the paling about the moat substantially and somewhat higher than before. Since that life in Maxey Castle Farm is for sale ask Mr Bimrose his landlady's name and where she lives and I will send to her. She lived in Westmorland Court in Great St Bartholomew's but I hear her husband is dead so she may have moved and I forget her name. [P.S.] I have writ you two warrants for my winter venison. Are my park does fat yet? Lay up the old pales for firewood.[1]

[1] This refers to the new paling of part of the park. On 9 November Guybon paid Robert Bursnoll and his labourer for 20 dayes building the park 'wall', £1 3s. He also paid 3s 6d to seven teams bringing wood from Etton to the sawpit; Disbursements 74.

## **348** FITZWILLIAM TO GUYBON

*[prob. November 1704]; F(M)C 1363*[1]

[P.S.] These very short days it's not good husbandry to do work by the day, especially with nobody to look after workmen, therefore do little more than necessity requires either about paling or anything else; but this is the right season to cut pales and other wood. We must scour ponds and moats now because they are dry and cannot be done any other time. Mrs Pendleton told me young Mr Selby has got a living in Sussex.[2] Let me know if it be so.

[1] Only a fragment of this letter survives but it has an archive number and does not belong to any of the complete letters on either side.

[2] Christopher Selby had gone to Suffolk not Sussex, see above **333** note 2.

## **349** FITZWILLIAM TO GUYBON

*[London,] 16 November 1704; F(M)C 1364*

Hope it's lack of business not lack of health that makes you not write but as you have had two bad fits this summer I fear the worst. Holland the salesman has sent £25 for his brother [Henry] in your parts. I hear nothing of Mr Duncomb your Stamford butcher but depending on his bringing me money I paid every penny I had and the £25 to Mr Colcutt for Manton's farm so have lived on credit all this week. Finding Colcutt had great occasions to sell I borrowed almost all the money I paid for it rather than go without it. Get up all the money you can from the tenants that I may repay this debt. If you had our heavy rain it will put you off cleaning the ponds. How far advanced is the cleaning of the brewhouse moat, Milton House well, etc.? (Hopes Guybon received previous letter with fee deer warrants, and encloses two more.)

## **350** JOHN CATLIN TO FITZWILLIAM

*Maxey, 18 November 1704; F(M)C 1365*

There is 36½ acres freehold land (with a little house in Deepingate let at about 20s a year) lying in Maxey East Field, commonly called Deepingate Field. Thomas Drury of Maxey and John Bolten of Northborough rent it at 9s 6d the acre. It is all arable land and in the best field belonging Maxey manor. It was lately Lord Torrington's and if you wish to buy it Mr Blackwell the attorney will sell it. He will be at his chamber in Clement's Inn from the 21st. Many offer for it, being good land and lying conveniently. I told Mr Guybon and he said he would mention it to you. Widow Rippon had Mr John Eldred, the Deeping St James attorney, write a letter concerning the mill, and she persuaded the jury to sign it but they did not see her copies. They also know the mills have been neglected and badly repaired so they are valued less than formerly.

## 351 FITZWILLIAM TO GUYBON

*London, 23 November 1704; F(M)C 1366*

Glad to receive yours of 21st because I hope you are in good health and understand so from Mr Pemberton and Goodman Dove, who was with me this evening. Rowland Morrice has paid £17, and Henry Hankin £7 12s 2d for Thomas Lawrence. I hope Henry Holland, Fearey and Exton will pay me a round sum for I need it badly. I am sorry Mr Selby's son stands on such high terms. Glad of your rains, but wish you had put me in mind of cleaning the moats two months ago.

Goodman Dove has prevailed with me to lett him plow up the 11 acres and the nineteene acres in Marrham in this manner: first he is to plow up the 11 acres for 4 yeares and the last yeare to sow it with what grass seed is suteable to the ground, as rye grass, clover and St Foile etc.; at 4 yeares end when he has laied that ground thus with grass seed he is then to plow up halfe the nineteene acres for 4 yeares and lay that downe with grass seed, and lastly to plow up the other halfe of the 19 acres and plow that up for 4 yeares more and lay that with grass seed. He is to take a new lease for 12 yeares. I must build him a small barne of 3 little baies and he is to covenant to lay all his mucke upon the plowed land, and the last yeare the same. He must not carry away any of it nor sell any if he goes off the farme. For building the barne he is to find stone and mortar and bring it to the worke and he is to thack it and find straw. I pay only the masons for their workemanship and the carpenter for makeing the roofe and doores and I must find timber.

Since the does are good send one next week, in a flag basket if the weather is cold enough. I wish you had sent Bimrose's landlady's name although I don't doubt to find her now. I don't know what use the 36 acres in Deepingate Field would be except to rent. If it was suitable for adding to a Maxey farm to make all the fields alike it would be something. I need a dozen acres to add to Carter's farm in the Maxey field next Weston's meadow. This 36 acres will not serve that purpose, so I hardly think it's worth buying unless it could be added to my farms to increase their acres in each field, but being in one field it can do me no service. It was Lord Carrington's[1], not Lord Torrington's,[2] and formerly Mr Levett's, and one Norton, a knave who married Levett's widow and cheated his children, mortgaging this and other land to Lord Carrington, who was also cheated and I fear cannot make a good title to it. But I have 'overpurchased myselfe' and cannot spare money save for buying William Joice's house and land in Etton if you can get it at 'a good pennyworth'. I hope Chesseldine will not leave his farm, as he says. He is a good tenant. I would not part with him. Tell him all his reckonings shall be set straight before Lady Day if that's his grievance. Send a considerable sum soon.

[1] Sir James Primrose, 3rd bart. The first baronet had claimed the title of Lord Carrington, but Sir James might more properly have been referred to as Lord Primrose, as he had been raised to the Scottish peerage in this title in 1703: *Complete Peerage*, x. 682.

[2] Arthur Herbert, 3rd Earl of Torrington (1647–1716). *Complete Peerage*, xii. 1, pp. 784–7.

## **352** FITZWILLIAM TO GUYBON

*London, 30 November 1704; F(M)C 1367*

Mr Hankin has paid £20 9s 10d for Mr Exton and Mr Thomas Lawrence has himself paid me £50. The 28th Mr Fearey's warehouse keeper brought me a bill to receive £100 on Sir Francis Child and told me her master had a £100 more to spare if I wished it. I refused at first saying to the woman I could not tell whether you were provided with sufficient money to repay it but, she pressing me saying her master Fearey would stay your own time to repay it and knowing you were concerned that returns were often hard to get I accepted it. Fearey has two notes for his £200, £100 paid the 28th, the other the 29th.[1] If you can get up enough money to buy the 36 acres in Deepingate Field which you say the tenants wish to add to their farms, I am willing to buy it if upon reasonable terms. Truly I am so much in debt for these late purchases that I would not think of it but that you say the tenants need that land. Let Chisseldine's farm to whoever you think the ablest tenant and a quiet, neighbourly man, but the new rent I stand upon. Goodman Chattris of Long Thorpe[2] came today wishing to have the Pear Tree Close as Robert Freeman leaves it next Ladyday. I told Chattris if it were so and you approved I would accept him for a tenant for ten years. He would plough it seven years, sow grass seed the seventh year and so hold it three years after. If Freeman leaves and you approve the bargain he shall pay £30 a year for seven years and £25 a year for the last three; he pays a fat turkey at Christmas or 5s. This is not an ill bargain if you approve of the man and think him able. He got £100 clear that year he was 'waggoner' besides what he was worth before. I had forgotten the warrants. Take what you will for yourself and divide the rest among Peterborough friends and Cousin Bellamy at 'Fawcett' (Farcet). I shall take my venison from the park. If the doe you kill prove well send another next week. My daughter is staying here so have not time to write to Mr Forster and Goodman Dove, but they shall hear next week. View Manton's Farm and let me know the state of repair of the houses, fences and the grove of trees behind the house and the wood near Belsis land. Discover if Mr Colcutt has informed Goodman Manton that he has sold me the farm and whether he has instructed him to pay the arrear of rent to you or not. Colcutt asked me for a copper in the house he says is his. See what Manton says about it. 'I would do all things that are faire between man and man'.

[1] Guybon repaid the first £100 on 8 December, the second on 26 January; Disbursements 74.

[2] Longthorpe manor belonged to Francis St John.

**353** FITZWILLIAM TO GUYBON
*London, 7 December 1704; F(M)C 1368*

I received no letter from you this week but hope you are in good health. I received the venison last Saturday but never had any so dirtily brought to me. I asked that it come up in a flag basket for then I pay for it by the weight since they don't know what is in it and at this season it comes sweet enough. The venison was not very fat but 'pretty meate'. Send another doe next week if none comes this. Send it in a flag basket that it may come clean for they throw it into every dirty place. (Repeats proposed terms of his agreement with Chattris set out in his previous letter.) I gave Mr Pemberton directions to draw his lease and Goodman Dove's but you know Dove's several rents better than I do so Pemberton must not draw them until you have given me your opinion. They must pay for drawing the leases. Fearey's £200 and Mr Lawrence's £50 being paid away I need money again. Tell Mrs Pendleton I wish Mr Pemberton to copy the counterpart of the lease her husband gave me when he first came to Marholm. The original is locked up at Milton. She shall have it again though it's no use now her husband is dead.

**354** FITZWILLIAM TO GUYBON
*London, 14 December 1704; F(M)C 1369*

Hankin has paid £24 5s for Mr Exton which came very seasonably, for these little purchases have put me out of money, but I was loath to lose the opportunity which might never have come again, 'at least in one age'. Business has fallen out 'very cross' besides my wife's illness which has prevented my coming down earlier, but my son and I intend to be at Milton for a short time soon after the holidays, and when the days grow longer, I hope at the latter end of February, we intend to come down 'for good and all'. I am sorry the drink is so spoiled. Dispose of the small beer if fit for anything and the strong, save one hogshead for when I come down. This weather it won't grow worse. If Goodman Dove won't thatch his new barn when built it won't be built by me. He made no scruple here in town. As to the tax, I will pay no window tax, parliament intending that for the tenants 'and I will not go about to breake a law'. So agree with [Dove] on all points and get Pemberton to draw a lease before he is allowed to 'putt plow into the ground'. I gave Pemberton pretty full instructions, but you were to supply the rents of the several grounds, third part of the taxes, rent fowls of the several grounds, with a good fat turkey cock or 5s for his ploughing, for he advances no rent but must give a New Year's gift. Have I let the Pear Tree Close dear enough? Give to the poor at Christmas as usual. Colcutt claims the copper at Manton's farm is his for he says he bought all the other sisters' rights out and Manton's wife died childless so he expects to use the copper himself. I hope to receive a good sum about Christmas for Marholm wool money. Don't let Goody Freeman of Milton run in arrear. 'You are too apt to forbeare people longer then does them good'. Hasten them at this time: I am so short of money. Thomas Freeman usually paid at this time from the money received for his wool and wether sheep at Christmas. You write to me about buying Lord Carrington's 36 acres in Deepinggate Field, but let me know which tenants hold it, how many acres each holds, and what they pay an acre. Also whether the land is arable or pasture, and whether 'good measure' or only 'feild measure' which is smaller. I will not buy William Joice's house unless he is at the charge of a fine. I will not take his bond for I fear he has made a purchase which will undo him.

## ANNE, LADY FITZWILLIAM TO GUYBON (1369 v)

Guybons, I disier you will giv 20ss at the sacrament at Crismas at Marham and for whot I iust to order you to lay out at Crismas I live it to you to doe as you think fitting.[1] Pray take care of youer health and keep yor self very worme this cold wether, soe I rest yor frend . . .

[1] A reference to almsgiving which was traditional at the Christmas celebration of Holy Communion.

## **355** FITZWILLIAM TO GUYBON

*London, 21 December 1704; F(M)C 1370*

Francis Guybon, Yours of the 19th I received yesterday and am glad to understand I shall receave some money this weeke though I feare it much. As to your tennant at Marrham Richard Burton's comeing up I shall be glad to see him when he comes but I assure you before hand I will not consent to plow any land till I come into the countrey and see the ground first and so he may save himselfe that labour and charge of comeing up unless he has other business, and as for Joseph Chamberlaine I say the same too. He shall plow up neither of those closes. I am sorry I gave my consent that Goodman Dove shall plow which has sett the rest upon demanding the same priviledge, and if he scruples in the least thacking the barne and doeing the rest of the worke that I mentioned in my letter [to] you, I hereby order you to discharge him from plowing at all. As to Richard Cox I know not the man in the least. You know best whither he be able or not to deale with a farme and you know what grounds are to lett at Marrham which I am ignorant off. What I say is this: have a care how you take any body into Marrham for feare of bringing a charge to the towne. You see what Allerton does as to Sowgate; you know what Castor does as to John Freeman and his wife who when they came first to Marrham were very unlikely to be a towne charge as this Richard Cox may be, but times change and so may men's conditions from riches to poverty. I say not this to undervallew the man. He may be as substantiall a man as most men in the towne but he's a stranger to me. I write this to you by way of precaution. If you like the man and know his circumstances do you make an agreement with him for as much as you can thinke he is able to deale with. Don't lett him come up to me for I know nothing of him nor the grounds he would hire. As to Mr Church[1] I am glad I know his mind. As he was first recommended to me so he is the first the liveing has been offered too. I do not want for candidates enough for those liveings so if he won't accept I know of another or two that will be glad on it on those termes. He may keep Maxey and Etton both, only keeping a curate, and can't he live upon Maxey liveing as he has done and lett the proffitts of Etton build the house? He shall be proffered it no more; there's another ready for it. As to young Mr Forster he may be very deserveing for all what I know of him but I thinke him yett too young to have a cure of souls. I will not dispose of Etton till I know Mr Church's mind further which I suppose I shall heare of soone one way or other . . .

[1] Rev. Richard Church of Norfolk (1657–1716) Vicar of Maxey 3 Oct 1701, Rector of Etton 12 Feb 1705; *Longden*, iii. 113.

## 356 FITZWILLIAM TO GUYBON

*London, 4 January 1704/5; F(M)C 1371*

> Did not write last week having no business nor a letter from you. Your tenant Richard Burton has paid me your £33 10s, and a Samuel Sylverwood of Long Thorpe paid £18 10s.

As to Mr Forster I can by no meanes approve of your choice of him for minister of Marrham. He is so young yett that he cannot be fitt for a cure of soules, and besides you formerly writt to me you thought him too young. The gentleman may deserve very well but my wife and selfe are now much advanc't in yeares and we desire to have a graver man for our conversation. I am sorry to deny you any thing but if you do but well consider his yeares and that he tooke orders but last midsummer you will be of my mind. I hope God Almighty will send freinds for the poore children[1] . . .

[1] Presumably referring to Mrs Pendleton's children.

## 357 JOHN CATLIN TO FITZWILLIAM

*Maxey, 6 January 1704/5; F(M)C 1372*

I received your honour's letter dated 25th of November on the 23rd of December, and the 36 acres of land I wrote of lying in Deepingate Feild is certainly the best feild belonging to Maxey and many of your lordship's tenants doth want land in that feild. John Carter wanteth land in the Parkhurne Feild that is next Westdeeping Meadow, but this feild would be as conveniant for him as that, it being sown every year and fallowed by parcels when the owners please, only they have the worst crops that sowe too often before they fallow. William Riddington, Thomas Druery, Robert Osborne and many others wanteth land in Deepingate Feild. This 36 acres was in the tennure of William Day, and Thomas Druery and John Bolton gave more rent to gett it from him. Thire is some small parcels in Deepingate Feild that is lett for 10 or 12 shillings an acre and most of it is lett for 8 shillings. Henry Vaughan lett all his arrable land except that in Deepingate Feild. The worst feild belonging to Maxey is the Church Feild, Bardyke Feild and the Mill Feild, and if the title was performed to your lordship it would be very conveniant. Thire is about 40 acres more in the same Deepingate Feild which I heard say is to be sold (since I writt the last letter) by a shopkeeper in Castlebiteham.[1] If your honour pleaseth to buy that I will know something about the price and write it to your lordship. Thire is a little cotage in Maxey with 4 acres of land which had been in lease for three lives and the two last died in the years 1693 and 1694. They were Widow Adington and her son John and after they died John Adington's wife having one son a child and two daughters elder then he, she with the help of her two daughters did pay Mr Vaughan tenn pounds who promised her a new lease of the cotage againe but he never brought them it, and now it is lett by Mary Adington, ever since the year 1696 when her mother dyed, for £2 18s a year and she is married (and lives at Langtauft[2] a mile beyond Market Deeping) to one Richard Ashlye. He pays 12s 6d a year for it and that hath been the rent from the year 1694 till now and when your lordship pleaseth it may be altered. Mrs Vaughan lives in her old house againe of your lordship's, late Eedesses. She hath lett her arrable land in Deepingate Feild to Thomas Druery and John Bimrose junior for 9s the acre. Her pasture land is not yet lett except the Little Park Close which is lett to Brown, a wheel right in Market Deeping for 7 pounds a year. I do not here she is likely to be married yet. I shall be ready to attend on Mr Guybon when he pleaseth to take her accompts and if your lordship would be pleased to make her shew her lease betwixt this and Ladyday next it might be known what land was not expressed in her lease and disposed of as your lordship pleaseth, and whensoever I hear or see any thing amiss I will write it to your lordship . . .

[1] Castle Bytham, Lincs.
[2] Langtoft, Lincs.

## 358 FITZWILLIAM TO GUYBON

*London, 11 January 1704/5; F(M)C 1373*

Joe Bull has paid £20 in part of rent, my son giving a receipt. Henry Hankin has paid £42 19s 1d for Mr Exton. I am glad Exton has promised to pay some money each week this month. I always allowed the minister who preached at Marholm before Mr Pendleton had it 10s a Sunday. Pay this to Mr Forster till he leaves the cure, and the rest due Michaelmas quarter pay to Mrs Pendleton. I will write about this Christmas quarter in my next, for I am in haste going to the burial of my old goldsmith, Mr Heriot. Let what money you send in future be brought to my house. Does Manton pay you any rent for Mr Colcutt? If he says he has sent it to Colcutt by any other hand tell him he must stir no copper nor anything else out of the house without my order, and see if the copper is there, and let me know it's worth.

## 359 FITZWILLIAM TO GUYBON

*London, 18 [January] 1704/5; F(M)C 1375*[1]

Received no letter this week so hope you are in good health. A Mr Brampston has paid £95 18s 8d for Henry and John Hollands. Allow any receipts signed by my son or my wife. I suppose you know their hands. [P.S.] Send all returns you can between now and the 26th when I am to pay away a great sum. I need an answer to my queries about Thomas Manton and his farm. I hope Mr Wright got down safe and has made a draft of the new Etton parsonage, and that Mr Church[2] can come up next week for his presentation and institution.

[1] The letter is damaged.
[2] See **355** note 1.

## 360 FITZWILLIAM TO GUYBON

*London, 25 January 1704/5; F(M)C 1376*

I received £22 11s 9d from James Dove and £82 11s 5d from Hankin for Mr Exton. These sums came mighty opportunely for tomorrow I am to pay a great sum to Mr Ballett's administrators. Have not seen Colcutt nor his son lately but will tell him Manton has his money for them. Before I let Mr Whitacre know you have received this £2 11s for his aunt's rent, due Michaelmas 1702, from Joe Clarke, discover if Clarke, who paid this rent to Mr Burman formerly, ever received it back again. If not I think it very hard Clarke should pay twice. When I know the truth I will discourse Whittacre about it. I have not heard lately from Mr Pemberton. What he does about the living he does by my direction. My wife is still very ill with her old distemper and my son and daughter much troubled with the toothache.

[P.S.] I forgott in my last letter to acquaint you that my Lord Mordaunt,[1] sonne to the Earle of Peterborough, intends to stand for knight of the shire of our county and we are all ingaged to serve him what we can, therefore when you ride out amungst the tennants speake to every one of them that is a freeholder to be for him and I shall take it kindly from them, and any others that are not my tennants, desire them from me to be for the Lord Mordaunt.[2] He is a person that has deservd so well from the nation that nobody can in reason refuse. He has been in our armies all these warrs, and in these two famous battells this last summer has been so wounded that he lost the use of one of his armes; besides his family has lived in our county with great honour and reputation above 200 yeares; has been all along one of the lord leuitenant of the county and his father the Earle of Peterborough is at this time sole lord leiutenant of it and has been so these 17 yeares together. The young lord is a person of great sobriety and prudence and much to be vallewed by all discreet and sober persons. Therefore pray do him what service lies in your power both in my severall townes likewise in Peterborough and elsewhere, speakes to all the ministers and they will secure their parishioners.

[1] John Mordaunt (1681–1710) eldest son of Charles, 3rd Earl of Peterborough and 1st Earl of Monmouth. He lost an arm at Blenheim, *Burke's Dormant . . . and Extinct Peerages* (1883) p. 381.

[2] The impact of Guybon's 'electioneering', or lack of it, is examined in the Introduction, above pp. xiv–xv.

## 361 FITZWILLIAM TO GUYBON

*[London, 1 February 170]4[/5]; F(M)C 1403*[1]

[Phea]sants came up very good. We sent my daughter the best of each sort and your health was drunk over them in both places. On 29 January a John Marshall paid me £8 5s 1d on Mr Henry Lawrence's account. I hope you will supply more soon. Had no letter this week but hope you are well. I wonder I hear nothing of Mr Church and believe he is sick for I have expected him in town this fortnight. Enquire of Maxey people on Saturday and write me word by Sunday's post why he is not come up. [P.S.] Enquire of some of Ufford how Willmott does, if he left home and how long gone. What interest have you and Mr Pemberton made among the freeholders for Lord Mordaunt?

[1] The letter is damaged, and this date is conjectural. It is filed between 21 June and 5 July 1705, but

the enquiry about Mr Church's non-appearance in London, and his appearance there by 8 February 1705 (see **362** below), suggests that that this is the 'missing' letter for the week of 1 February (since Fitzwilliam rarely omitted his weekly letter). Note also the reference to Lord Mordaunt.

## 362 FITZWILLIAM TO GUYBON

*London, 8 February 1704/5; F(M)C 1378*

Francis Guybon, I and all of us are much concerned to heare by yours that you have had a sharpe fitt of an ague. I hope you have heard no more of it since and you must take great care of yourselfe and not be out late of nights this winter season. Pray lett me have a letter from you this next post to lett us heare how you are and write as often as you can till you are quite gott ridd of this troublesome companion though yours only mentions how you are, and your name to it, which will be no great trouble besides the carriage of the letters which charge I will not vallew to have the sattisfaction of heareing how you are. Mr Church is in towne and finds some trouble about Maxey liveing, the continueing of which will be a great charge to him but it cannot be helpt.

> Mr Pemberton has not yet come to town. Send up Mr Halstead's notes. I fear I shall want money long before that is paid.

My wife would by all meanes have Mother Buttler lie in your chamber when you are any thing ill for feare you want any thing in the nights, and lett the pallett bedd be brought out of the wardrobes for her to lie in. Pray do not stirr out of your chamber of one weeke at least for feare the least cold should make your ague returne againe. Praying for your good recovery with all our kind loves to you I am your loveing freind . . .

## 363 FITZWILLIAM TO GUYBON

*London, 15 February 1704/5; F(M)C 1379*

> Mr Halstead has paid £23 off the four bills on Marholm tenants, amounting to £72 17s, but the bills not having then arrived he said he would pay the rest on the due date. In your letter of the 5th you reported you had paid Mr Exton all the money he had lately paid on returns amounting to £245 14s 2d.[1] In my books I find not near that sum returned by him either paid to me or to any goldsmith. I enclose an extract from my book from 1 March 1703[/4] to this day which amounts to about £245 16s 8d, but since Michaelmas the money he paid does not amount to above £87 13s 11d, unless what the Holland brothers paid was on his account, and that would only amount to £208 12s 7d. Look over the receipts Mr Exton gave you and if they amount to more than I set down they must be counterfeit. If my list is not right send a list of receipts received from him which I will compare with my book, to see where the mistake is and make enquiries.

We do all much rejoice to heare you have losst your ague. Pray do not stirr out but of warme daies. It's not so farr if the tennants brought their rents home to Milton. You may send Joe Chamberlaine to order them so to do. I writt this day sennight to Mrs Pendleton to write me an account how you were for feare you would not be able to do it and desired her to gett the pallatt bed into your chamber that Gooddy Butler might lie there to watch you when you were very ill. In your next lett me know if she had it. I am glad Harry Watts is married, if she proves but a good fortune to him at any time. You must talke to the old woman to be kind to her. I am much concerned for Mr Gascoigne, both for his owne, his father and mother sake, who were all very good people, but still hope he may recover. In your next lett me heare further about him and what his distemper is ... [P.S.] Mr Richard Church[2] I have presented to Etton liveing and he has had the bishop's institution and went out of towne last Tuesday afternoone and I suppose will be inducted this weeke so as to take possession next Sunday and preach on his owne account. Mr Paulin Phelips[3] I have presented to Marrham and the bishop has given him institution. He goes out of towne to morrow morning, that he cannot be inducted this weeke so you must take care to have some body preach at Marham next Sunday after which he will take care of it himselfe.

[1] Guybon noted this sum as 'returned to my lord' on 26 January, Disbursements 74.
[2] See **355** note 1.
[3] Pawling Phelips (1678–1735) Rector of Marholm 14 Feb 1705 and also Rector of Woolley, Hunts until death 22 Feb 1735; Longden, x. 261–3.

## 364 JOHN CATLIN TO FITZWILLIAM
*Maxey, 16 February 1704/5; F(M)C 1380*

(Had been at Stamford with Mr Huss of Castle Bytham, owner of the 40 acres, who had lost the chance to make his planned purchase at Castle Bytham, and so was in no hurry to sell, but would if he liked the price offered. Promised Catlin should hear further but Catlin had heard nothing yet. Mrs Stevens, a widow at Bourne [Lincolnshire], planned to sell speedily 30 acres of land in Maxey and two cottages, all freehold, let for £13 a year. Part was let to Richard Turnill, part to Widow Paddy, a cottage and some land to Robert Tyers; a small house and close to Edward Wise. One Briggs of Maxey and a kinsman had bid £200 for it and the tenants feared they would be turned out, especially Widow Paddy and Robert Tyers, who said they had spent much on the land and now must leave it 'except my lord buyeth it'. Widow Stevens had promised to do nothing for a week or more until Catlin could hear from Fitzwilliam. Asks Fitzwilliam not to let Guybon know it was Catlin who had mentioned this land lest he be angry, and to send word if he did not wish to buy the land for Mrs Stevens must sell speedily, it being mortgaged.)

## 365 FITZWILLIAM TO GUYBON
*London, 1 March 1704/5; F(M)C 1381*

I received your list of Exton's returns and we are both mistaken in our reckonings. Your mistake is £53 18s 5d paid 20 October 1703, five months before this reckoning begins. It was paid at Heriot's, and accounted for before Heriot's death. My mistake is the £82 11s 5d paid 24 January 1704[/5], which I ordered to be paid at a goldsmith's and being entered in his book did not enter in mine. All this makes £424 6s 9d paid by Exton's order by Henry Hankin, Halstead and the two Holland brothers since 1 March 1703[/4], a year today; your letter of the 20th mentioned that exact sum. I have been paid since my last: from Thomas Lawrence £40; from Hankin for Thomas Whitehead £27 4s 2d and for John Miller's son £4 9s 2d.[1] Since you are pleased I am satisfied with your choice of a tenant for Mr Exton's farm at Etton; only the two brothers Chamberlaine being unmarried their farm houses are not kept so handsomely within as if they had wives. If [young Adam Chamberlaine's][2] house and homestead at Northborough is that his father[3] bought I am willing to buy it, but his mother has it during her life. I cannot spare money at present but would set it off the rent. You and he contrive it as cheaply as you can. I will get cauliflower seed for Joe Chamberlaine. Take care Chisseldine pays all his rent and leaves all in repair before his stock is removed from the farm. Thank God this bout of my gout is over. [P.S.] My wife, poor woman, continues ill of her old distemper. Mrs Pendleton must sell her sheep, and let Joe Chamberlaine have the Old Park or I will take it in hand. I will have no sheep about Milton yards. Don't let Goodman Dove plough any of my land unless he provides stone and thatching for the barn as he proposed. If he does not I will charge him 5s an acre for all he ploughs. Take care Chatteris cuts no more bushes than he should near the hedges of Pear Tree Close which are needed to maintain the fences.

[1] Guybon noted it as 'returned by John Miller by order of Thomas Whitehead', Disbursements 74.
[2] Not named by Fitzwilliam but identified in postscript to **366** and by **369** below.
[3] Old Joseph Chamberlaine, Fitzwilliam's former gardener.

## **366** FITZWILLIAM TO GUYBON

*London, 8 March 1704/5; F(M)C 1382*

Francis Guybon, I received a letter from you dated the 6th instant. Mr Exton paid me last Munday nintyfive pounds for which he has my receipt and I was glad to heare by him how well you lookt and how well you were. As to Mrs Pendleton I am not to be told by you nor any one how farr I am to extend my kindness to her and hers. I know best my owne intentions and shall take my owne time. I was no waies obliged to her or Mr Pendleton but paid them for all services they did for me or mine, but I am sure he was obliged to me for all his wellbeing. As to the ground, who would have thought but she had putt off her stock last Michaelmass, her husband dieing a moneth before that time. She could not immagine she must alwaies live at Milton and we being comeing downe for these last 2 or 3 yeares, she could not thinke but it was fitt for her to remove before our comeing. We cannot spare those roomes she now makes use off and my wife and selfe being now advanc't in yeares and become sickly we must not be disturbed by the noise of children. If she has so many sheep undisposed off she may hold the ground another yeare. I have no halfe yeare's lands belonging to me. She must hold it a whole year or not at all because you mention she may hold it till Michaelmas but I cannot consent to that. My wife gave her good advise when she was last in towne and that was to take a little house in Peterborough and take boarders and then she would have the opportunity of educateing her children especially her sonn at the free schoole. We will do the poore woman no wrong in any respect but will countenance all we can. What I write to you is to go no farther I suppose. You mention I am like to have grounds enough in my hands at next Ladyday. I hope not so but if it be I desire to know in time which grounds they are and who are the tennants to them now. It is not the goeing of one poore ewe in the yards I vallew, it's a great many that cropps my greens about the court yard that does me the mischeife. The grass in the yards I vallew not so much as my laurell trees etc.

Young Colcutt tells me his father ordered him last November to tell Manton to pay the due rent to you and that I had bought the farm. They had no reply and came for the rent. Call on Manton for it, set all taxes right due last Michaelmas, and any repairs done to the house and cottages before the sale. Let the tenants sign the reckoning, and send it up so I can hand it to Colcutt with the rest of the money. I suppose you know that several of the Aylesworth tenancies that I bought off Dr Barber and Mr Weaver pay the king's taxes. When Joe Bull was in town with beasts before Christmas he told me he would rent Belham Field no longer if you would not forgive him £5 a year you had raised the rent above what Mr Phillips, the previous tenant, paid. If you would have to abate the £5 to another you might as well do it for him, if he is a good tenant and pays his rent. I mention this because you said I would have enough ground on my hands and perhaps this is one which you could prevent. He is willing to give the same rent as Mr Phillips. [P.S.] Is the house etc in Northborough that young Chamberlaine[1] would sell the same his father bought? I suppose his mother has it for life if she still lives?

[1] Adam Chamberlaine, see **369** and note to **365**.

## **367** FITZWILLIAM TO GUYBON

*London, 15 March 1704/5; F(M)C 1385*

I received today eight guineas, £8 12s, from Mrs Frances Strafford for Mr Forster and gave her my receipt. When he presents it pay him in guineas or silver as he chooses. I enclose a rental of Barber and Weaver's estate in Castor and Aylesworth. They are very cheap and therefore paid all taxes and the whole rent. None of the enclosure is ploughed so see it is kept so. You know next Lady Day's rents of Manton's farm and the cottages belonging to it are mine. If Mrs Bull and her son say nothing of leaving Belham Field, say nothing to them. 'I am as willing to save £5 a yeare as you can have me.' Tell Mr Church I have paid Mr Rocke the counsel two guineas as he desired, which he must repay you. Tell [George] Chamberlaine who rents the Etton tithes that I wish him to pay Church in full what is due him for serving the cure there to last Michaelmas, and to pay you the remainder of the tithes save parliamentary taxes. Did George Chamberlaine pay Pendleton his rent half yearly or quarterly?

If quarterly he must not part with that due at Christmas without my order. Let him pay Church for his curacy; I suppose it's £5.

## 368 JOHN CATLIN TO FITZWILLIAM

*Maxey, 20 March 1704/5; F(M)C 1386*

(Had received Fitzwilliam's answer about Widow Stevens' and a particular of Eaton's estate from Mr Church, and had carried out Fitzwilliam's commands. Had examined the town book to know some land more 'justly'. Eaton's property consisted of 15 acres 1½ rods in Maxey, comprising a house, orchard and close; closes in 'the Hurne', the Hurne Field, Deepingate Meadow, Deepingate Field, Church Field, March Field, Windmill Hill Field, South Field. Another half acre 'called a hempland' next the homestead he rented from Fitzwilliam for 4s rack rent. The four acre close in the Hurne was 'open with the Hurne Feild' and lay fallow once in four years. A rod in Millfield belonged to Maxey poor, and being close to the mill was often 'stroyed'. John Eaton had long rented it for a groat a year. All Eaton's estate was worth 7s an acre save an acre or so in the March and Church Field at 6s. Homestead and house, once repaired, could be rented for £3 a year, but would cost £40 to repair. Did not know what rent Edward Eaton paid, but the farm had been let for more when all the buildings were standing. Had asked Fitzwilliam not to let Guybon know he had written because he did not have his advice or permission to do so. Thanks Fitzwilliam for his promise of employment.)

## 369 FITZWILLIAM TO GUYBON

*London, 22 March 1704/5; F(M)C 1387*

If Adam Chamberlaine's Northborough house and homestead is not a very 'pretty thing', and all things in good repair, I will not value it, needing money for more urgent occasions, but do as you think most to my advantage. I am very sorry for honest Mr Whinyates. The last term that he dined with me I feared I should never see him more. Who is like to succeed him in the clerk of the peace's place, etc? I wish Lord Exeter would give it poor George Leaffeild. If you see Mr Exton at Peterborough next Saturday tell him I hear nothing of the coleseed chapman that promised to pay me £47 for him on the 17th. I hear nothing yet of Mr Halstead about Marholm wool money.[1] When you have money to spare I should be glad of it. I don't know which you mean by the 'Neither Goodlucks' but am glad you have let it. If you mean the Goodlucks the wheelwright of Aylesworth, Sechell, rented it was always called the 'Stoney' Goodlucks. What made Sechell leave it for he said he would take it with the farm? Has Mr 'Phellipps'[2] come to Marholm and if so does he live in the parsonage? If not let me know when you expect him to come for good and all. [P.S.] I wrote to Mr Pemberton a week ago. If you see him in Peterborough ask him if he had my letter.

[1] See below **371**.
[2] See note to **363** above.

## 370 FITZWILLIAM TO GUYBON

*London, 29 March 1705; F(M)C 1388*

If Adam Chamberlaine's house is a good house and improvable I will pay him ready money for it, but we have nobody there to search the title, so the writings must come up unless you can think of a lawyer. I am unwilling to pay any fine for it. I suppose old Goodman Chamberlaine made no other settlement on his wife and children than by his will so it must be inspected with the other writings. Let me know who made his will. 'I am sorry for that silly imprudent man Mr Leaffeild. He deserves to starve that knows not how to mannage his discourse at these yeares of his.' The Goodlucks Goody Freeman leaves was always called Middle Goodlucks. I thought her man who managed her concerns since Freeman died intended to rent that ground and the Marholm house where William Freeman lived, and then his widow and Tom Timpany. That fellow was here when Burton of Marholm was last in town and asked for it, but I referred him to you, being a stranger to his circumstances. Why does he not have it, and who lives in the house for it will 'take despaire' if it stands empty? I hope to be down before long. I am sorry we need so much stone for three places. I thought Ullitt's house, where old Hipwell lived, was a strong old house which might have stood long. Waldrum Hall being on a fenny, moory soil will not bear a heavy stone building, but it may be stone built as high as the beasts rub with their horns, 'horne high as the countrey man calls it'. It is a sorry inconsiderable house and not worth laying out much on it. Carter's Maxey house was a good strong, stone house, in good repair. A small part next the street bellied out. I don't know how you have neglected it but an easy charge could have repaired it with a few loads of stone. Employ John Catlin to report what is done in your absence there and at Etton and Waldrum Hall, for he can walk to those places once a day. I hear nothing of money from Halstead or anyone else and now want it very much. Take care of me next week.

## 371 FITZWILLIAM TO GUYBON

*London, 5 April 1705; F(M)C 1389*

A month ago you sent me four notes of John Halstead for the use of his father, Thomas Halstead, the Cambridge woolman: one to James Dove of Marholm for £25 3s; one to Mrs Bull for £16; one to Mr Joseph Bull for £10; one to Richard Burton for £21 14s. These he has now paid.

I hope you have made all the interest you can with the freeholders within my townes in behalfe of the Lord Mordaunt, the Earle of Peterborough's sonne. I named no other person to you because I reserved one vote for Sir Justinian Isham if he intended to stand, as many people thought he would not. Now I am sattisfied he will stand pray acquaint the freeholders I shall take it kindly they give Sir Justinian Isham their second vote but if it happins that Sir Justinian gives it up before the pole is taken then I desire they will give their votes to Sir Saint Andrew St John of whome I heare a great character. If Sir Justinian Isham comes into our parts waite of him and assure him from me that all the service you can do for him he may command, but withall you may tell him underhand he must joine with my Lord Mordaunt's agents in defrayeing the charges of the poore freeholders otherwaies few of them will go to Northampton and they make up the greatest number of the freeholders. Pray send me some more money soone for I am in want of it. Do not lett Sir Justinian Isham see this letter and if he asks for it lett him know there is other business of mine in it that you cannot part with it and is not fitting you should shew to any one, and I would not have him know that you are to order the freeholders from me to give the votes to Sir St Andrew St John in case Sir Justinian does not come to a pole, for everybody beleaves he will loose it and so will not come to a pole, and if not, I am then for Sir Saint Andrew St John but this is a secrett. I expect my 2 new parsons should go to the election when it is and give their votes. Tell them both so.

## 372 FITZWILLIAM TO GUYBON

*London, 12 April 1705; F(M)C 1390*

Yesterday Hankin paid me £37 3s 10d for Mr Exton, but I hear nothing of the £47 for coleseed to be paid above a month since. I hope Lord Mordaunt will be elected knight of the shire notwithstanding your contrary report. This is only noised abroad to discourage his party. Make sure our freeholders are for him. Tell Manton young Colcutt calls frequently for his rent. I suppose you don't intend pulling down William Ullitt's or Carter's houses at Maxey but only shoring up the roofs while you pull down the defective walls. A little stone will make all good. They make nothing here of taking down the whole side wall of a house almost as big as Milton, setting up props under the roof and lesser props under each floor and so build up the walls to them. The last Lord Exeter[1] intended to do this to Burleigh House had he lived. I was never at Waldrum Hall in my life so cannot judge, but if there must be a new house build it according to the rent it gives. If it will stand leave it until I come down. I wonder the new Aylesworth and Castor tenants are so backward in paying their rents. Their old landlords made them keep 'touch'[2] and in due time. Keep them to it and don't permit an ill habit as you have the other poorer tenants to my great loss. I am glad Mr Pemberton is better. His life is of great concern to his family. Send all the money possible for I must leave no debts behind. Have you had good rain in the country and will there be plentiful fruit?

[1] John Cecil, 5th Earl of Exeter, died 1700.
[2] To keep touch is to keep covenant, to keep faith.

## 373 FITZWILLIAM TO GUYBON

*London, 19 April 1705; F(M)C 1392*

Mr Colcutt wishes you would receive the rent for that little house next Mr Wright's and the 'farme backe gate' where Serjeant now lives, and that you would sell the copper and iron work at Manton's farm. I suppose Manton will buy it. I am sorry to hear Manton is so ill for if he dies I don't know where you will get so good a tenant. Yesterday a Wisbech man paid Mr Exton's

£47 for coleseed. I am heartily sorry to hear of John Webdale's death. He was a man 'like enough to live'. Don't slight the work at Ullitt's and John Carter's houses. I am glad you have had good rains but sorry you have a sickly time of it. [P.S.] We are all in good health but my wife is seldom well. Jack and daughter Barrington remember themselves kindly to you.

## 374 FITZWILLIAM TO GUYBON

*London, 3 May 1705; F(M)C 1393*

Received yours with the enclosed bill of £20 8s. Hankin has paid £16 19s 8d for a Marmaduke Tomlinson. I am very sorry Goodman Manton is dead and wish you a good tenant in his place. Mrs Bull is a good tenant and her rent safe. You should have done what she wants in reason as much as for any tenant belonging to my estate. Don't put her off to the last. If part of her little barn is fallen down it's proper to repair it before harvest that she may lay her grain in it. Her stable was strong and good when I left the country and part of it was rebuilt for William Rycraft. I wonder that should want rebuilding but the little barn was always a sorry thing standing in a wet place and if rebuilt it should be set on a drier soil nearer the great barn. It would be well placed between the great barn and the field gate next her ploughed ground and so be a fence to her yard, keeping it warm from the cold winterly winds for the benefit of 'the layer[1] of her beasts at straw', but at this distance I submit to yours and her better judgment. Take care of everything and return what money you can.

[1] Layer, an enclosure for animals to lie down.

## 375 FITZWILLIAM TO GUYBON

*London, 10 May 1705; F(M)C 1394*[1]

The merchant in Catteaton Street accepted the £20 bill you sent but will not pay it before June 10. I will then pay Mr Colcutt the money Thomas Manton paid you. Who are Thomas Manton's executors? Who is likely to take the farm and what are you likely to sell the copper for? Colcutt says Jackson the grocer, who married his wife's sister, received the last rent he had from the weaver living in the cottage next Mr Wright's house and my farmyard. He says there is three years' rent due since then. Mr Whittacre asks you to receive a year's rent from Ward and Clarke his Northborough tenants. On 24 October 1704 you sent up three tax receipts for those little things of Whittacre's, one for Ward, one for Clarke and one for 7s 6d from John Harrison. Whittacre knows nothing of Harrison and wishes to know why it should be placed to his account. I hear the election for knights of the shire is due in a week at Northampton. Go charge the freeholders to vote for Lord Mordaunt. What care is taken to carry the poorer freeholders there, bearing their charges there and back? You [formerly] wrote me that Sir Justinian Isham[2] had been among the [freeholders]. Let me know when the election is to be at Peterborough. [There are rumours] in town that Mr Charles Parker will stand but [I do] not believe it. Get the parsonage at Marholm ready for the new parson that he may have no excuse for not coming to live there. My daughter has gone to Essex for the summer and we are preparing to leave town speedily.

[1] Letter damaged, words in brackets conjectural.
[2] Sir Justinian Isham of Lamport Hall (1658–1730), 4th bart., a prominent Tory and member for Northamptonshire from 1698 to 1730.

## 376 FITZWILLIAM TO GUYBON

*London, 24 May 1705; F(M)C 1396*

Hankin has paid £14 19s 10d for Marmaduke 'Thomlinson'. I hear nothing from Mr Bevis as yet. Money will be very welcome. I hope you get a good tenant for Manton's farm next year, but this year the executor must hold it for no warning was given and Lady Day is passed. Send an account of the small estate at Maxey you say is convenient for Carter's farm and I will consider it. We passed the accounts with the county a little before I last left the country, about October 1696, and there remained only a very small sum in my hands. I suppose this £187 6s you say remains due the county is not in my hands but the tenants', and in that I shall not be much concerned; otherwise I should. I am sorry to hear Lord Mordaunt lost the election because I was engaged for him, but the two old ones who have carried it are very honest gentlemen. I am glad to hear you are all in good health at Milton. We are also but for my poor wife 'who is very ill most an end with the collicke in her stomach'. Sir Charles Barrington lost his election by a great deal of foul play from the 'fanaticke' party though we are [not] sorry for we hope now he will stay at home and mind his own business more.

## 377 JOHN CATLIN TO FITZWILLIAM

*Maxey, 29 May 1705; F(M)C 1398*

(Mr Hust of Castle Bitham has told Catlin to inform Fitzwilliam he will sell his Deepingate estate, let for £22 5s a year, for £420. He can be found at the Blue Boar, Stamford, any Friday. Encloses the particulars along with particular of Widow Stevens of Bourne's estate. Guybon had bargained a fortnight before but she asked £300, £50 more than she could sell it for, unless by parcels. Believes she will take £250. Doing some accounts for Mrs Webdale whose husband had died Catlin had found an acquittance of the rent John Bimrose paid his landlady for the [Maxey] castle farm. Money and tax made £29 6s 8d; Fitzwilliam's rent for it £33 17s 8d: in all £63 3s 4d[1] a year. Mrs Vaughan had let 12 acres of her 'lea ground' to Mr Sharp of Deeping St James for 25s an acre which he had ploughed and sowed with flax. She had told Guybon she would pay no more rent until her accounts were settled. If Fitzwilliam found Catlin an employment under Guybon it would be 'verry charitabley bestowed'; he would be a very faithful, obedient servant.)

[1] Catlin's addition is incorrect. The figure should be £63 4s 4d.

**378** FITZWILLIAM TO GUYBON
*[London, ? June] 1705; F(M)C 1399*[1]

(Regrets there is no mention of money in Guybon's last letter as his need is great. Brogden's £20 is yet unpaid. He had received a bill from Beales[2] that was not to be paid for three weeks or more.)

I hope wooll will be a better commodity then your letter mentions. I know not how to write to Mr Halstead else would be sure to do it, though I hope he will come to you without writeing to. I spake to one Thomas Busby, a Quaker and a draper in towne that I have dealt with many yeares. He may be trusted, if he comes for £150 worth of it for he is an able man and takes a fancy to buy wooll and other things and sells againe and getts money by it. He was to go into Lincolne shire at the beginning of next moneth, and he promist me to call and see Goody Freeman's wooll and the Marrham wooll and I gave him directions how to go to Milton and Marrham. Pray lett the tennants know of him. He is a little dapper man, weares his owne haire of a light browne, a man of 35 yeares of age.

I am sorry you want rain. We have occasional showers, and heavier rain 10 miles away. Captain Selby visited me last Tuesday. I was glad to see him. He was leaving town today. He has a suit in hand for his present wife's son.

[1] The letter is damaged.
[2] Steward of Fitzwilliam's Norfolk manors.

**379** FITZWILLIAM TO GUYBON
*London, 21 June 1705; F(M)C 1402*

I received yours of the 19th yesterday with the £30 bill enclosed on Mr Brogden, which won't be paid this fortnight because they take so many days grace, as they call it, after the appointed day. I want money extremely at this instant. You have the same dry weather we have here. God send rain for the cattle need it and hay grows dear, although there is much old hay hereabouts. I pity most my poor deer for they cannot be moved. Turn the horses and everything else into the woods to ease the park. We are all pretty well save my wife who is never well. We intend for the country soon so Mrs Pendleton must move from those rooms for we cannot spare them. If the rooms over the pantry and larders will serve her she may have them until she can 'stead'[1] herself better. Goody Butler, if still there, can lie in the maid's room at the top of the house. Let her get the brewing vessels ready. Return all you can to bring me down the sooner for I must not leave 'scores' unpaid. [P.S.] Send word if you hear when Parson Phellips comes to reside at Marholm, and if you have not paid him anything for the parsonage tender what is due to him for he is a modest man.

[1] Stead, to place.

## 380 FITZWILLIAM TO GUYBON

*[London,] 5 July 1705; F(M)C 1404*[1]

> I have received from a drover by Richard Burton's order £14 4s 8d and no more, and what is such a little sum compared to my wants?

I perceave you resolve to keep me in this towne otherwise you would send me such supplys of money as would enable me to pay my debts here to tradesmen and carry me home to Milton which when I once gett thither I hope I shall not returne hither againe in hast. Mr Busby was with me last Fryday for a letter of recommendation amung the tennants.[2] I told him I had writt one to you the day before, which was this day sennight, that they might trust him.[3] I perceave by him he intends to lay out 3 or 400 pounds with our tennants and in Lincolne shire but he will buy cheap. He is a notable man and I hope he and they are agreed for his money is ready. If the cottages in my purchace at Castor and Aylesworth are such pittyfull things I may thanke you for it. You, by your letters, incouraged me to it and told me the people were all substantiall people and their rents a good penny worth; there was no feare of the fall of rents for that they had leases, most of them for 21 yeares, and paid all the taxes and what not. You went into that estate severall times by my order to inquire the true rents and see in what condition the houses were, and alwaies gave me incouragement to go on. I have still your letters to produce. If they be othe[r]waies you have betrayed me by giveing me wrong information and that was not well done in you for who ought we to trust but our children and our stewards, and if they will be unfaithfull, the Lord reward them according to their merritt. As for this cottage of the Widdow Healey's, you have offered the wheeleright fairly. If he will take a lease of 21 yeares lett him lay out what he pleases to his owne mind so he leaves the house in as good condition as now it is, at the expiration of the terme. There's good land belongs to that cottage. It's a pretty thing enough and stands in a broad part of the towne street which is fitt for his trade, for to lay timber in etc. I shall not be willing to lay out much money on it for if this man dies we may not gett another of the same trade into the house so may come off as we did at the bakehouse, be at great charges in makeing an oven and the man broke soon after. I like not such projects. Reasonable repaires must be done but for £20 I shall lay out no such summe. You tell me you have laied out some money about those cottages. I know no necessity there was for it for the old tennants are in them all and they are obliged to mainteine and uphold. I ought to have known these matters before you had gone about them. As for Manton's farme you do not acquaint me that you have lett it and I know no necessity there was of repaireing before a farme is lett.

> Mr Colcutt wishes his rent from that weaver living in the cottage joining my farm where Goodman Serjeant lives, and wishes you to sell the copper and the ironwork to the next tenant of Manton's farm. [P.S.] Mr Whittacre can forbear his Northborough rents no longer. You say nothing of rain. How forward are things and how many fat bucks may I have from my park this season?

[1] Top of letter damaged.

[2] For Busby see above **378**.

[3] Text reads 'you him'. Apparently Fitzwilliam wrote 'you' in error, before realising he meant 'him'. Then having written 'him' forgot to cross out 'you'.

## 381 FITZWILLIAM TO GUYBON

*London, 19 July 1705; F(M)C 1406*[1]

> We are all much concerned to hear you have been ill, although rejoice that you hope to go to Peterborough next Saturday. I received yesterday £11 12s 7d from Henry Hankin from his sale of Marmaduke 'Thomlinson's' sheep. I cannot leave town until I have a considerable supply to pay my scores. I am sorry your drought continues. Occasionally we have pretty showers but not as much as we need. We hear they have had enough in Suffolk and parts of Leicestershire and regret you have not had your share. If the weather becomes more temperate send up a buck.

I went to Mr Busby, my Quaker draper, yesterday after I received your letter to know of him if he had bought our wooll. He told me not, and that the tennants did not know what to aske for their wooll considering the times. He said they ask't 18s a todd. I find he will not give above 13s 6d or 14s at most for it and he beleives they have a mind to sell it againe to their old chapman Mr Halstead else they would not have ask't that price. He bought a loade or two of wooll at Holbitch and Chatteris[2] for 11s and 6d a todd and beleives he shall gett more by that wooll then he should by yours at 14s. He did designe to lay out 3 or 400 pounds with you and thereabouts. He is goeing to Bristoll faire on Munday but promises me he will be as good a chapman as a[ny if they] sett him a markettable price. He buys fine cloath at Bristoll faire and will be backe ag[aine] ... He is a sharp man and has had as good fortune in dealeing ... [I] beleive him to be very wealthy and may safely be tru[sted] ... Goodman Dove and Richard Burton [were not] at home when he saw their wooll so he knows not their prices. I did not lett him know you had inf[ormed] me by letter he had not bought your wooll but went to him as if it were by chance, and talkt to him of other ma[tters] till he told me of himselfe what was done ...

[1] Bottom of letter badly damaged. Words in square brackets conjectural.
[2] Holbeach, Lincs. and Chatteris, Cambs.

## 382 FITZWILLIAM TO GUYBON

*London, 26 July 1705; F(M)C 1408*

> All glad to see your letter of the 24th, hoping your health is now reestablished. I am concerned you cannot supply me with money; even a small sum would help for the less I borrow the better. Don't send venison next week unless the weather cools. I spoke with an honest sensible man came up from Oundle side with sheep who told me he feared they should get no more for their wool this year than 16s which gave last 18s 6d. I am glad to hear it for my Quaker[1] frightened me by talking of 14s or under. I hope your old woolman of Cambridge will come among you again. I was sorry to hear from Mr Pemberton's letter of the sad accident at Marholm.[2] I wrote my thoughts to him but until I come down to examine my grants I cannot give a perfect answer. I rather believe the horse will fall to Lord Exeter. However, I wish Mr Pemberton to do what can be done to save my right, such as entering a protestation. But I hope the

horse got out of my lord's which will save all controversy. Secure me a buck from Lord Exeter this year. I enclose one warrant and will send the rest later.

[1] The draper, Busby.
[2] A horse killed a Mr Swain, see below **384**.

## 383 GUYBON TO FITZWILLIAM

*30 July 1705; F(M)C 1409*

(Has received Whittacre's rent due last Lady Day from his Northborough tenants, Joe Clarke, £4 16s, taxes allowed £1 4s, and Ward, £6 8s, taxes allowed £1 12s; will return it next week and some more with it. Weather too hot to send buck. Has not disposed of warrant sent earlier since Fitzwilliam had not specified who should receive it. They have heard nothing of Halstead [Cambridge woolman] yet although tenants would be glad to.)[1]

[1] Marginal note from F. reads 'To write to him I received 6 guyn. for Mrs Pendleton 20th of July.' The letter has further extensive annotation by Fitzwilliam relating to Whittacre's properties and arrears owed by widow of Thomas Griffin (receiver) from Michaelmas 1699 to Lady Day 1702, and from Whittacre to Fitzwilliam from Michaelmas 1702 to Lady Day 1705.

## 384 FITZWILLIAM TO GUYBON

*London, 2 August 1705; F(M)C 1410*

Yours of 30th received. Glad you sent no venison this hot weather. Send none until it abates and when you send let me know the preceding post so that I send for it and not have it lie in the carriers' hot warehouses. I hope you intend me a good sum with Whittacre's rents for I am in great need of it. There is time to decide on the warrants after I see what I shall need myself. I am glad Mr Phillip is come to Marholm. I wrote an angry letter when you sent word how the parish was neglected on Sundays. You have not said where the horse was found that killed Mr Swain. I hope Mr Halstead will yet come among you. I hear nothing of Busby who is now in the west of England. I forgot [to write] in my last that I had received six guineas for Mrs Pendleton from Mrs Frances Strafford. Pray pay her them. I gave my acquittance. It seems one Mrs Forster her cousin, who kept a school, is dead and long owed her £5. She could not die satisfied till her daughter Judah, who lives with the Duchess of Marlborough, promised she would pay Mrs Pendleton this money so she sent me these six guineas which is some recompence for the forbearance of £5 all this time. I am glad they are so honest for poor Mrs Pendleton's sake . . .[1]

[1] A badly damaged postscript reports the death of Francis St John, who had been ill for some months and 'had a mind to die at Battersea' at Sir Walter St John's house.

## 385 FITZWILLIAM TO GUYBON

*London, 9 August 1705; F(M)C 1411*

Glad you intend me money by Mr Pemberton next week. I need a good sum for my great wants and to pay Mr Whittacre's rent. To make it light of carriage for Pemberton get guineas in Peterborough. I am sorry no woolman comes but hope Mr Halstead will come. I hope they are not forced to sell at Mr Busby's price. Two days ago he told me he can buy cheaper wool at Leadenhall Market better than any at Marholm, and that is already in town. He bought two loads the last time he was with you; one of large, fine wool in Lincolnshire, the other about Chatteris in the Isle of Ely, of a very low price and yet as good as Marmaduke [Tomlinson's]. He bought more on his Bristol journey and will yet buy more. The weather has cooled so hope you will send a buck next week, and if it proves very cool send two bucks, shoulders and all. [P.S.] Mr Parker has an interest with Lord Exeter. Let him have Westhay warrant: himself a side, Mr Dickenson of Sexton Barnes[1] another, Charles Duce and Robert Newcomb half haunches. 'Sewley Walk' warrant give to Thomas Deacon of Swanspoole:[2] he a side, another for Cousin Henry Tryce; Cousin Bellamy and Mr Lowrey a haunch. The other warrant we will suspend for now. If Lowrey would rather delay his give it Robin Newcombe and let Mrs Whinyates have the haunch Whinyates should have had in Parker's Westhay warrant, for I suppose Lord Exeter has a respect for her for her husband's sake. When you wish for venison send word and I will join somebody with you in another warrant. I hear Mr St John's body was to be buried last night in Thorpe chapel. Tell me in your next if it was. I wish you could find a return for the money you send by Pemberton, for fear he might be robbed, unless he will secure the money.

[1] Sexton Barnes, a part of Peterborough, named for two fine monastic barns which stood there, known as 'the Sexton's and the Tithe Barn', *VCH Northamptonshire*, ii. 431.
[2] Swanspool, also a part of Peterborough, *ibid.*, p. 429.

## **386** FITZWILLIAM TO GUYBON

*London, 16 August 1705; F(M)C 1412*

Today Mr Pemberton brought me £60 from you in 56 guineas which came to £60 4s, so he demanded the 4s of me which I paid. Recollect if you paid him the 4s when you paid him the £60, and if not demand it off him. I will send for the buck on Saturday. Pray send another next week. We have had a terrible storm. Not much damage on land but I fear much has been done at sea. Let me know what damage Milton has suffered, and my estate and my neighbours. I am sorry Mr Halstead has not come among you. If you would send word how to address him at Cambridge I would write to him. I was told of another woolman who wishes to buy our wool, which I encouraged but hear nothing as yet. If he will come down I will send a letter with him or a post ahead giving my opinion of him. I have written another warrant which you may give Mr Deacon, if you think Sewley warrant will be better served for yourself and any who join with you.

## **387** FITZWILLIAM TO GUYBON

*London, 23 August 1705; F(M)C 1413*

Glad you are sending another buck. Send another next week. Take half a buck yourself, and share the other half between two who have not yet had venison. Don't forget Robin Newcomb. Take either Moorehay, Sewlehay, or Cross-a-hand warrant. I suppose you have disposed of one of these to Mr Deacon and his partners. The money you intend me this week by Mr Thomas Lawrence will be extremely welcome. I hope Mr Halstead or some other woolman has bought the tenants' wool. I heard from an intelligent farming man about Oundle side that Mr Halstead had been there and bought many parcels, paying ready money, two loads or better, and gave 17s a tod for the sort they sold last year for 18s and 18s 6d. I was glad to hear he paid so good a price and hope he has been with you since. His son was with him at Oundle. Let me know when harvest is in that I may have Adam Johnson brew. The farmer told me last week all their white corn was in about Oundle. I hope you are so forward.

### **388** FITZWILLIAM TO GUYBON

*London, 30 August 1705; F(M)C 1415*

The buck came very sweet and extraordinary good venison. I hope for another as good next Saturday, and if you have another very good buck left send it the next week. I hoped Lord Exeter would not deny me a buck this year, because he told you last year that if you sent in time he would give one out of his own park, and I hope he will yet if reminded of his promise. Since Robin Newcomb has such an occasion as his son taking a Cambridge degree let him have half a buck from Mr Arney's warrant, and dispose of the other half as you think fit. If you can get a buck from Lord Exeter give pieces to Mr Richard Dickenson and Mr Sparks who married Cousin Wardell's daughter, whom I had forgotten. Spend another piece at the ferry and invite Captain Selby to it. Give Captain Selby the other piece, for being newly married he may take it kindly. Try to get this buck from [Lord Exeter]. Harry Watts was here today making great complaints but I was too busy packing for the country so referred it to a Milton meeting. I expect to send 20 cwt next Monday, the rest the Monday after. Let Adam Johnson brew the week after next. I hope the drink won't be wasted this year, and be ripe enough to drink when I get down, but don't let him neglect hopping it. Brew two hogsheads of ale, at eight strike[1] of malt a hogshead, and four of small beer, one and a half strike a hogshead. Use good malt so the drink is clear else we shall not drink it, being used only to fine drink here. Keep account what hoops are put on, how many days cleaning vessels, how many brewing. I am greatly distressed for lack of money to pay my debts here. I have received nothing from Thomas Lawrence, nor anyone else since Pemberton paid the £60. I am sorry Mr Halstead forsook the tenants for I am certain he bought the Oundle wool. He was named, and described by his bigness and his son the same, and that they lived in the workhouse at Cambridge. Let the house be cleaned to receive us. Mrs Pendleton must remove elsewhere for we cannot spare the rooms she is in. I wrote you two months since that she could best be spared those rooms where Goody Butler is, and all to herself. Goody Butler can lie in the maid's chamber by the wardrobe. Mrs Bull must get us two maids and a man at Helpston or Castor statutes.[2]

[1] Strike: an antique measurement, which varied in size according to region but most commonly, as here, was equivalent to a bushel.

[2] Hiring fairs, see note to **230** above.

## **389** FITZWILLIAM TO GUYBON

*London, 1 September 1705; F(M)C 1416*

I forgot in my last to say that my wife and I wished Mrs Pendleton to pickle up for us as many mushrooms as she can get, if it's a right season to do them in, and likewise to pickle a great many cucumbers which either Mrs Pendleton or Mrs Bull may do, but for the mushrooms we depend upon Mrs Pendleton. If there are any fine young kidney beans to be had we desire some pickled also. They are an extraordinary fine pickle as they do them here in town. I hear nothing of Lawrence's money. The buck came sweet but ill killed, very bloody and not so fat as the others. If you have no better send no more this season. Today I sent to the Peterborough wagon seven boxes great and small, two trunks and one great copper 'sesterne' to set bottles in at the sideboard. They weighed they tell me 8cwt 1qtr 4lb. They will come to Milton next Wednesday or Thursday. More will come next week. [P.S.] I would not have Mrs Pendleton remove into the new buildings by your chamber but rather into her old chamber where she lay before she was married. When we come down we will contrive a place more convenient for her. Take care the boxes are carefully taken from the wagon at Milton, have people ready to help with them, and set them very carefully down for three are full of 'chinay' ware.

## **390** FITZWILLIAM TO GUYBON

*[London,] 6 September 1705; F(M)C 1417A*

... Let Adam Johnson brew the drink well. We have here so good and fine small beer that my servants will not like it if it is not clear. You and Mr Newcomb have the last warrant: that for Mr Arney's Walk. I hope you get a buck from Lord Exeter, half to spend at the ferry and give away the rest as you think fit, but give a piece to Captain Selby for I quite forgot him or he should have had a piece with the others, it being the first year of his marriage. Captain Styles and his son visited me, and he tells me of your good health ... [P.S.] Let Mrs Pendleton have all she needs for the 'pickling up' I ordered in my last. I spoke today with intelligent men from Lincolnshire and Huntingdonshire who both told me that wool which last year would have sold for 18s and 19s a tod they are glad to sell for 16s. I wish you had good chapmen who would pay you 16s for your Marholm, Milton and Woodcroft wool. I fear it will be your best price ...

## **391** FITZWILLIAM TO GUYBON

*London, 13 September 1705; F(M)C 1417B*

I have received £13 by Thomas Lawrence's order, a small sum compared with what I need to get out of town. Direct your next letter to my house in King's Street, Bloomsbury, over against the Black Mare, which is a very remarkable sign. I had to remove because the house I was in wanted much repairing. Let

Mrs Bull have money for things I have ordered her to buy at Brigg Fair next week. I shall send more boxes by Fearey's wagon next Monday.

## 392 FITZWILLIAM TO GUYBON

*London, 20 September 1705; F(M)C 1419*

In yours of the 17th you don't say how much you paid a bushel for malt, how many hoops were set on the hogsheads, how many days your brewer worked, if any helped him and for how long. Captain Styles when here lately told me your woodman, Tom Wootton, wished I would get another in his place next Michaelmas as he had lost too much blood to perform his place. I wonder he could not tell you of it as well as the captain. Seek a person fit for the place as I will be down the latter end of next week but keep this to yourself. I would have nobody know it. I hope Mrs Bull has got me a maid, and you have found a man for the gates etc. I sent last Monday by Fearey's wagon two great cases and three smaller boxes, weighing 4cwt 3qu. 18lbs. If they have not been sent to Milton get some Castor wagon which carries corn to Peterborough next Saturday to bring them back. I am sorry to hear you neglect slating Milton, for one that rode by the gates two months ago tells me it was pity I did not repair it. I told him probably the last storm did it but he said it was earlier. He described the damage as over the chapel end of the house. If so the best goods in my wardrobes must be wet in rainy weather, and the beds and hangings in the two chapel chambers. Let this be taken care of out of hand for you must expect rainy weather after your long drought. I don't know what to do for money, send some though only a little; all will help. My wife wishes Mrs Bull to enquire the prices of cinnamon, cloves, nutmegs, mace and Jamaica pepper and let me know the next post so we may decide to buy here or there. Also whether she can get good sugar and its price, or if she advises us to buy here; and let me know the price of your black pepper, that is round, which comes from the East Indies, which is the common pepper we use. [P.S.] Let her agree for soap, and let us know what she has done about maids.

## 393 GUYBON TO FITZWILLIAM

*24 September 1705; F(M)C 1420*

(Had received Fitzwilliam's of 20th. Had paid Mr Dickenson for 22 strike of malt at 2s 10d, £3 2s 4d and 7s 6d for 5 lbs hops at 18d. Had hooped no vessels this brewing. Adam Johnson was 4 days, his son 3 days, and Jonathan Watson 1 day helping to grind. Has been unable to fill woodman's place yet. Nobody suitable at Marholm. Had received the cases and boxes by Fearey. Sorry someone reports Milton wants slating. He must have been at a distance. Has done all he could short of reslating the roof, but leaves that for Fitzwilliam. Old and new buildings have had all necessary repairs. Can get no returns at present. Mrs Bull will report prices of spices, sugar and soap. She has hired two maids and a man is ready.)

**394** FITZWILLIAM TO GUYBON
*London, 27 September 1705; F(M)C 1422*

I am glad corn gives so good a price since I perceive you pay 2s 10d a strike for malt, and at that rate barley must give 2s, for the 10d is for the Queen's duty and the malting of it. I spoke again with the man who reported Milton House out of repair and he said it was the end of the new buildings next the road. Moreover he said looking at the great clock to learn the time he found there was no hand to it. Fit one before I come down. On Monday John Sisson of Northborough brought me £24, very welcome and I hope you will send more soon. I send no goods this week but a 'pretty many' on Monday. I hope Mr Pemberton and his wife got safe home to Peterborough, send them our respects and let them know we enquired after them. Mrs Bull wrote my wife about the maids. I will let her know a week in advance of our coming so that they may come and clean the house.

[P.S.] Since I writt this letter takeing a walke into Islington Feilds I spoke with an intelligent countrey man who came up to sell his sheep and lives between Brigstocke and Oundle; and askeing him about corne, malt and wooll he acquainted me: good wheate sold at Oundle markett for 2s 2d per strike, good barley for 18d and the choicest for 20d a strike and the best malt both at Oundle and Wellingborough for 2s 6d, so either you are imposed upon paying 2s 10d a strike or our markett run very high over the others doe, which if so I am glad off for the good of the tennants.

**395** FITZWILLIAM TO GUYBON
*London, 4 October 1705; F(M)C 1423*

I am glad the Pembertons got home safely. I know the old cart stable next the slaughter house has been down some time but hope the slaughter house is standing, for that room will be useful to the family, and also the other stable as far as where the 'grindlestone' used to stand, for the family must have those stables until the new stables are finished. I think the hand belonging to the best [clock] dial next the house was gilt like the dial, but the black dial next the carter's yard was only painted gold. I am glad to hear the tenants begin to make money for I cannot stir from here until a good sum is returned me. I am ashamed to leave town in debt when I have hitherto paid all my tradesmen when I bought their commodities and have saved much money by so doing. Speed your returns for I lie here at great charge and am afraid the winter will come on apace and make my journey the less pleasant besides dangerous for catching colds; but come I must because you told Mr Field my vintner the present state of your health which I was very sorry to hear. Pray God keep you in health to our next meeting and longer a good many years. [P.S.] My wife and son are in good health. I sent nothing last Monday and have nothing more to send but what we must make use of until the end but that will be 'a great loadeing' when we come away.

**396** FITZWILLIAM TO GUYBON
*London, 11 October 1705; F(M)C 1424*

Monday last a glover by Cripplegate brought me £50 on account of Thomas Rowell of Peterborough, very seasonably being drawn very low in cash, and another such sum will nearly send me out of town and out of debt. We are every day nearer and nearer to coming and hope to send more boxes next week.

**397** FITZWILLIAM TO GUYBON
*[London, c18 October 1705]; F(M)C 1400*[1]

I am glad you intend £50 for me next week. My wife read your letter and found she needed £50 so I fear I must let her have it and will want another £50 for myself. Hope the house is getting ready and the rooms aired for I intend to go down soon, God willing. You should receive today one trunk and five boxes. Keep them separate from the boxes and trunks already there, even if stored in the same room.

I am heartily sorry to heare of poore Mr Pemberton's illness. As soon as I received your letter I went to Dr Gold his physitian here in towne who he consulted with before he went to the Bath and I asked him what he would advise him to do. He told me at this distance 'twas impossible to direct. As his case may be, lime water may be good for him to take or milke and water. They were very good, both of them, for the diabetes, and for the quantity he referred that to his physitian to direct as he should find his condition required. I hope this will find him better but pray lett him know next Satturday what I write and recommend me to him. As he growes better pray lett him write to Dr Gold who I perceave takes it ill he neither saw him nor heard of him since he came from the Bath, and he does not know what occasion he may have of a good doctor considering his condition. [P.S.] I hope you will make the £50 you intend me a £100 because of this suddaine occasion.

[1] Top of letter damaged. This letter is filed before that of 21 June 1705. However, the letter's cover is postmarked 18 October, and the context, particularly the reference to Pemberton, who is described as recovering in the succeeding letter, also accords with this date.

**398** FITZWILLIAM TO GUYBON
*London, 25 October 1705; F(M)C 1426*

Received yours with the £12 bill for Goodman Dove's wool money, and glad you intend me more by Mr Holland, with more the week following. Rejoiced to hear Mr Pemberton is recovering. Let him know on Saturday that I saw Dr Gold at Westminster and told him of his recovery, but [Gold] told me plainly that he would not 'warrant him from another relapse soone; and if he vallewed his life as soone as he was able to travell he must drinke the Bristoll water.' This let him know. We have had much rain this past week, and I regret you intended to bring home the trunks and boxes only last Tuesday. I had hoped the carrier would have sent them to Milton the Thursday before, as he used to do, or that you would have brought them back in Castor corn wagons last Saturday. At the carrier's they would have stood in the yard or at best under a shed and God knows what harm the rain may have done. My wife is much concerned. Let none remain there henceforth, but get them home the Saturday after if the carrier won't deliver them earlier. I hope the tenants have sold their wooll well. They who have their wool unsold should have a better price because the taking of Barcelona will reopen the trade with Spain, the best trade England has with the 'woollen manufactor'. It's hoped all Spain will revolt now we have secured a great principality, but for fear of the worst I don't advise any that have their wool unsold to refuse a handsome price. Let me know for how much a tod Goodman Dove and the others sold their wool. Likewise what rain you have had at Milton, how the roads are, and if the ponds are low I would have the well at the pump emptied and cleaned to improve the water before I get down. It has been a very good year for cleaning all the ponds about the house and gardens. Keep the leads and gutters very clean for fear of sudden great showers.

**399** FITZWILLIAM TO GUYBON
*London, 1 November 1705; F(M)C 1428*

Mr Holland the salesman has paid £42 18s 11d, and John Sisson of Northborough £20 on his own account. I hear Woodcocke the drover was in town last Monday market but brought me no money. I sent Goodman Dove's note from Sowgate of Allerton to him that should pay it but he said he had had no money. He might have in a fortnight's time and might pay me then. If not I must stay his time which is uncertain. If I don't get the money before I leave I will bring the note back. Am glad Mr Pemberton mends and the six boxes and the trunk safe at Milton. Weigh the last lot I sent for fear I was 'cozened' in the weight. I sent an ignorant person and fear they were too hard with him. I am sorry you did not remind me of the dry year for I would have had the ponds cleansed with that part of the moat between the two orchards. Clean the pump well out of hand. Next week I will let you know the day I shall be at Milton but would not have it known. I sent down by Fearey's wagon last Monday three great stone bottles of oil, with a great watering pot for the garden, which Old Joseph complained he wanted before he died, and a box of glass lanterns for the house. Set the oil bottles in the new cellar with the wine, stopping the cellar window, etc, with straw that this frosty weather may not hurt them. Return what money you can for I shall need to use it soon even if I am then in the country.

**400** FITZWILLIAM TO GUYBON
*London, 8 November 1705; F(M)C 1429*

I am glad you intend me more money by Mr Holland next week. I have not received Dove's £12 bill yet. Gather rents as fast as you can and return them. I received the enclosed letter from Mr Whittwell to you for the fine of Colcutt's farm. It comes to just £1 15s but I thought Mr Leaffeild had taken all the post fines for our hundred as Lord Exeter's officer. Discover to whom I must pay it. Tell Mr William Leaffeild of Mr Whittwell's demands and hear what he says to it. I am glad Mr Pemberton mends but we are all very sorry to hear of the old gentlewoman's[1] illness fearing it may go hard with her at her great age. Call next Saturday to see how she and her son do. Glad the bottles and boxes are safe at Milton. I send nothing this week but shall next. Are the does in the park fat yet? If they are send one up by the wagon next week. [P.S.] Send me word when the forest does are warrantable, and if fat yet. Now the Peterborough coach is laid down for the winter they may alter the days the wagon comes up. Let me know on which days I may expect venison when you send any.

[1] Lawyer Pemberton's mother, apparently an old friend of the Fitzwilliams.

## 401 FITZWILLIAM TO GUYBON

*London, 15 November 1705; F(M)C 1430*

I have received nothing of the £60 or £80 you intended me by Mr Holland nor does the man at Lawrence Lane Corner pay Mr Dove's £12. I have sent 12 times but he always says he lacks money, says he will pay in a fortnight if he can but does not accept the bill. I have put it in Mr Heriot's hands to see if he can get either the money or his acceptance of the bill. If he fails I will send it back and Dove must get back his money from Mr Sowgate. I am glad you have ordered me money from Holland for Friday but expect it no earlier than next week 'for these salesmen love to keep money in their hands'. Many hogs are sold now for the Navy. You might get me returns from your hogmen, Mr Pancke, Rowland Morrice and another of Peterborough who used to pay me money. A year ago Mr Fearey paid me £200 in one payment. Peradventure he might supply a return for he is often receiving money from poulterers for ducks, etc. If the wagons are coming twice a week I had rather have the venison on Mondays than Wednesdays. I will be sending many things now the wagons are twice a week. Send a park doe next Monday, and if it is fat and good another the Thursday after. Am glad both Pemberton and his mother are 'on the mending hand'. Will he be well enough to come up next term?

## 402 FITZWILLIAM TO GUYBON

*London, 22 November 1705; F(M)C 1431*

(Repeats his appeals for money having received no returns. Hopes the brace of does coming from the park prove good as they are to be given away. Is glad Pemberton and old Mrs Pemberton get better daily but sorry to hear of the death of Mr Tryon of Bullicke 'who was a [good] man though a stranger to me'.[1] Refers to a terrible tempest of wind, 'God preserve us all'.)

[1] The Tryons were lords of the manor of Bulwick in Rockingham Forest. The word in brackets is conjectural, as the letter is damaged.

## 403 JOHN CATLIN TO FITZWILLIAM

*Maxey, 22 November 1705; F(M)C 1432*

(Thanks Fitzwilliam for two guineas which Mr Church had paid him on Fitzwilliam's instructions.) Mr Guybon bad me hasten some of the tenants and I do those in arrears but some take very little care to pay him, as Benjamin Wright shepherd, who is in arrear for about six years. Has very little stock, would not pay a quarter of [the arrear], only he has a bill from Mrs Vaughan for looking after sheep. Stephen Aldgate, Henry Butler, Widow Charlton and some others who owe a small rent for meadow will not pay until forced. Mrs Vaughan can spare Mr Guybon no money yet. She says she must buy some beasts to eat her hay stacks first.

## 404 FITZWILLIAM TO GUYBON

*London, 24 November 1705; F(M)C 1433*

I received your letter dated the 22nd this morning by the carrier's porter with a doe, very clean dressed which made it passable. I gave it away and wish it had been better for their sakes who had it. I am sorry you have not a man looking after the deer that understands to choose a good one. Don't trust that silly fellow John Freeman. I hoped the man that looked after Widow Freeman's stock since her husband died had been with her still or not far off, for he understood venison. Send me another to come up next Monday either out of the park or forest. At least send a good one from the park next Thursday by the carrier, larger than this, and cut out no shoulders for fear of spoiling the sides. I wonder you don't send the does in flag baskets for at this time of the year they won't taint and truly the does are hardly worth the carriage except by weight. If the forest does are no better than this was, dispose of them to those willing to pay the fees, but if better send one to see how I like it. I have here written my Westhay Walk warrant. Whether got or not I will certainly demand it. Three weeks since you wrote that Mr Holland should pay £60 or £80 that week and that Rudkin had 100 sheep on the road and their money should be paid me. The 12th of this month yours mentioned that Thomas Johnson and John Wattson had sent goods to Mr Holland, the salesman, and the money should be paid me, and that Holland the drover promised you to pay me here if he sold at St Ives. On the 19th you wrote you did not doubt these sums were paid and that I should receive more money this week. In fact I have not received one penny of these sums and am in great need of money.

## 405 FITZWILLIAM TO GUYBON

*London, 29 November 1705; F(M)C 1434*

Send a park doe next Monday. If the forest doe comes in time send it also but only if a good one. I have received no money since Sisson was here. You must find me more certain returns. Hankin was always careful to bring me my money as soon as he had sold the tenants' and neighbours' goods but this Holland is a man that keeps money in his hands. See my dressing room and the bed and bedding are well aired before good fires on Wednesday next, for a friend of mine, travelling north, will lie at Milton. Have a dish of meat ready for his supper.

### 406 FITZWILLIAM TO GUYBON

*London, 1 December 1705; F(M)C 1436*

My last letter answers yours concerning venison. No money has been paid since Sissons'.

My sonn is the bearer of this letter who I hope will gett safe to Milton next Wednesday. He would not be sattisfied till I gave him my consent to come and see you, so pray take care of him for a weeke that he intends to stay at Milton. I desire he may not be knowne to be in the countrey that he may have time to rest himselfe and injoy your company, and lett him not want for any money neither while he is there and at his comeing away. If the weather be tollerable I would have you shew him my estate that he may give me an account of everything. I hope you will take care to returne me some money soone or send it me up in specie. I hope Mr Church has a good horse to lend my sonn while he staies at Milton or you must gett one for him somewhere else while he staies in the countrey.

### 407 FITZWILLIAM TO GUYBON

*London, 6 December 1705; F(M)C 1437*

I received the doe from the park, handsome meat but not so clean as the last for the rainy weather spoiled it; send another from the park and a good forest doe with it if one comes in, and that will be all the venison I will have this season.

Pray lett my sonn have what venison he please to have and give away the rest of my fee deare as you thinke fitt. I hope he is safe at Milton and has gott no cold by the way. You are obliged to him for this vissitt for he came purposely to see you against my inclinations being much affraied of him for a winter journey and likewise his being there in a great cold house comeing from little warme roomes here in towne. Pray take all the care possibly you can of him and gett him a horse somewhere to ride about but I woud have him make no vissitts anywhere haveing no servants to waite of him.

With much ado and frequent sending I got last Monday the £12 on the bill Mr Sowgate gave James Dove in part of his wool money. On the 4th Mr John Holland's man Brampston paid for Edward Watson £3 1s 4d, for John Watson £11 16s 6d, for Thomas Johnson £18 8s 6d, for Thomas Rudkin £31 11s 5d, and for John Hicklin £22 1s 9d. In all £86 19s 6d for which I gave 5 several receipts. Mr Colcutt is very earnest for my arrears of rent due from a tenant living next door to William Serjeant's back gate and Mr Wright's house, late Jeffrey Gray's. He promised to pay you long since but Mr Colcutt threatens to trouble the man if he does not pay it at once. Mr Whittwell, the Oundle attorney, spoke to me about the post fine of £1 15s for Colcutt's estate. Send that money to him by somebody that shall take his receipt for it. [P.S.] Let the venison come in flag baskets for such venison is not worth the fee and is cheaper by weight; there's no danger of it stinking at this time of year.

## 408 FITZWILLIAM TO GUYBON

*London, [13] December [1705]; F(M)C 1438*[1]

Francis Guybon, I received yours dated the 11th yesterday and am extreame glad to heare that Jacke, and you, and everybody at Milton are in good health. I was very much affraied of his catching cold in his journey downe and in those wide roomes at Milton but I made him a promise last summer that he should see you before Christmass not doubting then but I should be downe myselfe long before, but matters falling out otherwaies I must have broke my word with him if I had not consented, and since he did go I ordered him to looke all over the house, gardens etc, and hope you will send him me up to towne in as good health as I sent him to you.

The very good doe by the carrier was the best I have had this year. I wish I could get such another. Since my son is so near returning send that other doe next Saturday week. Although Lord Exeter was not so civil and neighbourly as to send my son a doe at his first coming into the country, by warrant or otherwise, you might have killed one from the park for my son's table, either doe venison or young venison for roasting, stewing and boiling which, though not so fat, is excellent meat. Yesterday a Mr George Maure, a salesman, sent me £17 6s 3d on Joe Bull's account. I have great occasions for all you can get. [P.S.] Having kept the hay in the Meadow Close so long, and hay likely a dear commodity this winter, sell one of the cocks but keep the one best made and thatched.

[1] Letter damaged, dated from context.

## 409 FITZWILLIAM TO GUYBON

*London, 20 December 1705; F(M)C 1440*

Glad to hear my son has got no cold in the country. He is much pleased with his journey and especially finding you in such good health. Give to the poor people in the several towns as I used to allow in former years at Christmas. [P.S.] I wish you a merry Christmas and a happy new year. My wife is very ill.

## 410 FITZWILLIAM TO GUYBON

*London, 22 December 1705; F(M)C 1441*

Received your letter dated the 20th from Stilton intimating my son left Milton that day. He is now safely arrived, thank God, in very good health. If you have a good doe in the park have it cleanly killed and sent up next Thursday.

I hope to receive a doe from you on Wednesday. Send all venison in flag baskets. With our kind loves and thanks for your kindness to my son.

### 411 FITZWILLIAM TO GUYBON

*London, 3 January 1705/6; F(M)C 1442*

I had nothing to write last week unless I had renewed my complaints about money and yours complains as much. I can only say I receive no more than keeps the house in bread. I would have liked to pay a £500 debt off next month before I left town. I see I am not likely to, yet in former years I received four times as much at this season as I receive now. My son tells me the old ferry house is ready to fall. I am ready to rebuild the walls if it is any use to Harry Watts, but I heard it was not save perhaps the brewhouse. However, if the roof must be rebuilt I am unwilling, preferring to build anew along the bowling green hedge near their 'house of office'. I hope repairing the walls will serve for now. Let that little ash tree near the boat ferry road be cut down. My son says it has hindered the Lincoln carrier. I would not have the passengers disobliged.

They tell me that Jonas Styles of Helpston is lately dead by which meanes Harry Watts' wife is like to have a considerable fortune but there is a cross man he is to deale with woud make him compound for less then his share. Tell Harry I will stand by him and assist him that he shall receave no wrong from them, and if it may do him any kindness, will buy his share of the estate; at least, Harry Watts may tell them so and that may frighten them. I understand by my sonn that many of the trees are dead in the parke that I planted out in rowes or walks before I left the countrey and the occasion was because the cradles about them were not sufficient for they were too low built that the deare has barkt them and the horses has cropt off their heads. Pray tell Joseph Chamberlaine I woud have young trees sett in the roomes of them that are dead and spoiled and lett him have a labourer to digg the holes for the trees and help him in planting them and lett your carpenter be ready at the same time to fence them about with a good cradle and lett it be high enough against the horses and close enough against the deare, and now is the time to plant them out. If Joseph Chamberlaine wants roome to plant his young lime trees out he may make use of the old drying yard for to make a nursery off where his young lime trees may stand till they are growne bigg enough to plant out in walks. I understand that you have paled about the old drying yard which was never paled before but only hedgd and since it is done Joseph Chamberlaine may make a kittchin garden of it and plant out his young lime trees there besides, but he must be sure to kill the rabbits if there be any first or they will barke his lime trees.

Tell Mr Forster of Marholm I shall be down so soon it will not be worth his trouble and charge of coming up to reckon which I cannot do here, most of my papers being at Milton. [P.S.] My son thanks you for [your] letter and will reply soon. My poor wife is very ill.

## 412 FITZWILLIAM TO GUYBON

*London, 10 January 1705/6; F(M)C 1446*

Last Saturday John Holland the salesman paid me £32 12s 11d for Marmaduke Tomlinson; today George Maure, salesman, paid me £18 15s 8d for James Dove; and a Joseph Bodily paid £30 for Richard Burton. I am glad two others are to pay me money for these sums are almost all paid away to meet tradesmen's bills, 'for I find it a cruell thing to be in debt'. I am sorry money is scarce for I never wanted it more. Tell Joseph Chamberlaine he may make use of the old drying yard to plant his nuts and young lime trees if he can secure them against barking by rabbits. The worse the ground where trees are planted when young the more they thrive when planted out if that is better ground. Sell the copper for Mr Colcutt which was at Manton's old house for he tires me about it. Tell Mrs Bull my wife received her letter, her very good chine and black puddings for which we return her kind thanks. My wife will write when a little better but at present is very ill.

## 413 FITZWILLIAM TO GUYBON

*London, 17 January 1705/6; F(M)C 1448*

Mr Henry Hankin has paid me £18 6s 8d for Mr Exton. I hope I shall receive more. I am very much pressed by those I owe it to. My wife is a little mended, the rest of us in pretty good health. I hope you are all the same.

I heard last weeke but forgott to write it that James Ullitt died at the Bath this summer but of what I know not. One of my footmen learn't it accidentally at an ale house where he used to frequent when in towne. You may lett Goody Ullitt his mother know of it if you thinke fitt for she is often sending to inquire of him. If there be not rabbits frequent the old drieing yard I am sure the ground is good enough to plant the lime trees out in but I perceave Joseph Chamberlaine is not willing to bestow the charge of digging a trench to plant them out in because he will receave no bennefitt by it, but if the ground was fitt to raise peas and beanes and other garden stuff as would bring him in money he woud be ready enough then to digg it, but I see him plainly.

## 414 FITZWILLIAM TO GUYBON

*London, 24 January 1705/6; F(M)C 1450*

I sent Mr Rowell's £50 bill you enclosed to the man who promised he would pay next Wednesday, which will be good payment for they always take three days grace beyond the days mentioned in the bill. Don't sell Colcutt's copper until I have spoken with him again. A year ago you told me it would bring £3, and if I now tell him 15s or 20s he will think I cheat him. Consult Mr Knowles the brasier for it cannot be worth less than a shilling a pound, and new copper gives two shillings during this war. It must be sold by weight. You say there are no iron works but how could it be hung or used without? Manton used it all along. I am sorry Mrs Phillips was delivered of a dead child but hope she may do well again. [P.S.] Use the small beer, and tell me how it drinks, stale or otherwise, for I am unwilling it should be lost. Has Joe Chamberlaine planted out all the young lime trees he intends to this year? Does he want any seed for the garden as cauliflowers, or the like? I have extraordinarily good melon seed to bring down with me.

## 415 FITZWILLIAM TO GUYBON

*London, 31 January 1705/6; F(M)C 1453*

Francis Guybon, Yours of the 29th I received and am glad to heare I shall have some money next weeke by Mr Exton. Though I did not write you word last weeke of my wive's illness yett she is very seldome well but sometimes a little more at ease of her chollick in her stomach then at other times as she is now at this present, but yesterday was very ill with it. All the Christmass and a few daies before she was very bad. I am glad Mrs Phillips is like to do well againe. If Joe Chamberlaine does not plant out the lime trees soone he will loose the season for it. They should rather have been planted out before Christmass that they might have had the whole winter's soaking for after these raines we may have a drouth and then they will be all losst for want of moisture to nourish them. Therefore I desire he may loose no more time but go about them presently and do you take care he has a labourer to help him and lett the carpenters be ready to pale them about immediately. Lett Joe Chamberlaine know I have store of the best mellon seed already that I gott this last summer, but for collyflower seed and other seeds he must send me word how much of each sort I must gett him and when he would have them sent downe that he may sow them. He must name all the seeds to you that he wants and how much of each. For peas and beanes he has enough of them I suppose in the countrey or may gett them there. Sett downe every thing plaine and from his owne mouth for feare of mistakes. [P.S.] Mr Rowell's £50 was paid this day to a goldsmith's man. I sent for it.

## 416 FITZWILLIAM TO GUYBON

*London, 7 February 1705/6; F(M)C 1456*

Since I writ last Mr Hankin has paid £70 13s 4d for Mr Exton.

I am glad Joe Chamberlaine has seed enough for the garden of his owne, all but mellon seed and that I will send downe to him when Mr Pemberton returns back to Peterborough and sooner I cannot there being so small a parcell it may be losst should I send it by the carrier. He must mind the sorts of it that we may know which is which and you must write the names of it for him on little bitts of paper and sticke them downe on each bedd. Last yeare he gott you to write to me for some collyflower seed. If he will lett you know how much he wants I will send that downe also by Mr Pemberton for I suppose we have better here then he can have in the countrey, but for that as he thinks fitt.

(His wife continues very ill of the colic. Guybon to return money as he gets it.)

**417** FITZWILLIAM TO GUYBON
*London, 14 February 1705/6; F(M)C 1458*

I am sorry to hear Benjamin Burton is unlikely to continue tenant at Aylesworth. I presume you think him 'not able' or would not part with him. Secure my due rent and get a good tenant in his room. You may add that small farm Hullock rents to it if you cannot let it as it is, not that I have not kindness enough for Hullock. I would not part with him, being an old tenant, but I must have a regard to myself and Hullock's can be better spared than another's because it has no house on it. I leave it to your prudent management. Be earnest with the tenants and return as much as you can for I need to make up a sum.

**418** FITZWILLIAM TO GUYBON
*London, 20 February 1705/6; F(M)C 1459*

Francis Guybon, Yours of the 18th I received yesterday and I receaved on Tuesday by Mr Hankin by order of Thomas Whitehead £17 3s 1d just. I have sent you by Mr Pemberton a little parcell wherein is mellon seed for Joe Chamberlaine, of severall extraordinary good sorts. There is the names of every sort of them writt on the paper that incloses it and underneath on every paper is writt a figure of 2 or the figure of 4 which meanes how many yeares they are old, and this yeare they be a yeare older, so he must soake the oldest seeds before they be putt in the ground to plump them a little and order Joseph to putt the paper of each sort into a cleft stick and lett that stick be stuck downe at the head of the bedd where that sort is sowen that we may know what each sort is as to the goodness of it and then we may know what sort to save seed out of for another yeare. I have also sent downe amungst the seeds halfe an ounce of the best collyflower seed which cost 2s for feare he should not gett that which is so good in the countrey. As to Benjamin Burton, if you feare his condition is such as he cannot hold the farme pray part with him in time. It's a disparagement a tennant should faile under us. He has not been so long our tennant yett as to give our farme a disrepute for all Old Burton's sonns were lookt upon as druncken idle fellows but the old man was carefull of the maine chance though he loved a pott of ale too. I bought those cottages for the sake of the land belonging to them and if that farme wants more land it must be taken from the cottages rather then that should want, especially Hullock's land that has no house belonging to it, but I woud have you gett another tennant for it, but for abatement of rent I cannot do that. We are very sorry to heare of Mrs Bull's mischance. I hope all care was taken of her that could be at first, that she was lett blood and tooke some leucatellas balsam[1] inwardly to carry off any blood may be in her by reason of the bruise of her fall and that she has a good seare cloath[2] to her backe and her foot in case of any streine. Pray take care of her for her children are young and want sober heads to direct them, and if you thinke her in any danger lett her have a good physitian sent for to prescribe what is fitt for[3] her. Pray lett her want for nothing for her children are yett too young to be left to their owne mannagement.

(Pemberton's departure delayed until the next Monday so Joseph Chamberlaine to collect the seeds from Peterborough the next Thursday.)

[1] *Balsamum Locatelli*, a balsam devised by the Italian alchemist Ludovico Locatelli, author of *Theatro Arcani*, and which was considered, among other virtues, a specific for the plague until plague killed its originator in 1657: Charles H. LaWall, *Four Thousand years of Pharmacy* (London, 1927), p. 313.

[2] Cerecloth, cloth smeared with wax, etc., used as a plaster.

[3] 'for' accidentally repeated.

## 419 FITZWILLIAM TO GUYBON

*London, 28 February 1705/6; F(M)C 1460*

I am sorry to hear you were too unwell to go to Peterborough, but hope this will find you better. Let me know how you are. I am sorry also Mrs Bull has had so ill a bout. I had thought it not dangerous but perceive from yours that it was. I hope you have let her want for nothing, and have 'overlookt' her children to see they take due care of her; see she has everything fitting. I hope Joe Chamberlaine got the melon seed from Mr Pemberton who expected to be home by Sunday night or Monday for he went out of town Saturday morning 'betimes'. Considering what you write about Benjamin Burton I will abate not a penny of rent so as to be rid of him. If you hear of another very good tenant I hope you will get him to take it at the same rent for I am unwilling to reduce the rent, or at least not above 20s a year. Return money as fast as you can.

## 420 FITZWILLIAM TO GUYBON

*London, [7 March] 1705/6; F(M)C 1461*[1]

I sent to Mr Hankin to inform him about Benjamin Burton's farm for he spoke to me last year about John Burton's farm for Ned Gardiner. I believe they will give the old rent, and I am very unwilling to abate it, but if the Widow Thompson of Sutton would give the old rent I had rather she had it because she is a notable woman, while Gardiner I know not but I fear his management since he could not thrive on that farm where his father lived so many years. I am not much concerned about Harry Watt's not giving due warning. I never thought him a fit tenant for that farm.[2] If I mistake not it's a Lady Day not a Michaelmas farm, for although his parents came at Michaelmas they paid no rent for half a year. I am sorry there is no return this week for I am reduced to great straits. Do not fail next week. Let us know every letter how Mrs Bull does. [P.S.] Since I wrote this Mr George Mawre, salesman, brought me £26 7s 5d for James Dove to my great relief. I fear the small beer brewed for me last Michaelmas will soon be stale so use it when you think fit. I will order the brewing soon.

[1] Letter damaged. Postmark '7 M'.

[2] By 'farm' Fitzwilliam here means tenancy. The lease referred to is that of Gunwade Ferry.

## 421 GUYBON TO FITZWILLIAM

*14 March 1705/6; F(M)C 1464*

My lord, Since I wrott last to your honour there have happined a breach in our bridge at Lollam[1] but wee have gitten it mended againe for the present as well as wee can. There must be a new bridge soone either of stone or wood for this bridge is rutten. I had booth mason and carpenter with me for to see which would be the cheapest way and best. Hippie[2] will not turne an arch under £25 and he will finde the stone and lime but he will have all the carridges brought him, and the carpenter will build one for £4 if your honour will be pleased to lett him have a dozen of those plankes that are in the stable and 2 load of wood more that wee have at the pit, which will be the cheapest way a great deale and as good as the other. There must be one built soone. If the bridge should fall your honour would be fined which may cost more then 2 or 3 bridges building. Goe the cheapest way wee can, it will cost £10.

[1] Lolham Bridge carries Ermine Street across the Welland.

[2] Samuel Hibbons, a mason much employed by the estate. On 13 March Guybon paid Hibbons a total of £42 15s 5d for work done at Paradise farm, at William Ullitt's at Etton, at John Carter's at Maxey, at Robert Freeman's house, and at the Etton houses of Burr and Thomas Hall; Disbursements 74. Spelled 'Hibbons' in Guybon's accounts but 'Hibbens' in subsequent letters.

## **422** FITZWILLIAM TO GUYBON

*London, 14 March 1705/6; F(M)C 1465*

I am sorry you could not get me a return this week. You intimated I should have one so I paid some bills, and now am straitened for money to keep the house. You might have got one from George Woodcocke or another drover, even if only for £15 or £20, or else by the little Newark hogman, Rowland Morrice. He comes to town every week with hogs now they are victualling the fleet. Such a small sum would have served to keep house until you could return a greater sum by Mr Exton. I shall want a 'pretty deale', intending to come for Milton next month. We have clothes to buy for ourselves and servants, debts to pay, so I hope you will not keep me in town for want of money. We are glad Mrs Bull grows ever better. Let us know every week how she does. I have not seen Mr Hankin so suppose his friend Edward Gard[i]ner is accommodated with a farm. I shall not abate a penny to Benjamin Burton for I doubt he has been a good paymaster to you. Let him clear his arrears and be gone. We will take care not to let another tenant run in arrear. Let me know whether the weaver[1] in that house where lived Old Goody Lee, Mr Colcutt's wife's mother, has paid his arrears due Mr Colcutt so I can set the reckoning straight.

[1] William Mosley, see below **424**.

## **423** FITZWILLIAM TO GUYBON

*London, 16 March 1705/6; F(M)C 1466*

I received yours with the news of the bridge breaking at Lolham. Be well satisfied the bridge belongs to me as lord of Maxey, and whether it will be most prudent to repair with stone or timber. Both are equal to me. If it will cost £25 to turn an arch, that might last as long as three or four wooden bridges. If timber is thought suitable I cannot part with those planks in the stable for they were sawn for the gates. Ask Mr Wright how much plank he will need to make a pair of garden gates next the lane, another in the woodyard and another between the great garden and the little orchard where the ponds are.

Then I shall need a handsome pair at the entrance of the new stable yard and another for the backyard where the [old] stable and slaughterhouse are. If Wright can do this and have 12 planks spare, they may have the 12, but not otherwise for I shall never have such 'a parcell of good stuffe' together as long as I live. If there is not enough you must buy, for I can replace money but not such well seasoned planks. Ask Wright also if the two pair of old stable yard gates might not make gates for the entrances next the lane and next the woodyard. They need not be such choice workmanship though I would have them decent, one being in view. Ask Mr Wright to answer every particular of this letter.

## 424 GUYBON TO FITZWILLIAM

*19 March 1705/6; F(M)C 1467*

Yours of the 14th and 16th received. I have a return at last: John Walton of Burrough Fen[1] has beasts for next Monday market and what money they make he will order to be paid to you, and the week after Easter Mr Exton will be in town and will order you what money he makes. I received of William Mosley 12 October 1705 £2 2s 6d, with 17s 6d allowed him for two and a half years' taxes which makes one and a half year's rent due Mr Colcutt, Michaelmas 1704. He has paid nothing since.

William Kinge of Castor will be your honour's tennant for the ferry if your honour please. I know not where your honour will gitt a better tennant. He is a brisk man and she a very good weoman. He will be very usefull upon many occations. He desires to have a boote house built for the old one will not stand, and a shopp or 2 at the low ferry and desires to have thinges put in repaire and he will be tyed to keepe and leave them soe. I hope that he will bring the ferry to a good trad againe for now it is quieat gone. He desires your honour's answar soone that he may give his landlord word to provide himselfe, whoe have beene very kind to him. Mr Wright shall give your honour an answar of your letter this weeke.

[1] The Great Borough Fen comprised about 3,000 acres of fenland north of Peterborough, and anciently formed part of the waste attached to the hundred of Nassaburgh (the Soke of Peterborough) and was thus part of the lordship of the Abbey of Peterborough which came to the crown. In 1571 Elizabeth I granted it to Sir William Cecil, first Lord Burghley, and it descended from him to the Earls of Exeter: *VCH Northamptonshire*, ii. 472.

## 425 JOHN CATLIN TO FITZWILLIAM

*Maxey, 20 March 1705/6; F(M)C 1468*

Mr Guybon has ordered me to gather some of the small rents Mr Vaughan used to receive. I have made a book and write down all I receive, leaving room on every leaf for Mr Guybon to write his acquittance. If Mr Guybon comes not to Maxey I carry it to Milton within a week after receipt. I began Last Michaelmas and have received only about £30 for people are slow in paying, and I receive none but the smallest rents. If you come down in May people will not be so busy as at other times and I would call them to bring their arrears and reckonings. I will also write down Mrs Vaughan's accounts for I can do it better now than a year ago, because many tenants have brought in their receipts. The bridge at Lolham road is broken. It cost 10s mending this winter and was propped with a post last week. Samuel Hibbens will not make an arch under £20, paying no carriage. I know of no other estates to be sold, only 40 acres of 'dean and chapter land' Mr Church sells for a Mr Hunton. A Mr 'Larrans'[1] has bid Mr Eaton £160 for his estate and meets his brother about it again at Easter as I told your son when he was at Maxey. [P.S.][2] Mr Smith of Deepingate is in arrears for meadow and other land, which I have asked for (he is to pay some of it for Dr Wigmore), but he makes no haste about it although three or four years behind, and many others are also.

[1] Sic *for* Lawrence?
[2] This 'postscript' was written on the verso of the page containing the letter.

## **426** FITZWILLIAM TO GUYBON
*London, 21 March 1705/6; F(M)C 1469*

Received yours of the 19th yesterday. Am glad you have found some returns. I do not know the circumstances of [William] King of Castor, and should be sorry to bring a poor fellow to the ferry who could not furnish the house decently to accommodate guests. Also he should keep a handsome stock of coal to supply neighbours at their need. Enquire into his circumstances. I know nothing against him. I have heard the person of the man is fit for such a calling, 'being a jolly drinkeing fellow', but if he died has he a wife or son to succeed him, with substance to make good the rent? If you are satisfied on these points I am willing you and he should agree, but will abate no rent. Carter, Lord Exeter's coachman spoke several times for the ferry if Watts should leave. I don't know whether he lives with Lord Exeter still or has taken a farm. He has enough stock for such a place and is a notable fellow. When Watts gave warning you should have published it in Peterborough, Stamford and Oundle, and you would soon have had proffers, and may yet have proffers better than King's. But I may be mistaken and leave it to you to do for me what you can. I shall take care Watts does the repairs at the ferry. The house was new built for his parents, and the other buildings put in good repair and I will take care he leaves them so. The brewhouse was strong when I left the country although the house was decayed, and if Watts through penury has let the brewhouse decay for want of thatch he shall make it good. All shall be put into repair whoever takes it. I believe King's landlord will not part with him.

## **427** FITZWILLIAM TO GUYBON
*London, 28 March 1706; F(M)C 1471*

John Walton has not been as good as his promise to you for I have not heard from him and was forced to borrow £20 to buy bread for the house. I am not used to sending to market without money and am ashamed to begin now, and much wonder that I, who have so many thousands of pounds due to me, have to borrow to buy bread. It's high time to go into the country to see how things go. Let there be a speedy brewing of two hogsheads of ale and four of small beer, eight bushels of malt per hogshead of ale, one and a half to each of beer, 22 bushels in all. Take malt from those who have the best;

be not confined to Mr Dickenson. Mr Parker, Mr Deacon and Mr Whinyates when alive, always had the best malt, but I never heard Dickenson had good malt. My son complained of the 'smallness' of the last beer so Adam Johnson must cheat me of my measure for we used to have good drink with that allowance. Mr Wright has written saying it's a pity to use such good planks as those in the stable for Lolham Bridge, which he will need for the gates anyway, so advises building in stone if the ground be good and not 'moorey' or quick sands. If it is he recommends we build in wood, cutting down coarse pollards which will cut as good a plank for such a work as the finest we could get.[1] I have told him to view the ground, and also to send measurements of the henhouse windows so that I can get some 'wire lights' made here to keep out vermin. I will bring down all kinds of traps to kill them. I intend to build the bridge while in the country, and if it must be timber let the pollards be felled as soon as bark 'runns'. There is coarse pollards enough about the Far Lady Leas. We hope Mrs Bull grows better and better. She must hire us a maid in place of she who would not stay for our coming down. [P.S.] If John Carter is unwilling to leave his service you may close with King, if you think him able and his wife a gentle woman enough, and good enough cook, for now and then there may be occasion to 'dress victualls', and we may bring a guest to lodge at the house. I leave this to you for I know none of the people nor their qualifications.

[1] Wright's letter is at F(M)C 1470, dated 24 March.

## 428 FITZWILLIAM TO GUYBON

*London, 4 April 1706; F(M)C 1472*

On Friday I very 'seasonably' received £80 from one Plowright for John Walton.[1] I hear nothing yet of Mr Exton's money, but can wait a little longer now. I am glad you are brewing, it being fine weather for it. We thank Mrs Bull for her kind offer of her daughter until another maid can be had. I am sorry Harry Watt's wife is so ill. You don't say if she 'lies in' of a son or daughter. I hope Mr Pemberton has secured that estate to him which he was to levy a fine of last term. [P.S.] You don't say what you intend to do about the ferry. For the building at Waldrum Hall, if you have all the stone and timber together begin when you will this fine weather if the water is low enough. I have not heard from Mr Wright whether the ground will bear a stone bridge at Lolham. Give me your opinion which is the best 'husbandry' and best for the service of my family hereafter.

[1] Repaid 6 April, Disbursements 74.

## 429 JOHN CATLIN TO FITZWILLIAM

*Maxey, 5 April 1706; F(M)C 1473*

I have propped up Lolham bridge with three strong posts. I believe it will stand this summer without danger. There is but one arch. It has an old stone bottom that the wood lies on so that some parts seem strong but some places have holes and it is too thin to bear a new arch. Mr Wright says it will bear a rough arch of Helpston stone and be done cheaper, and that he can have lime from Castor for 3d a strike, and papers can be sent out that travellers may take another road till the bridge is finished. Mr Guybon had partly bargained with Samuel Hibbens to build this arch and find all materials but since your letter the bargain is void. Hibbens was to have £25, and to build it with free stone from Ketton pits, lime from Stamford and 'pendals'[1] to set the bottom and top, so that it might endure the weather and water. Hibbens was to pay Tippin the miller 50s to have a way through his yard while it was done and a piece of ground cut to turn the water. He is a good workman. He made four arches for the county in Lolham road employed by Sir St Andrew St John, Sir Matthew Dudlye and Mr Tryon[2] about six years since. He had £130 for two arches; and about £50 more to heighten the road. Those arches are 12 foot or better and this arch is to be 10 or better. The ground is very good hard gravel and will bear an arch but the old bridge cannot stand next winter, therefore best to have it done in summer when the water is low. Hibbens will do the workmanship and find no materials for £9 but maybe Mr Wright will find a cheaper way.

[1] A now obscure word, possibly dialect, which by the 19th century seemed to be 'a local term for various kinds of beds of stone'; *O.E.D.*, dates its earliest printed reference to 1808. The rock appears to have provided slabs or slates suitable for foundations, as here, or for floors (see **605** below).

[2] See note to **402**.

## **430** FITZWILLIAM TO GUYBON

*London, 11 April 1706; F(M)C 1476*

Since I wrote last a week ago Mr Exton paid at Heriot's £117. Today a Mr John Sampson paid me £10 11s for a Thomas Andrews of Peterborough, I suppose one of your tanners for bark.

I am sorry Harry Watts has losst his wife but hope Mr Pemberton has secured the estate. Lett him know I desire he will gett the bowleing green fitt for my sonn and I intend to bowle this summer. If you are sattisfied as to William King's ability to furnish the ferry house with handsome goods and that his wife is somewhat of a cooke and a cleanly woman fitt to accommodate strangers and passengers, I am sattisfied and you may agree with him but I expect the old rent. Mr Wright has sent me an estimate of the charge of Lolham Bridge new building which is a moderate and rationall estimate and does not amount to in all £15.[1] He has reckond the mason worke at £6; the rest is in the materialls. He thinks pendell stone may be the best to turne the arch with. He will acquaint you by word of mouth with the contents. I beleive it will be most prudent for me to find the materialls my selfe and I thinke it may be best for him to make the agreement and see the worke go on for I woud have it well done though I exceed the price he proposes and I would have the worke putt in hand as soon as the roades are dry enough for carriages.

You may begin at Waldrum Hall house when you like since you have already laid in stone and mortar. Build the house strong and well but not better than the tenant needs. Send what money you can.

[1] Wright had estimated: workmanship £6; 40 loads of pendle stone at 12d, £2; toll at 2d a load, 6s 8d; 16 quarters lime at 4s, £3 4s; 6 loads sand at 12d, 6s; 2 load large pendle slabs to pitch arch upon, 10s; 46 feet of coping stones at 1s, £2 6s; total: £14 12s 8d. (Wright incorrectly wrote £14 2s 8d.). Hibbens the builder had originally asked for £28, he finding all materials, Fitzwilliam paying carriage. Wright had counter offered that Fitzwilliam would find all materials and Hibbens would be paid for workmanship only. He had ordered Catlin to further prop the bridge which was very dangerous. Wright to Fitzwilliam, 7 April 1706, F(M)C 1474.

## 431 FITZWILLIAM TO GUYBON

*London, 18 April 1706; F(M)C 1477*

Since I wrote last Saturday, the 13th,[1] Henry Hankin brought £14 6s 1d for Marmaduke Tomlinson. I will be glad when Mr Exton's sheep come up for I would 'faine have' enough money to discharge some debts after which I would not need to return to town for a long time. Mr Whittacre asks that you call on his Northborough tenants for their rents. Don't forget it. I am glad to see what you write about William King for the ferry, and hope his goods to furnish the house match his qualifications for it. I hope you find a tenant for Benjamin Burton's house at the old rent. I am loath to reduce the rent on something bought so lately. Daughter Barrington is now in town and remembers herself kindly to you and to Mrs Pendleton. Don't let the work on Lolham Bridge be slighted, but well built and substantially. [P.S.] Spend the small beer you brewed last summer, and the ale also for fear it grow stale. Return what money you can. I am sure you can get returns by the hogmen for many hogs come up.

[1] Fitzwilliam dated the previous letter the 11th (a Thursday in 1706). If he wrote another two days later it has not survived.

## 432 GUYBON TO FITZWILLIAM

*23 April 1706; F(M)C 1479*

(Glad to hear by Fitzwilliam's of 18th that he received money from Thomas Andrews and Marmaduke Tomlinson, and hopes more has been paid since for Exton, who will have more sheep coming soon.)

I doe not question but that William King's ability in goods will be answarable to his other qualifications for such a house. His demands are these: he will have a brew house build, two shopps built at the low ferry and a well sunck by the brew house and to have things put in repaire and he will be tyed to keepe them and leave them soe; the rent he is willing to give which is a great rent as the times goe. I cannot gitt a tennant for Benjamin Burton's under £5 a year bate and soe Goody Tomson will give and not one penny more. Your honour had better lett it to her and abate her £5 then lett it to some for the rent. Your honour will be sure of your rent. Good tennants are hard to gitt. If these times hold there will be farmes enough to be lett; the tennants will not be able to hold them. I feare that wee shall have another drye sumer; if soe all the tennants will be undone. Mr Wright have put out Lolham bridge. They are agoeing about it next weeke and soe soone as that is done wee are for Waldrum Hall . . .

**433** FITZWILLIAM TO GUYBON
*London, 25 April 1706; F(M)C 1480*

I received yours of 23rd yesterday. On the 20th, Saturday, Mr Hankin paid for Mr Exton £25 1s 2d for sheep he had sent up. I am unwilling to abate Burton's farm by £5; it is too much to lose £100 in a purchase, which you greatly encouraged me to buy with the rest of that estate. However, since you say Goody Thompson is so good a tenant I will reduce the rent 40s a year for her, but for nobody else. If I find when I come down the ferry needs a new brewhouse I will build one for William King, and sink him a well but will not be bound to go as low as the river, and so will not guarantee him water all summer long. Mr Selby's well is an example for us, being dry most of the summer. For the shops Harry Watts shall be made to build them up. Let Lolham bridge be substantially built to last me and my children's time. Send what money you can.

**434** GUYBON TO FITZWILLIAM
*30 April 1706; F(M)C 1481*

My lord, Your honour's of the 25 I received. I am glad to heare Mr Exton ordred your honour some money. He will have more sheepe in the market soon and the money he will order to your honour. If your honour will not be pleased to abate £5 a year in Benjamin Burton's farme now, it will not be lett a good while for the land must be plowed and the medow looked after. Likewise the ferry, I wish your honour had no worse tennants then they will make; I would have your honour thinke that it is a rare thinge now adayes to gitt a good tennant, and to gitt them your honour must abate of the old rents for they are not able to give it these times, and when the times mend, your honour may rayse your rents againe. Lolham bridge is agoeing to be built and I hope substantially and well . . .

[Notes by Fitzwilliam]
[1] The ½ hoggshead of red wine conteines 34 gallons 3 quarts
The white conteines 32 gallons 1 pint
[2] May 4th 1706 Mr Hankin paid for Mr Exton £7 15s 7d
[3] To know what cheife rent he has received from Mr Feild of the Globe Taverne

**435** FITZWILLIAM TO GUYBON
*London, 2 May 1706; F(M)C 1482*

I am sorry to read in yours of the 30th what you write concerning abatement of rents. I would not have bought that estate had you not encouraged me by saying the land was worth the money even without a house on it, and then when I had bought it you wrote hoping I had them cheap for they were 'sorry, rotten houses'. I will not abate that farm £5 a year. I would rather take it in hand, for rent once abated never rises again. I will only abate 40s or £3 at most, and then only for three year leases. I forgot to write last time I was sending brandy and wine down by the carrier. I hope it takes no harm lying in the carrier's warehouse until next Saturday. Set them in the cellar apart from the others. The flag basket contains two wooden bottles of brandy, while another comes loose with the wine, all three sealed with my seal. There are 48 bottles of wine. More wine comes down on Monday. I am in great want of money after buying wine and clothes and liveries for myself and family. Don't let me wait for Exton's sheep coming up. Pay Robert Fearey the £20 for which he asked if you can. He presented a long bill. Check the brandy has not been pierced and stopped up again by the carrier's men. I threatened you should not pay the £20 if they did. [P.S.] Clean the cellar of last winter's straw. You could get a small 'bearestall'[1] into the cellar for I think to send wine in half hogsheads or tierces. I write tonight to Wright instructing him to direct John Wilkens to repair or rebuild the 'houses of offices' at Milton, my son saying they are dangerous to use, and the family cannot be without them when there. How many trees has Joseph Chamberlaine planted in the park this winter? Were they fenced in time against the deer? How many lime trees, how many walnut?

[1] Beer stall, a stand for a cask.

## **436** FITZWILLIAM TO GUYBON

*London, 4 May 1706; F(M)C 1483*

Francis Guybon, This morneing Mr Hankin brought me £7 15s 7d by order of Mr Exton and I had very ill luck yesterday for young John Figg my sonn's particular and old acquaintance of West Deeping brought me some money and I was not at home nor my sonn neither to give a receipt for it so I losst the opportunity of that returne which I perceave you sometimes want. I am very much putt to it for want of money, I intending to buy two or three quilts here in towne for the beds we ourselves are to lye in; I meane callicoes quilts to lie at topp of the bedds instead of the heavy ruggs. I desire Mrs Pendleton or Mrs Bull if she be able to come up to Milton, or both of them, would take exact measure of the nursery bedd, the bed in my bed chamber where my sonn lay last winter, and the bed where his man John Gray lay in my dressing roome. They must be so long and wide as to cover the whole bedds, tuck in also a little and hang downe a little besides though not to the very ground. I desire this may be done next Munday so soone as ever you receave this letter that you may write me an answer the next post that I may buy them to send downe as next Munday sevennight. Lett me know exactly how many feet long they must be, how many feet broad and lett me know to odd inches for we must be exact and you may have a carpenter to measure them to an odd inch.

I have today sent in Fearey's wagon two half hogsheads of wine, one red, one white. Also a small hamper of 21 bottles of wine, nine quart bottles, 12 pint bottles. One quart signed with globe seal, one with my seal, rest with a ship seal. Send a cart on Wednesday, and Joe Chamberlaine or some careful person with it to see them loaded, and unloaded at Milton into the new cellar. Rip the mats off the half hogsheads of wine and set them on a beer stall high enough for them to be bottled off when I am there. Set them bung uppermost, steady and apart so that one is not shaken when another is tilted to be drawn off. Set the bottles together on the cold cellar floor. I hope you have taken the straw from the cellar that kept the wine from the cold this winter. Keep the cellar clean and cool. Mr Field of the Globe Tavern who pays me yearly a chief rent at Maxey of £7 odd would know if any of his tenants have paid you any of that rent, how much and for what years. His tenants are a Day, a Measures and one or two whose names I forget. He wishes to know this soon for he will pay the remainder to me here. I would know what money he paid to the Vaughans on my account before they died. My daughter complains that she has not heard from you, having written two or three letters to you since your last to her. [P.S.] Send up all money you can.

## **437** JOHN CATLIN TO FITZWILLIAM

*Maxey, 8 May 1706; F(M)C 1484*[1]

May it please your honour, Mr Wright bar[g]ained with Samuel Hibben on Moonday the 29 of April last and at last made him yeild to do the workmanship for six pounds and four shillings towards a tub and things to carry lime in. He bargained with Tippen the miller of Lolham the same time for 50s to have the road through his ground till the bridg be finished. This last Moonday and Tusday Samuel Hibben took up the old bridg and to day he is about laying the foundation. Mr Wright was unwilling to be at charge of turning the watter into the next river by cutting the ground about 20 yards but the watter is risen and hinders them so that the watter must be damed some way or other till the foundation be laid. Waggons could not pass on to the miller's ground. I was forced to get two labourers two days to mend it that the road might not be stoped. The stones of the old foundation was decayed, some of them set on the edges too thin to bear a new arch and they are all taken up. They have brought 15 quarter of lime from Eason[2] and Samuel Hibbon saith he shall use more. They have six load of sand, 28 load of pendalls and slabbs for the bottom. The free stone is not come yet. The masons liketh the pendalls very well for endureing the watter but they take more lime being thiner then free stone and will be rougher work.

There is a small house of your lordship's at Northborough fallen down, held by one Edward Ward the younger. Rent is 20s a year and he is five and a half years in arrears. I often called on him for payment but he has paid nothing. The ground is hardly half an acre but with common [right], the wood and stone about it not worth 10s and hardly worth rebuilding. The ground might let for 6s 8d a year. The cowpastures were let on Thursday last, all but 18. This is the day it is 'broken' every year and if the 18 are not let by tonight they must be 'thrown in' which will raise the others 10d a pasture to 7s 6d to make the same rent as all would at 6s 8d. I will send a copy of Mrs Vaughan's accounts if you wish.

[1] Fitzwilliam noted on the cover of this letter 'worth reading'.

[2] Easton-on-the-Hill, 'much celebrated for its limestone' in the 18th century, *VCH Northamptonshire*, ii. 564.

## 438 FITZWILLIAM TO GUYBON

*London, 9 May 1706; F(M)C 1485*

I am sorry to hear times are so bad with the tenants. I hope they will mend and that this war will end soon. I hope all the wine came safe and regret the hamper and the brandy lay until Saturday at the carrier's for it was very hot. I am glad you have a return this week. I am sorry Mrs Bull is not well enough to come up to Milton yet, but Mrs Pendleton can measure the beds 'every jott as well', and let me know also the measure of the bed in Lady Newburgh's Chamber. Mrs Bull can send the key to the room by one of her daughters. [P.S.] Don't forget Field's tenants and his chief rent, and Whittacre wishes you to call for his rents. Let me know what they pay and what you set off for taxes.

## 439 FITZWILLIAM TO GUYBON

*London, 15[1] May 1706; F(M)C 1487*

(Repeats instructions about wine casks. Has received Mrs Bull's letter about the measurements of the beds for quilts. Will inform Whittacre about condition of his Northborough tenants' houses, and Field that his tenants have paid no chief rent. Has received no money from John Walton nor anybody else; is distressed for lack of money and wonders Guybon should fail him, when he had written so earnestly for money. Had sent to Smithfield to enquire about [Walton's] money but his salesman, Plowright, was out of town and not expected back until the next Saturday night. Fitzwilliam needs money to provision the house and Guybon must not depend on one man, but trust to two so that if one fails the other may 'hitt'. [P.S.] Had written Wright about repairing the 'houses of office' at once. They must have all stone, slates and pointing they need. Also boards for doors, expecially on the garden side)

[1] Either 15th or 16th, overwritten.

## 440 FITZWILLIAM TO GUYBON

*London, 23 May 1706; F(M)C 1489*

I have heard of no moneys from John Walton or any other. I wonder you trust to what that 'shattered brained' fellow Turner told you of a return from Walton, for I sent again to his salesman, Plowright, who sent word he had no orders from Walton to pay me money but rather to pay Mr Deepup £80 and the rest to an exciseman, Snow. I never needed money more and I 'strange'[1] you so neglect me. You say money is scarce and it will be if you never call on the tenants. I am told (I hope it's not true) that my small tenants are mostly five or six years in arrears. If it's so how can you answer the trust I place in you, for how can poor people ever pay such arrears? Don't let your forbearance endanger such a loss, but either make them pay or replace them with tenants who will.

[1] Strange, to be surprised.

## 441 FITZWILLIAM TO GUYBON

*London, 30 May 1706; F(M)C 1490*

(Has received £14 0s 8d from Hankin for Exton. Wishes John Walton's correspondents would get up the money Guybon mentions in time to supply him.)

I wish what you say likewise of the arre[ars] of rent due from the tennants that are so great be likewise so safe as you mention though others are of another opinion and so am I too especially of the poorer sort of tennants who ought never to be trusted above a yeare's rent at most. They have nothing to sell to pay it with but their cows and then how can they live? I am as mercifull as any can be but I must not be so imprudent as to leave so great arreares in tennants' hands as does them no manner of service and I want myselfe money in the meane time. Five or 6 yeares' rents for poore people to owe is a thing beyond immagination and I am laught at by all people of sense about this towne for suffering it. You have not writt me word how much money you received from Mr Colcutt tennant as was, between Mr Wright's house and the farme yard where Serjeant lives and how much he sett off in taxes, and lett me know how much you can sell the copper for at the Manton's farm house as was for I am teazed for these matters by old Colcutt. [P.S.] Do not forgett to returne me money.

## 442 FITZWILLIAM TO GUYBON

*London, 6 June 1706; F(M)C 1491*

Exton's £14 was paid three weeks since, very late. I find you have no mind for my coming to Milton or you would send returns more expeditiously. Walton's salesman, Plowright, has no orders to pay me money, and Thomas Chatteris cannot pay his rent yet, and claims to set off 40s for carrying venison. You see what people you deal with for returns, when I am satisfied there are more to be had than ever before in your parts now the drovers have changed their road, coming through Peterborough rather than the Red Inn and Wansford. Sir John Shaw,[1] Sir Charles Orby and others who have estates there tell me Deepup procures them returns. Doubtless he would do you the same kindness if you approached him. I wrote to you at least two months ago that since you approved of William King and his wife for the ferry, and since they had the wherewithal to stock it and furnish the house handsomely, I was willing to take them as tenants, but for the old rent, and the brewhouse and warehouses should be done to his content. I will build the new brewhouse on the bowling green side next the back door, but hope the old brewhouse will serve until next spring.

[1] Probably Sir John Shaw 2nd bart., died 1721.

## 443 JOHN CATLIN TO FITZWILLIAM

*Maxey, 11 June 1706; F(M)C 1493*[1]

Lolham bridge had the top of the arch turned 23 May. It cost 40s to turn the water. The foundations are 15 inches deeper than before. The arch is very strong but a little small and some say it will not carry the water away fast enough in a flood. Yet it is as big as the carpenters made the centre for it. The 'pendals' were broken very small but the work is strong if the lime and sand were beaten together enough. I feared it needed beating at times and asked them to well temper it. They have had 25 quarters of lime and some is left for when the freestone for the coping arrives. Edward Ward of Northborough has no stock on the Common. I visited him twice but he was both times from home so I left a note saying he must pay Mr Guybon. He has since paid 40s off his arrears and when the house is built promises to pay the rest before he enters. I have enclosed Mrs Vaughan's accounts in another letter. I hope it is done right. There are not so many arrears as Mr Cousens returned. The tax and poor assessment was £5 less than Mr Webdell reckoned, he being collector with John Alderman and John Bimrose for 1702 and overseer in 1701. Last year when the pastures were let there were 3 spare which I let to George Bo[w]man of Deeping for 9s a pasture. John Bimrose was angry and desired no more be let to Deeping lest the rent of the pastures was raised, for it was a showery spring and the pasture very hopeful, but it proved dear enough thanks to the dry summer. This year the tenants met on April 25 and concluded to hold all the spare pastures and so make up the rent. Only two or three were unwilling and Mr Church wished to leave it to the most votes and not concern himself. At last when Mr Church and John Bimrose saw the cowpastures were short they told me I should let all the rest to Deeping, but it was after the cows were in the pasture and in a dry year like this their fen is better than their pasture, so I could not let them. They should have told me sooner. They cannot be without the pastures at Maxey and will be glad to pay for their old pastures next year so that they may take new ones. I could not let them unless the rent had been under the rent the Maxey people pay but I did not let them know that. Mr Field is in arrears for seven years due last Lady Day 1706. The rent is £7 14s a year, total £53 18s. Only 50s is to be deducted, paid by Andrew Gunten of Deepingate, lately drowned coming home late from Stamford Market. His widow showed me that acquittance. I was with the other three tenants who told me they had paid no rent for Mr Field to Mr Vaughan. They only paid their own rent to Mr Pemberton for Mr Field's use. The tenants are John Measure, John Day, James Harington and Widow Gunten. There is still due to you from Mr Field £51 8s at Lady Day 1706.

[1] Fitzwilliam noted on the cover 'A letter of great concerne to me'.

## 444 FITZWILLIAM TO GUYBON

*London, 13 June 1706; F(M)C 1494*

On the 8th Marmaduke [Tomlinson] paid me £16 and Goodman Chattris £13 10s 6d. Before that I had to borrow money from my servant to go to market having none of my own. I hear nothing of Walton's money and know not where to send for it. Plowright, who sells Walton's beasts, is a Lincolnshire jobber who is only in town when he has goods of his own to sell besides Walton's and others' in those parts. I set off with Chattris for his carriages which made the money up £15 and that is his half year's rent. Marmaduke is still in town, for Mr Pemberton only came up last night, but I fear he will not be 'Duke's friend in renewing his lease of Sir John Brownlow's[1] land, for Mr Charles Parker put in for it and Pemberton will favour him over 'Duke. The scarcity of money in the country will bring me down sooner than anything else, but I am satisfied there is no lack of returns but you 'being growne now into yeares' cannot ride about as you used to getting in money or finding returns. If I had enough to pay my debts I would soon be down, but such small sums don't buy bread, meat and drink for the family. I hear Goody Freeman goes down hill every year. Take some of her land from her and make her sell stock so as to pay her arrears, for I fear you let her owe too much. Your forbearance will be her destruction, and I hear the same for many of my tenants, a great prejudice to me when I need money so much. Be sure to return a good sum next week and if you won't speak to Mr Deepup I will write to him myself. He has many returns to spare or Sir Charles Orby is mistaken, yet he is not steward to Sir Charles nor does any other business for him than returns, and Sir Charles has no kindness for him other than to serve his own turn. I hear nothing of Lolham Bridge, nor hear from 'Duke that you have begun Waldrum Hall, which do at once so that it may be finished at a good time of year.

[P.S.] You should do something at Richard Burton's house of Marrham who losst his wife last yeare in it by reason it rained downe upon the bed she lay in in. There should be a chimney build up in one of those roomes above staires in case a woman lies in at any time, and some ceileing worke don in the same roome to keep it warme. He is a good tennant and must have his house made a little convenient.

[1] Sir John Brownlow, 5th bart. (1690–1754) of Humby, was M.P. for Grantham, then for Lincolnshire, cr. Viscount Tyrconnel (Irish peerage) 1718: *The Commons 1715–1754*, i. 497.

## **445** FITZWILLIAM TO GUYBON

*London, 20 June 1706; F(M)C 1496*

Have received no money since my last. I found Plowright, John Walton's salesman, who said he had £10 of Walton's but no orders to pay me, so you see that Walton has sent no orders and I never wanted money more in my life. There are no such prices for wool as 11s or 12s a tod as yours mentions, but [even] if Goody Freeman sold her wool for no more, it gave just that price when Mr Blyeth and her husband took the farm so they have had a good time of it ever since. If Waldrum Hall can stand another year I am not against it but fear the worst. If the ways be good you should carry there all the stone, mortar and timber you will need to begin early next year. I received an open letter from Mr John Whittacre to you and to save you the post charge I am transcribing the contents. Tell his tenants he is angry at their not paying their rent, and must turn out if they pay no better. He will go down soon to see what repairs are needed and is angry Joe Clarke lets that house to a 'sorry' tenant who lets it decay. You may answer him that he should come down and see how the houses need much repairing, and how bad times are with his and others' tenants, and that nobody will buy the houses until repaired. He greatly wants to sell them. I would not buy Clarke's farm for that falls to me when Whittacre dies, but would buy Ward's but truly have no spare money at present. I have written you the contents of his letter and you must acknowledge you received it, directing your reply to Mr John Whittacre at Mr Pattison's, ironmonger, in High Holbourn near Southampton Street. This post I have instructed Mr Wright to repair the beam in the little parlour, and to make all ready to take down and rebuild the lucarne or bow window of the great house at the end near the new buildings. Mrs Bull must 'unfurnish' my dressing room until all is finished. My daughter is here and remembers herself to you, and will shortly reply to your letter of a fortnight ago. She goes to Essex in a fortnight.

### **446** FITZWILLIAM TO GUYBON

*London, [27 June] 1706; F(M)C 1507*[1]

I wonder you take no care of me for money. I wrote in my last John Walton had only £10 in Plowright's hands which he has no order to pay me. You could have spoken to Walton of this last Saturday. Plowright had only three bullocks of Walton's to sell which he sold at Stevenage and sent the money home by the drover. If the money had been brought to me it would only have been £12 or £13, and what is that compared to the money I need? Besides had the beasts been sold in town Plowright had no orders to pay me so I see how you do my business now. Fairly copy your accounts for my coming down for I have had none sent these two years. I wonder you complain for lack of rain. We have had nothing else this fortnight, very much spoiling the hay. If King is not content to have his brewhouse built when I think fit he may let the 'farme'[2] alone. I have nobody to look after anything there and must do it when I am on the spot. I will place it where I think fit and build it and the well as soon as can conveniently be done. The well must be sunk before the [brew]house is built if it must stand near it, otherwise it might bring it down. Although I intend to try it I fear the well will not 'quitt cost', witness Mr Selby's well at Castor. Nobody can think I will sink a well as low as the river. I am sorry you can get no more than £26 a year for Ben Burton's farm. £4 a year in £30 is a great loss. I believe you may prevail with her[3] to give the other 20s and don't forget a New Year's gift and boon days, and only let it for three years. I am glad you have written to Whittacre. I know Joe Clarke's farm is a lease for lives with Whittacre's the last but Ward's is copyhold which I have a mind to buy if I could spare the money, but I wish Whittacre to repair it first or allow for the repairs in the price. I hope to be at Milton soon to see what condition you are all in, and the grounds. If I have to borrow money to get out of town I will, as I have done these three weeks to buy bread. Leave this place I will and it's high time I did when I find the estate cannot maintain me when I am sure I don't spend half its revenue. I hope the prices of wool will mend, but Serjeant's is all fallow field wool and 11s is a handsome price considering pasture wool is not above 16s a tod. Fen wool never gave the price of our pasture wool.

[1] Letter damaged. Post mark on verso is 27 June.
[2] Meaning 'tenancy' (of Gunwade Ferry).
[3] Goody Thompson. See **432** and **433** above.

**447** GUYBON TO FITZWILLIAM
*1 July 1706; F(M)C 1499*

Yours of the 27th received. Marmaduke [Tomlinson] will have sheep in the market next Friday and what is made of them will be paid you, and hopefully even more. I cannot help it if people are so base as to break their promises. I did speak to Walton that Saturday and he promised you should be paid some money on the 21st or 22nd. I am glad we shall soon have you in the country. I wish you had never left it. I am sure it had been better for me by some pounds. You will find money hard to get, I never knew the like. I must pay £50 or £60 next week for the Queen's tax, the parson, etc. I do all I can to get you money although you say you see how I do your business but money is not to be got at present. If I could I would return a good sum. Because I don't you think I neglect your business. £100 was sooner got a few years since than is £20 now. I hope the times will be good again for they are bad enough. I have bargained with Goody Thomson for Burton's farm. She is to pay £27, a new year's gift but no boon days nor any Queen's taxes. I don't know what King will do but would not have you part with him for I don't know where you would get such another tenant.

**448** FITZWILLIAM TO GUYBON
*[London,] 4 July 1706; F(M)C 1500*[1]

I am glad I may depend on some money on Friday, but I fear it will be only a small sum for I find the tenants only send a few sheep at a time at this time of year. John Walton is a very knave to serve you so for his salesman, Plowright, has no order from him. Plowright was not in town for last Friday or Monday markets, being a kind of jobber for himself and salesman for Walton and a few others, so he is only in Smithfield now and then. I am sorry you have not got Goody Thompson to serve me some boon days. It is an ill precedent to other tenants in the same parish, and can be no prejudice to her for I never employ them at unseasonable times and when they have work to do for themselves. I don't wish to lose William King. It will be his own fault if he does not come to the ferry. I intend to build his brewhouse when I come down for I will be there to see it placed according to the design I have to make a backyard to the ferry. Everything reasonable shall be done for a good tenant. [P.S.] Mr Wright has written me of the finishing of Lolham Bridge and its cost, and of the Milton 'houses of offices'. I have ordered him to get all things ready for pulling down and repairing the 'lewcomb' by my dressing room when I come down. He tells me he has some Easton[2] lime at Castor to spare to buy sufficient strikes to repair the houses of office, but be sure it is Easton and not his own, for I hear he burns lime as Mr Selby did, and that's no better than my own used to be.

[1] Top of letter damaged.
[2] See **437** note 2 above.

## 449 GUYBON TO FITZWILLIAM

*8 July 1706; F(M)C 1501*

> I hope 'Duke ordered your money last week, and hope I shall get up some money to return next week.

William King is very unesie untill the well be sunck and brew house built for he would fill the cellar now full of good ale but cannot before the brew house be built and copper hung. He have a great deale of hay to carry and knowes not where to sett it he sayes, whether at the ferry, or Castor. He would not remove it againe for that will doe the hay harme. He sayes your honour have beene comeing this many years to Milton and he feares that your honour will not come yett. The bridge at Lolham was finisht last weeke. Mr Wright did come to Milton and see the lewcome and the beame in the little parlour but nothinge is done at them. I had some lime by me and have pointed the houses of office but there is no carpenters' worke done at them nor all the masons' worke yett. Mr Dickenson[1] of Peterborough was buried last Satterday night.

[1] Richard Dickenson, see below **450**.

## 450 FITZWILLIAM TO GUYBON

*London, 11 July 1706; F(M)C 1502*

Francis Guybon, Yours of the 8th I received yesterday. Last Munday evening Mr Hankin brought me £12 13s 6d by order of Duke, a very great supply of money after 6 weekes want of it! For William King's filling his cellar full of good ale, he has nothing to do with the ferry till Watts his time is up and I don't doubt but to have the well dugg and it may be the brew house built too. That will not be a worke so long a doeing by that time he comes to the ferry. In haysell and harvest, labourers are not to be had upon reasonable termes and to be sure I shall stay till towards Michaelmass when the springs are at lowest before I sincke the well, and after that build his brew house. King will find himselfe mistaken if he thinks I shall not come into the countrey before his worke is to be done, and if all he wants were now finisht he could not brew till Michaelmas time, for who brews at this time of the yeare drinke that is to be kept? I am heartily sorry to heare of the death of Mr Richard Dickenson. It was an honest family and now there's none left of it but his sonn if he be alive. I am sorry the houses of office and the beam in the little parlour are not secured before this. You did ill to point the houses of office or any thing at the slate worke there before the carpenters and masons had done their worke for to be sure knocking of the carpenters must needs make the lime fall out from between the slates. I should be glad to heare if there be any venison at Milton fitt to send me up for here's abundance about towne and very fatt ... [P.S.] My sonn has been gone from hence above a weeke haveing a mind to see the assizes at Winchester. From thence he went to Southampton, from thence to Portsmouth to see the great fleet before it goes out upon the descent in France. From thence he went by sea into the Isle of Wight to see our army that is there incampt. I hope he will come back againe now in a few daies.

## 451 FITZWILLIAM TO GUYBON

*London, 18 July 1706; F(M)C 1504*

I hope only want of business prevented you writing this week. A Mr Lawrence Parker, a dry salter in Southwark, brought me last Tuesday by order of Mr Charles Parker £300. Charles Parker's letter did not mention you so I doubted whether to receive it but finally I did, giving my receipt. The money shall remain untouched until I hear from you, being much more than you formerly returned and you giving no notice. If you ordered it I know well what to do with it and thank you for your care of me. I hope to be at Milton in a fortnight or so. Daughter Barrington left town last Monday, my son returning from Portsmouth that evening. [P.S.] I may send a large box by Monday's wagon. Let Joseph Chamberlaine get four new 'threepenny cords' for I fear the hoops on my halfhogsheads may fly this hot weather and the wine will be lost. Let him twist the cords tight at each end, but somebody must help him for he must not shake the vessels for fear of making the wine thick. If he thinks threepenny too small he must get fourpenny. I would have been glad to hear this week how fat the venison is.

## 452 FITZWILLIAM TO GUYBON

*London, 25 July 1706; F(M)C 1506*

I received yours of the 15th on Saturday the 20th, which should have come the Wednesday before. By the post stamp it came to town no sooner so the miscarriage must be by the neglect of those you trusted to carry it. Yours of the 22nd came yesterday. Last Monday by your order Heriot's received £79 15s 9d, I suppose paid by Bolton[1] since yours mention he had beasts coming for Smithfield. I am glad you will 'make a shift' to pay Mr Parker by degrees.[2] I hope he can stay so long for it, for I need it all. If not he must have some of it back. I hope you will 'stop his mouth'. Send your best buck next week by coach or wagon. If the weather is hotter than now defer until it cools. When the carpenters' work is done at the 'houses of office', if there needs 'sealeing worke' at the 'great house' on the garden side let it be done forthwith. I suppose the two little houses next the drying yard were never 'sealed'. If you have any, your own lime will be good enough for 'inward' work. Otherwise get a little from Peterborough which, being whiter, is fitter for 'sealeing worke'. Get all ready to pull down the 'lewcomb' but it shall not be stirred until I get there. I will read Joe Clarke's letter to Mr Whittacre and pay his last year's rent and get an acquittance. Seal all four pieces of venison that I may know I have my own. I hope you kept account of how many days Wright's men spent about the 'houses of office' and the parlour beam, and how often he was there himself. [P.S.] Give Mr Parker 'good words' desiring his forbearance for his money, for you see he can occasionally return you a good sum.

[1] A mistake for Walton. See previous and subsequent letters, **454** below.

[2] 'Paid Mr Parker which he returned to my lord, £300', 12 October; Disbursements 74.

## 453 FITZWILLIAM TO GUYBON

*London, 1 August 1706; F(M)C 1509*

Walton's money shall be repaid as soon as I receive that bill which you have written on desiring me to repay it, for such a man cannot forbear his money as Mr Parker can. It's very hot here, I hope the venison comes sweet. Put the box I sent this week in the matted chamber up the great stairs with the other boxes, etc, which were in the 'greate roome' over the 'great parlour'.

The Duke of Newcastle[1] is now at Orton[2] and Joe Chamberlaine may carry fruite thither who I know will want it every day for his table, and he has any very fine large fruite indeed worth makeing a present and some mellons with it that are ripe. He may present my humble service to the duke and lett him know I ordered him to waite upon him with it, but if his mellons are not extraordinary large and good as likewise his other fruite don't lett him carry it in my name but as if he came to sell it and not lett them know whence he came for I should be ashamed to have sorry small fruite come out of my garden. [P.S.] Lett me know when haysell was done and how forward you are in harvest, how much a todd wooll has sold for this yeare and if your Cambridge man has bought of the tennants this summer or not.

[1] John Holles, 1st Duke of Newcastle, *Complete Peerage*, iii. 249–51.

[2] Orton Longueville, Hunts, usually called Long Orton by Fitzwilliam, one of the duke's many manors. *VCH Huntingdonshire*, iii. 192.

## 454 FITZWILLIAM TO GUYBON

*London, 8 August 1706; F(M)C 1511*

Yours of the 5th I received yesterday. I repaid the £79 odd to John Walton's order. The hot weather much tainted the buck. Its flesh was thin and so small I took it for a 'sore' but I disposed of it. Send another next week when the weather will grow cooler. I hope it will prove better. I think Jack Freeman not very 'cunning' either at choosing a deer or shooting him and mistook his deer. You might get King to kill the next who my son says is very skilled in venison. Send the shoulders and stuff the [sockets] with straw and tell the carrier to lay the venison in a cool cellar and replace the straw with fresh every night. I enclose a warrant for Westhay Walk which send for as soon as possible. Lord Exeter has no restraint which expired at King William's death, and has since hindered me of many bucks unjustly. Discover if my lord will serve it and then send to the keeper. I send the sooner because my lord formerly said it came too late in the season.

## 455 FITZWILLIAM TO GUYBON

*London, 15 August 1706; F(M)C 1512*

I hope the buck comes sweeter than the last this cooler weather. I hope they will grow fatter every day now they begin to mend. I am obliged to Mr Parker for proffering you more money and his willingness to stay for it. If you could repay the money in a reasonable time I should like £100 more having several things to buy. Let him have a side of that buck I sent the warrant for from

Lord Exeter's walk, and if his lordship refuses to serve it I will ask Lord Westmorland to hunt it for me with his hounds as he did his own fee deer from that walk last year. Lord Exeter has 'cozened' me out of my fee deer ever since King William's death. Let Mr Pemberton have the other side and Cousins Tryce and Bellamy the two haunches. I think if Mr Parker has money in town and cannot get returns he may think it safer in my hands than with his kindred, who are tradesmen and might make use of it and he not know when to get it from them. Whatever causes his civility thank him from me and tell him whenever I have money to spare he may have it willingly. I am sorry no woolmen come among the tenants. I cannot advise them but believe wool will mend its price.

## **456** FITZWILLIAM TO GUYBON

*London, 22 August 1706; F(M)C 1513*

The buck came up somewhat green in places, elsewhere pretty well. I hope this cooler weather the next will come better. Next week I will send a great wicker bottle with wine and another bottle which send someone on horseback for and set them cool in the new cellar.

Pray lett Joe Chamberlaine or any body that has a large peircer make a hole with it in each of the halfe hoggs heads of wine I sent downe last, just neare the bung of each vessell to give them a little vent and then putt a round pegg in each of the holes and stopp it downe well againe and once in three daies pull out those peggs and give them a little vent and stopp them fast downe againe every time you vent them for at this time of the yeare wine is apt to frett especially what is in quantities in a vessell, and giveing it a little vent now and then preserves it from breaking the hoopes and the vessell too sometimes, especially when it is in pipes or great bodies. I am very sorry to heare you have so much dry weather. We have the same here about towne but it's convenient for to gett harvest in well which I suppose you have not yett done all round you. Pray God send us seasonable weather. I am glad to heare by the graziers that wooll rises for they tell me in Lincolnshire and Leicestershire that they who have sold make more of their wooll this yeare at least 2s in the pound already. I am sure I find cloath at least 3s in the pound dearer then it was in March last that I hope it will give a price againe soone.

[P.S.] Since Westhay warrant will be served give it to Mr Parker but tell him Mr Pemberton, cousins Tryce and Bellamy will be joined with him. Cross-a-hand give to Mr Deacon, with Mr Sparks and Mr Charles Duce for a haunch each, Mr Lowrey for the other side.

## **457** FITZWILLIAM TO GUYBON

*London, 24 August 1706; F(M)C 1514*

(The buck was the sweetest and fattest of the year. If another in the park was as good it should be sent the next Thursday. Wishes to know if Mrs Bull has her harvest in, and how forward harvest is with the other tenants.)

## 458 FITZWILLIAM TO GUYBON

*London, 29 August 1706; F(M)C 1515*

Francis Guybon, Yours of the 27th I received yesterday and am glad to heare the tennants have gott in their harvest before this rainy weather which began here with us on Bartholmew day[1] and has continued every day since by handsome showers that we have had here sufficient for the grass at present and hope you have had the same with you. I am sorry you have had no wooll man come amoung you as yett and wonder why the Cambridge chapman Mr Halstead has forsaken our parts. I am sure I entertained him kindly with wine every time he paid me any money that he cannot looke upon himselfe as affronted by me but he did tell me he gave to great a price for the wooll and losst £100 as he said one yeare but did not say it was by my tennants' wooll only. I am sorry to heare what you say about harvest, that a short horse is soone curried in your parts.[2] If so, I thinke my estate is plact in the most unfortunate place of all England for I do not heare that there has been sufficient of raine both in Lincolnshire and Leicester and the upper parts of Northamptonshire and most other countries, and besides noble cropps of corne, and with us you say there is neither hay, corne nor grass worth speaking on.

(Will send things weekly by the wagon and expects to be down in a fortnight. Test the small beer and ale brewed previous March and report how it is. [P.S.] Has Mr Pemberton gone to Bristol or the Bath as he intended and how long ago?)

[1] St Bartholomew's day, 24th August.

[2] To 'curry' a horse in this usage is to groom it with a comb. 'A short horse is soon curried' was a popular manner of speech, which here translates as 'a poor crop is quickly harvested'.

## 459 GUYBON TO FITZWILLIAM

*2 September 1706; F(M)C 1516*

I received no letter this week and hope your honours are all well. I hope the buck came well. You may have another as good this week. I received Mr Whittaker's letter yesterday, and will tell Joe Clarke the contents when I see him. Henry Watts goes up to town to see you, I suppose about his rent, he owing £170 for three years due Michaelmas 1706, all but £10. He wishes time to repay for he cannot make money at present, prices being low. Pray order him to leave the houses, fences, boat and roads belonging to the ferry in good repair. I hope we shall see you here before Michaelmas.

## 460 FITZWILLIAM TO GUYBON

*London, 5 September 1706; F(M)C 1517*

I wonder my letter sent a week today should miscarry.[1] I took great care in sending it to the posthouse, and have sent to inquire about it. They protest they take all imaginable care of their letters, so I hope you have received it by now. I will have no more bucks from my park this season so that there will be more next year. Dispose of Sewley and Moorehay warrants. Take a half yourself, and give pieces to Mr Whinyates and to Charles Duce. I think I named Robert Newcomb this summer already. You may have a piece dressed at the ferry where Mr Selby and Mr Wright would be glad to meet you and some of the country neighbours. You can give Mr Ash a piece from me which may be acceptable at this time he has newly married his son [but] I leave it to your discretion to give the venison where it will be most acceptable. Harry Watts brought your letter and complains of his losses and that King will buy none of his goods. I told him he must expect no abatement, but pay all arrears or give good security before he left. I had suffered too great losses by his neglect of the warehouses which are fallen, of part of the old house which a small charge in time could have preserved, and of the boat, which yearly repairing could have made last as long as boats used to last under former ferrymen. I told him it was a kindness I had taken back the ferry at Michaelmas rather than next Lady Day, for though his father entered at Michaelmas he paid no rent for the first half year and did not begin the toll until Lady Day after, John Chamberlaine renting the toll and living in the ferry house that winter. I won't take his single bond for what he owes. He told me of his brother Wright but I don't know whether he will be bondsman, but I expect a good one, or you must secure my rent from his stock and goods before they are removed from my ground. Be as secret as you can in what security you take for if the world thinks him much in debt it may hinder his marriage to another wife. I have written to Mr Wright to secure Milton House for this winter. It's too late to do anything this season. Let Mrs Bull secure me a good housemaid at Helpston statutes, and hire the cook maid for another year and pay her wages though she has done me no service for that was my fault not hers.[2] My son went yesterday to the Bath to divert himself. He had hopes of finding Mr Pemberton at Bristol but Harry Watts says he is still at Peterborough. [P.S.] Did my [missing] letter arrive, in which I asked you to test the ale and beer brewed last March? Did the bottles arrive safe?

[1] Letter **458** above.
[2] 'Paid Goody King of Alesworth her daughter's wages due Michaelmas last, £3', 5 October; Disbursements 74.

## **461** FITZWILLIAM TO GUYBON

*London, 12 September 1706; F(M)C 1518*

I am glad you received both my letters but sorry to hear of Mr Phillips'[1] and Mrs Bull's illnesses. Harry Watts told us Mrs Bull was very well at Peterborough market a week last Saturday. God send her well again to see her poor children well disposed of.

I am sorry you have no wooll chapmen come amung you. I find by Lincolneshire and Leicestershire grasiers that wooll is rather better by one shilling in the todd then it was last yeare and that's all though there is but very little sold yett I find by my intelligencers, for there being so great likely hood of a trade with Spaine againe if King Charles[2] does but succeed as we have great reason to beleive he will, wooll will rise very considerably soone, and corne the same, for they want much of those commodities in Spaine. I am glad to heare you have had raine with you. We have had enough here and the ground very green and full of grass. I hope you have secured the cooke maide, though the statutes be over at Castor and Helpston, for I would by no meanes part with her and send me word by your next whither she has hired herselfe any where else or not.[3] My sonn is very well at the Bath as we are the same here, thanke God.

[P.S.] Let me know when Mrs Bull was taken ill, what was her distemper and if so ill as to want a physician and who they had to her, and if she continues ill. Advise her children to take care of her and let her not want a phisician though she seems to oppose it. Go there often and see she wants for nothing.

[1] The Rev. Pawling Phelips is meant, see **464** below.

[2] England supported the Habsburg archduke, later Emperor Charles VI (1685–1740), in his claim to the throne of Spain.

[3] Goody King's daughter. See **460** and note 2 above.

## **462** FITZWILLIAM TO GUYBON

*London, 19 September 1706; F(M)C 1520*

I am willing to stay until Michaelmas come twelve months for the money Harry Watts owes me if Mr Wright will be bound for him. But if he sells any of his goods or cattle or wool and receives the money sooner I expect to be paid it, and give a receipt in part of the bond. That is fair to both and Mr Wright should see it done for his own security. Let Pemberton draw a substantial bond. We thank God Mrs Bull is on the mending hand. She must have a care she catches no cold and relapses. I am sorry Mr Phelips continues ill, and hope you visit him often. 'Company is great comfort to sicke people'. I don't doubt to raise his spirits again when I get down, and make so much of him at Milton he will visibly recover. Persuade him to make much of himself, and lack nothing necessary, for on him depends his family's welfare. I will not part with the cookmaid. I cannot be without her and she shall not long be a trouble to her father-in-law. I don't know where her mother is. I have not seen her since Easter or Whitsuntide and doubt she has been in town since.[1] I am sorry to hear about grain prices but hope the farmer has so much more grain as will make amends, for I hear from all hands what great crops grow round England. I am sorry Stourbridge Fair did not afford a good price for wool, but hope it's no worse than last year. If you have paid off Mr Parker the money he returned me, I would be glad of £100 more or what money you can spare. Rain and high winds for the past two days and nights have quite drowned the 'countreys' round about. [P.S.] You don't say to whom you disposed the fee deer warrants. If a Mr Feild, my vintner here in town, comes to Milton let him taste the claret and white wine I bought of him five or six years ago that he may see how sour it is, which my son told me of, and let him drink the bottle if he likes. He wishes to sell me a small estate in Northborough and Deeping Gate but I don't know how it lies to be joined to any of my farms. I told him till he could dispose of it you should receive his rents if it lay not out of your way. I believe I bought his wine seven years ago, the first I sent down after I left Milton last.[2] There was four dozen red, four dozen white, four dozen sa[ck].

[1] Goody King whose daughter is the cook-maid.

[2] Fitzwilliam underestimates the time since he was last at Milton.

## 463 FITZWILLIAM TO GUYBON
*London, 26 September 1706; F(M)C 1522*

I am sorry I am unlikely to have any money soon. I am glad Mrs Bull and Mr Phillips are 'on the mending hand', but sorry to hear of the death of William Sechell of Aylesworth. He was an industrious, careful man and we have lost a good tenant. I hope his wife knows how to manage the farm without him. Tell Mr Wright I wrote him a fortnight ago about propping up that lucarne over the great cellar, and securing that defective place in the great staircase, where I think the turret in great danger, for I feared I would not be down this season in time to do anything about them. These places must be well propped this winter for I fear the great rains of the past month have done great damage at Milton. Next week I expect my son home from the Bath and then I shall not be long from Milton, for now the weather has taken up the waters will soon go down and the roads be passable. I am sorry no woolmen come yet. I fear they will hardly come this year and so the tenants must be forced to sell to their neighbours. [P.S.] I wish Mr Wright to answer my letter because I also sought his advice about sinking the well at the ferry.

## 464 GUYBON TO FITZWILLIAM
*30 September 1706; F(M)C 1523*

Received yours of the 26th. I hope to pay Mr Parker all his money next Saturday and to return you more by him soon.[1] Mr Phillips is on 'the mending hand'. He preached last Sunday but Mrs Bull mends slowly. Mr Wright is now securing those places. He has so much business up and down the country he is seldom at home. There is much to do at Northborough church, new seats to be made and they would bring Marmaduke [Tomlinson] in to pay towards it. I think there is no reason when your honour has a 'chancell to yourself'[2] and are at all charge of repairing it. The parson says your seat is in the church. If so it must be removed to the 'chancell'. He wishes you to give the town the old clock and he will set it up at his own charge.

[1] Repaid the £300 on 12 October. He paid Parker a further £100 on 2 November; Disbursements 74.

[2] The parson was claiming that Fitzwilliam (or Tomlinson as his tenant at Northborough Castle) sat by right in the body of the church and therefore should contribute to the cost of the new seating. Guybon was pointing out the existence of a chapel within the church, a former chantry which contains Claypole and Cromwell monuments, which Fitzwilliam was responsible for maintaining, into which his seating could be removed. See Bridges, ii. 529 (where the chapel is 'called Claypole's ile or chancel').

## 465 FITZWILLIAM TO GUYBON
*London, 3 October 1706; F(M)C 1525*

Francis Guybon, Yours of the 30th past I received yesterday. I am glad to heare you intend me some more money soone and that Mr Phillips [Phelips] and Mrs Bull are both on the mending hand but am sorry she does not mend so fast as the parson but he is a young man and nature is more vigorous with such then elderly people. As to the old clocke at Milton I am willing to give it either to

Etton or Norborough provided the townes will repaire it and mainteine it there. I will preferr Etton first because that towne was mine before the other but if Etton refuse it then I will give it to Norborough towne but not to the parson for I understand he is a very pragmaticall and selfe ended[1] man and takes upon him more then he can justifie. Duke and old Jonathan Sisson the drover told me he obligd the towne to new pave his chancell which was alwaies done at the minister's charge and would make use of none of the old stone againe which would have helpt but some he made use off about the parsonage and some he sold. He does the same by the church but I will not consent he shall have any of the old stone but what is good lett it serve againe. The great house was never assess't to repaires of the church nor never shall by reason that chappell was kept in constant repaire by the great house and cost me £10 in new running some of the leads since I bought the estate. My seate in the church shall not be removed nor new built; it was a good seate and in good repaire last time I saw it and when it wants repaireing or new building it shall be done at the charge of the tennants of the great house and not by the towne. I will have no alteration in my seate; it shall stand where it is, and they as stirr it, lett it be at their perrills. This, pray acquaint the parson with all yourselfe and lett [it] be before some of the townes men. The parson must be curbd or he will domineer to much, though be civill in your discourse, but he must be told his owne.[2] I know not how they can sett up the clocke at Norboro there being no steeple to the church for if it must stand in the church they must make a handsome box case for it that may not looke undecent in the church and which may cost more then the towne are willing to lay out to have a clocke who have all along made a shift without one and the greatest conveniency of a clocke will be to the parsonage and a few houses neare the church. I do not say this against giving the towne the clocke if the townesmen have a mind to it and are willing to repaire and mainteine it when they have it which I leave wholly to them.

[1] Self-ended, characterised by self-centred actions or desires.
[2] To tell anyone his own, to tell him frankly of his faults.

## 466 FITZWILLIAM TO GUYBON

*London, 10 October 1706; F(M)C 1527*

(Glad Phelips is recovered and Mrs Bull recovering; also that Parker is to pay £100 that week. Those most earnest for the old clock should have it, provided they repaired and set it up. At Etton it would be heard all over the 'towne', but Northborough being so large, only half the town would hear it. [P.S.] His son returns from Bath in very good health.)

## 467 FITZWILLIAM TO GUYBON

*London, 17 October 1706; F(M)C 1529*

Mr Lawrence Parker brought me £100 last Tuesday for Mr Charles Parker of Peterborough. If the townsmen are not as desirous to have the clock, they shall never be imposed on to please their parsons who would, I am sure, bear little of the charge. I have written to Mr Wright about digging the ferry well now it is a fine, dry time. I leave it to him to let it out to good workmen who understand the business. Needham is a sorry fellow, not to be trusted, but I suppose would undertake it cheaper than any. I would rather pay somebody more who would do it well for his own credit. I am glad Mrs Bull mends daily and hope we shall see one another soon. I am sending a calesh[1] to use in the country. Have a place made fit for it in one of the coach houses by the middle of next week. You never told me how much Harry Watt's goods sold for at his French sale and where he and his family have gone to live; nor when King came to the ferry and how he has furnished his house there.

[1] A light carriage with folding hood.

## **468** FITZWILLIAM TO GUYBON

*London, 24 October 1706; F(M)C 1532*

I received no letter this week but hope you are well. One Stangar and Henry Lawrence of Walton have paid me £17 19s 10d between them. [P.S.] Let me know what was done at Maxey Court; whether the well is 'a digging'; how Mrs Bull is.

## **469** FITZWILLIAM TO GUYBON

*London, 31 October 1706; F(M)C 1534*

Glad to hear you and everyone are in good health. I am glad the ferry well is 'a digging'. Let it be dug at least 20 feet deep, with good stone for the walls and good slabs for the bottom to bear them. Let the masons have no money until Mr Wright tells you it's completed. I have written to him at length. Let him lack no good materials for the work. I find no tubs or buckets, nothing but good stone for walling and some small timbers to keep the earth from falling in while they dig. I am glad to hear so good an account from you of the new tenant at the ferry. He shall lack no encouragement, but his brewhouse cannot be built until next spring. I am sorry my black colt is dead but he was not over young for I believe he was got by the Holtham horse who has been dead almost 20 years. [P.S.] I have sent word to Mr Fearey by his wagoner to bring up a pair of horses to draw my calash down to Milton next week if he will take 40s for the journey. More I will not give. If the horses come I will send a manservant with the calash. Look after him until I come. I will allow you 4s a week for his board. I believe he will bring as much into the house with his gun as will maintain him, but I don't value that; you shall be allowed for his board notwithstanding. I enclose a warrant for Westhay Walk and will send the rest by degrees. Tell Mr Forster of Marholm I received his letter and would have answered it but I shall be down before Christmas. Bid him not to be discouraged by a few bad years. He shall find, if necessary, I will be kind to him.

## 470 FITZWILLIAM TO GUYBON

*London, 7 November 1706; F(M)C 1535*

I am sorry Mr Wright has hindered the work at the ferry by his multitude of business. If you had written of this sooner I would not have troubled him, but Castor being so near to the ferry, I thought it would not have hindered him to go there now and then. I suppose he has written you what he agreed with Robert Bursnoll.[1] I wrote him I feared they would weary of the work once they had got down 15 feet, and that the great rains we have had would make the water flow in upon them, making the work 'tiresome'. So I ordered him to tell you to keep money in your hand for fear they left the work half finished for it's more worth 10s a foot after 20 feet than it's worth 2s 6d for the first 10. I would have it no less than 20 feet deep and better 25, for it will be dry in summer if it is no deeper than the spring we pass going down to the boat ferry. So keep money in hand to make them finish the work well. 'For the placeing of the brewhouse I shall be convinct by reason and strive to please you all.' I am pleased you have such good company at the ferry as yours mentions. Staying here longer than I expected I begin to need money so remember me. [P.S.] Ask the new tenant King, who I hear is a good woodman, to look in the park and see if any deer are fat enough to kill and how many are worth sending up.

[1] After negotiating with several masons, Wright had agreed with Robert Bursnoll at a rate of 5s a foot for digging and walling the first 10 feet, 7s the next 10 feet, and 8s a foot if he needed to go beyond 20. The well to be 8 feet in diameter within the wall at the foot, 4 feet at the top. Wright reported that King wished the brewhouse to be built adjoining the house with a connecting door to the cellar passage. Wright to Fitzwilliam, 22 October 1706, F(M)C 1531.

## 471 FITZWILLIAM TO GUYBON

*London, 14 November 1706; F(M)C 1538*

Yours I received yesterday. Little Rowland Morrice cannot be depended on. He has failed often in payments after promising you faithfully. I have not yet heard of him but his market for hogs is always on Wednesdays, so fear he will disappoint me. Ask Mr Parker if he will return a sum next week that I can depend on. Give him the Westhay warrant. Since he has an interest with Lord Exeter he will have it better served. It shall be between him, Mr Sparks that married Mr Wardell's daughter, Mr Harry Tryce and Mr Bellamy of Farcet. Give the Cross-a-hand warrant to Mr Deacon, he taking what piece it pleases him best, the rest divided between Mr Lowrey, Mr Charles Duce and Robert Newcomb. For Sulehay [warrant] Mr Roger Pemberton to choose his piece, yourself another, and the rest to King at the ferry to dine his merry friends from Castor, as Mr Selby, Mr Wright, etc. I reserve Morehay Lawn warrant for further consideration. I don't think to have a doe from the park this season; it being so wet they cannot be good. I am glad [King] has such good company at the ferry. 'Pray God send it may hold'. I wish the well to be dug three feet after they find a spring, and Mr Wright writes to me they have not found one yet although they are past the third rock. I hope that work is not given over until they find a spring, for the water in it is only rainfall. Now we are about it let us do it well, with good materials. Let the workmen observe if they sink through any coal veins, for we struck a vein when digging a well at Woodcroft Farm about 18 years since. Glad you are all well, as are we here but my daughter in Essex complains much. I fear the air there is unhealthy.

## **472** FITZWILLIAM TO GUYBON

*London, 21 November 1706; F(M)C 1540*

I am glad you intend to supply me next week by Mr Parker. Rowland Morrice paid me £30 3s 5d late Saturday evening.

I am sorry to heare Robert Bursnell and his company were beate out from the well digging at the ferry by rainy weather but hope they are at worke againe now it is faire for such worke is not to be delayed but gone through with at once; should it lie all winter it will all fall in and be a perfect new peice of worke to begin againe. That was the reason I was against your paying them but very small subsistance money for feare of their leaveing it halfe done for I knew the deeper they went the worse worke it would prove and I wish it had been finished before the raine fell for now the very socke[1] of the ground after so much wett weather will bring water upon us, that we shall not know whither it be a spring or not. Pray lett them not rest till they fall to worke againe and finnish it and be sure to go deep enough. A worke well done is twice done.

I don't understand what repairs are needed to the old brewhouse walls at the ferry, for they are strong, the timber good. It only needs a little thatching for the winter, for we shall build the new brewhouse in the spring, but let the tenant have all that is necessary in the meantime. I saw Marmaduke [Tomlinson] this morning and he hopes to bring me some money tomorrow, but I don't know what he came up about for he sold his cattle in the country. If you think it will bring people to the ferry you may dispose of my warrant for a doe, giving the ferryman a piece and the rest to some of our friends, for I will have no venison up this winter. [P.S.] Mr Colcutt wishes the copper at Manton's at Castor taken up, irons and all, and carried to Fearey's at Peterborough to be brought up by wagon. He will pay for a mason to take it out, with Fearey paying carriage to Peterborough and Colcutt will repay him here. Let Fearey keep copper and irons until he is paid. It may be directed to Mr Thomas Colcutt to be delivered when called for, carriage to be paid.

[1] Sock, the boggy substratum of marshy soils.

## **473** FITZWILLIAM TO GUYBON

*London, 28 November 1706; F(M)C 1541*

Yours of the 25th received with Mr Rowell's bill for £50 but I fear I shall never get it for I can neither read the man's name nor the street where he lives, it's such a strange hand. Had he written whereabouts the street was I might have guessed it. However, tomorrow I will ask among the hackney coachmen and porters. 'Duke [Tomlinson] has paid me £50 rent. He was forced to stay in town until now because I was out of town five days on business. Neglect no time this fine weather to go on with the well at the ferry.

**474** FITZWILLIAM TO GUYBON

*London, 5 December 1706; F(M)C 1542*

Since I wrote last I have Mr Rowell's £50, for we made out his hand at last among us. I am glad the masons are back at work. Make a good well if you dig a mile deep, for I will have a good well now we are about it. I will write to Mr Wright about letting out the carpenters' and masons' work at Waldrum Hall. Mr Colcutt wishes to have the copper up because it was his father Lea's, and if it won't serve as a copper again thinks he can sell it better here than you can in the country, carriage charges and all. He is a notable man in his way. Let 'your Duke [Tomlinson] of Norborough' know that Mr Pemberton will not consent that he shall give [no?][1] more than 14 years' purchase for the house and land he wishes to buy; they ask 20 years' purchase, and having seen the writings I am of Mr Pemberton's opinion. I am very free that he shall buy it, and will not think of buying it myself. It is Joe Clarke's that I want and that will fall to me after one life.

[1] Fitzwilliam wrote 'more than', but the context makes it clear that 'no more than' (i.e. 'only') was intended.

**475** FITZWILLIAM TO GUYBON

*London, 9 December 1706; F(M)C 1543*

Mr Pemberton brought up a lease of one Osborne of Maxey. It's for three lives, one of which is dead I believe. Osborne wants money on the security of his lease; the estate falls to me on the determination of the lives. Pemberton advises me to lend the money rather than another, so let Osborne have what he needs and Pemberton will draw the writings to secure the loan. They only need £50 at present but if they need more let them have it.

**476** FITZWILLIAM TO GUYBON

*London, 12 December 1706; F(M)C 1544*

I am sorry Richard Burton has given warning. If he comes up with sheep I will speak with him about it, but you don't say what is his rent, nor whether he holds more land than that which he warns he will leave next Lady Day. I must not let my land without the houses which go with them. If Levitt's house needs repair you should do it for so good a tenant as you say he is. Let me know what he pays for Levitt's house and homestead and the 38 acres; how much you think the 38 acres too dear, and how much you advise me to reduce it. I will tell Mr Colcutt what he is offered for the copper in the country. However, you have trifled with him so long, proffering only 14s or 15s, and now rise so in price that he will think it worth more than it is and still have it up. However, do nothing until I send you his answer. [P.S.] Get a drawer from a Peterborough inn, or if Mr Taylor, the Lynn merchant, keeps a winecellar at Peterborough, ask him to send one of his men that understands filling wine hogsheads, to Milton to open my two halfhogsheads, and fill up what is wasted from the two great bottles I sent in August or September last. The biggest with wicker about it contains red wine; the three gallon stone bottle holds white. They need be opened only at the bungs, and stop them and the bottles well up again, for they may be used to refill again if I don't get down in time to have them bottled off. Take Mr Lowrey's advice for he lived with Sir Simon Taylor many years, and I suppose understands such a business better than anybody about Peterborough, and try to have him there when you fill up the halfhogsheads. With his directions anybody might do it. Write out your accounts for when I come down or send for them. I have had none for two or three years.

**477** FITZWILLIAM TO GUYBON
*London, 19 December 1706; F(M)C 1547*

Give to the poor this Christmas as I used to. Samuel Sylverwood has paid me £28 for Richard Burton; George Mawre has paid £6 16s 10d for James Dove; and today Henry Hankin has paid £74 11s 9d for Charles Parker. Keep them to their work at the well, and be sure they go three feet deeper after they come to water so we may always have three feet of water there. 'A worke once well done is twice done'. Keep the workmen as much in arrear of money as you can to ensure they finish it. [P.S.] I hope Mr Pemberton got well home. I have yet to hear from Mr Colcutt.

**478** GUYBON TO FITZWILLIAM
*23 December 1706; F(M)C 1548*

Mr Pemberton came home very well and glad to hear from him you are all in good health. The masons are about the well but the wet weather of the past 10 days beat them out of it. When the weather settles a little they will soon have it finished. Last Saturday Mr Osborne told me they need money. I promised him some next Saturday by which time Mr Pemberton will have done the writings. Richard Burton is willing to pay £30 for the cowpastures and Levitt's house and homestead, but paying no taxes. At present he pays £34 and the taxes, so that would reduce the rent by £6 a year. He is a good tenant and rents a great deal and the times are bad. He rents John Freeman's farm and the 22 acres by the mortar pits. If you and he agree he will take a lease of them all. If not he will leave the town which I would regret, for then you 'must abate to others'.

**479** FITZWILLIAM TO GUYBON
*London, 26 December 1706; F(M)C 1550*

Francis Guybon, Yours of the 23th I received yesterday. I am sorry to hear the well at the ferry is not yett done. We have had no raine here this fortnight to speake off and wonder to heare the worke is hindred by the raine when Mr Wright sent me word long since that the water in it which happens by the raine, though it be almost full over night is suncke all away the next morning which makes him beleive they are neare a spring that has passages under ground to the river. Pray lett it be gone on with as fast as may be that it may be finisht but be sure to go low enough after you have found the spring for you must conclude springs are now at the highest after so much raine and wett weather as we have had, that in a dry yeare must be much lower in water. As to Richard Burton, it's a great abatement he demands if it be sixe pounds in sixe and thirty. I shall not consent to lett a lease of it upon such an abatement though I will not stand with him for £3 or £4 a yeare if he takes from yeare to yeare as he has done I suppose. Times may mend after the warr is over which we hope will not last above a yeare longer and then there will be an open trade againe. If he goes on upon the old rent I will be kinder to him then he now demands for his losses last yeare and the yeare before but I cannot abide to abate of the old rent. Try what you can do with him to perswade him to reason. I heare he is to be in towne these hollydaies. If so, I hope I shall see him. I received a long letter from Mr Forster of Marrham and have writt him an answer and desird him to lett me know: if he was willing to hold the farme for one yeare longer from Ladyday next as he seemd to desire; how much he would give for the farme and not plow it at all, and if he did plow, how much then he was willing to give for the farme then; but to lett me know at the same time what part of the farme he intended to plow and how many acres the ground he plowd did conteine. Pray speake to him about this that he makes no mistake.

## 480 FITZWILLIAM TO GUYBON

*London, 2 January 1706/7; F(M)C 1551*

When the masons have dug as deep as they think fit I desire Mr Wright to see it before they lay a stone, that I may be sure they are deep enough, for I don't doubt they are so weary of it that the least water they find will lead them to say it's deep enough just 'to be ridd on't'. But I shall be the sufferer if they make a dry well and I have to begin again. I shall be glad to see Burton when he comes up; and glad if you have paid Mr Osborne £50 and that he shall want more, so that I may hope to have the lease come out sooner. [P.S.] We hear my daughter is very ill but hope she will do well again.

## 481 FITZWILLIAM TO GUYBON

*London, 16 January 1706/7; F(M)C 1555*

Glad to receive yours of 13th, for having no letter the week before I feared you might be ill. On Tuesday 14th Mr Hankin paid me £53 3s 6d for Mr Charles Parker. I wonder that the workmen are not yet through that rock at the well when Mr Wright wrote a fortnight since that they had made a little hole quite through it. Be sure to dig below where they find water for fear of dry summers for this long wet season must have thoroughly soaked the ground and springs must run 'quicke' after so much rain. If we once get a spring that will afford enough water I may think hereafter to lay pipes to Milton to mend the water there. I have had a long letter from Mr Forster which I will try to answer this post. My daughter is much better but 'no thoughts of breeding as I heare off'.

## 482 FITZWILLIAM TO GUYBON

*London, 23 January 1706/7; F(M)C 1556*

I shall be glad to see Richard Burton. Had you not paid the workmen at the well so much money the work would have been done before this, but they come to you pretending they have been at the work so many days, when they have been half the times they claim; you pay them and then they are overpaid, not underpaid. I wish you had let the work to Roles from the first and then it had been sooner done at less charge. Get everything ready to build at Waldrum Hall as soon as the season and weather permit. Are the half hogsheads of wine sent down last summer filled up as I ordered? Did Mr Lowrey watch them filled? Return me money as fast as you can.

## 483 FITZWILLIAM TO GUYBON

*London, 30 January 1706/7; F(M)C 1557*

Richard Burton has paid me £38 and Sam Sylverwood £17. Not having sent to Heriot's lately I did not know of Osborne's paying me there until you wrote. I do not know what to make of Richard Burton. He knows not his own mind half an hour. He told me his rent was £89 besides his rent fowls; that he paid a third of parliament taxes for his first farm, which is the house, homestead and 38 acres. For his other farm that was Jack Freeman's and the 22 acres he said I paid all taxes. I asked him what he wanted abated. He said £4 a year and those taxes amounting to 40s a year more. I agreed to his demand upon condition I might have the Freeman's farm house which would ease me of its repairing. He might be sure I would not let it for fear of bringing a charge to the 'towne' unless they were able to take a farm with it. Then he fell off from his first demand and said I must spread the hills in the 22 acres which would cost 40 shillings. At length I agreed to pay 40 shillings to spread the 'ants hills'. My son was by all the while. When Burton saw I met his terms he said they would cost £4 at least. Upon these terms we parted but I suppose he will consider better of it. I promised to do anything reasonable to make his house fit for a new wife. The more one complies with him the more he flies off. We talked about ploughing some of the 60 acres but could not agree for I said if I suffered him to plough I would abate no rent nor taxes. I am glad they are through the rock at the ferry well. Let them go deep enough.

## 484 GUYBON TO FITZWILLIAM

*4 February 1706/7; F(M)C 1558*

(Fitzwilliam's of the 31st[1] received. Glad Burton and Sylverwood paid him some money. Hoped to return more the next week. Sorry Fitzwilliam and Burton could not agree. Would not have Fitzwilliam part with him. Good tenants very hard to get. Burton's rent £89 a year besides rent fowls, a great rent in those times. They had not passed all the rocks at the well yet, having reached a third, very hard and thick. They hoped to meet with no more. The sinks about the [ferry] house were stopped. They opened them, the lower rooms were very wet and the cellars were unusable.)

[1] Error for 30th.

## 485 JOHN CATLIN TO FITZWILLIAM

*Maxey, 13 February 1706/7; F(M)C 1559*[1]

A Benjamin Wright of Maxey, shepherd, whose rent is £11 17s 8d a year has paid no rent since you bought the Maxey estate except for his cowpastures. Next Lady Day there will be due about £12. His substance will not pay half. He has a bill from Mrs Vaughan for looking after her sheep of about £5 but she stops it for rent he owes to Lady Sylvius so he goes on taking no care or notice. I told Mr Guybon two years ago and several times since but I believe he forgets, 'being anciant'. Mrs Vaughan says she will pay none of her husband's father's debts nor arrears he owed you when he died, saying she is advised to the contrary. She lets the land for advantage. Mr Guybon bids me ask her and I do often but she will not pay. She took about £40 the last time she paid Mr Guybon the £20. Mr Guybon is almost angry with me sometimes because I can gather him money no faster but it is very scarce where I go for it. Grain being so cheap breaks many tenants that have severe landlords but I think most of your tenants in Maxey manor are too far behind. Some have had no acquittances for several years and they will pay no more rent without an acquittance to that time, and I dare not meddle unless you have an account first of all their reckonings. I intend therefore if your honour pleases to come to London before 25th March next and, if you consent, will ask Mr Guybon for a colt to carry me, and I will bring the whole Maxey manor rental plainly written and inform you of everything and about the cowpastures, and I believe I can do the journey for about 20s if God and your honour please to give me leave.

[1] Fitzwilliam wrote on the cover: 'John Cattlins letter about what Mrs Vaughan sayes and severall things of consequence'.

## 486 FITZWILLIAM TO GUYBON

*London, 13 February 1706/7; F(M)C 1560*

Yours of the 4th received by Mr Pemberton who dined with us last Sunday. Have received Mrs Bull's order £7 7s 9d from a Robert Hardy. I suppose you and Burton will agree for the farm on the terms I offered him which were lower than he first demanded. The man knows not his own mind half an hour. Whenever I met his demand he asked for more, and so higher as he found me come up to his demands until in the end he knew not what reduction to ask. My son was by all the time. I said he could consider it on his way down but that I believed he had more a mind to strike a bargain with you but I told him he might not get as good terms as I offered. I wonder at the sinks being stopped up at the ferry. Both the sinks at the cellars of the house and the bowling green house were substantial and large, well slabbed at the top. There is no other sink there save one in the kitchen which runs above ground. Mr Pemberton says the well is sunk at the front between the house and the river, for he saw a heap of rubbish there, but I imagine he is mistaken and that they carried earth round from the back to get rid of it. I hope you will master the third rock, and find a good spring below, for I want a good well. [P.S.] I told Mr Wright to let out the building of Waldrum Hall.[1] Make sure it is raised so high that the low rooms are not drowned in flood time.

[1] Samuel Hibbens who had contracted for Lolham bridge, received the contract, see Disbursements 74 where an account with Hibbens of £35 12s on a separate sheet of paper is placed opposite the first half of 1707. Of this total his bill for Waldrum Hall was £23 19s.

## **487** GUYBON TO FITZWILLIAM

*17 February 1706/7; F(M)C 1561*

Richard Burton and I have not yet agreed. He stands to have the other 40s abated for 'cutting the hills' in the 22 acres, and to have his house 'made handsome'. He will spend £3 or £4 building outhouses that he needs. A Claypoole of Tallington has twice come to me about the castle farm at Maxey. Mr Bimrose leaves it this Lady Day. I tell him you have nothing to do with it to my knowledge. You must get the charter for the toll at Waldrum Hall renewed, else it will be lost for many refuse to pay. William Garner of Sutton would take your farm at Castor late Richard Lees', for the present tenant will sow no more than this crop. The two sinks at the ferry have been cleared; the well is dug between the stable and bowling green. They are walling the sides but are not yet sunk deep enough. The masons at Waldrum Hall are cutting stone and making all ready. Mr Parker will order you money next week.

## **488** FITZWILLIAM TO GUYBON

*London, 20 February 1706/7; F(M)C 1563*

Received yours of the 17th. I suppose Burton will not stand to that 40s since I agreed to all he demanded and more, and had I agreed to that 40s he would have demanded more still. I will do anything reasonable to his house. I am sorry Mr Bimrose leaves the Castle farm, fearing the rent will fall, but will not meddle in the letting of it, though Mrs Forster should seek my advise. I doubt Claypoole is able to deal with it, and would be glad to know if Bimrose is grown too poor to continue. I must seek among my Maxey writings to see how the charter runs for the toll.[1] They are at Milton and must await my return. I understand William Garner of Sutton is a very poor man. Mr Hankin was with me this morning to speak on his behalf. I told him if he [Hankin] would be bound for the rent [Garner] should have it; otherwise not. Hankin has money of Parker's in his hands but no order to pay me. I hope you will not lack a tenant for Manton's farm. Hankin says Garner wishes to take a piece of ground in Milton to plough, because the farm, he says, is too small to employ a team without other ploughland. I know of no small piece we have in our hands unless the Highway Close, and that Carnell ploughed not long since.

Poore Mr Pemberton was taken very ill last Tuesday in the afternoone of an appoplecticke fitt, just as I was 4 yeares agoe. He was lookt upon by the docters in great danger till this day but thanke God this day I thinke him much better and so do both his docters. My sonn and I are every day with him and I saw him cup't this evening myselfe. He is not quite out of danger yett but he being a very strong man I am not apprehensive he will die this bout. Pray waite upon Mrs Pemberton next Satturday from me and with my service tell her what I write to you and tell his mother the same for she may remember how I was, being with me severall times in my illness, and I take care he has the same meanes used to him as I had to me at that time which I hope he is the better for. You may assure Mrs Pemberton he shall want for no meanes that can be had for him for we send or go to him almost every two houres and his docters are with him twice a day or oftener if there be an occasion, but we hope after one day more we shall not have often occasion of them. So with all our kind services to the whole family of Mr Pemberton's and loves to yourselfe I am your loveing freind.

[1] Of the ferry at Waldrum Hall.

## 489 FITZWILLIAM TO GUYBON

*London, 27 February 1706/7; F(M)C 1564*

Mr Hankin brought me £66 6s. I am sorry Richard Burton is so ill but hope he will do well again and accept the terms I offered him. I am glad Claypoole is able to deal with Maxey Castle farm. I believe him honest and have sent to Mrs Forster your report of him. Until I see for what she lets Goodman Claypoole the farm I will not proceed with its purchase. Hankin will speak for young Garner but will not be bound for the rent nor lend him money, fearing things may be bad with him. Hankin told me [Garner's] father engaged him to pay many debts which were unknown at [Garner's] marriage. Now all is come out and Hankin fears Garner's circumstances are so low he cannot deal with much, otherwise Roger Standish would not have parted with him, so better you have nothing to do with him. Mr Colcutt would have his copper sent up by any wagon. Chattris could carry it to St Neot's and so up, or Fearey could bring it, after sending a cart to Castor for it. He will accept no such price as a guinea for it. When you send the woolman's bills I will do my best to get the money but you don't name him. Mr Pemberton, thank God, is better every day. He was taken with a great pain in his head last night, 'but Mrs Audriana with some lavender drops and vinegar removed the paine presently'. We don't doubt he will be well again soon.

**490** FITZWILLIAM TO GUYBON
*London, 6 March 1706/7; F(M)C 1566A*

(Is glad the money will be returned soon, and that Richard Burton has recovered. Unsafe to deal with Garner unless a responsible man was bound with him. Yet hoped Guybon would get a good tenant without reducing rent. Farm was 'pritty' as any in the 'towne', and considered a good 'pennyworth'. Fearey should take care to be satisfied for carrying up the copper before parting with it. Wishes to know who bought the tenants' wool the previous summer. Mr Pemberton 'mended' every day but would be too weak to go abroad for some time. Charles Turner of Lynn taken ill at his tavern but could not be dissuaded from setting out next morning. Hopes he got safe home. Would enquire price of bowls but under no obligation to buy them, being for the tenant's profit, and when he leaves his successor must pay him for them. Bowls at the green had been his father's when the green was at Milton. Fitzwilliam had sent them to the ferry when the green was set up but would not have bought any). Mrs Forster complains much of Bimrose for not paying his rent; he will owe a year at Lady Day. She expects it down because a tenant that leaves must clear his arrears before removing his stock. She asks me to secure that part of the rent due me, at the same time securing what is due her. Write me your views for I would do the woman any kindness I can. I perceive she has no kindness for Bimrose for he had much slighted her of late years, and he was no more at first than her father's ploughman. Her father trusted him, set him up with the farm ready stocked, so he has been very ungrateful to the poor woman if what she says is true. She would rather have Claypoole for tenant even if Bimrose would stay, but will not abate the old rent. It seems there's but 20 acres of arable and yet Bimrose claims he lacks barn room, when he has a slated barn which holds more than the arable will bear. [P.S.] Bimrose should secure her the arrears before he leaves, but she will not accept security but only the money for she needs it.

**491** JOHN CATLIN TO FITZWILLIAM
*Maxey, 13 March 1706[/7]; F(M)C 1567A*

(Has received Fitzwilliam's of 13th and 22nd February. Unless Fitzwilliam forbids it he intends to leave for London on 24th, bringing copies of rentals, arrears, and his book of receipts. Has Benjamin Wright's bill for £6 4s 10d from Mrs Vaughan, but written by Richard Ewen and unsigned by her. She acknowledges it, but claimed it was for money due Lady Sylvius whereas the particulars were all for 1700 and 1703, so Wright had assigned it for part of his arrears of rent if Fitzwilliam would accept it.) Many tenants in arrears go on carelessly, but most of them are able. Some promise to pay money at a time they appoint, but [even] with a two or three month delay, seldom perform it. I have told the tenants they must pay for their pastures on 3 April because there was not enough time before 'brake day'[1] last year. A few refuse to pay 7s 6d a pasture, fearing they will be raised in a wet year when they will be four times as good.

[1] Break day, an appointed time for payment.

## 492 FITZWILLIAM TO GUYBON

*London, 13 March 1706/7; F(M)C 1567B*

I am sorry I have had no money from Mr Parker this week for I need it much. There is no haste for the copper and no need to send a wagon specially from Peterborough, but take a time when it can be carried there for nothing for I shall get nothing from Colcutt.

Pray secure my rent due from Mr Bimrose before Ladyday as Mrs Forster desires for I heare by people in towne his circumstances are very meane and he very low in the world though he still makes a great show. What Bimrose is and has been worth he had gott it in Maxey Castle farme and I am sorry if Claypoole be able that he has given over the thoughts of taken it. I am sorry to heare times are so bad and that Mr Phillips and his daughter Webdale are gone off. Pray God send us better times which I hope we shall have after another yeare for in all probability this next summer will end the warr ... [P.S.] My sonn is sett out this morning for Essex to see his sister. Mr Pemberton is so finely well and recovers his strengths daily that he talks of leaving the towne this next weeke but I hope he will not so soon for feare of a relapse by catching cold. You mention nothing of the well at the ferry as if it was forgott.

## 493 FITZWILLIAM TO GUYBON

*London, 20 March 1706/7; F(M)C 1568*

(Fitzwilliam regrets he has had no return 'this week or last'. Will send Colcutt word his copper is coming. Is sorry for Mrs Forster who is worried about her farm if Bimrose really leaves it. He has given warning but not left, and she does not know how to secure her rent or what to do unless Guybon can find her a new tenant. Catlin is coming to town as Fitzwilliam had instructed him, but would not have time to talk to him next week. Catlin to delay his journey until Monday week, 31st March. Encloses letter for Catlin which Guybon must deliver the following Saturday night or early Sunday morning.) Seal his letter for I fold the two letters together with his unsealed to save the postage for one. Mr Pemberton is stronger each day and goes abroad for the air every day 'to use himselfe to it'. Yet I dissuade him from too soon a journey for fear of an ague. My son is with his sister in Essex, both very well. [P.S.] Whoever rents my fishing upon the river Neene must have it no longer being resolved to keep it in my own hands for I hear it has been very much abused by poachers. Let all those sort of people take notice to come there no more, no, not even with an angle for I will execute the laws against them. I shall appoint the same gamekeeper as the Duke of Newcastle appoints, Daniel Leadhead, who lives at Long Orton.[1] He shall enter that employment at Ladyday. I shall send down on Monday by Feary's wagon a box of grafts of choice pears for Joe Chamberlaine to graft. I will write by the next post what shall be done with them for now I have not time. Let Chamberlaine call next Wednesday for the box at Feary's and at the post for my letter.

[1] Above **453** and note.

## **494** FITZWILLIAM TO GUYBON

*London, 27 March 1707; F(M)C 1569*

I am extremely troubled you send me no money for I need it more than ever in my life. Send me what you can as quickly as possible.

As to William King's haveing the fishing I will by no meanes agree to it. He shall have liberty of fishing between the ferrys or thereabouts with a cast nett or so to get a dish of fish for his guests now and then, but to have the whole royalty I never will consent nor never lett it away from my one family. Robin Newcomb tooke it of me out of Mr Hinton['s] hands because he said it was abused and paid me 4 guyneys, if I mistake not, about 7 yeares' agoe, for 2 years rent then due. If he has not paid any rent since pray call of him for it for that I expect it from him. If he lett it to any one else the money I expect from him; it was without my knowledge or approbation. The Duke of Newcastle's gamekeeper[1] will terrifie strangers but King shall have leave to fish for his guess[2] but for no body else and now that we have severe lawes against poachers they shall be putt in execution and I intend to begin with Holmes the warrenar, Mr Richardson the petty cannon and parson of Eye,[3] and a minnister['s] sonn belonging to Mr Dreydon[4] and his father is a great huntsman and he an great shooter and lies much in my woods, and Parson Richardson is both for gunn and fishing. I am beholding to other people for this information and not to you who ought to informe me of all these poachers but you connive too much at all people that trespass on my royalties. Last Munday I sent downe by Fearey a box full of grafts for peares covered with horse dung and earth. I hope they be safe gott to Milton. There are the names to all the sorts tyed at the severall bundles but I question whither Joseph Chamberlane has stocks enough to plant a quarter of them. However, lett him graft all the stock he has; they ought to be all quince stocks and most of them for walls or dwarfe trees. Lett him be sure to graft that sort that is writt upon: the *burey du roy*,[5] *la chassary*,[5] the *virgolois*,[5] the orange burgamott, all the sorts of bergamotts and all the *bon cristian*,[5] peares both[6] winter and summer and lett every stocke when he has grafted them have a paper writt of the sort of it and tyed to the stocke till I gett downe and then I will putt them in better order. Pray order Joseph Chamberlaine to gett all the stocks he can against another yeares, especially quince stocks for peares I intend, God willing, to have amany trees grafted of the best sorts that are to be had of peares and every thing else. I hope he will raise me some mellons this yeare and all things else for the use of the house . . .

(In post script lists the pears again, emphasising that he would have Chamberlaine take particular care of them.)

[1] Daniel Leadhead.
[2] Guests.
[3] Eye, Northants, a village adjacent to Peterborough.
[4] I.e. of the household of John Dryden of Chesterton.
[5] Beurré du Roy, Leschasseries, Virgoulées, Bon Chrétien.
[6] 'Both' repeated in error.

## 495 FITZWILLIAM TO GUYBON

*London, 3 April 1707; F(M)C 1570*

I received yours by John Catlin and was glad Mr 'Plaw' [LePlaw] is to pay £30.[1] Yours yesterday brought the two bills for £50 which I sent to the man but he could not be found but his relatives said I could depend on their payment next Monday or the Friday following at latest. The bills are payable the 5th, but they always take three days more 'which they call dayes of grace', so I expect it no sooner than Friday. Being a salesman in Smithfield he is only there on market days. Get up as much money as you can for I need a great deal at this time of year for clothes for ourselves and servants, a new coach with harness and a calash besides.

[P.S.] I understand that 'Duke of Norborough[2] takes upon him to be lord parramount of all those parts and if any strayes are taken up and carried to pounds he fetches them out of Maxey pound, Deeping Gate pound and other pounds thereabouts and carries them to Norborough and takes what he pleases for their trespassing and gives me no account but keeps all the proffitt to himselfe. Upon this I have ordered John Cattlin that whatever strayes are taken in the North Fenn, in Deeping gate and all Maxey liberty should be carried to Maxey pound where they ought to be; and on the other side whatever stray is taken in Norborough closes or any of the feilds belonging to that towne shall be carried to Norborough pound and though the townes and the royalty of them are all mine yett I will preserve the priviledge of each parish and towneshipp to itselfe. I have ordered John Cattlin to take care of all the strayes belonging to Maxey, etc., and to see the cattle want for nothing and if there is any little matter to be gott by them he shall take it to himselfe but if any stray should not be owned of a yeare and a day that I expect a bennefitt off and also the same from Norborough. I heare nothing of Mr Phillips of Marrham that you said was comeing up.

[1] 'Aprill 5th: returned my lord by Mr Jacob LePla, £21 3s', Disbursements 74.
[2] Marmaduke Tomlinson who leased Northborough Castle from Fitzwilliam.

## 496 FITZWILLIAM TO GUYBON

*London, 10 April 1707; F(M)C 1572*

Had no letter this week so hope you are well. I wrote by John Catlin and hope he got safe home. I was paid by Mr 'Pla's' [LePlaw's] order £21 3s, and have received from Mr Crislow £50 with a promise he will pay the other £50 bill tomorrow – Good Friday. I believe we can depend on him for he has a fair reputation, so you may venture to pay Mr Checkley the first £50 on Saturday next and the second £50 next Monday, for if he pays not I shall write in time.[1] Return all the money you can. [P.S.] This ferry well has been long in digging and I hope to hear by your next it is finished. Before sealing this the post man brought me yours. I will see about bowls but expect King to pay for them. Get materials for building his brewhouse. I think to have it built onto the great house as you and Mr Wright have contrived. I was only against that place for fear of fire.

[1] There is no record of such a payment in Guybon's accounts.

## 497 FITZWILLIAM TO GUYBON

*London, 17 April 1707; F(M)C 1573*

I am sorry money is so hard to be got just when I most need it. God send us rain soon for we have a very dry time of it. Rain is prayed for in all the churches but I hoped it was not so dry with you. Mr Hankin brought me a bill of Sir Francis Child's for £36 18s 10d for Marmaduke Tomlinson.

I have been lookeing out for bowles for the ferry green. I cannot have good ones under 8s a paire. There are from 6s to a guyney a paire as they are turned with fine worke on them and the finest of wood but I thinke them of 8s a paire may do very well. I suppose my Lord Gainesborough, Mr Noell[1] and other gentlemen of quality may bring their owne bowles and leave them there for the bowling season, and my sonn and I will have each a paire. Those bowles as be now at the greene are all the fashion bowles now, and the great bowles are now most left off. Lett me heare when the first bowleing day is like to be and if they intend to keep two dayes in a weeke. I thinke Mundaies and Thursdaies may be the propperest daies but that must be as the gentlemen please.

I am sorry that after we have been so long about the well it must be deferred until Michaelmas. If it proves a wet time then it is never likely to be a well. Keep money in hand or Robert Bursnoll and his company will never more come at it, now they see what trouble they have at the well bottom. [P.S.] Please lend me two dozen quart bottles, or the largest you have. Let Joseph Chamberlaine scour them with shot, make them clean and hang them on the rack. Send word they are dry and fit for my use and I will tell you what to put in them. I had rather wine than ale bottles. Let none be fusty or ill smelling.

[1] Baptist Noel, 3rd Earl of Gainsborough (1684–1714) of Luffenham, Rutland. *Complete Peerage*, v. 600. 'Mr Noell' is probably his uncle, John Noel. See also **501** and **502**.

## 498 JOHN CATLIN TO FITZWILLIAM

*Maxey, 18 April 1707; F(M)C 1574*

The tenants of Maxey cowpastures met April 10th and concluded to put in only 150 cows and pay 7s 6d a pasture, which makes up the full rent. Mr Church has paid, and about seven more that had money when they met. So there will be none spare but all taken each year by Maxey people. When there were more than Maxey needed some made light of them, saying they would not all be let, but now there is only enough to serve Maxey they will be forced to speak in time for them before all are hired, for they cannot keep house without them. In dry years the pastures will be let with less trouble, and in wet it will be far better for your tenants because there will be none spare for Deeping. Mr Guybon is well pleased, but took not much money from them. They are warned to pay by Thursday next or have no new pastures. If you take Ben Wright's bill that I showed you he promises two more from John Carter and Robert Osborne, and then I shall have his rent. If I seize I will not get half his rent, but Mrs Vaughan will not pay her bill without forcing, so please order Mr Guybon to take it of me for Mrs Vaughan to pay, or let me know so that I may try some other method. I got home well on Sunday morning by the road you directed which was the best way. I give my humble thanks for your great kindness and the reward you gave me.

## 499 FITZWILLIAM TO GUYBON

*London, 24 April 1707; F(M)C 1577*[1]

I received yours yesterday with the subscription paper for the ferry. We have signed it and my son keeps it until this day week in hopes of getting some signatures here in town. Mr Phillips I saw last Sunday and today. If he will have a new seat in the chancel for his wife he must build it himself. Mr Hall of Collyweston offered to erect at his expense three new seats on his side the chancel if I would do the same on my side where the servants sat but I refused as my own seat is commodious enough, at least I thought so then. I don't know what I may do hereafter if Mr Phillips will build with me to make the chancel uniform. There really does want a good cushion and a communion table cloth, which must be a charge to the parish but I will prevail with him if I can to wait until there is a peace and money can be better spared. Recommend us kindly to Mr Pemberton and all that family and say we congratulate him on his daughter's marriage, and are extremely glad to hear by his son's letter that he 'has gott a good stomach againe and is otherwise so finely recovered by the help of the good aire'. You don't say if the bowls are approved of, the prices of which I sent down last Thursday's post.

[1] Letter unsigned, or else incomplete.

## 500 FITZWILLIAM TO GUYBON

*London, 8 May 1707; F(M)C 1578*

I received your letter of last week, my son another this week. Thank God I am much better than I was, but have been very ill with the stone and gravel. We are all extremely sorry to hear of the death of Mr Pemberton's son-in-law, and tell them we heartily condole with them in their great loss. The bottles I wished to borrow and have washed were to bottle some brandy in Milton new cellar in two large wooden bottles and one small. You had best get a drawer from a Peterborough tavern to fill them and he can also fill up the two half hogsheads of wine that were filled last winter. The red wine is in a great glass wickered bottle and the white wine is in a great three gallon stone bottle. Fearey's wagon will bring down on Wednesday six pair of new bowls and two jacks for the bowling green. The old bowls, if King rubs them well with oil, will look as well as the new, and I question if the new bowls will be better than the old. Mr Phelips of Marholm is well but cannot get his business dispatched. He dined with us today. I am heartily sorry the drought continues with you as with us. I should not be sorry if a great part of Westin's Meadow came into our hands for fear my old hay should be too old for the horses and my deer. Keep some of it unlet for fear of the worst. Be not too forward in letting the meadow under the usual prices. I want money so much I know not what to do and my illness has been chargeable.

## 501 FITZWILLIAM TO GUYBON
*London, 15 May 1707; F(M)C 1579*

Thank God I grow better every day and hope in a week to be quite well. This warmer weather remove the straw with which I suppose you covered my wine and brandy last winter. I hope the bowls are safe arrived, but if King should die don't send them to the bowling green until further order. I am extremely sorry to hear how ill he is. If he died I fear his wife could not hold the ferry for it's his acquaintance which brings custom there. You would better stop work on the new brewhouse. I yet hope for rain to make Westin's meadow grow better. We don't mow until the beginning of July. God knows how much rain we may have before then.

When I sent my warrant by my sonn to the Duke of Newcastle to be sent to one Daniell Leadhead of Long Orton the duke's gamekeeper and who I appoint to be mine upon the river, and my sonn informing the duke that the ferry man must have leave to fish to entertaine his guests now and then with a dish of fish, he answered the ferryman was the greatest poacher upon the water and that he made it his business to catch the best fish and carry presents of them both to the Earle of Gainesborough's and Mr Noell's, and that he uses an unlawfull nett and so must be restrained to fish only with a cast nett and angles which I thinke very well for I must not sufferr him to plunder the whole river to send away in presents to his old acquainteance, that maybe, may not come to the ferry twice in a yeare. Not that I grudge him fishing for what is dresst in his house for the bennefitt of his trade. Nor would I have any of Peterborough people or any others who may take a crowne's worth of fish or more under his patronage only for the spending 2d or a groat in ale, but if it be dresst at the ferry I shall not be against their leave to fish.

I see you have the workmen back at the ferry well and that they cannot draw it dry. If so they can never finish it properly, and had better give over until it be quite dry or until Michaelmas when the springs are at the lowest. You ask how Waldrum Hall is to be covered but do not say how it was covered before. I suppose a poor small rent like that does not deserve better than good thatch. I am sorry money is so scarce with you. I am sure it is with me. I have to draw from 'the maine stocke' for want of returns, and I think it a hard case if my land estate cannot maintain me. I hope you will quicken those who are most in arrears. Get the brewhouse and vessels clean and ready for I think next week to send word what drink I will have brewed. I expect to be down between now and midsummer. [P.S.] Give our kind respects to the Pemberton family. I am glad the small pox ceases in the family for I suppose all the children have not yet had them.

## 502 GUYBON TO FITZWILLIAM
*19 May 1707; F(M)C 1580*

Yours of the 15th received. The straw on the wine is removed and the cellar cleaned. I have the bowls safe at Milton. The half hogsheads of wine are filled and the brandy bottled. It made only 19 quart bottles. King, thank God, is better but puts off bowling yet. Your honour is misinformed of him being the greatest poacher on the water. I doubt he has sent the Earl of Gainsborough nor Mr Nowell a fish since he took the ferry, nor does he fish when the earl and Mr Nowell are there. He may have caught a dish of fish for them to eat there. He does not fish and keeps others from fishing and they it is, I believe, who have informed against him. The workmen are still at the well but cannot drain it dry. It's thought it is as dry as it will be at Michaelmas. Waldrum Hall will be reeded as it was before. I am sure it will be the cheapest thatching in the long run, for it will last many years, if the dearest at first. Money is very scarce in the country, it is the general complaint as you will have heard. I could sooner have gathered up £100 a few years ago than I now can gather £20. So fast as I can get up money I will return it. Mr Wright is very bad at present with sore eyes. The drought continues and if we have not rain soon it will come too late for Etton meadow and all the other hay ground.

### 503 FITZWILLIAM TO GUYBON

*London, 22 May 1707; F(M)C 1581*

Mr Whittacre greatly needs his Northborough rents and is particularly disposed to sell. Tell Marmaduke Tomlinson and his wife that I believe he will never have a better opportunity of buying. Whittacre needs £100 for a particular occasion. Mr Burman of Stamford once offered him 20 years' purchase for the copyhold estate, the part 'Duke wants most because there is a 'pritty deale' of land and meadow belonging to it. I told Whittacre he would have to come down and have got him down to 17 years. I will strive to get him to 16. If 'Duke won't buy on those terms tell Bolton of Northborough, but don't mention a price under 18 years for him for he is fond of buying there and will be a 'hearty chapman' if he has money to spare. Manage this as well as you can for Whittacre who will be beholden to you for it. I received yours of the 19th and am extremely glad King is much better, for I know when 'such sort of fatt drinkeing people fall ill it goes hard with them'. He does well to put off bowling until the warmer weather. He would have little company before then, and before the Earl of Gainsborough goes down, who promises my son to be often there, bringing what company he can with him. King must get another pair of good tables for one pair in such a house, especially on bowling days, will not be enough for it may be rainy and the company will go to tables. If he wishes us to buy him a pair we will do the best we can. A new pair of the newest fashion costs about 16s or 17s. I am sorry my brandy falls short of what I expected, for I sent five and a half gallons, and the bottles sealed down. There lacks three quarts if your bottles are all full quarts which I doubt, but if so my loss is more. I fear the carrier's men have used foul play which you may see by looking round the bottles. King shall not be debarred from taking fish for his guests to eat there but not to give away. The well is unlikely to be properly finished if you cannot draw it dry when the springs are at their lowest ebb, for how will you do it when it rains there as it has here since the change of the moon? We have had great showers since last night and hope 'in God' you have too, making the meadows and grounds grow for it is not too late. It will cost as much to reed Waldrum Hall as to slate it. It will last well and is a warm covering but take notice not every common thatcher knows how to lay on a reed thatch, and if not well done it will last no longer than common thatch, so get a thatcher from Spalding[1] for I am sure none nearer knows how to do it well. I don't doubt money is scarce, but not so scarce that I may not receive more than you send. I don't receive half the revenue of the estate under your jurisdiction and if you let tenants like Goody Freeman of Milton and Mr Forster of Marholm run so much in arrears in time I shall not receive a quarter. Such as they never think of paying their rents and others will follow their example if they are suffered. I hear Mrs Vaughan and other Maxey and Northborough tenants run in arrear, especially the small tenants whom you let run behind five or six years, which will be lost if they die before you get it. Since you have John Catlin to run about those 'townes' I wonder you should have any arrears there. Get up money as fast as you can for I am forced to spend from the 'maine stock' and it's hard if my land will not maintain me. Brew two hogsheads of ale and four of small beer, allowing 16 bushels of malt for the ale and eight for the beer, well hopped because it's warm weather. I hope last summer's beer is long since spent. Tell Mrs Bull I wish Milton House to be ready to receive me by the 20th of June. [P.S.] Send a good sum to pay my debts before I leave here. Mr Phelips has almost finished his business. I wish he was safely home for he begins to look very ill, his complexion much altered for the worse.

[1] Spalding, Lincs., 14 miles from Marholm.

## 504 FITZWILLIAM TO GUYBON

*London, 29 May 1707; F(M)C 1582*

Whittacre sends now to hear what 'Duke resolves to do, and would be glad of the tenants' Lady Day rent. I am very glad King is so well recovered. We will take care in buying him a pair of tables. I am sure slating is better than reeding for any landlord if the prices be alike. Reed will rot, slate won't, but will serve again, and will endure winds better being heavier. They use reed in the fens because they have no slate, but it's near us and we sent a great way for reeds. You were ill advised to buy this reed[1] but being bought it must be used.

I am much surprized to heare by yours you have entred on Goody Freeman's farme of Milton and given me no notice of it till this letter as if my advise was not worth haveing and I must know nothing of my owne business. I take this as ill as any thing you ever did. I was writt to about sixe moneths since that you had markt her sheep and stocke with my brand and was offered a tennant for the farme and woud buy all the stock but truely I did not beleive them but writt an answer you had given me no account of any such thing and I would not turne an old tennant out so long as they were able to hold. I have reason to beleive what I heard and I am sure you have dammified me above a hundred pounds by not letting me know it at first for I know you understand not how to mannage that farme, not being able to ride about as you have done, that what through want of care servants will be negligent that I am sure to loose halfe in halfe of every yeare I keep it in my hands. I know not how to be angry enough at this great miscarriage of yours and never so much as sent me an account what she was in my debt nor what her inventory came too for I suppose when you seized you had her goods in her house vallewed and inventoried and all her stocke the same and putt her out of the house otherwaies how do you know what she may have conveyed away to her children? Such a miscarriage as this is not to be expected from a man of your age and experience. I am sure that stocke would have sold as well at last Michaelmas as it will sell at next Midsummer and what a loss of rent is here since then. I could have lett the farme and have had security both for the rent and the stock if I would have beleived what was writt to me but where you take a kindness you care not what I sufferr and loose to gratifie your freinds. I expect forthwith that she leaves the house if she is not gone already and secure every thing in a legall manner which Mr Pemberton must direct you to do. You may remember what hapned to Sir John Cremer by Mrs Bond of the Crowne farme in Sechey:[2] how Sir John out of his kindness lett her remaine but a small time in the house and she conveyed away every thing to his great loss. This might be a sufficient warning to you if you vallewed my good. [P.S.] I am sorry to heare of Mrs Watts' illness but she is of a great age. I hope Mr Wright is not dangerously ill. I hope you will have more raine for it raines here every day and we have almost enough. You must incourage John Cattlin and chide him seemingly before those small tennants and tell him you are sure he does not call of them for money and must tell him before them that he shall distreine upon them if they don't pay him for you will not sufferr such arreares amungst them.

[1] Guybon paid Robert Wright £1 12s for reed 'by bill' about 20 June, Disbursements 74.

[2] Lady Fitzwilliam's uncle, Sir John Cremer of Setchey, Norfolk (died 1669). See note to **297**.

## 505 GUYBON TO FITZWILLIAM

*2 June 1707; F(M)C 1583*

Yours of the 29th received. Whittacre's Northborough tenants have no money but promise to pay soon. 'Duke has a mind to it but hopes you can persuade Whittacre to go below 16 years. We brew this week.[1] Mrs Watts was buried last Thursday. Mr Wright continues very ill of his eyes. Mr Phelips is home and well. I can get no money for you yet. I understand you are much surprised I have entered on Goody Freeman's farm. I hope you will have no cause to be angry. I am sure the stock is much better. Had it been sold last spring it would have given very little. I hope the farm will pay our keeping it and she was unable to go on with it. These many dry years have undone her with buying winter meat. I hope we shall have enough this winter having had some fine showers. I hope you may let the farm this year as well as last and sell the stock a great deal better. You will be at no great charge for servants, there being only Jack[2] who is a very careful, honest young man who minds his business.

[1] Guybon paid 5s for five pounds of hops on 14 June, Disbursements 74.

[2] Mrs Freeman's son, John.

**506** FITZWILLIAM TO GUYBON
*London, 5 June 1707; F(M)C 1584*

Yours of the 2nd received. Glad to hear of your fine showers, but by others come out of that country you have had abundance more than we have here. The roads are dirty from Lincolnshire to within 10 miles of London, which I rejoice at. Mr Whittacre is supplied with money and will not now sell at so low a price, so 'Duke must rest contented at present. We are all very sorry for the death of Mrs Watts, but 'she was in great yeares and we must all submitt to time'. I am sorry for Mr Wright's eyes but hope it will go off. I am not angry at your entering on Goody Freeman's farm at Milton, but at your not acquainting me you had done so, for I supposed it was but reasonable since the estate is mine that I should be acquainted with all transactions upon it and have my opinion before anything is done. This had been but good manners in you. I am sorry you send no money this week for I have many tradesmen to pay off, especially my coachmaker to whom I am greatly indebted. Speedily supply a great sum. Widow Freeman's farm cannot be let until Lady Day by which time the stock will be poor again, and how these past two years' rents must be paid I leave to your consideration. [P.S.] You do not report on the well. I hope you have given over working this wet weather for it cannot be properly finished until the springs are lowest about Michaelmas. You don't say what bowling you have had and what company there. I wish young Mr Pemberton was got well into Ireland for Lord Pembroke[1] told me yesterday he sets forward next Monday.

[1] Thomas Herbert, 8th Earl of Pembroke and 5th Earl of Montgomery, died 1733. *Complete Peerage*, x. 423–5.

**507** FITZWILLIAM TO GUYBON
*London, 12 June 1707; F(M)C 1587*

(Glad of showers which have caused grass to grow thick about town, which they cut as fast as they can. Troubled Guybon has no money for him.) Mr Whittacre greatly needs his rents. He would have gone to gaol if I had not borrowed money to lend him, for he was disappointed of the £100 loan he was promised, and his creditors would stay no longer, and he not knowing how to make me a security I was forced to buy his estate. I would not have done this if 'Duke [Tomlinson] had come up with his money in time to keep him out of gaol. Besides 'Duke seemed unwilling to meet his price so now that matter is ended, but I owe him Lady Day rent when you receive it from the tenants. I fear we shall never have a good well at the ferry. The work went badly at first. After such a dry summer last year they could have dug through that rock before the great rains of last October, and now they are but half through it and the water rises fast upon them. Give the work over until next Michaelmas. Give Mr Wright, if well enough, a great charge to go to Waldrum Hall to see the thatchers sew the reed well on. It was imprudent to thatch with reed when other thatch might have done as well, and slate would have been as cheap or cheaper. I hear from a Lincolnshire man who came over the ferry that King has had the small pox so no wonder you have had no bowling yet, for people will be unwilling to come to an infected house. However, you need not have concealed it from me. Gentlemen of no business are leaving town apace and after the end of term I hope to be soon at Milton. Don't forget a great sum of money for me next week.

### **508** FITZWILLIAM TO GUYBON

*London, 19 June 1707; F(M)C 1588*

God continue your fine rain until 'haysell'. I am sorry wool is like to be so very cheap. I still hope for the best. I have heard from Mr Wright about the well and Waldrum Hall. He recommends laying gravel about the house to keep off the water in flood times, especially the side where the floods most beat. Lay it with a good descent which he says will save the foundations. There is gravel enough so let it be dug and carried there before 'haysell', and let Mr Wright show them how to lay it to secure the house. Do not lose a day. I was much concerned you returned no money last week after promising to do so for three weeks or more. I am the poorer because I lent Mr Phelips £20 to pay his fees. Set off with him £12 10s this midsummer quarter and I suppose he will pay you the remainder in ready money. I am sorry to hear he has been ill since he returned. He wrote me 10 days ago but said nothing of it. (Seeks detailed report on the brewing.)

### **509** GUYBON TO FITZWILLIAM

*24 June 1707; F(M)C 1589*

This rain and hot weather will bring 'haysell' on apace. I cannot get a sum to return. If I could get but £50 or £60 I would send it, but I can hardly get money to pay the country charges. No gravel can be carried to Waldrum Hall until after harvest, the North Fen is too wet. We brewed as you ordered two hogsheads ale, four of beer. Adam Johnson was four days about it, his son three. We had the malt from Goodman Hullock, your tenant. Hops £5, hoops six and a new bottom for the great buck tub. Captain Selby is gone off.[1] Mr Philips continues ill.

[1] Is financially broken, see **510**.

### **510** FITZWILLIAM TO GUYBON

*London, 27 June 1707; F(M)C 1590*

I cannot but wonder that among all my tenants you cannot raise £50 or £60 in six weeks. I am surprised at Mr Selby's going off for I thought he married a rich woman. I hope we shall lose nothing by it, but am mightily sorry for him and that it falls out at this hay and harvest time. [P.S.] Let me know when it will be worth sending for venison from my park.

**511** FITZWILLIAM TO GUYBON
*London, 3 July 1707; F(M)C 1591*

I am glad you have returned me money but I hear nothing of it as yet. Get more quickly so that now the term is ended I may get out of town as soon as possible. I wonder Mr Phelips did not set off the £20 I lent him here just because I held his note. I would not have 'cousened' him. Tell him to repay me here soon. I lent him generously on an insignificant note, and doubt if he had died if I could ever have recovered on it, and told him he could set it off in his quarterly payments, but find he mistrusts me. I should have been as mistrustful of him. [P.S.] About town we have got our hay very well despite fine showers. I hope you have a good haymaking season. Is Westin's Meadow all let, and on good terms? Send any country news. I am glad Peterborough is to have so good a time, well diverted with cocking and horse racing.

**512** FITZWILLIAM TO GUYBON
*London, 10 July 1707; F(M)C 1593*

I have received no money from Mr Charles Parker. I sent to Henry Hankin who has none of Parker's money in his hands nor knows of any cattle or sheep on the road for Parker. Take better care of me. I am in great straits and design to be at Milton this month unless you keep me here for lack of money, which you have done for some years by failing to send money in time to pay my debts until the weather was so cold I dare not stir for fear of our healths. [P.S.] Run all the floors at Waldrum Hall with plaster instead of boards. Enquire for that plaster I used to pay 4d a cwt for, but better pay 5d than use boards when the rent is so small. I ordered the floors made very strong on purpose for the plaster. Ben Wright of Maxey owes me a deal of rent, Catlin tells me, and has a bill from Mrs Vaughan for work done. Take an assignment of that bill and I will make her pay me.

**513** FITZWILLIAM TO GUYBON
*London, 17 July 1707; F(M)C 1595*

I am much dissatisfied to receive no letters this week or last. If you are ill I wonder you could get nobody to write to me how you were, such as Mr Phelips or Mr Forster of Marholm, or Mr Wright of Castor, or any about Peterborough. Let me hear next post or I shall send somebody down to see how you are. Neither Mr Parker nor anyone has paid me money, so I have received none these three or four months, and cannot but wonder at your neglect of me.

**514** FITZWILLIAM TO GUYBON
*London, 24 July 1707; F(M)C 1597*

Have received your letters of the 19th and 21st gladly and the news that you are well. I have never had letters miscarry before, and my son's letter came safe to him. You often mistakenly write Moolesbury instead of Bloomsbury, but the postman knows where I live and brings them safe. I wonder you should write a month ago Mr Parker would pay me £50 at such a week if not already paid and now send word it will be in a fortnight. Don't write thus until you are certain. [P.S.] You don't write how Waldrum Hall and the ferry brewhouse go on, and what company you have had at the bowling green.

## 515 FITZWILLIAM TO GUYBON

*London, 31 July 1707; F(M)C 1598*

(Has received Guybon's of the 28th together with one that had miscarried dated 14th. Again complains of Guybon's writing 'Moolesbury', which is an actual place to which Fitzwilliam's letters are sometimes sent. Has not received Phelips' £20 which Kingston of Thorney Abbey is to pay.) Mr Lawrence Parker of Southwark has brought me £87 for his cousin Charles Parker of Peterborough.[1] I am sorry the smallpox has hindered people from coming to Peterborough and the ferry, and that you still have drought, for I heard reports that you had more rain there than we here. Ever since the 15th, St Swithin's Day, it has rained more or less every day. I am sorry the wind has harmed the corn. We had a severe blast for two or three hours but hoped it did not reach our 'countreyes'. I suppose the venison is as good as it will be and the weather not as hot now so send up next week the best buck, sealing every piece, and let me know who brings it, Fearey or Chattris.

[1] Guybon did not repay this until 8 October although the last return he had paid was dated 5 April, Disbursements 74.

## 516 JOHN CATLIN TO FITZWILLIAM

*Maxey, 6 August 1707; F(M)C 1599*

I only received yours of the 10th July last Monday. This harvest time few of 'our town' went to Peterborough market and I was not known at the Post House. They promise to send them sooner. Mrs Vaughan's Christian name is Amy. I have seen her write it in acquittances to tenants that hire land of her. I have told her she must pay both her father-in-law's arrears and Benjamin Wright's bill but 'she said she never would. I might make her if I could.' I believe it will be best to arrest her. Then she will be forced to submit. She has been arrested three or four times by a wheelwright, Brown, of Market Deeping, who has been her prisoner almost two years, he not being worth £5. I think he sued 'in forma pauperis'. Mr Guybon has been to her for money but she said she had none, but I went for Richard Ewen and Robert Osborne who paid her £10 each, so Mr Guybon gave her an acquittance for £20, but she would have it written for part of rent and will pay no other money. Nor would she let her husband's receipt book be seen. Robert Osborne, John Bimrose and Richard Ewen are to reckon with her; she is severe with her own accounts and will not allow any of theirs so they are almost out of love with her and will give up their land.

## 517 FITZWILLIAM TO GUYBON

*London, 7 August 1707; F(M)C 1600*

I am sorry you want rain when here we have rather too much. We are afraid it may harm the harvesting. I am glad you sent the shoulders of the buck. It's a dish I love very well. Send another next week for venison should be at its best and the weather pretty cool. I thought the Normans were very rich for I understood the father, who was Mr St John's fisherman, died worth at least £800 and this could not have been spent in so short a time. I hope you don't lose by them for they have not been long in that farm. The copper was sold here for £3 6s, and the carriage up cost only 4s 6d so you see how we are imposed on in the country when we have such things to sell. Serjeant's farm will let well enough being a good 'pennyworth'. I hope he has not taken a thing too big for him and so be forced shortly to follow Captain Selby, who I am mightily sorry for, and would like to hear what is likely to be lost by him and what he owed the bishop.[1] Have you followed my directions about buying 30 or 40 cwt of plaster and running the floors at Waldrum Hall?

[1] Serjeant had taken Selby's farm whose landlord was the Bishop of Peterborough.

## 518 FITZWILLIAM TO GUYBON

*London, 14 August 1707; F(M)C 1602*

The buck came sweet, clean, well killed and dressed, as if it had been mutton. I was never better pleased with any venison. I hope next Saturday's comes as well and since you say they are as good as they are like to be, send another to arrive the Saturday after. I think Northamptonshire a very unfortunate 'countrey' for rain. Northward they have had enough to spoil their harvests, my son writes that the roads about Tunbridge Wells are extremely bad, and it continues to rain every day here. If Mr Barlow was never paid the arrear of his bill he has got enough by me, but I will not wrong him of a shilling, if he has the patience to await my coming to Milton. There is not above 8s or 9s in arrear when necessary deductions are made. Here came last Tuesday morning Mr James Wallett to acquaint me his wife died the night before of a cancer in her breast and desiring something to help to bury her. I did not believe him until I sent to the house where my servant saw the dead corpse. Her life was the last in the Tyndall that Mr Bunning holds and at Michaelmas next I expect £40 from him instead of £15 which he usually paid half yearly. Mr Wallett says those grounds were never let under £80 a year and the warrener Robert Holmes used to give that rent. A Wyley married the other sister, the estate going to the longer liver of the two. Wyley's wife has been dead several years but Wallett sold his wife's share to the parson of Bourne[1] long before that for 50 guineas. I think the parson's name was Parsmore.[2] I wish you could return money soon.

[1] Bourne, Lincs.

[2] Possibly of the Pasmore or Passmore family of whom two were clergymen in the mid-seventeenth century: Longden, x. 193.

## 519 FITZWILLIAM TO GUYBON

*London, 21 August 1707; F(M)C 1603*

The buck came up sweet and clean. Send a buck next week unless I contradict it before. Richard Burton has been here complaining the work [on his house] must be last done. Go about it with all speed before winter. He must likewise have a small barn to hold ten loads of grain for we are almost resolved where he shall plough 10 or 12 acres. He pays nothing now for he cannot spare it until after Michaelmas so think of supplying me some other way soon. [P.S.] Burton will bring my forest deer warrants tomorrow.

## 520 FITZWILLIAM TO GUYBON

*London, 22 August 1707; F(M)C 1604*

(Sends this at Burton's urgent request. Also encloses four warrants for fee bucks from forest. Guybon to begin at once to set Burton's house in such condition that he may live comfortably in it when he marries. To send no buck until week after next when his son will be home to share it. Because Stourbridge Fair approaches, and many Peterborough people may be going there, Guybon to give Charles Parker Westhay Walk warrant, sharing with Pemberton, Henry Tryce, and Sparks; Cross-a-hand to Thomas Deacon with his associates written on the warrant; 'Moorehay Lawnce' to be kept until he knows what he will need himself.)

## 521 GUYBON TO FITZWILLIAM

*25 August 1707; F(M)C 1605*

(Had received letter and warrants by Burton and sent the two warrants to Parker and Deacon. Had not received Fitzwilliam's of 21st, however. Burton displeased Fitzwilliam had not ordered the building of the barn as well as repairing the house.) John Freeman asks what fine Fitzwilliam wants for a Maxey house, belonging to Northborough Court. Mr Hatton, a gentleman of Walsoken near Wisbech with an estate of £200 a year wished to borrow £1,000 from Fitzwilliam at 5% interest. Says it is a clear estate paying only Queen's taxes. In his next will send an account of Bunning's business.[1]

[1] In reply to Fitzwilliam's query, **518** above; see also **523**.

## 522 FITZWILLIAM TO GUYBON

*London, 28 August 1707; F(M)C 1606*

(Wonders Guybon never received his of the 21st. It had been carefully delivered into the post hours before the bag was shut. If it comes, Guybon must report what day it reached Peterborough; if it does not Fitzwilliam will complain about it. Last venison very ill killed, bloody, came up badly, hardly a piece untainted. Send none if weather continues very hot.) Burton needs no barn this year because we have not yet decided what ground he may plough. Next spring will be soon enough for that, and I hope to be down very soon. Let his house be put in order at once. I do not know this John Freeman that you ask what fine I will put on him. Is it for a death or an alienation? What is the yearly value? Mr Pemberton must send me a satisfactory account of what the last fine was and let him know the true yearly value. Thank the gentleman of Walsoken for his kind proffer but I have at present no money having given all I had to spare to the government.

## 523 GUYBON TO FITZWILLIAM

*1 September 1707; F(M)C 1607*

(Received Fitzwilliam's of 28th, but not that of 21st. Will send no venison until further order. Has enquired what rent of Tindalls was before Bunning had them). John Blackborne rented 24 acres 1 rod at £18 6s 8d a year, Thomas Bellars 22 acres 3 rods at £14 10s, Robert Wilson 15 acres, £9 and John Gee 8 acres £6 10s. Robert Holmes the warrener rented these lands formerly and says these are the highest rents ever given for them. Mr Bunning desires to know what you will ask for them till Lady day when if you and he can agree he will take a lease. You cannot have a better tenant. I gave you an account long since that part of George Chamberlaine's house at Etton was fallen, the roof and all the floors, nothing standing but bare walls. I hope it will be fit to slate, thatch or reed soon. The other part I fear will not stand long. We have many 'downefalls'. The whole year's rent of Tindalls is £48 6s 8d. There is 70 acres.

## 524 FITZWILLIAM TO GUYBON

*London, 4 September 1707; F(M)C 1608*[1]

Received yours of 1st yesterday. The weather proving very cool I am sorry you send no venison but my son does not come home until Wednesday next so it's no great mischance but send a buck next week. Dispose of Morehay Lawn warrant to my country friends, but let King have a piece so there can be another merry meeting at the ferry. I won't buy him another pair of tables until I hear from you. By now he will know whether the company that games in his house needs two pair of tables. I would not put him to a needless expense of 16s. Has Mr Pemberton paid you £3 owed by Mr Ash for interest on money lent him here? You never before wrote that part of George Chamberlaine's house had fallen. It's strange I cannot know such matters when you write every week, but your paper would hold three times what you write. I believe you think me unworthy to know my own business. Old Chamberlaine the father was a very 'sorry, worlin[2] sort of a man' who rather let the timbers lie bare and rot for want of [thatch] than put himself to any charge. I fear his son is [no better]. You must see [things as] well as I did when I lived there. You ought to [make my tenants do] their repairs in time, and not let [their houses] 'breake all to peices'. Chamberlaine's house shall be covered with slate, if reasonably priced, rather than thatch for fear of fire, but no inward work done. Mr Bunning shall rent Tindalls as soon as any, but I expect a whole year's rent at Lady Day next, for I must have the whole profits from the Lady Day before, and he shall have a lease on reasonable terms.

I cannot beleive the account you send of the present vallew of it to be true for why should Mr Wallett tell me that he and his brother[-in-law] Willy[3] has lett it to Robert Holmes the warrenar for £80 a yeare and now you say that he saies he gave no more then £48 6s 8d. I know Holmes is a very rascall and will say any thing to pleasure his neighbour rather then be true to me. All the countrey takes notice of his shooting pheasants and plundering my woods though you are passive and say nothing to him. I shall have spies upon him and all others that come into my woods or lordships to destroy the game and they shall have the penalty of the act of parliament[4] inflicted on them if they do more then they can justify but you sufferr all people to do what they will. If Mr Bunning will hire Tyndalls no longer then next Michaelmas and go off then I expect to receave of him two thirds of the yeare's rent, for the summer halfe yeare is alwaies vallewed at two thirds and the winter at one third. He and I will not fall out for a small matter. I shall make further inquiry into the vallew of that estate and Mr Bunning shall not be imposed upon for the rent but if he hires for no longer then next Ladyday he shall be obligd not to teare it up with horses as some tennants do that go off of land; from Candlemass to Ladyday he shall not keep a horse upon it. We cannot buy a partridge in London since this act of parliament lately pass't for security of the game. My wife haveing a great mind to eate a partridge pray gett Claypole and gett 2 or 3 brace of partridges and send them up in a little baskett with the venison next weeke for she almost longs, and her stomach is quite gone with her long illness and I am sure cannot eate above 2 wings of a partridge at a time.[5] I thinke woodcocks are not come in yett otherwise she loves a woodcocke better then anything or bird whatsoever and if a pheasant can be had pray send me up one for I love that bird very well . . .

> [P.S.] You don't mention how the well goes on nor whether you have had rain. I need money quickly. You may send a few guineas in the basket of partridges.

[1] Letter badly damaged. Words in brackets conjectural.
[2] Form of 'wirling', wretch.
[3] Wyley.
[4] An act for the better preservation of the game. Royal Assent 24 March 1706/7.
[5] Guybon paid 'Mr Claypoole' 4s for catching four brace of partridges, Disbursements 74.

## **525** FITZWILLIAM TO GUYBON

*London, 11 September 1707; F(M)C 1609*

> I had not sent for another buck if you had not said there were so many bucks in the park they would kill each other at rutting time. They are better killed than the forest deer which are hunted; mine are shot. Moreover mine are fatter, the best forest bucks having been killed by now. A forest deer will stink before it gets here. Ask Mr Pemberton for the £3 Ash paid him for me which Pemberton said he would pay the first time he saw you, 'but I see lawiers are all for receaving but their memoryes are bad when they are to pay it away againe'. I am glad to know King's mind else I had brought a pair of tables down. You only fancy you wrote to me that half Chamberlaine's house fell, for I have all your letters. If the rest is in danger prop it for the winter. We will take it down and rebuild next year. I am for slating it and Mrs Bull's also. [P.S.] Get me

money as fast as you can. It rains every day here and has for two months save for a fortnight about Bartholomew Fair. 'I thinke our part of Northamptonshire is the most unfortunate scituation in Europe'. In this dry time scour the moat from the wall next the horse pond in the lane by Milton stable yard gate through to the bridge between the orchards close to the best house of office. The filth badly needs removing from the houses of office and the drain from the drying yard cleaned at the same time. The muck will do well in the garden. It's 40 years since this place was scoured as far as the pales which divide the great moat.

## **526** JOHN CATLIN TO FITZWILLIAM

*Maxey, 11 September 1707; F(M)C 1611*

I have privately enquired about the rent of Tindalls when let to the full value but could never hear of their being let at near so much as Mr Wallett told you he let them to Holmes of Helpston Heath. Holmes and Webdale rented them together formerly but I know not their rent exactly. The Tindalls is five pasture closes, all 'greensword', none ploughed lately. Mr Bunning let [the 68 acres] singly to several tenants for £47 [thus:][1] 23 acres at £18, 22 at £14, 10 at £5 10s, 8 at £6 10s, 5 at £3. I believe Mr Guybon and Bunning are bargaining for them. Norborough Hills, now rented by William Bellows and 'Jiles' Young at rackrent, have not been leased this 12 years, as I hear. The next rental I write for Mr Guybon I intend to set all lease holders and all tenants at will by themselves. I will very shortly send an account of Waldrum Hall plaster floors, and other matters concerning Maxey manor. I would have written this answer sooner but about three weeks ago I fell sick of a fever and am but newly recovered it being a sickly time with many people about our 'towns'.

[1] Catlin set the following out in tabular form.

## **527** FITZWILLIAM TO GUYBON

*London, 18 September 1707; F(M)C 1612*

The buck came up tolerably well, good and young, and ate extremely well in the 'pasty'. I should have been glad of the partridges and pheasants last Saturday for an 'entertainement' I made, but they will be welcome whenever they come, but a few at a time so they can be eaten sweet. If Pemberton does not pay the £3 soon I shall demand it of Ash for I did not tell him to pay it to Pemberton. I leave it to you whether to thatch or slate George Chamberlaine's house but certainly slate the gutters. If you ever wrote about that house's downfall the letter must have miscarried. I have looked back through them and find no word of it. I am glad you at least received my letter of August 21st. Keep it to remind me of my agreement with Richard Burton. Mr Whittacre is very earnest to have his last year's rent from his former Northborough tenants. Let me know how much you receive and how much is set off for taxes so I may clear with him. I am sorry you still want rain. My son is safe home after his journey to 'Tunbridge' and travelling some hundreds of miles seeing the country and rarities round about.

## 528 FITZWILLIAM TO GUYBON

*London, 25 September 1707; F(M)C 1613*

Francis Guybon, Your letter dated the 17th I received as likewise the partridges which came to us very well and proved very good. Yesterday I received another letter from you dated the 22th instant and am sorry Mr Claypole asks more then the usuall price of catching[1] but I must submitt to it till you can find out another that will catch them cheaper for we must have some now and then. Pheasants I have had out of Essex from my daughter which were shott and wonder Holmes would not find me some when I know he does it to other families out of my woods. I shall have a great deale to say to him when I am in the countrey for all these matters but you connive at any thing though you know it's to my prejudice. Your last letter to me mentions that you are glad I want no money but if you looke into my letters I writt to you for these 2 months last past you will th[e]rein read how much I do want money and do at this time make use of other people's money left in my hands for a short time till I receave money from you to repay it. You say nothing will give money with you but I can heare from others that all sorts of graine rises of its price very handsomely and I hope will do more. Pray lett me know what horses or mares and colts were amungst the Widow Freeman stock for I shall want severall. I intend to have coach mares instead of horses and if there be any of them that are fitt pray preserve them for me or my son if there be any that serve his turne or mine for the saddle. I heare out of Islington Feilds that amungst others he had a very fine gray stoned coult that may make my sonn a fine horse another yeare. Pray take care he may be undisposed off till we see him. Pray be watchfull of Mr Forster for I heare he plowes Mr Styles' farme to halves this last yeare and intends to take it another yeare and all his muck that he should have layed on my land this yeare he has carried to Walton and laied it on Mr Styles' land and intends this Michaelmas time to drive his stock of[f] the land by stealth. You ought to know this better then I, being on the spott. Pray consider how to secure me what you can but medle with none of his goods till after Michaelmas day for feare of extinguishing my last halfe yeare's rent. Advise with Pemberton what course we had best take but do it very privatly. It may be what I have here writt may not be true and that such reports may be out of malice to him. However inquire well into the matter privatly and if true you had need begin with him in time ... [P.S.] Pray lett the well at the ferry be finnisht out of hand at this time or I shall never forgive you all. There is a way of blowing up of rocks though under water.

[1] A shilling a brace, see note to **524** above.

## 529 FITZWILLIAM TO GUYBON

*London, 2 October 1707; F(M)C 1614*

Francis Guybon, Yours of the 29th past I received and shall be glad of the partridges if they come. I am heartily sorry to heare how sad times it is with the poore tennants. I hope to see them soon and if I can but live out of the rents they are able to pay I care for no more. I will for beare them willingly what is reaso[n]able and fitting both for their good and mine, but to much forbearance makes many of them careless and begetts their ruine. If Richard Lea's farme cannot be lett you must then plow it halves for a year and it may fall out you may lett it better another yeare. I am sorry to perceave by yours that Mr Pemberton's health will not permitt him to keep Maxey court because yours mentions his clerke came to you about it. Lett it be kept however in its due time and I hope Mr Pemberton may be at it himselfe.

Let me know if Mr Pemberton has paid you the £3. If not I will write to Mr Ash to pay it you and let him recover it of Mr Pemberton. Ask Mr Pemberton for Mr Ash's bond that he took of him for my use. You say there are three mares and two colts among Widow Freeman's stock but not whether one colt is gray and is now kept in the park and was got by a fine horse. In time it may make my son a fine horse if well got. It being so late in the year that even if I were there nothing could be done at Milton House I wish Mr Wright to see that that place under the 'lanthorne' and that lucarne over my dressing room are secured to stand till the spring, doing anything he thinks is necessary to secure them from falling this winter.

## **530** FITZWILLIAM TO GUYBON

*London, 9 October 1707; F(M)C 1616*

I am glad you intend me more money next week. Mr Lawrence the carrier has paid £40 by your order. I am sorry Robert Mason of Northborough is gone off in my debt. You tempt them all to run away by letting them run so much in arrears that they think it worth their time to break for a great sum. Poor tenants are never to be trusted above two years' rent and that's too much. Let me know what Mason hired, how much he owed, and how much I shall lose by him. I am sorry to hear what a sorry fellow this Lawrence is to make mischief; if he told Mr Forster no more than what I said to him I value it not. I would not sell wool if it will lie dry. It will sell as well another year since it is so low now and nobody offers a price for it. Keep the maid 'in suspence' another week for I have earnest business now and cannot decide. Tell her you forgot to write to me about her or that I did not answer that part of your letter. Mr Phelips is now here and tells me a foolish story about Burton and Bevis. I perceive Mr Forster and old Adam Johnson show great malice against Burton. I shall find a way to order them all as you may let them know. Burton has law on his side and we fear nothing Bevis can do against him.

## **531** FITZWILLIAM TO GUYBON

*London, 12 October 1707; F(M)C 1617*

Francis Guybon, I herewith send you by Thomas Chattris my calesh[1] which should have been sent downe the last yeare but the raines fell sooner then I expected. Pray take care it be sett in the best place of the two coachhouses and lett the doores of the coach houses be kept constantly shutt to keep the weather from it. Joseph Chamberlaine must take care to cleane it well after the journey. I have sent downe a brush on purpose in the calesh to wash the armes and gilding and painting with about the body of the calesh. He must have a pale of cleane water and dipp the brush in it and so wash the painting and gilding with it and when he has cleaned it very well he must gett another pale of cleane water and wash it over againe. For the wheeles and perch and standard before and behind he may wash them with a mopp. Be sure he washes the durt of them very well for now we keep our wheeles as cleane as any other part of the coach. When he has done with the brush lett it be laied by till it is dry and then putt it under the seate of the calesh to be ready to cleane it when there is occasion. The seate of the calesh and box cloath, gett Mrs Bull to have then dustied well and laied by in some dry roome of the house. Lett Joseph Chamberlaine be carefull when he washes the gilding and painting worke of the calesh with the brush that the wooden part of the brush does [not] touch the painting worke for if it does it will scratch the armes and deface it. Pray read this letter well over to Joseph Chamberlaine that he may understand it well before he goes to cleane it ... [P.S.] My sonn sends downe his man's horse this weeke by Lawrence his wagon which he desires may be turnd to grass this winter but he must be turnd out a dayes and taken in a nights for one tenn daies or a fortnight and then turnd out for good and all. You need give him nothing but hay; he is fatt enough. If the parke be overstockt he may go in Lady Leas or the Goodlucks.

[1] See note to **467** above.

## **532** FITZWILLIAM TO GUYBON

*London, 16 October 1707; F(M)C 1618*

Received yours with the enclosed bill but cannot find George Mawre until tomorrow at the market when I will send and see if he will accept it. As to the Northborough farm late Preston's I am by no means for letting Marmaduke have it because surely he will only rent some poor man the house who will let house and barns run to ruin. I am for that other tenant you mention who will put everything in repair, but if he is one of my lesser tenants you may be at a loss to supply a good tenant for his lesser farm. Use your discretion. I don't remember I ever promised it to 'Duke, whatever he says. Perhaps some enclosure in the parks but never a farm like this which must be let to a man who will live in the house. Let me know this man's name, and, if he is my tenant, what he holds. Hire the cookmaid for I shall want her soon. I reckon there is no more than 8s or 9s owing on Barlow's bill, or I intended to abate his bill to that amount for reasons gone out of my head. I hope to be soon at Milton and will set it straight. Let me know if it is the old man who is in prison, or if he is dead or broke, and by what authority this man in prison comes to have title to the money in my hands. I must know before I pay anything. Mr Phelips is in town but does not know for how long for he has an intricate business in hand. [P.S.] I cannot spare Mrs Pendleton those rooms so she must move out in a fortnight. I hope my calash arrived safely with my directions to Chamberlaine. Let me know how it came and if it was not overturned in the journey for Chattris drove it himself.

**533** FITZWILLIAM TO GUYBON
*London, 21 October 1707; F(M)C 1620*

Marmaduke is here about Preston's farm. He says it's Thomas Rudkin the butcher that you have a mind to let this farm to. I have heard so much baseness of him formerly and now I hear how ill humoured he is to all my tenants and to my interest in particular that I will not consent he shall have any of my farms. I have ordered Duke to plough the land and sow it because it's time to do it. Whoever is put into it shall allow for it. Meanwhile do not dispose of it.

**534** FITZWILLIAM TO GUYBON
*London, 23 October 1707; F(M)C 1621*

The partridges came safe and good but send no more. We can buy them here for 12d a piece. The salesman Maure promises to pay your bill tomorrow.

Marmaduke Thomlinson has made such representations to me of the necessity he lay under of haveing more land laied to his farme for want of which his men and horses many times were idle and which he was forc't to keep for his great farme that to sattisfie him and my sonn who is much his freind I was forc't to promise him he should have it provided it was not disposed off before he gott downe. He is upon this consideration obligd to keep all the houses and fences and paleing and glass windows in good repaire and to be at the charge to putt them in repaire and leave them so as also the inside of the house with good floores whither they be earthen, tyled or boarden floores and the sealeing worke what there is or was, to mainteine them and leave them so. I expect besides the old rent 6 boone dayes with his wagon and 2 men yearely and a turkey cocke and turkey henn yearely or so much money as is usuall, besides some dozens of pidgeons which he promised me here when ever I pleased to send for them. I am sattisfied Rudkin is an ill man and has done many ill turns both to me and my tennants when he has had opportunities. That I have heard some yeares since. I am further sattisfied he never would have come to live in this farme house had he taken it, haveing a good house of his owne in the middle of the towne with all the conveniencies for his trade. In that regard I had better accommodate a tennant of my owne that putts in another man into the farme house as lett Rudkins do it. As to Mrs Pendleton she may continue where she is till further order but she cannot expect that I will sufferr any other family in Milton house then my owne when I am there. Therefore she must be thinking and prepared where to be ... [P.S.] No place like Peterborough for Mrs Pendleton for the education of her children.

**535** FITZWILLIAM TO GUYBON
*London, 30 October 1707; F(M)C 1623*

I shall be glad when you send pheasants to have a hare or two with them, but not by themselves. I find my son loves a hare which I did not know before. Mr Maure paid as he promised. I had rather Rudkin had Preston's farm if I could have been certain he would leave his own house to live in the farm house, and then my son was so much for 'Duke I could not be quiet until I promised it. [P.S.] Let me hear if [George] Chamberlaine's house at Etton is up again and what slating was done. You know 'Duke is a good tenant and pays his rent sooner than any tenant we have so should be encouraged.

### **536** FITZWILLIAM TO GUYBON

*London, 6 November 1707; F(M)C 1624*

Finish so much of the inside of George Chamberlaine's house as is necessary for his family but don't spend too much on it until I have seen it, which I thought to do before this but business has prevented. Then I shall see how he keeps it and deserves 'a good inside'. His father and mother kept it very nastily, but the tenant before, a Mr Wightman, kept it finely and deserved a good inside. I am very sorry to hear of honest Mr Willmott's death. Get Mr Whittacre's rents from his former Northborough tenants, or I must take a course with them on his behalf. I am sorry Mr Pemberton is unwell. I had hoped he would have quite 'worne out' his illness before now. God send his life for his children's sake. [P.S.] My son is out of town for a few days. He has bought a new horse, and intends to send you another to put to grass this winter. I believe the grass is as good in Lady Leas as in the park. Keep the park grass for the poor deer. Horses can be moved, deer cannot.

### **537** FITZWILLIAM TO GUYBON

*London, 13 November 1707; F(M)C 1627*

Last Saturday I received the basket with the two hares and rabbit by the carrier which came sweet, ate tender, and much pleased my son and all who ate them, so send some now and then. The £50 from Mr Parker would be very welcome. Thank you for intimating Mrs Dove's farm in Sutton[1] is to be sold but I know neither her husband's name nor where they live. You should first inform yourself of all particulars before you write: owners' names, where they live, yearly rent, how likely to hold it, and whether a good tenant thrives in it, and the condition of house and outhouses. They are great 'lights' to a purchaser who can bid accordingly. Goody Thompson, your tenant to Burton's farm at Aylesworth, lived in it several years and can give a good account of everything I want to know. Give Mr Ash this note for £315 I lent him last spring. I thought I had lost it. Here are my warrants for my winter fee deer. Let me know when the does will be at their best so I may send for some and dispose of the rest. You don't let me know how the well goes and what chance of it proving a good well. Let me know when Whittacre's other tenant pays, what you receive, what set off for taxes, that I may pay poor Whittacre without wronging myself, for I fear he needs it.

[1] A hamlet in Castor parish.

### **538** FITZWILLIAM TO GUYBON

*London, 20 November 1707; F(M)C 1629*

Mr Parker's correspondent, the Duke of Bedford's servant, Mr Pettyt, has paid the two amounts of £50 each.

You are very much misinformed as to the rent of Mrs Dove's farme and as to what is bid for it. The person as I am credibly informed asks no more for the farme then £1400 and the rent of it is but £55 per annum. I wonder when I gave you such a charge to give me a thorough information of it that you would not take the paines to ride over to Goody Thompson at Aylesworth or to her sonn at Sutton to know the truth of every thing yourselfe and not trust to what Joseph Chamberlaine tells you by hearsay only, or some such sorry fellow. You fare best that go of your owne errants. Pray informe yourselfe better and lett me have a true account by your next letter about every thing, what the farme really gives a yeare and if the rent will hold in these bad yeares. You say there is 7 score and 10 acres of arrable and 40 acres of medow and lea ground but mention nothing of pasture inclosed. If there be none what must that farme do in wett yeares if the medow be drowned? Lett me know how many acres of pasture, how many acres of medow and how many acres of lea ground and if the medow lies in good parts of the meadow or in low swampy parts of it. Do not informe any body what I write to you, about what the rent is of the farme or the price that is asked for it, not so much as the tennant himselfe, but heare what he sayes and write me word of it and take notice if the barnes and out houses are in repaire and good condition. If £1400 must be given for £55 a yeare, it's 25 yeares' purchase and a halfe, which is a mighty price. Pray know of the tennant if no small rent is paid out of it, either to the bishop or the deane and chapter or any body else and learne also what is become of a pretty little house belonging to this farme that I remember old Mr Pemberton lived in 40 yeares agoe and since before he went to live at Peterborough. That house is at some distan[c]e from the farme house, is nearer the meadow, a pretty stone house it was if not fallen downe.

Let Mr Ash know I shall need to make use of the £200 he owes me on his bond on 20 February next. Send up a park doe in flag basket next week. Give Charles Parker Westhay warrant for himself, Mr Pemberton, Harry Tryce and Mr Sparks; give Cross-a-Hand to Mr Thomas Deacon for himself, Mr Lowrey, Cousin Bellamy and Mr Charles Duce. I will use the other two myself. You ask for a horse for Will Serjeant who you hope will do well in Mr Selby's farm. I have no obligation to him if he leaves my farm. If he continues to hold my farm, and is able to manage both, which I doubt, I am willing to give him that old horse. I am glad the well is near finished. If it is not a good one I will dig on until it is. I am sorry Mr Willmott's circumstances are so bad but he has a good estate which will pay all. The halfhogsheads will need filling up. I think there is enough in the great bottles of red and white. Cover the wine bottles with straw, and straw up the windows against the cold air.

### **539** FITZWILLIAM TO GUYBON

*London, 27 November 1707; F(M)C 1631*

I have not heard from you this week so hope you are well and did not write because you were unable to inform yourself about the farm at Sutton. Be very particular about it by Wednesday post. Enquire if the dean and chapter receive a rent from it, and how much. The rest of the town is theirs.[1] I hope you send my doe this week; send a forest doe next week, or the week after if the notice is too short for the keepers.

[1] The manor of Sutton was granted to the Dean and Chapter of Peterborough 33 Henry VIII, and its sale in 1650 was rescinded at the Restoration: *VCH Northamptonshire*, ii. 481.

## 540 FITZWILLIAM TO GUYBON

*London, 11 December 1707; F(M)C 1632*

(Is 'finely recovered' again. Sorry to hear the wind has done much mischief. Considering Guybon's particulars of Mrs Dove's Sutton farm and the great price demanded he will send no more after it. Knows better how to deal with his money than to throw away three or four years' purchase. Guybon to have half the fourth warrant, the other to the ferry to 'make merry' with. Needs money soon.)

## 541 FITZWILLIAM TO GUYBON

*London, 18 December 1707; F(M)C 1633*

I continue very well in health but my fever was drawn down into one of my legs, which is still very painful; it will wear off in time. I received the doe and hare very sweet. I am glad you suffered no more damage in the great storm than to lose a tree. I hope the tenants don't conceal other trees fallen on their grounds and make use of the timber themselves. Send some young man to ride into every ground about Etton and Woodcroft to inspect, while you can see to Milton and Marholm. Since you wish it let Mr Parker have the Moorhay Lawn warrant, but I wonder what pretext Lord Exeter has to stop our warrants now. I doubt if your well will prove as good as you think. Dry years must prove that. My expense I know when I know the depth. It shall only be a draw well, so put me to no further expense. There shall be no pump set 'in the mind I am now in'. Give to the poor at Christmas as I used to do. Send all the money you can for I must pay away a great sum on 15 February which I cannot put off longer. Remind Mr Ash to pay the £200 by that time. Give our congratulations to Mrs Bull on her daughter's marriage, and hope she has a good husband, although sorry to hear she goes into the fens. I am sure she deserves a good husband. My wife wishes me to inform you she is very ill. Since the beer is stale spend it but I hope the ale will keep longer. Let me know if you filled up the wine hogsheads.

## 542 GUYBON TO FITZWILLIAM

*29 December 1707; F(M)C 1634*

Received yours of the 18th and hope you continue well, yet fear it for I had no letter last week. We have filled up the wine hogsheads long since. I will send all the money I possibly can against 15 February, and remind Mr Ash to send his £200. I enclose the bills for the well. Mr Wright will wait on you this week and give an account of it.

### 543 FITZWILLIAM TO GUYBON

*London, 1 January 1707/8; F(M)C 1635*

I have received yours enclosing the bills for the well which you might have sent by Wright for they cost me 9d by the post. I had no letter last week so did not write. I continue to mend daily but it takes longer because my doctor drew my fever out of my head into one of my legs where it turned into a St Anthony's fire, but in a few days I hope I shall be quite well if it does not turn to the gout which I have great symptoms of. Robert Sanders has paid £5 6s and Robert Hardy £14 12s 7d, both for James Dove. Hardy has paid £10 18s 11d for Richard Burton. Get up all you can. [P.S.] Cousin Thomas Bellamy was married yesterday. 'If his father does handsomly by him she may prove a good fortune to him'.

### 544 GUYBON TO FITZWILLIAM

*5 January 1707/8; F(M)C 1635v*

(Guybon hopes Wright had been with Fitzwilliam; that Fitzwilliam had received a brace of hares, and asks Fitzwilliam to send again the next Saturday in case he had found goods to send up. Would send all money he could by 15th February. Both meadows had been badly flooded the previous week.)

### 545 FITZWILLIAM TO GUYBON

*London, 8 January 1707/8; F(M)C 1636*

Francis Guybon, Yours dated the 5th I received yesterday. The hares came to us very well last Satturday but I have eaten much younger in my time. Mr Wright has been with me and intends to be goeing from hence next Satturday. He has much business about his new undertakeing of building a house for one Mr Trafford neare Wisbitch.[1] I wish he may gett by it but feare it, for it's a great undertakeing and he is to find all materialls. He has given me an account of the ferry well and the contracts he made with the workmen and wonder you should send me up bills of the men's daies' works when I have no body to reckon with but Robert Bursnoll and both Rolls and the other labourers must looke to him for their money for I have nothing to say to any of them, and pray do you part with no money to any of them till Mr Wright getts downe. If they will spend their time in drinking at the ferry instead of doeing good dayes' workes I cannt help it. I expect my bargaine and they shall not loose a farthing of the agreement made. Mr Wright tells me he intends to leave with me some bills to receave some small summs here for him and desires you may pay him in the countrey which I promised him. Pray do not forgett your promise of returning me what money you can by February 15th next.

[1] Wisbech, Cambs.

## 546 FITZWILLIAM TO GUYBON

*London, 15 January 1707/8; F(M)C 1637*

> I hope Mr Wright got safe home. We have had such terrible rains and some snow since I saw him, that I judged the waters unpassable and it has rained every day since, including 10 hours continuously last night. I wonder not at your great floods on both rivers. It has rained hereabouts almost every day for six or seven weeks. Mr Wright paid me £40, for you to repay in the country.

[Mr Wright] acquainted me with all passages about the ferry well and beleives the men had a hard bargaine but the agreement he made with them by the foot digging is in writeing which I expect their performance. Robert Bursnoll made a bargaine with Roles for £3 15s to digg through the rocks and though I perceave it is not done so well as it ought to be, I meane the rocke not dugg enough away to make a good passage for a buckett, yett I am willing to allow that £3 15s more then the bargaine though it is within the distance of 30 foot from the topp. If that summe will please them by way of their hard bargaine as they call it, well and good, if not, I recall this promise and lett them pay Roles, and if they do accept it, do not you pay Roles that money till I write againe to you about it for I have a long reckoning to make with Roles which you shall heare of hereafter. I quite forgott in my last to acquaint you of good Mr Dreydon['s] death.[1] He fell ill of the Munday after he had eaten a very good dinner and died of the Satturday following after he had settled all his affaires and given away large legacies. I heard not of his being ill till the Munday after he was dead. He has given away rings to all the gentlemen round about the countrey and adjacent. Pray go you to his funerall and present my service to the gentlemen that go downe to his buriall and lett them know I would have been sure to have been there my selfe had I been in the countrey and commanded you to be there to performe my last service to my very good freind. They carry his body out of towne to morrow and will rest at Huntingdon on Sunday where he is to lie in state. On Munday betimes they sett forward to Chasterton where he is to be buried about 12 or one of the clocke that day that the herse and coaches may returne that night to Huntingdon. If the waters are much out you may go by Wainsford bridge but take Joseph Chamberlaine with you to take care of you.

> You say you will return money by 15th February but if you wait until the day you may not get returns, so return every week to make up a good sum by the day. Tell Mr Ash he may continue his money three or four months if he pleases for the person I must pay the money to will accept his bond in part payment. Tonight I received £12 19s 3d from Robert Hardy.

[1] John Dryden of Chesterton.

## 547 FITZWILLIAM TO GUYBON

*London, 23 January 1707/8; F(M)C 1640*

> I am glad Mr Wright got safe home at last, and to hear you are so careful of yourself as not to stir out when you have a cold. Continue to do so and I hope you may live many years. I am very sorry for Mr Dove's death and

sorry Tom Wootton leaves Marholm. I hope you dissuade him but if not tell me who you think to put in his place. Mrs Bull got up to town and I send this by her. Robert Hardy has paid for James Dove £6 12s 8d, and £13 3s 2d for Richard Burton. Sam Sylverwood paid for Burton £10 17s 6d. Mr Forster has just come to town in good health.

## 548 FITZWILLIAM TO GUYBON

*London, 29 January 1707/8; F(M)C 1641*

I am sorry to hear by yours of the 27th that Mrs Bull was not yet home. She left Saturday early and hoped to be home by Monday noon. We are much 'dissatisfied' so send word in your next what time she got home. The two hares and two rabbits came safe last Saturday. Thank you for your kind remembrance of us. I hope Mr Forster got home well on Tuesday or Wednesday noon at furthest, and that he and Mrs Bull found the waters much abated.

Mr Forster is a much dissatisfied man and saies he will not stay any longer then Ladyday at Marrham. I told him I would be very kind to him and how much I would forgive him if he stayed, before my sonn. However I said I expected lawfull warning which was 6 months whereas it was but 3 months from the time he told me of his goeing. His reckoning my sonn and I computed and he made it appeare he had paid to you and me in money £1,046 13s 3½d. In taxes if he can make it out (which I much doubt) both for his farme my woods etc comes to £147 19s 3d. In assesments of the towne for my woods and straw he pretends you had to Milton some loads and some for thacking which comes too £14 3s 0¾d. All this together amounts too £1,208 15s 7¾d if he can make out his disbursments for taxes and towne rates by the severall assessments which he must produce or I will not allow them. The rent he will owe me next Lady day will come to £1,610 odd money out of which I proffered him before my sonn to abate him £200 provided he went on with the farme at £60 a yeare and he should plow on still but if he did not stay he lay at my discretion. I said moreover if the land should prove to deare at £60 I would still be kind to him but I hoped that times would mend and he would have the better pennyworth of it. Pray be watchfull of him and secure my rent without you perceave he beginns to plow againe and likely to continue. I expect he should lay my land 3 yeares from plowing before he leaves which his lease obliges him too. I am sorry to heare of Richard Burton's being so ill but Mr Forster tells me if he be well he is preparing to plow part of Burmer Leas up. Pray lett him know I will not give him leave to plow till he has signed a lease upon what terms I give leave to plow. My health has hinderd me from goeing downe this winter, otherwise this might have been dispatcht but since it falls out so I forbid him plowing till I go downe. Lett him know this very speedily if he is recovered as I hope he is. Mr Parker has paid me this very day £50. The 15th of February drawes on apace therefore you had need be speedy in returning me what money you can ... [P.S.] Do not forgett to lett Burton know speedily he must not plow till I see the land first that I will give leave to plow.

## 549 FITZWILLIAM TO GUYBON

*London, 5 February 1707/8; F(M)C 1642*

We are much concerned Mrs Bull only got home on Tuesday, of her miscarriage by the way, tiring her mare, etc. She could not be so long going home from here only, for she left at break of day on Saturday before. They claimed to have urgent business at Stamford Fair on the Tuesday. I perceive Mr Forster got home in due time for he only left at four o'clock after dinner on Monday. Thank God they are both safe home. You say had they not got home when they did they might be in London now, but don't explain why, which I should be glad to know for we have only a fine fair, frosty weather here with no snow. I am glad Goodman Burton of Marrham is recovering, but there must be no more ploughing in Burmore Leas till I get down to see it, and we have a lease drawn. Mr Parker has ordered his cousin Lawrence Parker to pay me another £50 which he sent me on Monday last. Send all you can between now and the 15th or 18th at furthest. I well remember my promise to Mrs Pemberton of one of the little saddles for her younger son, but they are locked in my wife's closet. He shall be sure of it whenever we get to Milton. My wife desires Mrs Bull will send her up three pots of the best honey we have at Milton.

## 550 FITZWILLIAM TO GUYBON

*London, 12 February 1707/8; F(M)C 1643*

I have received £5 18s 5d from Robert Hardy for James Dove of Marholm. I perceive Mr Ash intends to pay his money for I have received £129 of it by Thomas Deacon's order. I desire he will pay the remainder next week without fail, otherwise I shall be much disappointed. If he had paid none his bond would have gone in payment as I wrote to tell him a month ago. Return next week all money you can. I am glad I am to have some from Mr Charles Parker for he makes sure payment in good time. I am glad Mrs Bull is so well after her journey, but think she could not be four days going down unless she took some other journey besides. Mr Whittacre is often here for his last year's rents. I am ashamed to be thus dunned. If Joe Clarke has paid his rent tell me what it is, and if Ward is too poor get another tenant, but secure my year's rent due next Lady Day first before doing what you can for Whittacre. I wrote in my last how kind I would be to Mr Forster if he stayed; that he should still pay £60 per annum though I would be very kind to him out of that too, but 'I must keep up the reputation of my rents because I told him my sonn was upon his marriage[1] and it might hinder him'. I am sure he is as good if not better than when he came to Marholm. Considering he has lived, brought up his children and very well provided for some of them, he cannot have lost by the farm so much as he mentions nor anything at all I believe, but that's all one; I promise to be very kind to him yearly. Mr Eldred of Deeping an attorney is coming to me now and then for £50 he pretends the jury of Langdyke[2] has ordered me to pay to him for carrying on a suit with drovers who drive across our Great Fen[3] and come through 'Dosthorp'[4] and Peterborough with their droves. He brought me a paper[5] signed by Mr William Ash, Mr Robert Deepup and several others who seem inconsiderable people. I do not understand the 'countrey's' money should be spent this way. Mr Eldred is a busy man and would thrust himself into business at our charge. Lord Bedford[6], Captain Hyde, Mr Charles Bertie[7] want the toll of the cattle that used to pass through the Deepings and Wainsford and the 'country' [county] to be at the charge of doing this for them. Let them do it; it's their interest. Speak with Mr Ash about it. Those drovers would willingly pay a toll which would make amends for the damage they do the common and that money well laid out would do more good than the drovers can do harm. Let me know if Mr Osburne has taken the Maxey Castle farm and how much rent he gives for it. [P.S.] Mrs Pendleton must dispose of her stock. I cannot [spare] those grounds she hires nor the Meadow Close which I must lay for hay for my horses and deer.

1 In fact it was to be 10 years before John Fitzwilliam married.
2 The hundred court, see note to **220** above.
3 Variously called Borough Fen, Peterborough Great Fen.
4 Dogsthorpe, north of Peterborough, a former Fitzwilliam manor.
5 F(M)C 1639 23 January 1707/8.
6 Wriothesley Russell, 2nd Duke of Bedford (1680–1711). *Complete Peerage*, ii. 81–2.
7 Either Charles Bertie of Uffington, near Stamford (c 1641–1711), Tory M.P. for Stamford for 30 years, or his son: *House of Commons 1660–1690* i. 639–43.

## 551 FITZWILLIAM TO GUYBON

*London, 19 February 1707/8; F(M)C 1644*

I have neither heard of Mr Parker's money nor Mr Ash's yet. Feary's bookkeeper brought £30 on Mr Ash's account last Saturday and wished me to take a bill on one of Feary's poulterers in Newgate market for a fortnight or three weeks hence but I refused it. I have 'no occasion to run about adunning people for my owne'. [Ash] received my money altogether without trouble and it's hard I cannot get it again when I want it when he had fair notice. I know not what to do for tomorrow I am to pay the great sum I wrote I should want money for on the 15th. As to Mr Forster he knows my mind; I told him what I would do. If he ploughs any part of the farm the rent must stand in the books at £60 but I would be very kind to him unless the times mended very much, which I don't expect they will these two years. I am very unwilling to part with Mr Forster as an old tenant but I must not bring my rents too low and undervalue my estate. I can be kind considering hard times but Mr Forster is too imposing on my good nature. He may trust to my promise as I have trusted him with many a £100 which was worth £20 a year to him. Give him very good words. Tell him my son will intercede with me in his behalf which you had in a letter from [John] to you. He will not know where to do better. Neither Captain Styles nor anyone else can forbear his rents as I do, which is worth £5 a year in such a farm and to a careful tenant. Use the best arguments you can. [P.S.] I received the pot of honey and a letter from Mrs Bull. We are sorry for the loss of her mare. Ask Mr Wright if he goes on with the building Mr Trafford's house at Sutton in the fens[1] for we heard Mr Trafford was dead. Ask him also if old Mrs Dickenson of Westwinch[2] be dead or where she lives for I desired him to ask Mr Trafford about her.

1 Sutton or Long Sutton in South Holland, Lincs.
2 West Winch near King's Lynn, Norfolk.

## 552 GUYBON TO FITZWILLIAM

*23 February 1707/8; F(M)C 1645*

Received yours of the 19th. I hope you received the basket by the carrier last Saturday. I am surprised Mr Parker paid no money last week as he promised. I [can][1] do nothing with Mr Forster. He says he will not continue at Marholm unless you tell him his rent and soon. He has ploughed none nor will if he leaves it. I know not what you will do with it. Mr Wright I have not seen, being much abroad. He goes on with Mr Trafford's house at Sutton. Mr Osbourne took Maxey castle when he was in London for four years for £58 and gave Mrs Forster earnest.[2] He will pay within a month after Lady day and Michaelmas but now she demands security for his rent. Few tenants do that. I pray be pleased to speak to her in his behalf for he is a very honourable man, and if it should fall into your hands cannot have a better tenant. Richard Burton goes on with his ploughing. I spoke to him to forbear, but he tells me he has provided all for ploughing and intends going on as you and he agreed. He [wishes] a barn built and his house made 'handsome'. [I hope] his ploughing does him some good. 'Your honour must give [more] tennants leave to plow a little'. It would not be the worse for you. They will give the same rent as they did before they ploughed. It may [be] a means to get you some money which is very hard ... [P.S.] Pray let Mr Forster's rent be settled so he knows what to trust to. He is very uneasy and won't stay unless he knows soon. 'Gentlemen must be kinde and abate rents and give leave to plow or elce it will be worse for landlord and tennant.'

[1] Letter in places badly discoloured. This and subsequent words in brackets reconstructions.
[2] Earnest, money paid to secure a contract.

## 553 FITZWILLIAM TO GUYBON

*London, 26 February 1707/8; F(M)C 1647*

The basket came last Saturday with the pheasant, woodcock and hare very good, but send no more hares for they begin to breed and will not be as good. Mr Parker has paid no money yet. Mr Ash has paid by Mrs Bader, Robert Fearey's sister-in-law, £30 and £10 3s 4d. Hasten Mr Parker's promised return. You have not answered about Whittacre's rents. He needs them much I fear. You said some time ago you had Joe Clarke's rent; send word what it was and I will pay him. Take care neither he nor I lose by [Ward]. As to Mr Forster I know not what more to say. If he does not plough I expect the old rent Mrs Porter paid, £48 a year and yet I will be kind to him if times continue bad, but we have now a fine prospect both corn and meat prices rising. If he ploughs the rent must stand at £60 but still I will be kind. If nothing will prevail with him secure the money he owes me. He must not expect the same favour if he goes off as if he stayed. He may take it for a year longer if he will and see how we agree when I come down about the middle of May. As to Burton let him have a care; I know of no settled bargain we made. Let him acquaint you what it was and send me word. He went out of town in a huff and said he would not stay at Marholm upon those terms we talked of. If he has not a mind to be ruined let him leave off ploughing. I have law on my side and money enough to deal with 'any pragmaticall fellow that will plow my land up whither I will or no'. Tell Mr Phelips the parson, who is his great adviser, what I write. If he still persists before we have an agreement signed and sealed I shall take a course with him which will not please him. Let Mr Phelips talk with him about what I write and send his answer.

## 554 FITZWILLIAM TO GUYBON

*London, 4 March 1707/8; F(M)C 1648*

The hare and pheasant came very good. We will send every Saturday to the carriers to see if you have sent anything to save you writing twice, but if you don't think you will, send word by the letter that comes on Wednesdays.

I wish Mrs Pendleton may succeed in her business she comes to towne about. She might have done well to have advised with my sonn first about it before she came up for he saies they gennerally waite a yeare or two before they can gett into the house,[1] and if so and he comes to go to the schoole here he will not cost her less then neare £30 a yeare for his schooleing, his board and his cloaths but she may have better advise and know more then my sonn does. Though they gett a grant of a place amungst the foundation boyes yett they must wait for it till some boy dies or is removed to prentice or the university. It would be an act of charity in you to gett Ward's rent for poore Mr Whittacre for I feare he is in great want. Turner of Peterborough wrote a letter to my sonn this weeke to recommend him to Mr Pemberton about the bailiff's place of Peterborough. My sonn has writt this post to Mr Pemberton in his behalfe and pray do you speake with him together with my recommandations and how kindly we should all take it if he could do him that kindness. No place whatever is so fitt for him as this is and if I had any acquaintance with the deane I would write to him in his behalfe.

[1] Charterhouse School.

## 555 JOHN CATLIN TO FITZWILLIAM

*Maxey, 8 March 1707/8; F(M)C 1649*

I went about 14 days ago to view some fences of an estate of £16 a year belonging to the poor of Maxey at Aserby, Lincolnshire, where the tenant, one Sandy, was to be allowed to set the charge of repairing his fences against his first year's rent. Thomas Drury, one of your Maxey tenants, wished me to ask Mrs Stevens, as I went through Bourne, if she would sell the land rented by Widow Paddy, and I to buy it for him if under £57. She would set no lower price than £60 and a guinea in hand, but would sell at a lower rate if I would buy the whole estate. I thought of some persons who would buy that rented by Matthew Turnill, and John Carter had often wished Mr Guybon to buy the lea ground abutting the street croft and toft lying in his homestead between two of your leas. There is another rod of ground in the midst of your tenant William Dunstan's yard, which he pays 4s a year for, without which he has no passage to his homestead. So I ventured to give her a guinea earnest for £190 payable October 7th, she performing a good title. It is all the estate she has in Maxey, except two acres of lea which she has sold me for £20 payable the same day, if your honour will let me have it. If you like the estate or any part mentioned in the particular at those prices, you may have it or leave it. I gave the particulars a week ago to Mr Guybon who said he would send you them. If your honour would write what parts you approve of some neighbours may have the remainder. I cannot count it cheap but it is in small parcels and may [otherwise] be sold. With Mr Guybon's order I have let Benjamin Wright's house to a Tobias Love, lately a herdsman, but has had an estate of £35 a year fallen to him from a brother in Market Harborough. Benjamin Wright goes into a 'town' house at Lady Day. Worth little, he promises to leave money with some of his masters to pay his arrears. If Mrs Vaughan refuses to pay his £6 much longer I don't know how it will be got for it is above three years since this bill for wages was drawn, and some of the money was due three years before that. I am sorry I never knew exactly how much plaster came from Mr Williamards of Ufford for the floors at Waldrum Hall but I was sick at that time. Many tenants complain of the dearness of the cowpastures these past four years. Mrs Vaughan is going to plough Hurne Close, which has not been ploughed these 50 years, and sow flax. It is field ground but ploughing will impoverish it. I told her she should ask your leave but she said nobody could hinder her.

## **556** GUYBON TO FITZWILLIAM

*8 March 1707/8; F(M)C 1650*

Yours of the 4th received. I am sorry Mr Parker has not yet paid. He will soon. I can get no returns among the Peterborough men or the fen men. Mr Ash says he has paid all the bond I received from Mr Pemberton save some interest. When that is paid he desires to have his bond. Mrs Pendleton has written to Mr Fitzwilliam giving an account of her business. She asks that you let her continue the Old Park and Mulberry Close till her stock is in a condition to be put off. She will pay for the time she holds them, if not must give the stock away. William King desires your honour would write to Mr Wright that he should not make Milton Holme a wharf for it hinders the ferry very much. He lands all his timber and stone there for his building. Richard Burton has ploughed about 10 acres which he says you were content he should plough. If you are against it he says if you will allow him for ploughing and sowing you shall have the crop. He will plough no more. He wishes he had not ploughed this and will do anything you wish. I told Mr Forster what you wrote. He will not give £48, not above £40 a year. I wish your honour and he agreed and then he would bring his crop and all his things to Marholm again and there would be something to secure your rent. I have been several times at Ward's but could speak with him but once. He has no money yet but will have soon. Are those two farms yours this Lady Day? [P.S.] Mr Turner tells me the Dean of Peterborough and the minister of Allgate are in town. He desires you would do him what kindness you can about the bailiff of Peterborough's place. The dean shall have good security.

## 557 FITZWILLIAM TO GUYBON

*London, 11 March 1707/8; F(M)C 1652*

Mr Parker has not yet paid. I am in great need having paid away all my money and what I could raise on credit. I will send an account next week what Ash has repaid, and as soon as the principal and interest are paid will order you to deliver the bond. My son has done all that can be done for Mrs Pendleton. Her son cannot come in till Midsummer, if so soon. As to her holding the Old Park and Mulberry Close till her stock is in a condition to sell, that may be every year the same. She must leave them at some Ladyday; I do not make Michaelmas grounds of my closes. You wrote the same two or three years ago when I would have had her off. I must have my land and my house for my own convenience. I will have no family in [Milton] but my own when I am there. I told Mr Wright about his laying down timber at Milton Holme when he was here last. Tell his wife I will prefer my bill in chancery against her husband for laying his things in Castor Field and not bringing them to the ferry as he promised. I can make him spend a £100 so he will pay dearly for his wharfage. If I hear he has brought more goods to Milton Holme and does not pay King for the damage he has done him I will sue him next term. I shall allow Burton nothing for ploughing and sowing my ground. I gave him no leave but ordered him by you to give over the thoughts of it before he put the plough into the ground. He answered he had got all ready and would plough. I can produce your letter saying he gave this answer. I must now try at law whether he shall plough my land whether I will or no. He is too pragmatical and must be humbled. Had I granted him a lease as I intended I should not have been against it but nobody shall plough without a lease. Let him take what follows. Poor Mr Whittacre is in low circumstances. Since Lady Day 1707 the estate is mine and next Lady Day there will be a year's rent due. If Ward is so poor he cannot hold it, so secure my year's rent, do what you can for Mr Whittacre and get another tenant at Lady Day. I find Mr Pemberton no friend to Turner. The dean, a stranger, will do nothing without him. I don't know the dean but my son shall do what he can. I received a letter from John Catlin about some land which he has purchased for me.[1] Tell him I will stand to the bargain and he shall have what he likes for himself.

[1] Mrs Stevens' Maxey estate, see **555** above.

## 558 FITZWILLIAM TO GUYBON

*London, 18 March 1707/8; F(M)C 1653*

I am very sorry I am like to have no money from Mr Parker or any one else. To wait a month and now not have it for a fortnight longer and perhaps not then will be a great disappointment which you might have prevented had you not trusted wholly to Parker. For the foolish story of a pretended Prince of Wales there was nobody here anyway concerned about it, it being so ridiculous and the design so simple: the French king had a mind to be rid of the charge of keeping him and so sent him to be knocked on the head which I suppose he will be soon if not already.[1] I wonder people in our parts should be concerned when he was to land so far off us. We have cold weather but better now than later which would kill the fruit. We cannot expect warm weather at this season. I am sorry you have lambs already. You should have taken more care not to let the rams too soon to the ewes. After Ladyday would have been soon enough for lambing. I remember Thomas Freeman never expected lambs before Ladyday at soonest. I am content Mrs Pendleton should hold her closes another year and no longer. Let her dispose of her stock any time within this next year as may be most advantageous, but by mentioning her holding them till midsummer, you must take me for a fool or are one yourself to think I should be persuaded to let my land by the quarter, especially the best quarter of the year. I must take the Meadow Close in hand for hay for the stables. You may be deceived in thinking I shall not be at Milton soon. [P.S.] I believe you need not fear losing Mr Forster this year for Captain Styles will not let him his farm, hearing he is so much my debtor though lets him 'plow it to halfes'. I am sorry to find Mr Pemberton has so little value for me and my son as to oppose our desires in behalf of poor Turner. My son waited on the dean, though altogether a stranger to us, and he positively told my son he would be glad of Turner if Mr Pemberton approved, for he left it wholly to him. My son has written two letters to Mr Pemberton who has never had the manners to answer them. He is a knave and expects a bribe and values no man's friendship. This will certainly be remembered. Read my letters and answer them as you ought. I asked you what rent money you received from Joseph Clarke so I can pay Mr Whittacre who, I fear, is in great want.

[1] Louis XIV had supported James Stuart in his abortive attempt to land in Scotland.

## **559** FITZWILLIAM TO GUYBON

*London, 25 March 1708; F(M)C 1654*

I am glad you have got a £100 return, being in great need of it. I hope Mr Parker will return more soon. I will pay Mr Whittacre Joe Clarke's rent. This Lady Day rent from Clarke and Ward is due to me. I wish Ward's rent due to this poor man could be got but if Ward is not worth two years' rent I must take care of myself and secure my own year's rent now due. If he is not able to go on seize what he has and put in a new tenant; for both Clarke's and Ward's farms shall be put in repair but be not too costly. I told Mr Forster here that I expected £60 a year if he ploughed, and if it proved too dear I would be kind to him. If he did not plough he should pay £48, but I would be kind. I had hoped you would prevail with him for I don't wish him to leave Marholm, although he is an ill neighbour among the tenants, never keeping his fences in repair and occasioning trespasses on both sides. If his stock and goods are on the land today he must keep it another year.[1] In that time he and I can talk further, and I believe may agree for both our lives. He may do worse, not knowing what he takes with farms he has no experience of. I don't believe he has stock or experience to manage a great farm, having many fanciful ways of his own that others know he has lost much money by.

[1] If Forster's stock had been on the property on Lady Day, March 25th, he would have been required to keep the farm another year.

## 560 FITZWILLIAM TO GUYBON

*London, 1 April 1708; F(M)C 1656*

I am glad you have taken care of me for money, and will take further care soon. Since Mr Forster is gone I hope he has paid you the £400 he owes me for rent, or that you have secured his stock and goods and not allowed him to 'go off tamely'. He must not think to live quietly at Walton as long as 'there is law of my side'. If Burton will give £40 a year for that farm he shall have it for a year and 'see how we like one another' but he shall plough none of it at that rent. I will let it to no man for less than £40. I hope Mr Forster left fences, house and barn in repair. Next week I will write to Mr Ash about Mr Eldred[1] and likewise his bond.

Mr Eldred I find a very troublesome imposeing man on the countrey. I find he woud force himselfe on us the freeholders to be our attourney and run us into a sute at law when I hope there is no occation, for if the Lincolneshire drovers are forewarned driving their cattell and sheep over our common they will then take the road by the Red Inn as formerly. If they do not then we are to drive and impound them and that I suppose will frighton them from coming againe. If not we can but go to law with them at last. I had a great bundle of papers by the last post from Mr Eldred being orders of Langdyke court last year for payment of £50 when there is [no?] occasion. He wants to gett this money into his hands but I hope the jury at next Langdyke court will not order him to receave it. I writt him a sharpe letter about it but I suppose he will not shew that letter to any one. What money you have of the countrey's in your hand pay it to Mr Ash to be disposed off for the bennefitt of the common if the jury of Langdyke sends an order to you and desire Mr Ash and other of the best freeholders to putt themselves upon the next jury which is now soon to see the countrey's money is not fooled away. The Duke of Bedford, Captain Hyde, Mr Charles Bertie, Mr Dove and Mr Price,[2] these men loose their toles by the cattle goeing through Peterborough and if the countrey are not overforward in going to law these gentlemen that sufferr so much in their rents will make a purse amung themselves and try the cause for us which will save the countrey's money and our business will be done to our hands. These gentlemen joine and bribe Eldred to perswade our ignorant freeholders to spend the countrey's money to do them service. Pray read this part of my letter to Mr Ash.

[1] The Deeping Lawyer.
[2] Robert Apreece of Washingley.

## 561 GUYBON TO FITZWILLIAM

*5 April 1708; F(M)C 1658*

I hope you received the £100 I sent by Thomas Chattris and will send another £100 by him at his return for I know not how to return it. Mr Parker has no money at London yet. When he has I shall return by no other person. Mr Forster will put the fences, houses and barn in good repair before leaving them. He and I have agreed for this year for £40, £10 more than anyone else would give. Richard Burton offered £30 but no other did bid me a penny. Mr Forster says his lease has been out these 12 years. If you please to take £45 a year for 10 years of the 12 and £80 for the 2 last he will continue it this year at £40. He has paid £67 15s a year during his lease. I hope you both agree and he will pay all your money very honestly. I would not have you both part nor have him leave Marholm. I have none of the county's money in my hands. I gave Mr Pemberton the rent roll some years ago and he gathers it. The county asked me to give the rent roll to some attorney to sue the tenants for they were very backward in paying their rents so I thought I could not give it to a better man than Mr Pemberton. I went to Northborough to speak with [Ward but][1] he had not been at home for three weeks. His wife could not tell whether he would return so I made a seizure and took an account and today week will have a sale of what little there is. I fear there will be little more than will pay one year's rent, if that. We live in bad times and I know not when they will be better. We have so much water our fields are drowned. They cannot sow and what is sown in many grounds will be lost. I never knew the roads so bad in my life. We have much ado to ride from one 'towne' to another, the meadows and fens are drowned.

[1] The letter is damaged at this point.

## **562** FITZWILLIAM TO GUYBON

*London, 8 April 1708; F(M)C 1659*

I received your letter by Chattris and enclosed the new subscription for the ferry this year but I find the bowling day is altered from Monday to Thursday which I dislike though I would have King please the greatest part of the gentry. 'Sewley'[1] bowling day being Wednesday it may be any of our bowlers that go will be weary with bowling there and will be unwilling to come next day so the green will lose their company. I appointed Monday because it's nearest Saturday's market at Peterborough to buy provisions for the ordinary[2] and they would keep sweet enough until then. There's no market between Saturday and Thursday except Deeping which is far off. Besides, all gentlemen are fresh to bowl on Mondays and there is a day before Wednesday to rest or despatch any business. Gentlemen often cannot spare two days together for their recreations. Business must be minded as well as sports though I am very easy about the time appointed and the gentlemen may please themselves. Chattris paid me the £100. We reckoned that he has paid me £45 and £15 in money and carriages before. He has receipts for two years' rent to Lady Day 1707 and owes a year's rent due Lady Day last. He reckons he is obliged to bring me £100 gratis any time of year, so if you can get no sooner return send it by him. He will not be home to Thorpe for a fortnight but then will bring £100 or more if you have it. I am glad you have agreed again with Mr Forster for one year but I had rather had another tenant. He has such fancies in the managing his farm that he loses more than another man would and so I must abate more rent to him than to another. His sons leave him and go to service because he has such ways with him and will not be persuaded by them.

For the countreye's money I am sorry you lett Mr Pemberton receave the rents.

Lawiers I know love to receave money but cannot abide to part with it againe out of their hands but make use of it and then say they have not received it. There must be money gott ready soon for Mr Eldred will draw the countrey into a law suite whither we will or not; not but that we must defend our common and not sufferr a drift way over it because Mr Parker will improve his inclosure at Dosthorp[3] by that meanes. For one man's sake we must not injure all the other freeholders in our Soake and our tennants also. Pray take care the most substantiall men in the whole hundred be upon the jury and sensible men for I understand Mr Parker intends to be foreman of the jury and will gett as many of his freinds in it as he can. You must gett Mr Ash and as many good men as he knows to be jury men also and do what they thinke is most to the countrey advantage.

We cannot expect more from Ward than he has but let me know what it comes to that I may satisfy Mr Whittacre. I am sorry you have had too much rain but glad of the present fine weather. I sent King the subscription paper you sent up which my son and I signed. Be at Langdyke Court yourself.

[1] Sulehay was one of the forest walks for which Fitzwilliam received deer warrants (see **30**).
[2] Ordinary, a public meal regularly provided at fixed price in an eating house.
[3] Dogsthorpe, Northants.

## 563 FITZWILLIAM TO GUYBON

*London, 15 April 1708; F(M)C 1660*

The money Thomas Chattris paid was right save a Scots shilling, only a 2d loss. He will be at Peterborough next Saturday so may bring next week whatever you have gathered; it will be 'all a price to me', whether £100 or 'six or seven score'.[1] Let me know what was done at Langdyke Court, and whatever orders come to you from the court about paying money direct Mr Pemberton or the tenants to pay it, and keep the order as your justification. Your letter to the tenants is their justification for their payments. What do Ward's stock and goods amount to? Burton having ploughed my land without first acquainting me I shall build him no barn until I have considered it further. As you rightly say if Mr Forster leaves Marholm that house and barn may be fit for him if he will be a good chapman for the land also. You may do some inside work for him which may serve another tenant if he goes to Forster's. [P.S.] Did the soldiers that marched down from the north go through any part of my estate, and if so what harm was done? I understand they are to march to Colchester and so go overseas.

[1] Guybon returned £100 by 'Thomas Chattris' in late April, Disbursements 74, and see **565** below.

## 564 FITZWILLIAM TO GUYBON

*London, 22 April 1708; F(M)C 1661*

Glad of the money you intend me, but have not heard of Mr Miller's money yet.

Since the countrey will spend their money to advance the interest of the Duke of Bedford, Mr Bertie and Mr Hide who would have done it themselves and thereby saved our money which we are alwaies over prodigall off, I am glad the money is to be paid to Mr Ash who I hope will take care to see it laied out as it should and not pay attourneys what they call for before the business is done. I did heare that Mrs Hyde of Langtoff[1] did promise Mr Deepup £50 if he could make an interest whereby to stop the droves goeing through the fenn that they might keep the old roade by the Red Inne and now he has gott the point done for her. This I was told as a great secrett so you must have a care of speaking of it.

I wonder why Lord Exeter, Mr Bertie and Mr Hide should have paid £50 to them? Glad no mischief was done in the soldiers' march, and hope they will keep good order as they return. I am sorry Ward's inventory comes to no more for there will be nothing coming to Mr Whittacre. Get up what money you can. I expect to be down next month.

[1] Langtoft, Lincs.

**565** FITZWILLIAM TO GUYBON
*London, 29 April 1708; F(M)C 1663*

Thomas Chattris brought the £100 in two bags with a leaden shilling in one which I cannot get off yet. If you can get no returns send more by him a week on Saturday. Leave word with his wife in Thorpe to speak with you when he is next at Peterborough. Mr Miller's £50 9s was paid me last Tuesday. I perceive he borrows the money of Mr Maure, a Smithfield salesman, to get the money from you in the country to buy stock, and will repay [Maure] with the sale of fat sheep he sends up in a month, meanwhile 'allowing interest'. Thank God for this warm weather which will bring on grass, etc. Let Joseph Chamberlaine draw the calash from the coachhouse, rub clean the leatherwork and brasswork, and the next day oil the leatherwork and scour the brasswork, and let it dry in the sun a couple of hours. As to the ferry well don't cover it until I see it and find if it's deep enough to hold water in a dry year. I thought Mr Wright had had a frame made to draw water in buckets. I know many an inn on the road to town that pay at least £100 a year rent and have no pump, and I am not obliged to find King a pump. I don't say I won't set down a pump but I will take my own time for it. Let the walls be secured from wet and there will be no danger of their falling in again.

**566** FITZWILLIAM TO GUYBON
*London, 6 May 1708; F(M)C 1664*

I doubt I shall receive the £30 Mr Miller told you he would pay this week for he borrowed the last £50 at interest and received it from you to go to fair with. He will have no money of his own until he sends up fat goods, which is not for three weeks. You sent up some very bad money by Chattris which 'I have much ado to gett off' and fear I shall lose 3s 6d. He may be in town next Saturday, or Saturday after, and you may find him the surest man to send money by, unless Mr Parker, etc, but I had to pay him 5s for this last £200, and I fear he will expect more if I have any more by him, but I will try him once more and see how he deals with me. If you wash the calash's woodwork very clean there will be less to do when the weather is fair, and then draw it into the sun, clean the mould from the leather and oil it, and scour the brasswork, and let it dry in the sun but not for more than two hours if it's hot. I think to leave here the latter end of May, but with buying liveries and paying debts I shall need 'a pretty deale' of money before I leave town.

[P.S.] Mr Taylor one of our prebends of Peterborough who has been these 29 yeares amakeing his church at Harlow in Essex very fine that it was the neatest in all Essex, in an houre and halfes time it was consumed to ashes occasioned by lightening as they apprehend or else by mischeivous people as they feare. He had much adoe to save his owne life venturing in to save some of the things.

## 567 FITZWILLIAM TO GUYBON

*London, 13 May 1708; F(M)C 1665*

We are all extremely sorry to hear how ill Betty Bateman[1] is, but still hope 'her youth will beare her out from death this time.' My wife hopes it's 'a breeding fitt only', you mentioning no fever. I suppose her husband and mother will let her want for no good advice and means to be had. We all pray for her recovery. Chattris confessed he had made use of £16 of the last £100 he brought, but the false money my son got off at May Fair. We have had plenty of rain here and 'a hopefull haysell towards', and am extremely glad you have had the same. When I took Meadow Close in hand, they all said there was plenty of hay in it, which I hope will prove true for I shall need it for my stables this summer, even though I have failed to get down in former summers. I am sorry you lack company at your [bowling] green at Gunwade Ferry. I thought King's interest among the great men would have brought him company enough. Contrary to my expectation Miller's salesman, George Maure, brought me yesterday £16 14s 11d. [P.S.] I hope you will get me what money you can before haysell for they will not part with their money then. If this town can afford anything to do poor Betty good that is not to be had there let us know and we will endeavour to get it and send it.

[1] Mrs Bull's married daughter, see **568** below.

## 568 FITZWILLIAM TO GUYBON

*London, 20 May 1708; F(M)C 1666*

We are all extremely glad that Mrs Bull's daughter Bateman is recovering. I am glad of the money you are sending by Chattris and hope it comes safely. Mr Hankin has paid £16 14s 11d for 'Duke Tomlinson. I have promised my daughter one of my portraits at Milton and wish Mrs Bull to get it out for sending by the Peterborough carrier. The picture I will keep at Milton has a frame gilt with 'right gold', while the one to send has a differently 'fashioned' frame with holes right through and handsomely gilded but not as richly. Mr Wright must contrive to pack the picture so it won't 'joggle' which would spoil the gilding. After he has nailed pieces of wood to keep it tight hay must be laid under and over the picture.

## 569 JOHN CATLIN TO FITZWILLIAM

*Maxey, 21 May 1708; F(M)C 1667*

The house belonging to Mrs Stevens' estate will cost about 50s to repair, for it is strong. The barn was built about eight years ago at a cost of near £20. Mrs Stevens ordered me to let it at Lady Day which I did to Elias Goode, a tailor in our 'town', for 35s, with three acres and a rod of land at 18s: in all £2 13s a year. This was the worst part of the estate with fences out of repair, but Robert Tyers, carpenter, will give £26 for it and pay for all repairs. Shortly after I bargained with Mrs Stevens, Richard Turnill and his son, who are tenants for some of the land, went to Mrs Stevens and bid more for it, and would have made the bargain void, which put her into a 'fret', so I told him he would pay more rent for it if he held it after next Michaelmas. One of your tenants, William Riddington, will pay a guinea for the income of it, at £4 5s a year; so it may be let as you think best. The two acres of lea ground I beg for myself lie between two homesteads owned by the Earl of Exeter and John Grant. The house that was on it is almost all down, the materials worth scarce 20s and the fences very bad. When the house was there it was let for £2 7s a year to Edward Wise. I have had few 'astrays' as yet. When any come that are not 'owned' you shall know it. It's about half a year since I have the amercements[1] from Mr Pemberton, and Mr Guybon charged me to gather them. I have received some of the smallest, and others utterly refuse to pay, and Mr Pemberton will not make them do so without your order. Complaints are made because they are not gathered, saying nobody will fear to transgress on Maxey manor because they escape the penalty. I hope you will shortly order that they be forced to pay and observe your court leet, and I shall be less blamed.

[1] Fines imposed for offences charged in the manorial court, most commonly for acts of trespass.

## 570 FITZWILLIAM TO GUYBON

*London, 27 May 1708; F(M)C 1669*

Thomas Chattris paid me £100 last Saturday. He asks for more for carrying this money but I have paid him nothing yet. I am glad you intend me more at his next return but it grieves me to have so much specie sent out of our parts which will make it scarce but had rather this way than wait long for a return, wanting money badly. I hope some good people will carry money into the country. Repeats instructions for packing and sending the portrait for his daughter.[1] Though I hear very well of Mr Forster's second son, I don't know what substance he may have to manage such a farm. His father has taken it for this year. When I am at Milton I will see the young man, settle accounts with his father, and when he has paid me off we shall see what he will be able to give his son. I heard the young man was a coachman in a gentleman's service in 'our countrey' and he is to blame for leaving a good service. It's much too late to plough this year, and I am unwilling until I see what he would plough. Whoever ploughs my land shall lay it down with grass seed fit for that ground. Tell your friend Mr Turner of Peterborough that the letter he superscribed to me proved a letter to my wife from Mrs Dillingham, now

Mrs Johnson, to borrow money of her or of me to free her son from prison. Let Turner acquaint her neither of us have money spare at this time. Tell Mr Ash of Paston[2] I received his letter about his bond, that I expect to be at Milton by midsummer and when the interest is stated and paid he shall honestly have his bond delivered. I would have answered his letter but have a 'great rheume' in my eye and have much ado to write this.

[1] See **568** above.

[2] Paston, a hamlet of Peterborough, had been settled by Sir Henry Massingberd, bart., on his third wife, Elizabeth, who married William Ash in 1680: *VCH Northamptonshire*, ii.514.

## **571** FITZWILLIAM TO GUYBON

*London, 3 June 1708; F(M)C 1670*

My eye is almost well again. Daughter Barrington is in town and well. Sir Charles Barrington's mother is dead and left him her jointure to the value of £1,000 to £1,100 a year. My daughter asks kindly after you and wonders you never write to her. I excuse you by speaking of your 'much business' and your 'growing into yeares'. Get brewhouse, tubs and vessels very clean for I shall soon send word when to brew.

## **572** FITZWILLIAM TO GUYBON

*London, 10 June 1708; F(M)C 1671*

Brew two hogsheads of ale and four of small beer before 'haysell' begins. I allow 16 bushels malt for the ale, eight for the small beer. Use good malt for we have good small beer in town. I hope to be down by 'haysell' or a week after. Hop it well however. I received a letter from Mr Phelips about John Freeman's children who are likely to be a charge to Marholm. Let me know how the beadsmen's places are disposed of.[1] Take care John Freeman idles not his time away but works as he should to help to maintain the children. Otherwise I will look upon [him] as an idle fellow and will have him pressed for a soldier that he may bring no greater charge to the parish. We are very glad to hear of Mrs Bull's daughter Betty's being abroad again. [P.S.] Some of the old women may bring up the two youngest Freeman children, the youngest of all dry nursed. The boy being eight years old his father may take care of him. The picture came up very well. It's a sign you want no hay in the country for it had at least 50 pounds weight in it, most of it needless. Mr Hankin has paid £18 9s 7d on 'Duke Tomlinson's account.

[1] Beadsman, an inhabitant of an almshouse.

## **573** GUYBON TO FITZWILLIAM

*14 June 1708; F(M)C 1672*

Received yours of the 10th. Glad to hear picture came up well. We are brewing. I fear I shall hardly return you money before you are here.

John Freeman have buried his wife and she have left him three children.[1] He is a very poore man. He does follow his worke and doe what he can. Her father

I hope will take the eldest daughter and I hope Thomas Freeman in the fenn, his sonne. If soe there will be none but the youngest left for him to take care off. The beads men's places are disposed one as followeth: Good'y Goode one, Peggy Freeman and Good'y Butler one, the Widow Watson and Adam Johnson one, Francis Browne and Jonathan Watson one, they being sick and poore I gave it amongst them. There have beene bad times with the farmers and little to doe for the poore but I hope shall now have better. Your honour may take it away from Browne and Watson and dispose of it as your honour please. [P.S.] Since I wrott I am tould that Good'y Tomson of Aylesworth, John Freeman's sister of Marham, have taken his youngest child but desires some little mayntenance from the towne but I doe not heare what; soe now all his children are taken from him.

[1] The son of Thomas Freeman, Fitzwilliam's late gamekeeper and substantial tenant.

## 574 FITZWILLIAM TO GUYBON

*London, 17 June 1708; F(M)C 1673*

Francis Guybon, Yours of the 14th I received. I am glad to heare John Freeman's children are like to be disposed off without any charge to the towne. There is no reason to allow Jonathan Johnson[1] that is a young man any thing; though Francis Browne is a more elderly man then the other yett I would not use him nor any other to have shares of beadesmen places till they are past their worke. A little sickness they may labour under and recover againe and mind their worke but if they are incouraged with shares of those places they will alwaies be idle and a charge to the towne. I thought Adam Johnson had had a whole beedesman place since his mother died. He is a townes borne man and ever a great paines taker and had been a servant in our family and his predecessors had been the like before him but such as Browne and Jonathan Johnson and his mother they are able to worke. Goody Goude had her beadesman's place because she was a widdow and had young children to mainteine but after they were growne up to shift for themselves and are married away you might have taken halfe a place away from her and so pray do and lett Adam Johnson have it. Jonathan Wattson's mother is a hearty working woman and needs no releife yett. They can worke and are able if they have nothing else to support them and these places makes them all idle and pretend sickness. I hope you will be better then your word and returne me a little more money.

[1] Fitzwilliam confuses the names. Watson is meant; cf. **573**.

## 575 GUYBON TO FITZWILLIAM

*22 June 1708; F(M)C 1674*

Yours of the 17 instant received. John Freeman's children are disposed very well with little charge to the 'towne'. If you let them have a beadsmans' place it will pay for bringing up the child. Goody Watson is poor, weakly, and lame in an arm. She stands in as much need as any of them. The beadsmen's places are disposed on as follows: Adam Johnson one, Widow Goude and Widow Freeman one, Widow Watson and Widow Butler one, the 'towne' one for John Freeman's children; I think they cannot be better disposed, but as your honour pleases.[1] We begin to cut our hay today. I fear we shall have a 'catching' time. On Friday I intend to wash our sheep and the week after clip them. Wool is like to be but a bad commodity. There is a great deal brought into Peterborough market and sold for 11s 6d a tod. I hope we shall have the happiness to see you soon. If not I will return some money by Thomas Chattris.

[1] A beadsman's place was worth £2 10s a year, a half therefore was 25s. Guybon paid the money half yearly. In June 1708 Guybon also paid 10s to the overseer of the poor at Marholm for 'John Freeman's children'; Disbursements 74.

## **576** FITZWILLIAM TO GUYBON

*London, 24 June 1708; F(M)C 1675*

Sorry to hear you cut hay so soon since the weather is so 'catching'. It rains five or six showers every day here and spoils the colour of the hay. We did not use to cut hay in our parts until Fotheringay Fair time which is a fortnight hence, and by then we might have had fair weather. I am sorry wool bears no better price than 11s 6d the tod. I will venture to keep it another year but lay it up dry, and well covered from the dust. If near a wall be sure to put boards between wall and wool. I hope you note the number of fleeces clipped each year that I may know the number when I sell them. I am willing the beadsmen's places go as yours mentions for a year and then we may see how others deserve. I cannot be at Milton this month because of my wife's business, but hope to be there soon after. Take care to look after the haymakers for that 'must be tended as it should'. Return money by Chattris or somebody for I shall need it before I leave here. [P.S.] I see you were brewing last week. Let me know who brewed, how many days, how many strike of malt you had, how much a strike and how many hoops were set on the hogsheads. Your shepherd Freeman rents the Highway Close and his sheep are as much upon Gunworth Ground as in his own close, as people riding through the ground often notice, knowing his sheep by the brand.

## **577** GUYBON TO FITZWILLIAM

*28 June 1708; F(M)C 1676*

I received yours of 24th. Everybody is busy cutting hay, and I hope we shall have good weather to get it in. By the time hay is in harvest will be here. I have 'put out our hay to the mowing and makeing soe I know what the charge will be. I was tired with the haymakers last year, and was resolved would not be this.' We are cutting Meadow Close, Brooke Field and House Goodlucks at 1s 8d an acre for mowing and 12d an acre making. When brewing we had 24 strike of malt from Goodman Hullock who makes as good malt and sells as cheap as any. Adam Johnson brewed for five days and 17 hoops were set on the hogsheads and one on a tub. I cannot return by Chattris this time but will without fail the next. You are misinformed about Freeman's sheep being in Gunworth Ground. Those who ride through there cannot know his sheep by the brand for he uses none.

## **578** FITZWILLIAM TO GUYBON

*London, 1 July 1708; F(M)C 1677*

I received yours of 28th yesterday. Your haying is a fortnight early this year. Pray God you have fair weather but it rained daily here until last Sunday. Notwithstanding you have agreed by the acre for mowing and making yet they must be looked after to see they mow well and make the hay dry and handsome for horses, deer and sheep must have good hay but store beasts,[1] cows and oxen love 'mow burn't' hay. See the hay makers don't make it too hastily for their own profit for my horses must have good hay. I hope you soon return a good sum as yours promised. I perceive Mr Pemberton has 'played the knave with Turner at last'. He promised me and my son he should have the place. I assured him Turner would allow the widow yearly what Pemberton thought fit and would have as good security as should be required. I shall think of him when he thinks I have forgot it.

[1] Store beasts, those kept for fattening.

## **579** FITZWILLIAM TO GUYBON

*London, 8 July 1708; F(M)C 1678*

Glad you had fair weather for your hay. I hope it is pretty well in now. If not 'clapp on more hands' to finish it, but be careful they make it well and dry for 'they as worke by the great will make more hast then good speed'. Thomas Chattris dined here Sunday night and says he travels much at night with his meat and butter so I have agreed he shall bring up what venison I want before I go down. The goods he sends from Thorpe set out every Wednesday night about 11 [p.m.] so any venison you send must be at his house by 10 [p.m.] if cold enough to be packed by that time. No need to inform the Peterborough carrier that Chattris brings my venison. If good enough send a buck next week. [P.S.] Hope you had fair weather for clipping your sheep.

## **580** FITZWILLIAM TO GUYBON

*London, 15 July 1708; F(M)C 1679*

Sorry you have had 'catching' weather there; here it has been fair for 10 days until the change of the moon but showery since, and today also which is St Swithin's. Reassure Mr Ash about his bond; 'he shall not be wronged of a farthing'. I have not time to see about the interest being busy getting ready to come home, which I still hope will be this month. Glad you intend me a return by Mr Parker. Remember Chattris brings my venison which Lawrence[1] need not know. Tell Mr Pemberton on Saturday that I hear one Day of Deepingate intends to put some lives into his copyhold estate held of one of my manors. Tell him I always set my fines myself, and will not do so until I know whose life or lives are to be put in; what life or lives are in being; and the full improved value of the estate. Nothing shall be done until I have determined the fine. [P.S.] I believe Day is a copyholder of Northborough manor, and may be also for Maxey manor. Order John Catlin to find out for you the value of Day's estate both in Northborough and Maxey, what lives are in being and what to be put in.

[1] A rival carrier.

## 581 FITZWILLIAM TO GUYBON

*London, 22 July 1708; F(M)C 1680*

I am very sorry to hear King of the ferry is ill. I wish him a good recovery for he would be a great loss to us. Last Friday we had the same thunder and lightning that you had there. I was then abroad in the Fields[1] but found shelter and came home dry. Mr Pettyt has paid only £50 for Charles Parker, his servant saying he had no orders to pay me more. I hope you will order me the other £50. I send you this warrant you asked for but I had rather have my own than forest venison for we take greater care in killing it, and hope King will be well enough to kill me a buck next Wednesday if not this.

[1] Islington Fields.

## 582 JOHN CATLIN TO FITZWILLIAM

*Maxey, 24 July 1708; F(M)C 1681*

I was with John Day yesterday about his copyhold estate. He said he had written to his landlord Mr Field to ask that you would abate his fine of £10, which Mr Pemberton had set at Northborough Court in October 1704 when John Day and his wife Joan were admitted. William Day his father died the summer before. The estate has not been let these 50 or 60 years.[1] It is a good homestead of about an acre and a half with eight acres of land, some of it pasture. I judge it worth about £8 a year. The fine is at the will of the lord, and is not yet paid, but these two were admitted tenants about three years since.

[1] The farm had been in the hands of the Day Family for this period.

## 583 FITZWILLIAM TO GUYBON

*London, 29 July 1708; F(M)C 1682*

The fat buck I received from Chattris last Saturday had much ado to come sweet, it was so ill killed. I am sure it was pulled down by dogs, being very bloody, the haunches much torn and the bones broken. I thought King had been a better marksman. Mr Parker has paid by Hankin at Heriot's £103 18s 10d. I shall abate nothing of the fine Pemberton set on John Day of Deeping Gate, and were it set now it should be greater. He has set no more than one year's improved rent for two lives which is much too little. Since it is set it shall stand, but I wonder the fine was not paid long ago. My son wishes you to send by Chattris the eight guineas you got in selling his horse.

## 584 FITZWILLIAM TO GUYBON

*London, 31 July 1708; F(M)C 1683*

I received a brace of bucks and one pair of shoulders by Chattris's wagon or packhorses this morning. Send no more by him for his servants are careless, most of it is lost and it all 'stuncke'. The two haunches of the best buck were thrown away for carrion, and I fear the rest is too tainted to use. You were to blame in sending any up without my order. I fear King is an ill marksman, otherwise he would not have shot two bucks 'at a shoote'. The venison was run down by dogs as we could plainly see from its colour and the torn haunches. I am very angry at this miscarriage. I did not have such venison in Thomas Freeman's lifetime.

## 585 FITZWILLIAM TO GUYBON

*London, 5 August 1708; F(M)C 1685*

I will have no more venison until I can have it well killed and dressed. I never had so bad luck as this year. Chattris affirms the haunches of the best buck were green and the rest of it near stinking when he received it at St Neot's. Thomas Freeman used to stand in the little house and shoot out of the window where he had a good rest for his gun. They drove the deer up to him so that he could wait his opportunity while the deer stood singly and not shoot at the whole herd killing two at a time. I am sure there must be a dog to pull the deer down after shooting, else how could the haunches of the best buck be so torn and the bones in the first broken as well as the flesh torn off them. I do not intend giving away my fee deer. I am not to be told by the Peterborough people when I shall dispose it. I owe none of them anything nor am I obliged to any of them. I will use it myself if I think fit. God continue this fair, hot weather and you will have a good harvest.

## 586 FITZWILLIAM TO MR BETTS[1]

*London, 7 August 1708; F(M)C 1686*

Mr Betts, I received yours etc. As to the settling my estates in Northamptonshire and Norffolke on my son's marriage upon, I alwayes intended it (but not the whole in present possession) and soe beleive you mistooke me, but yet I never designed to receive any revenue of the whole more then the use of Milton house, the gardens, parke and some grounds about it to the value of about £250 per annum; the rest of the revenue I intended to give my sonn every yeare for a present designing him to live as well as any gentleman in that neighbourhood with his mannagement: but if Sir Henry will not leave that matter to my curtesy we will not breake off on that point. As to the joynture I told Sir Henry the last time we met I would give noe more then £2,400 which I thought sufficient being £200 more per annum then I at first offered for the £20,000 portion. My rents are old rents and my tenants and their ancestors have lived in most of my farmes these 60 and 80 yeares; very few of the rents have beene abated or raised. The tenants have noe leases, that they may be turned out at six monthes warning but my forefathers and I never thought fitt to doe it. The taxes are moderatly easy and in some of my mannors the tenants beare a third part of the taxes besides other honorary duties. For the pin money I can by noe meanes thinke of goeing higher then £400 per annum; more would be soe great a clogg to my sonne he could save nothing out of the estate and soe must run in debt. Consequently a lady that must spend more in her cloathes then £400 per annum will be to great for my estate. If these termes will be accepted by Sir Henry I shall think my son very happily placed in his family. If not, I must submitt to a more favorable oppertunity. However, I must alwayes owne your great civilities and kindness to me and my family.

[1] An intermediary, probably a lawyer, for Sir Henry Johnson, a wealthy Suffolk and London investor and landowner, long time M.P. for Aldburgh, with whom Lord Fitzwilliam was in treaty for a marriage for his son with Miss Johnson, and with whom negotiations were resumed, although unsuccessfully, in 1711; see Silas Petyt to Fitzwilliam 1 May 1711 and Fitzwilliam's reply (copy) 8 May 1711, F(M)Correspondence 1710–1740 (drawer 22). This letter, a copy written by an amanuensis, is included here because although not estate correspondence it contains valuable details about the estate itself.

## 587 FITZWILLIAM TO GUYBON[1]

*12 August 1708; F(M)C 1687*

(Sends these warrants because has little to write. The Pembertons have gone to Bath and Bristol. Prays they may find benefit there and return safe and well home. Wishes them fair harvest weather though a shower now and then would do little harm.)

[1] A note cut from the foot of a fee deer warrant.

## 588 FITZWILLIAM TO GUYBON

*London, 19 August 1708; F(M)C 1689*

Encloses fourth warrant. Glad he has sent money by Featherstone. Every little will help.)

My sonn has taken a journey of pleasure, went first to Northampton, thence to Leicester, Nottingham, Derby and will see all the gentlemen houses and rarities worth seeing. By what places he will come back I know not till I see him. He sett out last Fryday and gott to Nottingham on Munday night safe and well. I am glad to heare you have good harvest weather. Pray God continue it till all is done and that we may now and then have a good showre for sake of the edishes.

## 589 FITZWILLIAM TO GUYBON

*London, 26 August 1708; F(M)C 1690*

My son was well in Derbyshire last Monday and intends to return by Lichfield, Coventry and Warwick. From thence he goes to Woodstock by Oxford to see the Duke of Marlborough's new house[1] so he cannot see Milton this turn. I would have had him call going down but he wished to see Woburn,[2] Northampton, Leicester etc. Mr Featherstone I hear nothing of nor of any money paid by his order at any of my goldsmiths. It will be very welcome. I hope your good harvest weather continues to the end. Lend my calash to none. I sent it down new last year for my own use and I expect to 'weare it myselfe', not have it used by others. [P.S.] Mrs Pendleton told you last Lady day she could only put off her stock at a Michaelmas season. Remind her of it for I will not spare her closes after Lady day.

[1] Blenheim Palace.
[2] Woburn Abbey, the seat of the Duke of Bedford.

## 590 FITZWILLIAM TO GUYBON

*London, 2 September 1708; F(M)C 1691*

I have heard nothing yet of Featherstone's money. Make use yourself of the venison of my four warrants for I know of nobody who deserves any. If you think fit you may give the Checkleys a piece and the ferry man King three other pieces, a warrant between them. Take a warrant yourself and give Cousins Tryce and Bellamy a piece from the rest. I leave it to you. Mr Pemberton is from home, there needs none there. Checkleys were so kind as to visit me twice. 'Mrs Pemberton is a bold confident sort of a woman, and threw out some words as she had a mind to have my calash fetch her home from Oxford.' If her coachman comes for it you may say you have received no orders and dare not let it go. I shall not forget his carriage in the business of the Peterborough bailiff. This cooler weather if there be a good buck left in the park, send it up next week by Chattris. He tells me you need not kill the buck till Wednesday afternoon because he sends his butter, etc, on Thursday at 11 [p.m.] from Thorpe, but consult with Chattris first before you kill any venison because he may have altered his times since the cool weather. If you cannot speak with him next Saturday stay a week longer before you send any up. My son, thank God, came safe and well home last night.

## 591 FITZWILLIAM TO GUYBON

*London, 9 September 1708; F(M)C 1693*

I have heard nothing of Featherston but don't run after him for if he had brought any he would soon have been with you for it again. I begin to need money. There used to be various small sums paid me by people at or about Northborough at this time for sheep brought up from the fen sides and the North Fen. Speak to them and I am sure I shall not lack money. I am sorry rain has caused floods on both rivers. God send it fair to get the rest of the harvest in. I am sorry you doubt the buck this week by Chattris will prove well. I had rather no buck than an ill one. It is strange that when I lived there I could have five or six fat bucks from my park, and now only two, for the one shot by chance was only a 'sore', and though what was sweet was good meat, it was not fat. Tell me how you disposed of the warrants. I forgot Mr Lowrey for a piece and hope you did not.

**592** FITZWILLIAM TO GUYBON
*London, 11 September 1708; F(M)C 1694*

(The buck arrived well killed, dressed and very sweet so King can kill another, but only if there is one as good, for Fitzwilliam wishes to give venison to 'very good freinds'. Chattris will wait for it at Thorp until 11 [p.m.] that Thursday night.)

**593** FITZWILLIAM TO GUYBON
*London, 16 September 1708; F(M)C 1695*

You disposed of the venison very well. I hope Mr Parker has a piece because he is ready to return money when he can and I fear Lord Exeter may be cross and not serve the warrant though I hope for the best. For the man who desires to have Mr Foster's farm I am very well pleased with the thoughts of such a tenant for it if he is as substantial as you mention. Some enquiry should be made unless you will trust wholly to Richard Burton. He may plough up any of the old farm as Mr Forster did for £60 a year but if the 30 acres be added I expect not only the rent of that ground but £10 a year advance for ploughing it. I do not well understand you if you reckon no more than £40 a year for Mr Forster's farm without ploughing any of it. The rent of the 30 acres if I mistake not is £15 a year. Would you be willing to let this 30 acres to be ploughed for £5 a year more, which makes up the £60 per annum I perceive you would take rather than fail. I can never consent to take so little for it as £60 a year but hope you will get £70, or not above 40s a year less. He must have a lease of 21 years or 15 at least or he must plough but 10 acres at a time, and when that has been ploughed four years he must lay it with 'St Foile'[1] seed the last crop, so plough 10 acres more for four years, laying that in the same manner, and the last 10 acres the same, which makes 12 years. The three last years I expect he lay it to graze with some seed sown with the last crop and for the three years he shall pay no more than £60 a year. Upon these terms I will let this new tenant a lease for 15 years. If you come near an agreement insist the first 10 acres he ploughs shall be the lowest part of the ground next the eight acres, rising by degrees. Be sure the last 10 acres at the top of the hill next Burmer Lees be the last ploughed. I direct this in case the man dies or proves insolvent, as God knows what may happen in nine or 10 years, then the best part of my ground is not ploughed up. This may be some recompense to my successors for I cannot expect to live out such a lease. Under these terms I am unwilling to let it but must do as well as we can. I hope you will let 'Gunnard' [Gunwade] Ground, etc, late Tom Freeman's, at Milton and sell the stock. Strive to let Manton's farm at Castor and let me know what you can sell your wool for. There is two years' wool. I hope you keep account how many sheep you clipped each year. Return money soon. [P.S.] I fancy the two brothers Checkley will be chapmen for your wool. If they give security I will trust them till Lady day next for the money.

[1] Sainfoin, a herb much grown as a forage plant.

## 594 FITZWILLIAM TO GUYBON

*London, 23 September 1708; F(M)C 1697*

The buck came up very sweet last Saturday and we were very merry at eating it. We had Mr Berners of St Mary's Hall, etc. I hope soon you will let my farms that are in hand. The stock will be better put off at Michaelmas than Lady Day. I hope this fair weather has seen harvest in. I will never consent to building a good house so near Milton for when the family live there they cannot be without the land about it, and 'Gunworth' [Gunwade] Ground can be ploughed and then grazed again with sheep. Take care to pay Mrs Stevens the £190 for her land next October 7th, and John Catlin may go ask her where she will have the money, at Stamford, Peterborough or London. I don't know who to entrust to see the title and draw up the writings for all the attorneys about us are very blockheads and knaves too and Mr Snow of Stamford is little better. I have heard Blackwell of Stamford is an understanding man. I leave it to you to employ whom you think fit. You may try Snow though I have no great opinion of him as to the law but we must use what we can get. If the two Checkleys did not get down soon enough I hope their share of the venison was not lost. Let me know if Westhay warrant was served. You don't say what my wool will give a tod. Tell Joseph Chamberlaine I long to eat a peach out of the nursery. Now is the time they ripen so I would have him send me next week two or three dozen Newington peaches by Chattris. Buy a good basket for them with a cover. Wrap every peach in a paper, and give Chattris a great charge that the basket be not squeezed but don't let him know what is in it.

## 595 FITZWILLIAM TO GUYBON

*London, 30 September 1708; F(M)C 1698*

I am sorry you are not likely to let the farms but hope you may yet but glad to hear 'Gunworth' [Gunwade] Ground stock is better than when you entered on the farm. I can never believe Joseph Chamberlaine had no Newington peaches this year out of so many trees of that sort planted against several walls in the gardens. There was a great scarcity by reason of the blasting winds in the spring but he may as well say there was no wool clipped in England this year as no wallfruit in my gardens, for though some walls may fail others will not. I find he had rather sell them than pleasure me though I would not have died in his debt. I am glad to hear the Pembertons are returned to Peterborough. Let me know when they got home and how they do after their waters. I am glad you intend he shall look into the title and draw the writings of Mrs Stevens' land. I am sorry Mr Parker's wife is dead and poor William Leaffeild but we are more particularly concerned for good Old Mrs Pemberton but 'we must all take our turns and God Almighty prepare us for our ends'. I have here enclosed a bank bill for £100 which goes for ready money in any part of England. If Mrs Stevens scruples it any man in Peterborough will give ready money for it. I borrowed this of my wife for a fortnight or three weeks at most so return it again in that time or I shall forfeit my credit with her. The 5th of October is Tuesday and I was sure Chattris would not be at home until Wednesday if then, so I ran the venture of the post this once and hope you will have it safe on Saturday. Take no notice of your receiving it this way for fear of being waylaid another time.

### **596** FITZWILLIAM TO GUYBON

*London, 7 October 1708; F(M)C 1699*

I am much concerned I received no letter from you yesterday fearing you are not well. Besides in my letter I sent to you this day week enclosed a £100 bank bill to help you pay for Mrs Stevens' land because you desired Chattris to bring down £100. I thought this bill would go as safe by the post and be quicker than by Chattris. If you are not well have somebody write to me by the next post whether the bill came to your hand. I shall be in pain till I hear you have it and to hear how you are, and what is done in Mrs Stevens' business. My son is gone into Essex for a fortnight to be merry with his sister ... [P.S.] I am much in want of money, for I parted with all but £10 last Monday and am somewhat in debt for lack of the £100 I sent you. Relieve me as soon as possible.

### **597** FITZWILLIAM TO GUYBON

*London, 14 October 1708; F(M)C 1700*

I was relieved to have your letter of the 4th. I thought I had done mighty well when I sent you the £100 bank bill which I considered as good as money in the country as it is here. Mr Parker always paid me returns in bank bills, except once in guineas. I desire no better payments; they turn into money at any time. I will gladly receive it back again. When he was in town lately Mr Berners told me he had wall fruit this summer at St Mary's Hall, and threw up his hands when I told him what you had written that Joe Chamberlaine had said about wall fruit at Milton, considering how many more walls and garden room there was at Milton than St Mary's. I am glad Mrs Stevens' business is finished. When Mr Pemberton comes let him bring the writings that I may see they are substantially done. You write 'you would not have me be in paine for a little muck', meaning money I suppose, 'but without that muck in this towne we can neither gett bread nor cloaths' and I never wanted it more, but must have patience if it is not to be had. I am not against Mr Forster's son taking his father's farm, hoping he may do better than ever his father did. I look upon the old man as 'the most conceited man alive of his owne waies', although in talk he will argue rationally enough. I will never take less of the Forsters than £50 if they intend to plough as much as the enclosed paper mentions. At the end of the lease the ground must be sown with suitable grass seed. I will allow the land tax, but no meadow nor 'pole wood out of my sales' into the bargain. They may have what they please of it but for the price it sells at that year. I am very busy moving house back into Great Queen Street near Drury Lane so cannot consult my papers about Mr Ash's bond but will as soon as I am settled. He need not fear I shall ever call on him for the money again. I shall let him have the bond as soon as I am satisfied it is paid. I leave here the 5th of November.

## 598 FITZWILLIAM TO GUYBON

*London, 21 October 1708; F(M)C 1701*

The hares and rabbits came very good and sweet. I wished my son at the eating of them but he is at his sister's still. Let me know when the doe venison is best in season. I am glad Mr and Mrs Pemberton are in good health and the 'old gentlewoman' likely to do well again. Mr Ash need not be in such haste for his bond. Neither I nor mine intend him any injury. The trouble has been mine: he borrowed £315, and I received it back in £20 and £40, small sums it was a trouble 'to tell' out and in, and will be more trouble looking back through account books over a year or two. Let him send me a paper with the dates each sum was paid, while you send the date of the bond, and I shall soon set matters straight. I did not think you have new set those park pales next Brooke Field, but only those blown down in the great wind about five years since[1] otherwise I should have directed how I wished it done. Expecting to go down every summer has prevented me giving orders about them in the past, but by what you write things must be delayed no longer so set the work in hand. However, first consider with Mr Wright or another 'knowing' man whether it would be better to 'putt them out by the great', for John Wilkinson is a very slow workman and these short days will 'make poles worke' of it, and you are not able to oversee them as once you did. Unless you have wood cut already I believe oak pales would be best. We have pollard oaks enough at Milton Grounds about the Far Lady Leas, Pear Tree Close and 'Gunworth' [Gunwade] Ground. Don't leave the ground too naked but pick out some that won't be missed. Have two rails between post and post, not one as before which left the butt end of the pales in the ground where they rotted. With two rails the end of each pale need not touch the ground by an inch. It will be a greater charge at first but save that charge in time. Consult Mr Wright about putting it out, we supplying materials, they workmanship. This is a business where you ought to have a year to provide all materials. I fear it will be 'huddled up and not done as it should be'. This is a work to do once in 60 years but it was not done well in my father's time 'when I was child little'. I wish I could be there at the doing it. Old ferry boats make fine lasting pales.

[1] The 'Great Storm' of 26–27 November 1703; see **293** note.

## 599 FITZWILLIAM TO GUYBON

*London, 4 November 1708; F(M)C 1702*

I received yours yesterday enclosing young Forster's proposals. Since you say the forest venison will be the best, keep it all for me and send me a doe as soon as possible. Sew the four pieces in a flag basket and Chattris need not know what it is. I here enclose the two remaining warrants. [Here the warrants were cut from the letter dividing it into two halves.] I am glad you intend me money but it's a long time coming. I wonder you send none by such as John Sisson and others of Northborough and other 'townes' who bring up sheep in small parcels from the fen sides at this time of the year. As to young Augustine Forster I don't rightly understand his proposals, being in an unusual hand, but if he proposes to plough up Askinstalls, 22 acres and 20 acres a piece in the two 'hithermost' hills next Marholm, where I suppose he means always to have one piece lie fallow as if it were field land, then I will abate nothing of £50 a year, but will allow him 20 pole of wood. I expect a New Year's gift as his father gave, and boon days yearly. If he intends to plough but 20 acres I will take £45, but then why should he mention Askenstalls, and the two hills when any of them are more than 20 acres? Explain what he means in your next. If he ploughs but 20 acres I will allow no pole wood for fencing for his father is obliged to leave all in repair. He must take for six years.

### 600 FITZWILLIAM TO GUYBON

*London, 11 November 1708; F(M)C 1703*

I shall expect the doe by Chattris the next week, and send another the week after unless I forbid it. I am glad to hear 'Duke [Tomlinson] will be here this week, hoping he brings me money which I much need. If young Forster ploughs 60 acres in those three grounds you mention I will abate nothing of £50 a year, besides boon days and New Year's gifts, but then I will allow 20 poles of fencing wood yearly. Direct your next letter to my house in Great Queen Street near Drury Lane as you did formerly. Young Charles Turner is come to town. He had been better to stay at Peterborough, 'for he is a fatt young man and this towne will choake him' up especially if he drinks which I fear he may. He says he wishes to improve his skill in periwig making, and here he may do it if he minds business and his health permits him to stay.

### 601 GUYBON TO FITZWILLIAM

*22 November 1708; F(M)C 1705*

Received yours of the 18th. Enclosed is Mr Ash's note of the dates each sum was repaid. I hope you received the £50 by Thomas Chattris last Saturday. Mr Parker will order you £100 next week. The goods which should have come by Thomas Chattris last week I hope will come next. If you will not be at the charge of keeping the grey colt, you might as well let him 'goe to grass'. He was got by a good horse which was sold for £50, is stoned, about 14 hands, and is three years old at the end of June. He must be well kept; hay and chaff won't do it. 'He must have corne and [be] well dresst and tended'. Goodman Dove need not make a road through Goodman Burton's 60 acres which could do much damage. He is willing to let him through now and then but not make it a common road. We are cutting wood for the park pales, which will be double railed. The two Wilkinsons and Goodman Ricroft are doing it 'by the great' at 12d a yard.[1]

[Marginal note by Fitzwilliam:]

| | |
|---|---|
| Lent Mr Ash | £315 0s 0d |
| Paid | £115 0s 0d |
| Remains (for which he gave bond) | £200 0s 0d |
| Since paid | £199 19s 11d |
| 8 months int. at £5 per cent. | £6 13s 4d |

## 602 FITZWILLIAM TO GUYBON

*London, 25 November 1708; F(M)C 1706*

Received yours with Mr Ash's note. Received the £50 by Chattris.

As to the colt if he is like to make a fine horse for my son I leave it to you to have him kept as you thinke fitt but there must be great care in backing and mouthing him least he getts ill habitts and may make a vitious horse for what ill habitts or tricks he getts now he is young he will never be broken off afterwards. Great care must be taken he comes at no mares for that will make him vitious and unruly. If you thinke he is too young to be backt and trained I do not thinke he need to dress him but kept ruff and lye on his owne muck but for this I leave it to you to consult with them as understand it better and I know nobody you can consult better with then Old Robert Deepup who alwaies keeps a fine horse or two that he sells and makes money off. I thinke Dove is very unreasonable to thinke to cart all his mucke at this time of the yeare when the ground is soft through the 60 acres of Richard Burton's. In all Black's time there was nothing but a style and footway, but Dove is a good tennant so gett him a priveledge to cart there now and then. Since I writt this I am told that if you give this colt too much corne if he never had any given him formerly it will burne him and kill him since he can have no exercise to carry the corne off. If he were backt and coud be ridden then he might eate corne for it is hott in its nature. Pray advise well about what I write.

Your bargain for paling the park is reasonable for both sides.[1] See they double pin every pale to each rail. My daughter has been very ill with the colic, as Sir Charles writes us, but we hope she is better now.

[1] Guybon paid 'the carpenters' £19 7s on 11 March 1709 for 'paleing 329 yards about the parke at 12d a yard', Disbursements 74.

## 603 FITZWILLIAM TO GUYBON

*London, 27 November 1708; F(M)C 1707*

Received yours today with the hares and woodcocks which came sweet and good. I would have been glad of the venison this week but we must submit to disappointments. Send a doe every week until further order. Shoot one of our does and see how they prove.

## 604 GUYBON TO FITZWILLIAM

*30 November 1708; F(M)C 1709*

I am sorry Lady Barrington was ill but glad she is better. I would not have her ill nor any of our family, please God. Mr Parker's £100 will be paid this week. I have let to Mr Forster his father's farm for six years at £50 a year, six boon days and New Year's gift. He is to have 20 pole yearly and boards for his parlour. The floor is very bad. We have had a sharp weather here as ever I felt, the ferry river 'layd'.[1] If it is as sharp with you the Thames will be 'layd' again. I hope it won't hold long, it is so fierce. I have let Thomas Manton's farm for six years to William 'Sargint' for £22 a year, six boon days and a New Year's gift. Thomas Chattris will bring a doe next week, and [wood]-cocks if I can get them. [P.S.] Mr Feary wished me to let you know what I have paid him and what he owes for wood. I paid him £15 on 23 Feb. 1701[/2] and £20 11 May 1706. Belsis sale for oaks £8 15s: total £43 15s.

[1] Frozen

## 605 FITZWILLIAM TO GUYBON

*London, 2 December 1708; F(M)C 1710*

Yesterday Mr Charles Parker's correspondent, a Mr Smith, paid £100 by your order. My daughter is mending but has been dangerously ill. I am glad you have agreed with young Forster for his father's farm, but hope you have some security for the rent, for if the father could not deal with it how can his son be solvent unless his uncles have left him anything? Be sure he can manage it before he ploughs. Boarding that parlour would be to throw money away, for the ground is damp and will soon rot them. I would rather slab the floor with pendal stone[1] if he will fetch them. Boards are too dear during this war, and I will not consent to them until we have a peace which I hope is not far off. The weather has been sharp but not enough to freeze a river. The frost went last Monday and it has been 'wetting weather' since. You say you have let Manton's farm to William Serjeant for £22. I hope he has not too much already. He has my farm late Hinson's, the baker's house and close, Fracy's farm of Mr Ewing, all Mr Selby's farm rented from the bishop, and now Manton's. I hope he does not overreach himself. Which house will he live in? I don't want my house standing empty. How do you keep up my rent when you let the farm for only £22 when before it gave £24? At what rate do you let the cottage Serjeant does not have? I fear if you have this rainy weather it will make the venison lean. [P.S.] I was in bed when the £100 came. My son wrote the receipt but I signed it.

[1] For pendle stone see **429** note 1.

## 606 FITZWILLIAM TO GUYBON

*[London,] 9 [December] 1708; F(M)C 1711*

Send another doe next week if it can be well served, but if I don't like this doe you can give next week's to our Peterborough friends. They will be glad to have it and pay the fees.

I am glad I am like to have some money by my owne 40 weathers and likewise by Burton. I hope you have made Dove and him good freinds which you should informe me off that I may know the better how to discourse with Burton. As to these 40 good weathers as you call them they had need be good ones since they must pay me 3 yeare's rent of that farme of Freeman's for I have not heard of any others that were the product of that farme besides the wooll unless you have sold some sheep in the countrey. I know not who yett shall sell my sheep for Burton knows not the way of Smithfeild markett coming seldome to towne; he will be run downe by the salesmen; besides he knows not who to trust whereas the salesmen know all the butchers that they dare not cheate them whereas the butchers will laugh at a countrey fellow. He may do well enough with a few fenn sheep but must needs be to seeke in a great drove of good weather[s]. However I will consider what is best to be done against he comes up. Pray gett me up some moneys as fast as you can for I shall want more soon.

### **607** FITZWILLIAM TO GUYBON

*London, 11 December 1708; F(M)C 1713*

The doe was very good, but badly killed; shot through both haunches and bloody and had just begun to smell. With this rainy, muggy weather send the next doe loose so 'it may be hung out of nights to prevent the worst'.

### **608** FITZWILLIAM TO GUYBON

*[London, December 1708]; F(M)C 1717*[1]

I wish you had sold the sheep in the countrey for our grounds[2] will not make them thorough fatt, whereas they used to be sold to Cunnington Grounds and to the Coleseed Grounds in my time when I kept lands in my hands, and I am sure Thomas Freeman did use to sell his draught sheep, the cullings and likewise his weathers and lambs and never sent to towne as I remember. Both last Fryday and Munday's marketts were bad enough, and a great many sheep turnd out for this next Frydaie's markett. Richard Burton tells me the sheep are come safe to towne to a sheep, but feares they will not give above 16s or 16s 6d each. He expects 18s a peice for his because they are fatt with cole seed. I heare Dove has 30 sheep for this markett likewise. [P.S.] Pray tell Mr Turner of Peterborough to direct his letters to his sonn Charles at the Blew Perriwigg in Princess Street, neare Drewry Lane, because directing the letters to John Gray cost 4d every letter that comes and the poore fellow has not money to pay for any, for he owes John Grey for three letters already.

[1] This is probably the 16 December letter which fits with the sequence. The top is torn off with several lines missing including the superscription and date. The first part appears to have reiterated the instructions about venison of **606** above.

[2] Probably fattening grounds around London are meant.

### **609** FITZWILLIAM TO GUYBON

*London, 23 December 1708; F(M)C 1714*

The doe came up well and good meat. Keep half the Westhay doe yourself, and give the other to the ferryman for 'a merry meeting at his house'. If I had given it to some at Peterborough others would take it ill. This way I displease none by using it myself. Pay Mr Pemberton 40s for drawing the writings, perusing the title and sending to Bourne to see the deeds executed in Mrs Stevens' business. We had a very bad market for our sheep, yet last Monday's market was worse, as Jonathan Bateman told me, who paid me £40 but expected to have made at least £10 more. He is a very likely young man, talks 'pritty notable' and hope he will make Mrs Bull's daughter a good husband. You may drink one of my hogsheads of ale this Christmas that was brewed last spring and all but one hogshead of the small beer. I keep that to know whether it will keep a year for we used to drink in my father and mother's time no other than small beer a year old. Give to the poor this Christmas as I usually allowed.

I received a letter from Matthew Roles the stone digger upon Helpston's heath makeing sad complaints of his bargaine at the ferry well which is to be considered off so you may tell him that when he reckons with me and pays me for the many pitts he has suncke upon Helpston heath for each of which of 6 yards square I expect 20s for being the constant price in my father and mother's time, at that time he paies me that rent I will certainly throw him backe as much as will make him a saver by it for I do not desire he should loose by my worke if he make it appeare he did and I am sorry to heare of his fall downe the well which I hope was not altogether so bad as he represents it in his letter for I heard of it before and it was told in merriment as if done on purpose to laugh at and the rope lett slip by his fellow workmen who wore to lett him downe but he was pretty neare the bottom before they slipt the rope and had no great hurt. He magnifies the worke he has done to a great degree: that he has sunck it with his men only, since the masons left it off, nineteene foot; that it's now thirteen foot deep in water as good for brewing or any other use as can be.

I sent down two receipts by Richard Burton, one for what he paid me in part of rent, the other for what the sheep sold.[1] I sent by him the salesman's bill of the charges of selling the sheep and the drovers up to town. He was forced to make use of my salesman for notwithstanding his confidence in his own parts he knew not what to ask or do when he came into the market. We made a kind of agreement for his farm and for Jack Freeman's, all but the house and homestead which young Johnson lives in, which I am to receive rent for. My son wrote down the agreement which Burton carries with him. The rent was £85 or £86 a year and 10s in money for New Year's gifts for 10 years from last Lady Day. He is not to plough the last three years without a new bargain. The 12 acres he has ploughed in Burmore Leas he is to plough three years more; then lay it with grass seed, and plough 12 acres in the bottom of [Burmore Leas], next the 11 and 19 acres of Dove's for four years, laying it with grass seed suitable to the ground in the last year. The last three years nothing to be ploughed. He must have a little barn, his house made a little handsomer and a chimney put up in one of the chambers. Let Mr Pemberton draft a lease for 10 years and bring it up to me in Candlemas Term before it's engrossed. If he has taken other grounds of you as he says let them also be put in the lease and their rents and New Year gifts added.

[1] Burton's 40 sheep sold for £27 16s 8d, or at least that was what Fitzwilliam received; Disbursements 74.

## 610 FITZWILLIAM TO GUYBON

*London, 30 December 1708; F(M)C 1716*

I received yours dated 28th which should have come yesterday but I suppose the waters being out, and the frost and snow upon them, makes the ways 'unpassable'. We have here a very great snow, extreme frost and wind so that it could not be colder. Received your kind present of the pheasants last Saturday, and as for the doe we must expect ill luck sometimes. If it comes not this week we may have it the next which we still look upon as Christmas, until Plough Monday is over. However, if the doe is not handsome meat and well killed don't send it but dispose of it as you think fit. I am sorry the ale was so ill brewed that it was unfit to drink at Christmas. My coming down has been so uncertain for some years past that I thought Adam Johnson would have had the discretion to have hopped it so well as to last nine or ten months at least. I am sorry to hear poor Roles is so ill. I hope he recovered from the mischances and colds he got at the well and what he ails now is from another occasion. I truly thought I should be down this last summer else I had ordered a pump before this. If you think the walls are fallen in it may be convenient to have it cleansed before we cover it with a pump. Consult with Mr Wright or another 'knowing' person and let me know what they say. Inform yourself what a good pump will cost: how much a wooden pump and how much a leaden pump. Let me know the several prices and who and where they live that well understand how to make either. I doubt you must fetch a man from Lynn for we have only 'sorry' people about Peterborough.[1]

[1] Guybon paid James Cooke £6 14s for making the ferry pump, and Richard Peach £1 6s 9d for the iron work for the lead pump at the ferry, both on 12 October 1709; Disbursements 74.

## 611 FITZWILLIAM TO GUYBON

*London, 6 January 1708/9; F(M)C 1718*

On the 31st I received from John Webdale for James Dove £17 10s 9d for which I gave him my receipt. On Saturday last I received by Thomas Chattris the Cross-a-hand doe, the best from the forest this year and did me the most credit. [P.S.] Take care to throw the snow from the lewcombs in time for fear of a sudden thaw which would drown the house.

## 612 JOHN CATLIN TO FITZWILLIAM

*Maxey, 8 January 1708/9; F(M)C 1719*

Elias Goode's cottage (late Mrs Stevens') is now put in very good repair: house, barn and hovel new thatched, windows new glazed, and the [yard] against the street new fenced with pales; charge £4 10s. Mrs Stevens' estate paid you 1s 11d a year quit rent. There must be a rent still paid to you for my two acres; I believe about 2d which if you please I will write down in next year's rent roll and return you many thanks. There are two cottages of John Bimrose to be sold lying between the two houses you rent to Thomas Drury and Thomas Walter. The best of them came by his first wife Rose Ewen. Henry Alyen rents it for £4; the other was given him by his father at his marriage by deeds of lease and release and lets for £2 a year. They would cost £6 or £7 to repair. John Fitzwilliam esquire ordered me to give you an account of such estates. The wife of John Measure of Deepingate, who was Mr John Fitzwilliam's nurse, died yesterday and is to be buried tomorrow. Mr Pemberton tells me there will be no need to sue out a fine of recovery for the estate late Mrs Stevens', but I will act as you advise.

## 613 FITZWILLIAM TO GUYBON

*London, 13 January 1708/9; F(M)C 1720*

Yours dated the 3rd which should have come the 5th I received the 8th, the ways were so bad. I am sorry poor Roles continues so bad. If you find him in want pay him 40s. When I go down we will reckon the remainder of his bill. I won't have the pigs of lead at Milton meddled with until I am down because I know how many there are, and what each pig weighs, but I would be glad to know how many pounds of lead will be needed for the ferry pump, what the workmanship will cost, and what a wooden pump and its workmanship would cost. By no means stir abroad this terrible cold weather but keep warm at home. I had rather want money than you should endanger yourself. The Thames is almost frozen over. We had a great thaw Monday night and most of Tuesday, but now it freezes again very hard, with some small 'flights' of snow again today. I am sorry to hear of the mischances caused by the snowy weather. Goodman Dove has paid by his salesman £17 10s 9d on December 31, £15 0s 11d on January 11th. Joseph Bull sent my wife a very fine hen turkey and a fat goose for a present and a letter saying he will be at our house tomorrow. I suppose he brings beasts or sheep but the markets continue bad. Take care to feed well all your stock and the poor deer, for they are very tender. Some ash browse would be very acceptable to them. Take care of Milton House in case of thaw and keep yourself warm. [P.S.] I hope you take care of my wine by covering it with straw and stopping up the windows and doors.

## 614 FITZWILLIAM TO GUYBON

*London, 27 January 1708/9; F(M)C 1721*

I received yours of 24th today. The post could not come sooner because of the great snows. It began last Monday evening and continued all that night and all Tuesday. Do not stir abroad this cold weather. Send to the tenants to bring their money to you. Money will be very welcome.

I am glad to heare you think my money is so safe in the tennants' hands I writt to you off in my last. Pray God it proves so and am very glad to heare by yours Mr Pemberton is like to do well againe. I have been pestered with letters from people who hope to succeed him in my courts. Pray lett Mr Edmund Sparkes and Mr Orme know I received their letters and shall consider of their request when there is occasion but should he die it would not be yett these sixe months before I will settle my thoughts on any one.

## 615 FITZWILLIAM TO GUYBON

*London, 3 February 1708/9; F(M)C 1722*

I am sorry to hear that Mr Pemberton is unlikely to live. I had great hopes of him since he lived so long after he was first taken ill. I will take time who to pitch on to replace him in my courts; one that will do best service and that my son will approve for he is likely to have that estate when he thinks fit to choose a wife. No courts will be kept before Michaelmas so there is time enough. On the 31st Mr Hankin paid me £108 18s 9d for Mr Abraham Riss, but I hear nothing of your hogman Rowland Morrice who I believe will fail me as he used to do. Return money as fast as you can but care for your health, and be not out late at nights. It continues fine and warm in town so I hope the country will have a fine seed time.

## 616 FITZWILLIAM TO GUYBON

*London, 10 February 1708/9; F(M)C 1723*

I am extremely glad to hear Mr Pemberton is in a fine way to recovery. God continue it for the good of his family and service of his friends. I am glad I am to have more money for it will do me a particular service, and that you think of getting a tenant for Thomas Freeman's farm. However, I will not suffer an acre of it to be ploughed, nor am I willing to divide it unless you have other good tenants who would take some of the furthest grounds, such as Middle and House Goodlucks. Whoever takes it must buy the stock at the same time or I shall be a loser. Since Monday it has set in freezing and snowing again. It's terribly cold because of a high easterly wind. Take care of yourself and the poor deer who are a tender creature. You have not written whether Mr Pemberton's illness proceeded from his 'pissing distemper calld the diabetis' or his lethargy and sleepiness for he has had both, and this last was my last distemper.

## 617 JOHN CATLIN TO FITZWILLIAM

*Maxey, 17 February 1708/9; F(M)C 1724*

Before I received your honour's letter John Bimrose was gone to London so I have no price set on the estate. Yesterday his father came and told me he had had a letter from his son desiring me to send particulars of the estate to you, and he would come to you in London to sell it.

Henry Alyen's house is stone walls round as high as the thach. The west end is goveld[1] up to the ridgtree but not taveld[2] with free stone on the sides. The east end is studded up with wood and morter and plastered with limb[3] on the outside. The roofe is good; the cupples and spars are of oak very firm. The floor over the house is plastur with oak joyce tree and traceings very strong but the floor over the parler is a broken joycetree with a post or prop underit being of wyche or some such like wood much decayed; the post stands in the middle of the parlor. The barne is on the west side built up with stone to the top but the east side and the two ends are stone but halfe way and the rest studded and the studded walls wanteth mending. It is a large barne and will hold between 40 and 50 loads and the roofe is good. The fences about both the houses are very bad for the old quicks are almost quite destroyed. To write down all the defaults will take a great deal of room but in my oppinion Henry Alyen's house is worth £60, Thomas Wright's is worth £38 and his land worth £33; at this rate it is not dear. He must sell it. It is morgagd to John Bunning of Helpston, and now insted of paying off the morgage he hath occation for more money. He will (as his father told me) come to your honour's house and set a price on it soon after your honour receives this letter for his letter comes from his father this same post. I paid for my 2 acres of land to Mrs Stevens £17 1s 6d and three pounds charge in making a fence to inclose it; besids I spent £1 15s 0d at twice meeting to buy it and when it was paid for I never expended so much money for liquor or drink in two years' time neither before nor since for an attorney, one Mr Pedder, told me if I had not then bargain[ed] he would sell it by an juck of burning candle[4] who now is deceased. Mr Pemberton had £1 5s for my deeds drawing and parchments which is all I paid about that and Mrs Stevens had £190 for your honour's estate that she sold besides.[5] What Mr Pemberton is to have for your honour's deeds of writings I know not. Elias Goode hath but little stock (his father is in prison at Peterborough and hath been these 2 years and maintains him selfe there; when he will get out I know not). He is very dutyfull to his mother and hath only two cows and a few sheep but he minds his traid as yet, takes care to plow and sowe the 3 acres and roode of land as yet and will be confined to keep the house and fences in good repare as he finds them.

> Neither Mr Osborne nor his son are living in the castle yet; the house is in good repair, only the barn and stables need repair which he and his landlady dispute. He pays £58 a year rent. I believe 30s or 40s will repair the walls of the castle homestead.

[1] Gabled.

[2] To table the sloping sides of a gable with coping stones. Catlin means that while the walls of the house are stone to the thatch, the gables are not stone nor coped in stone.

[3] Lime.

[4] A form of auction terminated by the extinction of a lighted candle: *The Oxford Companion to Law* (1980), p. 94.

[5] Catlin means that Mrs Stevens, in addition to these sums, received £190 for that part of her estate which she sold to Fitzwilliam (which Guybon paid to her on 12 December 1708; Disbursements 74).

## **618** FITZWILLIAM TO GUYBON

*London, 17 February 1708/9; F(M)C 1725*

> We are all very glad Mr Pemberton is in so hopeful a way to recovery. I am concerned I shall have no money this week for I need some badly, and besides if I had £500 I could make 'a singular good advantage of it' as I have done already with what spare money I had. This opportunity will last until Lady Day but the sooner the better.

I reckoned with Robert Feary your late carrier last Satturday and he brought me a very unreasonable bill as I thought and plac't severall things to my account that I never heard off nor receavd. However for quiettness' sake I gave him a note to you to pay him three pounds more then what he has already had of you in money and wood. I have taken his discharge in full of all demands. He said there was 6 bucks brought up to towne more then what is in the bill and that Joseph Chamberlaine knows of them but lett him be sure not to remember them and say he knows nothing of them for he is overpaid at least £5. He had the ill conscience to sett downe 12s 6d for bringing me up 50 guyneas about 7 or 8 yeares since and sayes you agreed with him for that summe but I find him a great knave both in that and many other things. This cold season I hope will go over soone for the wise men say this frost will breake this very night about 12 of the clocke. We shall see by tomorrow morning whither they speake true or not. I heare you have severall trees blowne downe about Etton, Woodcraft etc this last stormy weather about a fortnight since. Pray take care to make the best of them or the tennants will take them. If this frost goes away handsomly I hope you may gett a horseback and see about them and gett up also what money possibly you can.

### 619 FITZWILLIAM TO GUYBON

*London, 24 February 1708/9; F(M)C 1726*

I am glad Mr Pemberton recovers daily. I heard by chance his son is in town but have not yet seen him. I hope this finer weather will permit you to go abroad and get me a large sum and that Mr Parker will return me a good sum this week. Keep the Meadow Close in hand this year for I shall want it this summer for hay fearing last summer's was 'ill gott'. [P.S.] Young Mr Pemberton has been here and goes for Peterborough tomorrow.

### 620 FITZWILLIAM TO GUYBON

*London, 3 March 1708/9; F(M)C 1728*

Francis Guybon ... I am glad to heare Mr Pemberton recovers more and more daily. I have received as yett no money for Mr Parker nor I beleive shall not if I may creditt Robert Fearey for he is obliged to pay him a considerable summe of money for a great quantity of oile he obligd Fearey to deliver him by such a day. It seems the bargaine was made when Fearey was in drinke and he would have given Mr Parker a handsome treate of some ginneas vallew the next day but could not be released of his bargaine and Fearey now hopes by the prizes of oile here and the great quantitys coming in from sea he shall gett money by the bargaine. If all this be true I beleive Mr Parker cannot spare much money but do not take any notice of what I write but keep it to yourselfe for I would not make difference amungst neighbours by carriing tales about.

By good fortune in my great straits for money 'Duke Tomlinson paid me £12 0s 3d by Mr Hankin, and today Charles Bull paid me £8 17s 11d by Mr Mawre. As to Mr Ash I writ you a month ago what sums I had received of him by return, and what was due in interest, upon payment of which you could deliver him his bond. Look for that letter; it will be a trouble to make it out again.

### 621 FITZWILLIAM TO GUYBON

*London, 10 March 1708/9; F(M)C 1729*

I received yours with Mr Rowell's bill for £50 which I hope I shall get but I have heard nothing of either Mr Parker or Robert Fearey nor their money, and both are engaged to lay out great sums for oil and Fearey asked me to lend him £100. I will send to this Marshall for Mrs Bull's money. I wrote you about Ash's interest and bond and if you lose my letters it's not my fault. By good fortune I found my account and his wrapped up together. Of £200 upon his bond I have received £199 19s 11d. I reckon there is eight months interest due at £5 per cent, which is £6 13s 4d, upon payment of which deliver him his bond.

Mr Turner upon his returne home will sattisfy you we are all in good health. His sonn Charles is gone into the Mediterranion sea with an officer who goes to Port Mahon in the island of Minorca where all our ships lies in the winter.[1] I hope he may do well but here he could not stay for the follies he had committed and besides would have been presst for a souldier or sea man. I writt the forepart of this letter in the morning and sending the note for £50 this afternoon that Mr Taylour might see it, my man in goeing thither loss't the note, but I have sent to stop payment and to acquaint him that I would have a new note by Mundaye's post. Pray desire Mr Rowell to write you a new note on halfe a sheet of paper which you fold up like a letter, seale it, superscribe it to me and putt it into the post house on Satturday next before you go home to Milton. Lett the note be writt as the last was 5 dayes after sight for feare of any miscarriage and then we have time enough to stop payment. Pray send this note away next Satturday for I am in great want of money. Feary I heare nothing of as yett, neither have I received Mrs Bull's £7 odd money. Duke of Montague of Boughton[2] died sudainly last night about 5 a clocke, well and dead in a minute, 71 yeares of age.

[1] Minorca had been captured by a fleet under Admiral Sir John Leake in 1708.

[2] Ralph Montagu, 1st Duke, of Boughton House, Northamptonshire, died at Montagu House, Bloomsbury, 9 March 1709. *Complete Peerage*, ix. 106–8

## 622 FITZWILLIAM TO GUYBON
*London, 17 March 1708/9; F(M)C 1731*

I received yours with the enclosed bill for £100 which I sent to the man who promised payment at due date next week. I have received of Marshall Mrs Bull's small sum and of Robert Fearey's daughter just £100, but because I would not pay her for bringing it she said I should never have any more of her money so you must not trust to his returns unless I pay an extravagant price which would prove of ill consequence for others will expect the same, making returns very chargeable. She was offered some good strong drink but nothing would serve her but a bottle of wine for she drank, as she said, no malt drink. Such people are come to a fine way of living. I heard Fearey was as angry as his daughter saying I should receive no more of his money since I refused to pay porterage when he brought up the money purposely to serve me. In this I know he told a great untruth for what need he bring money out of the country and receive it back in the country from you? He may alter his mind before you see him. Tell him I had rather send a goldsmith's man to receive it of him when he returns me any money if I may depend upon the time he will be at home and the money ready that the man may not lose his labour. I must send for this money of Mr Rowell's at the day which costs me nothing. I hope you will return a good sum as fast as you can for it will do me a great kindness.

## 623 FITZWILLIAM TO GUYBON
*London, 24 March 1708/9; F(M)C 1732*

(Has received Mr Rowell's £100. Glad more is coming which would do great service if in time. Glad Ash had his bond. Sorry to hear by his son of Captain Styles' death. Guybon should have sent word what he died of. Has great pain in right arm which prevents further writing. Bad weather stopped his son from going to Milton 10 days ago. Believes he will spend a fortnight or three weeks there in the spring.)

## 624 FITZWILLIAM TO GUYBON

*London, 31 March 1709; F(M)C 1733*

Sorry to hear you have so much rain. Here at the change of the moon the weather altered to fair, and continues still, so I hope we shall have fine weather for the lambs and the corn. Supply all returns possible as quickly as you can. Tell Marmaduke Tomlinson I received a letter from Thomas Rudkin, churchwarden of Northborough, complaining of the Hall Farm seats in the church - not those in the chapel belonging to the Hall. He intends to repair all the church seats and wishes to know if he shall repair the [Hall Farm] seats also. I replied saying he should leave them alone for they had always been repaired by those living in the Hall, not the churchwardens, and I would take care the tenants did any repairs needed. Tell 'Duke I expect him to repair the seats in the same way as the rest are done. He may buy materials and do them himself if that will save him money. If not he may let the churchwarden do it and pay his proportion to the town rate. The seats in the chapel are not to be meddled with.

## 625 FITZWILLIAM TO GUYBON

*London, 7 April 1709; F(M)C 1734*

April 2nd I received from Henry Hankin £79 19s 7d from Mr William Ash - but he knew not who Ash was nor where he lived—and on the 4th he paid £107 15s 11d for a Mr Warwick. This Mr Ash must be our neighbour who might adventure to pay me this without order knowing it will be secure to him as fast as you could raise it. I am glad Mr Pemberton is recovered of a second illness which I did not hear of before. Ask if he had a letter from me a fortnight ago and when I may expect a copy of those writings. (A reminder about 'Duke Tomlinson and the church seats.)

## 626 FITZWILLIAM TO GUYBON

*London, 14 April 1709; F(M)C 1735*

I have had no money since I last wrote. You say you told 'Duke about the church seats but do not say what answer he gave. If he does not wish to do them I will order the churchwarden to do them, and Duke must pay his proportion. What I suggested was just a kindness to him for he might do it cheaper out of his own pocket, but the pews must be like the rest. Let the house, gardens and yards be made decent for my son will soon be amongst you, and let my chamber be cleaned and bed aired. He has been unwell and needs a little 'aireing'. He will be down after Easter week. The fine weather has been followed by rain but all is for the best if it only falls 'leisurely'. [P.S.] Don't forget to ask Pemberton if he got my letter asking for copies of two writings in the hands of Mrs Stevens of Bourne. He can get any attorney there to do it, for until my counsel sees those writings they cannot tell whether it is necessary to have a fine on that small purchase. It's good to make all things sure.

### 627 FITZWILLIAM TO GUYBON

*[London,] 21 April 1709; F(M)C 1736*[1]

Francis Guybon, ... As to 'Duke since all the seates in the chur[ch need to be re]paired and his wants it as [muc]h as any, if he will not repaire his so that they may be all alike the church warden shall do it and then he must pay to the assessment. I would by no meanes have Mr Pemberton go on purpose to Bourne to gett the coppy of those deeds I want but only send to some attourney thereabouts to do it for him and if Mr Pedder be dead there is some other come thither by this time to do it for him. I do not know but Mr Pemberton is in the right that there will want no fine but I dare not trust to the opinion of an attourney only when I have choice of others. I am glad to heare I shall receav some more money next weeke. I beleive you mistake the names of the roomes at Milton for the great roome over the cellar was alwaies called my bed chamber and the roome that had the red cloath bed was called my dressing roome and that is the roome I suppose has the propps in it and my son's man lay in it last time he was downe and may do so againe for I presume the propps are safe. He may lie in the little roome called Doll's roome if Mrs Bull does not thinke fitt to lay my son's man in the roome with props. If it be rainy weather my sonn will not stirr from hence; if it be faire weather he may go downe about a fortnight after Easter, hardly before, though he talks of going downe the weeke after Easter weeke.[2] With all our kind loves to you I am your loveing friend, W. Fitzwilliam. [P.S.] I have much adoe to write, the paine being still very bad in my right arme.

[1] Part of the top of the letter torn off. Words in square brackets conjectural.

[2] John Fitzwilliam came to Milton and had probably left by June 24 for Guybon's accounts for that date show 'Paid Mr Fitzwilliam £16 and he spent the time that he was at Milton £15 16s 7d, £31 16s 7d; Disbursements 74.

## *EPILOGUE*

This was the last surviving letter of Lord Fitzwilliam to his steward. Two odd letters from Guybon, dated respectively 23 May and 19 September 1709,[1] have also survived. The first concerns payment of returns and describes what Fitzwilliam livestock are about Milton (468 sheep, 47 'beasts', with three mares, three colts, one filly and a foal); the shortage of hay and Guybon's strong desire that the farm should be let and the stock sold. Meanwhile 'Old Thomas Freman's widow' was buried last night. The second remarks that he would be very glad to see the Fitzwilliams, including John, and Lady Barrington, at Milton. Showers have held up the harvest, and flooded the meadows. The rest concerns the terms of a lease for a new tenant, a Mr Meares, for an unnamed farm. It is likely that Guybon fell ill the following winter for the entries between 25 February 1710 and 12 April 1710 in his account of disbursements are in another hand which resembles a more youthful and neater form of Lord Fitzwilliam's hand and may be by John Fitzwilliam. With the exception of a couple of entries for April 29 the entries continue in Guybon's hand until 26 May 1710 when the account ceases. It is likely that then, or shortly after, Guybon died. There is a continuously running account which is certainly in Lord Fitzwilliam's handwriting beginning on 11 March 1710 and ending (so far as the surviving sheets are concerned) in November 1710, recording disbursements at Milton which shows that Fitzwilliam and his son are in residence and that the household affairs are in Fitzwilliam's control and that Mrs Pendleton continued to act as housekeeper for the household as she had done for Guybon since her husband's death.[2] Why Fitzwilliam should be keeping this rough, loose sheet account while Guybon (for part of the time) kept his own account of disbursements is a mystery. However, the Guybon entries seem to be chiefly payments to tradesmen, and taxes, poor rates, etc, rather than household accounts. Certainly Guybon died during 1710, for there are surviving letters of his kinsmen to Fitzwilliam in September and October which specifically refer to his death and enquire about his estate.[3] Lord Fitzwilliam seems to have been as reluctant to leave Milton for London as he had formerly been to leave London for Milton for, despite his wife's isolation in London, he seems to have remained there for the whole of 1710 and indeed it is possible he had not returned to London by May 1711 when he was certainly at Milton whilst he was once more negotiating with Sir Henry Johnson's representative for a marriage between his son and Miss Johnson.[4] Lady Fitzwilliam was then still in London. On 28 September 1710 lady Fitzwilliam wrote a pathetic letter complaining that she had not heard from her husband since the previous month, and asking that she be informed where she must go for the winter, and that her husband would pay off her two maids for they should neither stay nor go with her.[5]

[1] F(M)C 1737, 1748.

[2] F(M)Correspondence Series B.

[3] Thomas Guybon, 18 September 1710, F(M)Correspondence, Drawer 22 1710–1744; John Pitts, Norwich, 4 October 1710, *ibid.*

[4] Sylvester Petyt to Fitzwilliam 1 and 6 May and Fitzwilliam's reply (fair copy) 8 May 1711, *ibid.* For evidence of earlier negotiations on this matter see **586** above.

[5] F(M)Correspondence, Drawer 22 1710–1744.

# INDEX

Numbers in roman indicate letters
Italics refer to page numbers


accidents, 45, 382, 384; *see also* Vaughan, Henry, death
Acts of Parliament, *xix–xx*, 1, 17, 18, 19, 41 & n, 56, 58, 90, 122 & n, 136, 163n, 354, 524 & n
Adington, family, 357
Ailsworth, Aylesworth, *ix, xviii*, 219, 220; estate, 211, 213, 214, 215, 216, 217, 218, 277, 286, 289, 290, 311, 316, 317, 366, 367, 380, 417; rents, 68; tenants, 372
Alconbury Weston, Hunts, 144
Aldeburgh, Suffolk, 586n
Alderman, John, tax collector, 443
Aldgate, Stephen, 403
Alexander, Gregory, 325, 326, 328
almsgiving, 45, 82, 122, 165, 186, 202, 203, 244, 293, 294, 354, 409, 541, 609
Alwalton, Allerton, Hunts, 313, 355, 399
Alyen, Henry, 612, 617
Andrew, Andrews, Charles, 54 & n, 163, 268 & n
  John, sr & jr, boatwrights, 90n, 144n
  Thomas, 54 & n, 163, 268 & n, 430, 432
Anne, Queen, *xix*, 234; accession, 216
Ap Price, Apreece, Appreece, Price, Robert of Washingley, Hunts, 121 & n, 156, 169, 184, 185, 560
  Mr, jr, 121 & n
apothecaries, 315; *see also* physicians; surgeons
army, 450, 563, 564; *see also* militia
Arney, Mr, gamekeeper, 242n, 388, 390
Arrasmith, Robert, jobber, 147
Ash, William, of Paston, 4 & n, 28, 29, 30, 32, 36, 39, 58, 61, 65, 72, 75, 76, 80, 82, 85, 90, 91, 117, 131, 146, 147, 158, 160, 161, 162, 165, 173, 177, 178, 191, 193, 194, 220, 226, 227, 228, 230, 237, 257, 260, 269, 271, 310, 460, 524, 525, 527, 529, 537, 538, 541, 542, 546, 550, 551, 553, 556, 557, 560, 562, 564, 570, 580, 597, 598, 601, 602, 620, 621, 623, 625; his wife, 4n, 570n
Ashly, Ashlye, Mrs Mary (née Addington), 357
  Richard, 357
  Thomas, 13, 172, 250, 251, 253
  William, 126, 127
Ashton, nr Bainton, 172
asses, 111, 144
Aswarby, Aserby, Lincs, 555
attorneys, *xiv*, 594, 615; *see also* Blackwell, Mr; Burman, Mr snr; Butler, Richard; Eldred, Mr; Pedder, Mr; Pemberton, Roger; Pigeon, Mr; Rocke, Mr; Snow, Mr; Whittwell, Mr; *under* Cambridgeshire; Peterborough

backgammon, 111n
Bader, Mrs, 553
Bagley, Henry, of Ecton, 205n
bailiffs, 301, 302, 305, 306; accounts, 301, 304, 306, 308, 313; *see also* Bennett, Mr; Catlin, John; Vaughan, Henry
Baily, Mr, poss. fenman of Thorney, 132, 133, 139
Bainton, 172; meadow, 38
Ballett, Ballat, Charles, lawyer, of Spalding, 27 & n, 28, 61, 73, 74, 102, 111, 184, 185, 192, 193, 276, 360; death, 304
bank bills, 2, 595, 596, 597
bankruptcy, 4, 225
Barber, Dr Gabriell, of Stamford, 277 & n, 286, 288, 289, 311, 316, 317, 318, 345, 366, 367
Barcelona, conquest of, 398
bark for tanning, 53, 54
Barlow, Mr, 289, 518, 532
Barnack, Barnicke, 172, 179, 185n
Barrett of Newburgh, 111n
Barrett, Thomas, of Heriot's goldsmiths, 206, 217, 299
Barrington, Lady Anna (née Fitzwilliam), *xiii, xv*, 140, 145, 150, 159, 160, 168, 180, 181, 186, 188, 189, 198, 200, 204, 205, 206, 210, 211, 212, 216, 223, 227, 232, 234, 251, 254, 265, 267, 288, 298, 307, 317, 318, 335, 347, 361, 373, 375, 436, 451, 492, 493, 528, 568, 596, 598, *296*; in London, 178, 219, 352, 431, 445, 571; ill, 166, 174, 219, 230, 249, 250, 360, 471, 480, 481, 602, 604, 605; marriage portion, 226, 227, 241, 242; *see also* Fitzwilliam, Anna
  Lady, sr, death, 571
  Sir Charles, 140n, 142, 143, 145, 147, 149, 150, 152, 153, 159, 160, 166, 198, 200, 202, 210, 241, 376, 571, 602
baskets, 39 & n

Bateman, Betty (née Bull) 541, 572, 609; ill, 567, 568
Jonathan, 541, 567, 609
Bates, Mr, 50, 163, 168
Thomas, 286
Bath, Somerset, 181, 397, 413, 460, 461, 463, 587
Baxter, Mr, 81, 246, 247, 248, 249, 250, 294, 295
beadsmen, 572, 573, 574, 575, 576
Beales, Edmund, steward of Norfolk estates, 56, 61, 138, 174, 187, 188, 267, 326n, 328, 378
beans, pickled, 389
Beaver, Thomas of Bainton, 38
Bedford, William Russell, 1st duke, 88
Wriothesley Russell, 2nd duke, 538, 550, 560, 564, 589n
beekeeping, 28, 104, 149, 257
beer, 194, 435
Bell, Henry, architect, of King's Lynn, 188n
Mr, 46, 54
Bellamy, cousin John, of Farcet, 2 & n, 44, 73, 81, 116, 119, 121, 282, 298, 330, 334, 352, 385, 455, 456, 471, 538, 543, 590
Mr, of Fletton, 53
Mrs John (née Tryce), 2n, 30, 74, 107; ill, 24, 106; death, 139
cousin Thomas, 330, 331; marriage, 543
Bellus, Bellars, Bellows, Thomas, of Helpston, 267, 523
William, 526
Belsize, Belsis farm, land, 221, 222, 228, 297, 352, 604
Bennett, Bennet, Mr, bailiff to Mr St John, 5n, 77, 102, 106, 107, 109, 118, 119, 120, 123, 124
Berners, Bermey, Mr, 181, 594, 597
Bertie, Charles, 5n, 90, 115, 309, 317, 550, 560, 564
Betts, William, 586
Bevill, Thomas, 217, 218, 301, 315, 316
Bevis, Miles, of Peterborough, 270n, 277, 279, 280, 281, 282, 283, 295, 297, 298, 299, 300, 306, 376
Mr, 530
Biggleswade, Beds, 222
bills of exchange, 3, 4
Bimrose, John, tax collector, 91, 103, 134, 153, 159, 161, 219, 301, 347, 351, 377, 443, 487, 488, 490, 492, 493, 516, 612, 617; his wife, 612
John jr, 357, 617
Bird, Mrs, 310, 311
Black, Mr, 602
Blackbourne, Blackborne, Daniel, of Pilsgate, 103, 104, 105; his wife, 103
John, 40, 523
Blackwell, Mr, attorney, of Stamford, 594
Mr, attorney, of Clement's Inn, 350
Bleckington, Mr, prebendary, 20, 221
Blenheim Palace, 589n
Bloofield, Mr, 229
Blyeth, Mr, 445
Boare, Mr, 292
boatwrights, 90, 117, 118, 119, 120, 131, 134; *see also* Andrew, John
Bodily, Joseph, 412
Bolton, Bolten, Alexander, 168n
John, of Northborough, 150, 168n, 224, 225, 238, 240, 350, 357, 503
Oliver, 168
Boman, George, 443
Bond, Mrs, 504
Bonnor, Anne, 301
Borough Fen *see* Peterborough Great Fen
Boughton House, Northants, 621
Bourne, Lincs, 364, 377, 518, 555, 609, 627
bowling greens, at Gunwade ferry, 430, 490, 497, 500, 501, 567; *see also under* Milton, Sulehay
bowls (sport), 490, 497, 500, 503, 562
Brampston, Mr, 359, 407
Bramson, Richard, 156
brandy, 500, 502
braziers *see* Hewson, Mr; Knowles, Mr
bread prices, 311
Brecknocke, Brecknock, Mr, 3, 47, 56, 75
brewing, at Milton, 100, 181, 195, 214, 271, 324, 325, 390, 392, 393, 427, 503, 509, 576, 577, 609; methods, 111, 141, 156, 239, 285, 321, 326, 388, 572
bribes, 114, 115
Briers, William, 163
Briggs, Mr, 364
Brightman, Stephen, of Northborough, 103, 114, 180, 193
Brigstock, 394
Brimble, William, 251, 253
Bristol, 381, 385, 398, 460, 587
Brogden, Mr, 17, 324, 325, 378, 379
Brookbancke, Mr, 259
Brooks, Mr, 257
Broughton, Mr, 24, 26, 29, 34, 35, 123
Brown, Browne, Francis, 573, 574
Mr, 4
Mr, wheelwright, of Market Deeping, 357, 516
Brownlow, Sir John, 3rd bart, 23
Sir John, 5th bart, 444 & n,
Brudenell, Brutnall, Mr, 30n, 153n
Bucke, William, 146
Buckle, Mr, Surveyor to the King's Stables, 8, 9, 12, 13, 14, 16, 20
Buddle, Richard, 220n
building, costs, 64, 421, 546; materials, 429, 430 & n, 437; rebuilding, 271, 272, 535, 617; repairs, 56, 57, 58, 133, 293, 372, 373, 380, 524, 526, 527, 612, 617; *see also under* Gunwade ferry, Milton House, Waldram Hall
Bull, Betty, 77, 220, 221; marriage, 541, *and see* Bateman, Betty
Charles, 620

Joseph, 42, 50, 77, 220n, 225, 236, 244, 252, 253, 254, 301, 358, 366, 367, 371, 408, 613
Mrs Joseph, 77, 78
Mrs, of Marholm, housekeeper at Milton, 4, 5 & n, 6, 9, 11, 16, 21, 28, 33, 42n, 44, 47, 48, 52n, 53, 60, 61, 63, 64, 69n, 74, 75, 77, 78, 79, 86, 91, 98, 100, 104, 129, 130, 131 & n, 137, 138, 142, 145, 156, 172, 204, 221, 223, 225, 231, 232, 233, 234, 236, 237, 238, 242, 243, 249, 257, 258, 282, 283, 284, 286, 289, 308, 331, 337, 340, 341, 367, 371, 374, 388, 389, 391, 392, 393, 394, 412, 420, 422, 427, 428, 436, 439, 445, 457, 460, 462, 486, 503, 525, 531, 541, 548, 549, 550, 551, 567, 568, 621, 622, 627; children of, 418, 419, 428, 463, 464, 465, 466, 467; goes to London, 219, 220, 547; ill, 66, 149, 285, 418, 419, 438, 461; mourning clothes for, 123, 124
Nanny, Nan, Nanne, 16 & n *see also* Hunt, Nanne
Bulwick, Bullicke, 402 & n
Bunning, Buninge, Buning, John, 220n, 617
Matthew, 181n
Mr, 269, 518, 523, 524, 526
Burbidge, Daniell, 220n
Burghley, Burleigh, 188, 282, 283, 334; House and park, 73, 372; venison from, 232, 233, 234, 282
Burley, old John, 103, 106
Robert, 103
Burman, Boreman, Mr, sr, steward of Maxey court, 51, 90, 113, 114, 116, 157, 161, 224, 229, 232, 289, 503; death, 290, 291
Mr, jr, 290, 330, 345, 360
Mrs, of Stamford, 330, 345
Burmer, Burmore, Mr, 87
Burr, Mr, of Etton, 421n
Burrows, John, 220n
Bursnoll, Bursnell, Robert, mason, 83, 121n, 347n, 470, 472, 497, 545, 546
Burton, Benjamin, of Ailsworth, 286, 288, 290, 308, 311, 312, 417, 418, 419, 420, 422, 431, 432, 433, 434, 446, 447, 537
John, of Ailsworth, 286, 309; death, 308
Mr, 182, 206, 211, 530
Richard, of Marholm, 251, 253, 332, 355, 356, 370, 371, 380, 381, 412, 444, 476, 477, 478, 479, 480, 482, 483, 484, 486, 487, 488, 490, 519, 520, 521, 522, 527, 543, 547, 549, 552, 553, 556, 557, 560, 561, 563, 593, 601, 602, 606, 608, 609; ill, 489, 548; wife's death, 444
Thomas, of Marholm, 253
William, 211, 213, 214, 218, 288, 290, 418
Busby, Thomas, draper, of London, 378, 380, 381, 382, 384, 385
butchers, 606
Butler, Buttler, Henry, 403
Richard, ? lawyer, 210n
Mother, Goody, widow, 78, 137, 345, 362, 363, 379, 388, 573, 575; mourning clothes for, 124

calash, 467, 531, 532, 565, 566, 589
Cambridge, Christ's College, *xix*, 267 & n, 269; Emmanuel College, 4n; university 388; woolman, *see* Halstead, Mr; workhouse, 388
Cambridgeshire, attorneys from, 316
Carborough, John, of Norborough, 238
Cardigan, Robert Brudenell, 2nd earl, 88
Carnell, Mr, 261, 488
William, 13
carpenters, 295; *see also* Ricroft, Edward; Tyers, Robert; Wilkinson, John; Wright, Robert
carriage, rates of, 14, 15, 161, 167, 176, 177, 180, 181; by sea, 177; methods, 335, 341
carriers, 14, 72, 75, 130, 147, 160, 161, 167, 168, 266, 277, 282, 298, 389, 400, 416, 503; snowbound, 79; *see also* Chatteris, T; Clarke, J; Feary, Mr; Lawrence, Mr; horse carriers; *under* Castor; Horncastle; Lincoln; Louth; Peterborough
Carrington, James Primrose, Lord, 351 & n, 354
Carter, John, 97, 134, 150, 165, 182, 351, 357, 370, 372, 373, 376, 421n, 426, 427, 498, 555
William, death, 57
Cartwright, Thomas, *xiv–xv*
Castle Bytham, Castlebiteham, Lincs, 357, 364, 377
Castor, *vii, ix, xv, xviii*, 12, 62, 65, 91, 97, 170, 172, 176, 355; baker's oven, 333, 334, 380; carrier, 392, 398; church bells, levy for, 203, 205; estate, 169, 213, 214, 215, 216, 217, 218, 229, 255, 259, 267, 277, 286, 289, 292, 303, 311, 316, 317, 367, 380, 487; Field, 557; inhabitants, 169, 171, 346; lime, 429; mill, 61; rents, 68; statutes, 388, 461; tenants, 372; *see also* baker's oven
Catlin, Cattlin, John, of Maxey, *xv*, 313, 315, 370, 430n, 493, 495, 496, 503, 504, 512, 557, 580, 594
cattle, 16, 92n; impounding, 495
Cecil, family, *see* Burghley
Chamberlaine, Adam, 365, 366, 369, 370
George, of Etton, 42, 49, 367, 523, 524, 525, 527, 535, 536; family of, 95, 524, 526
John, 460
Joseph sr, 42n, 48, 53, 92, 93, 169, 191, 193, 196, 214, 221, 222, 229, 239, 247, 248, 261, 262, 265, 286, 365 & n, 370, 399; blindness, 243, 244, 246; mourning clothes, for, 123, 124, death, 288; wife of, 47, 370
Joseph, jr, 102, 214, 239, 243, 244, 247, 255, 256, 288, 308, 312, 319, 338, 339, 341, 355, 363, 365, 411, 412, 413, 414, 415, 416, 418,

Chamberlaine (contd.)
Joseph, jr; (contd.)
419, 435, 436, 451, 453, 456, 493, 494, 497, 531, 532, 538, 546, 565, 594, 595, 597, 618; his house fire, 342n, 344n, 345, 346; mourning clothes for, 123, 124
Messrs, brothers, 365
Charles VI, Habsburg Emperor, 461 & n
Charles I, King 46n
Charles II, King, *xix–xx*
Charlton, Widow, 403
Charterhouse school, 334, 554
Chatteris, Chattris, Cambs, 381, 385
Chatteris, Chattris, Thomas, of Longthorpe, 277, 352, 353, 365, 442, 444, 489, 531, 532, 561, 562, 563, 565, 566, 567, 568, 570, 575, 576, 577, 579, 580, 583, 584, 585, 590, 591, 592, 594, 595, 596, 599, 600, 601, 602, 604, 611; wife of, 565
Checkly, Checkley, brothers, 590, 593, 594
Edward, 125, 126n
Mr, 496
William, 27, 74, 78, 125, 128
Chesterton, Chasterton, Hunts, 276, 494, 546
Child, Sir Francis, 124, 126, 127, 352, 497
Chisseldine, Chesseldine, Chiseldine, John, 11, 13, 42, 255, 295, 351, 365; wife's death, 255
Christopher, John, 40n
church wardens, *see* Rudkins, Thomas, of Northborough; levy, Castor, 203
Church, Mr, of Maxey, 265, 266n, 272, 290, 291, 367, 368, 403, 406, 425, 443, 498
Rev Richard, 339, 340, 355, 359, 361, 362, 363, 371
Clark, Edward, 220n
Clarke, John, carrier, 1n, 4, 15
John, of Glinton, 157
Joseph, of Northborough, 290, 293, 294, 295, 319, 320, 322, 323, 330, 336, 340, 342, 344, 345, 360, 375, 383, 445, 446, 452, 459, 474, 550, 553, 558, 559
Claypole, Claypoole, family, *xviii*; monuments, 464n
Mr, gamekeeper, 40, 524 & n, 528
Mr, Goodman, of Tallington, 487, 488, 489, 490, 492
John, *xviii*, 90n
Clement's Inn, 27n, 350
Clenchwarton, Norfolk, 104
clergy, 111, 335, 363, 371, 465, 494, 518, 556; appointments, 333, 334, 336, 339, 348 & n, 355, 359
Clerke, Mr, of Dogsthorpe, 212
Clitheroe, Clitherow, family, 90n, 140n
Mr, owner of Lolham, 90, 111, 126, 127, 139, 140, 146, 148, 150, 151, 262n, 264
Cloathier, Mr, surveyor, 22
clocks, 464, 465, 466, 467; *see also under* Milton House
coachmen, 277; *see also* Carter, John
coal, 56, 185, 186; prices, 61
coinage, reform, *xix–xxi*, 1, 3 & n, 14, 15, 16, 22, 35, 36
Colchester, Essex, 563
Colcutt, Thomas, 286, 292, 297, 303, 319, 320, 349, 352, 354, 358, 360, 366, 373, 375, 380, 400, 407, 412, 414, 422, 424, 441, 472, 474, 476, 489, 492, 493; his wife, 422
Mr jr, 300, 303, 319, 360, 366, 372
Cole, Coles, John, of Northborough, 62, 79, 144, 157, 179, 190, 191, 193, 206, 240, 249, 291
Randall, 103
Collins, John, 194
Richard, painter, of Peterborough, 248, 249, 289
Cooke, Anne, 84
James, 610n
John, 238
copper (vessel), 414, 472, 474, 476, 489, 492, 517
copyholders, 580, 582
corn, 309; harvest, 33; exports, 311; prices, 310, 394, 553
corn factors, 22, 26, 46, 270; *see also* Warner, Mr
coroner *see* Leaffeild, Mr
Cosins, Cozens, Cousens, John, 306 & n, 307, 308, 309, 313, 314, 443
Cotton, Sir Robert, 39, 40
courts, keeping, 113, 114, 157, 287, 290, 615; *see also under* Maxey
Coventry, Warwicks, 589
Cox, Richard, 355
Cremer, Sir John, 504 & n
crime *see* murders; robberies
Crislow, Mr, 496
Cromwell family, *xviii*, 464n
Crosen, William, 33
Cross a hand, forest walk, 107, 184, 231, 234, 242, 387, 456, 471, 520, 538, 611
Cross, John, 286
cucumbers, pickled, 231
Curtis, Rev, 301
widow, of Westdeeping, 146

Davies, Mr and Mrs, of Watlington, 181
Day, Joan, 582
John, of Deeping Gate, 436, 443, 580, 582, 583
William, of Deeping Gate, 134, 195, 203, 357; death, 582
Deacon, Thomas, of Peterborough, 22, 214, 226, 227, 239, 294, 385, 386, 387, 427, 456, 471, 520, 521, 538, 550
Death, Mr, 205n
deaths, by drowning, 159n; due to storms, 89, 293n
Deborough, John, 163
Deeping *see* Market Deeping
Deeping Fen, 85, 86, 205, 236
Deeping Gate, *xviii*, 83, 172, 195; chief men of, 114; estate, 116, 377, 462, 495; Field, 80,

137, 350, 351, 352, 354, 357, 368; Meadow, 80, 83, 84, 134, 368
Deeping St James, James Deeping, Deepin, 171, 290, 325, 326, 328
Deepings, the (towns), 107, 115, 550
Deepup, Mr, 220, 244, 440, 442, 444
Robert, 550, 602
deer, 22, 39, 70
management, 181, 185, 186, 187, 193, 222, 248, 279, 282, 294, 295, 296, 298, 307, 326, 327, 328, 379, 525, 536, 613
warrants, 30, 31, 102, 107, 146, 155, 160n, 184, 242, 243, 283, 292, 293, 328, 347, 385, 386, 387, 404, 454, 456, 460, 469, 471, 519, 520, 524, 538, 541, 562, 581, 590, 594, 609
*see also* venison
Denham, Mr, death, 133
Robert, 220n
Derby, 588
Derbyshire, 589
Dews, Mr, 126n
Dickinson, Dickenson, John, 163, 169, 171, 172, 184, 239, 270, 294
old Mrs, of West Winch, 551
Richard, 226, 283, 294, 385, 388, 393, 427, 449, 450
Dillingham, Mr, 266
Dolben, Dolbin, Gilbert, MP, *xiv*, 165 & n, 168, 169, 199
dogs, greyhounds, 116, 124, 125
Dogsthorpe, Dosthorp, 550 & n, 562 & n
Dove, James, Goodman of Marholm, 11, 13, 126, 127, 130, 131, 172, 248, 250, 251, 252, 254, 255n, 303, 332, 337, 351, 352, 353, 354, 355, 360, 365, 371, 381, 398, 399, 400, 401, 407, 412, 420, 477, 543, 547, 550, 560, 601, 602, 606, 608, 611, 613
Mr, death, 547
Mrs, death, 313
Mrs, of Sutton, 537, 538
Dowsett, Mr, keeper, 74
draper *see* Busby, Thomas
drove roads, 172 & n, 178 & n, 179, 442, 550, 560, 564
drovers, 46, 550; *see also* Broughton, Mr; *under* Lincolnshire
Drury, Drewry, Druery, Mr, 134
Thomas, of Maxey, 350, 357, 555, 612
dry salter *see* Parker, Lawrence
Dryden, Dreydon, Drayton, John, 14, 27 & n, 93 & n, 102, 169, 276, 494; death, 546
Duce, Charles, of Peterborough, 2, 6, 7, 30, 32, 33, 35, 36, 42, 44, 45, 46, 47, 50, 57, 81, 94, 99, 100, 101, 102, 119, 142, 163, 185, 232, 248, 249, 250, 283, 299, 300, 303, 304, 317, 318, 321, 322, 324, 385, 456, 460, 471, 538
Dudley, Dudlye, Sir Matthew, 429
Duncomb, Mr, 349
Dunstan, William, 555
Dymock, Dymoke, family, 257n
Eades, Richard, 286
Easton-on-the-Hill, Eason, 437 & n, 448
Eastrea, Estree, Cambs, 173
Eaton, Edward, 368
John, 368
Mr, 425
Ecton, 205n
Eddins, Edins, Edings, John, 157, 159, 179, 194, 202, 213, 216, 217, 218, 219, 221, 222, 223, 224, 238, 254, 271, 286, 318, 321
Edwards, Richard, 288
Eedess, Mr, 357
Eldred, John, attorney, 223, 224, 225n, 290, 350, 550, 560, 562
elections, 156 & n
Essex, 200, 202, 376
Higham Ferrers, *x*
Northamptonshire, *xiii, xiv*, 360, 371, 372, 375, 376
Peterborough, *x, xii, xiii*, 44, 68, 69, 70, 159, 163, 164, 165, 166, 168, 169, 170, 198, 199, 200, 201, 227, 375
Essex, *vii*, 5n, 493, 528, 596; *see also under* elections
Ette, Ettee, Richard, 36, 41, 130, 202
Etton, *vii, ix, xv, xviii*, 6, 47, 57, 62, 347n, 370, 421n, 465, 466, 535; cures, 335, 339, 340; estate, 351, 365, 541; living, 42, 43, 49, 58, 60, 61, 334, 339, 343, 355, 359, 363, 367; manor, *vii*; meadow, 263, 306, 502; neighbours at, 255; parish, 38; parsonage, 77, 359; rector of, 4n, 42n, 55n, 355n; storm damage, 295, 618; vicar of, 267n
Ewin, Ewing, Ewen, Mr, 605
Mr, of Church Hall, 87
Richard (1), 134, 137; death, 150, 159; his widow, 158, 159, 161, 162, 165, 167
Richard (2), 165 & n, 281n, 301, 303, 305, 491, 516
Thomas, 70, 160
Exeter, Anne, Countess, 111
Elizabeth, Countess, 229
John Cecil, 5th earl, 12 & n, 69, 73, 74, 97, 111, 116, 372; death 159
John Cecil, 6th earl, 12 & n, 185, 188, 228, 229, 232, 282, 334, 335, 369, 382, 385, 388, 390, 400, 408, 426, 454, 455, 471, 541, 564, 569, 593
Exton, Exon, William, 9, 11, 42, 46, 80, 126n, 130, 139, 144, 145, 146, 147, 220n, 230, 231, 308, 310, 311, 315, 316, 351, 352, 354, 358, 360, 363, 365, 366, 369, 372, 373, 413, 415, 416, 422, 424, 428, 430, 431, 432, 433, 434 & n, 436, 441, 442
fairs, 9, 48, 53, 90, 91, 92, 111, 129, 130, 142, 155, 230, 232, 234, 381, 462, 525, 576; *and see also* statutes, Peterborough Bridge fair
Farcet, Fawcett, Hunts, 2n, 172n, 352

Feary, Fearey, Robert, carrier, 14, 15, 22, 26, 28, 69, 72, 101, 102, 103, 124, 126, 130n, 163, 164, 166, 167, 176, 177, 178, 180, 181, 189, 190, 191, 212, 330, 335, 351, 352, 353, 391, 392, 393, 399, 401, 435, 436, 469, 489, 490, 493, 494, 500, 551, 553, 604, 618, 620, 621, 622; changes inns, 160
Featherstone, John, 124
Mr, 588, 589, 590, 591
fencing, hedging and plashing, paling, 9, 50, 93, 254, 346, 347, 411, 598, 602
fens, 252; adventurers in, 4, 86; depasturing in, 172 & n; drainage of, 4n, 85, 86n; *see also* North Fen; Peterborough Great Fen
ferries *see* Gunwade ferry; Waldram Hall ferry
ferry boats, 90, 116, 117, 118, 120, 126, 130, 131, 134, 136, 140, 144, 499
Field, Mr, vintner, 195, 199, 395, 434n, 436, 438, 439, 443, 462, 582
Thomas, 80
Figg, John, 436
fires, 46, 269, 271, 293, 342, 344n, 345, 346, 566
fish, sturgeon, 60, 61
Fisher, James, of Camberwell, *xviii*
fishing, leases, 50, 53, 54, 57, 493, 494; methods, 501; rents, 39
Fitzwilliam, family history, *vii–x, xvi–xix*
Anna Maria, *xii*, 25, 29, 31, 51, 61, 118; ill, 30; marriage, 140; *hence see* Barrington, Lady Anna
Anne, wife of 1st earl, *x, xiii, xv*, 29, 32, 46, 51, 53, 59, 61, 74, 92, 98, 102, 129, 130, 138, 166, 219, 223, 225, 231, 232, 234, 242, 257, 258, 263, 274, 275, 282, 283, 318, 339, 356, 359, 366, 389, 392, 395, 397, 398, 413, 504n, 549, 567, 570, 576, 595, 613, *296*; effigy of, *xviii*; godmother, 75; grief for son, 122, 123; ill, 48, 50, 63, 66, 75, 77, 82, 86, 97, 99, 100, 101, 126, 174, 201, 204, 205, 208, 237, 249, 250, 251, 254, 255, 278, 279, 280, 286, 288, 289, 290, 292, 297, 304, 315, 322, 325, 331, 341, 354, 360, 362, 365, 373, 376, 379, 409, 411, 412, 415, 416, 524, 541; letter from, 354 (part)
Jane, née Perry, 2nd baroness, *ix*, 289, 609
John, Jack, later 2nd earl, *x, xiii, xv, xvi*, 126, 144, 155, 199, 210, 223, 227, 274, 339, 354, 359, 373, 395, 411, 425, 427, 436, 450, 451, 460, 461, 462, 463, 466, 483, 486, 488, 492, 493, 497, 500, 501, 514, 518, 520, 524, 527, 528, 529, 531, 535, 536, 537, 548, 550, 551, 554, 556, 557, 558, 562, 567, 583, 590, 605, 609, 612, 615, 623, *296*; ill, 166, 360, 626; marriage treaty, 586; travels, 518, 527, 588, 589, 596, 598; visits Milton, 405, 406, 407, 408, 409, 410, 627 & n, *296*
William, 1st baron, *ix*, 267
William, 2nd baron, *ix*, 214, 490, 598, 609; debts, *ix*
William, 1st earl, *vii, ix, x, xiii, xviii*, 361n, 366; absentee landlord, *xi*; angry with steward, 11, 12, 18, 19, 34, 46, 56, 132, 133, 134, 186, 244, 248, 250, 300, 312, 333, 337, 366, 372, 380, 427, 435, 439, 440, 441, 446, 450, 494, 504, 506, 512, 513, 528, 538, 558; angry with tenants, 56; angry with tradesmen, carriers, 37, 618; at Milton, *296*; concerned for servants, *xv*, 61, 63, 66, 71, 74; disposition, *xii–xiii*; effigy of, *xviii*; genealogy, *vii–x*; house in London, 136, 391, 514, 597, 600; ill, 31, 52, 79, 80, 176, 177, 179, 180, 205, 211, 218, 219, 222, 249, 275, 365, 500, 540, 541, 542, 543, 548, 570, 616, 623, 627; income, *x*; living in London, *x*; portraits, 116, 568; Member of Parliament, *xi*; offices held, *xi & n*; views on elections, *xii, xiv, xv*
William, son of 1st earl, *xv*, 15, 53, 92, 106, 109, 110; death and burial, 121, 122, 125, 136; ill, 97, 98, 99, 100, 101, 107, 112, 116; mourning, 163
food prices, 11, 392
forest walks, 228; *see also* Cross a hand; Morehay; Sulehay; Westhay
Forster, Foster, Augustine, 570, 597, 599, 600, 604, 605
Mr, of Marholm, 6, 33, 40, 50, 248, 250 & n, 352, 367, 411, 469, 479, 481, 503, 528, 530, 547, 548, 549, 550, 551, 552, 553, 556, 558, 559, 560, 561, 562, 563, 570, 593, 597, 605
Mrs Judah, 384
Mrs, her chamber *see under* Milton House
Mrs, of Marholm, 488, 489, 490, 492, 493, 552
Mrs, schoolmistress, death, 384
Rev, 334, & n, 340, 343, 355, 356, 358
Fotheringhay, Fotheringay, fair, 576
Fracy, Mr, 605
Framlingham, Suffolk, 333n
Freeman, family, 282
Francis, of Etton, 38
John, Jack, 133, 355, 404, 454, 478, 483, 505, 521, 522, 572, 573, 574, 606, 609; marriage 57; children, 572, 573, 574, 575
Mr, 253
Mr, deceased, 370, 445
Mr, shepherd, 576, 577
Mrs John, 355; death, 573
Peggy, Goody, wife of Thomas, of Milton, 9, 133, 134, 136; Widow, 263, 265, 296, 354, 370, 378, 404, 444, 445, 503, 504, 505, 506, 528, 529, 573, 575; death, *296*
Mrs William 370
Robert, 352, 421n
Samuel, Dean of Peterborough, 14n
Thomas, gamekeeper, 2, 9n, 12, 26, 38, 39,

40, 42, 46, 50, 53, 54, 56, 69n, 78, 92, 93, 94, 107, 112, 117, 125, 128, 134, 136, 151, 181, 204, 241, 244, 248, 277, 354, 558, 584, 585, 593, 608, 616; ill, 133; death, 263, 272
Thomas in the fen, 573
William, of Marholm, 370
Fuller, Thomas, woolman, of Essex, 85, 90, 158, 161, 162
funerals, 121, 122 & n, 546

Gainsborough, Baptist Noel, 3rd earl, 497 & n, 501, 502, 503; *for* his kinsman *see* Noel, John
game, sent to London, 82, 88, 129, 134, 160, 200, 201, 259, 537, 545, 548, 553, 554, 598, 603
fowl, sent to London, 35, 36, 40, 41, 42, 50, 74, 76, 77, 82, 86, 110, 111, 147, 158, 188, 190, 200, 361, 524 & n, 527, 528, 534, 553
*see also* venison
gamekeepers, 146, 272, 275, 276, 277; *see also* Arney, Mr; Freeman, Thomas; Leadhead, Daniel
gaming, 524
Gardiner, Garner, Edward, Ned, 420, 422
Mr, sr, 489
William, of Sutton, 309, 310, 311, 487, 488, 489, 490
Gascoigne, Mary, 334
Mr, 181
Mr, jr, 363
Rev. George, 57, 334 & n
Gee, John, 523
George, Thomas, 43
glaziers *see* Willis, Mr
Glinton, 9, 172, 254, 255
glovers, 396
Gold, Dr, physician, of London, 397, 398
goldsmiths, 299; *see also* Barrett, Thomas; Heriot, Hardbord; Heriot, James; Shales, Charles; Sheppard, Mr
Goode, Goude, Elias, tailor, of Maxey, 569, 612, 617
Goody, Widow, 573, 574, 575
Mr sr, 617
Graham, Dorothy, *xviii*, 17n
grain prices, 51, 267, 462
Grant, John, 569
Grantchester, Cambs, 333n
Grantham, Lincs, 44n
Gray, Graie, Grey, Jeffrey, 286, 407
John, 608
John, manservant, 436
Great Fen, *see* Peterborough Great Fen
Griffin, Mrs, 330, 342
Thomas, deceased, 289, 383 & n
William, of Northborough, 103, 104, 293; deceased 319; his land, 107, 142; his lease, 105, 106
grocer *see* Jackson, Mr, grocer
Grosvenor, Mr, ? doctor, 273
Gunten, Andrew, of Deepingate, drowned, 443
Mrs Andrew, 443
Gunwade, Gunnard, Gunworth, 62, 295n, 576, 577, 593, 594, 595, 598
Gunwade ferry, *vii, xv, xvi*, 89, 90, 165, 176n, 448, 459, 460
brewhouse, 433, 496
ferry pump, 610, 613
ferryhouse, 411, 503, 524
lease, 420, 424, 426, 427, 430, 431, 432, 434, 442, 446, 449, 450
warehouse, 185
well, 433, 467, 469, 470, 471, 472, 477, 478, 479, 480, 481, 482, 483, 484, 486, 487, 497, 501, 502, 503, 507, 528, 541, 542, 543, 545, 546, 565, 609, 610
*see also under* bowling greens
Guybon, Francis, steward, Milton, *ix, xi, xii, xiii, xiv, xv*, 126n, 146n, 159n, 219n, 250n, 297n, 305n, 306n, 337, 340, 341, 360n, 361, 364, 377, 403, 407, 425, 429, 471, 485, 498, 516, 555, 569, *295–6*; career, *xv–xvi*; chief mourner, 121; disposition, *xv–xvi*; gifts to, 30, 44, 73, 119, 282; ill, 27, 273, 274, 275, 277, 278, 279, 280, 286, 339, 343, 345, 346, 349, 362, 363, 368, 381, 419, 547; death, *296*
Thomas, *xvi, 296n*

Hacke, Mr, 121
Hall, Burr, of Etton, 421n
Mr, of Collyweston, 499
Thomas, of Etton, 421n
Halstead, John, 289, 371, 387, 388
Thomas, woolman, of Cambridge, 232n, 234, 236, 237, 243, 245, 248, 257, 260, 308, 310, 311, 362, 363, 365, 369, 371, 378, 381, 382, 383, 384, 385, 386, 387, 388, 458
Hampden, John, 5n
Hankin, Hawkin, Henry, salesman, of Islington, 3 & n, 47, 56, 88, 156, 172, 185, 205, 211, 218, 248, 251, 270, 272, 278, 301, 306, 308, 309, 311, 315, 318, 322, 324, 334, 351, 352, 354, 358, 360, 365, 372, 374, 376, 381, 405, 413, 416, 418, 420, 422, 431, 433, 434n, 436, 441, 450, 477, 481, 488, 489, 497, 512, 568, 572, 583, 615, 620, 625
Hardy, Robert, 486, 543, 546, 547, 550
Harington, James, 443
Harlow, Essex, 566
Harrison, John, 375
Hascard, Dr, Dean of Windsor, 61, 102
Hatfield, Herts, coach stage, 145
Hatton, Mr, of Walsoken, 521, 522
Hawkins, Mr, death, 133
hay, 223, 226, 236, 261, 263, 273, 326, 408, 577, 578
prices, 224, 227
haymakers, 576, 577, 578, 579

Healy, Healey, Mr, 12, 13
widow, 286, 380
Helpston, *ix, xv, xviii, xix*, 6, 220n, 248; estate, 133, 134; storm damage in, 89; Heath, 526, 609; rents, 267, 269; statutes, 233, 234, 388, 460, 461; stone from, 429; tithes, 267, 269; Tyndales, Tindalls, also known as Clapham's, manor in, *ix, xix*, 38, 41, 51, 518, 523, 524, 526
hempdresser *see* Holmes, Mr
Henry, Robert, 220n
herdsman *see* Love, Tobias
Heriott, Herriott, Herriot, Heriot, George, goldsmith, 4n
Harbord, goldsmith, & shop, 299, 401, 430, 452, 483, 583
James (1629–1705), goldsmith, & shop, 4 & n, 15, 48, 58, 81, 99, 108n, 125, 126, 128, 134, 144, 145, 146, 150, 157, 159, 160, 168, 172, 176, 180, 181, 187, 190, 192, 194, 200, 201, 202, 205n, 206, 217, 218, 219, 220, 221, 226, 228, 243, 249, 251, 253, 255, 257, 258, 260, 265, 267, 268, 283, 304, 306, 311, 317, 324, 325, 334, 365; death, 358
Hertingfordbury, Hertingfordberry, Herts, 140n, 142, 166, 212
Hewson, Howson, Mr, brazier, 4, 6, 7, 163
Hibbons, Hibbens, Hippie, Samuel, mason, 421 & n, 425, 429, 430n, 437, 486n
Hide, Hyde, Mary (née Trollope), 140n
Mr, Capt, 550, 560, 564
Mrs, of Langtoft, 564
William, sr & jr, 140 & n
Hincon, Hinson, John, 258n; Mr, 605
Hinton, Mr, postmaster, 39, 40, 50, 53, 54, 56, 494
Hippwell, Hipwell, Richard, deceased, 159 & n, 370
Hoare, Francis, 218
hogmen, 1, 401; *see also* Morrice, R; Pank, Mr
hogs, 48, 50, 401, 422
Holbeach, Holbitch, Lincs, 381
Holland, Lincs, 110
Holland, The Netherlands, *xxi*, 311
Holland, Hollands, Henry, drover, 288, 298, 323, 328, 349, 351, 359, 363, 365, 404
John, salesman, 288, 298, 328, 349, 359, 363, 365, 399, 404, 407, 412
Mr, 321, 325, 326, 398, 400, 401, 405
Holman, Edward, Ned, of Castor, 97, 164, 248, 295, 346
John, 97
Holme, Hunts, 245
Holmes, Mr, hempdresser, 224
Robert, of Helpston Heath, warrener, 42, 494, 518, 523, 524, 526, 528
honey, 166, 257, 258, 259
Horncastle, Lincs, carriers, 177
Horner, John, Quaker, salesman, 11, 35, 45, 52, 54, 55, 62, 65, 72, 76, 78, 82, 85, 97, 101, 115, 132, 139, 150, 157, 159, 160, 190, 191, 193, 194, 211, 214, 216, 218; bankrupt, 225
horse carriers, 161, 167, 168, 177
Horseley, Horsley, Mr and Mrs, of Cliffords Inn, 3, 4, 6, 8
horses, 62, 111, 210, 469, 528, 529, 531, 536, 538, 601; distemper in, 94; for coach, 47, 48, 198; for muster, 138; forfeited, 306, 382; management, 185, 222, 602; prices, 583; racing, 511
Horwood, James, of Bainton, 38
household goods, 337; sent to Milton, 190, 191, 192, 193, 194, 389, 392, 398, 399, 436; linen, 53, 129, 130, 131
houses, prices, 617; *see also* building; Gunwade ferry house; Milton House; Waldram Hall
Hubbord, Mr, 218
Hullicke, Hullock, Hullocke, Goodman, maltster, 509, 577
John, husbandman, 270, 272, 288
Mr, 417, 418
Richard, 216, 217, 286
Humby, Lincs, 444n
Hunt (née Bull), Mr, 52
Nanne, 44, 47; ill, 59, 60, 61, 62; death, 63, 64
Huntingdon, 150
Huntingdonshire, 390
Hunton, Mr, 425
Huss, Hust, Mr, of Castle Bytham, 364, 377
Hycklin, Hicklyn, Hicklin, John, 407
Matthew, of Waldram Hall, 85, 90, 227

illness, 48, 59, 61, 79, 82, 94, 567; ague, 254, 362, 363; alcoholism, 71; apoplexy, 5, 205, 218, 315, 488; blindness, 243, 244, 246; bruises, 418; cancer, 174, 518; cold, 174, 230; colic, 288, 292, 297, 304, 325, 376, 415, 602; consumption, 97; convulsions/fits, 181; cough, 116; diabetes, 397, 616; distemper, 97, 315, 360, 365; fever, 97, 218, 219, 274, 541; gout, 176, 365; gravel, 500; gripes, 280; lameness, 176, 179; lethargy, 616; melancholy, 257; miscarriage, 219, 249; plague, 418n; rheum in the eye, 570; scurvy, 177, 256, 257; smallpox, 6, 21, 192, 199, 201, 501, 507, 515; sore eyes, 502; spleen, 257; sprains, 211; St Anthony's fire (erysipelas), 218, 219, 275, 543; stillbirth, 414; stone, 249, 500; toothache, 30, 208, 360
inns of court *see* Clement's Inn
inns, 317
Angel, Islington, 3n, 270, 272, 309
Black Mare, Bloomsbury, 391
Blue Board, Stamford, 377
Blue Periwig, Princess St, 608
Globe Tavern, 434, 436
Naked Boy, Fleet Street, 4n
Red Inn, 442, 460, 564
Swan, Welwyn, 149, 166
Unicorn, Lombard St, 189n

Ireland, Mr, tanner, 53, 54n
ironmonger *see* Pattison, Mr
Isham, Sir Justinian, *xiv–xv*, 371, 325 & n
Isle of Ely, 385
Isle of Wight, 450
Ixom, Ixem, Rev Thomas, 267 & n

Jackson, Mr, 15, 375
jobber *see* Plowright, Mr
Johnson, Adam sr, of Marholm, 121, 156, 194, 195, 239, 246, 248, 261, 283, 285, 325, 326, 387, 388, 390, 393, 427, 509, 530, 573, 574, 575, 577, 601; his sons, 236, 243, 245, 246, 393, 509
  Benjamin, 42, 50
  Miss, 586 & n, *296*
  Mrs, formerly Dillingham, 570
  Mrs, sr, deceased, 574
  Sir Henry, 586 & n, *296*
  Thomas, 404, 407
  young, 609
Joice, William, 351, 354
judges, 171
juries, 114
Justices of the Peace, 58
justices in eyre, 234

Kenwicke Farm, 173, 174, 193
Kettleborough, Mr, of Stamford, 15, 130
Ketton, stone, 429
King, Kinge, Mr, 310, 312
  William, of Castor, 424, 426, 427, 430, 431, 432, 433, 442, 446, 447, 448, 449, 450, 454, 460, 467, 470, 471, 494, 496, 500, 502, 503, 504, 524, 525, 556, 557, 562, 565, 583, 584, 590, 592; ill 501, 507, 581; his family, 424, 430, 460n, 461n, 462, 501
King's Lynn, Norfolk, 132, 176n, 181, 186, 476, 490, 610
Kingston, Mr, of Thorney Abbey, 3, 22, 37, 71, 72, 88, 515
Knowles, Mr, brazier, 414

Langdyke, Landike, Bush, 220n, 550; court, 210n, 220n, 550n, 560, 562, 563; jury, 220 & n
Langtoft, Lantauft, Lincs, 357 & n, 564 & n
law suits, 103, 516
Lawrence, Larrans, Henry, 338, 361, 468
  Mr, 207, 208, 286, 425, 530, 531, 580
  Mr, of Walton, 12, 226, 337
  Thomas, of Walton, 220n, 306, 334, 337, 351, 352, 353, 365, 387, 388, 389, 391
Lawson, Mr, of Bourne, 42
lawyers *see* attorneys
Laxton, Mr, of Thorney, 72
  Thomas, 220n
Le Plaw, Le Pla, Plaw, Pla, David, 6, 8, 12, 16, 46
  Jacob, 495 & n, 496
Leadhead, Daniel, gamekeeper, 493, 494, 501
Leaffeild, Leafield, George, 369, 370
  Mr, 4, 40, 41, 121, 306
  William, 342, 344n, 345, 400, 595
leases, 52, 54, 87, 150, 253, 286, 312, 370, 523, 552, 561, 593; ecclesiastical, 134; for lives, 159, 161, 162; terms violated, 262, 264; *see also* fishing leases
leather and tanning, 13, 16
Lee, Lea, Lees, Dr, 163
  Richard, of Castor, 474, 487, 529
  Widow, 286, 422
Leicester, 588, 589
Leicestershire, 381, 456, 461
Levett, Levitt, Mr, 195, 351, 476, 478; widow of, 195, 351
Lichfield, Staffs, 589
lime burning, 17, 186, 448
limestone, 437 & n
Lincoln, carriers, 176, 411
Lincolnshire, 378, 380, 44n; drovers, 560; wool, 385, 390, 456, 461
livestock, depasturing, 172 & n; diseases of, 94; management, 558; prices, 11
Lolham, Lollham, Lollam, bridge, rebuilding, 421 & n, 423, 425, 427, 428, 429, 430, 431, 432, 433, 434, 437, 443, 448, 449, 486n; estate, *ix*, 126, 127, 139, 146, 148, 264; timber on, 150; Mills, 159, 162
London, *xxi*; Aldersgate Street, 129; Battersea, 384n; Bear Quay, 267, 270; Bloomsbury, 514, 621n; Cateaton St, 375; Cripplegate, 396; Drury Lane, 136, 597, 600; Great Queen Street, 597, 600; High Holborn, Holbourn, 445; Islington Fields, *xi*, 334, 337, 339, 394, 528, 581; King's Street, Bloomsbury, 391; Lawrence Lane, 401; Leadenhall Market, 385; Lincolns Inn Fields, 88; Moore's Fields, 257; Newgate, market, 551; Princess St, 608; schools, 334; Smithfield, 439, 452, markets, 448, 495, 606; Southwark, 451, 515; Spitalfields, 160; St Giles in the Fields parish, 58, 68, 136; St James's Park, 88; Westminster Hall, 171; Westminster, 398; Westmorland Court, 347; Whitehall, 46; *see also* Bartholomew Fair; Clement's Inn; Thames, River; *under* inns; servants
Long Orton *see* Orton
Long Sutton, Sutton in the fens, Lincs, 551, 552
Longthorpe, Thorpe, 5n, 50, 73, 122, 352, 385
Louis XIV, King of France, 558
Louth, Lowth, Lincs, carriers, 176, 177
Love, Tobias, herdsman, 555
Lowrey, Mr, 30, 44, 73, 74, 77, 81, 116, 117, 119, 120, 130, 132, 134, 136, 144, 150, 163, 165, 219, 224, 226, 237, 276, 385, 456, 471, 476, 482, 538, 591; his wife, 7, 4, 77, 163, 164; remarriage, 270
Luff, Mr, porter, 160

Maidwell, Mr, 39, 54
malt, 214; mills, 239; prices, 181n, 394
maltsters, 214, 239, 427; *see also* Deacon, Thomas; Dickenson, John; Dickenson, Richard; Hullock, Goodman; Parker, Mr; Whinyates, Mr
Manton, Thomas, Goodman, 11, 53, 93, 292, 293, 319, 320, 352, 354, 358, 359, 360, 366, 372, 373, 414; death, 374, 375; farm of, 286, 292, 345, 346, 349, 352, 354, 367, 376, 380, 412, 441, 472, 488, 593, 604, 605
Mapletop, Mapletoft, Mappletopp, John, 32, 39, 46, 54, 134, 173, 174, 193, 213, 214
March, Cambs, 288
Marholm, Marham, Marrham, *vii, xv, xviii*, 33n, 57, 62, 103, 236, 254, 334, 382, 548; church, *vii, xviii*, 121, 123, 499; Fitzwilliam tombs, in, *xviii*
estate, 237, 351, 353, 355, 363, 541, 548, 551, 552, 553, 559, 561, 599, 600; living, 43, 333n, 334, 335, 339, 340, 356, 358, 363, 384; parsonage, 369, 375, 379; wool, 354, 369, 378, 385, 390
Market Deeping, 92 & n, 317, 498; bridge, 90, 91, 115
fair, 90, 91, 92 & n, 111
masons from, *see* masons
Market Harborough, Leics, 555
markets, 613; *see also under* London; Oundle; Peterborough; sheep; Stamford
Marlborough, Duchess of, 384
John Churchill, 1st duke of, 589
marriage portions, 50, 226, 227
Marshall, John, 328, 345, 361, 621, 622
Mason, Robert, 530
masons, 13, 14, 15 *see also* Bursnoll, Robert
Massingberd, Elizabeth (later Mrs Ash), 4n, 570n
Sir Henry, 4n, 570n
Matthews, Mathews, Mr, tax collector, 18
Mawre, Maure, George, salesman, 46, 253, 408, 412, 420, 477, 532, 534, 535, 565, 567, 620
Maxey, *ix, xv, xviii*, 17, 51, 52, 92, 106, 172, 333, 334, 364, 368, 569, 580
Castle and farm, *xviii*, 38, 113, 347, 377, 487, 488, 489, 492, 550, 552, 617; court dinner at, 114, 115, 157; royalties, 107
chief rents, 436
Church field, 357, 368
court, 113, 115, 116, 157, 159, 195, 287, 290, 291, 343, 529, 569
East Field, *see* 350 & Deepingate Field;
estate leases, 475
estate particular, 79, 80
estate rents, 126, 129, 224, 225, 245, 247, 251, 425, 485
estate settlement, 90, 91, 94, 98, 103, 105, 107, 115, 117, 120
estate tenants, 126, 237, 503
estate, 83, 84, 85, 87, 88, 89, 110, 111, 115, 116, 134, 160, 205, 289, 301, 302, 303, 305, 307, 309, 311, 340, 350, 351, 357, 364, 368, 376, 555, 557 & n, 612
jury, 114
liberty, 495
living, 355 & n, 359, 362
lord of, 423
Mills, 158, 159, 161, 162, 200, 202, 247, 350
pasture, cow pasture, cow commons in, 83, 84, 95, 96, 200, 202, 203, 261, 264, 271, 301, 306, 313, 314, 315, 443, 498, 555
people of, 114, 361, 516
poor of, 368, 555
pound, 495
rental, 306, 314
Meares, Meekes, Mr, 37, *296*
Seth, of Thorney, 126, 163
Measure, Measures, John, of Deepingate, 436, 443; his wife's death, 612
meat prices, 51, 553
medical treatment, 15, 53, 92, 181, 225, 275, 315, 397, 348, 418, 489; *see also* illness
midwives, 75n, 78
militia, 202; at Peterborough 47; horses for, 111, 200; *see also* army
Miller, John's son, 365
William, of Thorney fen, 39, 49, 50, 51, 53, 54, 97, 156, 176, 250, 269, 270, 172, 272, 275, 278, 564, 565, 566, 567
miller *see* Toby
Milton, *vii, xi, xv*, 65, 62, 93, 121, 122, 203, 363, 380, 386, 390, 425, 488, 541, 548, 556, 557, 594, 598; *296*; bowling green, 490; rents, 62, 68, 69
Milton House, *ix, x, xvi*, 5n, 89, 134, 337, 338, 346, 348, 349, 366, 372, 388, 389, 534, 557; cellar, 154, 156, 436; chimneys, 75, 82, 83, 85, 94, 131, 132, 255, 256, 257
clocks, 42, 131, 394, 395, 465, 466, 467
closet, 220
coach house, 248
coal house, 243
dining room, 192
doll's room, 627
dovecotes, 189
drying yard, 5, 35, 221, 222, 412, 413
fruit trees, 96, 221, 256, 411, 412, 493, 494, 594, 595, 597
gardens, 255, 261, 268, 346, 398, 411, 414, 415, 416, 418, 493, 494
gatehouse, 34n
gates, 423
glazing, 207, 208
henhouses, 427
Lady Newburgh's chamber, 111 & n, 192, 438
latrines, houses of office, 435, 439, 448, 450
lime house, 131
maintenance, 4, 29, 44, 124, 159, 170, 196, 221, 242, 245, 286, 346, 348, 349, 398, 460, 525, 529, 611, 613
moat, 346, 349, 525
Mrs Forster's chamber, 111

Mrs Lewellin's chamber, 111
new buildings, 4, 5 & n, 10, 11, 13, 14, 15, 17, 20, 24, 27, 29, 33, 34, 35, 37, 40, 57, 131, 132
painting work at, 248
park fences, 598, 602
park, *xvi*, 261
paving, 309
pictures sent to, 223, 337, 340, 341
pigeons, 96, 124, 161, 189, 190
poultry, 96
repairs, 22, 34, 132, 249, 256, 261, 286, 394, 445, 449, 450, 452, 463
roof, slating, 392, 393
stables, 131, 395
stone gallery, 249
storm damage, 293, 294
swans, 347
value of, 586
windows, lewcombs, 35 & n, 170, 196, 286, 445, 448, 449, 463, 529
Minorca, 621
money, *xxi*; loans, 130, 132, 220, 222, 226, 265, 266, 267, 292, 300, 521; returns, *passim*; returns, methods, 46; *see also* coinage
Montagu, Ralph, 1st duke of, death, 621 & n
Mordaunt, Charles *see* Peterborough, Earl of
John, Lord, *xiv–xv*, 360 & n, 361, 371, 372, 375, 376
Morehay, Moorehay, Lawn, forest walk, 387, 460, 471, 520, 524, 541
Morrice, Rowland, hogman, 1n, 2, 4, 7, 21, 41, 42, 45, 46, 48, 53, 108 & n, 154, 166, 177, 218, 221, 222, 223, 224, 249, 260, 261, 263, 270, 284, 351, 401, 422, 471, 472, 615
Mosley, William, weaver, 422n, 424
mourning customs, 121, 122 & n, 123, 124, 125, 126, 128, 130, 163, 294, 296, 546
murders, 229
mushrooms, pickled, 28, 231

napery, prices, 98
Nassaburgh hundred, 424n, court, 220n, 550 & n
Navy, 293n, 450, 621n
Neale, Noah, of Stamford, 6, 7, 8, 17, 136, 169, 170, 172, 176, 219, 220
Needham, Mr, 467
Nene, Neene, river, *vii, xvi*, 5n, 176n, 493
Newark, Notts, 422
Newcastle, John Holles, Duke of, 453 &n, 493, 494, 501
Newcomb, Newcombe, Robert, Robin, 17, 19, 20, 21, 22, 23, 26, 30, 35, 36, 44, 50, 54, 68, 69, 73, 116, 119, 184, 234, 246, 250, 270, 276, 282, 385, 387, 388, 390, 460, 471, 494; master of boat gangs, 116; his son, 388
Noel, Noell, Nowell, John, 44n, 497 & n, 501, 502
Baptist *see* Gainsborough, 3rd earl
Norfolk, *xi*, 191; Fitzwilliam estates in, *x*, 6, 8, 89, 173, 251, 504
Norman, family, 517
North Fen, 114, 115, 116, 117, 495, 591
North Runcton, Norf, church, 188
Northampton, 588, 589
Northamptonshire, *vii, xi*; county elections *see under* elections
Northborough, Norborough, *vii, ix, xviii*, 6, 57, 62, 106, 172, 366, 465, 466, 580; Barton hurn in, 271, 272; Castle, *xviii*, 328, 464n, 465; church, 326, 465; repairs, 464 & n; church seating, 624, 626, 627; court, 113, 114, 116, 117, 157, 159, 343, 582; estate, 14, 37, 90, 103, 105, 116, 133, 134, 160, 193, 290, 320, 322, 323, 340, 365, 366, 369, 380, 383, 437, 462, 495, 532, 534, 535, 561, 591, 624; Paradise farm in, 14, 20, 64, 142, 269, 271, 272, 284, 285, 421; rents, 340, 503, 536, 553; tenants, 114, 203, 237, 337, 431, 465, 467, 503, 505, 527
Norton, Mr and Mrs, 195, 351
Nottingham, 588
Nunnery, Mr, 271
nurses, 75n *see also* Measure, Mrs

Oagle, Robert, of Paradise, Northborough, 64, 271
oil, 620, 621
Old Park, 52, 53, 92, 93, 261, 262, 268, 280, 365, 556, 557
Old Sulehay forest *see* Sulehay forest
Orby, Sir Charles, 442, 444
Orme, Mr, 614
Orton Longueville, Long Orton, Orton, 453, 493, 501
Osborne, Osburne, Robert, of Maxey, 357, 475, 478, 480, 483, 498, 516, 550, 552, 617; his son, 617
Ossulston, John Bennet, 1st Lord, 12n
Oundle, 5n, 48, 382, 387, 388, 407, 426
Oxney farm, 173

Paddy, Widow, 364, 555
painter *see* Collins, Richard
Palmer, John, of Castor, 216, 217, 277, 346
Mrs, 169
Pank, Pancke, Mr, hogman, 46, 174, 175, 176, 202, 205, 306, 401
Parfaite, Mr, 103, 224
Parker, Charles, election agent, of Peterborough, 5n, 163, 375, 444, 451, 452, 453, 455, 456, 462, 464, 466, 467, 471, 472, 477, 481, 487, 488, 492, 512, 514, 515, 520, 521, 537, 538, 541, 548, 549, 550, 551, 552, 553, 556, 557, 558, 559, 561, 562, 566, 580, 581, 583, 593, 597, 601, 604, 605, 619, 620, 621; wife's death, 595
Lawrence, dry salter, of Southwark, 451, 467, 515, 549

Parker (contd.)
Mr, 5, 214, 220, 239, 294, 385, 427
William, of the Minster, 163, 252
Parliament *see* elections
Parsmore, Pasmore, Passmore, family, 518 & n
Parsons, Mr, 293, 294
Paston, 4n, 36, 334n, 570 & n
Pattison, Mr, ironmonger, London, 445
Paule, Mr, of Peterborough, 205
Pedder, Mr, attorney, 617, 627
Peach, Richard, 610n
peaches, 594, 595
Peakirk, *xv*, 117
pears, pear trees, 493, 494
Pemberton, Roger, lawyer, 7, 31, 44, 50, 62, 68, 73, 79, 80, 81, 103, 113, 114, 115, 116, 117, 119, 150, 157, 169, 171, 176, 195, 196, 199, 201, 210, 211, 212, 214, 221, 227, 242, 246, 257, 267, 290, 291, 292, 301, 303, 305, 313, 315, 327, 328, 337, 351, 353, 354, 360, 361, 362, 369, 372, 382, 385, 386, 388, 394, 395, 399, 400, 401, 402, 416, 418, 419, 428, 430, 443, 444, 455, 456, 458, 460, 462, 471 & n, 474, 475, 477, 478, 486, 499, 500, 504, 520, 522, 524, 525, 527, 528, 538, 554, 556, 557, 558, 561, 562, 563, 569, 578, 580, 582, 583, 590, 595, 597, 598, 609, 612, 617, 619, 620, 625, 626, 627; ill, 397, 398, 488, 489, 490, 492, 493, 529, 536, 614, 615, 616, 618; wife of, 251, 394, 395, 400, 401, 402, 488, 549, 590, 595, 598; sons of, 499, 506, 549, 619; daughter of, 251, 499
Pembroke, Thomas Herbert, 8th earl, 506 & n
Pendleton, Mr jr, 334, 554, 557
Mrs, housekeeper, 15, 23, 27, 28, 53, 56, 59, 62, 63, 66, 77, 92, 100, 102, 104, 116n, 223, 225, 231, 243, 256, 265, 268, 275, 333, 334, 339, 343, 344, 345, 346, 348, 353, 356n, 358, 363, 365, 366, 379, 383 & n, 384, 388, 389, 390, 431, 436, 438, 532, 534, 550, 554, 556, 557, 558, 589, *296*; pregnancy, 67, 74; childbirth, 75, 78; mourning clothes for, 123, 124
Rev Jeremiah, *xix*, 4 & n, 20, 22, 29, 30, 33, 34 & n, 35, 36, 37, 42, 43, 44, 53, 55, 56, 57, 58, 60, 61, 63, 66, 73, 74, 75, 77, 80, 81, 84, 85, 90, 92, 94, 103, 107, 111, 115, 119, 121, 122, 146, 147, 154, 182, 193, 212, 233, 243, 250, 262, 265, 273, 276, 282, 294, 334 & n, 339, 353, 358, 366, 367; letters from, 27, 256; ill, 51, 256, 257, 303, 315, 317, 318, 320, 321, 323, 324, 325, 326, 327, 330, 331; his nephew, 163, 168; morning clothes for, 123, 124; death, 333
pepper, prices, 289, 392
Peterborough, Charles Mordaunt, 3rd earl, 306 & n, 371
Peterborough, *xi*, 12, 58, 121, 122, 142, 143, 199, 369, 381, 385, 392, 400, 401, 426, 476, 500, 511, 520, 534, 550, 560, 610
Abbey, 424n
attorneys, 272
bailiffship, 554, 556, 590
Bishop of, 5n, 250, 517; his tenants, 5n, 6n, 605
Bridge, Brigg fair, 90, 91, 92, 142, 155, 190, 232, 236, 284, 337, 391
Canon of, 42n
carriers, 129, 277, 568, 579
Dean of, 14 & n, 20, 64, 221, 556, 557, 558
dean and chapter, *xviii*, 5n, 60, 425, 539 & n
election, *see* elections, Peterborough
Fitzwilliam's friends in, 130, 150, 198, 232, 233, 234, 244, 260, 283, 294, 352, 585, 606
freeholders, 562
gossip, 192
Great Fen, 116, 172 & n, 424 & n, 550
market, 461, 516, 562, 575
merchants, 266
people, 163n, 520, 556
post stage, 209
prebends of, 221, 566
prison, 617
school, 334, 366, 534
Soke, *vii, ix, xv n*, 92, 116, 219, 424n
Petty, Mr, of Bedford House, 196, 197
Pettyt, Petyt, Mr, 538, 581
Silas, 586n
Sylvester, *296 n*
Phelips, Phellips, Phellipps, Phillip, Phillips, Philips, Rev Pawling, 363 & n, 369, 371, 379, 384, 466, 495, 499, 500, 503, 505, 511, 515, 530, 532, 553, 572; ill, 461 & n, 462, 463, 464, 465, 503, 508, 509
Phillips, Henry, of Walton, 2, 9, 10, 11, 38, 90, 134, 173, 250, 251, 252, 366, 492
Mrs, 414, 415
Nicholas, 54
physicians *see* Gold, Dr; Wright, Dr; *also* apothecaries; surgeons
Pickering, Matthew, 5n, 47, 48, 50, 53, 54, 60, 73, 78, 82, 85, 87, 102, 106, 108, 114, 115, 116, 121, 124, 132, 139, 145, 160, 176, 177, 185, 187, 201
Pigeon, Pidgeon, Mr, lawyer, 17, 83n, 85, 90, 105, death, 126
Pilbort, Lawrance, 220n
Pilsgate, 172
Pitts, John, *296 n*
plashers, 93 & n, 254
plaster, prices, 512
plasterers *see* Tidd
ploughing, 5, 264, 300, 303, 309, 319, 320, 337, 351, 352, 355, 365, 479, 548, 549, 552, 556, 557, 593, 609
Plowright, Mr, salesman, jobber, of Lincs, 428, 439, 440, 442, 444, 445, 446, 448
poaching, 40, 41, 494, 502, 524
Pocklington, Mr, of Castor, 164, 165, 166, 203, 212
Popely, Griffin, 286

Port Mahon, Minorca, 621
Porter, Mrs, 553
Portsmouth, Hants, 450, 451
Portugal, 311
postal services, 7, 45, 77, 111, 171, 255, 319, 328, 452, 460, 514, 515, 516, 521, 522, 527, 595, 596, 608, 610, 613, 614
Preston, family and farm in Northborough, 56, 133, 134, 319, 532, 533, 535
Price, Mr, salesman, 278, *see also* Apreece
prices *see under* bread; building costs; coal; food; grain; hay; horses; houses; livestock; meat; napery; pepper; plaster; sheep; wool
Primrose, James, Lord, 351 & n, 354

Rainsford, Rainford, Nell, 7, 8
  Peter, 18, 47, 111, 113, 136n, 163, 168; his son, 163, 168
Read, Mr, 297, 298, 300
Rees, Ree, Ris, Riss, Abraham, 104, 106, 108 & n, 109, 110, 205 & n, 206, 251 &n, 615
rent rolls, rentals, 33, 292, 296, 301
rents, 5, 9, 11, 13, 50, 62, 64, 68, 80, 84, 85, 95, 103, 104, 146, 148, 159, 161, 165, 286, 289, 293, 303, 315, 320, 337, 340, 342, 366, 483, 484, 526, 534; abatement, 40, 435; arrears, 40, 248, 250, 261, 296, 307, 383n, 403, 440, 441, 443, 491, 503; chief, 134, 146, 436; gathering, 107, 239; rack, 83, 87
Richardson, Rev., of Eye, 494
Ricroft, Rycroft, Rycraft, Wricraft, Edward, 295n
  Goodman, 126n, 144n, 601, his son, 126n, 144n
  John, 11, 266, 300, 306, 322
  William, 374
Riddington, William, 357, 569
Ridley, Mr, surgeon, 275, 315
Rippon, Ripon, Alice (née Hipwell), wife of Thomas, 159, 161, 162, 200, 202, 247, 350
  Robert, of Lolham Mills, 159
  Thomas, death, 143
roads, levies for repair, 172, 176, 178, 179; *see also* drove roads
robberies, 77, 182 & n; compensation for, 183, 185 & n, 219, 220
Roberts, Jonathan, 261
Rocke, Mr, lawyer, 367
Rockingham, family estates in Yorks, *x*
Rockingham Forest, 30n, 160n, 234n, 402n
Roos, Mr jr, 121
Rowell, Roles, Thomas, of Peterborough, 396, 414, 415, 473, 474, 482, 545, 546
  Matthew, stone digger, of Helpston Heath, 609; ill, 610, 613
  Mr, 621, 622, 623
Rudkins, Rudkin, Thomas, 206, 291, 404, 407, 533, 534, 535, 624
Russell, Mr, undertaker, 126

Sampson, John, 430
Sanders, Robert, 543
Sandy, Mr, 555
Sargeant, Serjeant, Sargint, Josiah, 286
  William, 2, 6n, 18, 19, 69n, 166, 202, 205, 220n, 373, 380, 407, 441, 446, 517, 538, 604, 605
Scarbrow, John, of Northborough, 238n
schools *see* Charterhouse, *and under* London, Peterborough, Stamford
Sechell, William, 369, 463
Selby, Captain Michael, of Castor, 6 & n, 13, 18, 19, 52, 53, 77, 169, 171, 220n, 333n, 346, 378, 388, 390, 448, 460, 471, 509, 510, 517, 538, 605; his wife, 378, 510
  Rev Christopher, 333 & n, 348 & n, 351
servants, 75n, 103, clothes for, 32, 566
  concern for, 61, 63, 66, 74
  education of, 32; hiring, 100, 102, 230, 231, 233, 234, 235, 236, 237, 238, 282, 283, 331, 340, 341, 388, 392, 393, 394, 427, 460; London, 138, 145, 175, 176, 233, 341, 413, 469, *296*; Milton, 137, 138, 139, 141, 142, 145, 192, 436, 461, 462, 530; murdered, 229; paying off, 243, 245, 246; quitting, 175, 176; transfer to London, 39
Setchey, Sechey, Seche, Norfolk, *xv*, 6n, 297, & n, 504 & n
Shales, Charles, goldsmith, 189 & n
Sharpe, Mr, of Deeping St James, 305, 377
Shaw, Sir John, 442 & n
Sheate, William, 43
sheep, 606, 609; management, 558, 608; markets, 606, 608, 609; prices, 608, 609
Shelton, John, 206
shepherds *see* Freeman, Mr; Wright, Benjamin
Sheppard, Mr, goldsmith, Lombard Street, 73
shopkeepers, 357
Simpson, Mark, of Allerton, 77
Sisson, Sissons, Sesson, Sissenar, John, Goodman, of Northborough, 160, 168, 196, 197, 199, 200, 202, 203, 243, 289, 334, 341 & n, 342, 394, 399, 405, 406, 465, 599
  Mr, farmer, Rutland, 309, 311
slaters, 13; *see also under* Milton House
Slye, Walter, 196, 197
Smith, Mr, of London, 605
  Robert, tenant, of Deeping Gate, 83, 84, 96, 195, 203, 425
Snow, Mr, 15, 440, 594
Southampton, Hants, 450
Southwell, Thomas, 50n
Sowgate, Sougate, Mr, of Alwalton, 13, 14, 21, 313, 355, 399, 401, 407
Spain, trade with, 398, 461
Spalding, Lincs, 92, 185, 276, 503
Sparks, Sparkes, Edmund, 614
  Mr, 388, 456, 471, 520, 538
spectacles, 221
sports, 511

St Ives, Hunts, 404
St John, Francis, of Thorpe Hall, *xiv*, 5 & n, 47, 48, 50, 53, 56, 60, 68, 69, 70, 73, 77, 78, 85 & n, 87, 88, 91, 92, 93, 99, 102, 104, 105, 106, 107, 108, 109, 110, 117, 118, 120, 121, 124, 159, 163, 164, 165 & n, 166, 168, 170, 198, 200, 201, 352, 517; death, 384n, 385; his wife, 87, 88, 102; his sons, 110
Mrs Francis, 87, 88, 102
Sir St Andrew, 371, 429
Sir Walter, 93, 384n
St Neot's, St Need's, Hunts, 489, 585
Stamford, 68, 115, 142, 221, 316, 317, 426, 429, 443, 550n; Baron, 172, 179, 519
fair, 9, 53, 91, 129, 130, 549
people of, 289
school, 334
Stamford, Mr, 163, 179
Standish, David, of Peterborough, 309
Messrs, 163
Mr, jr, 49, 73, 74, 77, 111
Rev Francis, 42, 43, 49, 334
Roger, 489
Stangar, Mr, 468
Stasey, Stacey, Stacy, Richard, 326, 327, 328, 344, 346
statutes (fairs), 230 & n, *see also under* Castor; Helpston
Stevenage, Herts, 446
Stevens, Mr, 146, 148
Widow, of Bourne, 364, 368, 377, 555, 557n, 569, 594, 595, 596, 597, 609, 612, 617, 626
Stevenson, Mark, 78 (? = Simpson, Mark)
stewards, 313; *see also* Beales, Edmund; Guybon, Francis
accounts, *x*, *xxii*, 33, 34, 39, 78, 117, 127, 160, 180, 220, 242, 248, 250n, 292, 296, 306n, 337, 343, 363, 365, 425, 491, *296*
duties, *xii*, *xiv*, *xv–xvi*
of courts, 90n, 615; fees, 117; *see also* Burman, Mr, sr; Pemberton, Roger
Stilton, Hunts, 121, 122, 410
Stinton, Mr, 318
stone digger *see* Rowell, Matthew
storms, 293 & n, 294, 295, 386, 541, 544, 598, 618
Stourbridge, Sturbitch, Cambs, fair, 234, 462, 520
Strafford, Frances, 367, 384
Stuart, James, Pretender, 558 & n
Sturges, John, architect, *xvi*, 5n
Styles, Captain, of Walton, 40, 41, 81, 134, 135, 390, 392, 528, 551, 558; death, 623
Jonas, of Helpston, 411
Mr, jr, 390
Suffolk, 333n, 381
Sulehay, Sewley Hay, 160n, 562n; bowling at, 562; forest, 160n, 460, 471; walk, 276, 385, 386, 387
surgeons, 315; *see also* apothecaries; physicians
surveyor *see* Cloathier, Mr
Sussex, 348 & n
Sutton, 172, 219 & n, 220, 311, 537
farm at, 537, 538, 539, 540
Sutton in the fens *see* Long Sutton, Lincs
Sutton-on-Lound, Notts, *x*
Swain, Mr, death, 382n, 384
Sylverwood, Samuel, 356, 477, 483, 547
Sylvius, Lady Anne, (née Howard), *xviii*, 17, 38, 51, 52, 83, 107, 150, 180, 202, 224, 225, 247, 262n, 485, 491
Sir Gabriel, *xviii*, 17n, 107, 262n

tailor *see* Goode, Elias
Tallington, Lincs, 487
Tanner, Mr, 74
tanners, 53, 96; *see also* Andrew, Charles; Andrew, Thomas; Ireland, Mr
tanning *see* bark for tanning; leather and tanning
tax, *xix–xxi*, 1, 9, 15, 16, 23, 60, 65, 68, 77, 98, 101, 169, 228, 267, 320, 342, 366, 394, 447, 521, 548
assessors, *xix–xx*, 6, 8, 12
city, 58
collectors, 12, 17, 19, 59, 443; *see also* Alderman, John; Bimrose, John; Matthews, Mr; Webdale, Mr
commissioners, *xix–xx*, 6, 8, 17, 18, 19
country, 58
evasion of, 6, 7, 8, 62
land tax, *xix*, 6, 51, 91, 92, 220, 224, 286
methods of payment, *xix–xx*, 13, 14, 17, 18, 19, 68, 219
on deaths, 136 & n
receipts, 69
town assessments, 169, 170, 176
window tax, 90
Taylor, Taylour, Mr, prebend of Peterborough, 566
Mr, wine merchant, of King's Lynn, 476, 621
Sir Simon, 476
Temple, Mrs, 248
Thacker, Mr, 3, 4
Thames, River, 604, 613
thatchers, 503; *see also* Andrew, Charles; Andrew, Thomas
Thompson, Tomson, Henry, 318
Mr, 37
Widow, Goody, 420, 432, 433, 446n, 447, 448, 537, 538, 573; her son, 538
Thorney, Cambs, 250, 515
Thoughood, Nicolas, 220n
Tidd, family, plasterers, 11, 13, 15, 35 & n
timber, 150, 151, 347n; accounts, 34, 39, 45, 78, 160, 248, 292, 296, 343; planting, 146; sales, *x*, 294, 295; tithes, 135
Tinkerson, Edward, 40
Tippins, Tippin, Tippen, Thomas, 286, 429, 437